# Chambers
# FILM
# FACTS

*Compiled and edited by*
Allan Hunter

# Chambers

Published 1993 by Chambers Harrap Ltd
43–45 Annandale Street, Edinburgh EH7 4AZ

British Library Cataloguing in Publication Data

A catalogue record for this book is available
from the British Library.

ISBN 0 550 17257 2

Typeset by Pillans & Wilson Ltd
Printed in England by Clays Ltd, St Ives plc

# CONTENTS

# INTRODUCTION

Have you ever sat trying to recall the names of all the actors who formed *The Magnificent Seven*, or pondered just how many sequels have been made to *Dirty Harry* and what their titles were? Perhaps watching *Basic Instinct* has prompted a desire to know what other films Sharon Stone has appeared in or a crossword puzzle demands to know who provided the voice of Snow White in Disney's animated classic. All this information and more can be found in the pages of *Film Facts.*

*Film Facts* is a user-friendly reference volume packed with information on 65 years of world cinema conveniently classified under three sections devoted to films, actors and directors.

From Al Jolson's cry of 'wait a minute, wait a minute, you ain't heard nothing yet' in *The Jazz Singer* of 1927 the book comes right up to date with such recent titles as *Howard's End*, *The Crying Game* and *Scent Of A Woman*. The broad sweep of material covered within the volume ranges from the major Oscar winners and biggest box-offices successes of each year to enduring cult classics and the cream of international productions.

A readily accessible volume, the book should satisfy puzzle fans, film buffs and those in pursuit of reliable information, whether trivial or otherwise.

Comments, queries, suggestions and corrections will be welcomed care of the publishers.

Allan Hunter
*April 1993*

# HOW TO USE THIS BOOK

Conveniently divided into three sections, *Film Facts* provides a wealth of information on 65 years of world cinema, covering the period from the first talkie *The Jazz Singer* to the 1993 Best Picture Oscar-winner *Unforgiven*.

The first section consists of an alphabetical listing of film titles giving the film's country of origin, year of production, director and principal cast list. The second section provides biographical details and a comprehensive filmography for all the most important performers whose work is featured in the first section. The third section provides biographical details and a comprehensive filmography for every one of the directors whose work is featured in the first section.

An asterisk against a performer's name in the first section indicates that his or her career is covered by a filmography in section two. An asterisk against a film title in sections two and three indicates that fuller details of the particular film can be found in section one.

All foreign language films are listed under the title by which they are best known in Britain with a cross-reference to their original title or English equivalent. Thus *Last Tango In Paris* is described in full at that title and cross-referenced to *Ultima Tango A Parigi* but *La Dolce Vita* is described in full at its Italian title with the cross-reference to *The Sweet Life*.

Dates attached to films signify the film's original year of release in its country of origin and are consistent throughout. These may vary from the year of production or the year of the film's release in Britain.

Throughout section one additional information on sequels, prequels and remakes has been provided at the end of each relevant entry.

# Films

## A

***A Bout De Souffle*** see ***Breathless***

***Absence Of Malice*** (USA 1981)
Sydney Pollack

Gallagher (Paul Newman)*
Megan (Sally Field)*
Rosen (Bob Balaban)
Teresa (Melinda Dillon)
Malderone (Luther Adler)

***Absolute Beginners*** (UK 1986)
Julien Temple

Colin (Eddie O'Connell)
Crepe Suzette (Patsy Kensit)
Vendice Partners (David Bowie)*
Henley Of Mayfair (James Fox)

***The Accidental Tourist*** (USA 1988)
Lawrence Kasdan

Macon (William Hurt)*
Sarah (Kathleen Turner)*
Muriel (Geena Davis)*
Rose (Amy Wright)

***The Accused*** (USA 1988)
Jonathan Kaplan

Kathryn Murphy (Kelly McGillis)
Sarah Tobias (Jodie Foster)*
Ken Joyce (Bernie Coulson)
Cliff 'Scorpion' Albrecht (Leo Rossi)

***Adam's Rib*** (USA 1949)
George Cukor

Adam Bonner (Spencer Tracy)*
Amanda Bonner (Katharine Hepburn)*
Doris Attinger (Judy Holliday)*
Warren Attinger (David Wayne)

***The Addams Family*** (USA 1991)
Barry Sonnenfeld

Morticia Addams (Anjelica Huston)*
Gomez Addams (Raul Julia)*
Gordon (Christopher Lloyd)
Tully Alford (Dan Hedaya)

***The Adventures Of Baron
Munchausen*** (USA 1988)
Terry Gilliam

Baron Munchausen (John Neville)
Desmond/Berthold (Eric Idle)
Sally Salt (Sarah Polley)
Vulcan (Oliver Reed)*

***The Adventures Of Robin Hood***
(USA 1938)
Michael Curtiz and William Keighley

Sir Robin Of Locksley/Robin Hood (Errol
Flynn)*
Maid Marian (Olivia De Havilland)*
Sir Guy Of Gisbourne (Basil Rathbone)*
Prince John (Claude Rains)*

***An Affair To Remember***
(USA 1957)
Leo McCarey

Nickie Ferrante (Cary Grant)*
Terry McKay (Deborah Kerr)*
Kenneth (Richard Denning)
Lois (Neva Patterson)

***The African Queen*** (USA 1951)
John Huston

Charlie Allnut (Humphrey Bogart)*
Rose Sayer (Katharine Hepburn)*
Rev Samuel Sayer (Robert Morley)
Captain of the Louisa (Peter Bull)

**After Hours** (USA 1985)
Martin Scorsese

Paul Hackett (Griffin Dunne)
Marcy (Rosanna Arquette)
Kiki (Linda Fiorentino)
Julie (Teri Garr)

**Agnes Of God** (USA 1985)
Norman Jewison

Dr Martha Livingston (Jane Fonda)*
Mother Ruth Miriam (Anne Bancroft)*
Sister Agnes (Meg Tilly)
Dr Livingston's Mother (Anne Pitoniak)

**Aguirre, Der Zorn Gottes** see
   **Aguirre, Wrath Of God**

**Aguirre, Wrath Of God**
   (Germany 1972)
   (*Aguirre, Der Zorn Gottes*)
Werner Herzog

Don Lope De Aguirre (Klaus Kinski)
Inez De Atienza (Helena Rojo)
Don Pedro De Ursua (Ruy Guerra)
Brother Gaspar De Carvajal (Del Negro)

**Ai No Corrida** see **In The Realm
   Of The Senses**

**Airplane!** (USA 1980)
Jim Abrahams, David Zucker, Jerry
   Zucker

Ted Striker (Robert Hays)
Elaine (Julie Hagerty)
McCroskey (Lloyd Bridges)*
Capt Oveur (Peter Graves)
Dr Rumack (Leslie Nielsen)*

Sequel *Airplane II: The Sequel* (1982)

**Airport** (USA 1969)
George Seaton

Mel Bakersfield (Burt Lancaster)*
Vernon Demarest (Dean Martin)*
Tanya Livingston (Jean Seberg)
Gwen Meighen (Jacqueline Bisset)*

Joe Patroni (George Kennedy)
Ada Quonsett (Helen Hayes)*
D O Guerrero (Van Heflin)

Sequels *Airport 1975* (1974); *Airport '77*
   (1977); *Airport '79 — The Concorde*
   (1979)

**The Alamo** (USA 1960)
John Wayne

Col David Crockett (John Wayne)*
Col James Bowie (Richard Widmark)*
Col William Barret Travis (Laurence
   Harvey)*
Gen Sam Houston (Richard Boone)

**L'Albero Degli Zoccoli** see **The
   Tree Of Wooden Clogs**

**Alexander Nevsky** (USSR 1938)
Sergei Eisenstein

Prince Alexander Yaroslavich Nevsky
   (Nikolai Cherkassov)
Vassily Buslai (Nikolai P Okhlopov)
Gavrilo Olexich (Alexander L Abrikosov)
Ignat, Master Armourer (Dmitri N Orlov)

**Alexander's Ragtime Band**
   (USA 1938)
Henry King

Alexander(Roger Grant) (Tyrone
   Power)*
Stella Kirby (Alice Faye)*
Charlie Dwyer (Don Ameche)*
Jerry Allen (Ethel Merman)*

**Alfie** (UK 1966)
Lewis Gilbert

Alfie (Michael Caine)*
Ruby (Shelley Winters)*
Siddie (Millicent Martin)
Abortionist (Denholm Elliott)*

Sequel *Alfie Darling* (1974)

## Alice Doesn't Live Here Anymore
(USA 1974)
Martin Scorsese

Alice Hyatt (Ellen Burstyn)*
David (Kris Kristofferson)*
Flo (Dianne Ladd)
Audrey (Jodie Foster)*
Ben Everhart (Harvey Keitel)*

## Alien (USA 1979)
Ridley Scott

Dallas (Tom Skerritt)
Ripley (Sigourney Weaver)*
Lambert (Veronica Cartwright)
Brett (Harry Dean Stanton)
Kane (John Hurt)*

Sequels *Aliens* (1986); *Alien 3* (1992)

## Aliens (USA 1986)
James Cameron

Ripley (Sigourney Weaver)*
Newt (Carrie Henn)
Corporal Hicks (Michael Biehn)
Burke (Paul Reiser)

Sequel to *Alien* (1979), Sequel *Alien 3* (1992)

## All About Eve (USA 1950)
Joseph L Mankiewicz

Margo Channing (Bette Davis)*
Eve Harrington (Anne Baxter)*
Addison De Witt (George Sanders)*
Karen Richards (Celeste Holm)*
Miss Casswell (Marilyn Monroe)*

## All Of Me (USA 1984)
Rob Reiner

Roger Cobb (Steve Martin)*
Edwina Cutwater (Lily Tomlin)*
Terry Hoskins (Victoria Tennant)
Peggy Schuyler (Madolyn Smith)

## All Quiet On The Western Front
(USA 1930)
Lewis Milestone

Paul Baumer (Lew Ayres)*
Katczinsky (Louis Wolheim)
Himmelstoss (John Wray)
Tjaden (George 'Slim' Summerville)

Remake *All Quiet On The Western Front* (TV 1979)

## All That Jazz (USA 1979)
Bob Fosse

Joe Gideon (Roy Scheider)*
Angelique (Jessica Lange)*
Kate Jagger (Ann Reinking)
Audrey Paris (Leland Palmer)

## All The King's Men (USA 1949)
Robert Rossen

Willie Stark (Broderick Crawford)
Jack Burden (John Ireland)
Anne Stanton (Joanne Dru)
Sadie Burke (Mercedes McCambridge)

## All The President's Men
(USA 1976)
Alan J Pakula

Carl Bernstein (Dustin Hoffman)*
Bob Woodward (Robert Redford)*
Harry Rosenfeld (Jack Warden)
Ben Bradlee (Jason Robards)*

## Amadeus (USA 1984)
Milos Forman

Antonio Salieri (F Murray Abraham)
Wolfgang Amadeus Mozart (Tom Hulce)
Constanze Mozart (Elizabeth Berridge)
Emanuel Schikaneder (Simon Callow)

## Les Amants Du Pont-Neuf
(France 1991)
Leos Carax

Michèle (Juliette Binoche)
Alex (Denis Lavant)
Hans (Klaus Michael-Gruber)
Clochard's friend (Daniel Buain)

**America, America** (USA 1963)
Elia Kazan

Stavros Topouzoglou (Stathis Giallelis)
Vartan Damadian (Frank Wolff)
Isaac Topouzoglou (Harry Davis)
Vasso Topouzoglou (Elena Karam)

**American Gigolo** (USA 1980)
Paul Schrader

Julian Kay (Richard Gere)*
Michelle Stratton (Lauren Hutton)
Det Sunday (Hector Elizondo)
Anne (Nina van Pallandt)

**American Graffiti** (USA 1973)
George Lucas

Curt (Richard Dreyfuss)*
Steve (Ron Howard)
John (Paul Le Mat)
Terry (Charlie Martin Smith)
Falfa (Harrison Ford)*

Sequel *More American Graffiti* (1979)

**An American In Paris** (USA 1951)
Vincente Minnelli

Jerry Mulligan (Gene Kelly)*
Lise Bouvier (Leslie Caron)*
Adam Cook (Oscar Levant)
Henri Baurel (Georges Guetray)

**An American Werewolf In London**
   (USA 1981)
John Landis

David Kessler (David Naughton)
Alex Price (Jenny Agutter)*
Jack Goodman (Griffin Dunne)
Dr Hirsch (John Woodvine)

**The Amityville Horror** (USA 1979)
Stuart Rosenberg

George Lutz (James Brolin)
Kathleen Lutz (Margot Kidder)
Father Delaney (Rod Steiger)*
Father Bolen (Don Stroud)

Sequels *Amityville II: The Possession*
   (1982); *Amityville 3-D* (1983);
   *Amityville 4: The Evil Escapes* (TV
   1989); *Amityville 1992: It's About
   Time* (1992)

**Anatomy Of A Murder** (USA 1959)
Otto Preminger

Paul Biegler (James Stewart)*
Laura Manion (Lee Remick)*
Lt Frederick Manion (Ben Gazzara)*
Parnell McCarthy (Arthur O'Connell)

**Anchors Aweigh** (USA 1945)
George Sidney

Clarence Doolittle (Frank Sinatra)*
Susan Abbott (Kathryn Grayson)
Joseph Brady (Gene Kelly)*
Donald Martin (Dean Stockwell)

**And God Created Woman** see *Et
   Dieu Créa La Femme*

**Andrei Rublev** (USSR 1966)
Andrei Tarkovsky

Andrei Rublev (Anatoly Solonitsyn)
Dirill (Ivan Lapikov)
Daniel the Black (Nikolai Grinko)
Theophanes the Greek (Nikolai
   Sergeyev)

**An Angel At My Table**
   (New Zealand 1990)
Jane Campion

Janet Frame (Kerry Fox)
Teenage Janet (Karen Fergusson)
Young Janet (Alexia Keogh)
Myrtle Frame (Melina Bernecker)

**Angels With Dirty Faces**
   (USA 1938)
Michael Curtiz

Rocky Sullivan (James Cagney)*
Jerry Connolly (Pat O'Brien)
James Frazier (Humphrey Bogart)*
Laury Ferguson (Ann Sheridan)

Sequel *Angels Wash Their Faces* (1939)

**Animal Crackers** (USA 1930)
Victor Heerman

Capt Jeffrey Spaulding (Groucho Marx)*
Signor Emanuel Raveld (Chico Marx)*
The Professor (Harpo Marx)*
Horatio Jamison (Zeppo Marx)*
Mrs Rittenhouse (Margaret Dumont)

**Anna Christie** (USA 1930)
Clarence Brown

Anna Christie (Greta Garbo)*
Matt Burke (Charles Bickford)
Chris Christie (George F Marion)
Marthy Owen (Marie Dressler)

**Anna Karenina** (USA 1935)
Clarence Brown

Anna Karenina (Greta Garbo)*
Vronsky (Fredric March)*
Sergei (Freddie Bartholomew)
Kitty (Maureen O'Sullivan)

Remakes *Anna Karenina* (1948)(Vivien
Leigh*); *Anna Karenina* (TV 1985)
(Jacqueline Bisset)

**Anne Of The Thousand Days**
(USA 1969)
Charles Jarrott

King Henry VIII (Richard Burton)*
Anne Boleyn (Genevieve Bujold)
Queen Catherine of Aragon (Irene
Papas)
Cardinal Wolsey (Anthony Quayle)*

**Annie** (USA 1982)
John Huston

Daddy Warbucks (Albert Finney)*
Miss Hannigan (Carol Burnett)
Lily (Bernadette Peters)
Grace Farrell (Ann Reinking)
Annie (Aileen Quinn)

**Annie Get Your Gun** (USA 1950)
George Sidney

Annie Oakley (Betty Hutton)*
Frank Butler (Howard Keel)*
Buffalo Bill (Louis Calhern)
Chief Sitting Bull (J Carrol Naish)

**Annie Hall** (USA 1977)
Woody Allen

Alvy Singer (Woody Allen)*
Annie Hall (Diane Keaton)*
Rob (Tony Roberts)
Allison (Carol Kane)

**Another Woman** (USA 1988)
Woody Allen

Marion (Gena Rowlands)*
Hope (Mia Farrow)*
Ken (Ian Holm)
Larry (Gene Hackman)*

**The Apartment** (USA 1960)
Billy Wilder

Calvin Clinton 'Bud' Baxter (Jack
Lemmon)*
Fran Kubelik (Shirley MacLaine)*
J D Sheldrake (Fred MacMurray)*
Dr Dreyfus (Jack Kruschen)

**Apocalypse Now** (USA 1979)
Francis Coppola

Col Walter E Kurtz (Marlon Brando)*
Lt-Col Bill Kilgore (Robert Duvall)*
Capt Benjamin L Willard (Martin Sheen)*
Photojournalist (Dennis Hopper)*
Col Lucas (Harrison Ford)*

**Around The World In 80 Days**
(USA 1956)
Michael Anderson

Phineas Fogg (David Niven)*
Inspector Fix (Robert Newton)*
Passepartout (Cantinflas)
The Princess Aouda (Shirley MacLaine)*

**Arrowsmith** (USA 1931)
John Ford

Dr Martin Arrowsmith (Ronald Colman)*
Leora (Helen Hayes)*
Prof Gottlieb (A C Anson)
Sondelius (Richard Bennett)

**Arsenic And Old Lace** (USA 1944)
Frank Capra

Mortimer Brewster (Cary Grant)*
Elaine Harper (Priscilla Lane)
Jonathan Brewster (Raymond Massey)*
Dr Einstein (Peter Lorre)*
Abby Brewster (Josephine Hull)
Martha Brewster (Jean Adair)

**Arthur** (USA 1981)
Steve Gordon

Arthur Bach (Dudley Moore)*
Linda Marolla (Liza Minnelli)*
Hobson (John Gielgud)*
Martha Bach (Geraldine Fitzgerald)

Sequel *Arthur 2: On The Rocks* (1988)

**Ashes And Diamonds** (Poland 1958)
(*Popiol I Diament*)
Andrzej Wajda

Maciek Chelmicki (Zbigniew Cybulski)
Krystyna (Ewa Kryzjewska)
Szczuka (Waclaw Zastrzezynski)
Andrzej (Adam Pawlikowski)

**The Asphalt Jungle** (USA 1950)
John Huston

Dix Handley (Sterling Hayden)*
Alonzo D Emmerich (Louis Calhern)
Doll Conovan (Jean Hagen)
Gus Minissi (James Whitmore)
Angela Phinlay (Marilyn Monroe)*

**L'Atalante** (France 1934)
Jean Vigo

Père Jules (Michel Simon)
Juliette (Dita Parlo)
Jean (Jean Daste)
Pedlar (Gilles Margaritis)

**Atame!** see **Tie Me Up! Tie Me Down!**

**Atlantic City** (Canada/France 1980)
Louis Malle

Lou (Burt Lancaster)*
Sally (Susan Sarandon)*
Grace (Kate Reid)
Joseph (Michel Piccoli)

**Au Revoir Les Enfants**
(France/West Germany 1987)
Louis Malle

Julien Quentin (Gaspard Manesse)
Jean Bonnet (Raphael Fejto)
Mme Quentin (Francine Racette)
François Quentin (Stanislas Carre De Malberg)

**Auntie Mame** (USA 1958)
Morton Da Costa

Mame Dennis (Rosalind Russell)*
Beauregard Burnside (Forrest Tucker)
Vera Charles (Coral Browne)
Mr Babcock (Fred Clark)
Patrick Dennis (Roger Smith)

Musical version *Mame* (1973) (Lucille Ball)

**Avalon** (USA 1990)
Barry Levinson

Sam Krichinsky (Armin Mueller-Stahl)
Jules Kaye (Aidan Quinn)
Ann Kaye (Elizabeth Perkins)
Eva Krichinsky (Joan Plowright)

**Avanti!** (USA 1972)
Billy Wilder

Wendell Armbruster (Jack Lemmon)*
Pamela Piggott (Juliet Mills)
Carlo Carlucci (Clive Revill)
J J Blodgett (Edward Andrews)

***L'Avventura*** (Italy 1960)
Michelangelo Antonioni

Sandro (Gabriele Ferzetti)
Claudia (Monica Vitti)*
Anna (Lea Massari)
Giulia (Dominique Blanchar)

***Awakenings*** (USA 1990)
Penny Marshall

Leonard Lowe (Robert De Niro)*
Dr Malcolm Sayer (Robin Williams)*
Eleanor Costello (Julie Kavner)
Mrs Lowe (Ruth Nelson)

***The Awful Truth*** (USA 1937)
Leo McCarey

Jerry Warriner (Cary Grant)*
Lucy Warriner (Irene Dunne)*
Daniel Leeson (Ralph Bellamy)*
Armand Duvalle (Alex D'Arcy)

Musical remake *Let's Do It Again* (1953)
(Ray Milland*, Jane Wyman, Aldo
Ray)


## B

***Babes In Arms*** (USA 1939)
Busby Berkeley

Mickey Moran (Mickey Rooney)*
Patsy Barton (Judy Garland)*
Joe Moran (Charles Winninger)
Judge Black (Guy Kibbee)

***Babette's Feast*** (Denmark 1987)
(*Babettes Gaestebud*)
Gabriel Axel

Babette Hersant (Stéphane Audran)
Achille Papin (Jean-Philippe Lafont)
Swedish Royal Opera Patron (Bibi
Andersson)
Lorens Lowenhielm (Gudmar Wivesson)

***Babettes Gaestebud*** see
***Babette's Feast***

***Back To The Future*** (USA 1985)
Robert Zemeckis

Marty McFly (Michael J Fox)*
Dr Emmett Brown (Christopher Lloyd)
Lorraine Baines (Lea Thompson)
George McFly (Crispin Glover)

Sequels *Back To The Future Part II*
(1989); *Back To The Future Part III*
(1990)

***Backdraft*** (USA 1991)
Ron Howard

Stephen McCaffrey (Kurt Russell)*
Brian McCaffrey (William Baldwin)
Donald Rimgale (Robert De Niro)*
Ronald Bartel (Donald Sutherland)*

***The Bad And The Beautiful***
(USA 1952)
Vincente Minnelli

Georgia Lorrison (Lana Turner)*
Jonathan Shields (Kirk Douglas)*
Harry Pebbel (Walter Pidgeon)*
James Lee Bartlow (Dick Powell)*

***Bad Day At Black Rock*** (USA 1955)
John Sturges

John J Macready (Spencer Tracy)*
Reno Smith (Robert Ryan)*
Liz Wroth (Anne Francis)
Hector David (Lee Marvin)*

***The Bad News Bears*** (USA 1976)
Michael Ritchie

Coach Buttermaker (Walter Matthau)*
Manda Whurlitzer (Tatum O'Neal)
Roy Turner (Vic Morrow)
Cleveland (Joyce Van Patten)

Sequels *The Bad News Bears In
Breaking Training* (1977); *The Bad
News Bears Go To Japan* (1978)

**Bad Timing** (UK 1980)
Nicolas Roeg

Dr Alex Linden (Art Garfunkel)
Milena Flaherty (Theresa Russell)*
Inspector Frederich Netusil (Harvey
  Keitel)*
Stefan Vognic (Denholm Elliott)*

**Badlands** (USA 1973)
Terrence Malick

Kit (Martin Sheen)*
Holly (Sissy Spacek)*
Father (Warren Oates)
Caro (Roman Bieri)

**Ball Of Fire** (USA 1941)
Howard Hawks

Prof Bertram Potts (Gary Cooper)*
Sugarpuss O'Shea (Barbara Stanwyck)*
Prof Gurkakoff (Oscar Homolka)
Prof Jerome (Henry Travers)

Musical remake *A Song Is Born* (1948)
  (Danny Kaye*, Virginia Mayo)

**Bambi** (USA 1942)
James Algar, Bill Roberts, Norman
  Wright, Paul Satterfield, Sam
  Armstrong, Graham Heid

Voices of:
Bambi (Bobby Stewart)
Thumper (Peter Behn)
Flower (Stan Alexander)
Phylline (Cammie King)

**The Band Wagon** (USA 1953)
Vincente Minnelli

Tony Hunter (Fred Astaire)*
Gaby Berard (Cyd Charisse)*
Lester Marton (Oscar Levant)
Lily Marton (Nanette Fabray)
Jeffrey Cordova (Jack Buchanan)

**The Bank Dick** (USA 1940)
Edward Cline

Egbert Souse (W C Fields)*
Agatha Souse (Cora Witherspoon)
Myrtle Souse (Una Merkel)
Elsie May Adele Brunch Souse (Evelyn
  Del Rio)

**Barbarella** (USA 1968)
Roger Vadim

Barbarella (Jane Fonda)*
Pygar (John Philip Law)
Black Queen (Anita Pallenberg)
Concierge (Milo O'Shea)
Dildano (David Hemmings)*

**The Barefoot Contessa** (USA 1954)
Joseph L Mankiewicz

Harry Dawes (Humphrey Bogart)*
Maria Vargas (Ava Gardner)*
Oscar Muldoon (Edmond O'Brien)*
Alberto Bravano (Marius Goring)

**Barefoot In The Park** (USA 1967)
Gene Saks

Paul Bratter (Robert Redford)*
Corie Bratter (Jane Fonda)*
Victor Velasco (Charles Boyer)*
Mrs Ethel Banks (Mildred Natwick)

**The Barretts Of Wimpole Street**
  (USA 1934)
Sidney Franklin

Elizabeth Barrett (Norma Shearer)*
Robert Browning (Fredric March)*
Edward Moulton Barrett (Charles
  Laughton)*
Henrietta Barrett (Maureen O'Sullivan)

Remake *The Barretts Of Wimpole Street*
  (1957) (Jennifer Jones*, Bill Travers,
  John Gielgud*)

**Barry Lyndon** (UK 1975)
Stanley Kubrick

Barry Lyndon (Ryan O'Neal)*
Lady Lyndon (Marisa Berenson)
The Chevalier (Patrick Magee)
Capt Potzdorf (Hardy Kruger)


**Barton Fink** (USA 1991)
Joel Coen

Barton Fink (John Turturro)*
Charlie Meadows (John Goodman)*
Audrey Taylor (Judy Davis)*
Jack Lipnick (Michael Lerner)


**Basic Instinct** (USA 1992)
Paul Verhoeven

Det Nick Curran (Michael Douglas)*
Catherine Tramell (Sharon Stone)*
Gus (George Dzundza)
Dr Beth Garner (Jeanne Tripplehorn)
Hazel Dobkins (Dorothy Malone)*


**Batman** (USA 1989)
Tim Burton

Jack Napier/The Joker (Jack
  Nicholson)*
Bruce Wayne/Batman (Michael Keaton)*
Vicki Vale (Kim Basinger)*
Alexander Knox (Robert Wuhl)


**Batman Returns** (USA 1992)
Tim Burton

Bruce Wayne/Batman (Michael Keaton)*
Oswald Cobblepot/The Penguin (Danny
  De Vito)*
Selina Kyle/Catwoman (Michelle
  Pfeiffer)*
Max Schreck (Christopher Walken)*


**La Battaglia Di Algeri** see **The
  Battle Of Algiers**


**The Battle Of Algiers**
  (Italy/Algeria 1965)
(*La Battaglia Di Algeri*)
Gillo Pontecorvo

Col Mathieu (Jean Martin)
Saari Kader (Yacef Saadi)
Ali La Pointe (Brahim Haggiag)
Capt Dubois (Tommaso Neri)


**Beaches** (USA 1988)
Garry Marshall

C C Bloom (Bette Midler)*
Hillary Whitney Essex (Barbara
  Hershey)*
John Pierce (John Heard)
Dr Richard Milstein (Spalding Gray)


**Beau Geste** (USA 1939)
William Wellman

Beau Geste (Gary Cooper)*
John Geste (Ray Milland)*
Digby Geste (Robert Preston)*
Sgt Markoff (Brian Donlevy)
Isobel Rivers (Susan Hayward)*

Remake *Beau Geste* (1966) (Guy
  Stockwell, Doug McClure, Telly
  Savalas)


**Beauty And The Beast** (USA 1991)
Gary Trousdale, Kirk Wise

Voices of:
Belle (Paige O'Hara)
Beast (Robby Benson)
Gaston (Richard White)
Mrs Potts (Angela Lansbury)*


**Becket** (USA 1964)
Peter Glenville

Thomas Becket (Richard Burton)*
King Henry II (Peter O'Toole)*
Bishop Folliot (Donald Wolfit)
King Louis VII (Sir John Gielgud)*

**Becky Sharp** (USA 1935)
Rouben Mamoulian

Becky Sharp (Miriam Hopkins)*
Amelia Sedley (Frances Dee)
Marquis of Steyne (Cedric Hardwicke)
Lady Bareacres (Billie Burke)

**Beetlejuice** (USA 1988)
Tim Burton

Adam (Alec Baldwin)*
Barbara (Geena Davis)*
Betelgeuse (Michael Keaton)*
Lydia (Winona Ryder)*
Juno (Sylvia Sidney)*

**Belle De Jour** (France 1967)
Luis Bunuel

Sèverine Serizy (Catherine Deneuve)*
Pierre Serizy (Jean Sorel)
Madame Anais (Geneviève Page)
Henri Husson (Michel Piccoli)

**The Belles Of St Trinians**
(UK 1954)
Frank Launder

Miss Millicent Fritton/Clarence Fritton
(Alastair Sim)*
PW Sgt Ruby Gates (Joyce Grenfell)*
Flash Harry (George Cole)*
Miss Drownder (Hermoine Baddeley)

Sequels *Blue Murder At St Trinians*
(1958); *The Pure Hell Of St Trinians*
(1961); *The Great St Trinians Train
Robbery* (1966); *Wildcats Of St
Trinians* (1980)

**The Bells Of St Mary's** (USA 1945)
Leo McCarey

Father Chuck O'Malley (Bing Crosby)*
Sister Benedict (Ingrid Bergman)*
Mr Bogardus (Henry Travers)
Patsy (Joan Carroll)

**Ben-Hur** (USA 1959)
William Wyler

Judah Ben-Hur (Charlton Heston)*
Messala (Stephen Boyd)*
Esther (Haya Harareet)
Quintus Arrius (Jack Hawkins)*

**The Best Little Whorehouse In
Texas** (USA 1982)
Colin Higgins

Sheriff (Burt Reynolds)*
Mona Stangely (Dolly Parton)*
Melvin (Dom De Luise)
Governor (Charles Durning)

**The Best Years Of Our Lives**
(USA 1946)
William Wyler

Millie Stephenson (Myrna Loy)*
Al Stephenson (Fredric March)*
Fred Derry (Dana Andrews)*
Peggy Stephenson (Teresa Wright)
Homer Parrish (Harold Russell)

Remake *Returning Home* (TV 1975)

**Betty Blue** (France 1986)
(*37.2 Le Matin*)
Jean-Jacques Beineix

Betty (Béatrice Dalle)
Zorg (Jean-Hugues Anglade)
Lisa (Consuelo De Haviland)
Eddy (Gérard Darmon)

**Beverly Hills Cop** (USA 1984)
Martin Brest

Axel Foley (Eddie Murphy)*
Det Billy Rosewood (Judge Reinhold)
Sgt Taggart (John Ashton)
Jenny Summers (Lisa Eilbacher)

Sequel *Beverly Hills Cop II* (1987)

### The Bible...In The Beginning
(USA 1966)
John Huston

Cain (Richard Harris)*
Abraham (George C Scott)*
Sarah (Ava Gardner)*
The Three Angels (Peter O'Toole)*
Noah (John Huston)

### Bicycle Thieves (Italy 1948)
(*Ladri Di Biciclette*)
Vittorio De Sica

Antonio Ricci (Lamberto Maggiorani)
Bruno Ricci (Enzo Staiola)
Maria Ricci (Lianella Carell)
The Thief (Vittorio Antonucci)

### Big (USA 1988)
Penny Marshall

Josh Baskin (Tom Hanks)*
Susan (Elizabeth Perkins)
MacMillan (Robert Loggia)
Paul (John Heard)

### The Big Blue (France 1988)
(*Le Grand Bleu*)
Luc Besson

Joanna (Rosanna Arquette)
Jacques Mayol (Jean-Marc Barr)*
Enzo Molinari (Jean Reno)
Dr Laurence (Paul Shenar)

### The Big Chill (USA 1983)
Lawrence Kasdan

Sam (Tom Berenger)*
Sarah (Glenn Close)*
Michael (Jeff Goldblum)*
Nick (William Hurt)*
Harold (Kevin Kline)*
Meg (Mary Kay Place)
Chloe (Meg Tilly)
Karen (JoBeth Williams)

### The Big Country (USA 1958)
William Wyler

James McKay (Gregory Peck)*
Julie Maragon (Jean Simmons)*
Patricia Terrill (Carroll Baker)*
Steve Leech (Charlton Heston)*

### The Big Easy (USA 1987)
Jim McBride

Remy McSwain (Dennis Quaid)*
Anne Osborne (Ellen Barkin)*
Jack Kellom (Ned Beatty)
Andre De Soto (John Goodman)*

### The Big Heat (USA 1953)
Fritz Lang

Dave Bannion (Glenn Ford)*
Debby Marsh (Gloria Grahame)*
Katie Bannion (Jocelyn Brando)
Vince Stone (Lee Marvin)*

### The Big Sleep (USA 1946)
Howard Hawks

Philip Marlowe (Humphrey Bogart)*
Vivian Rutledge (Lauren Bacall)*
Eddie Mars (John Ridgley)
Carmen Sternwood (Martha Vickers)

Remake *The Big Sleep* (1978) (Robert
    Mitchum*, Sarah Miles*)

### The Big Trail (USA 1930)
Raoul Walsh

Breck Coleman (John Wayne)*
Ruth Cameron (Marguerite Churchill)
Gussie (El Brendel)
Zeke, Breck's pal (Tully Marshall)

### Bill And Ted's Excellent
   Adventure (USA 1989)
Stephen Herek

Ted 'Theodore' Logan (Keanu Reeves)*
Bill S Preston (Alex Winter)
Rufus (George Carlin)
Napoleon (Terry Camilleri)

Sequel *Bill And Ted's Bogus Journey*
    (1991)

**Bill Of Divorcement** (USA 1932)
George Cukor

Hilary Fairfield (John Barrymore)*
Sydney Fairfield (Katharine Hepburn)*
Margaret Fairfield (Billie Burke)
Kit Humphrey (David Manners)

Remake *A Bill Of Divorcement* (1940)
(Adolphe Menjou, Maureen O'Hara*)

**Billy Jack** (USA 1971)
T C Frank (Tom Laughlin)

Billy Jack (Tom Laughlin)
Jean Roberts (Delores Taylor)
Sheriff Cole (Clark Howat)
Posner (Bert Freed)

Sequels *The Trial Of Billy Jack* (1974);
*Billy Jack Goes To Washington* (1977)

**Billy Liar** (UK 1963)
John Schlesinger

Billy Fisher (Tom Courtenay)*
Liz (Julie Christie)*
Geoffrey Fisher (Wilfrid Pickles)
Alice Fisher (Mona Washbourne)

**Bird** (USA 1988)
Clint Eastwood

Charlie 'Bird' Parker (Forest Whitaker)*
Chan Parker (Diane Venora)
Red Rodney (Michael Zelniker)
Dizzy (Samuel E Wright)

**Bird On A Wire** (USA 1990)
John Badham

Rick Jarmin (Mel Gibson)*
Marianne Graves (Goldie Hawn)*
Eugene Sorenson (David Carradine)
Albert Diggs (Bill Duke)

**Birdman Of Alcatraz** (USA 1962)
John Frankenheimer

Robert Stroud (Burt Lancaster)*
Harvey Shoemaker (Karl Malden)*
Elizabeth Stroud (Thelma Ritter)
Stella Johnson (Betty Field)

**The Birds** (USA 1963)
Alfred Hitchcock

Mitch Brenner (Rod Taylor)*
Lydia Brenner (Jessica Tandy)*
Annie Hayworth (Suzanne Pleshette)
Melanie Daniels (Tippi Hedren)

**The Bishop's Wife** (USA 1947)
Henry Koster

Dudley (Cary Grant)*
Henry Brougham (David Niven)*
Julia Brougham (Loretta Young)*
Prof Wutheridge (Monty Woolley)

**The Black Hole** (USA 1979)
Gary Nelson

Dr Hans Reinhardt (Maximilian Schell)*
Dr Alex Durant (Anthony Perkins)*
Capt Dan Holland (Robert Forster)
Lt Charles Pizer (Joseph Bottoms)

**Blackmail** (UK 1929)
Alfred Hitchcock

Alice White (Anny Ondra)
Det Frank Webber (John Longden)
Tracy (Donald Calthrop)
The Artist (Cyril Ritchard)

**Black Narcissus** (UK 1947)
Michael Powell and Emeric
Pressburger

Sister Clodagh (Deborah Kerr)*
Dilip Rai (Sabu)
Mr Dean (David Farrar)
Sister Philippa (Flora Robson)*
Kanchi (Jean Simmons)*
Sister Ruth (Kathleen Byron)

**The Blackboard Jungle** (USA 1955)
Richard Brooks

Richard Dadier (Glenn Ford)*
Anne Dadier (Anne Francis)
Joshua Edwards (Richard Kiley)
Jim Murdock (Louis Calhern)
Gregory W Miller (Sidney Poitier)*

**Blade Runner** (USA 1982)
Ridley Scott

Deckard (Harrison Ford)*
Roy Batty (Rutger Hauer)*
Rachael (Sean Young)
Gaff (Edward James Olmos)
Pris (Daryl Hannah)*


**Der Blaue Engel** see **The Blue Angel**


**Blazing Saddles** (USA 1974)
Mel Brooks

Bart (Cleavon Little)
Jim (Gene Wilder)*
Taggart (Slim Pickens)
Olson Johnson (David Huddleston)


**Die Blechtrommel** see **The Tin Drum**


**Blithe Spirit** (UK 1945)
David Lean

Charles Condomine (Rex Harrison)*
Ruth Condomine (Constance
    Cummings)
Elvira (Kay Hammond)
Madame Arcati (Margaret Rutherford)*


**Blonde Venus** (USA 1932)
Josef Von Sternberg

Helen Faraday (Marlene Dietrich)*
Edward Faraday (Herbert Marshall)
Nick Townsend (Cary Grant)*
Johnny Faraday (Dickie Moore)


**Blood Simple** (USA 1984)
Joel Coen

Ray (John Getz)
Abby (Frances McDormand)
Julian Marty (Dan Hedaya)
Private Detective (M Emmet Walsh)


**Blow-Up** (UK 1966)
Michelangelo Antonioni

Thomas (David Hemmings)*
Jane (Vanessa Redgrave)*
Ron (Peter Bowles)
Patricia (Sarah Miles)*


**The Blue Angel** (Germany 1930)
(*Der Blaue Engel*)
Josef Von Sternberg

Prof Immanuel Rath (Emil Jannings)
Lola Frolich (Marlene Dietrich)*
Kiepert (Kurt Gerron)
Guste Kiepert (Rosa Valetti)

Remake *The Blue Angel* (1959) (Curt
    Jurgens, May Britt)


**The Blue Lagoon** (USA 1980)
Randal Kleiser

Emmeline (Brooke Shields)
Richard (Christopher Atkins)
Paddy Button (Leo McKern)
Arthur LeStrange (William Daniels)

Sequel *Return To The Blue Lagoon*
    (1991)
(Earlier version *The Blue Lagoon* (1948)
    (Jean Simmons*, Donald Houston))


**Blue Skies** (USA 1946)
Stuart Heisler

Johnny Adams (Bing Crosby)*
Jed Potter (Fred Astaire)*
Mary O'Hara (Joan Caulfield)
Tony (Billy De Wolfe)


**Blue Velvet** (USA 1986)
David Lynch

Jeffrey Beaumont (Kyle MacLachlan)
Dorothy Vallens (Isabella Rossellini)
Frank Booth (Dennis Hopper)*
Sandy Williams (Laura Dern)

**The Blues Brothers** (USA 1980)
John Landis

Joliet Jake (John Belushi)*
Elwood (Dan Aykroyd)*
Corrections Officer (Frank Oz)
Sister Mary Stigmata (Kathleen
   Freeman)

**Bob & Carol & Ted & Alice**
   (USA 1969)
Paul Mazursky

Carol (Natalie Wood)*
Bob (Robert Culp)
Ted (Elliott Gould)*
Alice (Dyan Cannon)*

**Bob Roberts** (USA 1992)
Tim Robbins

Bob Roberts (Tim Robbins)*
Bugs Raplin (Giancarlo Esposito)
Lukas Hart III (Alan Rickman)*
Chet MacGregor (Ray Wise)
Tawna Titan (Susan Sarandon)*

**Body Heat** (USA 1981)
Lawrence Kasdan

Ned Racine (William Hurt)*
Matty Walker (Kathleen Turner)*
Edmund Walker (Richard Crenna)
Peter Lowenstein (Ted Danson)*
Teddy Lewis (Mickey Rourke)*

**Bonfire Of The Vanities** (USA 1990)
Brian de Palma

Sherman McCoy (Tom Hanks)*
Peter Fallow (Bruce Willis)*
Maria Ruskin (Melanie Griffith)*
Judge White (Morgan Freeman)*

**Bonnie And Clyde** (USA 1967)
Arthur Penn

Clyde Barrow (Warren Beatty)*
Bonnie Parker (Faye Dunaway)*
C W Moss (Michael J Pollard)
Buck Barrow (Gene Hackman)*
Eugene Grizzard (Gene Wilder)*
Blanche Barrow (Estelle Parsons)

**Born On The 4th Of July**
   (USA 1989)
Oliver Stone

Ron Kovic (Tom Cruise)*
Donna (Kyra Sedgwick)
Recruiting Sergeant (Tom Berenger)*
Charlie (Willem Dafoe)*

**Born Yesterday** (USA 1950)
George Cukor

Billie Dawn (Judy Holliday)*
Paul Verrall (William Holden)*
Harry Brock (Broderick Crawford)
Jim Devery (Howard St John)

Remake *Born Yesterday* (1993)
   (Melanie Griffith*, Don Johnson,
   John Goodman)

**Le Boucher** (France/Italy 1969)
Claude Chabrol

Hélène Marcoux (Stéphane Audran)
Popaul Thomas (Jean Yanne)
Angelo (Antonio Passalia)
Léon Hamel (Mario Beccaria)

**Bound For Glory** (USA 1976)
Hal Ashby

Woody Guthrie (David Carradine)
Ozark Bule (Ronny Cox)
Mary Guthrie (Melinda Dillon)
Pauline (Gail Strickland)

**The Bounty** (USA 1984)
Roger Donaldson

Fletcher Christian (Mel Gibson)*
Lt William Bligh (Anthony Hopkins)*
Admiral Hood (Laurence Olivier)*
Capt Greetham (Edward Fox)
Fryer (Daniel Day Lewis)*

**Boys' Town** (USA 1938)
Norman Taurog

Father Edward Flanagan (Spencer
   Tracy)*
Whitey Marsh (Mickey Rooney)*

Dave Morris (Henry Hull)
Dan Farrow (Leslie Fenton)

Sequel *Men Of Boys' Town* (1940)


**Boyz N The Hood** (USA 1991)
John Singleton

Doughboy Baker (Ice Cube)
Tre Styles (Cuba Gooding Jnr)
Ricky Baker (Morris Chestnut)
Furious Styles (Larry Fishburne)


**Bram Stoker's Dracula** (USA 1992)
Francis Coppola

Count Dracula (Gary Oldman)*
Prof Van Helsing (Anthony Hopkins)*
Mina (Winona Ryder)*
Jonathan Harker (Keanu Reeves)*


**Brazil** (USA 1985)
Terry Gilliam

Sam Lowry (Jonathan Pryce)
Tuttle (Robert De Niro)*
Ida Lowry (Katherine Helmond)
Kurtzmann (Ian Holm)
Spoor (Bob Hoskins)*


**Breakfast At Tiffany's** (USA 1961)
Blake Edwards

Holly Golightly (Audrey Hepburn)*
Paul Varjak (George Peppard)*
'2E' (Patricia Neal)*
Mr Yunioshi (Mickey Rooney)*


**Breaking Away** (USA 1979)
Peter Yates

Dave Stohler (Dennis Christopher)
Mike (Dennis Quaid)*
Cyril (Daniel Stern)
Moocher (Jackie Earle Haley)


**Breathless** (France 1959)
(*A Bout De Souffle*)
Jean-Luc Godard

Patricia Franchini (Jean Seberg)
Michel Poiccard/'Laszlo Kovacs' (Jean-
   Paul Belmondo)*
Inspector Vital (Daniel Boulanger)
Antonio Berrutti (Henri-Jacques Huet)
Parvulesco (Jean-Pierre Melville)

Remake *Breathless* (1983) (Valerie
   Kaprisky, Richard Gere*)


**Bride Of Frankenstein** (USA 1935)
James Whale

The Monster (Boris Karloff)*
Henry Frankenstein (Colin Clive)
Elizabeth Frankenstein (Valerie Hobson)
Dr Septimus Pretorius (Ernest Thesiger)
Mary Wollstonecraft Shelley/The Bride
   (Elsa Lanchester)


**The Bridge On The River Kwai**
   (USA 1957)
David Lean

Shears (William Holden)*
Col Nicholson (Alec Guinness)*
Maj Warden (Jack Hawkins)*
Col Saito (Sessue Hayakawa)

Sequel *Return From The River Kwai*
   (1989)


**Brief Encounter** (UK 1945)
David Lean

Laura Jesson (Celia Johnson)*
Dr Alec Harvey (Trevor Howard)*
Fred Jesson (Cyril Raymond)
Albert Godby (Stanley Holloway)

Remake *Brief Encounter* (TV 1975)
   (Sophia Loren*, Richard Burton*)


**Bringing Up Baby** (USA 1938)
Howard Hawks

David Huxley (Cary Grant)*
Susan Vance (Katharine Hepburn)*
Aunt Elizabeth (May Robson)
Maj Horace Applegate (Charlie Ruggles)

**Broadcast News** (USA 1987)
James L Brooks

Tom Grunick (William Hurt)*
Aaron Altman (Albert Brooks)
Jane Craig (Holly Hunter)
Ernie Merriman (Robert Prosky)
Bill Rorich (Jack Nicholson)*

**Broadway Danny Rose** (USA 1984)
Woody Allen

Danny Rose (Woody Allen)*
Tina Vitale (Mia Farrow)*
Lou Canova (Nick Apollo Forte)
Himself (Milton Berle)

**The Broadway Melody** (USA 1929)
Harry Beaumont

Queenie (Anita Page)
Hank (Bessie Love)
Eddie (Charles King)
Uncle Jed (Jed Prouty)

Sequels *Broadway Melody Of 1936*
   (1935); *Broadway Melody Of 1938*
   (1937); *Broadway Melody of 1940*
   (1940)

**Bugsy Malone** (UK 1976)
Alan Parker

Bugsy Malone (Scott Baio)
Blousey (Florrie Dugger)
Tallulah (Jodie Foster)*
Fat Sam (John Cassissi)

**Bull Durham** (USA 1988)
Ron Shelton

Crash Davis (Kevin Costner)*
Annie Savoy (Susan Sarandon)*
Ebby Calvin 'Nuke' LaLoosh (Tim
   Robbins)*
Skip (Trey Wilson)

**Il Buono, Il Brutto, Il Cattivo** see
   **The Good, The Bad And The
   Ugly**

**Bullitt** (USA 1968)
Peter Yates

Frank Bullitt (Steve McQueen)*
Walter Chalmers (Robert Vaughn)
Cathy (Jacqueline Bisset)*
Weissberg (Robert Duvall)*

**Bus Stop** (USA 1956)
Joshua Logan

Cherie (Marilyn Monroe)*
Bo (Don Murray)
Virgil (Arthur O'Connell)
Grace (Betty Field)

**Butch Cassidy And The
   Sundance Kid** (USA 1969)
George Roy Hill

Butch Cassidy (Paul Newman)*
The Sundance Kid (Robert Redford)*
Etta Place (Katharine Ross)
Percy Garris (Strother Martin)

Prequel *Butch And Sundance: The
   Early Days* (1979) (Tom Berenger*,
   William Katt)

**Butterfield 8** (USA 1960)
Daniel Mann

Gloria Wandrous (Elizabeth Taylor)*
Weston Liggett (Laurence Harvey)*
Steven Carpenter (Eddie Fisher)
Emily Liggett (Dina Merrill)

# C

**Cabaret** (USA 1972)
Bob Fosse

Sally Bowles (Liza Minnelli)*
Brian Roberts (Michael York)*
Maximilian Von Heune (Helmut Griem)
Master of Ceremonies (Joel Grey)

**Cactus Flower** (USA 1969)
Gene Saks

Stephanie Dickinson (Ingrid Bergman)*
Julian Winston (Walter Matthau)*
Toni Simmons (Goldie Hawn)*
Harvey Greenfield (Jack Weston)

**La Caduta Degli Dei** see **The Damned**

**The Caine Mutiny** (USA 1954)
Edward Dmytryk

Capt Queeg (Humphrey Bogart)*
Lt Barney Greenwald (Jose Ferrer)
Lt Steve Maryk (Van Johnson)
Lt Tom Keefer (Fred MacMurray)*

Remake *The Caine Mutiny Court Martial*
  (TV 1988) (Brad Davis, Eric Bogosian,
  Jeff Daniels)

**California Suite** (USA 1978)
Herbert Ross

Bill Warren (Alan Alda)*
Sidney Cochran (Michael Caine)*
Dr Willis Panama (Bill Cosby)*
Hannah Warren (Jane Fonda)*
Marvin Michaels (Walter Matthau)*
Millie Michaels (Elaine May)
Dr Chauncy Gump (Richard Pryor)*
Diana Barrie (Maggie Smith)*

**Camelot** (USA 1967)
Joshua Logan

King Arthur (Richard Harris)*
Guenevere (Vanessa Redgrave)*
Lancelot Du Lac (Franco Nero)
Mordred (David Hemmings)*

**Camille** (USA 1936)
George Cukor

Marguerite Gautier (Greta Garbo)*
Armand (Robert Taylor)*
Monsieur Duval (Lionel Barrymore)*
Nichette (Elizabeth Allan)

Remake *Camille* (TV 1984) (Greta
  Scacchi)

**The Cannonball Run** (USA 1981)
Hal Needham

J J McClure (Burt Reynolds)*
Seymour (Roger Moore)*
Pamela (Farrah Fawcett)
Jamie Blake (Dean Martin)*
Fenderbaum (Sammy Davis Jnr)*

Sequel *Cannonball Run II* (1983)

**Cape Fear** (USA 1962)
J Lee Thompson

Sam Bowden (Gregory Peck)*
Max Cady (Robert Mitchum)*
Peggy Bowden (Polly Bergen)
Nancy Bowden (Lori Martin)

**Cape Fear** (USA 1991)
Martin Scorsese

Max Cady (Robert De Niro)*
Sam Bowden (Nick Nolte)*
Leigh Bowden (Jessica Lange)*
Danielle Bowdon (Juliette Lewis)

**Captain Blood** (USA 1935)
Michael Curtiz

Dr Peter Blood (Errol Flynn)*
Arabella Bishop (Olivia De Havilland)*
Capt Levasseur (Basil Rathbone)*
Hagthorpe (Guy Kibbee)

**Captains Courageous** (USA 1937)
Victor Fleming

Manuel (Spencer Tracy)*
Harvey (Freddie Bartholomew)
Disko (Lionel Barrymore)*
Mr Cheyne (Melvyn Douglas)*
Dan (Mickey Rooney)*

Remake *Captains Courageous* (TV 1977)
  (Ricardo Montalban, Jonathan Kahn)

**The Carpetbaggers** (USA 1964)
Edward Dmytryk

Jonas Cord Jr (George Peppard)*
Nevada Smith (Alan Ladd)*
Rina (Carroll Baker)*
Dan Pierce (Bob Cummings)

## *Carrie* (USA 1976)
Brian De Palma

Carrie White (Sissy Spacek)*
Margaret White (Piper Laurie)*
Billy Nolan (John Travolta)*
Sue Snell (Amy Irving)

## *Carry On Sergeant* (UK 1958)
Gerald Thomas

Sgt Grimshawe (William Hartnell)
Horace Strong (Kenneth Connor)
Peter Golightly (Charles Hawtrey)
James Bailey (Kenneth Williams)

Series *Nurse* (1958); *Teacher* (1959);
*Constable* (1960); *Regardless* (1961);
*Cruising* (1962); *Cabby* (1963); *Jack*
(1964); *Spying* (1964); *Cleo* (1964);
*Cowboy* (1965); *Screaming* (1966);
*Follow That Camel* (1967); *Don't Lose
Your Head* (1967); *Doctor* (1968);
*Camping* (1968); *Up The Kyber*
(1969); *Again Doctor* (1969); *Loving*
(1970); *Up The Jungle* (1970); *At
Your Convenience* (1971); *Henry*
(1972); *Abroad* (1972); *Girls* (1973);
*Dick* (1974); *Behind* (1975); *England*
(1976); *Emmannuelle* (1978);
*Columbus* (1992)

## *Casablanca* (USA 1942)
Michael Curtiz

Rick Blaine (Humphrey Bogart)*
Ilsa Lund Laszlo (Ingrid Bergman)*
Victor Laszlo (Paul Henreid)
Capt Louis Renault (Claude Rains)*

## *Cat Ballou* (USA 1965)
Elliot Silverstein

Cat Ballou (Jane Fonda)*
'Kid' Shelleen/Killer Tim Strawn (Lee
Marvin)*
Clay Boone (Michael Callan)
Jackson Two Bears (Tom Nardini)

## *Cat On A Hot Tin Roof* (USA 1958)
Richard Brooks

Maggie Pollitt (Elizabeth Taylor)*
Brick Pollitt (Paul Newman)*
Big Daddy Pollitt (Burl Ives)
Gooper Pollitt (Jack Carson)

## *Catch 22* (USA 1970)
Mike Nichols

Yossarian (Alan Arkin)*
Chaplain Tappman (Anthony Perkins)*
Lt Dobbs (Martin Sheen)*
Milo Minderbinder (Jon Voight)*
Gen Dreedle (Orson Welles)*

## *Cavalcade* (UK 1933)
Frank Lloyd

Jane Marryot (Diana Wynyard)
Robert Marryot (Clive Brook)
Fanny Bridges (Ursula Jeans)
Alfred Bridges (Herbert Mundin)

## *Cera Una Volta E West* see *Once Upon A Time In The West*

## *The Champ* (USA 1931)
King Vidor

Champ (Wallace Beery)*
Dink (Jackie Cooper)
Linda (Irene Rich)
Sponge (Rosco Ates)

Remake *The Champ* (1979) (Jon
Voight*, Ricky Schroder, Faye
Dunaway*)

## *Charade* (USA 1963)
Stanley Donen

Peter Joshua (Cary Grant)*
Reggie Lambert (Audrey Hepburn)*
Hamilton Bartholomew (Walter
Matthau)*
Tex Panthollow (James Coburn)*

**Chariots Of Fire** (UK 1981)
Hugh Hudson

Harold Abrahams (Ben Cross)
Eric Liddell (Ian Charleson)
Andrew Lindsey (Nigel Havers)
Sam Mussabini (Ian Holm)

**Charly** (USA 1968)
Ralph Nelson

Charly Gordon (Cliff Robertson)*
Alice Kinian (Claire Bloom)*
Dr Richard Nemur (Leon Janney)
Dr Anna Straus (Lilia Skala)

**Le Charme Discret De La
   Bourgeoisie see The Discreet
   Charm Of The Bourgeoisie**

**Cheaper By The Dozen** (USA 1950)
Walter Lang

Frank Bunker Gilbreth (Clifton Webb)*
Ann Gilbreth (Jeanne Crain)
Mrs Lillian Gilbreth (Myrna Loy)*
Dr Burton (Edgar Buchanan)

Sequel *Belles On Their Toes* (1952)

**Children Of A Lesser God**
   (USA 1986)
Randa Haines

James (William Hurt)*
Sarah (Marlee Matlin)
Mrs Norman (Piper Laurie)*
Dr Curtis Franklin (Philip Bosco)

**Children Of Paradise see Les
   Enfants Du Paradis**

**The China Syndrome** (USA 1979)
James Bridges

Kimberly Wells (Jane Fonda)*
Jack Godell (Jack Lemmon)*
Richard Adams (Michael Douglas)*
Herman De Young (Scott Brady)

**Chinatown** (USA 1974)
Roman Polanski

J J Gittes (Jack Nicholson)*
Evelyn Mulwray (Faye Dunaway)*
Noah Cross (John Huston)
Escobar (Perry Lopez)

Sequel *The Two Jakes* (1990) (see p91)

**Cimarron** (USA 1931)
Wesley Ruggles

Yancey Cravat (Richard Dix)
Sabra Cravat (Irene Dunne)*
Dixie Lee (Estelle Taylor)
Felice Venable (Nance O'Neil)

Remake *Cimarron* (1960) (Glenn Ford*,
   Maria Schell, Anne Baxter)

**The Cincinatti Kid** (USA 1965)
Norman Jewison

The Cincinnati Kid (Steve McQueen)*
Lancey Howard (Edward G Robinson)*
Melba (Ann-Margret)
Shooter (Karl Malden)*

**Cinderella** (USA 1949)
Wilfred Jackson, Hamilton Luske,
   Clyde Geronomi

Voices of:
Cinderella (Ilene Woods)
Prince Charming (William Phipps)
Stepmother (Eleanor Audley)
Fairy Godmother (Verna Felton)

**Cinema Paradiso** (Italy/France 1989)
Giuseppe Tornatore

Alfredo (Philippe Noiret)*
Salvatore Di Vita (Jacques Perrin)
Salvatore as a Child (Salvatore Cascio)
Salvatore as an Adolescent (Mario
   Leonardi)

**La Ciociara see Two Women**

**The Citadel** (UK 1938)
King Vidor

Andrew Manson (Robert Donat)*
Denny (Ralph Richardson)*
Owen (Emlyn Williams)
Christine Manson (Rosalind Russell)*
Dr Lawford (Rex Harrison)*

**Citizen Kane** (USA 1941)
Orson Welles

Charles Foster Kane (Orson Welles)*
Jedediah Leland (Joseph Cotten)*
Susan Alexander (Dorothy Comingore)
Mr Bernstein (Everett Sloane)
Kane's Mother (Agnes Moorehead)*

**City Lights** (USA 1931)
Charles Chaplin

The Tramp (Charles Chaplin)*
The Blind Girl (Virginia Cherrill)
The Millionaire (Harry Myers)
The Boxer (Hank Mann)

**City Slickers** (USA 1991)
Ron Underwood

Mitch Robbins (Billy Crystal)*
Phil Berquist (Daniel Stern)
Ed Furillo (Bruno Kirby)
Barbara Robbins (Patricia Wettig)
Curly (Jack Palance)*

**Cleopatra** (USA 1963)
Joseph L Mankiewicz

Cleopatra (Elizabeth Taylor)*
Mark Antony (Richard Burton)*
Julius Caesar (Rex Harrison)*
High Priestess (Pamela Brown)

**A Clockwork Orange** (UK 1971)
Stanley Kubrick

Alex (Malcolm McDowell)*
Mr Alexander (Patrick Magee)
Mrs Alexander (Adrienne Corri)
Chief Guard (Michael Bates)

**Close Encounters Of The Third Kind** (USA 1977)
Steven Spielberg

Roy Neary (Richard Dreyfuss)*
Claude Lacombe (François Truffaut)
Ronnie Neary (Teri Garr)
Jillian Guiler (Melinda Dillon)

**Coal Miner's Daughter** (USA 1980)
Michael Apted

Loretta Lynn (Sissy Spacek)*
Doolittle Lynn (Mooney) (Tommy Lee Jones)
Ted Webb (Levon Helm)
Clara Webb (Phyllis Boyens)

**Cocktail** (USA 1988)
Roger Donaldson

Brian Flanagan (Tom Cruise)*
Doug Coughlin (Bryan Brown)
Jordan Mooney (Elisabeth Shue)
Bonnie (Lisa Banes)

**Cocoon** (USA 1985)
Ron Howard

Art Selwyn (Don Ameche)*
Ben Luckett (Wilford Brimley)
Joe Finley (Hume Cronyn)*
Walter (Brian Dennehy)

Sequel *Cocoon: The Return* (1988)

**The Color Of Money** (USA 1986)
Martin Scorsese

Fast Eddie Felson (Paul Newman)*
Vincent (Tom Cruise)*
Carmen (Mary Elizabeth Mastrantonio)
Janelle (Helen Shaver)
Julian (John Turturro)*

**The Color Purple** (USA 1985)
Steven Spielberg

Albert (Danny Glover)*
Celie (Whoopi Goldberg)*
Shug Avery (Margaret Avery)
Sofia (Oprah Winfrey)

**Colors** (USA 1988)
Dennis Hopper

Danny McGavin (Sean Penn)*
Bob Hodges (Robert Duvall)*
Louisa Gomez (Maria Conchita Alonso)
Ron Delaney (Randy Brooks)

**Coming Home** (USA 1978)
Hal Ashby

Sally Hyde (Jane Fonda)*
Luke Martin (Jon Voight)*
Capt Bob Hyde (Bruce Dern)*
Sgt Dink Mobley (Robert Ginty)

**Coming To America** (USA 1988)
John Landis

Prince Akeem/Clarence/Saul/Randy
  Watson (Eddie Murphy)*
Semmi/Morris/Extremely Ugly Girl/Rev
  Brown (Arsenio Hall)
King Jaffe Joffer (James Earl Jones)*
Mortimer Duke (Don Ameche)*
Randolph Duke (Ralph Bellamy)*

**The Conversation** (USA 1974)
Francis Coppola

Harry Caul (Gene Hackman)*
Stan (John Cazale)
Bernie Moran (Allen Garfield)
Mark (Frederic Forrest)
Martin Stett (Harrison Ford)*

**The Cook, The Thief, His Wife
  And Her Lover** (UK 1989)
Peter Greenaway

Richard (Richard Bohringer)
Albert Spica (Michael Gambon)
Georgina (Helen Mirren)*
Michael (Alan Howard)

**Cool Hand Luke** (USA 1967)
Stuart Rosenberg

Luke Jackson (Paul Newman)*
Dragline (George Kennedy)
Society Red (J D Cannon)
The Captain (Strother Martin)

**The Country Girl** (USA 1954)
George Seaton

Frank Elgin (Bing Crosby)*
Georgie Elgin (Grace Kelly)*
Bernie Dodd (William Holden)*
Phil Cook (Anthony Ross)

**Cries And Whispers** (Sweden 1972)
(*Viskingar Och Rop*)
Ingmar Bergman

Agnes (Harriet Andersson)
Karin (Ingrid Thulin)
Maria (Liv Ullmann)*
Doctor (Erland Josephson)

**Crimes And Misdemeanours**
  (USA 1989)
Woody Allen

Lester (Alan Alda)*
Cliff Stern (Woody Allen)*
Miriam Rosenthal (Claire Bloom)*
Halley Reed (Mia Farrow)*
Dolores Paley (Anjelica Huston)*
Judah Rosenthal (Martin Landau)

**'Crocodile' Dundee** (Australia 1986)
Peter Faiman

Mick 'Crocodile' Dundee (Paul Hogan)*
Sue Charlton (Linda Kozlowski)
Walter Reilly (John Meillon)
Neville Bell (David Gulpilil)

Sequel *'Crocodile' Dundee II* (1988)

**Crossfire** (USA 1947)
Edward Dmytryk

Capt Finlay (Robert Young)*
Sgt Peter Keeley (Robert Mitchum)*
Monty Montgomery (Robert Ryan)*
Ginny Tremaine (Gloria Grahame)*

**Cry Freedom** (USA 1987)
Richard Attenborough

Donald Woods (Kevin Kline)*
Steve Biko (Denzel Washington)*
Wendy Woods (Penelope Wilton)
Dr Ramphele (Josette Simon)

**A Cry In The Dark**
  (USA/Australia 1988)
Fred Schepisi

Lindy (Meryl Streep)*
Michael (Sam Neill)*
Aidan 6 Years (Dale Reeves)
Aidan 8 Years (David Hoflin)

**The Crying Game** (UK 1992)
Neil Jordan

Jody (Forest Whitaker)*
Jude (Miranda Richardson)*
Fergus (Stephen Rea)
Dil (Jaye Davidson)

**Cyrano De Bergerac** (France 1990)
Jean-Paul Rappeneau

Cyrano De Bergerac (Gérard
  Depardieu)*
Roxane (Anne Brochet)
Christian De Neuvillette (Vincent Perez)
Count De Guiche (Jacques Weber)


# D

**The Damned** (Germany 1969)
(*La Caduta Degli Dei*)
Luchino Visconti

Friedrich Bruckmann (Dirk Bogarde)*
Baroness Sophie Von Essenbeck (Ingrid
  Thulin)
Aschenbach (Helmut Griem)
Martin Von Essenbeck (Helmut Berger)
Elisabeth Thallman (Charlotte
  Rampling)*

**Dances With Wolves**
  (USA/UK 1990)
Kevin Costner

Lt John J Dunbar (Kevin Costner)*
Stands With A Fist (Mary McDonnell)
Kicking Bird (Graham Greene)
Wind In His Hair (Rodney A Grant)

**Dangerous Liaisons** (USA 1988)
Stephen Frears

Marquise De Merteuil (Glenn Close)*
Vicomte De Valmont (John Malkovich)*
Madame De Tourvel (Michelle Pfeiffer)*
Chevalier Dancey (Keanu Reeves)*
Cecile De Volanges (Uma Thurman)

**Dark Victory** (USA 1939)
Edmund Goulding

Judith Traherne (Bette Davis)*
Dr Frederick Steele (George Brent)
Michael O'Leary (Humphrey Bogart)*
Ann King (Geraldine Fitzgerald)
Alec Hamin (Ronald Reagan)*

Remake *The Stolen Hours* (1963)
  (Susan Hayward*, Michael Craig)

**Darling** (UK 1965)
John Schlesinger

Robert Gold (Dirk Bogarde)*
Miles Brand (Laurence Harvey)*
Diana Scott (Julie Christie)*
Malcolm (Roland Curram)

**David Copperfield** (USA 1935)
George Cukor

David Copperfield (Freddie
  Bartholomew)
Mr Micawber (W C Fields)*
Dan Peggoty (Lionel Barrymore)*
Aunty Betsey (Edna May Oliver)

Remake *David Copperfield* (1970)
  (Robin Phillips, Laurence Olivier*,
  Ralph Richardson*, Richard
  Attenborough*)

**Day For Night** (France 1973)
(*La Nuit Americaine*)
François Truffaut

Ferrand (François Truffaut)
Julie (Jacqueline Bisset)*
Alphonse (Jean-Pierre Léaud)
Severine (Valentina Cortese)

***Daybreak*** see ***Le Jour Se Lève***

***Days Of Heaven*** (USA 1978)
Terrence Malick

Bill (Richard Gere)*
Abby (Brooke Adams)
The Farm Owner (Sam Shepard)
Linda (Linda Mantz)

***Days Of Thunder*** (USA 1990)
Tony Scott

Cole Trickle (Tom Cruise)*
Harry Hogge (Robert Duvall)*
Dr Claire Lewicki (Nicole Kidman)
Tim Daland (Randy Quaid)

***Days Of Wine And Roses***
(USA 1962)
Blake Edwards

Joe (Jack Lemmon)*
Kirsten (Lee Remick)*
Arnesen (Charles Bickford)
Jim Hungerford (Jack Klugman)

***Dead End*** (USA 1937)
William Wyler

Drina (Sylvia Sidney)*
Dave (Joel McCrea)*
'Baby Face' Martin (Humphrey Bogart)*
Kay (Wendy Barrie)

***Dead Poets Society*** (USA 1989)
Peter Weir

John Keating (Robin Williams)*
Neil Perry (Robert Sean Leonard)
Todd Anderson (Ethan Hawke)
Knox Overstreet (Josh Charles)

***Dead Ringers*** (Canada 1988)
David Cronenberg

Beverly Mantle/Elliot Mantle (Jeremy
Irons)*
Claire Niveau (Genevieve Bujold)
Cary (Heidi Von Palleske)
Danuta (Barbara Gordon)

***Death Becomes Her*** (USA 1992)
Robert Zemeckis

Madeline Ashton (Meryl Streep)*
Ernest Menville (Bruce Willis)*
Helen Sharp (Goldie Hawn)*
Lisle Von Rhuman (Isabella Rossellini)

***Death In Venice*** (Italy 1971)
(*Morte E Venezia*)
Luchino Visconti

Gustave Von Aschenbach (Dirk
Bogarde)*
Tadzio (Bjorn Andresen)
Tadzio's Mother (Silvana Mangano)
Frau Von Aschenbach (Marisa Berenson)

***The Deep*** (USA 1977)
Peter Yates

Romer Treece (Robert Shaw)*
Gail Berke (Jacqueline Bisset)*
David Sanders (Nick Nolte)*
Henn Cloche (Louis Gossett)

***The Deer Hunter*** (USA/UK 1978)
Michael Cimino

Michael (Robert De Niro)*
Stan (John Cazale)
Steven (John Savage)
Nick (Christopher Walken)*
Linda (Meryl Streep)*

***The Defiant Ones*** (USA 1958)
Stanley Kramer

John 'Joker' Jackson (Tony Curtis)*
Noah Cullen (Sidney Poitier)*
Sheriff Max Muller (Theodore Bikel)
Big Sam (Lon Chaney)

Remake *The Defiant Ones* (TV 1986)
(Robert Urich, Carl Weathers)

***Deliverance*** (USA 1972)
John Boorman

Ed (Jon Voight)*
Lewis (Burt Reynolds)*
Bobby (Ned Beatty)
Drew (Ronny Cox)

**Diamonds Are Forever** (USA 1971)
Guy Hamilton

James Bond (Sean Connery)*
Tiffany Case (Jill St John)
Blofeld (Charles Gray)
Plenty O'Toole (Lana Wood)

**The Diary Of Anne Frank**
(USA 1959)
George Stevens

Anne Frank (Millie Perkins)
Otto Frank (Joseph Schildkraut)
Mrs Van Daan (Shelley Winters)*
Peter Van Daan (Richard Beymer)

**Dick Tracy** (USA 1990)
Warren Beatty

Dick Tracy (Warren Beatty)*
Breathless Mahoney (Madonna)*
Big Boy Caprice (Al Pacino)*
Mumbles (Dustin Hoffman)*
Spaldoni (James Caan)*
D A Fletcher (Dick Van Dyke)

**Die Hard** (USA 1988)
John McTiernan

John McClane (Bruce Willis)*
Holly Gennaro McClane (Bonnie
Bedelia)
Hans Gruber (Alan Rickman)*
Sgt Al Powell (Reginald Veljohnson)

Sequel *Die Hard 2* (1990)

**The Dirty Dozen** (USA 1967)
Robert Aldrich

Maj Reisman (Lee Marvin)*
Col Everett Dasher-Breed (Robert
Ryan)*
Victor Franco (John Cassavetes)*
Joseph Wladislaw (Charles Bronson)*
Vernon Pinkley (Donald Sutherland)*

Sequels *The Dirty Dozen: The Next
Mission* (TV 1985); *The Dirty Dozen:
The Deadly Mission* (TV 1987); *The
Dirty Dozen: The Fatal Mission* (TV
1988)

**Dirty Harry** (USA 1971)
Don Siegel

Harry Callahan (Clint Eastwood)*
Lt Bressler (Harry Guardino)
Chico (Reni Santoni)
The Mayor (John Vernon)
Killer (Andy Robinson)
Sequels *Magnum Force* (1973); *The
Enforcer* (1976); *Sudden Impact*
(1983); *The Dead Pool* (1988)

**The Discreet Charm Of The
Bourgeoisie** (France/Italy 1972)
(*Le Charme Discret De La
Bourgeoisie*)
Luis Bunuel

Ambassador (Fernando Rey)
Mrs Thevenot (Delphine Seyrig)
Mrs Senechal (Stéphane Audran)
Florence (Bulle Ogier)

**Distant Voices, Still Lives**
(UK 1988)
Terence Davies

Mother (Freda Dowie)
Father (Peter Postlethwaite)
Eileen (Angela Walsh)
Tony (Dean Williams)

**Diva** (France 1981)
Jean-Jacques Beineix

Cynthia Hawkins (Wilhelmenia Wiggins
Fernandez)
Jules (Frederic Andrei)
Gorodish (Richard Bohringer)
Alba (Thuy An Luu)

**Do The Right Thing** (USA 1989)
Spike Lee

Sal (Danny Aiello)
Da Mayor (Ossie Davis)
Mother Sister (Ruby Dee)
Mookie (Spike Lee)
Pino (John Turturro)*

**Dr Jekyll And Mr Hyde** (USA 1932)
Rouben Mamoulian

Dr Henry Jekyll/Mr Hyde (Fredric
  March)*
Ivy Parsons (Miriam Hopkins)*
Muriel Carew (Rose Hobart)
Dr Lanyan (Holmes Herbert)

Remake *Dr Jekyll And Mr Hyde* (1941)
  (Spencer Tracy*)

**Dr No** (UK 1962)
Terence Young

James Bond (Sean Connery)*
Honey (Ursula Andress)
Dr No (Joseph Wiseman)
Felix Leiter (Jack Lord)

**Dr Strangelove: Or How I Learned
  To Stop Worrying And Love
  The Bomb** (USA 1964)
Stanley Kubrick

Group Capt Lionel Mandrake/President
  Merkin Mufftey/Dr Strangelove (Peter
  Sellers)*
Gen 'Buck' Turgidson (George C Scott)*
Gen Jack D Ripper (Sterling Hayden)*
Col 'Bat' Guano (Keenan Wynn)

**Doctor Zhivago** (USA 1965)
David Lean

Tonya (Geraldine Chaplin)
Lara (Julie Christie)*
Pasah/Strelnikoff (Tom Courtenay)*
Yevgraf (Alec Guinness)*
Alexander (Ralph Richardson)*
Yuri (Omar Sharif)*
Komarovsky (Rod Steiger)*

**Dodsworth** (USA 1936)
William Wyler

Sam Dodsworth (Walter Huston)*
Fran Dodsworth (Ruth Chatterton)
Edith Cortright (Mary Astor)*
Arnold Iselin (Paul Lukas)
Clyde Lockert (David Niven)*

**Dog Day Afternoon** (USA 1975)
Sidney Lumet

Sonny (Al Pacino)*
Sal (John Cazale)
Moretti (Charles Durning)
Leon (Chris Sarandon)

**La Dolce Vita** (Italy/France 1960)
(*The Sweet Life*)
Federico Fellini

Marcello Rubini (Marcello Mastroianni)*
Emma (Yvonne Furneaux)
Maddalena (Anouk Aimée)
Sylvia Rank (Anita Ekberg)

**Double Indemnity** (USA 1944)
Billy Wilder

Walter Neff (Fred MacMurray)*
Phyllis Dietrichson (Barbara Stanwyck)*
Barton Keyes (Edward G Robinson)*
Mr Jackson (Porter Hall)

Remake *Double Indemnity* (TV 1973)
  (Richard Crenna, Samantha Eggar,
  Lee J Cobb)

**Dracula** (USA 1931)
Tod Browning

Count Dracula (Bela Lugosi)*
John Harker (David Manners)
Nina Seward (Helen Chandler)
Dr Van Helsing (Edward Van Sloan)
Redfield (Dwight Frye)

Sequel *Dracula's Daughter* (1936)

**Dracula** (UK 1958)
Terence Fisher

Van Hesling (Peter Cushing)*
Count Dracula (Christopher Lee)*
Mina Holmwood (Melissa Stribling)
Arthur Holmwood (Michael Gough)

Sequels *Dracula — Prince Of Darkness*
  (1965); *Dracula Has Risen From The
  Grave* (1968); *Taste The Blood Of
  Dracula* (1970); *Dracula AD 1972* (1972);
  *The Satanic Rites Of Dracula* (1973)

## The Draughtsman's Contract
(UK 1982)
Peter Greenaway

Mr Neville (Anthony Higgins)
Mrs Herbert (Janet Suzman)
Mrs Talmann (Anne Louise Lambert)
Mr Talmann (Hugh Fraser)

## The Dresser (UK 1983)
Peter Yates

Sir (Albert Finney)*
Norman (Tom Courtenay)*
Oxenby (Edward Fox)
Her Ladyship (Zena Walker)

## Driving Miss Daisy (USA 1989)
Bruce Beresford

Hoke Colburn (Morgan Freeman)*
Daisy Werthan (Jessica Tandy)*
Boolie Werthan (Dan Aykroyd)*
Florine Werthan (Patti LuPone)

## Duck Soup (USA 1933)
Leo McCarey

Rufus T Firefly (Groucho Marx)*
Chicolini (Chico Marx)*
Pinkie (Harpo Marx)*
Bob Rolland (Zeppo Marx)*
Mrs Teasdale (Margaret Dumont)

## Duel In The Sun (USA 1946)
King Vidor

Pearl Chavez (Jennifer Jones)*
Lewt McCanles (Gregory Peck)*
Jesse McCanles (Joseph Cotten)*
Senator McCanles (Lionel Barrymore)*
Mrs McCanles (Lillian Gish)*

# E

## ET—The Extra-Terrestrial
(USA 1982)
Steven Spielberg

Mary (Dee Wallace)
Elliott (Henry Thomas)
'Keys' (Peter Coyote)
Gertie (Drew Barrymore)

## Earthquake (USA 1974)
Mark Robson

Graff (Charlton Heston)*
Remy Graff (Ava Gardner)*
Patrolman Slade (George Kennedy)
Royce (Lorne Greene)

## East Of Eden (USA 1955)
Elia Kazan

Caleb Trask (James Dean)*
Abra (Julie Harris)
Adam Trask (Raymond Massey)*
Kate Trask (Jo Van Fleet)

## Easter Parade (USA 1948)
Charles Walters

Hannah Brown (Judy Garland)*
Don Hewes (Fred Astaire)*
Jonathan Harrow III (Peter Lawford)
Nadine Hale (Ann Miller)

## Easy Rider (USA 1969)
Dennis Hopper

Wyatt (Peter Fonda)*
Billy (Dennis Hopper)*
Jesus (Antonio Mendoza)
George Hanson (Jack Nicholson)*

## Educating Rita (UK 1983)
Lewis Gilbert

Dr Frank Bryant (Michael Caine)*
Rita (Julie Walters)*
Brian (Michael Williams)
Trish (Maureen Lipman)

## Edward II (UK 1991)
Derek Jarman

Edward II (Steven Waddington)
Lightborn (Kevin Collins)
Piers Gaveston (Andrew Tiernan)
Isabella (Tilda Swinton)

**Edward Scissorhands** (USA 1990)
Tim Burton

Edward Scissorhands (Johnny Depp)*
Kim Boggs (Winona Ryder)*
Peg Boggs (Dianne Wiest)
The Inventor (Vincent Price)*
Bill Boggs (Alan Arkin)*

**8½** (Italy 1963)
(*Otto E Mezzo* )
Federico Fellini

Guido Anselmi (Marcello Mastroianni)*
Claudia (Claudia Cardinale)
Luisa Anselmi (Anouk Aimée)
Carla (Sandra Milo)

**El Cid** (USA 1961)
Anthony Mann

Rodrigo Diaz De Bivar/El Cid (Charlton
  Heston)*
Chimene (Sophia Loren)*
King Alfonso (John Fraeor)
Count Ordonez (Raf Vallone)

**El Dorado** (USA 1967)
Howard Hawks

Cole Thornton (John Wayne)*
J P Harrah (Robert Mitchum)*
Alan Bourdillon Traherne (James Caan)*
Maudie (Charlene Holt)

**The Electric Horseman** (USA 1979)
Sydney Pollack

Sonny Steele (Robert Redford)*
Hallie Martin (Jane Fonda)*
Charlotta (Valerine Perrine)
Wendell (Willie Nelson)

**The Elephant Man** (UK 1980)
David Lynch

Frederick Treves (Anthony Hopkins)*
John Merrick (John Hurt)*
Mrs Kendal (Anne Bancroft)*
Carr Gomm (John Gielgud)*
Mothershead (Wendy Hiller)*

**Elmer Gantry** (USA 1960)
Richard Brooks

Elmer Gantry (Burt Lancaster)*
Sister Sharon Falconer (Jean
  Simmons)*
Jim Lefferts (Arthur Kennedy)*
Lulu Bains (Shirley Jones)

**The Emigrants** (Sweden 1971)
(*Utvandrarna*)
Jan Troell

Karl Oskar (Max Von Sydow)*
Kristina (Liv Ullmann)*
Robert (Eddie Axberg)
Nils (Svenolof Bern)

Sequel *The New Land (Nybyggarna)*
(1972)

**Empire Of The Sun** (USA 1987)
Steven Spielberg

Jim (Christian Bale)
Basie (John Malkovich)*
Mrs Victor (Miranda Richardson)*
Dr Rawlins (Nigel Havers)

**The Empire Strikes Back**
  (USA 1980)
Irvin Kershner

Luke Skywalker (Mark Hamill)
Han Solo (Harrison Ford)*
Princess Leia (Carrie Fisher)
Lando Calrissian (Billy Dee Williams)

Sequel *Return of the Jedi* (1983) (see
  p72)
Sequel to *Star Wars* (1977) (see p82)

**Enemies, A Love Story** (USA 1989)
Paul Mazursky

Herman Broder (Ron Silver)
Tamara (Anjelica Huston)*
Masha (Lena Olin)
Yadwiga (Margaret Sophie Stein)

**Les Enfants Du Paradis**
   (France 1944)
(*Children Of Paradise*)
Marcel Carné

Garrance (Arletty)*
Baptiste Debureau (Jean-Louis Barrault)
Frederick Lemaitre (Pierre Brasseur)
Lacenaire (Marcel Herrand)

**The Entertainer** (UK 1960)
Tony Richardson

Archie Rice (Laurence Olivier)*
Phoebe Rice (Brenda De Banzie)
Billy (Roger Livesey)
Jean (Joan Plowright)
Frank (Alan Bates)*

Remake *The Entertainer* (TV 1975)
   (Jack Lemmon*, Ray Bolger)

**Et Dieu Créa La Femme**
   (France 1956)
(*And God Created Woman*)
Roger Vadim

Juliette (Brigitte Bardot)*
Eric Carradine (Curt Jurgens)
Michel Tardieu (Jean-Louis Trintignant)
Antoine Tardieu (Christian Marquand)

Remake *And God Created Woman*
   (1987) (Rebecca De Mornay*)

**Every Which Way But Loose**
   (USA 1978)
James Fargo

Philo Beddoe (Clint Eastwood)*
Lynn Halsey-Taylor (Sondra Locke)
Orville (Geoffrey Lewis)
Echo (Beverly D'Angelo)
Ma (Ruth Gordon)

Sequel *Any Which Way But Loose* (1980)

**The Evil Dead** (USA 1982)
Samuel M Raimi

Ash (Bruce Campbell)
Cheryl (Ellen Sandweiss)

Linda (Betsy Baker)
Scott (Hal Delrich)

Sequels *Evil Dead II: Dead By Dawn*
   (1987); *Army Of Darkness: The
   Medieval Dead* (1992)

**Excalibur** (USA 1981)
John Boorman

King Arthur (Nigel Terry)
Merlin (Nicol Williamson)
Morgana (Helen Mirren)*
Lancelot (Nicholas Clay)
Guenevere (Cherie Lunghi)

**Exodus** (USA 1960)
Otto Preminger

Ari Ben Canaan (Paul Newman)*
Kitty Fremont (Eva Marie Saint)
Gen Sutherland (Ralph Richardson)*
Maj Caldwell (Peter Lawford)

**The Exorcist** (USA 1973)
Wiliam Friedkin

Mrs MacNeil (Ellen Burstyn)*
Father Merrin (Max Von Sydow)*
Lieutenant Kinderman (Lee J Cobb)
Regan McNeil (Linda Blair)

Sequels *Exorcist II: The Heretic* (1977);
   *Exorcist III: Legion* (1990)

# F

**The Fabulous Baker Boys**
   (USA 1989)
Steve Kloves

Jack Baker (Jeff Bridges)*
Susie Diamond (Michelle Pfeiffer)*
Frank Baker (Beau Bridges)*
Nina (Ellie Raab)

**Fanny And Alexander**
   (Sweden 1982)
(*Fanny Och Alexander*)
Ingmar Bergman

Fanny Ekdahl (Pernilla Allwin)
Alexander Ekdahl (Bertil Guve)

Helena Ekdahl (Gunn Wallgren)
Oscar Ekdahl (Allan Edwall)

***Fanny Och Alexander*** see ***Fanny And Alexander***

***Fantasia*** (USA 1940)
Samuel Armstrong, James Algar, Bill Roberts, Paul Satterfield, Hamilton Luske, Jim Handley, Ford Beebe, T Hee (Walt Disney), Norman Ferguson, Wilfred Jackson

Himself (Deems Taylor)
Themselves (Leopold Stokowski and the Philadelphia Symphony Orchestra)
Sorcerer's Apprentice (Mickey Mouse)

***A Farewell To Arms*** (USA 1932)
Frank Borzage

Catherine Barkley (Helen Hayes)*
Lieutenant Fredric Henry (Gary Cooper)*
Major Rinaldi (Adolphe Menjou)
Helen Ferguson (Mary Philips)

Remake *A Farewell To Arms* (1957) (Jennifer Jones*, Rock Hudson*)

***Fatal Attraction*** (USA 1987)
Adrian Lyne

Dan Gallagher (Michael Douglas)*
Alex Forrest (Glenn Close)*
Beth Gallagher (Anne Archer)
Ellen Gallagher (Ellen Hamilton Latzen)

***Father Of The Bride*** (USA 1950)
Vincente Minnelli

Stanley T Banks (Spencer Tracy)*
Ellie Banks (Joan Bennett)
Kay Banks (Elizabeth Taylor)*
Buckley Dunstan (Don Taylor)

Sequel *Father's Little Dividend* (1951)
Remake *Father Of The Bride* (1991) (Steve Martin*, Diane Keaton*, Kimberly Williams)

***A Few Good Men*** (USA 1992)
Rob Reiner

Col Jessep (Jack Nicholson)*
Daniel Kaffee (Tom Cruise)*
Joanne Galloway (Demi Moore)*
Lt Kendrick (Kiefer Sutherland)

***Fiddler On The Roof*** (USA 1971)
Norman Jewison

Tevye (Chaim Topol)
Golde (Norma Crane)
Motel (Leonard Frey)
Yente (Molly Picon)

***Field Of Dreams*** (USA 1989)
Phil Alden Robinson

Ray Kinsella (Kevin Costner)*
Annie Kinsella (Amy Madigan)
Shoeless Joe Jackson (Ray Liotta)*
Terence Mann (James Earl Jones)*
Dr 'Moonlight' Graham (Burt Lancaster)*

***A Fish Called Wanda*** (UK 1988)
Charles Crichton

Archie Leach (John Cleese)*
Wanda Gershwitz (Jamie Lee Curtis)*
Otto West (Kevin Kline)*
Ken Pile (Michael Palin)*

***A Fistful Of Dollars*** (Italy/West Germany/France 1964)
(*Per Un Pugno Di Dollari*)
Sergio Leone

The Man With No Name (Clint Eastwood)*
Marisol (Marianne Koch)
Ramon Rojo (Gian Maria Volonte)
John Baxter (Wolfgang Lukschy)

Sequels *For A Few Dollars More* (1965) (see p30); *The Good, The Bad And The Ugly* (1966) (see p35)

***Five Easy Pieces*** (USA 1970)
Bob Rafelson

Robert Eroica Dupea (Jack Nicholson)*
Rayette Dipesto (Karen Black)
Partita Dupea (Lois Smith)
Catherine Van Ost (Susan Anspach)

**Five Star Final** (USA 1931)
Mervyn Le Roy

Randall (Edward G Robinson)*
Jenny Townsend (Marian Marsh)
Michael Townsend (H B Warner)
Rev T Vernon Isopod (Boris Karloff)*

Remake *Two Against The World* (1936)
(Humphrey Bogart*, Beverly Roberts)

**Flashdance** (USA 1983)
Adrian Lyne

Alex Owens (Jennifer Beals)
Nick Hurley (Michael Nouri)
Hanna Long (Lilia Skala)
Jeanie Szabo (Sunny Johnson)

**The Fly** (USA 1986)
David Cronenberg

Seth Brundle (Jeff Goldblum)*
Veronica Quaife (Geena Davis)*
Stathis Borans (John Getz)
Tawny (Joy Boushel)

Sequel *The Fly II* (1989)

**Footlight Parade** (USA 1933)
Roy Del Ruth

Chester Kent (James Cagney)*
Nan Prescott (Joan Blondell)*
Bea Thorn (Ruby Keeler)*
Scotty Blair (Dick Powell)*

**Footloose** (USA 1984)
Herbert Ross

Ren (Kevin Bacon)
Ariel (Lori Singer)
Rev Shaw Moore (John Lithgow)
Vi Moore (Dianne Wiest)

**For A Few Dollars More**
(Italy/France/West Germany 1965)
(*Per Qualche Dollari In Pui*)
Sergio Leone

The Man With No Name (Clint
Eastwood)*

Col Douglas Mortimer (Lee Van Cleef)
Indio (Gian Maria Volonte)
Hunchback (Klaus Kinski)

Sequel *The Good, The Bad And The
Ugly* (1966) (see p35)
Sequel to *A Fistful Of Dollars* (1964)
(see p29)

**For Whom the Bell Tolls**
(USA 1943)
Sam Wood

Robert Jordan (Gary Cooper)*
Maria (Ingrid Bergman)*
Pablo (Akim Tamiroff)
Agustin (Arturo De Cordova)

**For Your Eyes Only** (UK 1981)
John Glen

James Bond (Roger Moore)*
Melina (Carole Bouquet)
Columbo (Topol)
Bibi (Lynn-Holly Johnson)

**Forbidden Games** see **Les Jeux
Interdits**

**Foreign Correspondent**
(USA 1940)
Alfred Hitchcock

Johnny Jones/Huntley Haverstock (Joel
McCrea)*
Carol Fisher (Laraine Day)
Stephen Fisher (Herbert Marshall)
Scott Ffolliott (George Sanders)*

**Forever Amber** (USA 1947)
Otto Preminger

Amber St Clair (Linda Darnell)*
Bruce Carlton (Cornel Wilde)*
Lord Almsbury (Richard Greene)
King Charles II (George Sanders)*

**Fort Apache** (USA 1948)
John Ford

Capt Kirby York (John Wayne)*
Lt Colonel Owen Thursday (Henry
Fonda)*
Philadelphia Thursday (Shirley Temple)*
Sgt Major Michael O'Rourke (Ward
Bond)

**48 Hrs** (USA 1982)
Walter Hill

Jack Cates (Nick Nolte)*
Reggie Hammond (Eddie Murphy)*
Elaine (Annette O'Toole)
Haden (Frank McRae)

Sequel *Another 48 Hrs* (1990)

**49th Parallel** (UK 1941)
Michael Powell

Philip Armstrong Scott (Leslie Howard)*
Johnnie, The Trapper (Laurence
Olivier)*
Andy Brock (Raymond Massey)*
Peter (Anton Walbrook)

**42nd Street** (USA 1933)
Lloyd Bacon

Julian March (Warner Baxter)
Dorothy Brock (Bebe Daniels)
Peggy Sawyer (Ruby Keeler)*
Billy Lawler (Dick Powell)*
Ann Lowell (Ginger Rogers)*

**Foul Play** (USA 1978)
Colin Higgins

Gloria Mundy (Goldie Hawn)*
Tony Carlson (Chevy Chase)*
Hennessey (Burgess Meredith)*
Gerda (Rachel Roberts)*
Stanley Tibbets (Dudley Moore)*

**The Four Hundred Blows** see **Les
Quatres Cents Coups**

**The Fox** (USA 1968)
Mark Rydell

Jill (Sandy Dennis)
Paul (Keir Dullea)
Ellen March (Anne Heywood)
Realtor (Glyn Morris)

**Frances** (USA 1982)
Graeme Clifford

Frances Farmer (Jessica Lange)*
Harry York (Sam Shepard)*
Lillian Farmer (Kim Stanley)*
Ernest Farmer (Bart Burns)

**Frankenstein** (USA 1931)
James Whale

Frankenstein (Colin Clive)*
Elizabeth (Mae Clarke)
Victor (John Boles)
The Monster (Boris Karloff)*

Sequels *Bride Of Frankenstein* (1935)
(see p15); *Son Of Frankenstein*
(1939); *The Ghost Of Frankenstein*
(1942); *Frankenstein Meets The Wolf
Man* (1943); *House Of Frankenstein*
(1944); *House Of Dracula* (1945);
*Abbott And Costello Meet
Frankenstein* (1948)

**Frantic** (USA 1988)
Roman Polanski

Richard Walker (Harrison Ford)*
Sondra Walker (Betty Buckley)
Michelle (Emmanuelle Seigner)
Taxi Driver (Djiby Soumare)

**The French Connection**
(USA 1971)
William Friedkin

Jimmy 'Popeye' Doyle (Gene
Hackman)*
Alain Charnier (Fernando Rey)
Buddy Russo (Roy Scheider)*
Sal Boca (Tony LoBianco)

Sequel *The French Connection II* (1975)

**The French Lieutenant's Woman**
(UK 1981)
Karel Reisz

Sarah/Anna (Meryl Streep)*
Charles/Mike (Jeremy Irons)*
Sam (Hilton McRae)
Mary (Emily Morgan)

**Friendly Persuasion** (USA 1956)
William Wyler

Jess Birdwell (Gary Cooper)*
Eliza Birdwell (Dorothy McGuire)*
Josh Birdwell (Anthony Perkins)*
Widow Hudspeth (Marjorie Main)

**From Here To Eternity** (USA 1953)
Fred Zinnemann

Sgt Milton Warden (Burt Lancaster)*
Pvt Robert E Lee Prewitt (Montgomery
   Clift)*
Angelo Maggio (Frank Sinatra)*
Karen Holmes (Deborah Kerr)*
Alma Lorene (Donna Reed)*
Sgt 'Fatso' Judson (Ernest Borgnine)*

**From Russia With Love** (UK 1963)
Terence Young

James Bond (Sean Connery)*
Tatiana Romanova (Daniela Bianchi)
Kerim Bey (Pedro Armendariz)
Rosa Klebb (Lotte Lenya)
Red Grant (Robert Shaw)*

**From The Terrace** (USA 1960)
Mark Robson

Alfred Eaton (Paul Newman)*
Mary St John (Joanne Woodward)*
Natalie (Ina Balin)
Martha Eaton (Myrna Loy)*

**The Front Page** (USA 1931)
Lewis Milestone

Walter Burns (Adolphe Menjou)
Hildy Johnson (Pat O'Brien)
Peggy (Mary Brian)
Bensinger (Edward Everett Horton)

Remakes *His Girl Friday* (1940) (see
   p39) (Cary Grant*, Rosalind Russell*);
   *The Front Page* (1974) (Walter
   Matthau*, Jack Lemmon*); *Switching
   Channels* (1988) (Burt Reynolds*,
   Kathleen Turner*)

**Full Metal Jacket** (USA 1987)
Stanley Kubrick

Pvt Joker (Matthew Modine)*
Animal Mother (Adam Baldwin)
Pvt Pyle (Vincent D'Onofrio)
Gunnery Sgt Hartman (Lee Ermey)

**Funny Face** (USA 1956)
Stanley Donen

Jo Stockton (Audrey Hepburn)*
Dick Avery (Fred Astaire)*
Maggie Prescott (Kay Thompson)
Prof Emile Fiostre (Michel Auclair)

**Funny Girl** (USA 1968)
William Wyler

Fanny Brice (Barbra Streisand)*
Nick Arnstein (Omar Sharif)*
Rose Brice (Kay Medford)
Georgia James (Anne Francis)

Sequel *Funny Lady* (1975)

# G

**Gallipoli** (Australia 1980)
Peter Weir

Archy (Mark Lee)
Jack (Bill Kerr)
Frank Dunne (Mel Gibson)*
Wallace Hamilton (Ron Graham)

**Gandhi** (UK 1982)
Richard Attenborough

Mahatma Gandhi (Ben Kingsley)*
Margaret Bourke-White (Candice
   Bergen)*
Gen Dyer (Edward Fox)
Lord Irwin (John Gielgud)*

Judge Broomfield (Trevor Howard)*
The Viceroy (John Mills)*
Walker (Martin Sheen)*

## *Gaslight* (USA 1944)
George Cukor

Gregory Anton (Charles Boyer)*
Paula Alquist (Ingrid Bergman)*
Brian Cameron (Joseph Cotten)*
Miss Thwaites (Dame May Whitty)
Nancy Oliver (Angela Lansbury)*

## *Il Gattopardo* see *The Leopard*

## *The Gay Divorce* (USA 1934)
Mark Sandrich

Guy Holden (Fred Astaire)*
Mimi Glossop (Ginger Rogers)*
Aunt Hortense Ditherwell (Alice Brady)
Egbert Fitzgerald (Edward Everett
  Horton)

## *Genevieve* (UK 1953)
Henry Cornelius

Alan McKim (John Gregson)
Wendy McKim (Dinah Sheridan)
Ambrose Claverhouse (Kenneth More)*
Rosalind Peters (Kay Kendall)*

## *Gentleman's Agreement*
  (USA 1947)
Elia Kazan

Philip Green (Gregory Peck)*
Kathy (Dorothy McGuire)*
Dave (John Garfield)*
Anne (Celeste Holm)*

## *Gentlemen Prefer Blondes*
  (USA 1953)
Howard Hawks

Lorelei (Marilyn Monroe)*
Dorothy (Jane Russell)*
Sir Francis Beekman (Charles Coburn)
Malone (Elliott Reid)

Sequel *Gentlemen Marry Brunettes*
  (1955)

## *Georgy Girl* (UK 1966)
Silvio Narrizano

Georgy (Lynn Redgrave)*
James Leamington (James Mason)*
Jos (Alan Bates)*
Meredith (Charlotte Rampling)*

## *Get Carter* (UK 1971)
Mike Hodges

Jack Carter (Michael Caine)*
Eric Paice (Ian Hendry)
Anna Fletcher (Britt Ekland)*
Cyril Kinnear (John Osborne)

## *Ghost* (USA 1990)
Jerry Zucker

Sam Wheat (Patrick Swayze)*
Molly Jensen (Demi Moore)*
Carl Bruner (Tony Goldwyn)
Oda Mae Brown (Whoopi Goldberg)*

## *Ghostbusters* (USA 1984)
Ivan Reitman

Dr Peter Venkman (Bill Murray)*
Dr Raymond Stantz (Dan Aykroyd)*
Dana Barrett (Sigourney Weaver)*
Dr Egon Spengler (Harold Ramis)

Sequel *Ghostbusters II* (1989)

## *Giant* (USA 1956)
George Stevens

Lesley Benedict (Elizabeth Taylor)*
Bick Benedict (Rock Hudson)*
Jett Rink (James Dean)*
Vashti Snythe (Jane Withers)

## *Gigi* (USA 1958)
Vincente Minnelli

Gigi (Leslie Caron)*
Honoré Lachaille (Maurice Chevalier)*
Gaston Lachaille (Louis Jourdan)*
Madame Alvarez (Hermione Gingold)

**Gilda** (USA 1946)
Charles Vidor

Gilda Mundson (Rita Hayworth)*
Johnny Farrell (Glenn Ford)*
Ballin Mundson (George Macready)
Obregon (Joseph Calleia)

**The Glenn Miller Story** (USA 1953)
Anthony Mann

Glenn Miller (James Stewart)*
Helen Miller (June Allyson)*
Don Haynes (Charles Drake)
Si Schribman (George Tobias)

**Glory** (USA 1989)
Edward Zwick

Col Robert Gould Shaw (Matthew
  Broderick)*
Pvt Trip (Denzel Washington)*
Maj Cabot Forbes (Cary Elwes)
Sgt Major John Rawlins (Morgan
  Freeman)*

**The Go-Between** (UK 1971)
Joseph Losey

Marian, Lady Trimingham (Julie
  Christie)*
Ted Burgess (Alan Bates)*
'Leo' Colsten (Dominic Guard)
Mrs Maudsley (Margaret Leighton)*

**The Godfather** (USA 1972)
Francis Coppola

Don Vito Corleone (Marlon Brando)*
Michael Corleone (Al Pacino)*
Sonny Corleone (James Caan)*
Clemenza (Richard Castellano)
Tom Hagen (Robert Duvall)*

**The Godfather Part II** (USA 1974)
Francis Coppola

Michael Corleone (Al Pacino)*
Tom Hagen (Robert Duvall)*
Kay Corleone (Diane Keaton)*
Vito Corleone (Robert De Niro)*

**The Godfather Part III** (USA 1990)
Francis Coppola

Michael Corleone (Al Pacino)*
Kay Adams (Diane Keaton)*
Connie Corleone Rizzi (Talia Shire)
Vincent Mancini (Andy Garcia)*

**Going My Way** (USA 1944)
Leo McCarey

Father Chuck O'Malley (Bing Crosby)*
Genevieve Linden (Rise Stevens)
Father Fitzgibbon (Barry Fitzgerald)
Father Timothy O'Dowd (Frank
  McHugh)

Sequel *The Bells Of St Mary's* (1945)
  (see p10)

**Gold Diggers Of 1933** (USA 1933)
Mervyn LeRoy

J Lawrence Bradford (Warren William)
Carol King (Joan Blondell)*
Trixie Lorraine (Aline MacMahon)
Polly Parker (Ruby Keeler)*
Brad Roberts/Robert Treat Bradford
  (Dick Powell)*
Fay Fortune (Ginger Rogers)*

Sequels *Gold Diggers Of 1935* (1935);
  *Gold Diggers Of 1937* (1936)

**Goldfinger** (UK 1964)
Guy Hamilton

James Bond (Sean Connery)*
Pussy Galore (Honor Blackman)
Auric Goldfinger (Gert Frobe)
Jill Masterson (Shirley Eaton)

**Gone With The Wind** (USA 1939)
Victor Fleming, George Cukor, Sam
  Wood

Rhett Butler (Clark Gable)*
Scarlett O'Hara (Vivien Leigh)*
Ashley Wilkes (Leslie Howard)*
Melanie Hamilton (Olivia De Havilland)*

**The Good Earth** (USA 1937)
Sidney Franklin

Wang Lung (Paul Muni)*
O-Lan (Luise Rainer)*
Uncle (Walter Connolly)
Lotus (Tilly Losch)

**Good Morning, Vietnam** (USA 1987)
Barry Levinson

Adrian Cronauer (Robin Williams)*
Edward Garlick (Forest Whitaker)*
Tuan (Tung Thanh Tran)
Trinh (Chintara Sukapatana)

**The Good, The Bad And The Ugly**
   (Italy/France/West Germany 1966)
(*Il Buono, Il Brutto E Il Cattivo*)
Sergio Leone

Joe (Clint Eastwood)*
Tuco (Eli Wallach)*
Setenza (Lee Van Cleef)

Sequel to *A Fistful Of Dollars* (1964)
   (see p29); *For A Few Dollars More*
   (1965) (see p30)

**Goodbye Columbus** (USA 1969)
Larry Peerce

Neil Klugman (Richard Benjamin)
Brenda Patimkin (Ali McGraw)*
Mr Patimkin (Jack Klugman)
Mrs Patimkin (Nan Martin)

**The Goodbye Girl** (USA 1977)
Herbert Ross

Elliott Garfield (Richard Dreyfuss)*
Paula McFadden (Marsha Mason)
Lucy McFadden (Quinn Cummings)
Mark Morgenweiss (Paul Benedict)

**Goodbye Mr Chips** (USA 1939)
Sam Wood

Charles Chipping (Robert Donat)*
Katherine Ellis (Greer Garson)*
John/Peter Colley (Terry Kilburn)

Peter Colley as a Young Man (John
   Mills)*

Musical Remake *Goodbye Mr Chips*
   (1969) (Peter O'Toole*, Petula Clark)

**Goodfellas** (USA 1990)
Martin Scorsese

James Conway (Robert De Niro)*
Henry Hill (Ray Liotta)*
Tommy de Vito (Joe Pesci)*
Karen Hill (Lorraine Bracco)

**Gorillas In The Mist** (USA 1988)
Michael Apted

Dian Fossey (Sigourney Weaver)*
Bob Campbell (Bryan Brown)
Roz Carr (Julie Harris)
Sembagare (John Omirah Miluwi)

**The Graduate** (USA 1967)
Mike Nichols

Mrs Robinson (Anne Bancroft)*
Benjamin Braddock (Dustin Hoffman)*
Elaine Robinson (Katharine Ross)*
Mr Robinson (Murray Hamilton)

**Le Grand Bleu** see **The Big Blue**

**Grand Hotel** (USA 1932)
Edmund Goulding

Grusinskaya (Greta Garbo)*
The Baron (John Barrymore)*
Flaemmchen, the Typist (Joan
   Crawford)*
Preysing (Wallace Beery)*
Otto Kringelin (Lionel Barrymore)*

**Grand Prix** (USA 1967)
John Frankenheimer

Pete Aron (James Garner)*
Louise Frederickson (Eva Marie Saint)
Jean-Pierre Sarti (Yves Montand)*
Izo Yamura (Toshiro Mifune)

**La Grande Illusion** (France 1937)
Jean Renoir

Von Rauffenstein (Erich Von Stroheim)*
Marechal (Jean Gabin)*
Captain De Boeldieu (Pierre Fresnay)
Rosenthal (Marcel Dalio)

**The Grapes Of Wrath** (USA 1940)
John Ford

Tom Joad (Henry Fonda)*
Ma Joad (Jane Darwell)
Jim Casey (John Carradine)
Grandpa (Charles Grapewin)

**Grease** (USA 1978)
Randal Kleiser

Danny (John Travolta)*
Sandy (Olivia Newton-John)
Rizzo (Stockard Channing)
Kenickie (Jeff Conaway)

Sequel *Grease 2* (1982)

**The Great Dictator** (USA 1940)
Charles Chaplin

Hynkel, Dictator of Tomania/A Jewish
   Barber (Charles Chaplin)*
Napoloni, Dictator of Bacteria (Jack
   Oakie)
Hannah (Paulette Goddard)
Schultz (Reginald Gardiner)

**The Great Escape** (USA 1963)
John Sturges

'Cooler King' Hilts (Steve McQueen)*
'The Scrounger' Hendley (James
   Garner)*
'Big X' Bartlett (Richard Attenborough)*
Danny Velinski (Charles Bronson)*
'The Manufacturer' Sedgwick (James
   Coburn)*

Sequel *The Great Escape II: The Untold
   Story* (TV 1988)

**Great Expectations** (UK 1946)
David Lean

Pip Pirrip (John Mills)*
Estella/Her Mother (Valerie Hobson)
Joe Gargery (Bernard Miles)
Jaggers (Francis L Sullivan)
Miss Havisham (Martita Hunt)
Abel Magwitch (Finlay Currie)
Herbert Pocket (Alec Guinness)*

Subsequent version *Great Expectations*
   (1974) (Michael York*, Sarah Miles*,
   James Mason*)

**The Great Race** (USA 1965)
Blake Edwards

Leslie Gallant III (Tony Curtis)*
Professor Fate (Jack Lemmon)*
Maggie DuBois (Natalie Wood)*
Maximilian Mean (Peter Falk)

**The Great Ziegfeld** (USA 1936)
Robert Z Leonard

Florence Ziegfeld Jnr (William Powell)*
Billie Burke (Myrna Loy)*
Anna Held (Luise Rainer)*
Billings (Frank Morgan)

**The Greatest Show On Earth**
   (USA 1952)
Cecil B DeMille

Sebastian (Cornel Wilde)*
Holly (Betty Hutton)*
Brad Braden (Charlton Heston)*
Phyllis (Dorothy Lamour)*
Angel (Gloria Grahame)*
Buttons (James Stewart)*

**The Green Berets** (USA 1968)
John Wayne, Ray Kellogg

Col Mike Kirby (John Wayne)*
George Beckworth (David Janssen)
Sgt Petersen (Jim Hutton)
Sgt Muldoon (Aldo Ray)

**Green Card** (USA 1990)
Peter Weir

George Faure (Gérard Depardieu)*
Bronte Parrish (Andie MacDowell)
Lauren (Bebe Neuwirth)
Phil (Gregg Edelman)

**Gregory's Girl** (UK 1980)
Bill Forsyth

Gregory (Gordon John Sinclair)
Dorothy (Dee Hepburn)
Headmaster (Chic Murray)
Phil Menzies (Jake D'Arcy)

**Gremlins** (USA 1984)
Joe Dante

Billy (Zach Galligan)
Kate (Phoebe Cates)
Rand (Hoyt Axton)
Lynn (Frances Lee McCain)

Sequel *Gremlins 2: The New Batch*
(1990)

**Greystoke: The Legend Of Tarzan**
(UK 1984)
Hugh Hudson

Lord Greystoke (Ralph Richardson)*
John Clayton/Tarzan (Christopher
Lambert)*
Capt Philippe D'Arnot (Ian Holm)
Jane Porter (Andie MacDowell)

**The Grifters** (USA 1990)
Stephen Frears

Lilly Dillon (Anjelica Huston)*
Roy Dillon (John Cusack)
Myra Langtry (Annette Bening)
Guy at Bar (Jan Munroe)

**Guess Who's Coming To Dinner**
(USA 1967)
Stanley Kramer

Matt Drayton (Spencer Tracy)*
Christina Drayton (Katharine Hepburn)*
John Prentice (Sidney Poitier)*
Joey Drayton (Katharine Houghton)

**Gunfight At The OK Corral**
(USA 1957)
John Sturges

Wyatt Earp (Burt Lancaster)*
Doc Holliday (Kirk Douglas)*
Laura Denbow (Rhonda Fleming)
Kate Fisher (Jo Van Fleet)

**The Guns Of Navarone** (UK 1961)
J Lee Thompson

Capt Keith Mallory (Gregory Peck)*
Corp Miller (David Niven)*
Col Andrea Stavrou (Anthony Quinn)*
C P O Brown (Stanley Baker)*
Maj 'Lucky' Franklin (Anthony Quayle)*

Sequel *Force Ten From Navarone*
(1978) (Robert Shaw, Harrison Ford*,
Edward Fox)

**Guys And Dolls** (USA 1955)
Joseph L Mankiewicz

Sky Masterson (Marlon Brando)*
Sarah Brown (Jean Simmons)*
Nathan Detroit (Frank Sinatra)*
Adelaide (Vivian Blaine)

**Gypsy** (USA 1962)
Mervyn Le Roy

Rose (Rosalind Russell)*
Louise (Natalie Wood)*
Herbie Sommers (Karl Malden)*
Tulsa (Paul Wallace)

# H

**Hamlet** (UK 1948)
Laurence Olivier

Hamlet (Laurence Olivier)*
Gertrude (Eileen Herlie)
Claudius (Basil Sydney)
Horatio (Norman Wooland)
Ophelia (Jean Simmons)*

**Hamlet** (UK 1990)
Franco Zeffirelli

Hamlet (Mel Gibson)*
Gertrude (Glenn Close)*
Claudius (Alan Bates)*
The Ghost (Paul Scofield)*
Ophelia (Helena Bonham Carter)

**Hannah And Her Sisters**
(USA 1986)
Woody Allen

Mickey (Woody Allen)*
Elliot (Michael Caine)*
Hannah (Mia Farrow)*
April (Carrie Fisher)
Lee (Barbara Hershey)*
Frederick (Max Von Sydow)*
Holly (Dianne Wiest)

**Hans Christian Andersen**
(USA 1952)
Charles Vidor

Hans Christian Andersen (Danny Kaye)*
Niels (Farley Granger)
Doro (Jean Marie)
Peter (Joey Walsh)

**Harvey** (USA 1950)
Henry Koster

Elwood P Dowd (James Stewart)*
Veta Louise Simmons (Josephine Hull)
Miss Kelly (Peggy Dow)
Dr Sanderson (Charles Drake)

**The Harvey Girls** (USA 1946)
George Sidney

Susan Bradley (Judy Garland)*
Ned Trent (John Hodiak)
Chris Maule (Ray Bolger)
Em (Angela Lansbury)*

**Heathers** (USA 1989)
Michael Lehmann

Veronica Sawyer (Winona Ryder)*
J D (Jason Dean) (Christian Slater)*
Heather (Duke) (Shannen Doherty)
Heather (McNamara) (Lisanne Falk)

**Heaven Can Wait** (USA 1943)
Ernst Lubitsch

Henry Van Cleve (Don Ameche)*
Martha Van Cleve (Gene Tierney)
Hugo Van Cleve (Charles Coburn)
Mrs Strabel (Marjorie Main)

**Heaven Can Wait** (USA 1978)
Warren Beatty, Buck Henry

Joe Pendleton (Warren Beatty)*
Betty Logan (Julie Christie)*
Mr Jordan (James Mason)*
Max Corkle (Jack Warden)

**Heaven's Gate** (USA 1980)
Michael Cimino

James Averill (Kris Kristofferson)*
Nathan D Champion (Christopher
  Walken)*
William C Irvine (John Hurt)*
Ella Watson (Isabelle Huppert)*

**The Heiress** (USA 1949)
William Wyler

Catherine Sloper (Olivia De Havilland)*
Morris Townsend (Montgomery Clift)*
Dr Austin Sloper (Ralph Richardson)*
Lavinia Penniman (Miriam Hopkins)*

**Hello Dolly!** (USA 1969)
Gene Kelly

Dolly Levi (Barbara Streisand)*
Horace Vandergelder (Walter Matthau)*
Cornelius Hackl (Michael Crawford)
Orchestra Leader (Louis Armstrong)

**Henry V** (UK 1944)
Laurence Olivier

Henry V (Laurence Olivier)*
Ancient Pistol (Robert Newton)*
Chorus (Leslie Banks)
Princess Katherine (Renée Asherson)

**Henry V** (UK 1989)
Kenneth Branagh

Henry V (Kenneth Branagh)*
Chorus (Derek Jacobi)
Mistress Quickly (Judi Dench)
Falstaff (Robbie Coltrane)
French King (Paul Scofield)*
Princess Katherine (Emma Thompson)

**Here Comes Mr Jordan** (USA 1941)
Alexander Hall

Joe Pendleton (Robert Montgomery)
Mr Jordan (Claude Rains)*
Bette Logan (Evelyn Keyes)
Messenger No 7013 (Edward Everett
     Horton)

Sequel *Down To Earth* (1947)
Remake *Heaven Can Wait* (1978) (see
     p38)

**The High And The Mighty**
     (USA 1954)
William A Wellman

Dan Roman (John Wayne)*
May Holst (Claire Trevor)
Lydia Rice (Laraine Day)
Sullivan (Robert Stack)

**High Hopes** (UK 1988)
Mike Leigh

Cyril Bender (Philip Davis)
Shirley (Ruth Sheen)
Mrs Bender (Edna Dore)
Martin Burke (Philip Jackson)

**High Noon** (USA 1952)
Fred Zinnemann

Will Kane (Gary Cooper)*
Jonas Henderson (Thomas Mitchell)
Harvey Pell (Lloyd Bridges)*
Helen Ramirez (Katy Jurado)
Amy Kane (Grace Kelly)*

Sequel *High Noon II: The Return Of Will
     Kane* (TV 1980)

**High Sierra** (USA 1941)
Raoul Walsh

Roy Earle (Humphrey Bogart)*
Marie Garson (Ida Lupino)*
Babe Kozak (Alan Curtis)
Red Hattery (Arthur Kennedy)*
Louis Mendoza (Cornel Wilde)*

Remakes *Colorado Territory* (1949)
     (Joel McCrea*, Virginia Mayo); *I Died
     A Thousand Times* (1955) (Jack
     Palance*, Shelley Winters*)

**High Society** (USA 1956)
Charles Walters

C K Dexter Haven (Bing Crosby)*
Mike Connor (Frank Sinatra)*
Tracy Lord (Grace Kelly)*
Liz Imbrie (Celeste Holm)*

**Highlander** (UK 1986)
Rusell Mulcahy

Connor MacLeod (Christopher
     Lambert)*
Brenda Wyatt (Roxanne Hart)
Kurgen (Clancy Brown)
Ramirez (Sean Connery)*

Sequel *Highlander II: The Quickening*
     (1991)

**His Girl Friday** (USA 1940)
Howard Hawks

Walter Burns (Cary Grant)*
Hildy Johnson (Rosalind Russell)*
Bruce Baldwin (Ralph Bellamy)*
Sheriff Hartwell (Gene Lockhart)

Remake *Switching Channels* (1988)
     (Burt Reynolds*, Kathleen Turner*,
     Christopher Reeve*)

**Hoffa** (USA 1992)
Danny De Vito

James R Hoffa (Jack Nicholson)*
Bobby Ciaro (Danny De Vito)*
Carol D'Allesandro (Armand Assante)
Fitzsimmons (J T Walsh)

**Hold Back The Dawn** (USA 1941)
Mitchell Leisen

Georges Iscovescu (Charles Boyer)*
Emmy Brown (Olivia De Havilland)*
Anita Dixon (Paulette Goddard)
Van Den Luecken (Victor Francen)


**Holiday Inn** (USA 1942)
Mark Sandrich

Jim Hardy (Bing Crosby)*
Ted Hanover (Fred Astaire)*
Linda Mason (Marjorie Reynolds)
Lila Dixon (Virginia Dale)


**Home Alone** (USA 1990)
Chris Columbus

Kevin McAllister (Macaulay Culkin)*
Harry (Joe Pesci)*
Marv (Daniel Stern)
Peter McAllister (John Heard)

Sequel *Home Alone 2: Lost In New York*
(1992)


**Honey I Shrunk The Kids**
(USA 1989)
Joe Johnston

Wayne Szalinski (Rick Moranis)*
Big Russ Thompson (Matt Frewer)
Diane Szalinski (Marcia Strassman)
Mae Thompson (Kristine Sutherland)

Sequel *Honey I Blew Up The Baby*
(1992)


**Hook** (USA 1991)
Steven Spielberg

Captain Hook (Dustin Hoffman)*
Peter Banning/Peter Pan (Robin
  Williams)*
Tinkerbell (Julia Roberts)*
Smee (Bob Hoskins)*
Granny Wendy (Maggie Smith)*


**Hope And Glory** (UK 1987)
John Boorman

Bill Rohan (Sebastian Rice-Edwards)
Sue Rohan (Geraldine Muir)
Grace Rohan (Sarah Miles)*
Clive Rohan (David Hayman)
Bruce (Jean-Marc Barr)*
Grandfather George (Ian Bannen)


**Hot Shots!** (USA 1991)
Jim Abrahams

Sean 'Topper' Harley/Rhett Butler/
  Superman (Charlie Sheen)*
Kent Gregory (Cary Elwes)
Ramada Thompson/Scarlett O'Hara/
  Lois Lane (Valeria Golino)
Admiral Benson (Lloyd Bridges)*

Sequel *Hot Shots 2* (1993)


**How Green Was My Valley**
(USA 1941)
John Ford

Mr Gruffydd (Walter Pidgeon)*
Angharad (Maureen O'Hara)*
Gwilym Morgan (Donald Crisp)
Huw (Roddy McDowall)*


**How The West Was Won**
(USA 1962)
John Ford, Henry Hathaway,
  George Marshall, Richard Thorpe

Jethro Stuart (Henry Fonda)*
Cleve Van Valen (Gregory Peck)*
Linus Rawlings (James Stewart)*
Gen William T Sherman (John Wayne)*
Mike King (Richard Widmark)*


**How To Marry A Millionaire**
(USA 1953)
Jean Negulesco

Loco (Betty Grable)*
Pola (Marilyn Monroe)*
Schatze Page (Lauren Bacall)*
J D Hanley (William Powell)*

**Howard's End** (UK 1992)
James Ivory

Henry Wilcox (Anthony Hopkins)*
Ruth Wilcox (Vanessa Redgrave)*
Helen Schlegel (Helena Bonham Carter)
Margaret Schlegel (Emma Thompson)


**The Hucksters** (USA 1947)
Jack Conway

Victor Albee Norman (Clark Gable)*
Kay Dorrance (Deborah Kerr)*
Evan Llewellyn Evans (Sidney
    Greenstreet)
Jean Ogilvie (Ava Gardner)*


**Hud** (USA 1963)
Martin Ritt

Hud Bannon (Paul Newman)*
Alma Brown (Patricia Neal)*
Homer Bannon (Melvyn Douglas)*
Lon Bannon (Brandon De Wilde)


**The Hunchback Of Notre Dame**
    (USA 1939)
William Dieterle

The Hunchback (Charles Laughton)*
Frollo (Sir Cedric Hardwicke)
Clopin (Thomas Mitchell)
Esmeralda (Maureen O'Hara)*

Subsequent versions *The Hunchback Of
    Notre Dame* (1957) (Anthony Quinn*);
    *The Hunchback Of Notre Dame* (TV
    1982) (Anthony Hopkins*)


**The Hunt For Red October**
    (USA 1990)
John McTiernan

Marko Ramius (Sean Connery)*
Jack Ryan (Alec Baldwin)*
Bart Mancuso (Scott Glenn)
Capt Borodin (Sam Neill)*

Sequel *Patriot Games* (1992)


**The Hurricane** (USA 1937)
John Ford

Marama (Dorothy Lamour)*
Terangi (Jon Hall)
Madame Germains DeLaage (Mary
    Astor)*
Father Paul (C Aubrey Smith)

Remake *Hurricane* (1979) (Jason
    Robards*, Mia Farrow*, Max Von
    Sydow*)


**The Hustler** (USA 1961)
Robert Rossen

Eddie Felson (Paul Newman)*
Sarah Packard (Piper Laurie)*
Bert Gordon (George C Scott)*
Minnesota Fats (Jackie Gleason)*

Sequel *The Color Of Money* (1986)
    (p20)


# I

**I Am A Fugitive From A Chain
    Gang** (USA 1932)
Mervy Le Roy

James Allen (Paul Muni)*
Marie Woods (Glenda Farrell)
Helen (Helen Vinson)
Pete (Preston Foster)


**I Know Where I'm Going** (UK 1945)
Michael Powell, Emeric Pressburger

Joan Webster (Wendy Hiller)*
Torquil MacNeil (Roger Livesey)
Catriona Potts (Pamela Brown)
Mr Webster (George Carney)


**I Want To Live!** (USA 1958)
Robert Wise

Barbara Graham (Susan Hayward)*
Ed Montgomery (Simon Oakland)
Peg (Virginia Vincent)
Carl Palmberg (Theodore Bikel)

Remake *I Want To Live!* (TV 1983)
    (Lindsay Wagner)

## *I Was A Male War Bride*
(USA 1949)
Howard Hawks

Capt Henri Rochard (Cary Grant)*
Lt Catherine Gates (Ann Sheridan)
Capt Jack Rumsey (William Neff)
WACS (Marion Marshall/Randy Stuart)

## *I'll Cry Tomorrow* (USA 1955)
Daniel Mann

Lillian Roth (Susan Hayward)*
Tony Brademan (Richard Conte)
Burt McGuire (Eddie Albert)*
Katie Roth (Jo Van Fleet)

## *I'm All Right Jack* (UK 1959)
John Boulting

Stanley Windrush (Ian Carmichael)*
Fred Kite (Peter Sellers)*
Maj Hitchcock (Terry-Thomas)*
Sidney De Vere Cox (Richard
    Attenborough)*
Aunt Dolly (Margaret Rutherford)*

## *I'm No Angel* (USA 1933)
Wesley Ruggles

Tira (Mae West)*
Jack Clayton (Cary Grant)*
Bill Barton (Edward Arnold)
Benny Pinkowitz (Gregory Ratoff)

## *Imitation Of Life* (USA 1959)
Douglas Sirk

Lora Meredith (Lana Turner)*
Steve Archer (John Gavin)
Susie (age 16) (Sandra Dee)
Herself (Mahalia Jackson)

## *In Old Chicago* (USA 1938)
Henry King

Dion O'Leary (Tyrone Power)*
Belle Fawcett (Alice Faye)*
Jack O'Leary (Don Ameche)*
Molly O'Leary (Alice Brady)

## *In The Heat Of The Night*
(USA 1967)
Norman Jewison

Virgil Tibbs (Sidney Poitier)*
Bill Gillespie (Rod Steiger)*
Sam Wood (Warren Oates)
Quentin Dean (Delores Purdy)

Sequels *They Call Me MR TIBBS!*
    (1970); *The Organization* (1971)

## *In The Realm Of The Senses*
(France/Japan 1976)
(*Ai No Corrida*)
Nagisa Oshima

Kichizo (Tatsuya Fuji)
Sada (Eiko Matsuda)
Toku (Aoi Nakajima)
Maid Matsuko (Meika Seri)

## *In Which We Serve* (UK 1942)
Nöel Coward, David Lean

Capt Kinross (Nöel Coward)*
O/S 'Shorty' Blake (John Mills)*
CRO Walter Hardy (Bernard Miles)
Alix (Mrs Kinross) (Celia Johnson)*
Young Stoker (Richard Attenborough)*

## *Indiana Jones And The Last*
    *Crusade* (USA 1989)
Steven Spielberg

Indiana Jones (Harrison Ford)*
Prof Henry Jones (Sean Connery)*
Marcus Brody (Denholm Elliott)*
Young Indy (River Phoenix)*

## *Indiana Jones And The Temple*
    *Of Doom* (USA 1984)
Steven Spielberg

Indiana Jones (Harrison Ford)*
Willie Scott (Kate Capshaw)
Short Round (Ke Huy Quan)
Mola Ram (Amrish Puri)

**The Informer** (USA 1935)
John Ford

Gypo Nolan (Victor McLaglen)
Mary McPhillip (Heather Angel)
Dan Gallagher (Preston Foster)
Katie Madden (Margot Grahame)

Remake *Uptight* (1968) (Raymond St Jacques)

**Invasion Of The Bodysnatchers**
(USA 1956)
Don Siegel

Dr Miles Bennell (Kevin McCarthy)
Becky Driscoll (Dana Wynter)
Dr Danny Kauffman (Larry Gates)
Jack (King Donovan)

Remakes *Invasion Of The Bodysnatchers* (1978) (Donald Sutherland*, Brooke Adams); *Body Snatchers* (1993) (Forest Whitaker*, Meg Tilly)

**Irma La Douce** (USA 1963)
Billy Wilder

Nestor (Jack Lemmon)*
Irma La Douce (Shirley MacLaine)*
Moustache (Lou Jacobi)
Lefevre (Herschel Bernardi)

**Ironweed** (USA 1987)
Hector Babenco

Francis Phelan (Jack Nicholson)*
Helen (Meryl Streep)*
Annie Phelan (Carroll Baker)*
Billy (Michael O'Keefe)

**It Happened One Night** (USA 1934)
Frank Capra

Ellie Andrews (Claudette Colbert)*
Peter Warne (Clark Gable)*
Oscar Shapeley (Roscoe Karns)
Drunk Boy (Henry Wadsworth)

Musical remakes *Eve Knew Her Apples* (1945) (Ann Miller, William Wright); *You Can't Run Away From It* (1956) (Jack Lemmon*, June Allyson*)

**It's A Mad, Mad, Mad, Mad World**
(USA 1963)
Stanley Kramer

Capt C G Culpeper (Spencer Tracy)*
Mrs Marcus (Ethel Merman)*
Ding Bell (Mickey Rooney)*
Jimmy, the Crook (Buster Keaton)*

**It's A Wonderful Life** (USA 1946)
Frank Capra

George Bailey (James Stewart)*
Mary Hatch (Donna Reed)*
Dr Potter (Lionel Barrymore)*
Uncle Billy (Thomas Mitchell)
Clarence (Henry Travers)

Remake *It Happened One Christmas* (TV 1977) (Marlo Thomas, Wayne Rogers, Orson Welles*)

**Ivanhoe** (USA 1952)
Richard Thorpe

Wilfrid Of Ivanhoe (Robert Taylor)*
Rebecca (Elizabeth Taylor)*
Rowena (Joan Fontaine)*
Sir Brian De Bois-Guilbert (George Sanders)*

Subsequent version *Ivanhoe* (TV 1982) (Anthony Andrews, Sam Neill*, James Mason*)

# J

**JFK** (USA 1991)
Oliver Stone

Jim Garrison (Kevin Costner)*
Lee Harvey Oswald (Gary Oldman)*
Liz Garrison (Sissy Spacek)*
Clay Shaw (Tommy Lee Jones)
Jack Martin (Jack Lemmon)*
David Ferrie (Joe Pesci)*
Senator Russell Long (Walter Matthau)*
Willie O'Keefe (Kevin Bacon)
Col X (Donald Sutherland)*

**Jagged Edge** (USA 1985)
Richard Marquand

Teddy Barnes (Glenn Close)*
Jack Forrester (Jeff Bridges)*
Sam Ransom (Robert Loggia)
Thomas Krasny (Peter Coyote)

**Jaws** (USA 1975)
Steven Spielberg

Police Chief Martin Brody (Roy
  Scheider)*
Capt Quint (Robert Shaw)*
Matt Hooper (Richard Dreyfuss)*
Ellen Brody (Lorraine Gary)

Sequels *Jaws II* (1978); *Jaws 3-D*
  (1983); *Jaws — The Revenge* (1987)

**The Jazz Singer** (USA 1927)
Alan Crosland

Jakie Rabinowitz/Jack Robin (Al
  Jolson)*
Mary Dale (May McAvoy)
Cantor Rabinowitz (Warner Oland)
Chorus Girl (Myrna Loy)*

Remakes *The Jazz Singer* (1953)
  (Danny Thomas); *The Jazz Singer*
  (1980) (Neil Diamond)

**Jean De Florette** (France 1986)
Claude Berri

César Soubeyran (Yves Montand)*
Jean De Florette (Gérard Depardieu)*
Ugolin Soubeyran (Daniel Auteuil)
Aimée Cadoret (Elisabeth Depardieu)

Sequel *Manon Des Sources* (1986)

**The Jerk** (USA 1979)
Carl Reiner

Navin Johnson (Steve Martin)*
Marie (Bernadette Peters)
Patty Bernstein (Catlin Adams)
Mother (Mabel King)

Sequel *The Jerk Too* (TV 1984)
  (Mark Blankfield)

**Jesse James** (USA 1939)
Henry King

Jesse James (Tyrone Power)*
Frank James (Henry Fonda)*
Zerelda (Zee) (Nancy Kelly)
Will Wright (Randolph Scott)

Sequel *The Return Of Frank James*
  (1940)

**Jésus De Montréal** see **Jesus Of
Montreal**

**Jesus Of Montreal**
  (Canada/France 1989)
(*Jésus De Montréal*)
Denys Arcand

Daniel Colombe (Lothaire Bluteau)
Mireille (Catherine Wilkening)
Constance (Johanne-Marie Tremblay)
Martin (Rémy Girard)

**Les Jeux Interdits** (France 1952)
(*Forbidden Games*)
René Clément

Michel (Georges Poujouly)
Paulette (Brigitte Fossey)
Francis (Gouard Amédée
Berthe Dolle (Laurence Badie)

**The Jewel Of The Nile** (USA 1985)
Lewis Teague

Jack (Michael Douglas)*
Joan (Kathleen Turner)*
Ralph (Danny De Vito)*
Omar (Spiros Focas)

**Jezebel** (USA 1938)
William Wyler

Julie Morrison (Bette Davis)*
Preston Dillard (Henry Fonda)*
Buck Cantrell (George Brent)
Amy Bradford Dillard (Margaret Lindsay)

**Joan Of Arc** (USA 1948)
Victor Fleming

Jeanne D'Arc (Ingrid Bergman)*
The Dauphin, Charles II (José Ferrer)
Pierre Cauchon (Francis L Sullivan)
Count John of Luxembourg (J Carroll
   Naish)

**Joe** (USA 1970)
John G Avildsen

Joe Curran (Peter Boyle)
Melissa Compton (Susan Sarandon)*
Frank Russo (Patrick McDermott)
Kid in Soda Shop (Tim Lewis)

**Johnny Belinda** (USA 1948)
Jean Negulesco

Belinda McDonald (Jane Wyman)*
Dr Robert Richardson (Lew Ayres)*
Black McDonald (Charles Bickford)
Aggie McDonald (Agnes Moorehead)*

Remake *Johnny Belinda* (TV 1982)
   (Rosanna Arquette, Richard Thomas)

**The Jolson Story** (USA 1946)
Alfred E Green

Al Jolson (Larry Parks)
Julie Benson (Evelyn Keyes)
Steve Martin (William Demarest)
Tom Baron (William Goodwin)

Sequel *Jolson Sings Again* (1949)

**Le Jour Se Lève** (France 1939)
(*Daybreak*)
Marcel Carné

François (Jean Gabin)*
Clara (Arletty)*
Valentin (Jules Berry)
Françoise (Jacquelin Laurent)

**Ju Dou** (Japan/China 1989)
Zhang Yimou, Yang Fengliang

Yang Junshan (Li Wei)
Ju Dou (Gong Li)
Yang Tianqing (Li Baotian)
Yang Tianbai as a child (Zhang Yi)

**Judgement At Nuremberg**
   (USA 1961)
Stanley Kramer

Judge Dan Haywood (Spencer Tracy)*
Ernst Janning (Burt Lancaster)*
Col Tad Lawson (Richard Widmark)*
Madame Bertholt (Marlene Dietrich)*
Hans Rolfe (Maximilian Schell)*
Irene Hoffman (Judy Garland)*
Rudolf Petersen (Montgomery Clift)*

**Jules Et Jim** (France 1961)
François Truffaut

Catherine (Jeanne Moreau)*
Jules (Oskar Werner)
Jim (Henri Serre)
Gilberte (Vanna Urbino)

**Julia** (USA 1977)
Fred Zinnemann

Lillian Hellman (Jane Fonda)*
Julia (Vanessa Redgrave)*
Dashiell Hammett (Jason Robards)*
Johann (Maximilian Schell)*

**Julius Caesar** (USA 1953)
Joseph L Mankiewicz

Brutus (James Mason)*
Mark Antony (Marlon Brando)*
Julius Caesar (Louis Calhern)
Cassius (John Gielgud)*

Subsequent version *Julius Caesar*
   (1970) (Charlton Heston*, Jason
   Robards*, John Gielgud*)

**The Jungle Book** (USA 1967)
Wolfgang Reitherman

Voices of:
Baloo the Bear (Phil Harris)
Bagheera the Panther (Sebastian
   Cabot)
King Louie of the Apes (Louis Prima)
Shere Khan the Tiger (George
   Sanders)*
Mowgli, the Man Cub (Bruce
   Reitherman)

**Jungle Fever** (USA 1991)
Spike Lee

Flipper Purify (Wesley Snipes)*
Angie Tucci (Annabella Sciorra)
Cyrus (Spike Lee)
The Good Reverend Doctor Purify
  (Ossie Davis)

# K

**Kagemusha** (Japan 1980)
Akira Kurosawa

Shingen Takeda, Lord of Kai (Tatsuya
  Nakadai)
Kagemusha, Shingen's double (Tasuya
  Nakadai)
Nobukado Takeda, Shingen's younger
  brother (Tasuya Nakadai)
Katsuyori, Shingen's son (Kenichi
  Hagiwara)

**The Karate Kid** (USA 1984)
John G Avildsen

Daniel (Ralph Macchio)*
Miyagi (Noriyuki 'Pat' Morita)
Ali (Elisabeth Shue)
Kreese (Martin Kove)

Sequels *The Karate Kid, Part II* (1986);
  *The Karate Kid III* (1989)

**Key Largo** (USA 1948)
John Huston

Frank McCloud (Humphrey Bogart)*
Johnny Rocco (Edward G Robinson)*
Nora Temple (Lauren Bacall)*
James Temple (Lionel Barrymore)*
Gaye Dawn (Claire Trevor)

**The Killers** (USA 1946)
Robert Siodmak

Jim Reardon (Edmond O'Brien)*
Kitty Collins (Ava Gardner)*
Big Jim Colfax (Albert Dekker)
Swede (Burt Lancaster)*

Remake *The Killers* (1964) (Lee Marvin*,
  Angie Dickinson*, Ronald Reagan*)

**The Killing** (USA 1956)
Stanley Kubrick

Johnny Clay (Sterling Hayden)*
Marvin Ungar (Jay C Flippen)
Sherry Peatty (Marie Windsor)
George Peatty (Elisha Cook)

**The Killing Fields** (UK 1984)
Roland Joffe

Sydney Schanberg (Sam Waterston)
Dith Pran (Dr Haing S Ngor)
Al Rockoff (John Malkovich)*
Jon Swain (Julian Sands)

**Kind Hearts And Coronets**
  (UK 1949)
Robert Hamer

Louis Mazzini (Dennis Price)*
Edith D'Ascoyne (Valerie Hobson)
Duke Ethelred/Banker/Rev Henry/Gen
  Rufus/Admiral/Young D'Ascoyne/
  Young Henry/Agatha (Alec Guinness)*
Sibella (Joan Greenwood)*

**Kindergarten Cop** (USA 1990)
Ivan Reitman

Det John Kimble (Arnold
  Schwarzenegger)*
Joyce (Penelope Ann Miller)
Phoebe O'Hara (Pamela Reed)
Eleanor Crisp (Carroll Baker)*

**The King And I** (USA 1956)
Walter Lang

Anna Leonowens (Deborah Kerr)*
King of Siam (Yul Brynner)*
Tuptim (Rita Moreno)
Kralahome (Martin Benson)

**King Kong** (USA 1933)
Ernest B Schoedsack, Merian C
  Cooper

Ann Darrow (Fay Wray)
Carl Denham (Robert Armstrong)
Capt Engelhorn (Frank Reicher)
John Driscoll (Bruce Cabot)

Sequel *Son Of Kong* (1934)

**King Kong** (USA 1976)
John Guillermin

Jack Prescott (Jeff Bridges)*
Fred Wilson (Charles Grodin)
Dwan (Jessica Lange)*
Capt Ross (John Randolph)

Sequel *King Kong Lives* (1986)

**The King Of Comedy** (USA 1982)
Martin Scorsese

Rupert Pupkin (Robert De Niro)*
Jerry Langford (Jerry Lewis)*
Rita (Diahnne Abbott)
Masha (Sandra Bernhard)

**King Solomon's Mines** (USA 1950)
Andrew Marton, Compton Bennett

Elizabeth Curtis (Deborah Kerr)*
Allan Quartermain (Stewart Granger)*
John Goode (Richard Carlson)
Van Brun (Hugo Haas)

Subsequent version *King Solomon's Mines* (1985) (Richard Chamberlain, Sharon Stone*)

**King's Row** (USA 1942)
Sam Wood

Randy Monoghan (Ann Sheridan)
Parris Mitchell (Robert Cummings)
Drake McHugh (Ronald Reagan)*
Cassandra Tower (Betty Field)

**Kiss Of The Spiderwoman**
  (USA/Brazil 1985)
Hector Babenco

Luis Molina (William Hurt)*
Valentin Arregui (Raul Julia)*
Leni Lamaison/Marta/Spiderwoman
  (Sonia Braga)
Warden (José Lewgoy)

**Kitty Foyle** (USA 1940)
Sam Wood

Kitty Foyle (Ginger Rogers)*
Wynn Strafford (Dennis Morgan)
Mark (James Craig)
Giono (Eduardo Ciannelli)

**Klute** (USA 1971)
Alan J Pakula

Bree Daniels (Jane Fonda)*
John Klute (Donald Sutherland)*
Peter Cable (Charles Cioffi)
Frank Ligourin (Roy Scheider)*

**Kramer Vs Kramer** (USA 1979)
Robert Benton

Ted Kramer (Dustin Hoffman)*
Joanna Kramer (Meryl Streep)*
Margaret Phelps (Jane Alexander)
Billy Kramer (Justin Henry)

**The Krays** (UK 1990)
Peter Medak

Violet Kray (Billie Whitelaw)
Jack 'The Hat' McVitie (Tom Bell)
Ronald Kray (Gary Kemp)
Reginald Kray (Martin Kemp)

**Kumonosu-Jo** see **Throne Of Blood**

# L

**Ladri Di Biciclette** see **Bicycle Thieves**

**The Lady And The Tramp**
  (USA 1955)
Hamilton Luske, Clyde Geronimi,
  Wilfred Jackson

Voices of:
Darling/Peg/Si/Am (Peggy Lee)
Lady (Barbara Luddy)
Tramp (Larry Roberts)
Jock/Bull/Dachsie (Bill Thompson)

**The Lady Eve** (USA 1941)
Preston Sturges

Jean Harrington (Barbara Stanwyck)*
Charles Pike (Henry Fonda)*
Col Harrington (Charles Coburn)
Mr Pike (Eugene Pallette)

Remake *The Birds And The Bees*
(1956) (Mitzi Gaynor, George Gobel,
David Niven*)

**Lady For A Day** (USA 1933)
Frank Capra

Dave The Dude (Warren William)
Apple Annie (May Robson)
Judge Blake (Guy Kibbee)
Missouri Martin (Glenda Farrell)

Sequel *Lady By Choice* (1934)
Remake *Pocketful Of Miracles* (1961)

**The Lady From Shanghai**
(USA 1948)
Orson Welles

Michael O'Hara (Orson Welles)*
Elsa Bannister (Rita Hayworth)*
Arthur Bannister (Everett Sloane)
George Grisby (Glenn Anders)

**The Lady Vanishes** (UK 1938)
Alfred Hitchcock

Iris Henderson (Margaret Lockwood)*
Gilbert Redman (Michael Redgrave)*
Dr Hartz (Paul Lukas)
Miss Froy (Dame May Whitty)
Caldicott (Naunton Wayne)
Charters (Basil Radford)

Remake *The Lady Vanishes* (1979)
(Cybill Shepherd, Elliott Gould*)

**The Ladykillers** (UK 1955)
Alexander Mackendrick

The Professor (Alec Guinness)*
The Major (Cecil Parker)*
Louis (Herbert Lom)
Harry (Peter Sellers)*
Mrs Wilderforce (Katie Johnson)

**The Last Emperor**
(Italy/UK/China 1987)
Bernardo Bertolucci

Pu Yi (Adult) (John Lone)
Wan Jung (Joan Chen)
Reginald Johnston (R J) (Peter
O'Toole)*
The Governor (Ying Ruocheng)

**The Last Of The Mohicans**
(USA 1992)
Michael Mann

Hawkeye (Daniel Day-Lewis)*
Cora Munro (Madeleine Stowe)
Chingachgook (Russell Means)
Uncas (Eric Schweig)

**The Last Picture Show** (USA 1971)
Peter Bogdanovich

Sonny Crawford (Timothy Bottoms)
Duane Jackson (Jeff Bridges)*
Jacy Farrow (Cybill Shepherd)
Sam the Lion (Ben Johnson)

Sequel *Texasville* (1990)

**Last Tango In Paris**
(Italy/France 1972)
(*Ultimo Tango A Parigi*)
Bernardo Bertolucci

Paul (Marlon Brando)*
Jeanne (Maria Schneider)
Tom (Jean-Pierre Leaud)
Concierge (Darling Legitimus)

**The Last Temptation Of Christ**
(USA 1988)
Martin Scorsese

Jesus (Willem Dafoe)*
Judas (Harvey Keitel)*
Zealot (Paul Greco)
Mary Magdalene (Barbara Hershey)*

**Laura** (USA 1944)
Otto Preminger

Laura Hunt (Gene Tierney)
Mark McPherson (Dana Andrews)*
Waldo Lydecker (Clifton Webb)*
Shelby Carpenter (Vincent Price)*

**The Lavender Hill Mob** (UK 1951)
Charles Crichton

Mr Henry Holland (Alec Guinness)*
Mr Pendlebury (Stanley Holloway)
Lackery (Sidney James)
Shorty (Alfie Bass)
Chiquita (Audrey Hepburn)*

**Lawrence Of Arabia** (UK 1962)
David Lean

T E Lawrence (Peter O'Toole)*
Price Feisal (Alec Guinness)*
Auda Abu Tayi (Anthony Quinn)*
Gen Allenby (Jack Hawkins)*
Sherif Ali (Omar Sharif)*

**Lenny** (USA 1974)
Bob Fosse

Lenny Bruce (Dustin Hoffman)*
Honey Bruce (Valerie Perrine)
Sally Marr (Jan Miner)
Artie Silver (Stanley Beck)

**The Leopard** (Italy/France/USA 1963)
(*Il Gattopardo*)
Luchino Visconti

Don Fabrizio (Burt Lancaster)*
Tancredi (Alain Delon)*
Angelica Sedara (Claudia Cardinale)
Don Calogero Sedara (Paolo Stoppa)

**Les Misérables** (USA 1935)
Richard Boleslawski

Jean Valjean (Fredric March)*
Javert (Charles Laughton)*
Bishop Bienvenu (Cedric Hardwicke)
Cosette (Rochelle Hudson)

Subsequent versions *Les Misérables*
(1952) (Michael Rennie, Robert
Newton); *Les Misérables* (1957) (Jean
Gabin*, Bernard Blier); *Les
Misérables* (TV 1978) (Richard
Jordan, Anthony Perkins*)

**Lethal Weapon** (USA 1987)
Richard Donner

Martin Riggs (Mel Gibson)*
Roger Murtaugh (Danny Glover)*
Joshua (Gary Busey)
The General (Mitchell Ryan)

Sequels *Lethal Weapon 2* (1989) (Joe
Pesci*); *Lethal Weapon 3* (1992)

**The Letter** (USA 1940)
William Wyler

Leslie Crosbie (Bette Davis)*
Robert Crosbie (Herbert Marshall)
Howard Joyce (Henry Stephenson)
Mrs Hammond (Gale Sondergaard)

Remake *The Letter* (TV 1982) (Lee
Remick*)

**A Letter To Three Wives**
(USA 1949)
Joseph L Mankiewicz

Deborah Bishop (Jeanne Crain)
Lora May Hollingsway (Linda Darnell)
Rita Phipps (Ann Sothern)
George Phipps (Kirk Douglas)*

Remake *A Letter To Three Wives* (TV
1985) (Loni Anderson, Michele Lee,
Stephanie Zimbalist)

**Licence To Kill** (UK 1989)
John Glen

James Bond (Timothy Dalton)*
Pam Bouvier (Carey Lowell)
Franz Bouvier (Robert Davi)
Lupe Lamora (Talisa Soto)

**The Life And Death Of Colonel Blimp** (UK 1943)
Michael Powell, Emeric Pressburger

Theo Kretschmar-Schuldorff (Anton Walbrook)
Edith Hunter/Barbara Wynne/Angela Cannon (Deborah Kerr)*
Gen Clive Wynne-Candy (Roger Livesey)
Col Betteridge (Roland Culver)

**Life Is Sweet** (UK 1990)
Mike Leigh

Wendy (Alison Steadman)
Andy (Jim Broadbent)
Natalie (Claire Skinner)
Nicola (Jane Horrocks)

**The Life Of Emile Zola** (USA 1937)
William Dieterle

Emile Zola (Paul Muni)*
Capt Alfred Dreyfus (Joseph Schildkraut)
Alexandrine Zola (Gloria Holden)
Lucie Dreyfus (Gale Sondergaard)

**Life With Father** (USA 1947)
Michael Curtiz

Clarence Day (William Powell)*
Vinnie Day (Irene Dunne)*
Mary (Elizabeth Taylor)*
The Reverend Dr Lloyd (Edmund Gwenn)

**Lilies Of The Field** (USA 1963)
Ralph Nelson

Homer Smith (Sidney Poitier)*
Mother Maria (Lilia Skala)
Sister Gertrude (Lisa Mann)
Sister Agnes (Isa Crino)

Sequel *Christmas Lilies Of The Field* (TV 1979) (Billy Dee Williams, Maria Schell)

**Limelight** (USA 1952)
Charles Chaplin

Calvero (Charles Chaplin)*
Terry (Claire Bloom)*
Neville (Sydney Chaplin)
Calvero's Partner (Buster Keaton)*

**The Lion In Winter** (USA 1968)
Anthony Harvey

King Henry II (Peter O'Toole)*
Queen Eleanor of Aquitaine (Katharine Hepburn)*
Princess Alais (Jane Merrow)
Prince Geoffrey (John Castle)
King Philip of France (Timothy Dalton)*
Prince Richard the Lion-Hearted (Anthony Hopkins)*

**Little Big Man** (USA 1970)
Arthur Penn

Jack Crabb (Dustin Hoffman)*
Mrs Pendrake (Faye Dunaway)*
Allardyce T Merriweather (Martin Balsam)
Gen George Armstrong Custer (Richard Mulligan)

**Little Caesar** (USA 1930)
Mervyn Le Roy

'Rico' Bandello (Edward G Robinson)*
Joe Massara (Douglas Fairbanks Jnr)
Olga Strassof (Glenda Farrell)
The 'Big Boy' (Sidney Blackmer)

**The Little Foxes** (USA 1941)
William Wyler

Regina Giddens (Bette Davis)*
Horace Giddens (Herbert Marshall)
Alexandra Giddens (Teresa Wright)
David Hewitt (Richard Carlson)

Prequel *Another Part Of The Forest* (1948) (Fredric March, Dan Duryea)

**The Little Mermaid** (USA 1989)
John Musker, Ron Clements

Voices of:
Louis (Rene Auberjonois)
Eric (Christopher Daniel Barnes)
Ariel (Jodi Benson)
Ursula (Pat Carroll)


**Little Women** (USA 1933)
George Cukor

Jo (Katharine Hepburn)*
Amy (Joan Bennett)
Prof Fritz Bhaer (Paul Lukas)
Aunt March (Edna May Oliver)
Beth (Jean Parker)
Meg (Frances Dee)

Subsequent versions *Little Women*
(1949) (June Allyson*, Elizabeth
Taylor*); *Little Women* (TV 1978)
(Meredith Baxter Birney, Susan Dey)


**Live And Let Die** (UK 1973)
Guy Hamilton

James Bond (Roger Moore)*
Kananga/Mr Big (Yaphet Kotto)
Solitaire (Jane Seymour)
Sheriff Pepper (Clifton James)


**The Lives Of A Bengal Lancer**
(USA 1935)
Henry Hathaway

Lt McGregor (Gary Cooper)*
Lt Forsyth (Franchot Tone)
Maj Hamilton (C Aubrey Smith)
Lt Stone (Richard Cromwell)


**The Living Daylights** (UK 1987)
John Glen

James Bond (Timothy Dalton)*
Kara Milovy (Maryam D'Abo)
Gen Georgi Koskov (Jeroen Krabbe)
Brad Whitaker (Joe Don Baker)


**Local Hero** (UK 1983)
Bill Forsyth

Felix Happer (Burt Lancaster)*
MacIntyre (Peter Riegert)
Gordon Urquhart (Denis Lawson)
Danny Oldsen (Peter Capaldi)


**Lolita** (UK 1962)
Stanley Kubrick

Humbert Humbert (James Mason)*
Charlotte Haze (Shelley Winters)*
Clare Quilty (Peter Sellers)*
Lolita Haze (Sue Lyon)


**The Long Day Closes** (UK 1992)
Terence Davies

Mother (Marjorie Yates)
Bud (Leigh McCormack)
Kevin (Anthony Watson)
John (Nicholas Lamont)


**Long Day's Journey Into Night**
(USA 1962)
Sidney Lumet

Mary Tyrone (Katharine Hepburn)*
James Tyrone Snr (Ralph Richardson)*
James Tyrone Jnr (Jason Robards Jnr)*
Edmund Tyrone (Dean Stockwell)


**The Long Good Friday** (UK 1980)
John Mackenzie

Harold Shand (Bob Hoskins)*
Victoria (Helen Mirren)*
Charlie (Eddie Constantine)
Parky (Dave King)


**The Long Voyage Home**
(USA 1940)
John Ford

Ole Olson (John Wayne)*
Aloysius Driscoll (Thomas Mitchell)
Smithy (Ian Hunter)
Cocky (Barry Fitzgerald)

**The Longest Day** (USA 1962)
Ken Annakin, Andrew Marton,
 Bernhard Wicki

RAF Pilot (Richard Burton)*
Pvt Flanagan (Sean Connery)*
Brig Gen Theodore Roosevelt (Henry
 Fonda)*
Brig Gen Norman Cota (Robert
 Mitchum)*
Lt Col Benjamin Vandervoort (John
 Wayne)*

**The Longest Yard** (USA 1974)
Robert Aldrich

Paul Crewe (Burt Reynolds)*
Warden Hazen (Eddie Albert)*
Capt Knauer (Ed Lauter)
Nate Scarboro (Michael Conrad)

**Longtime Companion** (USA 1990)
Norman René

Willy (Campbell Scott)
Fuzzy (Stephen Caffrey)
Sean (Mark Lamos)
David (Bruce Davidson)

**Look Who's Talking** (USA 1989)
Amy Heckerling

James (John Travolta)*
Mollie (Kirstie Alley)
Rosie (Olympia Dukakis)
Albert (George Segal)*
Voice of Mikey (Bruce Willis)*

Sequel *Look Who's Talking Too* (1990)

**Lorenzo's Oil** (USA 1992)
George Miller

Augusto Odone (Nick Nolte)*
Michaela Odone (Susan Sarandon)*
Professor Nikolais (Peter Ustinov)*
Deirdre Murphy (Kathleen Wilhoite)

**Lost Horizon** (USA 1937)
Frank Capra

Robert Conway (Ronald Colman)*
Sondra (Jane Wyatt)
Alexander Plovett (Edward Everett
 Horton)
George Conway (John Howard)

Musical remake *Lost Horizon* (1973)
 (Peter Finch*, Liv Ullmann*)

**The Lost Weekend** (USA 1945)
Billy Wilder

Don Birnam (Ray Milland)*
Helen St James (Jane Wyman)*
Nick Birnam (Phillip Terry)
Nat the Bartender (Howard Da Silva)

**Love Affair** (USA 1939)
Leo McCarey

Terry McKay (Irene Dunne)*
Michael Marnet (Charles Boyer)*
Grandmother Janou (Maria
 Ouspenskaya)
Kenneth Bradley (Lee Bowman)

Remake *An Affair To Remember* (1957)
 (see p1)

**The Love Bug** (USA 1969)
Robert Stevenson

Jim Douglas (Dean Jones)*
Carol (Michele Lee)
Thorndyke (David Tomlinson)
Tennessee Steinmetz (Buddy Hackett)

Sequels *Herbie Rides Again* (1974);
 *Herbie Goes To Monte Carlo* (1977);
 *Herbie Goes Bananas* (1980)

**Love Is A Many Splendored
 Thing** (USA 1955)
Henry King

Mark Elliot (William Holden)*
Han Suyin (Jennifer Jones)*
Mr Palmer-Jones (Torin Thatcher)
Adeline Palmer-Jones (Isobel Elsom)

**Love Me Or Leave Me** (USA 1955)
Charles Vidor

Ruth Etting (Doris Day)*
'The Gimp' Martin Snyder (James
    Cagney)*
Johnny Alderman (Cameron Mitchell)
Bernard V Loomis (Robert Keith)

**The Love Parade** (USA 1929)
Ernst Lubitsch

Count Alfred Renard (Maurice
    Chevalier)*
Queen Louise (Jeanette McDonald)*
Jacques (Lupino Lane)
Lulu (Lillian Roth)

**Love Story** (USA 1970)
Arthur Hiller

Jenny Cavilleri (Ali MacGraw)*
Oliver Barrett IV (Ryan O'Neal)*
Phil Cavilleri (John Marley)
Oliver Barrett III (Ray Milland)*

Sequel *Oliver's Story* (1978)

**Lust For Life** (USA 1956)
Vincente Minnelli

Vincent Van Gogh (Kirk Douglas)*
Paul Gauguin (Anthony Quinn)*
Theo Van Gogh (James Donald)
Christine (Pamela Brown)

# M

**M** (Germany 1931)
Fritz Lang

Franz Becker (Peter Lorre)*
Mother (Ellen Widmann)
Child (Inge Landgot)
Safe-Breaker (Gustav Grundgens)

Remake *M* (1951) (David Wayne)

**Mad Max** (Australia 1979)
George Miller

Mad Max (Mel Gibson)*
Jessie (Joanne Samuel)
Toecutter (Hugh Keays-Byrne)
Goose (Steve Bisley)

**Mad Max II — The Road Warrior**
    (Australia 1981)
George Miller

Mad Max (Mel Gibson)*
Gyro Captain (Bruce Spence)
Wez (Vernon Wells)
Feral Kid (Emil Minty)

**Mad Max—Beyond Thunderdome**
    (Australia/USA 1985)
George Miller, George Ogilvie

Mad Max (Mel Gibson)*
Jedediah (Bruce Spence)
Jedediah Jnr (Adam Cockburn)
Aunty Entity (Tina Turner)

**Madame Curie** (USA 1943)
Mervyn Le Roy

Madame Marie Curie (Greer Garson)*
Pierre Curie (Walter Pidgeon)*
David Le Gros (Robert Walker)
Eugène Curie (Dame May Whitty)

**The Magnificent Ambersons**
    (USA 1942)
Orson Welles

Eugene Morgan (Joseph Cotten)*
Isabel Amberson Minafer (Dolores
    Costello)
Lucy Morgan (Anne Baxter)*
George Amberson Minafer (Tim Holt)
Fanny Amberson (Agnes Moorehead)*

**Magnificent Obsession** (USA 1954)
Douglas Sirk

Helen Phillips (Jane Wyman)*
Bob Merrick (Rock Hudson)*

**Magnificent Obsession** (USA 1954)
(cont.)
Joyce Phillips (Barbara Rush)
Nancy Ashford (Agnes Moorehead)*

Previous version *Magnificent Obsession*
(1935) (Irene Dunne*, Robert Taylor*)


**The Magnificent Seven** (USA 1960)
John Sturges

Chris (Yul Brynner)*
Calvera (Eli Wallach)*
Vin (Steve McQueen)*
Chico (Horst Buchholz)
O'Reilly (Charles Bronson)*
Lee (Robert Vaughn)
Harry Luck (Brad Dexter)
Britt (James Coburn)*

Sequels *Return Of The Seven* (1966);
*Guns Of The Magnificent Seven*
(1969); *The Magnificent Seven Ride!*
(1972)


**Malcolm X** (USA 1992)
Spike Lee

Malcolm X (Denzel Washington)*
Shorty (Spike Lee)
Betty Shabazz (Angela Bassett)
Baines (Albert Hall)
Elijah Mohammad (Al Freeman Jnr)


**The Maltese Falcon** (USA 1941)
John Huston

Sam Spade (Humphrey Bogart)*
Brigid O'Shaughnessy (Mary Astor)*
Iva Archer (Gladys George)
Joel Cairo (Peter Lorre)*
Casper Gutman (Sydney Greenstreet)

Other versions *The Maltese Falcon*
(1931) (Ricardo Cortez, Bebe
Daniels); *Satan Met A Lady* (1936)
(Warren William, Bette Davis*)
Spoof remake *The Blackbird* (1975)
(George Segal*, Stéphane Audran)

**A Man For All Seasons** (UK 1966)
Fred Zinnemann

Thomas More (Paul Scofield)*
Alice More (Wendy Hiller)*
Cromwell (Leo McKern)
King Henry VIII (Robert Shaw)*
Cardinal Wolsley (Orson Welles)*
Margaret More (Susannah York)*
Richard Rich (John Hurt)*

Remake *A Man For All Seasons* (TV
1988) (Charlton Heston*, Vanessa
Redgrave*)


**The Man In The White Suit**
(UK 1951)
Alexander Mackendrick

Sidney Stratton (Alec Guinness)*
Daphne Birnley (Joan Greenwood)*
Alan Birnley (Cecil Parker)*
Michael Cornland (Michael Gough)


**The Man Who Shot Liberty
Valance** (USA 1962)
John Ford

Ransom Stoddart (James Stewart)*
Tom Doniphon (John Wayne)*
Hallie Stoddart (Vera Miles)
Liberty Valance (Lee Marvin)*


**The Man Who Would Be King**
(USA 1975)
John Huston

Daniel Dravot (Sean Connery)*
Peachy Carnehan (Michael Caine)*
Rudyard Kipling (Christopher Plummer)
Billy Fish (Saeed Jaffrey)


**The Manchurian Candidate**
(USA 1962)
John Frankenheimer

Bennet Marco (Frank Sinatra)*
Raymond Shaw (Laurence Harvey)*
Eugenie Rose 'Rosie' (Janet Leigh)*
Eleanor Iselin (Angela Lansbury)*

**Manhattan** (USA 1979)
Woody Allen

Isaac Davis (Woody Allen)*
Mary Wilke (Diane Keaton)*
Yale (Michael Murphy)
Tracy (Mariel Hemingway)
Jill (Meryl Streep)*

**Marty** (USA 1955)
Delbert Mann

Marty (Ernest Borgnine)*
Clara (Betsy Blair)
Mrs Pilletti (Esther Minciotti)
Virginia (Karen Steele)

**Mary Poppins** (USA 1964)
Robert Stevenson

Mary Poppins (Julie Andrews)*
Bert/Mr Dawes Snr (Dick Van Dyke)
Mr Banks (David Tomlinson)
Mrs Banks (Glynis Johns)

**M*A*S*H** (USA 1970)
Robert Altman

Hawkeye (Donald Sutherland)*
Trapper John (Elliott Gould)*
Duke (Tom Skeritt)
Maj Hot Lips (Sally Kellerman)
Maj Frank Burns (Robert Duvall)*

**A Matter Of Life And Death**
(UK 1946)
Michael Powell, Emeric Pressburger

Squadron Leader Peter Carter (David
   Niven)*
June (Kim Hunter)
Conductor 71 (Marius Goring)
Dr Reeves (Roger Livesey)
Abraham Farlan (Raymond Massey)*
English Pilot (Richard Attenborough)*

**Mean Streets** (USA 1973)
Martin Scorsese

Johnny Boy (Robert De Niro)*
Charlie (Harvey Keitel)*
Tony (David Proval)
Teresa (Amy Robinson)

**Meet Me In St Louis** (USA 1944)
Vincente Minnelli

Esther Smith (Judy Garland)*
'Tootie' Smith (Margaret O'Brien)
Mrs Anna Smith (Mary Astor)*
Rose Smith (Lucille Bremer)

**Memphis Belle** (UK 1990)
Michael Caton-Jones

Dennis Dearborn (Matthew Modine)*
Danny Daly (Eric Stolz)
Luke Sinclair (Tate Donovan)
Phil Rosenthal (D B Sweeney)

**Mephisto** (Hungary 1981)
Istvan Szabo

Hendrik Hofgen (Klaus Maria
   Brandauer)*
Nicoletta Von Niebuhr (Ildiko Bansagi)
Barbara Bruckner (Krystyna Janda)
General (Rolf Hoppe)

**Midnight Cowboy** (USA 1969)
John Schlesinger

Joe Buck (Jon Voight)*
Enrico 'Ratso' Rizzo (Dustin Hoffman)*
Cass (Sylvia Miles)
Shirley (Brenda Vaccaro)

**Midnight Express** (USA 1978)
Alan Parker

Billy Hayes (Brad Davis)
Jimmy (Randy Quaid)
Tex (Bo Hopkins)
Max (John Hurt)*

**Midnight Run** (USA 1988)
Martin Brest

Jack Walsh (Robert De Niro)*
Jonathan Mardukas (Charles Grodin)
Alonzo Mosely (Yaphet Kotto)
Marvin Dorfler (John Ashton)

## A Midsummer Night's Dream
(USA 1935)
William Dieterle

Bottom (James Cagney)*
Hermia (Olivia De Havilland)*
Puck (Mickey Rooney)*
Lysander (Dick Powell)*

## Mildred Pierce (USA 1945)
Michael Curtiz

Mildred Pierce (Joan Crawford)*
Wally Fay (Jack Carson)
Monty Beragon (Zachary Scott)
Ida (Eve Arden)
Veda Pierce (Ann Blyth)

## Miller's Crossing (USA 1990)
Joel Coen

Tom Reagan (Gabriel Byrne)
Verna (Marcia Gay Harden)
Bernie Bernbaum (John Turturro)*
Leo (Albert Finney)*

## Miracle On 34th Street (USA 1947)
George Seaton

Doris Walker (Maureen O'Hara)*
Fred Gailey (John Payne)
Kris Kringle (Edmund Gwenn)
Susan Walker (Natalie Wood)

Remake *Miracle On 34th Street* (TV 1973) (Jane Alexander, David Hartman, Sebastian Cabot)

## Misery (USA 1990)
Rob Reiner

Paul Sheldon (James Caan)*
Annie Wilkes (Kathy Bates)*
Buster (Richard Farnsworth)
Virginia (Frances Sternhagen)
Marcia Snidell (Lauren Bacall)*

## The Misfits (USA 1960)
John Huston

Gay Langland (Clark Gable)*
Roslyn Taber (Marilyn Monroe)*
Perce Howland (Montgomery Clift)*
Isabelle Steers (Thelma Ritter)

## Missing (USA 1981)
Costa-Gavras

Ed Horman (Jack Lemmon)*
Beth Horman (Sissy Spacek)*
Terry Simon (Melanie Mayron)
Charles Horman (John Shea)

## Mississippi Burning (USA 1988)
Alan Parker

Anderson (Gene Hackman)*
Ward (Willem Dafoe)*
Mrs Pell (Frances McDormand)
Deputy Pell (Brad Dourif)

## Mrs Miniver (USA 1942)
William Wyler

Mrs Kay Miniver (Greer Garson)*
Clem Miniver (Walter Pidgeon)*
Carol Beldon (Teresa Wright)
Lady Beldon (Dame May Whitty)

Sequel *The Miniver Story* (1950)

## Mr Deeds Goes To Town (USA 1936)
Frank Capra

Longfellow Deeds (Gary Cooper)*
Babe Bennett (Jean Arthur)*
MacWade (George Bancroft)
Cornelius Cobb (Lionel Stander)

## Mister Roberts (USA 1955)
John Ford

Lt Doug Roberts (Henry Fonda)
The Captain (James Cagney)*
Ensign Frank Thurlowe Pulver (Jack Lemmon)*
Doc (William Powell)*

Sequel *Ensign Pulver* (1964) (Robert Walker Jnr, Burl Ives, Walter Matthau*)

## Mr Smith Goes To Washington
(USA 1939)
Frank Capra

Jefferson Smith (James Stewart)*
Saunders (Jean Arthur)*
Senator Joseph Payne (Claude Rains)*
Jim Taylor (Edward Arnold)

**Modern Times** (USA 1936)
Charles Chaplin

A Tramp (Charles Chaplin)*
A Gamin (Paulette Goddard)
A Café Proprietor (Henry Bergman)
A Mechanic (Chester Conklin)

**Mona Lisa** (UK 1986)
Neil Jordan

George (Bob Hoskins)*
Simone (Cathy Tyson)
Mortwell (Michael Caine)*
Anderson (Clarke Peters)

**Monsieur Hulot's Holiday**
(France 1952)
Jacques Tati

Monsieur Hulot (Jacques Tati)*
Martine (Nathalie Pascaud)
Old Maid (Valentine Camax)
The Aunt (Michela Rolla)

**Moonraker** (USA 1979)
Lewis Gilbert

James Bond (Roger Moore)*
Holly Goodhead (Lois Chiles)
Drax (Michael Lonsdale)
Jaws (Richard Kiel)

**Moonstruck** (USA 1987)
Norman Jewison

Loretta Castorini (Cher)*
Ronny Cammareri (Nicolas Cage)*
Cosmo Castorini (Vincent Gardenia)
Rose Castorini (Olympia Dukakis)
Mr Johnny Cammareri (Danny Aiello)

**Morte E Venezia** see **Death In Venice**

**Moulin Rouge** (UK 1952)
John Huston

Toulouse Lautrec/His Father (Jose
  Ferrer)
Marie Charlet (Colette Marchand)
Myriamme Hayem (Suzanne Flon)
Jane Avril (Zsa Zsa Gabor)

**Mujeres Al Borde De Un Ataque De Nervios** see **Women On The Verge Of A Nervous Breakdown**

**The Muppet Movie** (USA 1979)
James Frawley

Kermit the Frog/Rowlf/Dr Teeth/Waldorf
  (Jim Henson)
Miss Piggy/Fozzie Bear/Animal/Sam the
  Eagle (Frank Oz)
Floyd Pepper/Crazy Harry/Robin the
  Frog/Lew Zealand (Jerry Nelson)
Scooter/Statler/Janice/Sweetums/
  Beaker (Richard Hurt)

**Murder On The Orient Express**
(UK 1974)
Sidney Lumet

Hercule Poirot (Albert Finney)*
Mrs Hubbard (Lauren Bacall)*
Greta Ohlsson (Ingrid Bergman)*
Countess Andronyi (Jacqueline Bisset)*
Col Arbuthnot (Sean Connery)*
Beddoes (John Gielgud)*
Princess Dragomiroff (Wendy Hiller)*
Hector McQueen (Anthony Perkins)*
Mary Debenham (Vanessa Redgrave)*
Hildegarde Schmidt (Rachel Roberts)*
Ratchett (Richard Widmark)*
Count Andrenyi (Michael York)*

**The Music Man** (USA 1962)
Morton Dacosta

Harold Hill (Robert Preston)*
Marian Paroo (Shirley Jones)
Marcellus Washburn (Buddy Hackett)
Eulalie MacKechnie Shinn (Hermione
  Gingold)

**Mutiny On The Bounty** (USA 1935)
Frank Lloyd

Capt William Bligh (Charles Laughton)*
Fletcher Christian (Clark Gable)*
Roger Byam (Franchot Tone)
Burkitt (Donald Crisp)

**Mutiny On The Bounty** (USA 1962)
Lewis Milestone

Fletcher Christian (Marlon Brando)*
Capt William Bligh (Trevor Howard)*
John Mills (Richard Harris)*
Alexander Smith (Hugh Griffith)


**My Beautiful Laundrette** (UK 1985)
Stephen Frears

Johnny (Daniel Day-Lewis)*
Nasser (Saeed Jaffrey)
Papa (Roshan Seth)
Omar (Gordon Warnecke)


**My Darling Clementine** (USA 1946)
John Ford

Wyatt Earp (Henry Fonda)*
Chihuahua (Linda Darnell)*
Doc Holliday (Victor Mature)*
Old Man Clanton (Walter Brennan)


**My Fair Lady** (USA 1964)
George Cukor

Eliza Doolittle (Audrey Hepburn)*
Prof Henry Higgins (Rex Harrison)*
Alfred P Doolittle (Stanley Holloway)
Col Hugh Pickering (Wilfrid Hyde-White)


**My Left Foot** (UK 1989)
Jim Sheridan

Christy Brown (Daniel Day-Lewis)*
Mrs Brown (Brenda Fricker)
Sheila (Alison Whelan)
Mr Brown (Ray McAnally)


**My Own Private Idaho** (USA 1991)
Gus Van Sant

Mike Waters (River Phoenix)*
Scott Favor (Keanu Reeves)*
Richard Waters (James Russo)
Bob Pigeon (William Richert)

# N

**The Naked Gun: From The Files Of Police Squad!** (USA 1988)
David Zucker

Frank Drebin (Leslie Nielsen)*
Jane Spence (Priscilla Presley)
Vincent Ludwig (Ricardo Montalban)
Ed Hocken (George Kennedy)

Sequels *The Naked Gun 2½: The Smell Of Fear* (1991); *The Naked Gun 33⅓ (1993)*


**Nashville** (USA 1975)
Robert Altman

Connie White (Karen Black)
Barbara Jean (Ronee Blakely)
Tom Frank (Keith Carradine)
Opal (Geraldine Chaplin)
Linnea Reese (Lily Tomlin)*


**National Lampoon's Animal House** (USA 1978)
John Landis

Larry 'Pinto' Kroger (Thomas Hulce)
Kent 'Flounder' Dorfman (Stephen Furst)
Chip Diller (Kevin Bacon)
John 'Bluto' Blutarsky (John Belushi)*


**National Velvet** (USA 1944)
Clarence Brown

Mi Taylor (Mickey Rooney)*
Mr Brown (Donald Crisp)
Velvet Brown (Elizabeth Taylor)*
Mrs Brown (Anne Revere)
Edwina Brown (Angela Lansbury)*

Sequel *International Velvet* (1978)
(Tatum O'Neal)


**Network** (USA 1976)
Sidney Lumet

Diane Christenson (Faye Dunaway)*
Max Schumacher (William Holden)*
Howard Beale (Peter Finch)*
Frank Hackett (Robert Duvall)*
Louise Schumacher (Beatrice Straight)

**Never Say Never Again** (UK 1983)
Irvin Kershner

James Bond (Sean Connery)*
Maximilian Largo (Klaus Maria
  Brandauer)*
Ernst Blofeld (Max Von Sydow)*
Fatima Blush (Barbara Carrera)
Domino (Kim Basinger)*

**New York, New York** (USA 1977)
Martin Scorsese

Francine Evans (Liza Minnelli)*
Jimmy Doyle (Robert De Niro)*
Tony Harwell (Lionel Stander)
Paul Wilson (Barry Primus)

**Night And Day** (USA 1946)
Michael Curtiz

Cole Porter (Cary Grant)*
Linda Lee Porter (Alexis Smith)
Himself (Monty Woolley)
Carole Hill (Ginny Simms)

**A Night At The Opera** (USA 1935)
Sam Wood

Otis B Driftwood (Groucho Marx)*
Fiorello (Chico Marx)*
Tomasso (Harpo Marx)*
Mrs Claypool (Margaret Dumont)

**The Night Of The Hunter** (USA 1955)
Charles Laughton

Preacher Harry Powell (Robert Mitchum)*
Willa Harper (Shelley Winters)*
Rachel Cooper (Lillian Gish)*
Birdie (James Gleason)

Remake *Night Of The Hunter* (TV 1991)
  (Richard Chamberlain)

**Night Of The Iguana** (USA 1964)
John Huston

Rev T Lawrence Shannon (Richard
  Burton)*
Maxine Faulk (Ava Gardner)*
Hannah Jelkes (Deborah Kerr)*
Charlotte Goodall (Sue Lyon)

**Night Of The Living Dead**
  (USA 1968)
George A Romero

Barbara (Judith O'Dea)
Ben (Duane Jones)
Harry Cooper (Karl Hardman)
Tom (Keith Wayne)

Sequels *Dawn Of The Dead* (1978); *Day
  Of The Dead* (1985)
Remake *Night Of The Living Dead*
  (1990)

**A Nightmare On Elm Street**
  (USA 1984)
Wes Craven

Lt Thompson (John Saxon)
Margee (Ronee Blakely)
Nancy (Heather Langenkamp)
Glen (Johnny Depp)*
Freddie Krueger (Robert Englund)*

Sequels *A Nightmare On Elm Street 2:
  Freddy's Revenge* (1985); *A
  Nightmare On Elm Street 3: Dream
  Warriors* (1987); *A Nightmare On Elm
  Street 4: The Dream Master* (1988); *A
  Nightmare On Elm Street 5: The
  Dream Child* (1989); *Freddy's Dead:
  A Nightmare On Elm Street 6* (1991)

**The Nights Of Cabiria** (Italy 1957)
(*Le Notti Di Cabiria*)
Federico Fellini

Cabiria (Giulietta Masina)
Oscar D'Onofrio the Accountant
  (François Perier)
Alberto Lazzari the Movie Star (Amedeo
  Nazzari)
Hypnotist (Aldo Silvani)

**Nine To Five** (USA 1980)
Colin Higgins

Judy Bernly (Jane Fonda)*
Violet Newstead (Lily Tomlin)*
Doralee Rhodes (Dolly Parton)*
Franklin Hart Jnr (Dabney Coleman)

*1941* (USA 1979)
Steven Spielberg

Sgt Tree (Dan Aykroyd)*
Ward Douglas (Ned Beatty)
Wild Bill Kelso (John Belushi)*
Joan Douglas (Lorraine Gary)
Gen Stilwell (Robert Stack)

*1900* (Italy/France/Germany 1976)
(*Novocento*)
Bernardo Bertolucci

Alfredo Berlinghieri (Robert De Niro)*
Olmo Dalco (Gérard Depardieu)*
Attila (Donald Sutherland)*
Alfredo Berlinghieri (Burt Lancaster)*

*Ninotchka* (USA 1939)
Ernst Lubitsch

Lena Yakushova 'Ninotchka' (Greta
  Garbo)*
Count Leon D'Algout (Melvyn Douglas)*
Duchess Swana (Ina Claire)
Michael Iranoff (Sig Rumann)

Musical remake *Silk Stockings* (1957)
  (Cyd Charisse*, Fred Astaire*)

*No Way Out* (USA 1987)
Roger Donaldson

Tom Farrell (Kevin Costner)*
David Brice (Gene Hackman)*
Susan Atwell (Sean Young)
Scott Pritchard (Will Patton)

*Norma Rae* (USA 1979)
Martin Ritt

Norma Rae (Sally Field)*
Sonny (Beau Bridges)*
Reuben (Ron Leibman)
Vernon (Pat Hingle)

*North By Northwest* (USA 1959)
Alfred Hitchcock

Roger Thornhill (Cary Grant)*
Eve Kendall (Eva Marie Saint)
Phillip Vandamm (James Mason)*
Clara Thornhill (Jessie Royce Landis)

*Not As A Stranger* (USA 1955)
Stanley Kramer

Lucas Marsh (Robert Mitchum)*
Kristina Hedvigson (Olivia De
  Havilland)*
Alfred Boone (Frank Sinatra)*
Harriet Lang (Gloria Grahame)*

*Notorious* (USA 1946)
Alfred Hitchcock

Nick Devlin (Cary Grant)*
Alicia Huberman (Ingrid Bergman)*
Alexander Sebastian (Claude Rains)*
Paul Prescott (Louis Calhern)

*Le Notti Di Cabiria* see *Nights Of
  Cabiria*

*Novocento* see *1900*

*Now Voyager* (USA 1942)
Irving Rapper

Charlotte Vale (Bette Davis)*
Jerry Durrance (Paul Henreid)
Dr Jaquith (Claude Rains)*
June Vale (Bonita Granville)

*La Nuit Americaine* see *Day For
  Night*

*The Nun's Story* (USA 1959)
Fred Zinnemann

Sister Luke (Audrey Hepburn)*
Dr Fortunati (Peter Finch)*
Mother Emmanuel (Edith Evans)*
Mother Mathilde (Peggy Ashcroft)*

*Nuts* (USA 1987)
Martin Ritt

Claudia Draper (Barbra Streisand)*
Aaron Levinsky (Richard Dreyfuss)*
Rose Kirk (Maureen Stapleton)
Arthur Kirk (Karl Malden)*

# O

## Oceans Eleven (USA 1960)
Lewis Milestone

Danny Ocean (Frank Sinatra)*
Sam Harmon (Dean Martin)*
Josh Howard (Sammy Davis Jnr)*
Jimmy Foster (Peter Lawford)

## Octopussy (UK 1983)
John Glen

James Bond (Roger Moore)*
Octopussy (Maud Adams)
Kamal (Louis Jourdan)*
Magda (Kristina Wayborn)

## The Odd Couple (USA 1967)
Gene Saks

Felix Unger (Jack Lemmon)*
Oscar Madison (Walter Matthau)*
Cecily Pigeon (Monica Evans)
Gwendolyn Pigeon (Carole Shelley)

## Odd Man Out (UK 1946)
Carol Reed

Johnny McQueen (James Mason)*
Lukey (Robert Newton)*
Dennis (Robert Beatty)
Shell (F J McCormick)

Remake *The Lost Man* (1969) (Sidney Poitier*)

## Of Mice And Men (USA 1939)
Lewis Milestone

George (Burgess Meredith)*
Mae (Betty Field)
Lennie (Lon Chaney Jnr)
Slim (Charles Bickford)

Remake *Of Mice And Men* (1992) (Gary Sinise, John Malkovich*)

## An Officer And A Gentleman
(USA 1982)
Taylor Hackford

Zack Mayo (Richard Gere)*

Paula Pokrifki (Debra Winger)*
Sid Worley (David Keith)
Byron Mayo (Robert Loggia)
Sgt Emil Foley (Louis Gossett Jnr)

## Offret see The Sacrifice

## Oh, God! (USA 1977)
Carl Reiner

God (George Burns)*
Jerry Landers (John Denver)
Bobbie Landers (Teri Garr)
Dr Harmon (Donald Pleasence)
Sam Raven (Ralph Bellamy)*

Sequels *Oh, God! Book II* (1980); *Oh, God! You Devil* (1984)

## Oh, Mr Porter! (UK 1937)
Marcel Varnel

William Porter (Will Hay)*
Jeremiah Harbottle (Moore Marriott)
Albert Brown (Graham Moffatt)
Charles Trimbletow (Sebastian Smith)

## Oklahoma! (USA 1956)
Fred Zinnemann

Curly (Gordon Macrae)
Ado Annie (Gloria Grahame)*
Laurey (Shirley Jones)
Jud Fry (Rod Steiger)*

## Old Gringo (USA 1989)
Luis Puenzo

Harriet Winslow (Jane Fonda)*
Ambrose Bierce (Bitter) (Gregory Peck)*
Tomas Arroyo (Jimmy Smits)
Col Frutos Garcia (Patricio Contreras)

## The Old Maid (USA 1939)
Edmund Goulding

Charlotte Lovell (Bette Davis)*
Delia Lovell Ralston (Miriam Hopkins)*
Clem Spender (George Brent)
Tina (Jane Bryan)

***Oliver!*** (UK 1968)
Carol Reed

Fagin (Ron Moody)
Nancy (Shani Wallis)
Bill Sikes (Oliver Reed)*
Mr Bumble (Harry Secombe)
Oliver Twist (Mark Lester)
The Artful Dodger (Jack Wild)

***Oliver Twist*** (UK 1948)
David Lean

Bill Sykes (Robert Newton)*
Fagin (Alec Guinness)*
Nancy (Kay Walsh)
Oliver Twist (John Howard Davies)

***The Omen*** (UK 1976)
Richard Donner

Robert Thorn (Gregory Peck)*
Katherine Thorn (Lee Remick)*
Jennings (David Warner)
Mrs Baylock (Billie Whitelaw)

Sequels *Damien—Omen II* (1978); *The Final Conflict* (1981); *Omen IV: The Awakening* (TV 1991)

***On Golden Pond*** (USA 1981)
Mark Rydell

Ethel Thayer (Katharine Hepburn)*
Norman Thayer Jnr (Henry Fonda)*
Chelsea Thayer Wayne (Jane Fonda)*
Billy Ray (Doug McKeon)

***On Her Majesty's Secret Service***
(UK 1969)
Peter Hunt

James Bond (George Lazenby)
Tracy Draco (Diana Rigg)
Ernest Stavro Blofeld (Telly Savalas)
Marc Ange Draco (Gabriele Ferzetti)

***On The Town*** (USA 1949)
Gene Kelly, Stanley Donen

Gabey (Gene Kelly)*
Chip (Frank Sinatra)*

Brunhilde Esterhazy (Betty Garrett)
Claire Huddesen (Ann Miller)
Ozzie (Jules Monshin)
Ivy Smith (Vera-Ellen)

***On The Waterfront*** (USA 1954)
Elia Kazan

Terry Malloy (Marlon Brando)*
Edie Doyle (Eva Marie Saint)
Father Barry (Karl Malden)*
Johnny Friendly (Lee J Cobb)
Charles Malloy (Rod Steiger)*

***Once Upon A Time In America***
(USA 1983)
Sergio Leone

Noodles (Robert De Niro)*
Max (James Woods)*
Deborah (Elizabeth McGovern)
Carol (Tuesday Weld)*

***Once Upon A Time In The West***
(Italy 1968)
(*Cera Una Volta E West*)
Sergio Leone

Harmonica (Charles Bronson)*
Frank (Henry Fonda)*
Cheyenne (Jason Robards)*
Jill McBain (Claudia Cardinale)

***One-Eyed Jacks*** (USA 1961)
Marlon Brando

Rio (Marlon Brando)*
'Dad' Longworth (Karl Malden)*
Louisa (Pina Pellicer)
Maria (Katy Jurado)

***One Flew Over The Cuckoo's Nest*** (USA 1975)
Milos Forman

Randle Patrick McMurphy (Jack Nicholson)*
Nurse Mildred Ratched (Louise Fletcher)
Harding (William Redfield)
Ellis (Michael Berryman)

**One Hundred And One Dalmatians** (USA 1961)
Wolfgang Reitherman, Hamilton S Luske, Clyde Geronimi

Voices of:
Pongo (Rod Taylor)*
Anita (Lisa Davis)
Perdita (Cate Bauer)
Roger Radcliff (Ben Wright)

**One Hundred Men And A Girl** (USA 1937)
Henry Koster

Patricia Cardwell (Deanna Durbin)*
Himself (Leopold Stokowski)
John Cardwell (Adolphe Menjou)
Mrs Frost (Alice Brady)

**One, Two, Three** (USA 1961)
Billy Wilder

C R MacNamara (James Cagney)*
Otto Ludwig Piffl (Horst Buchholz)
Scarlett Hazeltine (Pamela Tiffin)
Phyllis MacNamara (Arlene Francis)

**Operation Petticoat** (USA 1959)
Blake Edwards

Admiral Matt Sherman (Cary Grant)*
Lt Nick Holden (Tony Curtis)*
Lt Dolores Crandall (Joan O'Brien)
Lt Barbara Duran (Dina Merrill)

Remake *Operation Petticoat* (TV 1977)
(John Astin, Richard Gilliland, Jamie Lee Curtis*)

**Orphée** see **Orpheus**

**Ordinary People** (USA 1980)
Robert Redford

Calvin (Donald Sutherland)*
Beth (Mary Tyler Moore)
Conrad (Timothy Hutton)*
Berger (Judd Hirsch)

**Orpheus** (France 1950)
(*Orphée*)
Jean Cocteau

Orphée (Jean Marais)
The Princess (Maria Casares)
Eurydice (Marie Dea)
Heurtebise (François Perier)

**Ossessione** (Italy 1942)
Luchino Visconti

Giovanna (Clara Calamai)
Gino (Massimo Girotti)
The Husband (Juan De Landa)
Lo Spagnuolo (Elia Marcuzzo)

**Othello** (USA 1952)
Orson Welles

Othello (Orson Welles)*
Iago (Micheal MacLiammoir)
Desdemona (Suzanne Cloutier)
Roderigo (Robert Coote)

Subsequent version *Othello* (1965)
(Laurence Olivier*, Maggie Smith*)

**Otto E Mezzo** see **8½**

**Our Town** (USA 1940)
Sam Wood

Mr Morgan, the Narrator (Frank Craven)
George Gibbs (William Holden)*
Emily Webb (Martha Scott)
Mrs Gibbs (Fay Bainter)

**Out Of Africa** (USA 1985)
Sydney Pollack

Karen Blixen (Meryl Streep)*
Denys Finch Hatton (Robert Redford)*
Baron Bror Blixen (Klaus Maria Brandauer)*
Berkeley (Michael Kitchen)

**The Outlaw** (USA 1943/1946)
Howard Hughes

Rio (Jane Russell)*
Billy the Kid (Jack Buetel)

**The Outlaw** (USA 1943/1946) (cont.)
Pat Garrett (Thomas Mitchell)
Doc Holliday (Walter Huston)*

**The Outlaw Josey Wales**
(USA 1976)
Clint Eastwood

Josey Wales (Clint Eastwood)*
Lone Watie (Chief Dan George)
Laura Lee (Sondra Locke)
Terrill (Bill McKinney)

Sequel *The Return of Josey Wales*
(1986) (Michael Parks)

**The Outsiders** (USA 1983)
Francis Coppola

Dallas Winston (Matt Dillon)*
Johnny Cade (Ralph Macchio)*
Ponyboy Curtis (C Thomas Howell)*
Darrel Curtis (Patrick Swayze)*
Sodapop Curtis (Rob Lowe)*
Two-Bit Mathews (Emilio Estevez)*
Steve Randle (Tom Cruise)*

**The Owl And The Pussycat**
(USA 1970)
Herbert Ross

Doris (Barbra Streisand)*
Felix (George Segal)*
Barney (Robert Klein)
Dress Shop Proprietor (Allen Garfield)

**The Ox-Bow Incident** (USA 1943)
William A Wellman

Gil Carter (Henry Fonda)*
Donald Martin (Dana Andrews)*
Rose Mapen (Mary Beth Hughes)
Juan Martines (Anthony Quinn)*

# P

**Paint Your Wagon** (USA 1969)
Joshua Logan

Ben Rumson (Lee Marvin)*
Pardner (Clint Eastwood)*
Elizabeth (Jean Seberg)
Rotten Luck Willie (Harve Presnell)

**The Paleface** (USA 1948)
Norman Z McLeod

'Painless' Peter Potter (Bob Hope)*
Calamity Jane (Jane Russell)*
Terris (Robert Armstrong)
Pepper (Iris Adrian)

Sequel *The Son Of Paleface* (1952)

**Pale Rider** (USA 1985)
Clint Eastwood

Preacher (Clint Eastwood)*
Hull Barret (Michael Moriarty)
Sarah Wheeler (Carrie Snodgress)
Josh La Hood (Christopher Penn)

**The Palm Beach Story** (USA 1942)
Preston Sturges

Jerry Jeffers (Claudette Colbert)*
Tom Jeffers (Joel McCrea)*
Princess Centimillia (Mary Astor)*
J B Hackensacker III (Rudy Vallee)

**Paper Moon** (USA 1973)
Peter Bogdanovich

Moses Pray (Ryan O'Neal)*
Addie Loggins (Tatum O'Neal)
Trixie Delight (Madeline Kahn)
Deputy Hardin (John Hillerman)

**Papillon** (USA 1973)
Franklin J Schaffner

Henri Charrière, 'Papillon' (Steve
  McQueen)*
Louis Dega (Dustin Hoffman)*
Indian Chief (Victor Jory)
Julot (Don Gordon)

**Parenthood** (USA 1989)
Ron Howard

Gil Buckman (Steve Martin)*
Karen Buckman (Mary Steenburgen)
Helen (Dianne Wiest)
Frank Buckman (Jason Robards)*
Tod (Keanu Reeves)*

**Paris, Texas** (USA 1984)
Wim Wenders

Travis Anderson (Harry Dean Stanton)
Walter R Anderson (Dean Stockwell)
Jane (Nastassja Kinski)*
Hunter Anderson (Hunter Carson)

**A Passage To India** (UK 1984)
David Lean

Adela Quested (Judy Davis)*
Dr Aziz (Victor Banerjee)
Mrs Moore (Peggy Ashcroft)*
Richard Fielding (James Fox)

**Pat And Mike** (USA 1952)
George Cukor

Mike Conovan (Spencer Tracy)*
Pat Pemberton (Katharine Hepburn)*
Davie Hucko (Aldo Ray)
Collier Weld (William Ching)

**Pather Panchali** (India 1955)
(*Song Of The Little Road*)
Satyajit Ray

Harihar (Kanu Banerjee)
Sarbajaya (Karuna Banerjee)
Durga (Uma Das Gupta)
Apu (Subir Banerjee)

Sequels *Aparajito* (1956); *Apu Sansar* (1959)

**Paths Of Glory** (USA 1957)
Stanley Kubrick

Col Dax (Kirk Douglas)*
Corp Paris (Ralph Meeker)
Gen Broulard (Adolphe Menjou)
Gen Mireau (George Macready)

**Patton: Lust For Glory** (USA 1970)
Franklin J Schaffner

Gen George S Patton Jnr (George C Scott)*
Gen Omar N Bradley (Karl Malden)*
Capt Chester B Hansen (Stephen Young)
Brig Gen Hobart Carver (Michael Strong)

Sequel *The Last Days of Patton* (TV 1986)

**The Pawnbroker** (USA 1965)
Sidney Lumet

Sol Nazerman (Rod Steiger)*
Marilyn Birchfield (Geraldine Fitzgerald)
Rodriguez (Brock Peters)
Jesus Ortiz (Jaime Sanchez)

**Peeping Tom** (UK 1959)
Michael Powell

Mark Lewis (Carl Boehm)
Helen Stephens (Anna Massey)
Mrs Stephens (Maxine Audley)
Vivian (Moira Shearer)

**Peggy Sue Got Married** (USA 1986)
Francis Coppola

Peggy Sue (Kathleen Turner)*
Charlie Bodell (Nicolas Cage)*
Richard Norvik (Barry Miller)
Carol Heath (Catherine Hicks)

**Per Qualche Dollare In Pui** see **For A Few Dollars More**

**Pur Un Pugno Di Dollari** see **A Fistful Of Dollars**

**Persona** (Sweden 1966)
Ingmar Bergman

Elisabeth Vogler (Liv Ullmann)*
Nurse Alma (Bibi Andersson)
The Woman Doctor (Margarethe Krook)
Mr Vogler (Gunnar Bjornstrand)

**Personal Services** (UK 1987)
Terry Jones

Christine Painter (Julie Walters)*
Wing Commander Morton (Alec McCowen)
Shirley (Shirley Stelfox)
Dolly (Danny Schiller)

**Peter Pan** (USA 1953)
Hamilton Luske, Clyde Geronimi,
  Wilfred Jackson

Voices of:
Peter Pan (Bobby Driscoll)
Wendy (Kathryn Beaumont)
Captain Hook/Mr Darling (Hans Conreid)
Mr Smee (Bill Thompson)

**Peter's Friends** (UK 1992)
Kenneth Branagh

Roger (Hugh Laurie)
Mary (Imelda Staunton)
Peter (Stephen Fry)
Maggie (Emma Thompson)
Andrew (Kenneth Branagh)*
Sarah (Alphonsia Emmanuel)
Carol (Rita Rudner)

**The Petrified Forest** (USA 1936)
Archie L Mayo

Alan Squier (Leslie Howard)*
Gabrielle Maple (Bette Davis)*
Mrs Chisholm (Genevieve Tobin)
Duke Mantee (Humphrey Bogart)*

**Peyton Place** (USA 1957)
Mark Robson

Constance MacKenzie (Lana Turner)*
Selena Cross (Hope Lange)
Dr Matthew Swain (Lloyd Nolan)
Lucas Cross (Arthur Kennedy)*

Sequel *Return To Peyton Place* (1961);
  *Murder In Peyton Place* (TV 1977);
  *Peyton Place: The Next Generation*
  (TV 1985)

**The Philadelphia Story** (USA 1940)
George Cukor

C K Dexter Haven (Cary Grant)*
Tracy Lord (Katharine Hepburn)*
Macaulay Connor (James Stewart)*
Elizabeth Imbrie (Ruth Hussey)

Musical remake *High Society* (1956)
  (see p39)

**Pickpocket** (France 1959)
Robert Bresson

Michel (Martin Lassalle)
Jeanne (Marika Green)
Jacques (Pierre Leymarie)
Police Inspector (Jean Pelegri)

**Picnic** (USA 1955)
Joshua Logan

Hal Carter (William Holden)*
Rosemary Sydney (Rosalind Russell)*
Madge Owens (Kim Novak)*
Flo Owens (Betty Field)
Alan (Cliff Robertson)*

**Picnic At Hanging Rock**
  (Australia 1975)
Peter Weir

Mrs Appleyard (Rachel Roberts)*
Michael Fitzhubert (Dominic Guard)
Dianne De Poitiers (Helen Morse)
Minnie (Jacki Weaver)

**Pillow Talk** (USA 1959)
Michael Gordon

Brad Allen (Rock Hudson)*
Jan Morrow (Doris Day)*
Jonathan Forbes (Tony Randall)
Alma (Thelma Ritter)

**The Pink Panther** (USA 1963)
Blake Edwards

Sir Charles Lytton (David Niven)*
Inspector Jacques Clouseau (Peter
  Sellers)*
George Lytton (Robert Wagner)
Simone Clouseau (Capucine)
Princess Dala (Claudia Cardinale)

Sequels *A Shot In The Dark* (1964);
  *Inspector Clouseau* (1969); *The Return
  Of The Pink Panther* (1974); *The Pink
  Panther Strikes Again* (1976); *Revenge
  Of The Pink Panther* (1978); *The Trail
  Of The Pink Panther* (1982); *The Curse
  Of The Pink Panther* (1982); *Son Of
  The Pink Panther* (1993)

**Pinocchio** (USA 1940)
Ben Sharpsteen, Hamilton Luske

Voices of:
Pinocchio (Dickie Jones)
Geppeto (Christian Rub)
Jiminy Cricket (Cliff Edwards)
The Blue Fairy (Evelyn Venable)


**A Place In The Sun** (USA 1951)
George Stevens

George Eastman (Montgomery Clift)*
Angela Vickers (Elizabeth Taylor)*
Alice Tripp (Shelley Winters)*
Hannah Eastman (Anne Revere)


**Places In The Heart** (USA 1984)
Robert Benton

Edna Spalding (Sally Field)*
Margaret Lomax (Lindsay Crouse)
Wayne Lomax (Ed Harris)
Viola Kelsey (Amy Madigan)
Mr Will (John Malkovich)*
Moze (Danny Glover)*


**Planes, Trains And Automobiles**
(USA 1987)
John Hughes

Neal Page (Steve Martin)*
Del Griffith (John Candy)*
Susan Page (Laila Robbins)
State Trooper (Michael McKean)


**Planet Of The Apes** (USA 1967)
Franklin J Schaffner

George Taylor (Charlton Heston)*
Cornelius (Roddy McDowall)*
Dr Zira (Kim Hunter)
Dr Zaius (Maurice Evans)

Sequels *Beneath The Planet Of The
Apes* (1969); *Escape From The
Planet Of The Apes* (1971); *Conquest
Of The Planet Of The Apes* (1972);
*Battle For The Planet Of The Apes*
(1973)


**Platoon** (USA 1986)
Oliver Stone

Sgt Barnes (Tom Berenger)*
Sgt Elias (Willem Dafoe)*
Chris (Charlie Sheen)*
Big Harold (Forest Whitaker)*


**Play It Again Sam** (USA 1972)
Herbert Ross

Allan Felix (Woody Allen)*
Linda Christie (Diane Keaton)*
Dick Christie (Tony Roberts)
Humphrey Bogart (Jerry Lacy)


**Play Misty For Me** (USA 1971)
Clint Eastwood

Dave Garland (Clint Eastwood)*
Evelyn Draper (Jessica Walter)
Tobie Williams (Donna Mills)
Sgt McCallum (John Larch)


**The Player** (USA 1992)
Robert Altman

Griffin Mill (Tim Robbins)*
June Gudmundsdottir (Greta Scacchi)
Walter Stuckel (Fred Ward)
Det Susan Avery (Whoopi Goldberg)*


**Point Blank** (USA 1967)
John Boorman

Walker (Lee Marvin)*
Chris (Angie Dickinson)*
Yost (Keenan Wynn)
Brewster (Carroll O'Connor)


**Point Break** (USA 1991)
Kathryn Bigelow

Bodhi (Patrick Swayze)*
Johnny Utah (Keanu Reeves)*
Angelo Pappas (Gary Busey)
Tyler (Lori Petty)

**Police Academy** (USA 1984)
Hugh Wilson

Carey (Steve Guttenberg)
Karen (Kim Cattrall)
Lt Harris (G W Bailey)
Moses (Bubba Smith)

Sequels *Police Academy 2: Their First Assignment* (1985); *Police Academy 3: Back In Training* (1986); *Police Academy 4: Citizens On Patrol* (1987); *Police Academy 5: Assignment Miami Beach* (1988); *Police Academy 6: City Under Siege* (1989)

**Poltergeist** (USA 1982)
Tobe Hooper

Steve (Craig T Nelson)
Diane (JoBeth Williams)
Dr Lesh (Beatrice Straight)
Dana (Dominique Dunne)

Sequels *Poltergeist II* (1986); *Poltergeist III* (1988)

**Popeye** (USA 1980)
Robert Altman

Popeye (Robin Williams)*
Olive Oyl (Shelley Duvall)
Poopdeck Pappy (Ray Walston)
Bluto (Paul Smith)

**Popiol I Diament** see **Ashes And Diamonds**

**The Poseidon Adventure**
(USA 1972)
Ronald Neame

Rev Frank Scott (Gene Hackman)*
Mike Rogo (Ernest Borgnine)*
James Martin (Red Buttons)
Nonnie Parry (Carol Lynley)
Acres (Roddy McDowall)*
Linda Rogo (Stella Stevens)
Belle Rosen (Shelley Winters)*

Sequel *Beyond The Poseidon Adventure* (1979) (Michael Caine*, Sally Field*)

**The Postman Always Rings Twice** (USA 1946)
Tay Garnett

Cora Smith (Lana Turner)*
Frank Chambers (John Garfield)*
Nick Smith (Cecil Kellaway)
Arthur Keats (Hume Cronyn)*

**The Postman Always Rings Twice** (USA 1981)
Bob Rafelson

Frank Chambers (Jack Nicholson)*
Cora Papadakis (Jessica Lange)*
Nick Papadakis (John Colicos)
Salesman (Christopher Lloyd)

**Postcards From The Edge**
(USA 1990)
Mike Nichols

Suzanne Vale (Meryl Streep)*
Doris Mann (Shirley MacLaine)*
Jack Falkner (Dennis Quaid)*
Lowell (Gene Hackman)*
Dr Frankenthal (Richard Dreyfuss)*

**Predator** (USA 1987)
John McTiernan

Dutch (Arnold Schwarzenegger)*
Dillon (Carl Weathers)
Anna (Elpidia Carrillo)
Mac (Bill Duke)

Sequel *Predator 2* (1990) (Danny Glover*)

**Presumed Innocent** (USA 1990)
Alan J Pakula

Rusty Sabich (Harrison Ford)*
Raymond Horgan (Brian Dennehy)
Sandy Stern (Raul Julia)*
Barbara Sabich (Bonnie Bedelia)
Carolyn Polhemus (Greta Scacchi)

**Pretty Woman** (USA 1990)
Garry Marshall

Edward Lewis (Richard Gere)*

Vivian Ward (Julia Roberts)*
James Morse (Ralph Bellamy)*
Philip Stuckey (Jason Alexander)


**Prick Up Your Ears** (USA 1987)
Stephen Frears

Joe Orton (Gary Oldman)*
Kenneth Halliwell (Alfred Molina)
Peggy Ramsey (Vanessa Redgrave)*
John Lahr (Wallace Shawn)


**The Pride Of The Yankees**
(USA 1942)
Sam Wood

Lou Gehrig (Gary Cooper)*
Eleanor Gehrig (Teresa Wright)
Sam Blake (Walter Brennan)
Hank Hannemann (Dan Duryea)


**The Prime Of Miss Jean Brodie**
(UK 1969)
Ronald Neame

Jean Brodie (Maggie Smith)*
Teddy Lloyd (Robert Stephens)
Sandy (Pamela Franklin)
Gordon Lowther (Gordon Jackson)
Miss Mackay (Celia Johnson)*


**The Prince And The Showgirl**
(UK 1957)
Laurence Olivier

Elsie Marina (Marilyn Monroe)*
The Prince Regent (Laurence Olivier)*
The Queen Dowager (Sybil Thorndike)
Northbrook (Richard Wattis)


**The Prince Of Tides** (USA 1991)
Barbra Streisand

Tom Wingo (Nick Nolte)*
Susan Lowenstein (Barbra Streisand)*
Sallie Wingo (Blythe Danner)
Lila Wingo Newbury (Kate Nelligan)

**The Prisoner Of Zenda** (USA 1937)
John Cromwell

Rudolf Rassendyl/King Rudolf V (Ronald
Colman)*
Princess Flavia (Madeleine Carroll)
Rupert of Hentzau (Douglas Fairbanks
Jnr)
Antoinette De Mauban (Mary Astor)*

Subsequent versions *The Prisoner Of
Zenda* (1952) (Stewart Granger*,
Deborah Kerr*, James Mason*); *The
Prisoner Of Zenda* (1979) (Peter
Sellers*)


**Private Benjamin** (USA 1980)
Howard Zeiff

Judy Benjamin (Goldie Hawn)*
Capt Doreen Lewis (Eileen Brennan)
Henri Tremont (Armand Assante)
Col Clay Thornbrush (Robert Webber)


**The Private Life Of Henry VIII**
(UK 1933)
Alexander Korda

Henry VIII (Charles Laughton)*
Thomas Culpepper (Robert Donat)*
Catherine Howard (Binnie Barnes)
Anne of Cleves (Elsa Lanchester)
Anne Boleyn (Merle Oberon)*


**The Private Lives Of Elizabeth
And Essex** (USA 1939)
Michael Curtiz

Queen Elizabeth (Bette Davis)*
Earl of Essex (Errol Flynn)*
Lady Penelope Grey (Olivia De
Havilland)*
Francis Bacon (Donald Crisp)
Sir Walter Raleigh (Vincent Price)*


**Prizzi's Honor** (USA 1985)
John Huston

Charley Partana (Jack Nicholson)*
Irene Walker (Kathleen Turner)*
Eduardo Walker (Robert Loggia)
Maerose Prizzi (Anjelica Huston)*

**The Professionals** (USA 1966)
Richard Brooks

Bill Dolworth (Burt Lancaster)*
Henry Fardan (Lee Marvin)*
Hans Ehrengard (Robert Ryan)*
Jacob Sharp (Woody Strode)

**Psycho** (USA 1960)
Alfred Hitchcock

Norman Bates (Anthony Perkins)*
Marion Crane (Janet Leigh)*
Lila Crane (Vera Miles)
Sam Loomis (John Gavin)

Sequels *Psycho II* (1983); *Psycho III*
(1986); *Psycho IV: The Beginning*
(1990 TV)

**The Public Enemy** (USA 1931)
William A Wellman

Tom Powers (James Cagney)*
Gwen Allen (Jean Harlow)*
Matt Doyle (Edward Woods)
Mamie (Joan Blondell)*

**Punchline** (USA 1988)
David Seltzer

Lilah Krytsik (Sally Field)*
Steven Gold (Tom Hanks)*
John Krytsik (John Goodman)*
Romeo (Mark Rydell)

**The Purple Rose Of Cairo**
(USA 1985)
Woody Allen

Cecilia (Mia Farrow)*
Tom Baxter/Gil Shepherd (Jeff Daniels)
Monk (Danny Aiello)
Larry (Van Johnson)

**Pygmalion** (UK 1938)
Anthony Asquith, Leslie Howard

Prof Henry Higgins (Leslie Howard)*
Eliza Doolittle (Wendy Hiller)*
Alfred P Doolittle (Wilfrid Lawson)
Col Pickering (Scott Sunderland)

Musical remake *My Fair Lady* (1964)
(see p58)

# Q

**Les Quatres Cents Coups**
(France 1959)
(*The Four Hundred Blows*)
François Truffaut

Antoine Doinel (Jean-Pierre Leaud)
His Mother (Claire Maurier)
His Father (Albert Remy)
Schoolmaster (Guy Decomble)

Sequels *L'Amour A Vingt Ans* (Love At
Twenty) (1962); *Baisers Volés* (Stolen
Kisses) (1968); *Domicile Conjugale*
(Bed And Board) (1970); *L'Amour En
Fuite* (Love On the Run) (1979)

**Queen Christina** (USA 1933)
Rouben Mamoulian

Queen Christina (Greta Garbo)*
Don Antonio De La Prada (John Gilbert)
Magnus (Ian Keith)
Chancellor Oxenstierna (Lewis Stone)

**The Quiet Man** (USA 1952)
John Ford

Sean Thornton (John Wayne)*
Mary Kate Danaher (Maureen O'Hara)*
Michaeleen Flynn (Barry Fitzgerald)
Father Peter Lonergan (Ward Bond)

**Quo Vadis** (USA 1951)
Mervyn Le Roy

Marcus Vinicus (Robert Taylor)*
Lygia (Deborah Kerr)*
Petronius (Leo Genn)
Nero (Peter Ustinov)*
Extra (Sophia Loren)*
Guest (Elizabeth Taylor)*

# R

**Rachel, Rachel** (USA 1968)
Paul Newman

Rachel Cameron (Joanne Woodward)*
Nick Kazlik (James Olson)
Mrs Cameron (Kate Harrington)
Calla Mackie (Estelle Parsons)

**Raging Bull** (USA 1980)
Martin Scorsese

Jake La Motta (Robert De Niro)*
Vickie La Motta (Cathy Moriarty)
Joey (Joe Pesci)*
Salvy (Frank Vincent)

**Ragtime** (USA 1981)
Milos Forman

Police Commissioner Waldo (James
  Cagney)*
Younger Brother (Brad Dourif)
Booker T Washington (Moses Gunn)
Coalhouse Walker Jnr (Howard E
  Rollins)

**Raiders Of The Lost Ark**
  (USA 1981)
Steven Spielberg

Indiana Jones (Harrison Ford)*
Karen Allen (Marion Ravenswood)
Belloq (Paul Freeman)
Toht (Ronald Lacey)

Sequels *Indiana Jones And The Temple
  Of Doom* (1984) (see p42); *Indiana
  Jones And The Last Crusade* (1989)
  (see p42)

Sequels *Indiana Jones And The Temple Of Doom* (1984) (see p42); *Indiana Jones And The Last Crusade* (1989) (see p42)

**The Railway Children** (UK 1970)
Lionel Jeffries

Mother (Dinah Sheridan)
Perks (Bernard Cribbins)
Old Gentleman (William Mervyn)
Bobbie (Jenny Agutter)*

**Rain Man** (USA 1988)
Barry Levinson

Raymond Babbitt (Dustin Hoffman)*
Charlie Babbitt (Tom Cruise)*
Susanna (Valeria Golino)
Dr Bruner (Jerry Molen)

**Raising Arizona** (USA 1987)
Joel Coen

H I (Nicolas Cage)*

Ed (Holly Hunter)
Nathan Arizona Snr (Trey Wilson)
Gale (John Goodman)*

**Ran** (Japan 1985)
Akira Kurosawa

Hidetora Ichimonji (Tatsuya Nakadai)
Taro (Akira Terao)
Jiro (Jimpachi Nezu)
Saburo (Daisuke Ryu)

**Random Harvest** (USA 1942)
Mervyn Le Roy

Charles Rainer (Ronald Colman)*
Paula (Greer Garson)*
Dr Jonathan Benet (Philip Dorn)
Kitty (Susan Peters)

**Rashomon** (Japan 1951)
Akira Kurosawa

Tajomaru (Toshiro Mifune)
Masago (Machiko Kyo)
Takehiro (Masayuki Mori)
Firewood Dealer (Takashi Shimura)

**The Razor's Edge** (USA 1946)
Edmund Goulding

Larry Darrell (Tyrone Power)*
Isabel Bradley (Gene Tierney)
Sophie Nelson (Anne Baxter)*
Elliott Templeton (Clifton Webb)*

Remake *The Razor's Edge* (1984) (Bill
  Murray*, Theresa Russell*)

**Reap The Wild Wind** (USA 1942)
Cecil B DeMille

Capt Jack Stuart (John Wayne)*
Drusilla Alston (Susan Hayward)*
Stephen Tulliver (Ray Milland)*
Loxi Claiborne (Paulette Goddard)

**Rear Window** (USA 1954)
Alfred Hitchcock

L B Jeffries (James Stewart)*
Lisa Fremont (Grace Kelly)*
Thomas J Doyle (Wendell Corey)
Stella (Thelma Ritter)

**Rebecca** (USA 1940)
Alfred Hitchcock

Maxim De Winter (Laurence Olivier)*
Rebecca De Winter (Joan Fontaine)*
Mrs Danvers (Judith Anderson)
Jack Favell (George Sanders)*


**Rebel Without A Cause** (USA 1955)
Nicholas Ray

Jim Stark (James Dean)*
Judy (Natalie Wood)*
Jim's Father (Jim Backus)
Jim's Mother (Ann Doran)
Plato (Sal Mineo)
Goon (Dennis Hopper)*


**The Red Badge Of Courage**
(USA 1951)
John Huston

Henry Fleming, the Youth (Audie
Murphy)*
Tom Wilson, the Loud Soldier (Bill
Mauldin)
The Lieutenant (Douglas Dick)
The Tattered Man (Royal Dano)


**Red River** (USA 1948)
Howard Hawks

Thomas Dunson (John Wayne)*
Matthew Garth (Montgomery Clift)*
Tess Millay (Joanne Dru)
Groot Nadine (Walter Brennan)

Remake *Red River* (TV 1988) (James
Arness, Bruce Boxleitner)


**The Red Shoes** (UK 1948)
Michael Powell, Emeric
Pressburger

Boris Lermontov (Anton Walbrook)
Victoria Page (Moira Shearer)
Julian Craster (Marius Goring)
Ivan Boleslawsky (Robert Helpmann)


**Red Sorghum** (People's Republic
of China 1987)
Zhang Yimou

Grandmother, Nine (Gong Li)
Grandfather (Jiang Wen)
Luohan (Teng Ru-Jun)
Sanpao (Ji Cun Hua)


**Reds** (USA 1981)
Warren Beatty

John Reed (Warren Beatty)*
Louise Bryant (Diane Keaton)*
Eugene O'Neil (Jack Nicholson)*
Emma Goldman (Maureen Stapleton)
Pete Van Wherry (Gene Hackman)*


**Regarding Henry** (USA 1991)
Mike Nichols

Henry Turner (Harrison Ford)*
Sarah Turner (Annette Bening)
Bradley (Bill Nunn)
Rachel Turner (Mikki Allen)


**La Règle Du Jeu** (France 1939)
(*The Rules Of The Game*)
Jean Renoir

André Jurieux (Roland Toutain)
Genevieuve (Mila Parley)
Lisette (Paulette Dubost)
Robert (Marcel Dalio)
Octave (Jean Renoir)


**Repulsion** (UK 1965)
Roman Polanski

Carol Ledoux (Catherine Deneuve)*
Helen Ledoux (Yvonne Furneaux)
Colin (John Fraser)
Michael (Ian Hendry)


**Return Of The Jedi** (USA 1983)
Richard Marquand

Luke Skywalker (Mark Hamill)
Han Solo (Harrison Ford)*
Princess Leia (Carrie Fisher)
Lando Calrissian (Billy Dee Williams)

Sequel to *Star Wars* (1977) (see p82) and *The Empire Strikes Back* (1980) (see p27)

## Return Of The Secaucus Seven
(USA 1980)
John Sayles

Jeff (Mark Arnott)
Chip (Gordon Clapp)
Frances (Maggie Cousineau)
Ron (David Strathairn)
Katie (Maggie Renzi)

## Reversal Of Fortune (USA 1990)
Barbet Schroeder

Sunny Von Bulow (Glenn Close)*
Claus Von Bulow (Jeremy Irons)*
Alan Dershowitz (Ron Silver)
Carol (Annabella Sciorra)

## Revolution (UK 1985)
Hugh Hudson

Tom Dobb (Al Pacino)*
Sgt Maj Peasy (Donald Sutherland)*
Daisy (Nastassja Kinski)*
Mrs McConnahay (Joan Plowright)

## Richard III (UK 1955)
Laurence Olivier

Richard III (Laurence Olivier)*
Clarence (John Gielgud)*
Buckingham (Ralph Richardson)*
Edward IV (Cedric Hardwicke)
Lady Anne (Claire Bloom)*

## Riff-Raff (UK 1990)
Ken Loach

Stevie (Robert Carlyle)
Susan (Emer McCourt)
Shem (Jimmy Coleman)
Mo (George Moss)

## The Right Stuff (USA 1983)
Philip Kaufman

Chuck Yeager (Sam Shepard)*

Alan Shepard (Scott Glenn)
John Glenn (Ed Harris)
Gordon Cooper (Dennis Quaid)*
Glennis Yeager (Barbara Hershey)*
Bancho Barnes (Kim Stanley)*

## Rio Bravo (USA 1959)
Howard Hawks

John T Chance (John Wayne)*
Dude (Dean Martin)*
Colorado Ryan (Ricky Nelson)
Feathers (Angie Dickinson)*

## Riot In Cell Block 11 (USA 1954)
Don Siegel

Dunn (Neville Brand)
The Warden (Emile Meyer)
Haskell (Frank Faylen)
Crazy Mike (Leo Gordon)

## Risky Business (USA 1983)
Paul Brickman

Joel (Tom Cruise)*
Lana (Rebecca De Mornay)*
Guido (Joe Pantoliano)
Rutherford (Richard Masur)

## River's Edge (USA 1986)
Tim Hunter

Layne (Crispin Glover)
Matt (Keanu Reeves)*
Clarissa (Ione Skye Leitch)
Feck (Dennis Hopper)*

## Road To Singapore (USA 1940)
Victor Schertzinger

Josh Mallon (Bing Crosby)*
Ace Lanigan (Bob Hope)*
Mima (Dorothy Lamour)*
Joshua Mallon IV (Charles Coburn)

Sequels *Road To Zanzibar* (1941); *Road To Morocco* (1942); *Road To Utopia* (1945); *Road To Rio* (1947); *Road To Bali* (1952); *Road To Hong Kong* (1961)

**The Roaring Twenties** (USA 1939)
Raoul Walsh

Eddie Bartlett (James Cagney)*
George Hally (Humphrey Bogart)*
Jean Sherman (Priscilla Lane)
Lloyd Hart (Jeffrey Lynn)

**The Robe** (USA 1953)
Henry Koster

Marcellus Gallio (Richard Burton)*
Diana (Jean Simmons)*
Demetrius (Victor Mature)*
Peter (Michael Rennie)

**Robin Hood: Prince Of Thieves**
  (USA 1991)
Kevin Reynolds

Robin of Locksley (Kevin Costner)*
Azeem (Morgan Freeman)*
Marian (Mary Elizabeth Mastrantonio)
Will Scarlett (Christian Slater)*
Sheriff of Nottingham (Alan Rickman)*
King Richard (Sean Connery)*

**Robocop** (USA 1987)
Paul Verhoeven

Murphy/Robocop (Peter Weller)*
Lewis (Nancy Allen)
The Old Man (Daniel O'Herlihy)
Jones (Ronny Cox)

Sequels *Robocop 2* (1990); *Robocop 3*
  (1992)

**Rocky** (USA 1976)
John G Avildsen

Rocky Balboa (Sylvester Stallone)*
Adrian (Talia Shire)
Paulie (Burt Young)
Apollo Creed (Carl Weathers)
Mickey (Burgess Meredith)*

Sequels *Rocky II* (1979); *Rocky III* (1982);
  *Rocky IV* (1985); *Rocky V* (1990)

**Roma, Città Aperta** see **Rome—
  Open City**

**Rome—Open City** (Italy 1945)
(*Roma, Città Aperta*)
Roberto Rossellini

Pina (Anna Magnani)*
Don Pietro Pellegrini (Aldo Fabrizi)
Manfredi (Marcello Pagliero)
Marina (Maria Michi)

**Roman Holiday** (USA 1953)
William Wyler

Joe Bradley (Gregory Peck)*
Princess Ann (Audrey Hepburn)*
Irving Radovich (Eddie Albert)*
Countess Vereberg (Margaret Rawlings)

Remake *Roman Holiday* (TV 1987)
  (Tom Conti*, Catherine Oxenberg)

**Roman Scandals** (USA 1933)
Frank Tuttle

Eddie (Eddie Cantor)*
Olga (Ruth Etting)
Princess Silvia (Gloria Stuart)
Josephus (David Manners)

**Romancing The Stone** (USA 1984)
Robert Zemeckis

Jack Colton (Michael Douglas)*
Joan Wilder (Kathleen Turner)*
Ralph (Danny De Vito)*
Ira (Zack Norman)

Sequel *The Jewel Of The Nile* (1985)
  (see p44)

**Romeo And Juliet** (UK 1968)
Franco Zeffirelli

Juliet (Olivia Hussey)
Romeo (Leonard Whiting)
Tybalt (Michael York)*
Mercutio (John McEnery)

Other versions *Romeo And Juliet* (1936)
  (Norma Shearer*, Leslie Howard*);
  *Romeo And Juliet* (1954) (Susan
  Shentall, Laurence Harvey*)

**Room At The Top** (UK 1959)
Jack Clayton

Alice Aisgill (Simone Signoret)*
Joe Lampton (Laurence Harvey)*
Susan Brown (Heather Sears)
Mr Brown (Donald Wolfit)

Sequels *Life At The Top* (1965); *Man At the Top* (1973)

**A Room With A View** (UK 1985)
James Ivory

Charlotte Bartlett (Maggie Smith)*
Lucy Honeychurch (Helena Bonham Carter)
Mr Emerson (Denholm Elliott)*
George Emerson (Julian Sands)
Cecil Vyse (Daniel Day Lewis)*

**The Rose** (USA 1979)
Mark Rydell

Rose (Bette Midler)*
Rudge (Alan Bates)*
Dyer (Frederic Forrest)
Billy Ray (Harry Dean Stanton)

**Rose Marie** (USA 1936)
W S Van Dyke

Marie De Flor (Jeanette MacDonald)*
Sgt Bruce (Nelson Eddy)*
John Flower (James Stewart)*
Teddy (David Niven)*

Remake *Rose Marie* (1954) (Ann Blyth, Howard Keel*)

**The Rose Tattoo** (USA 1955)
Daniel Mann

Serafina Delle Rose (Anna Magnani)*
Alvaro Mangiacavallo (Burt Lancaster)*
Rosa Delle Rose (Marisa Pavan)
Jack Hunter (Ben Cooper)

**Rosemary's Baby** (USA 1968)
Roman Polanski

Rosemary Woodhouse (Mia Farrow)*
Guy Woodhouse (John Cassavetes)*
Minnie Castevet (Ruth Gordon)
Roman Castevet (Sidney Blackmer)

Sequel *Look What's Happened To Rosemary's Baby* (TV 1976) (Patty Duke Astin, Stephen McHattie)

**Roxanne** (USA 1987)
Fred Schepisi

C D Bales (Steve Martin)*
Roxanne (Daryl Hannah)*
Chris (Rick Rossovich)
Dixie (Shelley Duvall)

**Ruggles Of Red Gap** (USA 1935)
Leo McCarey

Marmaduke Ruggles (Charles Laughton)*
Effie Floud (Mary Boland)
Egbert Floud (Charles Ruggles)
Mrs Judson (Zasu Pitts)

**The Rules Of The Game** see **La Règle Du Jeu**

**The Russians Are Coming, The Russians Are Coming**
(USA 1966)
Norman Jewison

Walt Whittaker (Carl Reiner)
Elspeth Whittaker (Eva Marie Saint)
Lieutenant Rozanov (Alan Arkin)*
Link Mattocks (Brian Keith)

**Ryan's Daughter** (UK 1970)
David Lean

Rose Ryan (Sarah Miles)*
Charles Shaughnessy (Robert Mitchum)*
Father Collins (Trevor Howard)*
Maj Randolph Doryan (Christopher Jones)
Michael (John Mills)*

# S

**The Sacrifice** (Sweden 1986)
(*Offret*)
Andrei Tarkovsky

Alexander (Erland Josephson)
Adelaide (Susan Fleetwood)
Julia (Valerie Mairesse)
Otto (Allan Edwall)

**Salvador** (USA 1986)
Oliver Stone

Richard Boyle (James Woods)*
Dr Rock (James Belushi)
Ambassador Thomas Kelly (Michael Murphy)
John Cassady (John Savage)

**Samson And Delilah** (USA 1949)
Cecil B DeMille

Samson (Victor Mature)*
Delilah (Hedy Lamarr)*
Saran of Gaza (George Sanders)*
Semadar (Angela Lansbury)*

**San Francisco** (USA 1936)
W S Van Dyke

Blackie Norton (Clark Gable)*
Mary Blake (Jeanette McDonald)*
Father Tim Mullin (Spencer Tracy)*
Jack Burley (Jack Holt)

**The Sand Pebbles** (USA 1966)
Robert Wise

Jake Holman (Steve McQueen)*
Frenchy Burgoyne (Richard Attenborough)*
Capt Collins (Richard Crenna)
Shirley Eckert (Candice Bergen)*

**Sands Of Iwo Jima** (USA 1949)
Allan Dwan

Sgt John M Stryker (John Wayne)*
PFC Peter Conway (John Agar)
Allison Bromley (Adele Mara)
Corp Al Thomas (Forrest Tucker)

**Saturday Night And Sunday Morning** (UK 1960)
Karel Reisz

Arthur Seaton (Albert Finney)*
Doreen Gretton (Shirley Anne Field)
Brenda (Rachel Roberts)*
Aunt Ada (Hylda Baker)

**Saturday Night Fever** (USA 1977)
John Badham

Tony Manero (John Travolta)*
Stephanie (Karen Lynn Gornley)
Bobby C (Barry Miller)
Joey (Joseph Call)

Sequel *Staying Alive* (1983)

**Save The Tiger** (USA 1973)
John G Avildsen

Harry Stoner (Jack Lemmon)*
Janet Stoner (Patricia Smith)
Phil Green (Jack Gilford)
Myra (The Hitchhiker) (Laurie Heineman)

**Sayonara** (USA 1957)
Joshua Logan

Maj Lloyd Gruver (Marlon Brando)*
Hana-Ogi (Miiko Taka)
Eileen Webster (Patricia Owens)
Joe Kelly (Red Buttons)

**Scandal** (UK 1989)
Michael Caton-Jones

Stephen Ward (John Hurt)*
Christine Keeler (Joanne Whalley-Kilmer)
Mandy Rice-Davies (Bridget Fonda)*
John Profumo (Ian McKellen)

**Scarface** (USA 1932)
Howard Hawks

Tony Camonte (Paul Muni)*
Casca Camonte (Ann Dvorak)
Poppy (Karen Morley)
Gaffney (Boris Karloff)*
Guido Rinaldo (George Raft)*

**Scarface** (USA 1983)
Brian De Palma

Tony Montana (Al Pacino)*
Manny Ray (Steven Bauer)
Elvira (Michelle Pfeiffer)*
Gina (Mary Elizabeth Mastrantonio)

**Scent Of A Woman** (USA 1992)
Martin Brest

Lt Col Frank Slade (Al Pacino)*
Charlie Simms (Chris O'Donnell)
Mr Trask (James Rebhorn)
Donna (Gabrielle Anwar)

**The Sea Hawk** (USA 1940)
Michael Curtiz

Capt Geoffrey Thorpe (Errol Flynn)*
Donna Maria Alvarez de Cordoba
   (Brenda Marshall)
Don Jose Alvarez de Cordoba
   (Claude Rains)*
Sir John Burleson (Donald Crisp)

**Sea Of Love** (USA 1989)
Harold Becker

Frank Keller (Al Pacino)*
Helen Cruger (Ellen Barkin)*
Sherman Trouhy (John Goodman)*
Terry (Michael Rooker)

**The Searchers** (USA 1956)
John Ford

Ethan Edwards (John Wayne)*
Martin Pawley (Jeffrey Hunter)
Laurie Jorgensen (Vera Miles)
Capt Rev Samuel Johnson Clayton
   (Ward Bond)
Debbie Edwards (Natalie Wood)*

**Separate Tables** (USA 1958)
Delbert Mann

Sybil Railton-Bell (Deborah Kerr)*
Ann Shankland (Rita Hayworth)*
Maj Pollock (David Niven)*
Miss Pat Cooper (Wendy Hiller)*
John Malcolm (Burt Lancaster)*

**Sergeant York** (USA 1941)
Howard Hawks

Alvin C York (Gary Cooper)*
Pastor Rosier Pile (Walter Brennan)
Gracie Williams (Joan Leslie)
Michael T 'Pusher' Ross (George Tobias)

**Serpico** (USA 1973)
Sidney Lumet

Frank Serpico (Al Pacino)*
Bob Blair (Tony Roberts)
Chief Sidney Green (John Randolph)
Tom Keough (Jack Kehoe)
Capt McClain (Biff McGuire)

Sequel *Serpico: The Deadly Game* (TV
   1976) (David Birney)

**The Servant** (UK 1963)
Joseph Losey

Hugo Barrett (Dirk Bogarde)*
Vera (Sarah Miles)*
Susan (Wendy Craig)
Tony (James Fox)

**Seven Brides For Seven Brothers**
   (USA 1954)
Stanley Donen

Adam Pontipee (Howard Keel)*
Milly (Jane Powell)
Benjamin Pontipee (Jeff Richards)
Gideon Pontipee (Russ Tamblyn)

**Seven Days In May** (USA 1963)
John Frankenheimer

Gen James M Scott (Burt Lancaster)*
Col Martin 'Jiggs' Casey (Kirk Douglas)*
President Jordan Lyman (Fredric March)*
Eleanor Holbrook (Ava Gardner)*

**Seven Samurai** (Japan 1954)
(*Shichinin No Samurai*)
Akira Kurosawa

Kambei (Takashi Shimura)
Kikuchiyo (Toshiro Mifune)
Gorobei (Yoshio Inaba)
Kyuzo (Seiji Miyaguchi)

Remake *The Magnificent Seven* (1960)
   (see p54)

**The Seven Year Itch** (USA 1955)
Billy Wilder

The Girl (Marilyn Monroe)*
Richard Sherman (Tom Ewell)
Helen Sherman (Evelyn Keyes)
Tom McKenzie (Sonny Tufts)

**The Seventh Seal** (Sweden 1957)
(*Det Sjunde Inseglet*)
Ingmar Bergman

Antonius Block (Max Von Sydow)*
Jons (Gunnar Bjornstrand)
Death (Bengt Ekerot)
Jof (Nils Poppe)

**sex, lies and videotape** (USA 1989)
Steven Soderbergh

Graham Dalton (James Spader)*
Ann Millaney (Andie MacDowell)
John Millaney (Peter Gallagher)
Cynthia Bishop (Laura San Giacomo)

**Shadow Of A Doubt** (USA 1943)
Alfred Hitchcock

Uncle Charlie (Joseph Cotten)*
Young Charlie (Teresa Wright)
Jack Graham (MacDonald Carey)
Emma Newton (Patricia Collinge)

Remake *Shadow Of A Doubt* (TV 1991)
(Mark Harmon, Margaret Webb)

**Shadows** (USA 1958–9)
John Cassavetes

Lelia (Lelia Goldoni)
Ben (Ben Carruthers)
Hugh (Hugh Hurd)
Tony (Anthony Ray)

**Shampoo** (USA 1975)
Warren Beatty

George Roundy (Warren Beatty)*
Jackie Shawn (Julie Christie)*
Jill (Goldie Hawn)*
Felicia Carr (Lee Grant)

**Shane** (USA 1953)
George Stevens

Shane (Alan Ladd)*
Marian Starrett (Jean Arthur)*
Joe Starrett (Van Heflin)
Slick Wilson (Jack Palance)*
Joey Starrett (Brandon De Wilde)

**Shanghai Express** (USA 1932)
Josef Von Sternberg

Shanghai Lily (Marlene Dietrich)*
Capt Harvey (Clive Brook)
Hui Fei (Anna May Wong)
Henry Chang (Warner Oland)

**She Done Him Wrong** (USA 1933)
Lowell Sherman

Lady Lou (Mae West)*
Capt Cummings 'The Hawk' (Cary
  Grant)*
Chick Clark (Owen Moore)
Serge Stanieff (Gilbert Roland)

**She's Gotta Have It** (USA 1986)
Spike Lee

Nola Darling (Tracy Camilla Johns)
Jamie Overstreet (Tommy Redmond
  Hicks)
Greer Childs (John Canada Terrell)
Mars Blackman (Spike Lee)

**Shichinin No Samurai** see **Seven
  Samurai**

**The Shining** (USA 1980)
Stanley Kubrick

Jack Torrance (Jack Nicholson)*
Wendy Torrance (Shelley Duvall)
Danny (Danny Lloyd)
Halloran (Scatman Crothers)

**Ship Of Fools** (USA 1965)
Stanley Kramer

Mary Treadwell (Vivien Leigh)*
La Condesa (Simone Signoret)*
Bill Tenny (Lee Marvin)*
Dr Schuman (Oskar Werner)

**Shirley Valentine** (UK 1989)
Lewis Gilbert

Shirley Valentine (Pauline Collins)*
Costas (Tom Conti)*
Gillian (Julia McKenzie)
Jane (Alison Steadman)


**The Shootist** (USA 1976)
Don Siegel

John Bernard Books (John Wayne)*
Bond Rogers (Lauren Bacall)*
Gillom Rogers (Ron Howard)
Dr Hostetler (James Stewart)*


**The Shop Around The Corner**
(USA 1940)
Ernst Lubitsch

Klara Novak (Margaret Sullavan)*
Alfred Kralik (James Stewart)*
Hugo Matuschek (Frank Morgan)
Ferencz Vadas (Joseph Schildkraut)

Remake *In the Good Old Summertime*
(1949) (Judy Garland*, Van Johnson)


**Showboat** (USA 1951)
George Sidney

Magnolia Hawks (Kathryn Grayson)
Julie La Verne (Ava Gardner)*
Gaylord Ravenal (Howard Keel)*
Capt Andy Hawks (Joe E Brown)

Previous versions *Showboat* (1929)
(Laura La Plante, Joseph Schildkraut);
*Showboat* (1936) (Irene Dunne*, Allan
Jones)


**The Silence Of The Lambs**
(USA 1991)
Jonathan Demme

Clarice Starling (Jodie Foster)*
Dr Hannibal Lecter (Anthony Hopkins)*
Jack Crawford (Scott Glenn)
Jame Gumb (Ted Levine)


**Silkwood** (USA 1983)
Mike Nichols

Karen Silkwood (Meryl Streep)*
Drew Stephens (Kurt Russell)*
Dolly Pelliker (Cher)*
Winston (Craig T Nelson)


**Silver Streak** (USA 1976)
Arthur Hiller

George Caldwell (Gene Wilder)*
Hilly Burns (Jill Clayburgh)*
Grover Muldoon (Richard Pryor)*
Roger Devereau (Patrick McGoohan)


**Silverado** (USA 1985)
Lawrence Kasdan

Paden (Kevin Kline)*
Emmett (Scott Glenn)
Jake (Kevin Costner)*
Mal (Danny Glover)*
Sheriff Langston (John Cleese)*


**Since You Went Away** (USA 1944)
John Cromwell

Anne Hilton (Claudette Colbert)*
Jane (Jennifer Jones)*
Bridget 'Brig' Hilton (Shirley Temple)*
Lt Anthony Willett (Joseph Cotten)*


**Singin' In The Rain** (USA 1952)
Stanley Donen, Gene Kelly

Don Lockwood (Gene Kelly)*
Cosmo Brown (Donald O'Connor)*
Kathy Selden (Debbie Reynolds)*
Lina Lamont (Jean Hagen)


**Det Sjunde Insegelt** see **The
Seventh Seal**


**Sleeper** (USA 1973)
Woody Allen

Miles Monroe (Woody Allen)*
Luna Schlosser (Diane Keaton)*
Erno Windt (John Beck)
Dr Nero (Marya Small)

**Sleeping Beauty** (USA 1959)
Clyde Geronimi, Eric Larson,
 Wolfgang Reitherman, Les Clark

Voices of:
Maleficent (Eleanor Audley)
Flora (Verna Felton)
Fauna (Barbara Jo Allen (Vera Vague))
Merryweather (Barbara Luddy)

**Sleeping With The Enemy**
(USA 1991)
Joseph Ruben

Sara Walters/Laura Burney (Julia
 Roberts)*
Martin Burney (Patrick Bergin)
Ben Woodward (Kevin Anderson)
Chloe (Elizabeth Lawrence)

**Sleuth** (UK 1972)
Joseph L Mankiewicz

Andrew Wyke (Laurence Olivier)*
Milo Tindle (Michael Caine)*
Inspector Doppler (Alec Cawthorne)
Marguerite (Margo Channing)

**Smokey And The Bandit**
(USA 1977)
Hal Needham

Bandit (Burt Reynolds)*
Carrie (Sally Field)*
Sheriff Buford T Justice (Jackie
 Gleason)*
Cledus Snow (Jerry Reed)

Sequels *Smokey And The Bandit II*
 (1980); *Smokey And The Bandit 3*
 (1983)

**Smultronstället** see *Wild
 Strawberries*

**The Snake Pit** (USA 1948)
Anatole Litvak

Virgina Stuart Cunningham (Olivia De
 Havilland)*
Robert Cunningham (Mark Stevens)
Dr Mark Kirk (Leo Genn)
Grace (Celeste Holm)*

**Snow White And The Seven
 Dwarfs** (USA 1937)
Walt Disney

Voices of:
Snow White (Adriana Casselotti)
Prince Charming (Harry Stockwell)
The Queen (Lucile La Verne)
Magic Mirror (Moroni Olsen)
Sneezy (Billy Gilbert)

**The Snows Of Kilimanjaro**
(USA 1952)
Henry King

Harry Street (Gregory Peck)*
Helen (Susan Hayward)*
Cynthia (Ava Gardner)*
Countess Liz (Hildegard Neff)

**A Soldier's Story** (USA 1984)
Norman Jewison

Capt Davenport (Howard E Rollins Jnr)
Sgt Waters (Adolph Caesar)
Corp Ellis (Robert Townsend)
PFC Peterson (Denzel Washington)*

**Some Like It Hot** (USA 1959)
Billy Wilder

Sugar Kowalczyk (Marilyn Monroe)*
Joe/Josephine (Tony Curtis)*
Jerry/Daphne (Jack Lemmon)*
Spats Columbo (George Raft)
Osgood Fielding Jnr (Joe E Brown)

**The Song Of Bernadette**
(USA 1943)
Henry King

Bernadette Soubirous (Jennifer Jones)*
Peyramale (Charles Bickford)
Vital Dutour (Vincent Price)*
Dr Dozous (Lee J Cobb)

**Song Of The Little Road** see
 *Pather Panchali*

**Sons And Lovers** (UK 1960)
Jack Cardiff

Walter Morel (Trevor Howard)*
Mrs Morel (Wendy Hiller)*
Paul Morel (Dean Stockwell)
Clara Dawes (Mary Ure)

**Sophie's Choice** (USA 1982)
Alan J Pakula

Sophie Zawistowska (Meryl Streep)*
Nathan Landau (Kevin Kline)*
Stingo (Peter MacNicol)
Narrator (Josef Sommer)

**The Sound Of Music** (USA 1965)
Robert Wise

Maria (Julie Andrews)*
Capt Von Trapp (Christopher Plummer)*
The Baroness (Eleanor Parker)
Max Detweiler (Richard Haydn)

**Sounder** (USA 1972)
Martin Ritt

Rebecca Morgan (Cicely Tyson)
Nathan Lee Morgan (Paul Winfield)
David Lee Morgan (Kevin Hooks)
Mrs Boatwright (Carmen Mathews)

Sequel *Sounder Part 2* (1976) (Ebony
    Wright, Harold Sylvester)

**South Pacific** (USA 1958)
Joshua Logan

Nellie Forbush (Mitzi Gaynor)
Emile De Becque (Rossano Brazzi)
Lt Joseph Cable (John Kerr)
Liat (France Nuyen)
Bloody Mary (Juanita Hall)

**Spartacus** (USA 1960)
Stanley Kubrick

Spartacus (Kirk Douglas)*
Marcus Licinius Crassus (Laurence
    Olivier)*
Varinia (Jean Simmons)*
Antoninus (Tony Curtis)*
Gracchus (Charles Laughton)*
Lentulus Batiatus (Peter Ustinov)*

**Spellbound** (USA 1945)
Alfred Hitchcock

Dr Constance Peterson (Ingrid
    Bergman)*
John J B Ballantine (Gregory Peck)*
Dr Murchison (Leo G Carroll)
Mary Carmichael (Rhonda Fleming)

**Splash** (USA 1984)
Ron Howard

Allen Bauer (Tom Hanks)*
Madison (Daryl Hannah)*
Walter Kornbluth (Eugene Levy)
Freddie Bauer (John Candy)*

Sequel *Splash, Too* (TV 1988) (Todd
    Waring, Amy Yassbeck)

**The Spy Who Loved Me** (UK 1977)
Lewis Gilbert

James Bond (Roger Moore)*
Maj Anya Amasova (Barbara Bach)
Karl Stromberg (Curt Jurgens)
Jaws (Richard Kiel)

**Stage Door** (USA 1937)
Gregory La Cava

Terry Randall (Katharine Hepburn)*
Joan Maitland (Ginger Rogers)*
Anthony Powell (Adolphe Menjou)
Linda Shaw (Gail Patrick)

**Stagecoach** (USA 1939)
John Ford

The Ringo Kid (John Wayne)*
Dallas (Claire Trevor)
Hatfield (John Carradine)
Dr Josiah Boone (Thomas Mitchell)
Buck Rickabaugh (Andy Devine)

Remakes *Stagecoach* (1966) (Alex
    Cord, Ann-Margret, Bing Crosby*);
    *Stagecoach* (TV 1986) (Kris
    Kristofferson*, Elizabeth Ashley)

**Stalag 17** (USA 1953)
Billy Wilder

Sefton (William Holden)*
Dunbar (Don Taylor)
Hoffy (Richard Erdman)
Von Sherbach (Otto Preminger)


**A Star Is Born** (USA 1937)
William A Wellman

Esther Blodgett/Vicki Lester (Janet
 Gaynor)
Norman Maine (Fredric March)*
Oliver Niles (Adolphe Menjou)
Lettie (May Robson)


**A Star Is Born** (USA 1954)
George Cukor

Esther Blodgett/Vicki Lester (Judy
 Garland)*
Norman Maine (James Mason)*
Matt Libby (Jack Carson)
Oliver Niles (Charles Bickford)


**A Star Is Born** (USA 1976)
Frank Pierson

Esther Hoffman (Barbra Streisand)*
John Norman (Kris Kristofferson)*
Bobby Ritchie (Gary Busey)
Gary Danziger (Oliver Clark)


**Star Trek—The Motion Picture**
 (USA 1979)
Robert Wise

Capt James Tiberius Kirk (William
 Shatner)*
Mr Spock (Leonard Nimoy)*
Dr Leonard 'Bones' McCoy (DeForest
 Kelley)
Chief Engineer Montgomery 'Scotty'
 Scott (James Doohan)
Sulu (George Takei)
Chekov (Walter Koenig)
Uhura (Nichelle Nichols)

Sequels *Star Trek II: The Wrath Of Khan*
 (1982); *Star Trek III: The Search For
 Spock* (1984); *Star Trek IV: The
 Voyage Home* (1986); *Star Trek V:
 The Final Frontier* (1989); *Star Trek
 VI: The Undiscovered Country* (1991)


**Star Wars** (USA 1977)
George Lucas

Luke Skywalker (Mark Hamill)
Han Solo (Harrison Ford)*
Princess Leia Organa (Carrie Fisher)
Grand Moff Tarkin (Peter Cushing)*
Ben Obi-Wan Kenobi (Alec Guinness)*

Sequels *The Empire Strikes Back*
 (1980) (see p27); *Return of The Jedi*
 (1983) (see p72)


**Steel Magnolias** (USA 1989)
Herbert Ross

M'Lynn Eatenton (Sally Field)*
Truvy Jones (Dolly Parton)*
Ouiser Boudreaux (Shirley MacLaine)*
Annelle Dupuy Desoto (Daryl Hannah)*
Clairee Belcher (Olympia Dukakis)
Shelby Eatenton Latcherie (Julia
 Roberts)*


**Stella Dallas** (USA 1937)
King Vidor

Stella Martin Dallas (Barbara Stanwyck)*
Stephen Dallas (John Boles)
Laurel Dallas (Anne Shirley)
Helen Morrison (Barbara O'Neil)

Remake *Stella* (1990) (Bette Midler*,
 Stephen Collins)


**The Sting** (USA 1973)
George Roy Hill

Henry Gondorff (Paul Newman)*
Johnny Hooker (Robert Redford)*
Doyle Lonnegan (Robert Shaw)*
Lt Snyder (Charles Durning)

Sequel *The Sting II* (1983) (Jackie
 Gleason*, Mac Davis)

**Stir Crazy** (USA 1980)
Sidney Poitier

Skip Donahue (Gene Wilder)*
Harry Monroe (Richard Pryor)*
Rory Schultebrand (Georg Stanford
   Brown)
Meredith (JoBeth Williams)


**The Story Of Louis Pasteur**
   (USA 1936)
William Dieterle

Louis Pasteur (Paul Muni)*
Madame Pasteur (Josephine
   Hutchinson)
Annette Pasteur (Anita Louise)
Jean Matchel (Donald Woods)


**La Strada** (Italy 1954)
Federico Fellini

Zampano (Anthony Quinn)*
Gelsomina (Giulietta Masina)
Matto 'The Fool' (Richard Basehart)
Columbiani (Aldo Silvani)


**Strangers On A Train** (USA 1951)
Alfred Hitchcock

Guy Haines (Farley Granger)
Anne Morton (Ruth Roman)
Bruno Anthony (Robert Walker)
Senator Morton (Leo G Carroll)

Remake *Once You Kiss A Stranger*
   (1969) (Paul Burke, Carol Lynley)


**A Streetcar Named Desire**
   (USA 1951)
Elia Kazan

Blanche Du Bois (Vivien Leigh)*
Stanley Kowalski (Marlon Brando)*
Stella Kowalski (Kim Hunter)
Mitch (Karl Malden)*

Remake *A Streetcar Named Desire* (TV)
   (1984) (Ann-Margret, Treat Williams)


**Strictly Ballroom** (Australia 1992)
Baz Luhrmann

Scott Hastings (Paul Mercurio)
Fran (Tara Morice)
Barry Fife (Bill Hunter)
Shirley Hastings (Pat Thomson)


**Stromboli** (Italy 1950)
(*Stromboli, Terra Di Dio*)
Roberto Rossellini

Karin Bjiorsen (Ingrid Bergman)*
Antonio (Mario Vitale)
The Priest (Renzo Cesana)
The Lighthouse Keeper (Mario Sponza)


**Stromboli, Terra Di Dio** see
   **Stromboli**


**The Stuntman** (USA 1980)
Richard Rush

Eli Cross (Peter O'Toole)*
Cameron (Steve Railsback)
Nina Franklin (Barbara Hershey)*
Sam (Allen Goorwitz)


**Subway** (France 1985)
Luc Besson

Helena (Isabelle Adjani)*
Fred (Christopher Lambert)*
The Florist (Richard Bohringer)
Inspector Gesberg (Michel Galabru)


**Suddenly Last Summer**
   (USA 1959)
Joseph L Mankiewicz

Catherine Holly (Elizabeth Taylor)*
Dr John Cukrowicz (Montgomery Clift)*
Mrs Violet Venable (Katharine
   Hepburn)*
Dr Hockstader (Albert Dekker)


**Sullivan's Travels** (USA 1941)
Preston Sturges

John L Sullivan (Joel McCrea)*
The Girl (Veronica Lake)
Mr Lebrand (Robert Warwick)
Mr Jones (William Demarest)

**Sunday Bloody Sunday** (UK 1971)
John Schlesinger

Alex Greville (Glenda Jackson)*
Dr Daniel Hirsh (Peter Finch)*
Bob Elkin (Murray Head)
Mrs Greville (Peggy Ashcroft)*


**The Sundowners** (USA 1960)
Fred Zinnemann

Ida Carmody (Deborah Kerr)*
Paddy Carmody (Robert Mitchum)*
Venneker (Peter Ustinov)*
Mrs Firth (Glynis Johns)


**Sunset Boulevard** (USA 1950)
Billy Wilder

Joe Gillis (William Holden)*
Norma Desmond (Gloria Swanson)*
Max Von Mayerling (Erich Von
  Stroheim)*
Betty Schaefer (Nancy Olson)


**Superman** (USA 1978)
Richard Donner

Jor-El (Marlon Brando)*
Lex Luthor (Gene Hackman)*
Superman/Clark Kent (Christopher
  Reeve)*
Perry White (Jackie Cooper)
Pa Kent (Glenn Ford)*
Lois Lane (Margot Kidder)
Lara (Susannah York)*

Sequels *Superman II* (1980); *Superman
  III* (1983); *Superman IV: The Quest
  For Peace* (1987)


**Suspect** (USA 1987)
Peter Yates

Kathleen Riley (Cher)*
Eddie Sanger (Dennis Quaid)*
Carl Wayne Anderson (Liam Neeson)
Judge Matthew Helms (John Mahoney)

**Suspicion** (USA 1941)
Alfred Hitchcock

Johnnie Aysgarth (Cary Grant)*
Lina McLaidlaw (Joan Fontaine)*
Gen McLaidlaw (Cedric Hardwicke)
Beaky Thwaite (Nigel Bruce)

Remake *Suspicion* (TV 1987) (Anthony
  Andrews, Jane Curtin)


**Sweet Bird Of Youth** (USA 1962)
Richard Brooks

Chance Wayne (Paul Newman)*
Alexandra Del Lago (Geraldine Page)
Heavenly Finley (Shirley Knight)
'Boss' Finley (Ed Begley)

Remake *Sweet Bird Of Youth* (TV 1989)
  (Mark Harmon, Elizabeth Taylor*)


**Sweet Charity** (USA 1968)
Bob Fosse

Charity Hope Valentine (Shirley
  MacLaine)*
Big Daddy (Sammy Davis Jnr)*
Vittorio Vitale (Ricardo Montalban)
Oscar Lindquist (John McMartin)
Nickie (Chita Rivera)


**Sweet Dreams** (USA 1985)
Karel Reisz

Patsy Cline (Jessica Lange)*
Charlie Dick (Ed Harris)
Hilda Hensley (Ann Wedgeworth)
Randy Hughes (David Clennon)


**The Sweet Life** see **La Dolce Vita**


**Sweet Smell Of Success**
  (USA 1957)
Alexander Mackendrick

J J Hunsecker (Burt Lancaster)*
Sidney Falco (Tony Curtis)*
Susan Hunsecker (Susan Harrison)
Steve Dallas (Marty Milner)

**Swing Time** (USA 1936)
George Stevens

John 'Lucky' Garnett (Fred Astaire)*
Penelope Carrol (Ginger Rogers)*
Dr Cardetti 'Pop' (Victor Moore)
Mabel Anderson (Helen Broderick)

**Swiss Family Robinson**
(USA 1960)
Ken Annakin

Father (John Mills)*
Mother (Dorothy McGuire)*
Fritz (James MacArthur)
Roberta (Janet Munro)


# T

**A Tale Of Two Cities** (USA 1935)
Jack Conway

Sydney Carton (Ronald Colman)*
Lucie Manette (Elizabeth Allan)
Miss Pross (Edna May Oliver)
Stryver (Reginald Owen)

Remake *A Tale Of Two Cities* (1958)
(Dirk Bogarde*, Dorothy Tutin); *A Tale
Of Two Cities* (TV 1980) (Chris
Sarandon, Alice Krige)

**Talk Radio** (USA 1988)
Oliver Stone

Barry Champlain (Eric Bogosian)
Ellen (Ellen Greene)
Laura (Leslie Hope)
Dan (Alec Baldwin)*

**The Taming Of The Shrew**
(USA 1967)
Franco Zeffirelli

Katharina (Kate) (Elizabeth Taylor)*
Petruchio (Richard Burton)*
Baptista (Michael Hordern)
Lucentio (Michael York)*

**Tarzan The Apeman** (USA 1932)
W S Van Dyke

Tarzan (Johnny Weissmuller)*
Jane Parker (Maureen O'Sullivan)
Harry Holt (Neil Hamilton)
James Parker (C Aubrey Smith)

Weissmuller Sequels *Tarzan And His
Mate* (1934); *Tarzan Escapes* (1936);
*Tarzan Finds A Son!* (1939); *Tarzan's
Secret Treasure* (1941); *Tarzan's
New York Adventure* (1942); *Tarzan
Triumphs* (1943); *Tarzan's Desert
Mystery* (1943); *Tarzan And The
Amazons* (1945); *Tarzan And The
Leopard Woman* (1946); *Tarzan And
The Huntress* (1947); *Tarzan And
The Mermaids* (1948)

**Taxi Driver** (USA 1976)
Martin Scorsese

Travis Bickle (Robert De Niro)*
Betsy (Cybill Shepherd)
Iris Steensman (Jodie Foster)*
Wizard (Peter Boyle)
Sport (Harvey Keitel)*
Tom (Albert Brooks)

**The Teahouse Of The August
Moon** (USA 1956)
Daniel Mann

Sakini (Marlon Brando)*
Capt Fisby (Glenn Ford)*
Lotus Blossom (Machiko Kyo)
Capt Mclean (Eddie Albert)*

**Teenage Mutant Ninja Turtles**
(USA 1990)
Steve Barron

April O'Neil (Judith Hoag)
Casey Jones (Elias Koteas)
Raphael/Passenger in Cab (Josh Pais)
Michaelangelo/Pizza Man (Michelan
Sisti)
Donatello/Foot Messenger (Leif Tilden)
Leonardo/Gang Member (David
Forman)

**Teenage Mutant Ninja Turtles**
(USA 1990) (cont.)

Sequels *Teenage Mutant Ninja Turtles II: The Secret Of The Ooze* (1991); *Teenage Mutant Ninja Turtles III* (1993)


**'10'** (USA 1979)
Blake Edwards

George (Dudley Moore)*
Sam (Julie Andrews)*
Jenny (Bo Derek)*
Hugh (Robert Webber)


**The Ten Commandments** (USA 1956)
Cecil B DeMille

Moses (Charlton Heston)*
Rameses II (Yul Brynner)*
Nefertiti (Anne Baxter)*
Dathan (Edward G Robinson)*


**Tender Mercies** (USA 1983)
Bruce Beresford

Mac Sledge (Robert Duvall)*
Rosa Lee (Tess Harper)
Dixie (Betty Buckley)
Sue Anne (Ellen Barkin)*


**Tequila Sunrise** (USA 1988)
Robert Towne

McKussic (Mel Gibson)*
Jo Ann (Michelle Pfeiffer)*
Frescia (Kurt Russell)*
Carlos/Escalante (Raul Julia)*


**The Terminator** (USA 1984)
James Cameron

The Terminator (Arnold Schwarzenegger)*
Kyle Reese (Michael Biehn)
Sarah Connor (Linda Hamilton)
Traxler (Paul Winfield)


**Terminator 2: Judgment Day**
(USA 1991)
James Cameron

The Terminator (Arnold Schwarzenegger)*
Sarah Connor (Linda Hamilton)
John Connor (Edward Furlong)
T-1000 (Robert Patrick)


**Terms Of Endearment** (USA 1983)
James L Brooks

Emma Horton (Debra Winger)*
Aurora Greenway (Shirley MacLaine)*
Garrett Breedlove (Jack Nicholson)*
Vernon Dahlart (Danny De Vito)*


**Tess** (UK/France 1979)
Roman Polanski

Tess Durbeyfield (Nastassja Kinski)*
Angel Clare (Peter Firth)
Alec D'Urberville (Leigh Lawson)
John Durbeyfield (John Collin)


**Test Pilot** (USA 1938)
Victor Fleming

Jim Lane (Clark Gable)*
Ann Barton (Myrna Loy)*
Gunnar Sloane (Spencer Tracy)*
Howard B Drake (Lionel Barrymore)*


**Thelma & Louise** (USA 1991)
Ridley Scott

Louise Sawyer (Susan Sarandon)*
Thelma Dickinson (Geena Davis)*
Hal Slocombe (Harvey Keitel)*
J D (Brad Pitt)*


**They Shoot Horses Don't They?**
(USA 1969)
Sydney Pollack

Gloria Beatty (Jane Fonda)*
Robert Syverton (Michael Sarrazin)
Alice (Susannah York)*
Rocky (Gig Young)

**The Thief Of Bagdad** (UK 1940)
Ludwig Berger, Michael Powell, Tim Whelan

Jaffar (Conrad Veidt)*
Abu (Sabu)
Princess (June Duprez)
Ahmed (John Justin)
Djinni (Rex Ingram)

Other versions *The Thief Of Bagdad* (1924) (Douglas Fairbanks Snr); *The Thief Of Baghdad* (TV 1978) (Kabir Bedi)

**The Thin Man** (USA 1934)
W S Van Dyke

Nick Charles (William Powell)*
Nora Charles (Myrna Loy)*
Dorothy Wynant (Maureen O'Sullivan)
Lt John Guild (Nat Pendleton)

Sequels *After The Thin Man* (1936); *Another Thin Man* (1939); *Shadow Of The Thin Man* (1941); *The Thin Man Goes Home* (1944); *Song Of The Thin Man* (1947)

**The Third Man** (UK 1949)
Carol Reed

Holly Martins (Joseph Cotten)*
Harry Lime (Orson Welles)*
Anna Schmidt (Alida Valli)
Maj Calloway (Trevor Howard)*

**The Thirty-Nine Steps** (UK 1935)
Alfred Hitchcock

Pamela (Madeleine Carroll)
Richard Hannay (Robert Donat)*
Miss Smith/Annabella (Lucie Mannheim)
Prof Jordan (Godfrey Tearle)
Margaret (Peggy Ashcroft)*

Remakes *The 39 Steps* (1959) (Kenneth More*, Taina Elg); *The Thirty-Nine Steps* (1978) (Robert Powell, Karen Dotrice)

**37.2 Le Matin** see **Betty Blue**

**This Is Spinal Tap** (USA 1984)
Rob Reiner

Marti DiBerti (Rob Reiner)
David St Hubbins (Michael McKean)
Nigel Tufnel (Christopher Guest)
Derek Smalls (Harry Shearer)

**The Thomas Crown Affair** (USA 1968)
Norman Jewison

Thomas Crown (Steve McQueen)*
Vicky Anderson (Faye Dunaway)*
Eddie Malone (Paul Burke)
Erwin Weaver (Jack Weston)

**Thoroughly Modern Millie** (USA 1967)
George Roy Hill

Millie Dillmount (Julie Andrews)*
Dorothy Brown (Mary Tyler Moore)
Mrs Meers (Beatrice Lillie)
Jimmy Smith (James Fox)

**Three Coins In The Fountain** (USA 1954)
Jean Negulesco

Shadwell (Clifton Webb)*
Miss Frances (Dorothy McGuire)*
Anita (Jean Peters)
Prince Dino Di Cessi (Louis Jourdan)*

Remake *Coins In The Fountain* (TV 1990) (Loni Anderson, Stefanie Kramer, Shanna Reed)

**Three Days Of The Condor** (USA 1975)
Sydney Pollack

Joe Turner (Robert Redford)*
Kathy Hale (Faye Dunaway)*
Higgins (Cliff Robertson)*
Joubert (Max Von Sydow)*

**Three Men And A Baby** (USA 1987)
Leonard Nimoy

Peter (Tom Selleck)*
Michael (Steve Guttenberg)
Jack (Ted Danson)*
Sylvia (Nancy Travis)

Sequel *Three Men And A Little Lady*
(1990)

**The Three Musketeers** (USA 1948)
George Sidney

D'Artagnan (Gene Kelly)*
Constance Bonacieux (June Allyson)*
Lady De Winter (Lana Turner)*
Cardinal Richelieu (Vincent Price)*

**The Three Musketeers** (UK 1973)
Richard Lester

Athos (Oliver Reed)*
Constance (Raquel Welch)
Aramis (Richard Chamberlain)
D'Artagnan (Michael York)*
Porthos (Frank Finlay)
Milady (Faye Dunaway)*
Richelieu (Charlton Heston)*

Sequels *The Four Musketeers* (1974);
*Return of The Musketeers* (1989)

**Three Smart Girls** (USA 1936)
Henry Koster

Penny Craig (Deanna Durbin)*
Judson Craig (Charles Winninger)
Donna Lyons (Binnie Barnes)
Michael Stuart (Ray Milland)*

Sequel *Three Smart Girls Grow Up*
(1939)

**Throne Of Blood** (Japan 1957)
(*Kumonosu-Jo*)
Akira Kurosawa

Taketoki Washizu (Toshiro Mifune)
Asaji, his Wife (Isuzu Yamada)
Noriyasu Odagura (Takashi Shimura)
Yoshaki Miki (Minoru Chiaki)

**Throw Momma From The Train**
(USA 1987)
Danny De Vito

Owen (Danny De Vito)*
Larry (Billy Crystal)*
Beth (Kim Greist)
Momma (Anne Ramsey)

**Thunderball** (UK 1965)
Terence Young

James Bond (Sean Connery)*
Domino Derval (Claudine Auger)
Emilio Largo (Adolfo Celi)
Fiona Volpe (Luciana Paluzzi)

**Tie Me Up! Tie Me Down!**
(Spain 1990)
(*Atame!*)
Pedro Almodovar

Marina (Victoria Abril)*
Ricky (Antonio Banderas)*
Maximo Espejo (Francisco Rabal)
Lola (Loles Leon)

**Till The Clouds Roll By** (USA 1946)
Richard Whorf

Jerome Kern (Robert Walker)
Marilyn Miller (Judy Garland)*
Sally (Lucllle Bremer)
Sally, as a Girl (Joan Wells)

**Time Bandits** (UK 1980)
Terry Gilliam

Robin Hood (John Cleese)*
King Agamemnon (Sean Connery)*
Pansy (Shelley Duvall)
Mrs Ogre (Katherine Helmond)
Supreme Being (Ralph Richardson)*

**The Tin Drum**
(France/West Germany 1979)
(*Die Blechtrommel*)
Volker Schlöndorff

Oskar Matzerath (David Bennent)
Alfred Matzerath (Mario Adorf)
Agnes Matzerath (Angela Winkler)
Jan Bronski (Daniel Olbrychski)

**Tin Men** (USA 1987)
Barry Levinson

BB (Richard Dreyfuss)*
Tilley (Danny De Vito)*
Nora (Barbara Hershey)*
Moe (John Mahoney)


**To Be Or Not To Be** (USA 1942)
Ernst Lubitsch

Maria Tura (Carole Lombard)*
Josef Tura (Jack Benny)*
Stanislav Sobinski (Robert Stack)
Greenberg (Felix Bressart)
Col Ehrhardt (Sig Ruman)

Remake *To Be Or Not To Be* (1983)
(Anne Bancroft*, Mel Brooks*)


**To Catch A Thief** (USA 1955)
Alfred Hitchcock

John Robie (Cary Grant)*
Frances Stevens (Grace Kelly)*
Mrs Stevens (Jessie Royce Landis)
H H Hughson (John Williams)


**To Have And Have Not** (USA 1944)
Howard Hawks

Harry Morgan (Humphrey Bogart)*
Eddie (The Rummy) (Walter Brennan)
Marie (Lauren Bacall)*
Helene De Bursac (Dolores Moran)

Remakes *The Breaking Point* (1950)
(John Garfield*, Patricia Neal*); *The
Gun Runners* (1958) (Audie Murphy*,
Patricia Owens)


**To Hell And Back** (USA 1955)
Jesse Hibbs

Himself (Audie Murphy)*
Johnson (Marshall Thompson)
Kerrigan (Jack Kelly)
Brandon (Charles Drake)


**To Kill A Mockingbird** (USA 1962)
Robert Mulligan

Atticus Finch (Gregory Peck)*
Scout Finch (Mary Badham)
Jem Finch (Phillip Alford)
Dill Harris (John Megna)
Boo Radley (Robert Duvall)*


**To Sir With Love** (UK 1967)
James Clavell

Mark Thackeray (Sidney Poitier)*
Denham (Christian Roberts)
Pamela Dare (Judy Geeson)
Barbara Pegg (Lulu)


**Tokyo Monogatari** see **Tokyo Story**


**Tokyo Story** (Japan 1953)
(*Tokyo Monogatari*)
Yasujiro Ozu

Shukishi Hirayama (Chishu Ryu)
Tomi Hirayama (Chiyeko Higashiyama)
Koichi Hirayama (So Yamamura)
Fumiko (Kuniko Miyake)


**Tom Jones** (UK 1963)
Tony Richardson

Tom Jones (Albert Finney)*
Sophie Western (Susannah York)*
Squire Western (Hugh Griffith)
Miss Western (Edith Evans)*


**Tootsie** (USA 1982)
Sydney Pollack

Michael Dorsey/Dorothy Michaels
(Dustin Hoffman)*
Julie (Jessica Lange)*
Sandy (Teri Garr)
Ron (Dabney Coleman)


**Top Gun** (USA 1986)
Tony Scott

Maverick (Tom Cruise)*
Charlie (Kelly McGillis)
Ice (Val Kilmer)
Goose (Anthony Edwards)

**Top Hat** (USA 1935)
Mark Sandrich

Jerry Travers (Fred Astaire)*
Dale Tremont (Ginger Rogers)*
Horace Hardwick (Edward Everett
  Horton)
Madge Hardwick (Helen Broderick)

**Torch Song Trilogy** (USA 1988)
Paul Bogart

Ma (Anne Bancroft)*
Alan (Matthew Broderick)*
Arnold (Harvey Fierstein)
Ed (Brian Kerwin)

**Total Recall** (USA 1990)
Paul Verhoeven

Doug Quaid (Arnold Schwarzenegger)*
Melina (Rachel Ticotin)
Lori (Sharon Stone)*
Cohaagen (Ronny Cox)

**Touch Of Evil** (USA 1958)
Orson Welles

Ramon Miguel Vargas (Charlton
  Heston)*
Susan Vargas (Janet Leigh)*
Hank Quinlan (Orson Welles)*
Tanya (Marlene Dietrich)*

**The Towering Inferno** (USA 1974)
John Guillermin, Irwin Allen

Michael O'Hallorhan (Steve McQueen)*
Doug Roberts (Paul Newman)*
James Duncan (William Holden)*
Susan Franklin (Faye Dunaway)*
Harlee Claiborne (Fred Astaire)*
Lisolette Mueller (Jennifer Jones)*

**Trading Places** (USA 1983)
John Landis

Louis Winthorpe III (Dan Akyroyd)*
Billy Ray Valentine (Eddie Murphy)*
Coleman (Denholm Elliott)*
Randolph Dale (Ralph Bellamy)*
Mortimer Duke (Don Ameche)*

**The Train** (USA 1964)
John Frankenheimer

Labiche (Burt Lancaster)*
Von Waldheim (Paul Scofield)*
Christine (Jeanne Moreau)*
Mademoiselle Villard (Suzanne Flon)
Papa Boule (Michel Simon)

**Trapeze** (USA 1956)
Carol Reed

Mike Ribble (Burt Lancaster)*
Tino Orsini (Tony Curtis)*
Lola (Gina Lollobrigida)
Bouglione (Thomas Gomez)

**The Treasure Of The Sierra
  Madre** (USA 1948)
John Huston

Fred C Dobbs (Humphrey Bogart)*
Howard (Walter Huston)*
Curtin (Tim Holt)
Cody (Bruce Bennett)

**The Tree Of Wooden Clogs**
  (Italy 1978)
(*L'Albero Degli Zoccoli*)
Ermanno Olmi

Batisti (Luigi Ornaghi)
Batistina, his Wife (Francesa Moriggi)
Minek (Omar Brignoli)
Tuni (Antonio Ferrari)

**Trop Belle Pour Toi!** (France 1989)
Bertrand Blier

Bernard (Gérard Depardieu)*
Colette (Josiane Balasko)
Florence (Carole Bouquet)
Marcello (Roland Blanche)

**True Grit** (USA 1969)
Henry Hathaway

Reuben J 'Rooster' Cogburn (John
  Wayne)*
La Boeuf (Glen Campbell)
Mattie Ross (Kim Darby)

Ned Pepper (Robert Duvall)*
Moon (Dennis Hopper)*

Sequel *Rooster Cogburn* (1975); *True Grit* (TV 1978) (Warren Oates)

## Tucker: The Man And His Dream
(USA 1988)
Francis Coppola

Preston Tucker (Jeff Bridges)*
Vera (Joan Allen)
Abe (Martin Landau)
Eddie (Frederic Forrest)

## Tugboat Annie (USA 1933)
Mervyn Le Roy

Annie Brennan (Marie Dressler)
Terry Brennan (Wallace Beery)*
Alec Brennan (Robert Young)*
Pat Severn (Maureen O'Sullivan)

Sequel *Tugboat Annie Sails Again* (1940) (Marjorie Rambeau)

## Tunes Of Glory (UK 1960)
Ronald Neame

Lt Col Jock Sinclair (Alec Guinness)*
Lt Col Basil Barrow (John Mills)*
Maj Charlie Scott (Dennis Price)*
Capt Jimmy Cairns (Gordon Jackson)
Morag Sinclair (Susannah York)*

## Turner And Hooch (USA 1989)
Roger Spottiswoode

Scott Turner (Tom Hanks)*
Emily Carson (Mare Winningham)
Chief Hyde (Craig T Nelson)
David Sutton (Reginald VelJohnson)

## The Turning Point (USA 1977)
Herbert Ross

Emma Jacklin (Anne Bancroft)*
Deedee Rodgers (Shirley MacLaine)*
Yuri Kopeikine (Mikhail Baryshnikov)
Emilia Rodgers (Leslie Browne)

## Twelve Angry Men (USA 1957)
Sidney Lumet

Juror No 8 (Henry Fonda)*
Juror No 3 (Lee J Cobb)
Juror No 10 (Ed Begley)
Juror No 4 (E G Marshall)

## Twelve O'Clock High (USA 1949)
Henry King

Gen Frank Savage (Gregory Peck)*
Lt Col Ben Gately (Hugh Marlowe)
Col Davenport (Gary Merrill)
Gen Pritchard (Millard Mitchell)
Maj Harvey Stovall (Dean Jagger)

## 20,000 Leagues Under The Sea
(USA 1954)
Richard Fleischer

Ned Land (Kirk Douglas)*
Capt Nemo (James Mason)*
Prof Aronnax (Paul Lukas)
Conseil (Peter Lorre)*

## Twins (USA 1988)
Ivan Reitman

Julius Benedict (Arnold Schwarzenegger)*
Vincent Benedict (Danny De Vito)*
Marnie Mason (Kelly Preston)
Linda Mason (Chloe Webb)

## The Two Jakes (USA 1990)
Jack Nicholson

Jake Gittes (Jack Nicholson)*
Jake Berman (Harvey Keitel)*
Kitty Berman (Meg Tilly)
Lillian Bodine (Madeleine Stowe)

## 2001: A Space Odyssey (UK 1968)
Stanley Kubrick

David Bowman (Keir Dullea)
Frank Poole (Gary Lockwood)
Dr Heywood Floyd (William Sylvester)
Moonwatcher (Daniel Richter)

Sequel *2010* (1984) (Roy Scheider*, Helen Mirren*)

**Two Women** (Italy 1961)
(*La Ciociara*)
Vittorio De Sica

Cesira (Sophia Loren)*
Rosetta (Eleanora Brown)
Giovanni (Raf Vallone)
Michel (Jean-Paul Belmondo)*

# U

**Ugetsu Monogatari** (Japan 1953)
Kenji Mizoguchi

Lady Wakasa (Machiko Kyo)
Genjuro (Masayuki Mori)
Miyagi, Genjuro's Wife (Kinuyo Tanaka)
Tobei (Sakae Ozawa)

**Ultimo Tango A Parigi** see **Last Tango In Paris**

**Under Fire** (USA 1983)
Roger Spottiswoode

Russell Price (Nick Nolte)*
Oates (Ed Harris)
Alex Grazier (Gene Hackman)*
Claire (Joanna Cassidy)

**Unforgiven** (USA 1992)
Clint Eastwood

William Munny (Clint Eastwood)*
'Little Bill' Daggett (Gene Hackman)*
Ned Logan (Morgan Freeman)*
English Bob (Richard Harris)*

**An Unmarried Woman** (USA 1978)
Paul Mazursky

Erica (Jill Clayburgh)*
Saul (Alan Bates)*
Martin (Michael Murphy)
Charlie (Cliff Gorman)

**The Untouchables** (USA 1987)
Brian De Palma

Eliot Ness (Kevin Costner)*
Jim Malone (Sean Connery)*

Oscar Wallace (Charles Martin Smith)
George Stone (Andy Garcia)*
Al Capone (Robert De Niro)*

**Urban Cowboy** (USA 1980)
James Bridges

Bud (John Travolta)*
Sissy (Debra Winger)*
Wes (Scott Glenn)
Pam (Madolyn Smith)

**Utvandrarna** see **The Emigrants**

# V

**The Verdict** (USA 1982)
Sidney Lumet

Frank Galvin (Paul Newman)*
Laura Fischer (Charlotte Rampling)*
Mickey Morrissey (Jack Warden)
Ed Concannon (James Mason)*

**Vertigo** (USA 1958)
Alfred Hitchcock

John 'Scottie' Ferguson (James Stewart)*
Madeleine Elster/Judy Barton (Kim Novak)*
Midge (Barbara Bel Geddes)
Gavin Elster (Tom Helmore)

**Victim** (UK 1961)
Basil Dearden

Melville Farr (Dirk Bogarde)*
Laura Farr (Sylvia Syms)
Calloway (Dennis Price)*
Lord Fullbrook (Anthony Nicholls)

**A View To A Kill** (UK 1985)
John Glen

James Bond (Roger Moore)*
Max Zorin (Christopher Walken)*
Stacey Sutton (Tanya Roberts)
May Day (Grace Jones)

**The Vikings** (USA 1958)
Richard Fleischer

Einar (Kirk Douglas)*
Eric (Tony Curtis)*
King Ragnar (Ernest Borgnine)*
Princess Morgana (Janet Leigh)*

**Viskingar Och Rop** see **Cries And Whispers**

# W

**Wall Street** (USA 1987)
Oliver Stone

Gordon Gekko (Michael Douglas)*
Bud Fox (Charlie Sheen)*
Darien Taylor (Daryl Hannah)*
Lou Mannheim (Hal Holbrook)

**War And Peace** (USA 1956)
King Vidor

Natasha Rostov (Audrey Hepburn)*
Pierre Bezukhov (Henry Fonda)*
Prince Andrey (Mel Ferrer)
Anatole Kuragin (Vittorio Gassman)

Subsequent version *War And Peace*
(1968) (Lyudmila Savelyeva, Sergei
Bondarchuk)

**The War Of The Roses** (USA 1989)
Danny De Vito

Oliver Rose (Michael Douglas)*
Barbara Rose (Kathleen Turner)*
Gavin D'Amato (Danny De Vito)*
Susan (Marianne Sägebracht)

**Wargames** (USA 1983)
John Badham

David (Matthew Broderick)*
McKittrick (Dabney Coleman)
Falken (John Wood)
Jennifer (Ally Sheedy)

**Way Out West** (USA 1937)
James W Horne

Stan (Stan Laurel)*
Ollie (Oliver Hardy)*
Mickey Finn (James Finlayson)
Lola Marcel (Sharon Lynne)

**The Way We Were** (USA 1973)
Sydney Pollack

Katie Morosky (Barbra Streisand)*
Hubbell Gardiner (Robert Redford)*
J J (Bradford Dillman)
Carol Ann (Lois Chiles)

**Wayne's World** (USA 1992)
Penelope Spheeris

Wayne Campbell (Mike Myers)
Garth Algar (Dana Carvey)
Benjamin Oliver (Rob Lowe)*
Cassandra (Tia Carrere)

**West Side Story** (USA 1961)
Robert Wise, Jerome Robbins

Maria (Natalie Wood)*
Tony (Richard Beymer)
Riff (Russ Tamblyn)
Anita (Rita Moreno)

**What Ever Happened To Baby Jane?** (USA 1962)
Robert Aldrich

Jane Hudson (Bette Davis)*
Blanche Hudson (Joan Crawford)*
Edwin Flagg (Victor Buono)
Mrs Bates (Anna Lee)

**What's Up Doc?** (USA 1972)
Peter Bogdanovich

Judy Maxwell (Barbra Streisand)*
Howard Bannister (Ryan O'Neal)*
Eunice Burns (Madeline Khan)
Hugh Simon (Kenneth Mars)

**When Harry Met Sally...** (USA 1989)
Rob Reiner

Harry Burns (Billy Crystal)*
Sally Albright (Meg Ryan)
Marie (Carrie Fisher)
Jess (Bruno Kirby)

**Where Eagles Dare** (USA 1968)
Brian G Hutton

Maj John Smith (Richard Burton)*
Lt Morris Schaffer (Clint Eastwood)*
Mary Ellison (Mary Ure)
Col Wyatt-Turner (Patrick Wymark)

**Whisky Galore** (UK 1948)
Alexander Mackendrick

Capt Paul Waggett (Basil Radford)
Mrs Waggett (Catherine Lacey)
Sgt Odd (Bruce Seaton)
Peggy Macroon (Joan Greenwood)*

Sequel *Rockets Galore!* (1958)

**White Christmas** (USA 1954)
Michael Curtiz

Bob Wallace (Bing Crosby)*
Phil Davis (Danny Kaye)*
Betty Haynes (Rosemary Clooney)
Judy Haynes (Vera-Ellen)

**White Heat** (USA 1949)
Raoul Walsh

Arthur Cody Jarrett (James Cagney)*
Verna Jarrett (Virginia Mayo)
Hank Fallon/Vic Pardo (Edmond
    O'Brien)*
Ma Jarrett (Margaret Wycherly)

**Who Framed Roger Rabbit**
    (USA 1988)
Robert Zemeckis

Eddie Valiant (Bob Hoskins)*
Judge Doom (Christopher Lloyd)
Dolores (Joanna Cassidy)
And voices of:
Roger Rabbit (Charles Fleischer)
Jessica Rabbit (Kathleen Turner)*
Jessica's Singing Voice (Amy Irving)

**Who's Afraid Of Virginia Woolf?**
    (USA 1966)
Mike Nichols

Martha (Elizabeth Taylor)*
George (Richard Burton)*
Nick (George Segal)*
Honey (Sandy Dennis)

**Wild At Heart** (USA 1990)
David Lynch

Sailor Ripley (Nicolas Cage)*
Lula Pace Fortune (Laura Dern)
Marietta Fortune (Diane Ladd)
Bobby Peru (Willem Dafoe)*

**The Wild Bunch** (USA 1969)
Sam Peckinpah

Pike Bishop (William Holden)*
Dutch Engstrom (Ernest Borgnine)*
Deke Thornton (Robert Ryan)*
Sykes (Edmond O'Brien)*

**The Wild One** (USA 1953)
Laslo Benedek

Johnny (Marlon Brando)*
Chino (Lee Marvin)*
Kathie (Mary Murphy)
Harry Bleeker (Robert Keith)

**Wild Strawberries** (Sweden 1957)
(*Smultronstället*)
Ingmar Bergman

Prof Isak Borg (Victor Sjöström)
Sara (Bibi Andersson)
Marianne Borg (Ingrid Thulin)
Evald Borg (Gunnar Björnstrand)

**Wilson** (USA 1944)
Henry King

Woodrow Wilson (Alexander Knox)
Edith Wilson (Geraldine Fitzgerald)
Prof Holmes (Charles Coburn)
Joseph Tumulty (Thomas Mitchell)
Wiliam G McAdoo (Vincent Price)*

**Wish You Were Here** (UK 1987)
David Leland

Lynda (Emily Lloyd)
Eric (Tom Bell)
Dave (Jesse Birdsall)
Aunt Millie (Pat Heywood)

**The Witches Of Eastwick**
(USA 1987)
George Miller

Daryl Van Horne (Jack Nicholson)*
Alexandra Medford (Cher)*
Jane Spofford (Susan Sarandon)*
Sukie Ridgemont (Michelle Pfeiffer)*

**Witness For The Prosecution**
(USA 1957)
Billy Wilder

Leonard Vole (Tyrone Power)*
Christine Vole (Marlene Dietrich)*
Sir Wilfrid Robarts (Charles Laughton)*
Miss Plimsoll (Elsa Lanchester)

Remake *Witness For The Prosecution*
(TV 1982) (Beau Bridges*, Diana
Rigg, Ralph Richardson*, Deborah
Kerr*)

**The Wizard Of Oz** (USA 1939)
Victor Fleming

Dorothy Gale (Judy Garland)*
Hunk/The Scarecrow (Ray Bolger)
Zeke/The Cowardly Lion (Bert Lahr)
Hickory/The Tin Man (Jack Haley)
Glinda (Billie Burke)
Miss Gulch/The Wicked Witch (Margaret
Hamilton)
The Wizard (Frank Morgan)

Remake *The Wiz* (1978) (Diana Ross)
Sequel *Return To Oz* (1985) (Fairuza
Balk)

**Woman Of The Year** (USA 1942)
George Stevens

Sam Craig (Spencer Tracy)*
Tess Harding (Katharine Hepburn)*

Ellen Whitcomb (Fay Bainter)
Clayton (Reginald Owen)

Remake *Woman Of The Year* (TV 1976)
(Joseph Bologna, Judd Taylor)

**The Women** (USA 1939)
George Cukor

Mary Haines (Norma Shearer)*
Crystal Allen (Joan Crawford)*
Sylvia Fowler (Rosalind Russell)*
Countess De Lave (Mary Boland)

Musical remake *The Opposite Sex*
(1956) (June Allyson*, Joan Collins,
Dolores Gray, Ann Sheridan)

**Women In Love** (UK 1969)
Ken Russell

Rupert Birkin (Alan Bates)*
Gerald Crich (Oliver Reed)*
Gudrun Brangwen (Glenda Jackson)*
Ursula Brangwen (Jennie Linden)

Sequel *The Rainbow* (1989)

**Women On The Verge Of A
Nervous Breakdown** (Spain 1988)
(*Mujeres Al Borde De Un Ataque
De Nervios*)
Pedro Almodovar

Pepa Marcos (Carmen Maura)*
Carlos (Antonio Banderas)*
Lucia (Julieta Serrano)
Candela (Maria Barranco)

**Working Girl** (USA 1988)
Mike Nichols

Jak Trainer (Harrison Ford)*
Katharine Parker (Sigourney Weaver)*
Tess McGill (Melanie Griffith)*
Mick Dugan (Alec Baldwin)*

**Wuthering Heights** (USA 1939)
William Wyler

Cathy Linton (Merle Oberon)*
Heathcliff (Laurence Olivier)*

**Wuthering Heights** (USA 1939) (cont.)
Edgar (David Niven)*
Ellen Dean (Flora Robson)*

Subsequent versions *Wuthering Heights*
(1970) (Anna Calder-Marshall,
Timothy Dalton*); *Wuthering Heights*
(1992) (Juliette Binoche, Ralph
Fiennes)


# Y

**Yankee Doodle Dandy** (USA 1942)
Michael Curtiz

George M Cohan (James Cagney)*
Mary (Joan Leslie)
Jerry Cohan (Walter Huston)*
Sam Harris (Richard Whorf)

**The Year Of Living Dangerously**
(Australia 1982)
Peter Weir

Guy Hamilton (Mel Gibson)*
Jill Bryant (Sigourney Weaver)*
Billy Kwan (Linda Hunt)
Pete Curtis (Michael Murphy)

**The Yearling** (USA 1946)
Clarence Brown

Pa Baxter (Gregory Peck)*
Ma Baxter (Jane Wyman)*
Jody Baxter (Claude Jarman Jnr)
Buck Forrester (Chill Wills)

**Yentl** (USA 1983)
Barbra Streisand

Yentl (Barbra Streisand)*
Avigdor (Many Patinkin)
Hadass (Amy Irving)
Papa (Nehemiah Persoff)

**You Can't Take It With You**
(USA 1938)
Frank Capra

Alice Sycamore (Jean Arthur)*
Martin Vanderhof (Lionel Barrymore)*
Tony Kirby (James Stewart)*
Anthony P Kirby (Edward Arnold)

**You Only Live Twice** (UK 1967)
Lewis Gilbert

James Bond (Sean Connery)*
Blofeld (Donald Pleasence)
Aki (Akiko Wakabayashi)
Tiger Tanaka (Tetsuro Tamba)

**Young Frankenstein** (USA 1974)
Mel Brooks

Dr Frankenstein (Gene Wilder)*
Monster (Peter Boyle)
Igor (Marty Feldman)
Elizabeth (Madeline Khan)
Blind Man (Gene Hackman)*

**Young Guns** (USA 1988)
Christopher Cain

William H Bonney (Emilio Estevez)*
Doc Scurlock (Kiefer Sutherland)*
Chavez Y Chavez (Lou Diamond
Phillips)
Dick Brewer (Charlie Sheen)*
'Dirty Steve' Stephens (Dermot
Mulroney)
Charley Bowdre (Casey Siemaszko)

Sequel *Young Guns II* (1990)


# Z

**Z** (France/Algeria 1968)
Constantin Costa-Gavras

'Z' (Yves Montand)*
The Magistrate (Jean-Louis Trintignant)
The Journalist (Jack Perrin)
The Public Prosecutor (François Perier)

**Zelig** (USA 1983)
Woody Allen

Leonard Zelig (Woody Allen)*
Dr Eudora Fletcher (Mia Farrow)*
Dr Sindell (John Buckwater)
Glandular Diagnosis Doctor (Marvin
  Chatinover)

**Ziegfeld Follis** (USA 1944)
Vincente Minnelli

Florence Ziegfeld (William Powell)*
Fred Astaire*
Gene Kelly*
Judy Garland*

**Zorba The Greek** (Greece 1964)
Michael Cacoyannis

Alexis Zorba (Anthony Quinn)*
Basil (Alan Bates)*
The Widow (Irene Papas)
Madame Hortense (Lila Kedrova)

**Zulu** (UK 1964)
Cy Endfield

Lt John Chard (Stanley Baker)*
Rev Otto Witt (Jack Hawkins)*
Pvt Henry Hook (James Booth)
Lt Gonville Bromhead (Michael Caine)*

Prequel *Zulu Dawn* (1979)

# Actors

## A

### ABRIL, Victoria
(1959– ) Spain

1975 *Obsession; Robin Hood; Caperucite Roja; Cambion De Sexo*
1976 *Robin And Marian; La Bien Plantada; Dona Perfecta*
1977 *Esposa Y Amante*
1979 *La Muchacha De Las Bragas De Oro; Mater Amatissima*
1980 *Ma Vale Pajaro En Mano Que Ciento Volando*
1981 *Asesinato En El Comite Central; La Guerrillera*
1982 *La Colmena; La Batalla Del Porro; Le Bastard; La Lune Dans Le Caniveau* (UK: *The Moon In The Gutter*); *Sem Sombra De Pecado; I Married A Dead Man; Rio Abajo*
1983 *Bajo El Singo De Piscis; Le Voyage; L'Bicicletas Son Para El Verano; L'Addition; Rouge George*
1984 *La Noche Mas Hermosa; Padre Nuestro; After Dark*
1985 *La Hora Bruja; Tiempo De Silencio; Vado E Torno*
1986 *Max, Mon Amour* (UK: *Max, My Love*)
1987 *El Lute; El Placer De Matar; Barrios Altos; El Juego Mas Divertido*
1988 *Ada Dans La Jungle; Baton Rouge; Sans Peur Et Sans Rapproche*
1989 *Sandino; Si Te Dicen Que Cai*
1990 *Atame!** (UK: *Tie Me Up! Tie Me Down!*); *A Solas Contigo*
1991 *Une Epoque Formidable; Amantes* (UK: *Lovers*); *Tacones Lejanos** (UK: *High Heels*)
1992 *Demasiado Corazon*

### ADJANI, Isabelle
(1955– ) France

1969 *Le Petit Bougnat*
1971 *Faustine Et Le Bel Eté* (UK: *Faustine*)
1974 *La Gifle* (UK: *The Slap*)
1975 *L'Histoire D'Adèle H* (UK: *The Story Of Adèle H*)
1976 *Le Locataire* (UK: *The Tenant*); *Barocco; Violette Et François*
1978 *The Driver; Les Soeurs Bronte*
1979 *Nosferatu: Phantom Der Nacht* (UK: *Nosferatu The Vampyre*)
1980 *Possession; Clara Et Les Chic Types*
1981 *Quartet; L'Année Prochaine Si Tout Va Bien*
1982 *Tout Feu, Tout Flamme; Antonieta; Mortelle Randonée*
1983 *L'Eté Meutrier* (UK: *One Deadly Summer*)
1985 *Subway**
1986 *Maladie D'Amour*
1987 *Ishtar*
1988 *Camille Claudel*
1993 *Toxic Affair*

### AGUTTER, Jenny
(1952– ) UK

1964 *East Of Sudan*
1965 *Ballerina*
1966 *A Man Could Get Killed*
1968 *The Gates Of Paradise; Star!*
1969 *I Start Counting*
1970 *The Railway Children**
1971 *Walkabout; The Snow Goose* (TV)
1972 *A War Of Children* (TV)
1976 *Logan's Run; The Eagle Has Landed; The Man In The Iron Mask* (TV)
1977 *Equus; Sois Belle Et Tais-Toi*
1978 *China 9, Liberty 37; Dominique; The Riddle Of The Sands*
1979 *Mayflower: The Pilgrims Adventure* (TV); *Sweet Wiliam*
1980 *Miss Right*

1981 *The Survivor; Amy; An American Werewolf In London; Late Flowering Love* (short)
1984 *Secret Places*
1987 *Dark Tower*
1989 *King Of The Wind*
1990 *Child's Play 2; The Outsiders* (TV); *Darkman*
1992 *Freddy FRO7* (voice only)

## ALBERT, Eddie
real name: Edward Albert Heimberger
(1908– ) USA

1938 *Brother Rat*
1939 *On Your Toes; Four Wives*
1940 *An Angel From Texas; My Love Came Back; A Dispatch From Reuter's* (UK: *This Man Reuter*): *Brother Rat And A Baby* (UK: *Baby Be Good*)
1941 *Four Mothers; The Wagons Roll At Night; Thieves Fall Out; Out Of The Fog; The Great Mr Nobody*
1942 *Treat'Em Rough; Eagle Squadron*
1943 *Ladies' Day; Lady Bodyguard, Bombardier*
1945 *Strange Voyage*
1946 *Rendezvous With Annie; The Perfect Marriage*
1947 *Smash-Up* (UK: *A Woman Destroyed*); *Time Out Of Mind; Hit Parade Of 1947*
1948 *Every Girl Should Be Married; The Dude Goes West; You Gotta Stay Happy*
1950 *The Fuller Brush Girl* (UK: *The Affairs Of Sally*)
1951 *You're In The Navy Now; Meet Me After The Show*
1952 *Actors And Sin; Carrie*
1953 *Roman Holiday**
1955 *The Girl Rush; I'll Cry Tomorrow**
1956 *Attack!; Oklahoma!*; The Teahouse Of The August Moon**
1957 *The Sun Also Rises; The Joker Is Wild*
1958 *The Gun Runners; The Roots Of Heaven; Orders To Kill*
1959 *Beloved Infidel; The Dingaling Girl* (TV)

1961 *The Young Doctors; The Two Little Bears*
1962 *Madison Avenue; The Longest Day*; Who's Got The Action?; The Party's Over; The Miracle Of The White Stallions* (UK: *Flight Of The White Stallions*)
1963 *Captain Newman MD*
1965 *Seven Women*
1971 *See The Man Run* (TV)
1972 *Fireball Foward* (TV); *The Heartbreak Kid*
1974 *The Take; McQ; The Borrowers* (TV); *The Longest Yard** (UK: *The Mean Machine*); *Escape To Witch Mountain*
1975 *The Devil's Rain; Hustle; Promise Him Anything* (TV); *Switch* (TV); *Whiffs* (UK: *C*A*S*H*)
1976 *Birch Interval*
1977 *Moving Violation*
1978 *Crash* (TV); *Foolin' Around*
1979 *Yesterday; Airport'79–The Concorde*
1980 *How To Beat Tho High Cost Of Living; Scoring; The Border*
1981 *Take This Job And Shove It; The Oklahoma City Dolls* (TV)
1982 *Yes, Giorgio; Trouble In The High Timber Country* (TV)
1983 *The Dream Murder Case* (TV); *The Act*
1984 *Dreamscape; Burning Rage* (TV)
1985 *In Like Flynn* (TV); *Stitches*
1986 *Turnaround; Head Office*
1987 *Brenda Starr*
1988 *The Big Picture*
1990 *Return To Green Acres* (TV)
1991 *The Girl From Mars* (TV)

## ALDA, Alan
(1936– ) USA

1963 *Gone Are The Days*
1968 *The Extraordinary Seaman; Paper Lion*
1970 *Catch 22*; The Moonshine War; Jenny*
1971 *The Mephisto Waltz; To Kill A Clown*

**ALDA, Alan** (cont.)

1972 *The Glass House* (TV);
*Playmates*(TV)
1973 *Isn't It Shocking?* (TV)
1977 *Kill Me If You Can* (TV)
1978 *California Suite\*; Same Time,
Next Year*
1979 *The Seduction Of Joe Tynan*
1981 *The Four Seasons* (also directed)
1986 *Sweet Liberty* (also directed)
1988 *A New Life* (also directed)
1989 *Crimes And Misdemeanours\**
1990 *Betsy's Wedding* (also directed)
1992 *Whispers In The Dark*
1993 *Manhattan Murder Mystery; And
The Band Played On* (TV)

**ALLEN, Woody**
real name: Allen Stewart Konigsberg
(1935–   ) USA

1965 *What's New Pussycat?*
1967 *Casino Royale*
1969 *Take The Money And Run*
1971 *Bananas*
1972 *Everything You Always Wanted
To Know About Sex But Were
Afraid To Ask; Play It Again, Sam*
1973 *Sleeper\**
1975 *Love And Death*
1976 *The Front*
1977 *Annie Hall\**
1979 *Manhattan\**
1980 *Stardust Memories; To Woody
Allen, From Europe With Love*
(documentary)
1982 *A Midsummer Night's Sex
Comedy*
1983 *Zelig*
1984 *Broadway Danny Rose\**
1986 *Hannah And Her Sisters\**
1987 *Radio Days* (narrator); *King Lear*
1989 *New York Stories; Crimes And
Misdemeanours\**
1991 *Scenes From The Mall*
1992 *Shadows And Fog; Husbands
And Wives*
1993 *Manhattan Murder Mystery*

See also directors listing

**ALLYSON, June**
real name: Eleanor Geisman
(1917–   ) USA

1937 *Swing For Sale; Pixilated; Dime
For Dance* (all shorts)
1938 *Dates And Nuts; The Prisoner Of
Swing; Sing For Sweetie* (all
shorts)
1939 *Rollin' In Rhythmn*
1943 *Best Foot Forward; Girl Crazy;
Thousands Cheer*
1944 *Two Girls And A Sailor; Meet The
People*
1945 *Her Highness And The Bellboy;
The Sailor Takes A Wife; Music
For Millions*
1946 *Two Sisters From Boston; Till The
Clouds Roll By\*; The Secret Heart*
1947 *High Barbaree; Good News*
1948 *The Bride Goes Wild; The Three
Musketeers\*; Words And Music*
1949 *Little Women; The Stratton Story;
The Reformer And The Redhead*
1950 *Right Cross*
1951 *Too Young To Kiss*
1952 *The Girl In White* (UK: *So Bright
The Flame*)
1953 *Battle Circus; Remains To Be
Seen; The Glenn Miller Story\**
1954 *Executive Suite; Woman's World*
1955 *Strategic Air Command; The
McConnell Story* (UK: *Tiger In
The Sky*); *The Shrike*
1956 *The Opposite Sex; You Can't Run
Away From It*
1957 *Interlude; My Man Godfrey*
1959 *Stranger In My Arms*
1971 *See The Man Run* (TV)
1972 *They Only Kill Their Masters*
1973 *The Letters* (TV)
1977 *Curse Of The Black Widow* (TV)
1978 *Vega$* (TV); *Blackout*
1979 *Three On A Date* (TV)
1982 *The Kid With The Broken Halo*
(TV)

**AMECHE, Don**
real name: Dominic Amici
(1908–   ) USA

1933 *Beauty At The World's Fair* (short)

1935 *Clive Of India; Dante's Inferno*
1936 *Sins Of Man; Ramona; Ladies In Love; One In A Million*
1937 *Love Is News; Fifty Roads To Town; You Can't Have Everything; Love Under Fire*
1938 *In Old Chicago\*; Happy Landing; Josette; Alexander's Ragtime Band\*; Gateway*
1939 *Midnight; Hollywood Cavalcade; Swanee River; The Three Musketeers* (UK: *The Singing Musketeer*); *The Story Of Alexander Graham Bell* (UK: *The Modern Miracle*)
1940 *Lillian Russell; Four Sons; Down Argentine Way*
1941 *That Night In Rio; Moon Over Miami; Kiss The Boys Goodbye; The Feminine Touch*
1942 *Confirm Or Deny; The Magnificent Dope; Girl Trouble*
1943 *Heaven Can Wait\*; Happy Land; Something To Shout About*
1944 *Wing And A Prayer; Greenwich Village*
1945 *It's In The Bag* (UK: *The Fifth Chair*); *Guest Wife*
1946 *So Goes My Love* (UK: *A Genius In The Family*)
1947 *That's My Man* (UK: *Will Tomorrow Ever Come?*)
1948 *Sleep My Love*
1949 *Slightly French*
1952 *Hollywood Night At 21 Club* (short)
1954 *Phantom Caravan; Fire One*
1961 *A Fever In The Blood*
1966 *Rings Around The World; Picture Mommy Dead*
1968 *Shadow Over Elveron* (TV)
1970 *Suppose They Gave A War And Nobody Came; The Boatniks*
1971 *Gidget Gets Married* (TV)
1975 *Won Ton Ton, The Dog Who Saved Hollywood*
1983 *Trading Places\**
1985 *Cocoon\**
1986 *A Masterpiece Of Murder* (TV); *Pals* (TV)
1987 *Harry And The Hendersons* (UK: *Bigfoot And The Hendersons*)

1988 *Coming To America\*; Cocoon: The Return; Things Change*
1990 *Odd Ball Hall*
1991 *Oscar*
1992 *Folks!*
1993 *Homeward Bound* (voice only)


## ANDREWS, Carver Dana
(1909–92) USA

1939 *Lucky Cisco Kid*
1940 *The Westerner; Sailor's Lady; Kit Carson*
1941 *Tobacco Road; Belle Starr; Ball Of Fire\*; Swamp Water* (UK: *The Man Who Came Back*)
1942 *The Berlin Correspondent*
1943 *The Ox-Bow Incident\** (UK: *Strange Incident*); *December Seventh; Crash Dive; North Star*
1944 *The Purple Heart; Wing And A Prayer; Up In Arms; Laura\**
1945 *State Fair; Fallen Angel; Walk In The Sun; Know Your Enemy: Japan* (narrator only)
1946 *Canyon Passage; The Best Years Of Our Lives\**
1947 *Boomerang; Night Song; Daisy Kenyon*
1948 *The Iron Curtain; Deep Waters; No Minor Vices*
1949 *Sword In The Desert; Britannia Mews*
1950 *My Foolish Heart; Where The Sidewalk Ends; Edge Of Doom* (UK: *Stronger Than Fear*)
1951 *The Frogmen; Sealed Cargo; I Want You*
1952 *Assignment–Paris!*
1953 *Elephant Walk*
1954 *Duel In The Jungle; Three Hours To Kill*
1955 *Smoke Signal; Strange Lady In Town; While The City Sleeps*
1956 *Comanche; Beyond A Reasonable Doubt; Hollywood Goes A-Fishing* (short)
1957 *Night Of The Demon* (US: *Curse Of The Demon*); *Spring Reunion; Zero Hour*

**ANDREWS, Carver Dana** (cont.)
1958  The Fearmakers; Enchanted
       Island; The Right Hand Man (TV)
1960  The Crowded Sky; Alas, Babylon
       (TV)
1962  Madison Avenue
1964  The Satan Bug
1965  Crack In The World; Brainstorm;
       The Woman Who Wouldn't Die; In
       Harm's Way; Town Tamer; The
       Loved One; Battle Of The Bulge;
       Berlin, Appuntamento (UK: Spy In
       Your Eye)
1966  Johnny Reno; Supercolpo Da 7
       Miliardi (UK: The 1,000 Carat
       Diamond)
1967  Hot Rods To Hell; The Frozen
       Dead; The Cobra; I Diamenti Che
       Nassuno Voleva Rubare
1968  The Devil's Brigade
1971  The Failing Of Raymond (TV)
1972  Innocent Bystanders
1974  Airport'75
1975  The First 36 Hours Of Dr Durant
       (TV); Take A Hard Ride; Shadow
       In The Streets
1976  The Last Tycoon
1977  Good Guys Wear Black; The Last
       Hurrah (TV)
1978  Born Again
1979  The Pilot
1984  Prince Jack

**ANDREWS, Julie**
real name: Julia Wells
(1935–  ) UK

1952  Rose Of Baghdad (voice only)
1956  High Tor (TV)
1958  The Reluctant Debutante (extra)
1964  Mary Poppins*: The
       Americanization Of Emily
1965  The Sound Of Music*
1966  Torn Curtain; Hawaii
1967  Thoroughly Modern Millie*; The
       Singing Princess (voice only)
1968  Star!
1970  Darling Lili
1974  The Tamarind Seed; The Return
       Of The Pink Panther (footage
       deleted)

1979  10*; Little Miss Marker
1981  SOB
1982  Victor/Victoria
1983  The Man Who Loved Women
1986  Duet For One; That's Life!
1990  Tchin Tchin
1991  Our Sons (TV)

**ARKIN, Alan**
(1934–  ) USA

1957  Calypso Heat Wave
1962  That's Me (short)
1963  The Last Mohican (short)
1966  The Russians Are Coming, The
       Russians Are Coming*
1967  Woman Times Seven; Wait Until
       Dark
1968  The Heart Is A Lonely Heart;
       Inspector Clouseau
1969  Popi; The Monitors; People Soup
       (short)
1970  Catch 22*
1971  Little Murders
1972  Last Of The Red Hot Lovers;
       Deadhead Miles
1974  Freebie And the Bean
1975  Rafferty And The Gold Dust
       Twins; Hearts Of The West (UK:
       Hollywood Cowboy)
1976  The Defection Of Simas Kudirka
       (TV); The Seven-Per-Cent
       Solution
1977  Fire Sale
1978  The Other Side Of Hell (TV)
1979  The In-Laws; The Magician Of
       Lublin; Improper Channels
1980  Simon
1981  Full Moon High; Chu Chu And
       The Philly Flash; The Last
       Unicorn (voice only)
1982  The Return Of Captain Invincible
1985  Joshua Then And Now; Bad
       Medicine
1986  Big Trouble; A Deadly Business (TV)
1987  Escape From Sobibor (TV)
1988  Necessary Parties (TV)
1989  Coupe De Ville
1990  Havana; Edward Scissorhands*
1991  The Rocketeer
1992  Glengarry Glen Ross

## ARLETTY
real name: Léonie Bathiat
(1898–1992) France

1931 *Un Chien Qui Rapporte; Mais N'Te Promène Donc Pas Toute Nue* (UK: *Don't Walk About In The Nude*)
1932 *Enlevez Moi; Un Fil A La Patte; Feue La Mère De Madame; La Belle Aventure*
1933 *Une Idée Folle; Un Soir De Réveillon; Je Te Confie Ma Femme*
1934 *Le Voyage De Monsieur Perrichon*
1935 *La Guerre Des Valses; Pension Mimosas; La Fille De Madame Angot; L'Ecole Des Concottes; Amants Et Voleurs; Le Vertige*
1936 *La Garçonne; Un Mari Revé; Aventure A Paris; Faisons Un Rêve; Messieurs Les Ronds-De-Cuir*
1937 *Les Perles De La Couronne; Aloha Le Chant Des Iles; Mirages; Désire*
1938 *Le Petit Chose; La Chaleur Du Sein; Hotel Du Nord*
1939 *Le Jour Se Lève\** (UK: *Daybreak*); *Fric Frac; Circonstances Atténuantes*
1940 *Tempête*
1941 *Madame Sans Gêne*
1942 *La Femme Que J'Ai Le Plus Aimée* (UK: *The Woman I Loved The Most*); *Boléro; L'Amant De Bornéo; Les Visiteurs Du Soir*
1944 *Les Enfants Du Paradis\**
1949 *Portrait D'Un Assassin*
1952 *L'Amour, Madame; Gibier De Potence*
1953 *Le Père De Mademoiselle*
1954 *Le Grand Jeu*
1955 *L'Air De Paris; Huis Clos*
1956 *Mon Curé Chez Les Pauvres*
1957 *Vacances Explosives*
1958 *Le Passager Clandestin*
1959 *Et Ta Soeur?; Maxime*
1960 *Drôle De Dimanche*
1961 *La Gamberge; Les Petits Matins; La Loi Des Hommes*

1962 *The Longest Day\**
1963 *Tempo Di Roma; Le Voyage A Biarritz*

## ARTHUR, Jean
real name: Gladys Greene
(1905–91) USA

1923 *Somebody Lied* (short); *Cameo Kirby*
1924 *Spring Fever; Case Dismissed; The Powerful Eye* (all shorts); *The Temple Of Venus; Fast And Fearless; Biff Bang Buddy; Bringin' Home The Bacon; Travelin' Fast; Thundering Romance*
1925 *The Fighting Smile; Seven Chances; The Drug Store Cowboy; A Man Of Nerve; Tearin' Loose*
1926 *Hello Lafayette; Eight Cylinder Bull; The Mad Racer* (all shorts); *Thundering Through; Born To Battle; The Hurricane Horseman; Twisted Triggers; Roaring Rider; The Fighting Cheat; Riding Rivals; The College Boob; Lightning Bill; Double Daring; Under Fire; The Cowboy Cop* (UK: *Broke To The Wide*)
1927 *Bigger And Better Blondes* (short); *The Block Signal; Husband Hunters; The Broken Gate; Horseshoes; Winners Of The Wilderness; The Poor Nut; Flying Luck; The Masked Menace*
1928 *Wallflowers; Easy Come, Easy Go; Warming Up; Brotherly Love; Sins Of The Fathers*
1929 *The Canary Murder Case; The Mysterious Dr Fu Manchu; The Saturday Night Kid; The Greene Murder Case; Halfway To Heaven; Stairs Of Sand*
1930 *Street Of Chance; The Record Run; Young Eagles; Paramount On Parade; The Return Of Dr Fu Manchu; Danger Lights; The Silver Horde*

**ARTHUR, Jean** (cont.)
1931 *The Gang Buster; The Lawyer's Secret; Ex-Bad Boy; Virtuous Husband* (UK: *What Wives Don't Want*)
1933 *Get That Venus; The Past Of Mary Holmes*
1934 *Whirlpool; The Defense Rests; The Most Precious Things In Life*
1935 *The Whole Town's Talking* (UK: *Passport To Fame*); *Public Hero Number One; Party Wire; Diamond Jim; The Public Menace; If You Could Only Cook*
1936 *Mr Deeds Goes To Town\*; The Plainsman; More Than A Secretary; The Ex-Mrs Bradford; Adventure In Manhattan* (UK: *Manhattan Madness*)
1937 *History Is Made At Night; Easy Living*
1938 *You Can't Take It With You\**
1939 *Only Angels Have Wings; Mr Smith Goes To Washington\**
1940 *Arizona; Too Many Husbands* (UK: *My Two Husbands*)
1941 *The Devil And Miss Jones*
1942 *The Talk Of The Town*
1943 *The More The Merrier; A Lady Takes A Chance*
1944 *The Impatient Years*
1948 *A Foreign Affair*
1953 *Shane\**

**ASHCROFT, Peggy**
(1907–91) UK

1933 *The Wandering Jew*
1935 *The 39 Steps\**
1936 *Rhodes Of Africa*
1940 *Channel Incident* (short)
1941 *Quiet Wedding*
1959 *The Nun's Story\**
1967 *Tell Me Lies; October Revolution* (narrator only)
1968 *Secret Ceremony*
1969 *Three Into Two Won't Go*
1971 *Sunday Bloody Sunday\**
1973 *Der Füssganger* (UK: *The Pedestrian*)
1976 *Joseph Andrews*

1978 *Hullabaloo Over Georgie And Bonnie's Pictures*
1984 *A Passage To India\**
1986 *When The Wind Blows* (voice only)
1988 *Madame Sousatzka*
1989 *She's Been Away* (TV)

**ASTAIRE, Fred**
real name: Frederick Austerlitz
(1899–1987) USA

1915 *Fanchon The Cricket*
1931 *Municipal Bandwagon* (short)
1933 *Dancing Lady; Flying Down To Rio*
1934 *The Gay Divorcee\** (UK: *The Gay Divorce*); *Rebecca*
1935 *Top Hat\**
1936 *Follow The Fleet; Swing Time\**
1937 *Shall We Dance?; Damsel In Distress*
1938 *Carefree*
1939 *The Story Of Vernon And Irene Castle*
1940 *Broadway Melody Of 1940; Second Chorus*
1941 *You'll Never Get Rich*
1942 *You Were Never Lovelier; Holiday Inn\**
1943 *The Sky's The Limit*
1944 *Ziegfeld Follies\**
1945 *Yolanda And The Thief*
1946 *Blue Skies\**
1948 *Easter Parade\**
1949 *The Barkleys Of Broadway*
1950 *Three Little Words; Let's Dance*
1951 *Royal Wedding* (UK: *Wedding Bells*)
1952 *The Belle Of New York*
1953 *The Band Wagon\**
1954 *Deep In My Heart*
1955 *Daddy Long Legs*
1956 *Funny Face\**
1959 *On The Beach*
1961 *The Pleasure Of His Company*
1962 *The Notorious Landlady*
1964 *Paris When It Sizzles* (voice only)
1968 *Finian's Rainbow*
1969 *Midas Run* (UK: *A Run On Gold*)

1971 *The Over-The-Hill Gang Rides Again* (TV)
1972 *Imagine*
1974 *The Towering Inferno\*; That's Entertainment*
1976 *That's Entertainment, Part Two*
1977 *Taxi Mauve* (UK: *Purple Taxi*); *The Amazing Dobermans*
1978 *A Family Upside Down* (TV); *The Man In The Santa Claus Suit* (TV)
1981 *Ghost Story*

## ASTOR, Mary
real name: Lucille Langhanke
(1906–87) USA

1921 *Sentimental Journey* (scenes deleted); *The Beggar Maid; Bullets Or Ballots; Brother Of The Bear; My Lady O' The Pines; The Bashful Suitor* (all shorts)
1922 *The Young Painter* (short); *Hope; The Angelus; The Man Who Played God; John Smith*
1923 *Second Fiddle; Success; The Scarecrow; The Bright Shawl; Puritan Passions; To The Ladies; The Rapids; The Marriage Maker; Hollywood; Woman Proof*
1924 *Beau Brummell; The Fighting Coward; Unguarded Woman; Inez From Hollywood* (UK: *The Good Bad Girl*); *The Fighting American; The Price Of A Party*
1925 *Oh, Doctor; Enticement; Playing With Souls; Don Q Son Of Zorro; The Pace That Thrills; The Scarlet Saint*
1926 *Don Juan; The Wise Guy; Forever After; High Steppers*
1927 *No Place To Go; The Sea Tiger; Sunset Derby; Rose Of The Golden West; Two Arabian Knights; The Rough Riders* (UK: *The Trumpet Calls*)
1928 *Heart To Heart; Sailors' Wives; Dressed To Kill; Three-Ring Marriage; Dry Martini*
1929 *Romance Of The Underworld; New Year's Eve; Woman From Hell; Ladies Love Brutes*

1930 *The Runaway Bride; Holiday; The Lash* (UK: *Adios*); *The Royal Bed* (UK: *The Queen's Husband*)
1931 *Behind Office Doors; Sin Ship; Other Men's Women; White Shoulders; Smart Woman*
1932 *Men Of Chance; The Lost Squadron; A Successful Calamity; Those We Love; Red Dust*
1933 *The Little Giant; Jennie Gerhardt; The World Changes; Convention City; The Kennel Murder Case*
1934 *Easy To Love; Upperworld; The Man With Two Faces; Return Of The Terror; The Case Of The Howling Dog; The Hollywood Gad-About* (short)
1935 *I Am A Thief; Straight From The Heart; Dinky; Page Miss Glory; Man Of Iron; Red Hot Tires* (UK: *Racing Luck*)
1936 *The Murder Of Dr Harrigan; And So They Were Married; Trapped By Television* (UK: *Caught By Television*); *Dodsworth\**
1937 *The Lady From Nowhere; The Prisoner Of Zenda\*; Hurricane\**
1938 *No Time To Marry; There's Always A Woman; Woman Against Woman; Listen, Darling; Paradise For Three* (UK: *Romance For Three*)
1939 *Midnight*
1940 *Turnabout; Brigham Young*
1941 *The Maltese Falcon\*; The Great Lie*
1942 *In This Our Life; Across The Pacific; The Palm Beach Story\**
1943 *Young Ideas; Thousands Cheer*
1944 *Meet Me In St Louis\*; Blonde Fever*
1946 *Claudia And David; Cynthia* (UK: *The Rich, Full Life*)
1947 *Fiesta; Desert Fury; Cass Timberlane*
1948 *Act Of Violence*
1949 *Little Women; Any Number Can Play*
1956 *A Kiss Before Dying; The Power And The Prize; The House Without A Name* (short)

**ASTOR, Mary** (cont.)
1957 *The Devil's Hairpin; Mr And Mrs McAdam* (TV): *The Troublemakers* (TV)
1958 *This Happy Feeling; The Return Of Ansel Gibbs* (TV)
1959 *Stranger In My Arms; Diary Of A Nurse* (TV)
1960 *Journey To The Day* (TV)
1961 *Return To Peyton Place*
1964 *Youngblood Hawke; Hush...Hush, Sweet Charlotte*

**ATTENBOROUGH, Richard**
(1923–   ) UK

1942 *In Which We Serve**
1943 *Schweik's New Adventures; The Hundred-Pound Window*
1945 *Journey Together*
1946 *A Matter of Life And Death*; School For Secrets*
1947 *The Man Within; Dancing With Crime; Brighton Rock*
1948 *London Belongs To Me; The Guinea Pig*
1949 *The Lost People; Boys In Brown*
1950 *Morning Departure*
1951 *Hell Is Sold Out; The Magic Box*
1952 *Sports Page No 6 — Football* (short); *Gift Horse; Father's Doing Fine*
1953 *Eight O'Clock Walk*
1955 *The Ship That Died Of Shame; Private's Progress*
1956 *The Baby And The Battleship; Brothers-In-Law*
1957 *The Scamp*
1958 *Dunkirk; Sea Of Sand; The Man Upstairs*
1959 *Danger Within; I'm All Right Jack*: Jet Storm; SOS Pacific*
1960 *The Angry Silence; The League Of Gentlemen*
1961 *Only Two Can Play*
1962 *All Night Long; The Dock Brief*
1963 *The Great Escape**
1964 *Seance On A Wet Afternoon; The Third Secret; Guns At Batasi; A Boy's Day* (short, narrator)
1965 *The Flight Of The Phoenix*

1966 *The Sand Pebbles**
1967 *Dr Dolittle*
1968 *Only When I Larf; The Bliss Of Blossom*
1969 *David Copperfield* (TV); *The Magic Christian*
1970 *A Severed Head; The Last Grenade; Loot; Don't Make Me Laugh* (narrator only)
1971 *10 Rillington Place; Cup Glory* (narrator only)
1974 *Rosebud*
1975 *And Then There Were None; Brannigan; Conduct Unbecoming*
1977 *Shatranj Ke Khilari* (UK: *The Chess Players*)
1979 *The Human Factor*
1993 *Jurassic Park*

See also directors listing

**AYKROYD, Dan**
real name: Daniel Agraluscarsacra
(1951–   ) Canada

1974 *Love At First Sight*
1979 *Mr Mike's Mondo Video; 1941**
1980 *The Blues Brothers**
1981 *Neighbors*
1982 *It Came From Hollywood*
1983 *Doctor Detroit; Trading Places*; The Twilight Zone — The Movie*
1984 *Ghostbusters*; Nothing Lasts Forever; Indiana Jones And The Temple Of Doom**
1985 *Into The Night; Spies Like Us*
1986 *One More Saturday Night* (executive producer only)
1987 *Dragnet*
1988 *The Couch Trip; My Stepmother Is An Alien; The Great Outdoors; Caddyshack II*
1989 *Ghostbusters II; Driving Miss Daisy**
1990 *Loose Cannons*
1991 *Nothing But Trouble* (also director); *My Girl*
1992 *This Is My Life; Sneakers; Chaplin*
1993 *The Coneheads; My Girl 2*

## AYRES, Lew
full name: Lewis Ayer
(1908– ) USA

1929 *The Sophomore; Big News; The Shakedown; The Kiss*
1930 *Compromised; All Quiet On The Western Front*; Common Clay; The Doorway To Hell* (UK: *A Handful Of Clouds*; *East Is West*
1931 *Iron Man; Up For Murder; Many A Slip; Heaven On Earth; Spirit Of Notre Dame* (UK: *Vigour Of Youth*)
1932 *The Impatient Maiden; Night World; The Cohens And Kellys In Hollywood; Okay America!* (UK: *Penalty Of Fame*)
1933 *State Fair; Don't Bet On Love; My Weakness*
1934 *Cross Country Cruise; She Learned About Sailors; Let's Be Ritzy* (UK: *Millionaire For A Day*)
1935 *Servants' Entrance; Lottery Lover; Silk Hat Kid; Spring Tonic*
1936 *The Leathernecks Have Landed* (UK: *The Marines Have Landed*) (also director); *Panic On The Air; Shakodown; Murder With Pictures; Hearts In Bondage* (director only)
1937 *Lady Be Careful; The Crime Nobody Saw; Last Train From Madrid; Hold'Em Navy*
1938 *Scandal Street; Holiday; King Of The Newsboys; Rich Man — Poor Girl; Young Dr Kildare; Spring Madness*
1939 *Ice Follies Of 1939; Broadway Serenade; Calling Dr Kildare; Three Glamour Girls; Remember?; Secret Of Dr Kildare*
1940 *Dr Kildare's Strange Case; The Golden Fleecing; Dr Kildare's Crisis; Dr Kildare Goes Home*
1941 *Maisie Was A Lady; The People Versus Dr Kildare* (UK: *My Life Is Yours*)
1942 *Dr Kildare's Wedding Day* (UK: *Mary Names The Day*); *Dr Kildare's Victory* (UK: *The Doctor And The Debutante*); *Fingers At The Window*

1946 *The Dark Mirror*
1947 *The Unfaithful*
1948 *Johnny Belinda**
1950 *The Capture*
1951 *New Mexico*
1953 *No Escape; Donovan's Brain*
1956 *The Family Nobody Wanted* (TV)
1962 *Advise And Consent*
1964 *The Carpetbaggers**
1971 *She Waits* (TV); *Earth II* (TV); *The Last Generation*
1972 *The Man; The Stranger* (TV); *The Biscuit Eater*
1973 *Battle For The Planet Of The Apes; The Questor Tapes* (TV)
1974 *Heatwave* (TV)
1977 *End Of The World; Francis Gary Powers — The True Story Of The U2 Incident* (TV)
1978 *Damien — Omen II; Suddenly Love* (TV); *Battlestar Galactica* (TV)
1979 *Letters From Frank; Salem's Lot* (TV)
1980 *Of Mice And Men* (TV)
1985 *Limo Street* (TV)
1986 *Under Siege* (TV)
1989 *Cast the First Stone* (TV)

# B

## BACALL, Lauren
real name: Betty Joan Perske
(1924– ) USA

1944 *To Have And Have Not**
1945 *Confidential Agent*
1946 *The Big Sleep*; Two Guys From Milwaukee* (UK: *Royal Flush*)
1947 *Dark Passage*
1948 *Key Largo**
1950 *Bright Leaf; Young Man With A Horn* (UK: *Young Man Of Music*)
1953 *How To Marry A Millionaire**
1954 *Woman's World*
1955 *The Cobweb; Blood Alley; Salute To The Theatre* (documentary)
1956 *Written On The Wind*
1957 *Designing Women*
1958 *The Gift Of Love*

**BACALL, Lauren** (cont.)
1959 *Northwest Frontier*
1964 *Shock Treatment; Sex And The Single Girl*
1966 *Harper* (UK: *The Moving Target*)
1974 *Murder On The Orient Express\**
1976 *The Shootist\**
1978 *Perfect Gentlemen* (TV)
1980 *Health*
1981 *The Fan*
1987 *Appointment With Death*
1988 *Mr North; Dinner At Eight* (TV); *Tree Of Hands; John Huston* (documentary)
1990 *A Star For Two; Misery\**
1991 *All I Want For Christmas*
1992 *The Painting* (TV)

## BAKER, Carroll
(1931– ) USA

1953 *Easy To Love*
1956 *Baby Doll; Giant\**
1958 *The Big Country\**
1959 *The Miracle; But Not For Me*
1961 *Something Wild; Bridge To The Sun*
1962 *How The West Was Won\*; Station Six Sahara*
1964 *The Carpetbaggers\*; Cheyenne Autumn*
1965 *Sylvia; The Greatest Story Ever Told; Mister Moses; Harlow*
1967 *The Harem; Jack Of Diamonds*
1968 *Orgasmo* (UK: *Paranoia*); *Paranoia* (UK: *A Quiet Place To Kill*); *The Sweet Body Of Deborah*
1969 *Cose Dolce...Cosi Perversa* (UK: *So Sweet...So Perverse*)
1970 *The Spider*
1971 *At The Bottom Of The Pool; Captain Apache; The Fourth Mrs Anderson*
1972 *The Devil Has Seven Faces; Behind The Silence; Bloody Mary*
1973 *Baba Yaga—Devil Witch; The Flower With The Deadly Sting; Il Coltello Di Ghiaccio; The Madness Of Love*
1974 *Take This My Body*

1975 *James Dean—The First American Teenager* (documentary); *The Private Lesson; The Lure; The Sky Is Falling; La Moglie Vergine* (UK: *Virgin Wife*)
1976 *Il Corpo; La Moglie Di Mio Padre* (UK: *Confessions Of A Frustrated Housewife*); *Zerschossene Traüme; Bad*
1977 *Cyclone*
1978 *Ab Morgen Sind Wir Reich Und Ehrlich*
1979 *The World Is Full Of Married Men*
1980 *The Watcher In The Woods*
1983 *Red Monarch* (TV); *The Secret Diary Of Sigmund Freud; Star 80*
1985 *Hitler's SS: Portrait In Evil* (TV); *What Mad Pursuit?* (TV)
1986 *Native Son; On Fire* (TV)
1987 *Ironweed\**
1989 *Fatal Spell*
1990 *Kindergarten Cop; Gipsy Angel*
1991 *Blonde Fist*

## BAKER, Sir Stanley
(1927–76) UK

1943 *Undercover*
1948 *All Over Town*
1949 *Obsession*
1950 *Your Witness; Lilli Marlene*
1951 *The Rossiter Case; Captain Horatio Hornblower RN; Home To Danger; Cloudburst; Whispering Smith Hits London*
1953 *The Cruel Sea; The Red Beret; The Tell Tale Heart* (short)
1954 *Hell Below Zero; The Good Die Young; Knights Of The Round Table; The Beautiful Stranger; Helen Of Troy*
1955 *Richard III\**
1956 *Alexander The Great; A Hill In Korea; Checkpoint; Child In The House*
1957 *Hell Drivers; Campbell's Kingdom; Violent Playground*
1958 *Sea Fury*
1959 *The Angry Hills; Blind Date; Jet Storm; Yesterday's Enemy*

1960 *Hell Is A City; The Criminal*
1961 *The Guns Of Navarone**
1962 *A Prize Of Arms; Sodom And Gomorrah; The Man Who Finally Died; In The French Style: Eva*
1963 *Zulu**
1965 *Dingaka; Sands Of The Kalahari; Who Has Seen The Wind?; One Of Them Is Brett* (narrator only)
1967 *Accident; Robbery: Code Name Heraclitus* (TV)
1969 *The Games; Where's Jack?; La Ragazza Con La Pistola* (UK: *Girl With A Pistol*)
1970 *Perfect Friday; The Last Grenade; Popsy Pop* (UK: *The 21 Carat Snatch*)
1971 *Una Lucertola Con La Pelle De Donna* (UK: *A Lizard In A Woman's Skin*)
1972 *Innocent Bystanders*
1975 *Zorro; Orzowei; Pepita Jiminez* (aka *Bride To Be*)

## BALDWIN, Alec
(1958– ) USA

1984 *Sweet Revenge* (TV)
1985 *Love On The Run* (TV)
1986 *Forever, Lulu*
1987 *The Alamo: 13 Days To Glory* (TV); *She's Having A Baby*
1988 *Beetlejuice*; Talk Radio; Married To The Mob; Working Girl**
1989 *Miami Blues; Great Balls Of Fire*
1990 *The Hunt For Red October*; Alice*
1991 *The Marrying Man* (UK: *Too Hot To Handle*)
1992 *Prelude To A Kiss*
1993 *Damages*

## BANCROFT, Anne
real name: Anna Maria Italiano
(1931– ) USA

1952 *Don't Bother To Knock; Tonight We Sing*
1953 *The Robe*; The Treasure Of The Golden Condor; The Kid From The Left Field*

1954 *Demetrius And The Gladiators; The Raid; Gorilla At Large*
1955 *A Life In The Balance; New York Confidential; The Naked Street; The Last Frontier*
1956 *Walk The Proud Land; Nightfall*
1957 *The Restless Breed; Invitation To A Gunfighter* (TV); *The Girl In Black Stockings; So Soon To Die* (TV)
1962 *The Miracle Worker*
1963 *The Girl Of The Via Flaminia*
1964 *The Pumpkin Eater*
1965 *The Slender Thread; Seven Women*
1967 *The Graduate**
1970 *Arthur Penn, 1922: Themes And Variations* (documentary)
1972 *Young Winston*
1974 *The Prisoner Of Second Avenue*
1975 *The Hindenburg*
1976 *Silent Movie; Lipstick*
1977 *Jesus Of Nazareth* (TV); *The Turning Point**
1979 *Fatso* (also directed)
1980 *The Elephant Man**
1983 *To Be Or Not To Be*
1984 *Garbo Talks!*
1985 *Agnes Of God**
1986 *'Night, Mother; 84 Charing Cross Road*
1988 *Torch Song Trilogy**
1989 *Bert Rigby, You're A Fool*
1992 *Neil Simon's Broadway Bound* (TV); *Honeymoon In Vegas*
1993 *Point Of No Return; Mr Jones*

## BANDERAS, Antonio
(1960– ) Spain

1982 *Laberinto De Pasiones* (UK:*Labyrinth Of Passions*); *Pestanas Postizas*
1983 *El Señor Galindez*
1984 *El Caso Almeria; Los Zancos* (UK: *Stilts*)
1985 *Cassa Cerrado; 27 Horas; Requiem Por Un Campesino Espanol* (UK: *Requiem For A Spanish Peasant*); *La Corte De Faraón* (UK: *Pharoah's Court*)

**BANDERAS, Antonio** (cont.)

1986 *Matador; Así Combo Habían Sida*
1987 *La Ley Del Deseo* (UK: *The Law Of Desire*); *El Placér De Matar* (UK: *The Pleasure Of Killing*)
1988 *Mujeres Al Borde De Un Ataque De Nervios** (UK: *Women On The Verge Of A Nervous Breakdown*); *Baton Rouge*
1989 *Si Te Dicen Que Caí*
1990 *Contra El Viento; Atame!** (UK: *Tie Me Up! Tie Me Down!*)
1991 *Truth Or Dare* (UK: *In Bed With Madonna*) (documentary)
1992 *The Mambo Kings*
1993 *Philadelphia; The House Of The Spirits*

## BARDOT, Brigitte
(1934– ) France

1952 *Le Trou Normand; Les Dents Longues; Manina* (UK: *The Lighthouse Keeper's Daughter*)
1953 *Le Portrait De Son Père; Act Of Love; Si Versailles M'Etait Contée* (UK: *Royal Affairs At Versailles*)
1954 *Tradita; Helen Of Troy; Le Fils De Caroline Chérie*
1955 *Futures Vedettes* (UK: *Sweet Sixteen*); *Doctor At Sea*; *Les Grands Manouevres* (UK: *Summer Manouevres*); *La Lumière D'En Face* (UK: *The Light Across The Street*): *Cette Sacrée Gamine* (UK: *Mam'zelle Pigalle*)
1956 *Mio Figlio Nerone* (UK: *Nero's Weekend*); *En Effeuillant La Marguerite* (UK: *Mam'selle Striptease*): *Et Dieu Créa La Femme** (UK: *And God Created Woman*); *La Mariée Etait Trop Belle* (UK: *The Bride Is Too Beautiful*)
1957 *Une Parisienne* (UK: *Parisienne*); *Les Bijoutiers Du Clair De Lune* (UK: *Heaven Fell That Night*)
1958 *En Cas De Malheur* (UK: *Love Is My Profession*); *La Femme Et Le Pantin* (UK: *A Woman Like Satan*)

1959 *Babette S'En Va-t-En Guerre* (UK: *Babette Goes To War*); *Le Testament D'Orphée; Voulez-Vous Danser Avec Moi?* (UK: *Come Dance With Me*)
1960 *L'Affaire D'Une Nuit* (UK: *It Happened At Night*); *La Vérité* (UK: *The Truth*)
1961 *La Bride Sur Le Cou* (UK: *Please, Not Now!*): *Amours Célèbres; Vie Privée* (UK: *A Very Private Affair*)
1962 *Le Repos Du Guerrier* (UK: *Warrior's Rest*)
1963 *Le Mépris* (UK: *Contempt*); *Paparazzi* (documentary); *Tentazioni Proibite; Une Ravissante Idiote* (UK: *A Ravishing Idiot*)
1964 *Marie Soleil*
1965 *Dear Brigitte; Viva Maria!*
1966 *Masculin–Féminin; A Coeur Joie* (UK: *Two Weeks In September*)
1967 *Histoires Extraordinaires* (UK: *Tales Of Mystery*)
1968 *Shalako*
1969 *Les Femmes*
1970 *L'Ours Et La Poupée; Les Novices; Boulevard Du Rhum* (UK: *Rum Runner*)
1971 *Les Pétroleuses* (UK: *The Legend Of Frenchie King*)
1973 *Don Juan 1973 Ou Et Si Don Juan Etait Une Femme* (UK: *Don Juan, Or If Don Juan Were A Woman*): *L'Histoire Très Bonne Et Très Joyeuse De Colinot Trousse-Chemise* (UK: *Colinot, The Petticoat-Lifter*)

## BARKIN, Ellen
(1954– ) USA

1981 *We're Fighting Back* (TV)
1982 *Diner; Parole* (TV)
1983 *Tender Mercies*; Daniel; Enormous Changes At The Last Minute; Eddie And The Cruisers*
1984 *Harry And Son; Terrible Joe Moran* (TV); *The Adventures Of Buckaroo Banzai Across The Eighth Dimension*

1985 *Terminal Choice*
1986 *Desert Bloom; Down By Law; Act Of Vengeance* (TV)
1987 *The Big Easy*\*; *Made In Heaven; Siesta*
1988 *Clinton And Nadine* (aka *Blood Money*)
1989 *Sea Of Love*\*; *Johnny Handsome*
1991 *Switch*
1992 *Man Trouble; Mac; Into The West*
1993 *This Boy's Life*

## BARR, Jean-Marc
(1960– ) USA

1985 *King David*
1987 *Hope And Glory*\*
1988 *Le Grand Bleu*\* (UK: *The Big Blue*)
1989 *Le Brasier*
1991 *Europa*
1992 *The Plague*

## BARRYMORE, John
real name: John Blythe
(1002–1942) USA

1914 *An American Citizen; The Man From Mexico*
1915 *The Dictator; Are You A Mason; The Incorrigible Dukane*
1916 *Nearly A King; The Lost Bridegroom; The Red Widow*
1917 *Raffles, The Amateur Cracksman*
1918 *On The Quiet; Here Comes The Bride*
1919 *The Test Of Honor*
1920 *Dr Jekyll And Mr Hyde*
1921 *The Lotus Eater*
1922 *Sherlock Holmes* (UK: *Moriarty*)
1924 *Beau Brummell*
1926 *The Sea Beast*
1927 *Life In Hollywood No 4; Twenty Minutes At Warner Brothers' Studios* (both shorts); *The Beloved Rogue; When A Man Loves* (UK: *His Lady*)
1928 *Tempest*
1929 *Eternal Love; Show Of Shows; General Crack*

1930 *The Man From Blankley's; Moby Dick*
1931 *Svengali; The Mad Genius*
1932 *Arsene Lupin; Grand Hotel*\*; *A Bill Of Divorcement*\*; *State's Attorney* (UK: *Cardigan's Last Case*); *Rasputin And The Empress* (UK: *Rasputin The Mad Monk*)
1933 *Topaze; Reunion In Vienna; Dinner At Eight; Night Flight; Scarlet River; Counsellor-At-Law*
1934 *Long Lost Father; Twentieth Century*
1936 *Romeo And Juliet*
1937 *Maytime; Bulldog Drummond Comes Back; Night Club Scandal; True Confession; Bulldog Drummond's Revenge*
1938 *Bulldog Drummond's Peril; Spawn Of The North; Romance In The Dark; Marie Antoinette; Hold That Co-Ed* (UK: *Hold That Gal*)
1939 *The Great Man Votes; Midnight*
1940 *The Great Profile*
1941 *The Invisible Woman; World Premiere*
1942 *Screen Snapshots No 107* (short); *Playmates*

## BARRYMORE, Lionel
real name: Lionel Blythe
(1878–1954) USA

1911 *Fighting Blood; The Battle* (both shorts)
1912 *An Adventure In The Autumn Woods; Brutality; The Chief's Dilemma; Friends; The Chief's Blanket; A Cry For Help; Fate; The God Within; Gold And Glitter; Home Folks; The Informer; Love In An Apartment Hotel; The Massacre; The Musketeers Of Pig Alley; My Baby; The New York Hat; Oil And Water; The One She Loved; So Near And Yet So Far; The Burglar's Dilemma; My Hero; The Telephone Girl And The Lady; Three Friends* (all shorts)
1913 *The Battle Of Elderbrush Gulch; Death's Marathon; The House Of*

**BARRYMORE, Lionel** (cont.)
*Darkness; Brute Force; Just Gold; The Lady And The Mouse; A Misunderstood Boy; Near To Earth; The Perfidy Of Mary; The Rancher's Revenge; The Sheriff's Baby; The Wrong Bottle; A Girl's Stratagem; The Switch Tower; A Timely Interception; The Wanderer; The Yaqui Cur; Her Father's Silent Partner; Pa Says; A Welcome Intruder; Woman Against Woman; The Fatal Wedding; Father's Lesson; His Inspiration; Mister Jefferson Green; So Runs The Way; The Suffragette Minstrels; The Vengeance Of Galora; Classmates; The House Of Discord; The Power Of The Press; The Stolen Treaty* (all shorts); *The Well; The Crook And The Girl*

1914 *Men And Women; The Span Of Life; Judith Of Bethulia; Strongheart; The Woman In Black; The Seals Of The Mighty; Under The Gaslight*

1915 *Wildfire; The Romance Of Elaine; A Modern Magdalen; The Curious Life Of Judge Legarde; The Flaming Sword; Dora Thorne; A Yellow Streak*

1916 *Dorian's Divorce; The Quitter; The Upheaval; The Brand Of Cowardice*

1917 *The End Of The Tour; His Father's Son; The Millionaire's Double; Life's Whirlpool* (also directed)

1919 *The Valley Of Night*

1920 *The Copperhead; The Master Mind; The Devil's Garden*

1921 *The Great Adventure; Jim The Pen Man*

1922 *Boomerang Bill; The Face In The Fog*

1923 *The Enemies Of Women; Unseeing Eyes*

1924 *The Eternal City; Decameron Nights; America; Meddling Women*

1925 *I Am The Man; Die Frau Mit Dem Sclechten Ruf; The Iron Man; Children Of The Whirlwind; The Girl Who Wouldn't Work; The Wrongdoer; Fifty–Fifty; The Splendid Road*

1926 *The Barrier; Brooding Eyes; The Lucky Lady; Paris At Midnight; The Bells; The Temptress; Wife Tamers* (short)

1927 *The Show; Women Love Diamonds; Body And Soul; The Thirteenth Hour*

1928 *Sadie Thompson; Drums Of Love; West Of Zanzibar; The Lion And The Mouse; Road House; The River Woman; Love* (UK: *Anna Karenina*)

1929 *Madame X; His Glorious Night; The Unholy Night; Confession* (short) (all director only); *Alias Jimmy Valentine; Hollywood Revue Of 1929; Mysterious Island*

1930 *The Rogue Song* (director only); *Free And Easy*

1931 *Ten Cents A Dance* (director only); *A Free Soul; Mata Hari; Guilty Hands; The Yellow Ticket* (UK: *The Yellow Passport*)

1932 *Broken Lullaby* (UK: *The Man I Killed*); *Arsene Lupin; Washington Masquerade* (UK: *Mad Masquerade*); *Grand Hotel\*; Rasputin And The Empress* (UK: *Rasputin The Mad Monk*)

1933 *Sweepings; Dinner At Eight; Stranger's Return; Night Flight; One Man's Journey; Scarlet River; The Late Christopher Bean; Should Ladies Behave; Looking Forward* (UK: *Service*)

1934 *This Side Of Heaven; Cardboard City; Treasure Island; The Girl From Missouri* (UK: *100 Per Cent Pure*); *Carolina* (UK: *The House Of Connelly*)

1935 *Mark Of The Vampire; The Little Colonel; Public Hero Number One; The Return Of Peter Grimm; Ah, Wilderness!*

1936 *The Voice Of Bugle Ann; The Road To Glory; The Devil Doll; The Gorgeous Hussy; Camille**

1937 *A Family Affair; Captains Courageous*; Saratoga; Navy Blue And Gold*

1938 *A Yank At Oxford; Test Pilot*; You Can't Take It With You*; Young Dr Kildare*

1939 *Let Freedom Ring; Calling Dr Kildare; On Borrowed Time; Secret Of Dr Kildare*

1940 *Dr Kildare's Strange Case; Dr Kildare Goes Home; Dr Kildare's Crisis*

1941 *The Bad Man* (UK: *Two Gun Cupid*); *The Penalty; Cavalcade Of The Academy Awards* (short); *The People Versus Dr Kildare* (UK: *My Life Is Yours*); *Lady Be Good; Dr Kildare's Wedding* (UK: *Mary Names The Day*)

1942 *Dr Kildare's Victory* (UK: *The Doctor And The Debutante*): *Calling Dr Gillespie; Dr Gillespie's New Assistant*

1943 *Tennessee Johnson* (UK: *The Man On America's Conscience*); *Thousands Cheer; Dr Gillespie's Criminal Case* (UK: *Crazy To Kill*); *A Guy Named Joe; The Last Will And Testament Of Tom Smith* (short)

1944 *Three Men In White; Since You Went Away*; Between Two Women; Dragon Seed* (narrator only)

1945 *The Valley Of Decision*

1946 *Three Wise Fools; The Secret Heart; It's A Wonderful Life*; Duel In The Sun**

1947 *Dark Delusion* (UK: *Cynthia's Secret*)

1948 *Key Largo**

1949 *Down To The Sea In Ships; Malaya* (UK: *East Of The Rising Sun*)

1950 *Right Cross; The Screen Actor* (short)

1951 *Bannerline*

1952 *Lone Star*

1953 *Main Street To Broadway*

## BASINGER, Kim
(1954– ) USA

1977 *Dog And Cat* (TV)

1978 *The Ghost Of Flight 401* (TV); *Katie: Portrait Of A Centrefold* (TV)

1981 *Killjoy* (TV); *Hard Country*

1982 *Mother Lode*

1983 *Never Say Never Again*; The Man Who Loved Women*

1984 *The Natural*

1985 *Fool For Love*

1986 *9½ Weeks; No Mercy*

1987 *Blind Date; Nadine*

1988 *My Stepmother Is An Alien*

1989 *Batman**

1991 *The Marrying Man* (UK: *Too Hot To Handle*)

1992 *Final Analysis; Cool World*

1993 *The Real McCoy*

## BATES, Alan
(1934– ) UK

1960 *The Entertainer**

1961 *Whistle Down The Wind*

1962 *A Kind Of Loving*

1963 *The Running Man; The Caretaker*

1964 *Nothing But The Best; Zorba The Greek**

1965 *Insh'Allah* (narrator only)

1966 *Georgy Girl*; King Of Hearts*

1967 *Far From The Madding Crowd*

1968 *The Fixer*

1969 *Women In Love**

1970 *Three Sisters*

1971 *The Go-Between*

1972 *A Day In The Death Of Joe Egg; Second Best* (short)

1973 *Impossible Object*

1974 *Mikis Theodorakis: A Profile Of Greatness; Butley; The Story Of Jacob And Joseph* (TV)

1975 *In Celebration; Royal Flash*

1977 *The Shout*

1978 *An Unmarried Woman**

1979 *The Rose**

1980 *Nijinsky; Very Like A Whale* (TV)

1981 *Quartet; The Trespasser; Rece Do Gory* (UK: *Hands Up!*)

**BATES, Alan** (cont.)
1982 *Return Of The Soldier; Britannia Hospital*
1986 *Duet For One*
1987 *A Prayer For The Dying; Pack Of Lies* (TV)
1988 *Force Majeure*
1989 *We Think The World Of You*
1990 *Doctor M; Mister Frost; Hamlet**
1991 *102 Boulevard Haussmann* (TV); *Secret Friends*
1992 *Shuttlecock; The Silent Tongue*

## BATES, Kathy
(1948–   ) USA

1971 *Taking Off*
1977 *Straight Time*
1982 *Come Back To The Five And Dime, Jimmy Dean, Jimmy Dean*
1986 *Johnny Bull* (TV)
1987 *Summer Heat*
1988 *Arthur 2: On The Rocks*
1989 *Roe Vs Wade* (TV)
1990 *Men Don't Leave; Dick Tracy*; White Palace; Misery**
1991 *At Play In The Fields Of The Lord; Fried Green Tomatoes At The Whistle Stop Café*
1992 *Shadows And Fog; Used People*
1993 *A Home Of Our Own*

## BAXTER, Anne
(1923–85) USA

1940 *Twenty Mule Team; The Great Profile*
1941 *Charley's Aunt; Swamp Water* (UK: *The Man Who Came Back*)
1942 *The Magnificent Ambersons*; The Pied Piper*
1943 *Crash Dive; Five Graves To Cairo; The North Star*
1944 *The Sullivans; The Eve Of St Mark; Guest In The House; Sunday Dinner For A Soldier*
1945 *A Royal Scandal* (UK: *Czarina*)
1946 *Smoky; Angel On My Shoulder; The Razor's Edge**
1947 *Blaze Of Noon; Mother Wore Tights* (narrator only)

1948 *Homecoming; The Luck Of The Irish; The Walls Of Jericho; Yellow Sky*
1949 *You're My Everything*
1950 *A Ticket To Tomahawk; All About Eve**
1951 *Follow The Sun*
1952 *The Outcasts Of Poker Flat; My Wife's Best Friend; O'Henry's Full House; Screen Snapshots No 206* (short)
1953 *I Confess; The Blue Gardenia*
1954 *Carnival Story*
1955 *One Desire; The Spoilers*
1956 *The Come-On; The Ten Commandments*; Three Violent People*
1958 *Chase A Crooked Shadow; The Right Hand Man* (TV)
1960 *Cimarron; Summer Of The 17th Doll* (UK: *Season Of Passion*)
1961 *Mix Me A Person*
1962 *A Walk On The Wild Side*
1965 *The Family Jewels*
1966 *The Tall Women*
1967 *The Busy Body; Stranger On The Run* (TV)
1968 *The Challengers* (TV); *Companions In Nightmare* (TV)
1970 *Ritual Of Evil* (TV)
1971 *If Tomorrow Comes* (TV); *The Catcher* (TV); *Fools' Parade* (UK: *Dynamite Man From Glory Jail*)
1972 *The Late Liz; Lisa Bright And Dark* (TV); *Lapin 360*
1977 *Nero Wolfe* (TV)
1978 *Little Mo* (TV)
1980 *Jane Austen In Manhattan* (TV)
1983 *The Architecture Of Frank Lloyd Wright* (narrator only)
1984 *The Masks Of Death* (TV)

## BEATTY, Warren
real name: Henry Warren Beaty
(1937–   ) USA

1961 *Splendor In The Grass; The Roman Spring Of Mrs Stone*
1962 *All Fall Down*
1964 *Lilith*
1965 *Mickey One*

1966 *Promise Her Anything;*
*Kaleidoscope*
1967 *Bonnie And Clyde\**
1969 *The Only Game In Town*
1970 *Arthur Penn, 1922: Themes And*
*Variations* (documentary)
1971 *McCabe And Mrs Miller; $* (UK:
*The Heist*)
1973 *Year Of The Woman*
(documentary)
1974 *The Parallax View; The Fortune*
1975 *Shampoo\**
1978 *Heaven Can Wait\** (also co-
director)
1981 *Reds\** (also director)
1987 *Ishtar*
1990 *Dick Tracy\** (also director)
1991 *In Bed With Madonna*
(documentary); *Bugsy*

See also directors listing

## BEERY, Wallace
(1885–1949) USA

1014 *Sweedie And The Lord; Sweedie*
*And The Double Exposure;*
*Sweedie's Skate; Sweedie*
*Springs A Surprise; The*
*Fickleness Of Sweedie; Sweedie*
*Learns To Swim; She Landed A*
*Big One; Sweedie And The*
*Trouble Maker; Sweedie At The*
*Fair; Madame Double X; The*
*Plum Tree; Sweedie the Swatter;*
*The Fable Of The Bush League*
*Lover Who Failed To Qualify; The*
*Broken Pledge; Chick Evans*
*Links With Sweedie* (all shorts)
1915 *Sweedie's Suicide; Sweedie And*
*The Dog; Two Hearts That Beat*
*As Ten; Sweedie's Hopeless*
*Love; Sweedie Goes To College;*
*Love And Trouble; Sweedie*
*Learns To Ride; Sweedie's Hero;*
*The Slim Princess; Sweedie In*
*Vaudeville; Sweedie's Finish* (all
shorts)
1916 *Sweedie The Janitor; Teddy At*
*The Throttle; A Dash Of Courage*
(all shorts)

1917 *Cactus Nell; The Clever Dummy;*
*Maggie's First False Step* (all
shorts); *Patria; The Little*
*American*
1918 *Johanna Enlists*
1919 *The Love Burglar; The*
*Unpardonable Sin; Life Line;*
*Soldier Of Fortune; Behind The*
*Door; Victory; The Virgin Of*
*Stamboul*
1920 *The Mollycoddle; The Round Up;*
*The Last Of The Mohicans; The*
*Rookies Return*
1921 *The Four Horsemen Of The*
*Apocalypse; 813; Patsy; A Tale Of*
*Two Worlds; The Golden Snare;*
*The Last Trail*
1922 *Wild Honey; The Man From Hell's*
*River; The Rosary; The*
*Sagebrush Trail; Ridin' Wild; I Am*
*The Law; Robin Hood; Trouble*
*Associated; Hurrican's Gal; Only*
*A Shop Girl*
1923 *Stormswept; The Flame Of Life;*
*Bavu; Ashes Of Vengeance;*
*Drifting; The Eternal Struggle; The*
*Spanish Dancer; The Three Ages;*
*Richard, The Lion Hearted; Drums*
*Of Jeopardy; White Tiger*
1924 *The Sea Hawk; Unseen Hands;*
*Madonna Of The Streets;*
*Dynamite Smith; Another Man's*
*Wife; The Red Lily; The Signal*
*Tower; So Big*
1925 *Let Women Alone; The Great*
*Divide; Coming Through; The*
*Devil's Cargo; Adventure; The*
*Lost World; The Night Club;*
*Rugged Water; In The Name Of*
*Love; Pony Express*
1926 *Behind The Front; Volcano; We're*
*In The Navy Now; The Wanderer;*
*Old Ironsides* (UK: *Sons Of The*
*Sea*)
1927 *Casey At The Bat; Fireman,*
*Save My Child; Now We're In*
*The Navy*
1928 *Wife Savers; Partners In Crime;*
*The Big Killing; Beggars Of Life*
1929 *Chinatown Nights; Stairs Of Sand;*
*River Of Romance*

**BEERY, Wallace** (cont.)
1930  *Way For A Sailor; Billy The Kid; The Big House; Min And Bill; A Lady's Morals* (UK: *Jenny Lind*)
1931  *The Secret Six; Hell Divers; The Champ\**
1932  *Grand Hotel\*; Flesh; The Stolen Jools* (UK: *The Slippery Pearls*) (short)
1933  *Dinner At Eight; Tugboat Annie\*; The Bowery*
1934  *The Mighty Barnum; Viva, Villa!; Treasure Island*
1935  *West Point Of The Air; China Seas; O'Shaughnessy's Boy; Ah, Wilderness!*
1936  *A Message To Garcia; Old Hutch*
1937  *Good Old Soak; Slave Ship*
1938  *Bad Man Of Brimstone; Port Of Seven Seas; Stablemates*
1939  *Stand Up And Fight; Sergeant Madden; Thunder Afloat; Screen Snapshots No 77* (short)
1940  *Twenty Mule Team; Wyoming* (UK: *Bad Man Of Wyoming*); *The Man From Dakota* (UK: *Arouse And Beware*)
1941  *Barnacle Bill; The Bugle Sounds; The Bad Man* (UK: *Two Gun Cupid*)
1942  *Jackass Mail*
1943  *Salute To The Marines*
1944  *Rationing; Barbary Coast Gent*
1945  *This Man's Navy*
1946  *Bad Bascomb; The Mighty McGurk*
1948  *Alias A Gentleman; A Date With Judy*
1949  *Big Jack*

**BELLAMY, Ralph**
(1904–91) USA

1931  *The Secret Six; The Magnificent Lie; Surrender; West Of Broadway; Disorderly Conduct*
1932  *Young America* (UK: *We Humans*); *Forbidden; Rebecca Of Sunnybrook Farm; The Woman In Room 13; Wild Girl* (UK: *Salomy Jane*); *Air Mail; Almost Married*

1933  *Second Hand Wife; Parole Girl; Destination Unknown; Picture Snatcher; The Narrow Corner; Below The Sea; Headline Shooter* (UK: *Evidence In Camera*); *Blind Adventure; Ace Of Aces; Flying Devils* (UK: *The Flying Circus*)
1934  *Ever In My Heart; Spitfire; This Man Is Mine; Once To Every Woman; One Is Guilty; Before Midnight; The Crime Of Helen Stanley; Girl In Danger*
1935  *Woman In The Dark; Helldorado; The Wedding Night; Rendezvous At Midnight; Air Hawks; Eight Bells; The Healer; Navy Wife; Gigolette* (UK: *Night Club*)
1936  *Hands Across The Table; Dangerous Intrigue; The Final Hour; Roaming Lady; Straight From The Shoulder; Wild Brian Kent*
1937  *Counterfeit Lady; The Man Who Lived Twice; The Awful Truth\*; Let's Get Married*
1938  *The Crime Of Dr Hallet; Fools For Scandal; Boy Meets Girl; Carefree; Girls' School; Trade Winds*
1939  *Let Us Live; Blind Alley; Smashing The Spy Ring; Flight Angels; Coast Guard*
1940  *His Girl Friday\*; Brother Orchid; Queen Of The Mob; Dance, Girl, Dance; Public Deb No 1; Ellery Queen, Master Detective; Meet The Wildcat*
1941  *Ellery Queen's Penthouse Mystery; Footsteps In The Dark; Affectionately Yours; Ellery Queen And The Perfect Crime* (UK: *The Perfect Crime*); *Dive Bomber; Ellery Queen And The Murder Ring* (UK: *The Murder Ring*); *The Wolf Man*
1942  *The Ghost Of Frankenstein; Lady In A Jam; Men Of Texas* (UK: *Men Of Destiny*): *The Great Impersonation*
1943  *Stage Door Canteen*
1944  *Guest In The House*

1945 *Delightfully Dangerous; Lady On A Train*
1955 *The Court Martial Of Billy Mitchell* (UK: *One Man Mutiny*)
1956 *Heritage Of Anger* (TV)
1960 *Sunrise At Campobello*
1966 *The Professionals**
1967 *Wings Of Fire* (TV)
1968 *Rosemary's Baby**
1969 *The Immortal* (TV)
1971 *Doctors' Wives*
1972 *Something Evil* (TV); *Cancel My Reservation*
1973 *Owen Marshall, Counsellor At Law* (TV)
1974 *Log Of The Black Pearl* (TV)
1975 *Murder On Flight 502* (TV); *Adventures Of The Queen* (TV); *Search For The Gods* (TV)
1976 *McNaughton's Daughter* (TV); *Return To Badham County* (TV); *Return To Earth* (TV); *The Boy In The Plastic Bubble* (TV)
1977 *Oh, God!**; *Charlie Cobb: Nice Night For A Hanging* (TV)
1978 *The Clone Master* (TV); *The Millionaire*
1979 *The Billion Dollar Threat* (TV); *Power* (TV)
1980 *The Memory Of Eva Ryker* (TV)
1983 *Trading Places**
1984 *Love Leads The Way*
1987 *Amazon Women On The Moon; Disorderlies*
1988 *Coming To America**; *The Good Mother*
1989 *Christine Cromwell: Things That Go Bump In The Night* (TV)
1990 *Pretty Woman**

## BELMONDO, Jean-Paul
(1933– ) France

1955 *Molière* (short)
1956 *Dimanche Nous Volerons*
1957 *A Pied, A Cheval Et En Voiture*
1958 *Sois Belle Et Tais-Toi* (UK: *Blonde For Danger*); *Drôle De Dimanche; Les Tricheurs* (UK: *Youthful Sinners*); *Charlotte Et Son Jules* (short); *Les Copains De Dimanche*
1959 *Mademoiselle Ange; A Bout De Souffle** (UK: *Breathless*); *A Double Tour* (UK: *Web Of Passion*)
1960 *Moderato Cantabile* (UK: *Seven Days...Seven Nights*); *Lettere Di Una Novizia; La Française Et L'Amour* (UK: *Love And The Frenchwoman*); *Les Distractions* (UK: *Trapped By Fear*); *Class Tous Risques* (UK: *The Big Risk*)
1961 *La Viaccia; La Ciociara** (UK: *Two Women*); *Léon Morin, Priest; Une Femme Est Une Femme; Amours Célèbres; Un Nommé La Rocca*
1962 *Un Singe En Hiver* (UK: *It's Hot In Hell*); *Cartouche* (UK: *Swords Of Blood*); *Le Doulos; I Don Giovanni Della Costa Azzurra; L'Ainé Des Ferchaux*
1963 *Mare Matto; I Giorno Piu Corto* (UK: *The Shortest Day*); *Dragées Au Poivre* (UK: *Sweet And Sour*); *Peau De Banane*
1964 *L'Homme De Rio* (UK: *That Man From Rio*); *Cent Mille Dollars Au Soleil; Echappement Libre; La Chasse A L'Homme* (UK: *The Gentle Art Of Seduction*); *Weekend A Zuydcoote* (UK: *Weekend At Dunkirk*)
1966 *Les Tribulations D'Un Chinois En Chine* (UK: *Up To His Ears*); *Tendre Voyou; Paris, Brûle T'Il?* (UK: *Is Paris Burning?*)
1967 *Casino Royale; Le Voleur* (UK: *The Thief*); *La Bande A Bébel* (short)
1968 *Ho!*
1969 *Dieu A Choisi Paris; Le Cerveau* (UK: *The Brain*); *La Sirène Du Mississippi* (UK: *Mississippi Mermaid*); *Un Homme Qui Me Plait* (UK: *A Man I Like*)
1970 *Borsalino*
1971 *Les Mariés De L'An Deux* (UK: *The Scoundrel*); *Le Casse* (UK: *The Burglars*)
1972 *Docteur Popaul* (UK: *Scoundrel In White*); *La Scoumoune*
1973 *L'Héritier* (UK: *The Inheritor*)

**BELMONDO, Jean-Paul** (cont.)
1974 *Stavisky; Le Magnifique* (UK: *How To Destroy The Reputation Of The Greatest Secret Agent*)
1975 *Peur Sur La Ville* (UK: *Night Caller*)
1977 *L'Animal; Le Corps De Mon Ennemi*
1979 *Flic Ou Voyou*
1980 *Le Guignolo; I Piccioni Di Piazza San Marco*
1981 *Le Professionel*
1982 *L'As Des As*
1983 *Le Marginal*
1984 *Les Morfalous; Joyeuses Paques*
1985 *Hold Up*
1987 *Le Solitaire*
1988 *Itineraire D'Un Enfant Gâté*
1992 *Inconnu Dans La Maison*


**BELUSHI, John**
(1949–82) USA

1975 *Shame Of The Jungle* (UK: *Jungle Burger*)
1978 *National Lampoon's Animal House\*; Goin' South*
1979 *Old Boyfriends; 1941\**
1980 *The Blues Brothers\**
1981 *Neighbors; Continental Divide*


**BENNY, Jack**
real name: Benjamin Kubelsky
(1894–1974) USA

1928 *Bright Moments* (short)
1929 *The Songwriters' Revue* (short); *Hollywood Revue Of 1929*
1930 *The Rounder* (short); *Strictly Modern; Chasing Rainbows; Medicine Man*
1931 *A Broadway Romeo; Cab Waiting; Taxi Tangle* (all shorts)
1933 *Mr Broadway*
1934 *Transatlantic; Merry-Go-Round*
1935 *Broadway Melody Of 1936; It's In The Air*
1936 *The Big Broadcast Of 1937; College Holiday*

1937 *Artists And Models; Manhattan Merry-Go-Round* (UK: *Manhattan Music Box*)
1938 *Artists And Models Abroad* (UK: *Stranded In Paris*)
1939 *Man About Town*
1940 *Buck Benny Rides Again; Love Thy Neighbor*
1941 *Charley's Aunt*
1942 *To Be Or Not To Be\*; George Washington Slept Here*
1943 *Show Business At War; Screen Snapshots No 109* (both shorts); *The Meanest Man In The World*)
1944 *Hollywood Canteen*
1945 *It's In The Bag!* (UK: *The Fifth Chair*); *The Horn Blows At Midnight*
1946 *Without Reservations*
1948 *Screen Snapshots No 166; Radio Broadcasting Today* (both shorts)
1949 *The Lucky Stiff; The Great Lover; A Rainy Day In Hollywood* (short)
1952 *Somebody Loves Me; Memorial To Al Jolson* (narrator only)
1953 *Hollywood's Pair Of Jacks* (short)
1954 *Susan Slept Here*
1955 *The Seven Little Foys*
1957 *Beau James*
1958 *Fabulous Hollywood; The Mouse That Jack Built* (both shorts)
1959 *Who Was That Lady?*
1963 *It's A Mad, Mad, Mad, Mad World\**
1967 *A Guide For The Married Man*
1972 *The Man*


**BERENGER, Tom**
(1949– ) USA

1976 *The Sentinel*
1977 *Johnny, We Hardly Knew Ye* (TV); *Looking For Mr Goodbar*
1978 *In Praise Of Older Women*
1979 *Butch And Sundance: The Early Days*
1980 *The Dogs Of War*
1982 *Oltre La Porta* (UK: *Beyond The Door*)
1983 *Eddie And The Cruisers; The Big Chill\**

1984 *Fear City*
1985 *Rustlers' Rhapsody*
1986 *If Tomorrow Comes; La Sposa Americana; Platoon**
1987 *Someone To Watch Over Me; Dear America* (voice only)
1988 *Shoot To Kill* (UK: *Deadly Pursuit*); *Last Rites; Betrayed; Beyond Obsession*
1989 *Major League; Love At Large; Born On The 4th Of July**
1990 *The Field*
1991 *Shattered; At Play In The Fields Of The Lord*
1992 *Sniper*
1993 *Sliver*

## BERGEN, Candice
(1946– ) USA

1966 *The Group; The Sand Pebbles**
1967 *The Day The Fish Came Out; Vivre Pour Vivre*
1968 *The Magus*
1070 *Getting Straight; Soldier Blue, The Adventurers*
1971 *Carnal Knowledge; The Hunting Party; T R Baskin* (UK: *A Date With A Lonely Girl*)
1974 *11 Harrowhouse*
1975 *Bite The Bullet; The Wind And The Lion*
1976 *The Domino Principle* (UK: *The Domino Killings*)
1977 *The End Of The World, In Our Usual Bed, In A Night Full Of Rain; Oliver's Story*
1979 *Starting Over*
1981 *Rich And Famous*
1982 *Gandhi**
1983 *Arthur The King*
1985 *Stick; Murder: By Reason Of Insanity* (TV)
1987 *Mayflower Madam* (TV)

## BERGMAN, Ingrid
(1915–82) Sweden

1934 *Munkbrogreven* (UK: *The Count Of Monk's Bridge*)

1935 *Brannigar* (UK: *The Surf*); *Swedenhielms* (UK: *The Swedenhielm Family*); *Valborgsmassoafton* (UK: *Walpurgis Night*)
1936 *Pa Solsidan* (UK: *On The Sunny Side*); *Intermezzo*
1938 *Dollar; En Kvinnas Ansikte* (UK: *A Woman's Face*); *Die Vier Gesellen* (UK: *The Four Companions*)
1939 *En Enda Natt* (UK: *Only One Night*); *Intermezzo: A Love Story* (UK: *Escape To Happiness*)
1940 *Juninatten* (UK: *A June Night*)
1941 *Adam Had Four Sons; Rage In Heaven; Dr Jekyll And Mr Hyde*
1942 *Casablanca**
1943 *Swedes In America* (documentary) (UK: *Ingrid Bergman Answers*); *For Whom The Bell Tolls**
1944 *Gaslight** (UK: *The Murder In Thornton Square*)
1945 *The Bells Of St Mary's**; *Spellbound*; Saratoga Trunk*
1946 *Notorious**; *The American Creed* (documentary)
1948 *Arch Of Triumph; Joan Of Arc**
1949 *Under Capricorn*
1950 *Stromboli*
1951 *Europa 51*
1953 *Siamo Donne* (UK: *We The Women*)
1954 *Viaggio In Italia* (UK: *Journey To Italy*); *Giovanna D'Arco Al Rogo* (UK: *Joan At The Stake*)
1955 *Angst* (UK: *Fear*)
1956 *Elena Et Les Hommes* (UK: *Elena And Men*); *Anastasia*
1958 *Indiscreet; The Inn Of The Sixth Happiness*
1960 *The Camp* (documentary)
1961 *Aimez-Vous Brahms?* (UK: *Goodbye Again*)
1964 *The Visit; The Yellow Rolls-Royce*
1967 *Stimulantia*
1969 *Cactus Flower**
1970 *A Walk In The Spring Rain; Henri Langlois* (documentary)

**BERGMAN, Ingrid** (cont.)
1973 *From The Mixed-Up Files Of Mrs Basil E Frankweiler* (UK: *The Hideaways*)
1974 *Murder On The Orient Express**
1976 *A Matter Of Time*
1978 *Hostsonaten* (UK: *Autumn Sonata*)
1981 *A Woman Called Golda* (TV)

**BISSET, Winifred Jacqueline**
(1944– ) UK

1965 *The Knack And How To Get It*
1966 *Drop Dead Darling; Cul-De-Sac*
1967 *Two For The Road; Casino Royale; The Sweet Ride; The Cape Town Affair*
1968 *The Detective; Bullitt**; La Promesse* (UK: *Secret World*); *The First Time* (UK: *You Don't Need Pyjamas At Rosie's*)
1969 *L'Echelle Blanche; Airport**
1970 *The Grasshopper; The Mephisto Waltz*
1971 *Believe In Me*
1972 *Secrets; Stand Up And Be Counted; The Life And Times Of Judge Roy Bean*
1973 *The Thief Who Came To Dinner; La Nuit Americaine** (UK: *Day For Night*); *Le Magnifique* (UK: *How To Destroy The Reputation Of The Greatest Secret Agent*)
1974 *Murder On The Orient Express**
1975 *The Spiral Staircase*
1976 *Der Richter Und Sein Henker* (UK: *End Of The Game*); *St Ives; The Sunday Woman*
1977 *The Deep**
1978 *The Greek Tycoon; Who Is Killing The Great Chefs Of Europe?* (UK: *Too Many Chefs*)
1979 *Amo Non Amo* (UK: *I Love You I Love You Not*)
1980 *Inchon!; When Time Ran Out*
1981 *Rich And Famous; Together?*
1982 *Forbidden*
1983 *Class*
1984 *Under The Volcano*
1985 *Anna Karenina* (TV)

1986 *Choices* (TV)
1987 *High Season*
1988 *La Maison De Jade*
1989 *Amoureuse; Scenes From The Class Struggle In Beverly Hills*
1990 *Wild Orchid; The Maid*
1993 *Crime Broker; Hoffman's Hunger*

**BLONDELL, Joan**
(1909–79) USA

1930 *Devil's Parade; Broadway's Like That* (both shorts); *The Office Wife; Sinner's Holiday; Other Men's Women*
1931 *Illicit; Millie; My Past; Public Enemy** (UK: *Enemies Of The Public*); *God's Gift To Women* (UK: *Too Many Women*); *Big Business Girl; Night Nurse; The Reckless Hour; Blonde Crazy* (UK: *Larceny Lane*)
1932 *Big City Blues; The Greeks Had A Word For Them; The Crowd Roars; The Famous Ferguson Case; Make Me A Star; Miss Pinkerton; Three On A Match; Central Park; Lawyer Man; Union Depot* (UK: *Gentleman For A Day*)
1933 *Blondie Johnson; Gold Diggers Of 1933**; *Goodbye Again; Footlight Parade**; *Havana Widows; Convention City; I've Got Your Number; Broadway Bad* (UK: *Her Reputation*)
1934 *He Was Her Man; Dames; Kansas City Princess; Smarty* (UK: *Hit Me Again*)
1935 *Traveling Saleslady; Broadway Gondolier; We're In The Money; Miss Pacific Fleet*
1936 *Colleen; Sons O' Guns; Bullets Or Ballots; Stage Struck; Three Men On A Horse; Gold Diggers Of 1937; Talent Scout* (UK: *Studio Romance*)
1937 *Back In Circulation; The Perfect Specimen; A Day At Santa Anita* (short); *The King And The Chorus Girl* (UK: *Romance Is Sacred*)

1938 *Stand-In; There's Always A Woman*
1939 *Off The Record; East Side Of
Heaven; The Kid From Kokomo*
(UK: *The Orphan Of The Ring*);
*Good Girls Go To Paris; The
Amazing Mr Williams*
1940 *I Want A Divorce; Two Girls On
Broadway* (UK: *Choose Your
Partner*)
1941 *Topper Returns; Model Wife;
Three Girls About Town; Lady For
A Night*
1943 *Cry Havoc*
1944 *A Tree Grows In Brooklyn*
1945 *Don Juan Quilligan; Adventure*
1946 *Christmas Eve*
1947 *The Corpse Came COD;
Nightmare Alley*
1950 *For Heaven's Sake*
1951 *The Blue Veil*
1956 *The Opposite Sex*
1957 *Lizzie; This Could Be The Night;
Child Of Trouble* (TV); *The Desk
Set* (UK: *His Other Woman*); *Will
Success Spoil Rock Hunter* (UK:
*Oh For A Man*)
1959 *A Marriage Of Strangers* (TV)
1960 *Angel Baby*
1964 *Advance To The Rear* (UK:
*Company Of Cowards*)
1965 *The Cincinnati Kid\**
1966 *Paradise Road; Ride Beyond
Vengeance; The Spy In The
Green Hat*
1967 *Winchester 73* (TV); *Waterhole
Number 3*
1968 *Stay Away Joe; Kona Coast*
1969 *The Delta Factor*
1970 *The Phynx; Battle At Gannon's
Bridge* (TV)
1971 *Support Your Local Gunfighter*
1974 *The Dead Don't Die* (TV)
1975 *Winner Takes All* (TV); *Big Daddy;
Won Ton Ton — The Dog Who
Saved Hollywood*
1976 *Death At Love House* (TV)
1977 *Opening Night*
1978 *Grease\*; Battered* (TV)
1979 *The Champ; The Glove; Family
Secrets* (TV)
1980 *The Woman Inside*

## BLOOM, Claire
real name: Claire Blume
(1931– ) UK

1948 *The Blind Goddess*
1952 *Limelight\**
1953 *Innocents In Paris; The Man
Between*
1955 *Richard III\*; Ballet Girl* (narrator
only)
1956 *Alexander The Great*
1958 *The Brothers Karamazov; The
Buccaneer*
1959 *Look Back In Anger; Adventures
Of Mr Wonderbird* (voice only)
1960 *Schachnovelle* (UK: *Three Moves
To Freedom*)
1962 *The Chapman Report; The
Wonderful World Of The Brothers
Grimm*
1963 *The Haunting; 80,000 Suspects; Il
Maestro Di Vigevano*
1964 *The Outrage; Alta Infidelta* (UK:
*High Infidelity*)
1965 *The Spy Who Came In From The
Cold*
1968 *Charly; The Illustrated Man*
1969 *Three Into Two Won't Go*
1970 *A Severed Head*
1971 *Red Sky At Morning*
1973 *A Doll's House*
1976 *Islands In The Stream*
1981 *Clash Of The Titans*
1984 *Ellis Island* (TV)
1985 *Always; Florence Nightingale* (TV)
1986 *Promises To Keep* (TV); *Liberty*
(TV)
1987 *Sammy And Rosie Get Laid*
1989 *The Lady And The Highwayman*
(TV); *Crimes And
Misdemeanours\**
1991 *The Princess And The Goblin*
(voice only)

## BOGARDE, Dirk
real name: Derek Niven Van Den
Bogaerde
(1921– ) UK

1939 *Come On George* (extra)
1947 *Dancing With Crime*

**BOGARDE, Dirk** (cont.)

1948 *Esther Waters; Quartet; Once A Jolly Swagman*

1949 *Dear Mr Prohack; Boys In Brown; The Blue Lamp*

1950 *So Long At The Fair; The Woman In Question; Blackmailed*

1952 *Hunted; Penny Princess; The Gentle Gunman*

1953 *Appointment In London; Desperate Moment*

1954 *They Who Dare; Doctor In The House; The Sleeping Tiger; For Better, For Worse; The Sea Shall Not Have Them; Simba*

1955 *Doctor At Sea; Cast A Dark Shadow*

1956 *The Spanish Gardener; Ill Met By Moonlight*

1957 *Doctor At Large; Campbell's Kingdom*

1958 *A Tale Of Two Cities; The Wind Cannot Read*

1959 *The Doctor's Dilemma; Libel!*

1960 *Song Without End; The Angel Wore Red; The Singer Not The Song*

1961 *Victim\**

1962 *HMS Defiant; The Password Is Courage; We Joined The Navy*

1963 *The Mindbenders; I Could Go On Singing; Hot Enough For June; The Servant\**

1964 *Doctor In Distress; King And Country; The High Bright Sun*

1965 *Darling\**

1966 *Modesty Blaise*

1967 *Accident; Our Mother's House*

1968 *Sebastian; The Fixer; Return To Lochaver* (documentary)

1969 *Oh! What A Lovely War; Justine; La Cadula Degli Dei\** (UK: *The Damned*)

1970 *Upon This Rock* (documentary)

1971 *Morte A Venezia\** (UK: *Death In Venice*)

1973 *The Serpent*

1974 *Il Portier Di Notte* (UK: *The Night Porter*)

1975 *Permission To Kill*

1977 *Providence; A Bridge Too Far*

1978 *Despair*

1981 *The Patricia Neal Story* (TV)

1986 *May We Borrow Your Husband?* (TV)

1987 *The Vision* (TV)

1990 *Daddy Nostalgie* (UK: *These Foolish Things*)

**BOGART, Humphrey De Forest**
(1899–1957) USA

1930 *Broadway's Like That* (documentary); *Up The River; A Devil With Women*

1931 *Body And Soul; Bad Sister; Women Of All Nations; A Holy Terror; Big City Blues*

1932 *Love Affair; Three On A Match*

1934 *Midnight*

1936 *The Petrified Forest\*; Bullets or Ballots; Two Against The World* (UK: *The Case Of Mrs Pembrook*); *China Clipper; Isle Of Fury; Black Legion*

1937 *The Great O'Malley; Marked Woman; Kid Galahad; San Quentin; Dead End\*; Stand In*

1938 *Swing Your Lady; Men Are Such Fools; Crime School; Racket Busters; The Amazing Dr Clitterhouse; Angels With Dirty Faces\**

1939 *King Of The Underworld; The Oklahoma Kid; Dark Victory\*; You Can't Get Away With Murder; The Roaring Twenties\*; The Return Of Dr X; Invisible Stripes*

1940 *Virginia City; It All Came True; Brother Orchid; They Drive By Night* (UK: *The Road To Frisco*)

1941 *The Maltese Falcon\*; High Sierra\*; The Wagons Roll At Night*

1942 *Across the Pacific; In This Our Life; All Through The Night; The Big Shot; Casablanca\**

1943 *Action In The North Atlantic; Thank Your Lucky Stars; Sahara; Showbusiness At War* (documentary)

1944 *Passage To Marseille; To Have And Have Not\**

1945 *Conflict; Hollywood Victory Caravan* (documentary)
1946 *Two Guys From Milwaukee* (UK: *Royal Flush*); *The Big Sleep\**
1947 *Dead Reckoning; The Two Mrs Carrolls; Dark Passage*
1948 *Always Together; The Treasure Of The Sierra Madre\*; Key Largo\**
1949 *Knock On Any Door; Tokyo Joe*
1950 *Chain Lightning; In A Lonely Place; The Enforcer* (UK: *Murder Inc*)
1951 *Sirocco; The African Queen\**
1952 *Deadline USA* (UK: *Deadline*)
1953 *Battle Circus; Beat The Devil; The Love Lottery*
1954 *The Caine Mutiny\*; Sabrina* (UK: *Sabrina Fair*); *The Barefoot Contessa\*; A Star Is Born\** (voice only)
1955 *We're No Angels; The Left Hand Of God; The Desperate Hours*
1956 *The Harder They Fall*

## BORGNINE, Ernest
real name: Ermes Burgnino
(1915– ) USA

1951 *China Corsair; The Whistle At Eaton Falls* (UK: *Richer Than The Earth*); *The Mob* (UK: *Remember That Face*)
1953 *From Here To Eternity\*; The Stranger Wore A Gun*
1954 *Demetrius And The Gladiators; The Bounty Hunter; Johnny Guitar; Vera Cruz; Run For Cover; Bad Day At Black Rock\**
1955 *Marty\*; Violent Saturday; The Last Command; The Square Jungle*
1956 *Jubal; The Catered Affair* (UK: *Wedding Breakfast*); *The Best Things In Life Are Free*
1957 *Three Brave Men*
1958 *The Badlanders; Torpedo Run; The Vikings\**
1959 *The Rabbit Trap*
1960 *Pay Or Die!; Man On A String* (UK: *Confessions Of A Counterspy*); *Summer Of The Seventeenth Doll*

1961 *Seduction Of The South; Los Guerrilleros; Go Naked In The World; Il Guidizio Universale*
1962 *Barabbas; Il Re Di Poggioreale*
1964 *McHale's Navy*
1965 *The Flight Of The Phoenix*
1966 *The Oscar*
1967 *The Dirty Dozen\*; Cuka*
1968 *Ice Station Zebra; The Split; The Legend Of Lylah Clare*
1969 *The Wild Bunch\*; Vengeance Is Mine; Rain For A Dusty Summer*
1970 *Suppose They Gave A War And Nobody Came; The Adventurers; A Bullet For Sandoval*
1971 *The Trackers* (TV); *Bunny O'Hare; Hannie Caulder; Willard; Sam Hill—Who Killed The Mysterious Mr Foster?* (TV)
1972 *The Revengers; Guns Of The Revolution; Tough Guy; The Poseidon Adventure\**
1973 *Emperor Of The North Pole; The Neptune Factor*
1974 *Law And Disorder; Sunday In The Country; Twice In A Lifetime* (TV)
1975 *The Devil's Rain; Hustle*
1976 *Future Cop* (TV); *Shoot; Cleaver And Haven* (TV); *Natale In Casa Di Appuntamento*
1977 *Fire!* (TV); *The Prince And The Pauper; The Greatest*
1978 *Convoy; The Double McGuffin; Ravagers; The Cops And Robin* (TV); *The Ghost Of Flight 401* (TV)
1979 *The Black Hole\*; All Quiet On The Western Front* (TV)
1980 *When Time Ran Out...; Super Snooper*
1981 *Deadly Blessing; High Risk; Escape From New York*
1982 *The Graduates Of Malibu High; Hollywood Hookers; Blood Feud* (TV)
1983 *Young Warriors; Masquerade* (TV); *Carpool* (TV); *Airwolf* (TV)
1984 *The Last Days Of Pompeii* (TV); *White Stallion; Man Hunt Warning; Codename Wildgeese; Love Leads The Way*

**BORGNINE, Ernest** (cont.)
1985 *The Dirty Dozen: The Next Mission* (TV); *Blood Hunt; Alice In Wonderland* (TV)
1987 *Treasure Island; The Dirty Dozen: The Deadly Mission* (TV); *Skeleton Coast; Throwback; Qualcuna Paghera; The Opponent*
1988 *The Dirty Dozen: The Fatal Mission* (TV); *Any Man's Death; San Francisco Bridge; Spike Of Bensonhurst*
1989 *Music City Blues; Captain Henkel/ Tides Of War; Turnaround; Ski School; Laser Mission; Jake Spanner—Private Eye* (TV); *Real Men Don't Eat Gummy Bears*
1990 *Any Man's Death; Moving Target; Appearances* (TV)


**BOWIE, David**
real name: David Jones
(1947– ) USA

1967 *The Image* (short)
1969 *The Virgin Soldiers*
1976 *The Man Who Fell To Earth*
1978 *Just A Gigolo*
1981 *Christiane F*
1982 *Ziggy Stardust And The Spiders From Mars*
1983 *Merry Christmas Mr Lawrence; The Hunger; Yellowbeard*
1985 *Into The Night*
1986 *Labyrinth; Absolute Beginners**
1987 *In My Life: The Story Of John Lennon*
1988 *The Last Temptation Of Christ**
1992 *The Linguini Incident; Twin Peaks: Fire Walk With Me*


**BOYD, Stephen**
real name: William Millar
(1928–77) UK

1955 *Born For Trouble; An Alligator Named Daisy*
1956 *The Man Who Never Was; A Hill In Korea*

1957 *Seven Waves Away; Island In The Sun; Seven Thunders: Les Bijoutiers Du Clair De Lune* (UK: *Heaven Fell That Night*)
1958 *The Bravados*
1959 *Ben-Hur*; A Woman Obsessed; The Best Of Everything*
1960 *The Big Gamble*
1962 *The Inspector; Billy Rose's Jumbo*
1963 *Imperial Venus; The Fall Of The Roman Empire*
1964 *The Third Secret*
1965 *Gengis Khan*
1966 *The Bible...In The Beginning*; The Oscar; Fantastic Voyage; The Poppy Is Also A Flower* (UK: *Danger Grows Wild*)
1967 *Assignment K; The Caper Of The Golden Bulls* (UK: *Carnival Of Thieves*)
1968 *Shalako*
1969 *Slaves*
1970 *Marta*
1971 *Hannie Caulder*
1972 *Carter's Army* (TV); *Kill; Bloody Mary; The Hands Of Cormac Joyce* (TV); *Key West* (TV); *The Big Game; The Devil Has Seven Faces*
1973 *The Man Called Noon*
1974 *One Man Against The Organization; The Left Hand Of The Law*
1975 *Of Men And Women II; Those Dirty Dogs; The Lives Of Jenny Dolan* (TV)
1976 *Impossible Love; Potato Fritz/ Montana Trap; Lady Dracula; Evil In The Deep; Frauenstation*
1977 *The Squeeze*


**BOYER, Charles**
(1899–1978) France

1920 *L'Homme Du Large; Le Grillon Du Foyer*
1921 *Chantelouve*
1922 *L'Esclave*
1927 *La Ronde Infernale*
1928 *Le Capitain Fracasse*
1929 *Le Procès De Mary Dugan*

1930 *Barcarole D'Amour; Révolte Dans La Prison*
1931 *Tumultes; IFI Ne Réponde Pas; The Magnificent Lie*
1932 *The Man From Yesterday; Red-Headed Woman*
1933 *L'Epervier; The Only Girl; Liliom*
1934 *The Battle; Caravan; Le Bonheur*
1935 *Private Worlds; Break Of Hearts; Shanghai*
1936 *Mayerling; The Garden Of Allah*
1937 *Tovarich; Conquest* (UK: *Marie Walewska*); *History Is Made At Night; Orage*
1938 *Algiers*
1939 *Love Affair*: When Tomorrow Comes*
1940 *All This And Heaven Too; The Heart Of A Nation* (narrator only)
1941 *Back Street; Hold Back The Dawn; Appointment For Love*
1942 *Tales Of Manhattan*
1943 *The Constant Nymph; Flesh And Fantasy; Little Isles Of Freedom* (narrator only)
1944 *Together Again; Gaslight** (UK. *The Murder In Thornton Square*)
1945 *Bataille De Russie; Le Combattant* (both narrator only); *Confidential Agent*
1946 *Cluny Brown*
1947 *A Woman's Vengeance*
1948 *Arch Of Triumph*
1949 *On Stage* (short)
1950 *Hollywood-Sur-Seine* (narrator only)
1951 *The First Legion; Thunder In The East; The Thirteenth Letter*
1952 *The Happy Time*
1953 *Madame De..*
1954 *Nana*
1955 *The Cobweb*
1956 *La Fortuna Di Essera Donna* (UK: *Lucky To Be A Woman*); *Paris — Palace Hotel; Around The World In 80 Days**
1957 *Une Parisienne; C'Est Arrivé A 36 Chandelles*
1958 *The Buccaneer; Maxime; Le Grand Recontre* (narrator only)
1960 *Fanny*

1961 *The Four Horsemen Of The Apocalypse; Adorable Julia; Son Et Lumière* (narrator only); *Les Démons De Minuit* (UK: *Demons At Midnight*)
1965 *A Very Special Favour*
1966 *Paris Brûle T'Il?* (UK: *Is Paris Burning?*); *How To Steal A Million*
1967 *Casino Royale; Barefoot In The Park**
1969 *The April Fools; The Madwoman Of Chaillot; The Day The Hot Line Got Hot*
1973 *Lost Horizon*
1974 *Stavisky*
1976 *A Matter Of Time*

## BRANAGH, Kenneth
(1960– ) UK

1987 *High Season; A Month In The Country*
1989 *Henry V**
1991 *Dead Again*
1992 *Peter's Friends*; Swing Kids*
1993 *Much Ado About Nothing*

See also directors listing

## BRANDAUER, Klaus Maria
(1944– ) Austria

1972 *The Salzburg Connection*
1980 *Mephisto**
1983 *Never Say Never Again**
1984 *Colonel Redl*
1985 *The Lightship; Out Of Africa*; Quo Vadis?* (TV)
1986 *Streets Of Gold*
1988 *Hanussen; Burning Secret*
1989 *La Revolution Française; Georg Elser–Einer Aus Deutschland* (UK: *Seven Minutes*) (also director); *The Spider's Web*
1990 *The Russia House*
1991 *White Fang; Becoming Colette*

## BRANDO, Marlon
(1924– ) USA

1950 *The Men*
1951 *A Streetcar Named Desire**

**BRANDO, Marlon** (cont.)
1952 *Viva Zapata!*
1953 *Julius Caesar\*; The Wild One\**
1954 *On The Waterfront\*; Desirée*
1955 *Guys And Dolls\**
1956 *The Teahouse Of The August Moon\**
1957 *Sayonara\**
1958 *The Young Lions*
1959 *The Fugitive Kind*
1961 *One-Eyed Jacks\**
1962 *Mutiny On The Bounty\**
1963 *The Ugly American*
1964 *Bedtime Story; Tiger By The Tail* (documentary)
1965 *Morituri* (UK: *The Saboteur, Code Name Morituri*)
1966 *The Chase; The Appaloosa* (UK: *Southwest To Sonora*); *Meet Marlon Brando* (documentary); *A Countess From Hong Kong*
1967 *Reflections In A Golden Eye*
1968 *The Night Of The Following Day; Candy*
1969 *Burn!* (UK: *Queimada!*)
1971 *The Nightcomers*
1972 *The Godfather\*; Ultima Tango A Parigi\** (UK: *Last Tango In Paris*)
1976 *The Missouri Breaks*
1978 *Superman\**
1979 *Apocalypse Now\**
1980 *The Formula*
1989 *A Dry White Season*
1990 *The Freshman*
1991 *Hearts Of Darkness* (documentary)
1992 *Christopher Columbus: The Discovery*

**BRIDGES, Beau**
(1941–   ) USA

1948 *No Minor Vices; Force Of Evil*
1949 *The Red Pony; Zamba* (UK: *Zamba The Gorilla*)
1950 *The Company She Keeps*
1961 *The Explosive Generation*
1965 *Valley Of The Giants*
1967 *The Incident; Attack On The Iron Coast*
1968 *For Love Of Ivy*

1969 *Gaily, Gaily* (UK: *Chicago, Chicago*); *Adam's Woman*
1970 *The Landlord*
1971 *The Christian Licorice Store*
1972 *Hammersmith Is Out; Child's Play*
1973 *Lovin' Molly; Your Three Minutes Are Up; The Man Without A Country* (TV)
1974 *The Stranger Who Looks Like Me*
1975 *Medical Story* (TV); *The Other Side Of The Mountain*
1976 *One Summer Love* (TV); *Swashbuckler* (UK: *The Scarlet Buccaneer*); *Two Minute Warning*
1977 *Greased Lightning; Behind The Iron Mask* (UK: *The Fifth Musketeer*)
1978 *The Four Feathers; Something Light; The President's Mistress* (TV)
1979 *Norma Rae\*; The Runner Stumbles; The Child Stealer* (TV)
1980 *Silver Dream Racer*
1981 *Honky Tonk Freeway; The Kid From Nowhere* (TV) (also director)
1982 *Night Crossing; Love Child; Witness For The Prosecution* (TV)
1983 *Heart Like A Wheel*
1984 *The Hotel New Hampshire; The Red-Light Sting* (TV)
1986 *Outrage* (TV); *A Fighting Chance* (TV); *The Thanksgiving Promise* (TV) (also director)
1987 *Devil's Odds/The Wild Pair* (also director); *Seven Hours To Judgement* (also director); *Perfect Stranger*
1988 *The Iron Triangle*
1989 *Signs Of Life; The Fabulous Baker Boys\*; The Wizard; Everybody's Baby: The Rescue Of Jessica McClure* (TV); *Just Another Secret* (TV)
1990 *Daddy's Dyin'—Who's Got The Will; Women & Men: Stories Of Seduction* (TV)
1991 *Married To It; Without Warning: The James Brady Story* (TV); *Wildflower* (TV)

## BRIDGES, Jeff
(1949–  ) USA

1950 The Company She Keeps
1969 Silent Night, Lonely Night (TV);
     Halls Of Anger
1970 In Search Of America; The Yin
     And The Yang Of Dr Go
1971 The Last Picture Show*
1972 Fat City; Bad Company
1973 The Last American Hero; Lolly
     Madonna XXX (UK: The Lolly
     Madonna War); The Iceman
     Cometh
1974 Thunderbolt And Lightfoot;
     Rancho De Luxe
1975 Hearts Of The West (UK:
     Hollywood Cowboy); Tilt
1976 King Kong*; Stay Hungry
1977 Winter Kills
1978 Somebody Killed Her Husband
1979 The American Success Company
1980 Heaven's Gate*
1981 Cutter And Bone (UK: Cutter's
     Way); The Last Unicorn (voice
     only)
1982 Kiss Me Goodbye; Tron
1984 Against All Odds; Starman
1985 8 Million Ways To Die; Jagged
     Edge*
1986 The Morning After; The
     Thanksgiving Promise (TV)
1987 Nadine
1988 Tucker: The Man And His Dream*
1989 See You In The Morning; Cold
     Feet; The Fabulous Baker Boys*
1990 Texasville; Capital News (TV)
1991 The Fisher King
1992 American Heart; The Vanishing
1993 Fearless; The Firm

## BRIDGES, Lloyd
(1913–  ) USA

1944 Two Man Submarine; Louisiana
     Hayride; Once Upon A Time;
     She's A Soldier Too; The Master
     Race; Saddle Leather Law (UK:
     The Poisoner)
1945 A Walk In The Sun; Strange
     Confession; Secret Agent X-9

1946 Miss Susie Slagle's; Abilene
     Town; Canyon Passage
1947 Ramrod; The Trouble With
     Women; Unconquered
1948 Secret Service Investigator;
     Sixteen Fathoms Deep; Moonrise;
     Mr Whitney Had A Notion
1949 Red Canyon; Hide-Out; Home Of
     The Brave; Calamity Jane And
     Sam Bass; Trapped
1950 Colt 45; Rocketship XM; The
     White Tower; The Sound Of Fury
     (UK: Try And Get Me)
1951 Three Steps North; Little Big Horn
     (UK: The Fighting 7th); The
     Whistle At Eaton Falls (UK: Richer
     Than The Earth)
1952 High Noon*; Plymouth Adventure;
     The Tall Texan; Last Of The
     Comanches (UK: The Sabre And
     The Arrow)
1953 City Of Bad Men; The Kid From
     Field; The Limping Man
1954 Pride Of The Blue Grass (UK:
     Prince Of The Blue Grass)
1955 Wichita; Apache Woman; Third
     Party Risk
1956 Wetbacks; The Rainmaker
1957 Ride Out For Revenge
1958 The Goddess
1966 Around The World Under The Sea
1967 The Daring Game; Attack On The
     Iron Coast
1969 The Happy Ending; Lost Flight
     (TV); The Love War (TV); The
     Silent Gun (TV); Silent Night,
     Lonely Night (TV)
1970 Do You Take This Stranger? (TV)
1971 A Tattered Web (TV); To Find A
     Man; The Deadly Dream (TV)
1972 Crime Club (TV); Haunts Of The
     Very Rich (TV); Trouble Comes
     To Town (TV); Scuba (narrator
     only)
1973 Running Wild; Death Race (TV)
1974 Stowaway To The Moon (TV);
     Deliver Us From Evil
1975 The Return Of Joe Forrester (TV)
1977 Behind The Iron Mask (UK: The
     Fifth Musketeer); The Force Of
     Evil

**BRIDGES, Lloyd** (cont.)

1978 *Something Light; The Great Wallendas* (TV); *Telethon* (TV)
1979 *Disaster On The Coastliner* (TV); *Bear Island; Mission Galactica* (TV); *The Critical List* (TV)
1980 *Airplane!\**
1982 *Airplane 2: The Sequel; Life Of The Party: The Story of Beatrice* (TV)
1983 *Grace Kelly* (TV)
1984 *Paper Dolls* (TV)
1985 *Weekend Warriors; Hollywood Air Force*
1986 *The Thanksgiving Promise* (TV)
1987 *Devil's Odds/The Wild Pair*
1988 *Tucker: The Man And His Dream\**
1989 *Winter People; Cousins*
1990 *Joe Vs The Volcano; Capital News* (TV); *Leona Helmsley— The Queen Of Mean* (TV)
1991 *Hot Shots!*
1992 *Honey, I Blew Up The Baby*
1993 *Hot Shots 2*

**BRODERICK, Matthew**
(1961–   ) USA

1983 *Max Dugan Returns; War Games\**
1984 *1918; Ladyhawke*
1985 *Master Harold...And The Boys* (TV)
1986 *Ferris Bueller's Day Off; On Valentine's Day*
1987 *Project X*
1988 *Biloxi Blues; Torch Song Trilogy\**
1989 *Family Business\*; Glory\**
1990 *The Freshman*
1992 *Welcome To Buzzsaw*
1993 *The Night We Never Met*

**BRONSON, Charles**
real name: Charles Buchinski
(1921–   ) USA

1951 *You're In The Navy Now; The People Against O'Hara; The Mob* (UK: *Remember That Face*)
1952 *Red Skies Of Montana; My Six Convicts; The Marrying Kind; Pat And Mike; Diplomatic Courier*

1953 *House Of Wax; The Clown; Miss Sadie Thompson*
1954 *Tennessee Champ; Riding Shotgun; Apache; Vera Cruz; Drum Beat; Crime Wave* (UK: *The City Is Dark*)
1955 *Big House USA; Target Zero*
1956 *Explosion; Jubal*
1957 *Run Of The Arrow*
1958 *Machine Gun Kelly; Gang War; Showdown At Boot Hill; When Hell Broke Loose*
1959 *Never So Few*
1960 *The Magnificent Seven\**
1961 *Masters Of The World; A Thunder Of Drums; X-15*
1962 *Kid Galahad; This Rugged Land*
1963 *The Great Escape\*; Four For Texas*
1964 *Guns Of Diablo*
1965 *The Sandpiper; Battle Of The Bulge*
1966 *This Property Is Condemned*
1967 *The Dirty Dozen\*; Guns For San Sebastian*
1968 *Adieu L'Ami* (UK: *Farewell Friend*); *Villa Rides; C'Era Una Volta Il West\** (UK: *Once Upon A Time In The West*)
1969 *Twinky; Rider On The Rain*
1970 *You Can't Win'Em All; Violent City; De La Part Des Copains* (UK: *Cold Sweat*)
1971 *Red Sun; Quelqu'un Derrière La Porte* (UK: *Two Minds For Murder*)
1972 *Chato's Land; The Mechanic; The Valachi Papers*
1973 *The Stone Killer; Valdez, The Halfbreed* (UK: *The Valdez Horses*)
1974 *Mr Majestyk; Death Wish\**
1975 *Breakout; Hard Times* (UK: *The Streetfighter*); *From Noon Till Three*
1976 *Breakheart Pass; St Ives; Raid On Entebbe*
1977 *Telefon; The White Buffalo*
1978 *Love And Bullets*
1979 *Cabo Blanco*
1980 *Death Hunt; Borderline*

1981 *Death Wish II*
1982 *10 To Midnight*
1984 *The Evil That Men Do*
1985 *Death Wish 3; Act Of Vengeance* (TV)
1986 *Murphy's Law*
1987 *Assassination; Death Wish 4: The Crackdown*
1988 *Messenger Of Death*
1989 *Kinjite: Forbidden Subjects*
1991 *The Indian Runner*
1993 *Death Wish V*

## BRYNNER, Yul
real name: Youl Bryner
(1915–85) Swiss-Mongolian

1949 *The Port Of New York*
1956 *The King And I\*; The Ten Commandments\*; Anastasia*
1958 *The Brothers Karamazov; The Buccaneer; The Journey*
1959 *Le Testament D'Orphée; Solomon And Sheba; The Sound And The Fury*
1960 *Once More With Feeling; The Magnificent Seven\*; Surprise Package; Profile Of A Miracle* (narrator)
1961 *Aimez-Vous Brahms? (UK: Goodbye Again); Escape From Zahrain)*
1962 *Taras-Bulba*
1963 *Kings Of The Sun*
1964 *Flight From Ashiya; Invitation To A Gunfighter*
1965 *Morituri (UK: The Saboteur, Code Name Morituri)*
1966 *Paris Brûle T'Il? (UK: Is Paris Burning?); Return Of The Seven; Triple Cross; The Poppy Is Also A Flower (UK: Danger Grows Wild)*
1967 *The Long Duel; The Double Man*
1968 *Villa Rides!*
1969 *The Picasso Summer; The Battle Of Neretva; The File Of The Golden Goose; The Magic Christian; The Madwoman Of Chaillot*
1970 *Indio Black (UK: The Bounty Hunters)*

1971 *Romance Of A Horsethief; Catlow; The Light At The Edge Of The World*
1972 *Fuzz*
1973 *The Serpent; Westworld*
1975 *The Ultimate Warrior*
1976 *Con La Rabbia Agli Occhi (UK: Anger In His Eyes); Futureworld)*

## BURNS, George
real name: Nathan Birnbaum
(1896–   ) USA

1929 *Lamb Chops* (short)
1930 *Fit To Be Tied; Pulling A Bone* (both shorts)
1931 *The Antique Shop; Once Over, Light; One Hundred Percent Service* (all shorts)
1932 *Oh My Operation; The Babbling Brook* (both shorts); *The Big Broadcast*
1933 *Hollywood On Parade; Patents Pending; Let's Dance; Walking The Baby* (all shorts); *International House; College Humor*
1934 *We're Not Dressing; Six Of A Kind; Many Happy Returns*
1935 *Love In Bloom; Here Comes Cookie; The Big Broadcast Of 1936*
1936 *College Holiday; The Big Broadcast Of 1937*
1937 *A Damsel In Distress*
1938 *College Swing (UK: Swing, Teacher, Swing)*
1939 *Honolulu*
1944 *Two Girls And A Sailor*
1954 *Screen Snapshots No 224* (short)
1956 *The Solid Gold Cadillac* (narrator only)
1975 *The Sunshine Boys*
1977 *Oh, God!\**
1978 *Sergeant Pepper's Lonely Hearts Club Band; Movie Movie; The Comedy Company* (TV)
1979 *Just You And Me, Kid; Going In Style*
1980 *Oh, God! Book II*
1982 *Two Of A Kind* (TV)

**BURNS, George** (cont.)
1984 *Oh God, You Devil!*
1988 *18 Again*


**BURSTYN, Ellen**
real name: Edna Gillooley
(1932– ) USA

1964 *Goodbye Charlie; For Those Who Think Young*
1969 *Pit Stop; Tropic Of Cancer*
1970 *Alex In Wonderland*
1971 *The Last Picture Show\**
1972 *The King Of Marvin Gardens*
1973 *The Exorcist\**
1974 *Harry And Tonto; Thursday's Game* (TV); *Alice Doesn't Live Here Anymore\**
1977 *Providence; A Dream Of Passion*
1978 *Same Time, Next Year*
1980 *Resurrection; The Silence Of The North*
1981 *The People Vs Jean Harris* (TV)
1984 *In Our Hands; The Ambassador*
1985 *Twice In A Lifetime; Surviving* (TV); *Act Of Vengeance* (TV); *Into Thin Air* (TV)
1986 *Brian Walker, Please Come Home* (TV); *Something In Common*
1987 *Pack Of Lies* (TV); *Dear America* (voice only)
1988 *Hanna's War*
1990 *When You Remember Me* (TV)
1991 *Dying Young; Mrs Lambert Remembers Love* (TV)
1992 *Earth And The American Dream* (voice only)


**BURTON, Richard**
real name: Richard Jenkins
(1925–84) UK

1948 *The Last Days Of Dolwyn*
1949 *Now Barabbas Was A Robber*
1950 *Waterfront; The Woman With No Name*
1951 *Green Grow The Rushes*
1952 *My Cousin Rachel*
1953 *The Desert Rats; The Robe\**
1954 *Prince Of Players*

1955 *The Rains Of Ranchipur; Thursday's Children* (narrator only)
1956 *Alexander The Great*
1957 *Sea Wife; Bitter Victory*
1958 *March To Aldermaston; A Midsummer Night's Dream* (both voice only)
1959 *Look Back In Anger*
1960 *The Bramble Bush; The Ice Palace*
1961 *Dylan Thomas* (documentary)
1962 *The Longest Day\**
1963 *Cleopatra\*; The VIPs; Zulu\*; Inheritance* (narrator only)
1964 *Becket\*; The Night Of The Iguana\*; Hamlet*
1965 *Eulogy To 5.02; The Days Of Wilfred Owen* (both narrator only); *The Spy Who Came In From The Cold; The Sandpiper; What's New Pussycat?*
1966 *Who's Afraid Of Virginia Woolf?\**
1967 *The Taming Of The Shrew\*; Doctor Faustus* (also directed); *The Comedians; The Comedians In Africa* (documentary)
1968 *Boom!; Candy; Where Eagles Dare\*; The Rime Of The Ancient Mariner* (narrator only); *A Wall In Jerusalem* (narrator only)
1969 *Anne Of The Thousand Days\*; Staircase*
1971 *Villain; Raid On Rommel; Under Milk Wood*
1972 *The Assassination Of Trotsky; Hammersmith Is Out; Bluebeard*
1973 *Massacre In Rome; Sujetska* (UK: *The Fifth Offensive*); *Divorce His, Divorce Hers* (TV)
1974 *Il Viaggio* (UK: *The Voyage*); *The Klansman*
1975 *Brief Encounter* (TV)
1976 *Resistance; Volcano* (narrator only)
1977 *Exorcist II — The Heretic; Equus*
1978 *Absolution; Breakthrough; Tristan And Isolt*
1980 *Circle Of Two*
1982 *Wagner* (TV); *To The End Of The Earth* (narrator only)
1984 *1984; Ellis Island* (TV)

# C

## CAAN, James

real name: James Cahn
(1938–  ) USA

1963 Irma La Douce*
1964 Lady In A Cage
1965 The Glory Guys; Red Line 7000
1967 El Dorado*; Countdown; Journey
To Shiloh; Submarine X-1; Games
1969 The Rain People; Man Without
Mercy
1970 Rabbit Run
1971 T R Baskin (UK: A Date With A
Lonely Girl); Brian's Song (TV)
1972 The Godfather*
1973 Slither; Cinderella Liberty
1974 Freebie And The Bean; The
Conversation*; The Gambler; The
Godfather Part II*
1975 Funny Lady; Rollerball; The Killer
Elite
1976 Harry And Walter Go To New
York; Silent Movie
1977 A Bridge Too Far; Un Autre
Homme, Une Autre Chance (UK:
Another Man, Another Woman)
1978 Comes A Horseman
1979 Chapter Two
1980 Hide In Plain Sight (also director)
1981 Thief; Les Uns Et Les Autres (UK:
The Ins And The Outs)
1982 Kiss Me Goodbye
1987 Gardens Of Stone
1988 Alien Nation
1990 Dick Tracy*; Misery*
1991 For The Boys; The Dark
Backward
1992 Honeymoon In Vegas
1993 Flesh And Bone; The Program

## CAGE, Nicolas

real name: Nicholas Coppola
(1964–  ) USA

1981 The Best Of Times (TV)
1982 Fast Times At Ridgemont High;
Valley Girl
1983 Rumblefish
1984 Racing With The Moon; The
Cotton Club; Birdy

1985 The Boy In Blue
1986 Peggy Sue Got Married*
1987 Raising Arizona*; Moonstruck*
1988 Vampire's Kiss
1989 Time To Kill (aka Short Cut)
1990 Wild At Heart; Fire Birds (UK:
Wings Of The Apache
1991 Zandalee
1992 Honeymoon In Vegas; Red Rock
West
1993 Amos And Andrew

## CAGNEY, James Francis

(1899–1986) USA

1930 Sinner's Holiday; Doorway To Hell
(UK: A Handful Of Clouds); Other
Men's Women (UK: Steel
Highway)
1931 How I Play Golf (documentary);
The Public Enemy* (UK: Enemies
Of The Public); The Millionaire;
Smart Money; Blonde Crazy (UK:
Larceny Lane)
1932 Taxi!; The Crowd Roars; Winner
Takes All; James Cagney
(documentary)
1933 Hollywood On Parade No 8
(documentary); Hard To Handle;
Lady Killer; Picture Snatcher; The
Mayor Of Hell; Footlight Parade*
1934 Screen Snapshots No 11; The
Hollywood Gad-About (both
documentaries); Jimmy The Gent;
He Was Her Man; Here Comes
The Navy; The St Louis Kid (UK:
A Perfect Weekend)
1935 A Trip Through A Hollywood
Studio (documentary); Devil Dogs
Of The Air; 'G'Men; The Irish In
Us; The Frisco Kid; A Midsummer
Night's Dream*; Ceiling Zero
1936 Great Guy (UK: Pluck Of The
Irish)
1937 Something To Sing About
1938 Boy Meets Girl; Angels With Dirty
Faces*; For Auld Lang Syne
(documentary)
1939 The Oklahoma Kid; Each Dawn I
Die; The Roaring Twenties*

**CAGNEY, James Francis** (cont.)

1940 *The Fighting 69th; Torrid Zone; City For Conquest*
1941 *Strawberry Blonde; The Bride Came COD*
1942 *Captains Of The Clouds; Yankee Doodle Dandy\**
1943 *You, John Jones; Showbusiness At War* (both documentaries); *Johnny Come Lately* (UK: *Johnny Vagabond*)
1944 *Battle Stations* (narrator only)
1945 *Blood On The Sun*
1946 *13 Rue Madeleine*
1948 *The Time Of Your Life*
1949 *White Heat\**
1950 *Kiss Tomorrow Goodbye; West Point Story* (UK: *Fine And Dandy*)
1951 *Come Fill The Cup; Starlift*
1952 *What Price Glory?*
1953 *A Lion Is In The Streets*
1955 *Run For Cover; The Seven Little Foys; Love Me Or Leave Me\*; Mister Roberts\**
1956 *Tribute To A Bad Man; These Wilder Years*
1957 *Man Of A Thousand Faces; Short Cut To Hell* (director only)
1958 *Never Steal Anything Small*
1959 *Shake Hands With The Devil*
1960 *The Gallant Hours*
1961 *One Two Three*
1962 *Road To The Wall* (narrator only)
1966 *Ballad Of Smokey The Bear* (narrator only)
1968 *Arizona Bushwackers* (narrator only)
1975 *Brother, Can You Spare A Dime?* (documentary)
1981 *Ragtime\**
1984 *Terrible Joe Moran* (TV)

## CAINE, Michael

real name: Maurice Joseph Micklewhite
(1933–  ) UK

1956 *A Hill In Korea*
1957 *How To Murder A Rich Uncle*
1958 *The Key; Carve Her Name With Pride; The Two-Headed Spy; Blind Spot*

1959 *Danger Within; Passport To Shame*
1960 *Foxhole In Cairo; The Bulldog Breed*
1961 *The Day The Earth Caught Fire*
1962 *Solo For Sparrow; The Wrong Arm Of The Law*
1963 *Zulu\**
1965 *The Ipcress File*
1966 *Gambit; Alfie\*; The Wrong Box; Funeral In Berlin; Hurry Sundown*
1967 *Billion Dollar Brain; Woman Times Seven; Tonite Let's All Make Love In London*
1968 *Deadfall; Play Dirty; The Magus*
1969 *The Italian Job; The Battle Of Britain; Too Late The Hero*
1970 *The Last Valley; Simon, Simon* (short)
1971 *Get Carter; Zee And Co; Kidnapped*
1972 *Sleuth\*; Pulp*
1974 *The Marseille Contract; The Black Windmill; The Wilby Conspiracy*
1975 *The Man Who Would Be King\*; The Romantic Englishwoman; Peeper*
1976 *Harry And Walter Go To New York; The Eagle Has Landed*
1977 *A Bridge Too Far; The Silver Bears*
1978 *The Swarm; California Suite\**
1979 *Ashanti; Beyond The Poseidon Adventure*
1980 *The Island; Dressed To Kill*
1981 *The Hand; Escape To Victory*
1982 *Deathtrap; The Jigsaw Man*
1983 *Educating Rita\*; The Honorary Consul; Blame It On Rio*
1984 *Water*
1985 *The Holcroft Covenant*
1986 *Sweet Liberty; Half Moon Street; The Whistle Blower; Mona Lisa\*; Hannah And Her Sisters\**
1987 *Surrender; The Fourth Protocol; Jaws 4 — The Revenge; Hero* (narrator only)
1988 *John Huston* (documentary); *Without A Clue; Dirty Rotten Scoundrels; Jack The Ripper* (TV)

1990 *A Shock To The System;
Bullseye!; Mr Destiny; Jekyll &
Hyde* (TV)
1992 *Noises Off; Blue Ice; The Muppets
Christmas Carol*

## CANDY, John
(1951–   ) Canada

1975 *It Sounded Like A Good Idea At
The Time; The Clown Murders*
1976 *Find The Lady*
1977 *Faceoff*
1978 *The Silent Partner*
1979 *Lost And Found; 1941\**
1980 *The Blues Brothers\**
1981 *Heavy Metal* (voice only); *Stripes*
1982 *It Came From Hollywood*
1983 *Strange Brew; National
Lampoon's Vacation; Going
Beserk*
1984 *Splash\**
1985 *Sesame Street Presents Follow
That Bird; Brewster's Millions;
Volunteers; Summer Rental*
1986 *Armed And Dangerous; Little
Shop Of Horrors; Rocket Boy* (TV)
1987 *Spaceballs; Really Weird Tales*
(TV); *Planes, Trains And
Automobiles\**
1988 *The Great Outdoors*
1989 *Who's Harry Crumb?; Hot To Trot*
(voice only); *Speed Zone; Uncle
Buck*
1990 *Home Alone\*; Masters Of
Menace; The Rescuers Down
Under* (voice only)
1991 *Delirious; Nothing But Trouble;
Only The Lonely; JFK\*; Career
Opportunities*
1992 *Once Upon A Crime; Boris And
Natasha; Bartholomew Vs Neff*

## CANNON, Dyan
real name: Samille Leisen
(1937–   ) USA

1959 *This Rebel Breed*
1960 *The Rise And Fall Of Legs
Diamond*
1969 *Bob & Carol & Ted & Alice\**

1970 *Doctors' Wives*
1971 *The Anderson Tapes; The Love
Machine; Le Casse* (UK: *The
Burglars*); *Such Good Friends*
1972 *Shamus*
1973 *The Last Of Sheila*
1974 *Child Under A Leaf; The Virginia
Hill Story* (TV)
1975 *Number One* (short, director only)
1978 *Lady Of The House* (TV); *The
Revenge Of The Pink Panther;
Heaven Can Wait\**
1979 *For The First Time* (also director)
1980 *Coast To Coast; Honeysuckle
Rose*
1982 *Deathtrap; Author! Author!;
Having It All*
1983 *Arthur The King* (TV)
1984 *Master Of The Game* (TV)
1988 *Caddyshack II; Rock'n'Roll Mom*
(TV)
1989 *One Point Of View*
1991 *The End Of Innocence* (also
director)
1992 *Christmas In Connecticut* (TV)
1993 *The Pickle*

## CANTOR, Eddie
real name: Edward Iskowitz
(1892–1964) USA

1926 *Kid Boots*
1927 *The Speed Hound* (short); *Follies;
Special Delivery*
1928 *That Party In Person* (short);
*Glorifying The American Girl*
1930 *Insurance* (short); *Whoopee!*
1931 *Palmy Days*
1932 *The Kid From Spain*
1933 *Roman Scandals\**
1934 *Hollywood Cavalcade; Screen
Snapshots No 11* (both shorts);
*Kid Millions*
1936 *Strike Me Pink*
1937 *Ali Baba Goes To Town*
1940 *Forty Little Mothers*
1943 *Thank Your Lucky Stars*
1944 *Hollywood Canteen; Show
Business*
1945 *Rhapsody In Blue*

133

**CANTOR, Eddie** (cont.)
1948 *If You Knew Susie*
1952 *The Story Of Will Rogers*
1953 *The Eddie Cantor Story*


## CARMICHAEL, Ian
(1920– ) UK

1948 *Bond Street*
1949 *Trottie True; Dear Mr Prohack*
1952 *Time Gentlemen Please!; Ghost Ship; Miss Robin Hood*
1953 *Meet Mr Lucifer*
1954 *The Colditz Story; Betrayed*
1955 *Storm Over The Nile; Simon And Laura*
1956 *Private's Progress; The Big Money; Brothers-In-Law*
1957 *Lucky Jim; Happy Is The Bride!*
1959 *Left, Right And Centre; I'm All Right Jack\**
1960 *School For Scoundrels; Light Up The Sky*
1961 *Double Bunk*
1962 *The Amorous Prawn*
1963 *Heavens Above!; Hide And Seek*
1964 *The Case Of The 44s*
1967 *Smashing Time*
1971 *The Magnificent Seven Deadly Sins*
1973 *From Beyond The Grave*
1979 *The Lady Vanishes*
1989 *Diamond Skulls*


## CARON, Leslie
(1931– ) France

1951 *An American In Paris\*; The Man With A Cloak*
1952 *Glory Alley*
1953 *Lili; The Story Of Three Loves*
1954 *The Glass Slipper*
1955 *Daddy Long Legs*
1956 *Gaby*
1958 *Gigi\**
1959 *The Doctor's Dilemma; The Man Who Understood Women; Austerlitz* (UK: *The Battle Of Austerlitz*)
1960 *The Subterraneans*
1961 *Fanny*

1962 *Guns Of Darkness; The L-Shaped Room; Les Quatres Vérités* (UK: *Three Fables Of Love*)
1964 *Father Goose*
1965 *A Very Special Favor*
1966 *Promise Her Anything; Paris Brule T'Il?* (UK: *Is Paris Burning?*)
1967 *Il Padre Di Famiglia*
1970 *Madron*
1971 *Chandler*
1972 *Purple Night*
1974 *QB VII* (TV)
1976 *Sérail*
1977 *Valentino; L'Homme Qui Aiment Les Femmes* (UK: *The Man Who Loved Women*)
1979 *Goldengirl; Tous Vedettes*
1980 *Kontrakt*
1981 *Chanel Solitaire*
1982 *The Imperative; Die Unerreichbare* (TV)
1985 *La Diagonale Du Fou* (UK: *Dangerous Moves*); *Reel Horror*
1987 *The Sealed Train*
1989 *Courage Mountain; Guerriers Et Captives*
1990 *Blue Notte/Dirty Night*
1992 *Damage*


## CASSAVETES, John
(1929–89) USA

1951 *Fourteen Hours*
1953 *Taxi*
1955 *The Night Holds Terror*
1956 *Crime In The Streets*
1957 *Affair In Havana; Edge Of The City* (UK: *A Man Is Ten Feet Tall*)
1958 *Saddle The Wind; Virgin Island*
1959 *Shadows\**
1962 *The Webster Boy*
1964 *The Killers*
1967 *The Dirty Dozen\*; The Devil's Angels*
1968 *Rosemary's Baby\*; Gli Intoccabili* (UK: *Machine Gun McCain*); *Roma Coma Chicago* (UK: *The Violent Four*)
1969 *If It's Tuesday, This Must Be Belgium*
1970 *Husbands*

1971 *Minnie And Moskowitz*
1975 *Capone*
1976 *Two Minute Warning; Mickey And Nicky*
1977 *Opening Night*
1978 *The Fury; Brass Target*
1979 *Flesh And Blood* (TV)
1981 *Incubus; Whose Life Is It Anyway?*
1982 *Tempest; The Haircut* (short)
1983 *Marvin And Tige; Love Streams; I'm Almost Not Crazy: John Cassavetes — The Man And His Work*

See also directors listing

## CHAPLIN, Sir Charles
(1889–1977) UK

1914 *Making A Living; Kid Auto Races At Venice; Mabel's Strange Predicament; Between Showers; A Film Johnnie; Tango Tangles; His Favourite Pastime; Cruel, Cruel Love; The Star Boarder; Mabel At The Wheel; Twenty Minutes Of Love; The Knockout; Tillie's Punctured Romance; Caught In A Cabaret; Caught In The Rain; A Busy Day; The Fatal Mallet; Her Friend The Bandit; Mabel's Busy Day; Mabel's Married Life; Laughing Gas; The Property Man; The Face On The Bar-Room Floor; Recreation; The Masquerader; His New Profession; The Rounders; The New Janitor; Those Love Pangs; Dough And Dynamite; Gentlemen Of Nerve; His Musical Career; His Trysting Place; Getting Acquainted; His Prehistoric Past*
1915 *His New Job; A Night Out; The Champion; In The Park; A Jitney Elopement; The Tramp; By The Sea; His Regeneration; Work; A Woman; The Bank; Shanghaied; A Night In The Show; Carmen*

1916 *Police; The Floorwalker; The Fireman; The Vagabond; One AM; The Count; The Pawn Shop; Behind The Screen; The Rink*
1917 *Easy Street; The Cure; The Immigrant; The Adventurer*
1918 *How To Make Movies; The Bond; A Dog's Life; Triple Trouble; Shoulder Arms; Charlie Chaplin In A Liberty Loan Appeal*
1919 *Sunnyside; A Day's Pleasure*
1920 *The Kid; The Mollycoddle*
1921 *The Nut; The Idle Class*
1922 *Pay Day; Nice And Friendly*
1923 *The Pilgrim; Souls For Sale*
1924 *The Gold Rush*
1928 *The Circus; Show People; The Woman Disputed*
1931 *City Lights**
1936 *Modern Times**
1940 *The Great Dictator**
1947 *Monsieur Verdoux*
1952 *Limelight**
1957 *A King In New York*
1966 *A Countess From Hong Kong*

See also directors listing

## CHARISSE, Cyd
real name: Tula Finklea
(1921– ) USA

1941 *Rhumba Serenade; Poème; I Knew It Would Be This Way; Did Anyone Call?* (all shorts)
1942 *This Love Of Mine* (short); *Something To Shout About; Mission To Moscow*
1943 *Thousands Cheer*
1944 *Ziegfeld Follies**
1946 *The Harvey Girls*; Three Wise Fools; Till The Clouds Roll By**
1947 *Fiesta; The Unfinished Dance*
1948 *On An Island With You; Words And Music; The Kissing Bandit*
1949 *Tension; East Side, West Side*
1951 *Mark Of The Renegade*
1952 *The Wild North; Singin' In The Rain**
1953 *Sombrero; The Band Wagon*; Easy To Love*

## CHARISSE, Cyd (cont.)

1954 *Deep In My Heart; Brigadoon*
1955 *It's Always Fair Weather*
1956 *Meet Me In Las Vegas* (UK: *Viva Las Vegas*); *Invitation To The Dance*
1957 *Silk Stockings*
1958 *Twilight For The Gods; Party Girl*
1960 *Black Tights*
1961 *Five Golden Hours*
1962 *Something's Gotta Give* (unfinished); *Two Weeks In Another Town*
1963 *Il Segreto Del Vestito Rosso* (UK: *Assassin...Made In Italy*)
1966 *The Silencers; Maroc 7*
1972 *Call Her Mom* (TV)
1975 *Won Ton Ton, The Dog Who Saved Hollywood*
1978 *Warlords Of Atlantis*
1980 *Portrait Of An Escort* (TV)
1989 *Swimsuit* (TV); *Private Screenings*

## CHASE, Chevy

real name: Cornelius Chase
(1944–   ) USA

1974 *The Groove Tube*
1976 *Tunnelvision*
1978 *Foul Play**
1980 *Caddyshack; Oh Heavenly Dog; Seems Like Old Times*
1981 *Modern Problems; Under The Rainbow*
1983 *Deal Of The Century; National Lampoon's Vacation*
1985 *Fletch; National Lampoon's European Vacation; Sesame Street Presents Follow That Bird; Spies Like Us*
1986 *Three Amigos*
1987 *Rolling In The Aisles*
1988 *The Couch Trip; Funny Farm; Caddyshack II*
1989 *Fletch Lives; National Lampoon's Christmas Vacation* (UK: *National Lampoon's Winter Holiday*)
1991 *Nothing But Trouble; LA Story*
1992 *Memoirs Of An Invisible Man; Hero* (UK: *Accidental Hero*)
1993 *Cops And Robbersons*

## CHER

real name: Cherylin Sarkisian
(1946–   ) USA

1965 *Wild On The Beach*
1967 *Good Times*
1969 *Chastity*
1982 *Come Back To The Five And Dime, Jimmy Dean, Jimmy Dean*
1983 *Silkwood**
1985 *Mask*
1987 *Suspect*; The Witches Of Eastwick*; Moonstruck**
1990 *Mermaids*
1992 *The Player**

## CHEVALIER, Maurice

(1888–1972) France

1908 *Trop Crédule* (short)
1911 *Un Marie Qui Se Fait Attendre; La Mariée Recalcitrante; Per Habitude* (all shorts)
1912 *La Valse Renversante* (short)
1917 *Une Soirée Mondaine* (short)
1921 *Le Mauvais Garçon*
1922 *Le Match Criqui-Ledoux* (short); *Gonzague*
1923 *L'Affaire De La Rue De Lourcine; Jim Bougne, Boxeur*
1924 *Per Habitude*
1928 *Bonjour New York!*
1929 *Innocents Of Paris; The Love Parade**
1930 *Paramount On Parade; The Big Pond; Playboy Of Paris*
1931 *The Smiling Lieutenant; El Cliente Seductor* (short)
1932 *One Hour With You; Make Me A Star; Love Me Tonight; Hollywood On Parade No 5* (short); *The Stolen Jools* (UK: *The Slippery Pearls*); *Stopping The Show* (voice only); *Battling Georges* (short)
1933 *A Bedtime Story; The Way To Love*
1934 *The Merry Widow*
1935 *Folies Bergère* (UK: *The Man From The Folies Bergère*)

1936 *The Beloved Vagabond;
L'Homme Du Jour; Avec Le
Sourire*
1938 *Break The News*
1939 *Pièges*
1946 *Paris 1900; Le Silence Est D'Or*
1949 *Le Roi*
1950 *Ma Pomme*
1952 *Jouons Le Jeu . . . L'Avarice*
(short)
1953 *Chevalier De Ménilmontant*
(short); *Schlager-Parade*
1954 *A Hundred Years Of Love; I Had
Seven Daughters; Caf'Conc*
(short)
1955 *Sur Toute La Gamme* (narrator
only)
1957 *Love In The Afternoon; The Heart
Of Showbusiness; Rendez-Vous
Avec Maurice Chevalier* (series of
shorts)
1958 *Gigi**
1959 *Count Your Blessings*
1960 *Can-Can; Black Tights; A Breath
Of Scandal; Pepe*
1961 *Jessica; Fanny*
1962 *In Search Of The Castaways*
1963 *Panic Button; A New Kind of Love*
1964 *I'd Rather Be Rich; La Chance Et
L'Amour*
1967 *Monkeys, Go Home!*
1970 *The Aristocats* (voice only)

## CHRISTIE, Julie
(1940– ) UK

1962 *Crooks Anonymous; The Fast
Lady*
1963 *Billy Liar**
1964 *Young Cassidy*
1965 *Darling*; Doctor Zhivago**
1966 *Fahrenheit 451*
1967 *Far From The Madding Crowd;
Tonite Let's All Make Love In
London* (documentary)
1968 *Petulia*
1969 *In Search Of Gregory*
1971 *The Go-Between; McCabe And
Mrs Miller*
1973 *Don't Look Now*
1975 *Shampoo*; Nashville**

1977 *Demon Seed*
1978 *Heaven Can Wait**
1981 *Memoirs Of A Survivor; The
Animals Film* (narrator only); *Les
Quarantièmes Rugissants* (UK:
*The Roaring Forties*)
1982 *The Return Of The Soldier*
1983 *Heat And Dust; The Gold Diggers*
1985 *Power*
1986 *Miss Mary; La Mémoir Tatouée*
(UK: *Secret Obsession*); *The Sins
Of The Fathers* (TV)
1988 *The Control Room; Dadah Is
Death* (TV)
1990 *Fools Of Fortune*
1991 *The Railway Station Man*

## CLAYBURGH, Jill
(c1944– ) USA

1966 *The Wedding Party*
1971 *The Telephone Book*
1972 *Portnoy's Complaint; The Snoop
Sisters* (TV)
1973 *The Thief Who Came To Dinner;
Tiger On A Chain* (TV); *Shock-A-
Bye Baby* (TV)
1974 *The Terminal Man*
1975 *Roman Grey* (TV); *Hustling* (TV)
1976 *Silver Streak*; Gable And
Lombard*
1977 *Semi-Tough; Griffin And Phoenix*
(UK: *Today Is Forever*)
1978 *An Unmarried Woman**
1979 *La Luna; Starting Over*
1980 *It's My Turn*
1981 *First Monday In October*
1982 *I'm Dancing As Fast As I Can*
1983 *Hanna K*
1985 *Where Are The Children?*
1986 *Miles To Go* (TV)
1987 *Shy People*
1988 *Who Gets The Friends?* (TV)
1989 *Unspeakable Acts* (TV); *Fear
Stalk* (TV)
1990 *Beyond The Ocean*
1991 *Pretty Hattie's Baby*
1992 *Le Grand Pardon 2; Rich In Love*

## CLEESE, John
(1939–  ) UK

1967 *Interlude*
1968 *The Bliss Of Mrs Blossom*
1969 *The Best House In London; The Magic Christian*
1970 *The Rise And Rise Of Michael Rimmer; The Statue*
1971 *And Now For Something Completely Different*
1972 *The Love Ban*
1974 *Romance With A Double Bass; Monty Python And The Holy Grail*
1976 *Pleasure At Her Majesty's*
1979 *Monty Python's Life Of Brian; The Secret Policeman's Ball; Away From It All* (narrator only)
1980 *Time Bandits**
1981 *Monty Python Live At The Hollywood Bowl; The Great Muppet Caper*
1982 *The Secret Policeman's Other Ball; Privates On Parade*
1983 *Monty Python's Meaning Of Life; Yellowbeard*
1985 *Silverado**
1986 *Clockwise*
1987 *The Secret Policeman's Third Ball*
1988 *A Fish Called Wanda*; The Big Picture*
1989 *Erik The Viking*
1990 *Bullseye!*
1991 *An American Tail: Fievel Goes West* (voice only)
1993 *Splitting Heirs*

## CLIFT, Edward Montgomery
(1920–66) USA

1948 *Red River*; The Search*
1949 *The Heiress**
1950 *The Big Lift*
1951 *A Place In The Sun**
1953 *I Confess; From Here To Eternity**
1954 *Stazione Termini* (UK: *Indiscretion*)
1957 *Raintree County*
1958 *The Young Lions; Lonelyhearts*
1959 *Suddenly Last Summer**
1960 *Wild River; The Misfits**

1961 *Judgement At Nuremberg**
1962 *Freud* (UK: *Freud — The Secret Passion*)
1966 *L'Espion* (UK: *The Defector*)

## CLOSE, Glenn
(1947–  ) USA

1979 *Orphan Train* (TV); *Too Far To Go* (TV)
1982 *The World According To Garp*
1983 *The Big Chill**
1984 *Something About Amelia* (TV); *The Natural; The Stone Boy; Greystoke: The Legend Of Tarzan, Lord Of The Apes** (voice only)
1985 *Jagged Edge*; Maxie*
1987 *Fatal Attraction**
1988 *Dangerous Liaisons*; Stones For Ibarra* (TV); *Light Years* (voice only)
1989 *Immediate Family*
1990 *Reversal Of Fortune*; Hamlet**
1991 *Sarah Plain And Tall* (TV); *Meeting Venus; Hook**
1992 *Skylark* (TV)
1993 *Once Upon A Forest* (voice only); *The House Of The Spirits*

## COBURN, James
(1928–  ) USA

1959 *Ride Lonesome; Face Of A Fugitive*
1960 *The Magnificent Seven**
1962 *Hell Is For Heroes; The Murder Men*
1963 *The Great Escape*; Charade*; The Man From Galveston*
1964 *The Americanization Of Emily*
1965 *Major Dundee; High Wind In Jamaica; The Loved One*
1966 *Our Man Flint; What Did You Do In The War Daddy?; Dead Heat On A Merry-Go-Round*
1967 *In Like Flint; Waterhole No 3; The President's Analyst*
1968 *Duffy; Candy; Hard Contract*
1969 *Last Of The Mobile Hot Shots* (UK: *Blood Kin*)

1971 *Giu La Testa* (UK: *A Fistful Of Dynamite!*)
1972 *The Honkers; The Carey Treatment; A Reason To Live, A Reason To Die*
1973 *Pat Garrett And Billy The Kid; The Last Of Sheila; Harry Never Holds* (UK: *Harry In Your Pocket*)
1974 *The Internecine Project*
1975 *Hard Times* (UK: *The Streetfighter*); *Bite The Bullet*
1976 *Sky Riders; The Last Hard Men; White Rock; Midway* (UK: *The Battle Of Midway*); *A Fast Drive In The Country*
1977 *Cross Of Iron*
1978 *The Dain Curse* (TV); *California Suite\*; Crimes Obscurs En Extrème-Occident*
1979 *The Muppet Movie\*; The Baltimore Bullet; Goldengirl; Firepower*
1980 *Loving Couples; The Fall Guy* (TV); *Mr Patman* (UK: *Crossover*)
1981 *Jacqueline Susann's Valley Of The Dolls* (TV); *Looker; High Risk*
1983 *Malibu* (TV); *Digital Dreams*
1984 *Martin's Day; Draw!* (TV)
1985 *Sins of The Father* (TV)
1986 *Death Of A Soldier; Phoenix Fire*
1988 *Walking After Midnight*
1989 *Train To Heaven*
1990 *Young Guns II*
1991 *Hudson Hawk; Helicon; The Doorman*
1992 *The Player\**

## COLBERT, Claudette
real name: Lily Claudette Chauchoin
(1903– ) France

1927 *For The Love Of Mike*
1929 *The Hole In The Wall; The Lady Lies*
1930 *The Big Pond; Young Man Of Manhattan; Manslaughter; L'Enigmatique; Monsieur Parkes*
1931 *The Smiling Lieutenant; Honor Among Lovers; Secrets Of A Secretary; His Woman*

1932 *The Wiser Sex; The Misleading Lady; The Man From Yesterday; Make Me A Star; The Phantom President; The Sign Of The Cross*
1933 *Tonight Is Ours; I Cover The Waterfront; Three Cornered Moon; Torch Singer* (UK: *Broadway Singer*)
1934 *Four Frightened People; It Happened One Night\*; Cleopatra; Imitation of Life*
1935 *The Gilded Lily; Private Worlds; She Married Her Boss; The Bride Comes Home*
1936 *Under Two Flags*
1937 *Maid Of Salem; Tovarich; I Met Him In Paris*
1938 *Bluebeard's Eighth Wife; Zaza*
1939 *Midnight; Drums Along The Mohawk; It's A Wonderful World*
1940 *Boom Town; Arise, My Love*
1941 *Skylark; Remember The Day*
1942 *The Palm Beach Story\**
1943 *So Proudly We Hail!; No Time For Love*
1944 *Since You Went Away\**
1945 *Practically Yours; Guest Wife; Tomorrow Is Forever*
1946 *Without Reservations; The Secret Heart*
1947 *The Egg And I*
1948 *Sleep My Love; Family Honeymoon*
1949 *Bride For Sale*
1950 *Three Came Home; The Secret Fury*
1951 *Let's Make It Legal; Thunder On The Hill* (UK: *Bonaventure*)
1952 *The Planter's Wife*
1953 *Destinées* (UK: *Love And The Frenchwoman*)
1954 *Si Versailles M'Etait Conté* (UK: *Versailles*)
1955 *Texas Lady*
1961 *Parrish*
1987 *The Two Mrs Grenvilles* (TV)

## COLE, George
(1925– ) UK

1941 *Cottage To Let*

139

**COLE, George** (cont.)

1942 *Those Kids From Town*
1943 *The Demi-Paradise; Fiddling Fuel* (short)
1944 *Henry V\**
1945 *Journey Togetherr*
1948 *My Brother's Keeper; Quartet*
1949 *The Spider And The Fly*
1950 *Morning Departure; Gone To Earth*
1951 *Flesh And Blood; Laughter In Paradise; Scrooge; Lady Godiva Rides Again*
1952 *The Happy Family; Who Goes There?; Top Secret; Folly To Be Wise*
1953 *Will Any Gentleman?; The Intruder; Our Girl Friday; The Clue Of The Missing Ape*
1954 *The Belles Of St Trinians\*; An Inspector Calls; A Prize of Gold; Happy Ever After*
1955 *Where There's A Will; The Constant Husband; The Adventures Of Quentin Durward*
1956 *It's A Wonderful World; The Green Man; The Weapon*
1958 *Blue Murder At St Trinian's*
1959 *Too Many Crooks; Don't Panic Chaps!; The Bridal Path*
1961 *The Pure Hell Of St Trinian's; The Anatomist*
1963 *Dr Syn, Alias The Scarecrow; Cleopatra\**
1964 *One Way Pendulum*
1965 *The Legend Of Young Dick Turpin*
1966 *The Great St Trinian's Train Robbery*
1968 *The Green Shoes* (short)
1970 *The Vampire Lovers*
1971 *Fright*
1973 *Take Me High*
1976 *The Bluebird*
1983 *Perishing Solicitors* (short)

**COLLINS, Pauline**
(1940– ) UK

1965 *Secrets Of A Windmill Girl*
1989 *Shirley Valentine\**
1992 *City Of Joy*

**COLMAN, Ronald**
(1891–1958) UK

1917 *The Live Wire* (short)
1919 *The Toilers; A Daughter Of Eve; Sheba; Snow In The Desert*
1920 *A Son Of David; Anna The Adventuress; The Black Spider*
1921 *Handcuffs Or Kisses*
1923 *The Eternal City; The White Sister; Twenty Dollars A Week*
1924 *Tarnish; Her Night Of Romance; Romola; A Thief In Paradise*
1925 *His Supreme Moment; The Sporting Venus; Her Sister From Paris; The Dark Angel; Stella Dallas; Lady Windermere's Fan*
1926 *Kiki; Beau Geste; The Winning Of Barbara Worth*
1927 *The Night Of Love; The Magic Flame*
1928 *Two Lovers*
1929 *The Rescue; Bulldog Drummond; Condemned* (UK: *Condemned To Devil's Island*)
1930 *Raffles; The Devil To Pay*
1931 *The Unholy Garden; Arrowsmith\**
1932 *Cynara*
1933 *The Masquerader*
1934 *Bulldog Drummond Strikes Back*
1935 *Clive Of India; The Man Who Broke The Bank At Monte Carlo; A Tale Of Two Cities\**
1936 *Under Two Flags*
1937 *Lost Horizon\*; The Prisoner Of Zenda\**
1938 *If I Were King*
1940 *Lucky Partners; The Light That Failed*
1941 *My Life With Caroline*
1942 *The Talk Of The Town; Random Harvest\**
1944 *Kismet*
1946 *The Late George Apley*
1947 *A Double Life*
1950 *Champagne For Caesar*
1953 *The Globe Playhouse* (narrator only)
1956 *Around The World In 80 Days\**
1957 *The Story Of Mankind*

## CONNERY, Sean
real name: Thomas Connery
(1930–  ) UK

1954 *Lilacs In The Spring*
1956 *No Road Back*
1957 *Time Lock; Hell Drivers; Action Of The Tiger*
1958 *Another Time, Another Place; A Night To Remember*
1959 *Darby O'Gill And The Little People; Tarzan's Greatest Adventure*
1961 *The Frightened City; On The Fiddle*
1962 *The Longest Day\*; Dr No\**
1963 *From Russia With Love\**
1964 *Woman Of Straw; Goldfinger\*; Marnie*
1965 *The Hill; Thunderball\**
1966 *A Fine Madness*
1967 *You Only Live Twice\*; The Castles Of Scotland* (narrator only)
1968 *Shalako*
1969 *The Molly Maguires; The Red Tent; The Bowler And The Bunnet* (also director)
1971 *The Anderson Tapes; Diamonds Are Forever\**
1972 *The Offence*
1973 *Zardoz*
1974 *Murder On The Orient Express\*; Ransom; The Vocation* (narrator only)
1975 *The Wind And The Lion; The Man Who Would Be King\**
1976 *Robin And Marian; The Next Man*
1977 *A Bridge Too Far*
1978 *The First Great Train Robbery*
1979 *Meteor; Cuba*
1980 *Time Bandits\**
1981 *Outland*
1982 *Wrong Is Right* (UK: *The Man With The Deadly Lens*); *Five Days One Summer; Burning* (narrator only)
1983 *Sword Of The Valiant; Never Say Never Again\**
1986 *Highlander\*; The Name Of The Rose\**

1987 *The Untouchables\**
1988 *The Presidio; Memories Of Me*
1989 *Indiana Jones And The Last Crusade\*; Family Business\**
1990 *The Hunt For Red October\*; The Russia House; Wake-Up Call* (short)
1991 *Highlander II — The Quickening; Robin Hood — Prince Of Thieves\**
1992 *Medicine Man*
1993 *The Rising Sun*

## CONTI, Tom
(1942–  ) UK

1974 *Flame; Galileo*
1976 *Eclipse; Full Circle*
1977 *The Duellists*
1980 *Blade On The Feather* (TV)
1981 *The Wall* (TV)
1983 *Reuben, Reuben; Merry Christmas Mr Lawrence*
1985 *American Dreamer; Saving Grace*
1986 *Miracles; Io E D'Annunzio; Nazi Hunter: The Beate Klarsfeld Story* (TV); *Heavenly Pursuits*
1987 *Beyond Therapy; The Quick And The Dead* (TV); *Roman Holiday* (TV)
1988 *Fatal Judgement* (TV); *Two Brothers, Running*
1989 *That Summer Of White Roses; Shirley Valentine\**
1990 *Shattered*
1991 *The Siege Of Venice*

## COOPER, Gary
real name: Frank James Cooper
(1901–61) USA

1923 *Blind Justice*
1925 *The Thundering Herd; Wild Horse Mesa; The Lucky Horseshoe; Tricks* (short); *The Eagle; Poverty Row; Lightnin' Wins* (short); *The Vanishing American* (UK: *The Vanishing Race*); *The Enchanted Hill; Three Pals*
1926 *Watch Your Wife; Old Ironsides; Lightning Justice; The Winning Of Barbara Worth*

**COOPER, Gary** (cont.)

1927 *Arizona Bound; The Last Outlaw; Nevada; Wings; Children Of Divorce; It; Quicksands*

1928 *Beau Sabreur; The Legion Of The Condemned; Half A Bride; The First Kiss; Lilac Time* (UK: *Love Never Dies*)

1929 *The Shopworn Angel; Wolf Song; The Betrayal; The Virginian*

1930 *Seven Days Leave* (UK: *Medals*); *Only The Brave; Paramount On Parade; The Texan* (UK: *The Big Race*); *A Man From Wyoming; The Spoilers; Morocco\**

1931 *Fighting Caravans; City Streets; I Take This Woman; His Woman*

1932 *Make Me A Star; The Devil And The Deep; If I Had A Million; A Farewell To Arms\*; Voice Of Hollywood* (short); *The Stolen Jools* (UK: *The Slippery Pearls*) (short)

1933 *Today We Live; One Sunday Afternoon; Design For Living; Alice In Wonderland*

1934 *Operator 13* (UK: *Spy 13*); *Now And Forever; Hollywood Cavalcade* (short)

1935 *The Wedding Night; Lives Of A Bengal Lancer\*; Peter Ibbetson; La Fiesta De Santa Barbara* (short); *Star Night At The Cocoanut Grove* (short)

1936 *Mr Deeds Goes To Town\*; The General Died At Dawn; The Plainsman*

1937 *Lest We Forget* (short); *Souls At Sea*

1938 *The Adventures Of Marco Polo; Bluebeard's Eighth Wife; The Cowboy And The Lady*

1939 *Beau Geste\*; The Real Glory*

1940 *The Westerner; Northwest Mounted Police*

1941 *Meet John Doe\*; Sergeant York\*; Ball Of Fire\**

1942 *The Pride Of The Yankees\*; Hedda Hopper's Hollywood No 3* (short)

1943 *For Whom The Bell Tolls\**

1944 *The Story Of Dr Wassell; Casanova Brown; Memo For Joe* (short)

1945 *Along Came Jones; Saratoga Trunk*

1946 *Cloak And Dagger*

1947 *Variety Girl; Unconquered*

1948 *Good Sam*

1949 *The Fountainhead; It's A Great Feeling; Task Force; Snow Carnival* (short)

1950 *Bright Leaf; Dallas*

1951 *You're In The Navy Now; Starlift; It's A Big Country; Distant Drums*

1952 *High Noon\*; Springfield Rifle*

1953 *Return To Paradise; Blowing Wild*

1954 *Vera Cruz; Garden Of Evil*

1955 *The Court Martial Of Billy Mitchell* (UK: *One Man Mutiny*); *Hollywood Mothers* (short)

1956 *Friendly Persuasion\**

1957 *Love In The Afternoon*

1958 *Ten North Frederick; Man Of The West; Glamorous Hollywood* (short)

1959 *The Hanging Tree; Alias Jesse James; They Came To Cordura; The Wreck Of The Mary Deare*

1961 *The Naked Edge*

**COSBY, Bill**
(1937–  ) USA

1971 *To All My Friends On Shore* (TV); *Man And Boy*

1972 *Hickey And Boggs*

1974 *Uptown Saturday Night*

1975 *Let's Do It Again; Mother, Jugs And Speed*

1977 *A Piece Of The Action*

1978 *California Suite\*; Top Secret* (TV)

1981 *The Devil And Max Devlin*

1983 *Bill Cosby—Himself*

1987 *Leonard—Part VI*

1990 *Ghost Dad*

1993 *Meteor Man*

**COSTNER, Kevin**
(1955–  ) USA

1974 *Sizzle Beach USA*

1981 *Shadows Run Black*
1982 *Night Shift; Chasing Dreams; Frances\*; Winning Streak* (aka *Stacy's Knights*)
1983 *Table For Five; The Big Chill\*; Testament*
1984 *The Gunrunner*
1985 *Fandango: American Flyers; Silverado*
1987 *Amazing Stories; The Untouchables\*; No Way Out\**
1988 *Bull Durham\**
1989 *Field Of Dreams\**
1990 *Revenge; Dances With Wolves\** (also director)
1991 *Robin Hood—Prince Of Thieves\*; Truth Or Dare* (UK: *In Bed With Madonna*) (documentary); *JFK\**
1992 *The Bodyguard*
1993 *Perfect World; Rapa Nui* (co-producer only)


## COTTEN, Joseph
(1905–  ) USA

1938 *Too Much Johnson*
1941 *Citizen Kane\*; Lydia*
1942 *The Magnificent Ambersons\*; Journey Into Fear*
1943 *Hers To Hold; Shadow Of A Doubt\**
1944 *Gaslight\** (UK: *The Murder In Thornton Square*); *Since You Went Away\*; I'll Be Seeing You*
1945 *Love Letters*
1946 *Duel In The Sun\**
1947 *The Farmer's Daughter*
1948 *Portrait Of Jennie*
1949 *The Third Man\*; Under Capricorn; Beyond The Forest; Walk Softly Stranger*
1950 *Gone To Earth* (narrator only); *Two Flags West; September Affair*
1951 *Half Angel; Peking Express; The Man With A Cloak*
1952 *Untamed Frontier; The Steel Trap*
1953 *Niagra; A Blueprint For Murder; Egypt By Three* (narrator only)

1955 *Special Delivery; The Killer Is Loose*
1956 *The Bottom Of The Bottle* (UK: *Beyond The River*); *Nobody Runs Away* (short)
1957 *The Halliday Brand*
1958 *Touch Of Evil\*; From The Earth To The Moon*
1960 *The Angel Wore Red*
1961 *The Last Sunset*
1964 *Hush, Hush . . . Sweet Charlotte*
1965 *The Money Trap; The Great Sioux Massacre; Krakatoa* (narrator only)
1966 *The Oscar; Some May Live* (TV); *Gli Uomini Dal Passo Pesante* (UK: *The Tramplers*); *I Crudeli* (UK: *The Hellbenders*); *Brighty Of Grand Canyon*
1967 *Jack Of Diamonds*
1968 *Rio Hondo* (UK: *White Comanche*); *Petulia; Gangster 70*
1969 *The Lonely Profession* (TV); *Cutter's Trail* (TV); *Latitude Zero; Keene*
1970 *The Grasshopper; Tora! Tora! Tora!; E Venne L'Ora Della Vendetta; Do You Take This Stranger* (TV); *Assault On The Wayne* (TV)
1971 *Lady Frankenstein; The Abominable Dr Phibes; City Beneath The Sea* (UK: *One Hour To Doomsday*)
1972 *The Screaming Woman* (TV); *Lo Scopone Scientifico* (UK: *The Scientific Cardplayer*); *The Devil's Daughter* (TV); *Doomsday Voyage; Gli Orrori Del Castello Di Norimberga* (UK: *Baron Blood*)
1973 *Soylent Green; F For Fake; Timber Tramp*
1974 *A Delicate Balance*
1975 *Il Giustiziere Sfida La Citta* (UK: *Syndicate Sadists*)
1976 *The Lindbergh Kidnapping Case* (TV); *A Whisper In The Dark*
1977 *Airport '77; Twilight's Last Gleaming*
1978 *L'Ordre Et La Securité Du Monde; Caravans; Fish Men*

**COTTEN, Joseph** (cont.)

1979 *Guyana: The Crime Of The Century; The House Where Evil Dwells; Island Of Mutations; Casino* (TV); *Trauma; The Concorde Affair*
1980 *The Hearse; Heaven's Gate\*; Delusion*
1981 *The Survivor*

**COURTENAY, Tom**
(1937–  ) UK

1962 *The Loneliness Of The Long Distance Runner; Private Potter*
1963 *Billy Liar\**
1964 *King And Country*
1965 *Operation Crossbow; King Rat; Doctor Zhivago\**
1966 *The Night Of The Generals*
1967 *The Day The Fish Came Out*
1969 *A Dandy In Aspic*
1969 *Otley*
1971 *Catch Me A Spy; One Day In The Life Of Ivan Denisovitch*
1972 *Today Mexico — Tomorrow The World* (short)
1973 *I Heard The Owl Call My Name* (TV)
1983 *The Dresser\**
1985 *Happy New Year*
1987 *Leonard Part VI*
1990 *The Last Butterfly*
1991 *Let Him Have It*

**COWARD, Nöel**
(1899–1973) UK

1918 *Hearts Of The World*
1935 *The Scoundrel*
1942 *In Which We Serve\**
1945 *Blithe Spirit\** (narrator only)
1950 *The Astonished Heart*
1956 *Around The World In 80 Days\**
1960 *Our Man In Havana; Surprise Package*
1963 *Paris When It Sizzles*
1965 *Bunny Lake Is Missing*

1968 *Boom!*
1969 *The Italian Job*

See also directors listing

**CRAWFORD, Joan**
real name: Lucille Fay Le Sueur
(1904–77) USA

1925 *Miss MGM* (documentary); *Lady Of The Night; Proud Flesh; Pretty Ladies; The Merry Widow; The Circle; Old Clothes; Sally, Irene And Mary; The Only Thing* (UK: *Four Flaming Days*)
1926 *The Boob* (UK: *The Yokel*); *Paris* (UK: *Shadow Of Paris*); *Tramp, Tramp, Tramp*
1927 *Winners Of The Wilderness; The Taxi Dance; West Point* (UK: *Eternal Youth*); *The Understanding Heart; The Unknown; Twelve Miles Out; Spring Fever*
1928 *The Law Of The Range; Rose Marie; Across To Singapore; Dream Of Love; Four Walls; Our Dancing Daughters*
1929 *The Duke Steps Out; Our Modern Maidens; Untamed; Hollywood Revue Of 1929*
1930 *Montana Moon; Our Blushing Brides*
1931 *Paid* (UK: *Within The Law*); *Dance, Fools, Dance; Laughing Sinners; This Modern Age; Possessed*
1932 *Grand Hotel\*; The Stolen Jools* (UK: *The Slippery Pearls*) (short); *Letty Lynton; Rain*
1933 *Today We Live; Dancing Lady*
1934 *Sadie McKee; Forsaking All Others; Chained*
1935 *No More Ladies; I Live My Life*
1936 *The Gorgeous Hussy; Love On The Run*
1937 *The Last Of Mrs Cheyney; The Bride Wore Red; Mannequin*
1938 *The Shining Hour*
1939 *Ice Follies Of 1939; The Women\**

1940 *Strange Cargo; Susan And God*
(UK: *The Gay Mrs Trexel*)
1941 *When Ladies Meet; Woman's
Face*
1942 *They All Kissed The Bride;
Reunion In France* (UK:
*Mademoiselle France*)
1943 *Above Suspicion*
1944 *Hollywood Canteen*
1945 *Mildred Pierce**
1946 *Humoresque*
1947 *Possessed; Daisy Kenyon*
1949 *Flamingo Road; It's A Great
Feeling*
1950 *The Damned Don't Cry; Harriet
Craig*
1951 *Goodbye My Fancy; This Woman
Is Dangerous*
1952 *Sudden Fear*
1953 *Torch Song*
1954 *Johnny Guitar*
1955 *Hollywood Mothers*
(documentary); *Female On The
Beach; Queen Bee*
1956 *Autumn Leaves*
1957 *The Story Of Esther Costello*
1959 *The Best Of Everything*
1962 *What Ever Happened To Baby
Jane?**
1963 *Caretakers* (UK: *Borderlines*)
1964 *Della* (TV); *Straitjacket*
1965 *I Saw What You Did*
1967 *Beserk!; The Karate Killers*
1969 *Night Gallery* (TV)
1970 *Trog*

## CRONYN, Hume
(1911–   ) USA

1943 *Shadow Of A Doubt*; Phantom Of
The Opera; The Cross Of Lorraine*
1944 *The Ziegfeld Follies*; The
Seventh Cross; Main Street After
Dark; Blonde Fever; An American
Romance; Lifeboat*
1945 *A Letter For Evie; The Sailor
Takes A Wife*
1946 *The Green Years; The Postman
Always Rings Twice*; The Secret
Heart* (voice only)

1947 *The Beginning Or The End; Brute
Force*
1948 *The Bride Goes Wild*
1949 *Top O' The Morning*
1951 *People Will Talk*
1956 *The Crowded Paradise*
1960 *Sunrise At Campobello*
1963 *Cleopatra**
1964 *Hamlet*
1969 *Gaily, Gaily; The Arrangement*
1970 *There Was A Crooked Man*
1974 *The Parallax View; Conrack*
1981 *Rollover; Honky Tonk Freeway*
1982 *The World According To Garp*
1984 *Impulse*
1985 *Brewster's Millions; Cocoon*; The
Thrill Of Genius*
1987 *batteries not included; Foxfire*
(TV)
1988 *Cocoon: The Return*
1992 *Neil Simon's Broadway Bound*
(TV)

## CROSBY, Bing
real name: Harry Lillis Crosby
(1901–77) USA

1930 *Ripstitch, The Tailor; Two Plus
Fours* (both shorts); *King Of Jazz;
Check And Double Check;
Reaching For The Moon*
1931 *I Surrender Dear; One More
Chance; At Your Command* (all
shorts); *Confessions Of A Co-Ed*
(UK: *Her Dilemma*)
1932 *The Billboard Girl; Hollywood On
Parade No 2; Dream House;
Hollywood On Parade No 4* (all
shorts); *The Big Broadcast*
1933 *Blue Of The Night; Please; Sing,
Bing, Sing* (all shorts); *College
Humor; Too Much Harmony;
Going Hollywood*
1934 *Just An Echo* (short); *We're Not
Dressing; Here Is My Heart; She
Loves Me Not*
1935 *Star Night At The Cocoanut Grove*
(documentary); *Mississippi; Two
For Tonight; The Big Broadcast Of
1936*

**CROSBY, Bing** (cont.)

1936 *Anything Goes; Rythmn On The Range; Pennies From Heaven*

1937 *Waikiki Wedding; Double Or Nothing*

1938 *Don't Hook Now* (short); *Sing You Sinners; Dr Rythmn*

1939 *Paris Honeymoon; The Star Maker; East Side Of Heaven*

1940 *Swing With Bing* (short); *Rythmn On The River; Road To Singapore\*; If I Had My Way*

1941 *Birth Of The Blues; Road To Zanzibar*

1942 *Angels Of Mercy* (short); *My Favourite Blonde; Holiday Inn\*; Road To Morocco; Star Spangled Rythmn*

1943 *Dixie*

1944 *The Road To Victory* (short); *The Princess And The Pirate; The Shining Future; Going My Way\*; Here Come The Waves*

1945 *All Star Bond Rally; Hollywood Victory Caravan* (both shorts); *Out Of This World* (voice only); *Road To Utopia; Duffy's Tavern; The Bells Of St Mary's\**

1946 *Monsieur Beaucaire; Blue Skies\**

1947 *Welcome Stranger; My Favourite Brunette; Road To Rio; Variety Girl*

1948 *The Emperor Waltz; Rough But Hopeful* (short)

1949 *The Road To Peace; It's In The Groove; Honor Caddie; You Can Change The World* (all shorts); *A Connecticut Yankee In King Arthur's Court; Top O' The Morning; The Adventures Of Ichabod And Mr Toad* (voice only)

1950 *Riding High; Mr Music*

1951 *Here Comes The Groom; Angels In The Outfield* (UK: *Angels And The Pirates*); *A Millionaire For Christy* (voice only)

1952 *The Greatest Show On Earth\*; Son Of Paleface; Just For You; Road To Bali*

1953 *Little Boy Lost; Off Limits* (UK: *Military Policeman*); *Scared Stiff; Faith, Hope And Hogan* (short)

1954 *White Christmas; The Country Girl\**

1955 *Bing Presents Orieste; Hollywood Fathers* (both shorts)

1956 *Anything Goes; High Society\*; High Tor* (TV)

1957 *The Heart Of Showbusiness* (narrator); *Man On Fire*

1958 *Showdown At Ulcer Gulch* (short)

1959 *This Game Of Golf; Your Caddie Sir* (both shorts); *Alias Jesse James; Say One For Me*

1960 *Let's Make Love; High Time; Pepe*

1961 *Kitty Caddy* (voice only); *Road To Hong Kong*

1964 *Robin And The Seven Hoods*

1965 *Bing Crosby In Cinerama's Russian Adventure* (narrator only)

1966 *Stagecoach*

1968 *Bing Crosby's Washington State* (documentary)

1970 *Golf's Golden Years* (narrator only); *Goldilocks* (TV); *Dr Cook's Garden* (TV)

1972 *Cancel My Reservation*

1974 *That's Entertainment*

**CRUISE, Tom**
real name: Tom Cruise Mapother IV
(1962– ) USA

1981 *Endless Love; Taps*

1982 *The Outsiders\**

1983 *Risky Business; Losin' It; All The Right Moves*

1985 *Legend*

1986 *Top Gun\*; The Color Of Money\**

1988 *Cocktail\*; Rain Man\*; Young Guns\** (cameo only)

1989 *Born On The 4th Of July\**

1990 *Days Of Thunder\**

1992 *Far And Away; A Few Good Men\**

1993 *The Firm*

## CRYSTAL, Billy
(1948–   ) USA

1977  SST—Death Flight (TV)
1978  Rabbit Test; Human Feelings (TV)
1979  Animalympics (voice only);
      Breaking Up Is Hard To Do (TV)
1980  Enola Gay: The Men, The
      Mission, The Atomic Bomb (TV)
1984  This Is Spinal Tap
1986  Running Scared
1987  The Princess Bride; Throw
      Momma From The Train*
1988  Memories Of Me
1989  When Harry Met Sally*
1991  City Slickers*
1992  Mr Saturday Night (also director)

## CULKIN, Macaulay
(1980–   ) USA

1988  Rocket Gibraltar
1989  Uncle Buck; See You In The
      Morning
1990  Jacob's Ladder; Home Alone*
1991  Only The Lonely; My Girl
1992  Home Alone 2: Lost In New York
1993  The Good Son; The Pagemaster
      (voice only)

## CURTIS, Jamie Lee
(1958–   ) USA

1977  Operation Petticoat (TV)
1978  Halloween*
1979  The Fog
1980  Terror Train; Prom Night
1981  Halloween II; Roadgames; She's
      In The Army Now (TV); Death Of
      A Centrefold (TV)
1982  Coming Soon (TV); Money On
      The Side (TV)
1983  Trading Places*; Love Letters
1984  Grandview USA
1985  Perfect; Annie Oakley (TV)
1986  As Summers Die (TV)
1987  Amazing Grace And Chuck (UK:
      Silent Voice); A Man In Love
1988  A Fish Called Wanda*; Dominick
      And Eugene (UK: Nicky And
      Gino)

1990  Blue Steel
1991  Queen's Logic; My Girl
1992  Forever Young
1993  Mother's Boys

## CURTIS, Tony
real name: Bernard Schwartz
(1925–   ) USA

1948  Criss Cross
1949  City Across The River; Take One
      False Step; The Lady Gambles;
      Johnny Stool Pigeon
1950  Francis; Sierra; I Was A
      Shoplifter; Winchester '73;
      Kansas Raiders; The Prince Who
      Was A Thief
1951  Flesh And Fury
1952  No Room For The Groom; Son Of
      Ali Baba
1953  All-American (UK: The Winning
      Way); Forbidden; Houdini
1954  Beachhead; Johnny Dark; The
      Black Shield Of Falworth; So This
      Is Paris
1955  Six Bridges To Cross; The Purple
      Mask; The Square Jungle
1956  The Rawhide Years; Trapeze
1957  Mister Cory; The Midnight Story
      (UK: Appointment With A
      Shadow); Sweet Smell Of
      Success*
1958  The Vikings*; The Defiant Ones*;
      Kings Go Forth; The Perfect
      Furlough (UK: Strictly For
      Pleasure)
1959  Some Like It Hot*; Operation
      Petticoat*
1960  Who Was That Lady?;
      Spartacus*; Pepe; The Young
      Juggler (TV); The Rat Race
1961  The Great Imposter; The Outsider
1962  40 Pounds Of Trouble; Taras
      Bulba
1963  Captain Newman MD; The List Of
      Adrian Messenger; Paris When It
      Sizzles
1964  Wild And Wonderful; Goodbye
      Charlie; Sex And The Single Girl
1965  The Great Race*; Boeing, Boeing

**CURTIS, Tony** (cont.)

1966 *Chamber Of Horrors; Not With My Wife You Don't; Drop Dead Darling*
1967 *La Cintura Di Castita* (UK: *The Chastity Belt*); *Don't Make Waves*
1968 *The Boston Strangler; Rosemary's Baby\** (voice only)
1969 *Monte Carlo Or Bust!*
1970 *You Can't Wim'Em All; Suppose They Gave A War And Nobody Came*
1973 *The Third Girl From The Left* (TV)
1974 *Lepke; The Count Of Monte Cristo*
1975 *The Big Rip-Off* (TV)
1976 *The Last Tycoon*
1977 *Casanova And Co* (UK: *The Rise And Rise Of Casanova*); *Sextette; The Manitou*
1978 *Vega$* (TV); *The Bad News Bears Go To Japan; The Users* (TV); *It Rained All Night The Day I Left*
1979 *Little Miss Marker; Titleshot*
1980 *The Million Dollar Face* (TV); *The Mirror Crack'd; Moviola: The Scarlett O'Hara War* (TV)
1981 *Inmates: A Love Story* (TV)
1982 *Brainwaves; Othello, The Black Commando; Portrait Of A Showgirl* (TV); *Balboa*
1984 *Where Is Parsifal?; King Of The City*
1985 *Insignificance; Half-Nelson* (TV)
1986 *Mafia Princess* (TV); *The Last Of Philip Banter*
1987 *Club Life*
1988 *Midnight; Der Passagier* (UK: *Welcome To Germany*)
1989 *Lobster Man From Mars; The High-Flying Mermaid; Tarzan In Manhattan* (TV); *Walter And Carlo In America*
1990 *Thanksgiving Day* (TV)
1991 *Prime Target; Blood Law; Center Of The Web*
1992 *Christmas In Connecticut* (TV)
1993 *Naked In New York*


**CUSHING, Peter**
(1913–   ) UK

1939 *The Man In The Iron Mask*

1940 *Dreams; The Hidden Master* (both shorts); *A Chump At Oxford; Vigil In The Night; Women In War; Laddie; The Howards Of Virginia* (UK: *The Tree Of Liberty*)
1941 *We All Help; The New Teacher; Safety First* (all shorts); *They Dare Not Love*
1947 *It Might Be You* (short)
1948 *Hamlet\**
1952 *Moulin Rouge*
1954 *The Black Knight*
1955 *The End Of The Affair*
1956 *Magic Fire; Alexander The Great; Time Without Pity; The Curse Of Frankenstein*
1957 *The Abominable Snowman; Violent Playground*
1958 *Dracula\*; The Revenge Of Frankenstein*
1959 *John Paul Jones; The Hound Of The Baskervilles; The Mummy; The Flesh And The Fiends*
1960 *Suspect; Cone Of Silence; Brides Of Dracula; Sword Of Sherwood Forest*
1961 *Fury At Smugglers Bay; The Naked Edge*
1962 *The Hellfire Club; Cash On Demand; The Devil's Agent; Captain Clegg; The Man Who Finally Died*
1964 *Tho Evil Of Frankenstein; The Gorgon*
1965 *Dr Terror's House Of Horrors; She; Dr Who And The Daleks; The Skull*
1966 *Island Of Terror; Some May Live* (TV); *Daleks — Invasion Earth 2150 AD*
1967 *Frankenstein Created Woman; Night Of The Big Heat; Torture Garden; Caves Of Steel; The Blood Beast Terror; The Mummy's Shroud* (narrator only)
1968 *Corruption*
1969 *One More Time; Frankenstein Must Be Destroyed; Scream And Scream Again*
1970 *The Vampire Lovers; I, Monster; The House That Dripped Blood;*

**CUSHING, Peter** (cont.)
Incense For The Damned; Death
Corps (UK: *Almost Human*)
1971 *Twins Of Evil*
1972 *Fear In The Night; Asylum; Dr
Phibes Rises Again; Dracula AD
1972; Nothing But The Night;
Tales From The Crypt; The
Creeping Flesh; Panico En El
Transiberio* (UK: *Horror Express*)
1973 *The Satanic Rites Of Dracula;
Frankenstein And The Monster
From Hell; And Now The
Screaming Starts; From Beyond
The Grave*
1974 *The Beast Must Die; The Legend
Of The Seven Golden Vampires;
Madhouse; Tendre Dracula/La
Grande Trouille; The Ghoul;
Shatter; Legend Of The Werewolf*
1976 *The Devil's Men; At The Earth's
Core; Trial By Combat*
1977 *The Uncanny; Star Wars\*; Die
Standarte; The Great Houdinis*
(TV)
1978 *Touch Of The Sun; I litlei 's Son;
The Detour* (narrator only)
1979 *Arabian Adventure*
1980 *Monster Island*
1981 *A Tale Of Two Cities* (TV); *Black
Jack*
1982 *House Of The Long Shadows*
1983 *Sword Of The Valiant; Helen
Keller...The Miracle Continues*
(TV)
1984 *The Masks Of Death* (TV); *Top
Secret!*
1986 *Biggles*

# D

**DAFOE, Willem**
real name: William Dafoe
(1955–   ) USA

1980 *Heaven's Gate\**
1982 *The Loveless*
1983 *The Hunger*
1984 *Roadhosue 66; New York Nights;
Streets Of Fire*

1985 *To Live And Die In LA; The
Communists Are Comfortable*
1986 *Platoon\**
1987 *Dear America* (voice only); *Off
Limits* (UK: *Saigon*)
1988 *The Last Temptation Of Christ\*;
Mississippi Burning\**
1989 *Born On The 4th Of July\*;
Triumph Of The Spirit*
1990 *Wild At Heart; Cry Baby; Flight Of
The Intruder*
1992 *Light Sleeper; White Sands; Body
Of Evidence*

**DALTON, Timothy**
(1946–   ) UK

1968 *The Lion In Winter\**
1970 *Cromwell; Wuthering Heights;
Giochi Particolari* (UK: *The
Voyeur*)
1971 *Mary, Queen Of Scots*
1972 *Lady Caroline Lamb*
1975 *Permission To Kill*
1977 *Sextette*
1978 *Agatha*
1979 *The Flame Is Love*
1980 *Flash Gordon*
1981 *Chanel Solitaire*
1984 *The Master Of Ballantrae* (TV)
1985 *The Doctor And The Devils;
Florence Nightingale* (TV)
1987 *Brenda Starr; The Living
Daylights\**
1988 *Hawks*
1989 *Licence To Kill\**
1990 *The King's Whore*
1991 *The Rocketeer*
1993 *Hot Shots 2*

**DANSON, Ted**
(1947–   ) USA

1979 *The Onion Field*
1980 *The Women's Room* (TV); *Once
Upon A Spy* (TV)
1981 *Our Family Business* (TV); *Body
Heat\**
1982 *The Good Witch Of Laurel
Canyon* (TV); *Creepshow*
1983 *Cowboy* (TV)

**DANSON, Ted** (cont.)
1984 *Something About Amelia* (TV)
1985 *Little Treasure*
1986 *Just Between Friends; When The Bough Breaks* (TV); *A Fine Mess*
1987 *We Are The Children* (TV); *Three Men And A Baby**
1989 *Cousins; Dad*
1990 *Three Men And A Little Lady*
1993 *Made In America*


**DARNELL, Linda**
real name: Manetta Darnell
(1921–65) USA

1939 *Elsa Maxwell's Hotel For Women; Daytime Wife*
1940 *Brigham Young — Frontiersman; Star Dust; Chad Hanna; The Mark Of Zorro*
1941 *Blood And Sand; Rise And Shine*
1942 *The Loves Of Edgar Allan Poe*
1943 *City Without Men; The Song Of Bernadette*; Showbusiness At War* (short)
1944 *Buffalo Bill; It Happened Tomorrow; Summer Storm; Sweet And Low Down*
1945 *All-Star Bond Rally* (short); *The Great John L* (UK: *A Man Called Sullivan*); *Hangover Square; Fallen Angel*
1946 *Anna And The King Of Siam; My Darling Clementine*; Centennial Summer*
1947 *Forever Amber*
1948 *The Walls Of Jericho; Unfaithfully Yours*
1949 *A Letter To Three Wives*; Everybody Does It; Slattery's Hurricane*
1950 *No Way Out; Two Flags West*
1951 *The Thirteenth Letter; The Lady Pays Off; The Guy Who Came Back*
1952 *Blackbeard The Pirate; Night Without Sleep; Saturday Island*
1953 *Donne Proibite* (UK: *Forbidden Women*); *Second Chance*
1954 *This Is My Love*
1955 *Gli Ultimi Cinque Minuti*

1956 *Dakota Incident*
1957 *Zero Hour*
1963 *El Valle De Las Espados*
1965 *Black Spurs*


**DAVIS, Bette**
real name: Ruth Elizabeth Davis
(1908–89)

1931 *Bad Sister; Seed; Waterloo Bridge; Way Back Home* (UK: *Old Greatheart*)
1932 *Hell's House; So Big; The Dark Horse; The Menace; The Man Who Played God* (UK: *The Silent Voice*); *The Rich Are Always With Us; Cabin In The Cotton; Three On A Match*
1933 *20,000 Years In Sing Sing; Parachute Jumper; Ex-Lady; The Working Man; Bureau Of Missing Persons*
1934 *Fashions Of 1934* (UK: *Fashion Follies Of 1934*); *The Big Shakedown; Jimmy The Gent; Fog Over Frisco; Housewife; Of Human Bondage*
1935 *Bordertown; Front Page Woman; Special Agent; Dangerous*; The Girl From Tenth Avenue* (UK: *Men On Her Mind*)
1936 *The Petrified Forest*; The Golden Arrow; Satan Met A Lady; A Day At Santa Anita* (short)
1937 *Kid Galahad; Marked Woman; That Certain Woman; It's Love I'm After*
1938 *Jezebel*; The Sisters*
1939 *The Private Lives Of Elizabeth And Essex*; Dark Victory*; Juarez; The Old Maid**
1940 *All This And Heaven Too; The Letter**
1941 *The Little Foxes*; The Great Lie; Shining Through; The Bride Came COD; The Man Who Came To Dinner*
1942 *In This Our Life; Now Voyager**
1943 *Watch On The Rhine; Thank Your Lucky Stars; Showbusiness At War* (documentary); *A Present*

With A Future (documentary);
Stars On Horseback
(documentary); Old Acquaintance
1944 Mr Skeffington; Hollywood
Canteen
1945 The Corn Is Green
1946 Deception; A Stolen Life
1948 Winter Meeting; June Bride
1949 Beyond The Forest
1950 All About Eve*
1951 Another Man's Poison; Payment
On Demand
1952 Phone Call From A Stranger; The
Star
1955 The Virgin Queen
1956 The Catered Affair (UK: The
Wedding Breakfast); Storm
Center
1959 The Scapegoat; John Paul Jones
1961 A Pocketful Of Miracles
1962 What Ever Happened To Baby
Jane?*
1963 La Noia (UK: The Empty Canvas)
1964 Dead Ringer (UK: Dead Image);
Hush...Hush, Sweet Charlotte;
Where Love Has Gone
1965 The Nanny
1967 The Anniversary
1969 Connecting Rooms
1971 Bunny O'Hare
1972 Madame Sin (TV); The Judge And
Jake Wyler (TV); La Scopone
Scientifico (UK: The Scientific
Cardplayer)
1973 Scream, Pretty Peggy (TV)
1976 Burnt Offerings; The
Disappearance Of Aimee (TV)
1978 The Dark Secret Of Harvest
Home (TV); Return To Witch
Mountain; Death On The Nile
1979 Strangers: The Story Of A Mother
And A Daughter (TV)
1980 White Momma (TV); The Watcher
In The Woods
1981 Skyward (TV); Family Reunion
(TV)
1982 A Piano For Mrs Cimino (TV);
Little Gloria...Happy At Last (TV)
1983 Right Of Way (TV)
1985 Murder With Mirrors (TV); Hotel
(TV)

1986 As Summers Die (TV); Directed
By William Wyler (documentary)
1987 The Whales Of August
1989 The Wicked Stepmother; Hairway
To The Stars (documentary)

## DAVIS, Geena
real name: Virginia Davis
(1959– ) USA

1982 Tootsie*
1985 Fletch; Secret Weapons (TV);
Transylvania 6-5000
1986 The Fly*
1988 Beetlejuice*; The Accidental
Tourist*
1989 Earth Girls Are Easy
1990 Quick Change
1991 Thelma & Louise*
1992 A League Of Their Own; Hero
(UK: Accidental Hero)

## DAVIS, Judy
(1956– ) Australia

1977 High Rolling
1979 My Brilliant Career
1981 Hoodwink; The Winter Of Our
Dreams
1982 Who Dares Wins
1984 A Passage To India*
1986 Kangaroo
1987 High Tide
1988 Georgia
1990 Alice
1991 Impromptu; Barton Fink; One
Against The Wind (TV); Where
Angels Fear To Tread; The Naked
Lunch
1992 Husbands And Wives; On My
Own

## DAVIS, Sammy (Jnr)
(1925–90) USA

1933 Rufus Jones For President (short)
1934 Season's Greetings (short)
1956 The Benny Goodman Story
1958 Anna Lucasta
1959 Porgy And Bess
1960 Ocean's Eleven*; Pepe

**DAVIS, Sammy (Jnr)** (cont.)
1962 *The Threepenny Opera; Convicts Four* (UK:*Reprieve!*); *Sergeants Three*
1963 *Johnny Cool*
1964 *Robin And The Seven Hoods; Nightmare In The Sun*
1966 *A Man Called Adam*
1968 *Salt And Pepper; Sweet Charity\**
1969 *Man Without Mercy; The Pigeon* (TV)
1970 *One More Time*
1971 *The Trackers* (TV)
1973 *Poor Devil* (TV); *Save The Children*
1979 *Sammy Stops The World*
1981 *The Cannonball Run\**
1982 *Heidi's Song* (voice only)
1983 *The Cannonball Run II*
1984 *Cry Of The City*
1985 *Alice In Wonderland* (TV); *That's Dancing*
1986 *The Perils Of PK*
1988 *Moon Over Parador*
1989 *Tap*
1990 *The Kid Who Loved Christmas* (TV)

## DAY, Doris
real name: Doris Kappelhoff
(1924– ) USA

1941 *Les Brown And His Orchestra* (short)
1948 *Romance On The High Seas* (UK: *It's Magic*)
1949 *My Dream Is Yours; It's A Great Feeling*
1950 *Young Man With A Horn* (UK: *Young Man Of Music*); *The West Point Story* (UK: *Fine And Dandy*); *Tea For Two; Storm Warning*
1951 *Lullaby Of Broadway; Starlift; On Moonlight Bay; I'll See You In My Dreams*
1952 *The Winning Team; April In Paris; Screen Snapshots No 206* (documentary)
1953 *By The Light Of The Silvery Moon; Calamity Jane; So You Want A Television* (documentary)

1954 *Lucky Me; Young At Heart*
1955 *Love Me Or Leave Me\**
1956 *The Man Who Knew Too Much; Julie*
1957 *The Pajama Game*
1958 *Teacher's Pet; The Tunnel Of Love*
1959 *It Happened To Jane; Pillow Talk\**
1960 *Midnight Lace; Please Don't Eat The Daisies*
1961 *Lover Come Back*
1962 *That Touch Of Mink; Billy Rose's Jumbo*
1963 *The Thrill Of It All; Move Over Darling*
1964 *Send Me No Flowers*
1965 *Do Not Disturb*
1966 *The Glass Bottom Boat*
1967 *Caprice; The Ballad Of Josie*
1968 *Where Were You When The Lights Went Out; With Six You Get Egg Roll*

## DAY-LEWIS, Daniel
(1958– ) UK

1971 *Sunday, Bloody Sunday\**
1982 *Gandhi\**
1984 *The Bounty\**
1985 *My Beautiful Laundrette\*; A Room With A View\*; The Insurance Man* (TV)
1986 *Nanou*
1988 *The Unbearable Lightness Of Being; Stars And Bars*
1989 *My Left Foot\*; Eversmile New Jersey*
1992 *The Last Of The Mohicans\**
1993 *Age Of Innocence*

## DEAN, James Byron
(1931–55) USA

1951 *Fixed Bayonets*
1952 *Sailor Beware; Has Anybody Seen My Gal?*
1955 *East Of Eden\*; Rebel Without A Cause\**
1956 *Giant\**

## DE HAVILLAND, Olivia Mary
(1916–  ) UK

1935 *A Midsummer Night's Dream\*; Alibi Ike; The Irish In Us; Captain Blood\**
1936 *Anthony Adverse; The Charge Of The Light Brigade; A Day At Santa Anita* (documentary)
1937 *Call It A Day; The Great Garrick; It's Love I'm After*
1938 *Gold Is Where You Find It; The Adventures Of Robin Hood\*; Four's A Crowd; Hard To Get*
1939 *Wings Of The Navy; Dodge City; The Private Lives Of Elizabeth And Essex\*; Gone With The Wind\**
1940 *Raffles; My Love Came Back; Santa Fe Trail*
1941 *The Strawberry Blonde; Hold Back The Dawn\*; They Died With Their Boots On*
1942 *The Male Animal; In This Our Life*
1943 *Thank Your Lucky Stars; Stars On Horseback* (documentary); *Princess O'Rourke; Government Girl*
1946 *The Well-Groomed Bride; To Each His Own; Devotion; The Dark Mirror*
1948 *The Snake Pit\**
1949 *The Heiress\**
1952 *My Cousin Rachel*
1955 *That Lady; Not As A Stranger\**
1956 *The Ambassador's Daughter*
1958 *The Proud Rebel*
1959 *Libel!*
1962 *Light In The Piazza*
1964 *Hush, Hush...Sweet Charlotte; Lady In A Cage*
1970 *The Adventurers*
1972 *The Screaming Woman* (TV); *Pope Joan*
1977 *Airport '77*
1978 *The Swarm; The Fifth Musketeer*
1982 *Murder Is Easy; The Royal Romance Of Charles And Diana* (TV)
1986 *Anastasia: The Mystery Of Anna* (TV)
1988 *The Woman He Loved* (TV)

## DELON, Alain
(1935–  ) France

1956 *Quand La Femme S'En Mêle* (UK: *Send A Woman When The Devil Fails*)
1958 *Sois Belle Et Tais-Toi* (UK: *Blonde For Danger*); *Christine; Faible Femmes* (UK: *Women Are Weak*)
1959 *Le Chemin Des Ecoliers; Plein Soleil* (UK: *Purple Noon*)
1960 *Rocco And His Brothers*
1961 *Che Gioia Vivere; Les Amours Célèbres; The Eclipse*
1962 *The Devil And The Ten Commandments; Mélodie En Sous-Sol* (UK: *The Big Snatch*); *Il Gattopardo\** (UK: *The Leopard*); *Carambolages*
1963 *The Black Tulip*
1964 *Les Félins* (UK: *The Love Cage*); *L'Insoumis; The Yellow Rolls-Royce; L'Amour A La Mer*
1965 *Once A Thief*
1966 *Paris Brûle T'Il?* (UK: *Is Paris Burning?*); *Lost Command; Texas Across The River; Les Aventuriers* (UK: *The Last Adventure*)
1967 *Le Samourai; Histoires Extraordinaires* (UK: *Tales of Mystery*); *Diabolically Yours*
1968 *Girl On A Motorcycle; Adieu L'Ami* (UK: *Farewell Friend*); *La Piscine* (UK: *The Sinners*)
1969 *Jeff; The Sicilian Clan*
1970 *Borsalino; Le Cercle Rouge; Madly*
1971 *Doucement Les Basses!; Red Sun; Fantasia Chez Les Ploucs; La Veuve Couderc*
1972 *The Assassination Of Trotsky; Un Flic* (UK: *Dirty Money*); *Le Prima Notte Di Quiete; Traitement Du Choc* (UK: *The Doctor In The Nude*); *Il Etait Une Fois Un Flic*
1973 *Tony Arzenta/Big Guns; Deux Hommes Dans La Ville; Les Granges Brûlées* (UK: *The Investigator*)
1974 *La Race Des 'Seigneurs'; Les Seins De Glace; Borsalino & Co*

**DELON, Alain** (cont.)
(UK: *Blood On The Streets*); *Le Gifle*
1975 *Zorro; Le Gitan; Flic Story; Creezy*
1976 *Mr Klein; Le Gang; Comme Un Boomerang*
1977 *America At The Movies* (narrator only); *L'Homme Pressé* (UK: *The Hurried Man*); *Armageddon; Mort D'Un Pourri; Attention, Les Enfants Regardent*
1978 *Le Toubib*
1979 *Harmonie; The Concorde—Airport '79; Teheran Incident/Teheran 1943*
1980 *Trois Hommes A Abattre* (UK: *Three Men To Kill*)
1981 *Pour Le Peau D'Un Flic* (also director)
1982 *Le Choc*
1983 *Le Battant* (UK: *The Fighter*); *Swann In Love*
1984 *Notre Histoire* (UK: *Our Story*); *Separate Rooms*
1985 *The Untouchable; Parôle De Flic; Les Mocassins Italiens*
1986 *Le Passage*
1988 *Ne Reveillez Pas Un Flic Qui Dort* (UK: *Let Sleeping Cops Lie*)
1990 *Nouvelle Vague; Dancing Machine*
1992 *Le Retour De Casanova*
1993 *Dérapage*

**DE MORNAY, Rebecca**
(1962– ) USA

1982 *One From The Heart*
1983 *Risky Business\*; Testament*
1985 *The Trip To Bountiful; The Slugger's Wife; Runaway Train*
1986 *The Murders In The Rue Morgue* (TV)
1987 *Crack; And God Created Woman; Beauty And The Beast*
1988 *Feds*
1989 *Dealers*
1990 *By Dawn's Early Light* (TV); *Grand Tour(TV)*
1991 *Backdraft\*; An Inconvenient Woman* (TV)

1992 *The Hand That Rocks The Cradle*
1993 *Beyond Innocence*

**DENEUVE, Catherine**
real name: Catherine Dorléac
(1943– ) France

1956 *Les Collégiennes*
1959 *Les Petits Chats*
1960 *L'Homme A Femmes; Les Portes Claquent; Ce Soir Ou Jamais*
1961 *Les Parisiennes*
1962 *La Vice Et La Vertu* (UK: *Vice And Virtue*); *Et Satan Conduit Le Bal; Vacances Portugaises*
1963 *Les Plus Belles Escroqueries Du Monde*
1964 *Les Parapluies Du Cherbourg* (UK: *The Umbrellas Of Cherbourg*); *La Chasse A L'Homme; Un Monsieur De Compagnie; Le Costanza Della Ragione*
1965 *Repulsion\*; Le Chant Du Monde; La Vie De Château; Das Liebeskarusell* (UK: *Who Wants To Sleep?*)
1966 *Les Créatures*
1967 *Belle De Jour\*; Les Desmoiselles De Rochefort* (UK: *The Young Girls Of Rochefort*)
1968 *Benjamin; Manon 70; Mayerling; La Chamade*
1969 *The April Fools; La Sirène Du Mississippi* (UK: *Mississippi Mermaid*); *Don't Be Blue*
1970 *Tristana; Peau D'Ane* (UK: *Once Upon A Time*); *Henri Langlois* (documentary)
1971 *Liza; Ça N'Arrive Qu'Aux Autres*
1972 *Un Flic* (UK: *Dirty Money*); *Melampo*
1973 *L'Evènement Le Plus Important Depuis L'Homme A Marché Sur La Lune* (UK: *The Slightly Pregnant Man*); *Touche Pas La Femme Blanche*
1974 *Fatti Di Gente Perbene; Zig-Zag; La Femme Aux Bottes Rouges*
1975 *Hustle; Le Sauvage; L'Agression*

1976 *Il Cassotto; Si C'Etait A Refaire* (UK: *Second Chance*)
1977 *March Or Die!*
1978 *Ecoute Voir; L'Argent Des Autres; Si Je Suis Comme Ça, C'Est La Faute De Papa; Anima Persa*
1979 *A Nous Deux; Ils Sont Grands, Ses Petits*
1980 *Courage Fuyons; Le Dernier Métro* (UK: *The Last Metro*); *Je Vous Aime*
1981 *Le Choix Des Armes; Reporters; Hotel Des Amériques; Daisy Chain*
1982 *Le Choc; L'Africain*
1983 *The Hunger; Bon Plaisir*
1984 *Fort Saganne; Parôles Et Musiques*
1985 *Speriamo Che Sia Femina* (UK: *Let's Hope It's A Girl*)
1986 *Le Mauvaise Herbe; Le Lieu De Crime*
1987 *Agent Trouble*
1988 *Drôle Endroit Pour Une Rencontre* (UK: *Strange Place To Meet*); *Hotel Panique; The Man Who Loves Zoos; Frequence Meurtre*
1989 *Helmut Newton: Frames From The Edge* (documentary)
1991 *La Reine Blanche*
1992 *Indochine*
1993 *Ma Saison Préférée*

## DE NIRO, Robert
(1943– ) USA

1965 *Trois Chambres A Manhattan*
1966 *The Wedding Party*
1968 *Greetings*
1969 *Bloody Mama*
1970 *Hi, Mom!*
1971 *Jennifer On My Mind; The Gang That Couldn't Shoot Straight; Born To Win*
1973 *Bang The Drum Slowly; Mean Streets*
1974 *Sam's Song* (aka *The Swap*); *The Godfather Part II**
1976 *Taxi Driver*; Novecento** (UK: *1900*); *The Last Tycoon*
1977 *New York, New York**

1978 *The Deer Hunter**
1980 *Raging Bull**
1981 *True Confessions*
1982 *The King Of Comedy*; Elia Kazan, Outsider* (documentary)
1983 *Once Upon A Time In America**
1984 *Falling In Love*
1985 *Brazil**
1986 *The Mission*
1987 *Angel Heart; The Untouchables*; Dear America* (voice only); *Hello Actors Studio* (documentary)
1988 *Midnight Run*; Jacknife*
1989 *Stanley And Iris; We're No Angels*
1990 *Goodfellas*; Awakenings**
1991 *Guilty By Suspicion; Backdraft*; Cape Fear**
1992 *The Mistress; Night And The City; Mad Dog And Glory*
1993 *This Boy's Life; A Bronx Tale* (also director)

## DEPARDIEU, Gérard Xavier
(1947– ) France

1965 *Le Beatnik Et Le Minet*
1967 *Rendez-Vous A Badenberg* (TV)
1971 *Nathalie Granger; Le Cri Du Cormoran Le Soir Au-Dessus Des Jonques; Un Peu Du Soleil Dans L'Eau Froide*
1972 *Le Viager; Le Tueur; La Scoumoune* (UK: *The Scoundrel*); *Au Rendez-Vous De La Mort Joyeuse; L'Affaire Dominici; Deux Hommes Dans La Ville*
1973 *Un Monsieur Bien Rangé; Rude Journée Pour La Reine; Les Gaspards; Les Valseuses* (UK: *Making It*); *La Femme Du Gange; L'Inconnu* (TV)
1974 *Stavisky; Vincent, François, Paul Et Les Autres*
1975 *Pas Si Méchant Que Ça; Sept Morts Sur Ordonnance; Maitresse; La Dernière Femme* (UK: *The Last Woman*); *Je T'Aime Moi Non Plus* (UK: *I Love You, I Don't*)
1976 *Barocco; René La Canne; Vera Baxter; Novecento** (UK: *1900*)

**DEPARDIEU, Gérard Xavier** (cont.)
1977 *Le Camion; Dites-Lui Que J'Aime* (UK: *This Sweet Sickness*); *La Nuit, Tous Les Chats Sont Gris; Préparez Vos Mouchoirs* (UK: *Get Out Your Handkerchiefs*); *Rêve De Singe; Die Linkshandige Frau* (UK: *The Left-Handed Woman*)
1978 *Violenta; Le Sucre; Les Chiens; Le Grand Embouteillage*
1979 *Loulou; Rosy La Bourrasque; Buffet Froid*
1980 *Mon Oncle D'Amérique; Le Dernier Métro* (UK: *The Last Metro*); *Je Vous Aime; Inspector La Bavure*
1981 *Le Choix Des Armes; La Femme D'A Côté* (UK: *The Woman Next Door*); *La Chèvre*
1982 *Le Retour De Martin Guerre; Le Grand Frère; Danton\**
1983 *La Lune Dans Le Caniveau* (UK: *The Moon In The Gutter*); *Le Compères* (UK: *Father's Day*)
1984 *Fort Saganne; Le Tartuffe* (also director); *Rive Droite, Rive Gauche*
1985 *Police; Une Femme Ou Deux*
1986 *Tenuee De Soirée; Jean De Florette\*; Les Fugitifs*
1987 *Sous Le Soleil De Satan* (UK: *Under Satan's Sun*)
1988 *Drôle Endroit Pour Une Recontre* (UK: *Strange Place To Meet*); *Camille Claudel; Deux*
1989 *Trop Belle Pour Toi\*; I Want To Go Home*
1990 *Cyrano De Bergerac\*; Green Card\*; Uranus*
1991 *Merci La Vie; Mon Père, Ce Héros; Tous Les Matins Du Monde*
1992 *1492: The Conquest Of Paradise*
1993 *Germinal; Hélas Pour Moi; A Simple Formality*

**DEPP, Johnny**
(1963– ) USA

1984 *A Nightmare On Elm Street\**
1985 *Private Resort*

1986 *Platoon\*; Slow Burn* (TV)
1990 *Cry Baby; Edward Scissorhands\**
1991 *Freddy's Dead: A Nightmare On Elm Street 6*
1992 *Arizona Dream*
1993 *Benny And Joon; Gilbert Grape*

**DEREK, Bo**
real name: Mary Collins
(1956– ) USA

1975 *And Once Upon A Time*
1977 *Orca–Killer Whale*
1978 *Love You*
1979 *'10'\**
1980 *A Change Of Seasons*
1981 *Tarzan — The Apeman*
1984 *Bolero*
1990 *Ghosts Can't Do It*
1992 *Chocolate; California Dreaming*
1993 *Woman Of Desire*

**DERN, Bruce**
(1936– ) USA

1960 *Wild River*
1961 *The Crimebusters*
1964 *Bedtime Story; Marnie; Hush, Hush...Sweet Charlotte*
1967 *The St Valentine's Day Massacre; The War Wagon; The Wild Angels; Waterhole No 3; Will Penny; The Trip; Rebel Rousers; Hang 'Em High*
1968 *Psych-Out*
1969 *Support Your Local Sheriff; Castle Keep; Number One; They Shoot Horses Don't They?\*; Bloody Mama*
1970 *Drive, He Said; Cycle Savages; Sam Hill — Who Killed The Mysterious Mr Foster?* (TV)
1971 *The Incredible Two-Headed Transplant; Silent Running*
1972 *The Cowboys; Thumb Tripping; The King Of Marvin Gardens*
1973 *The Laughing Policeman* (UK: *An Investigation Of Murder*)
1974 *The Great Gatsby*

1975 *Smile; Posse; Won Ton Ton — The Dog Who Saved Hollywood*
1976 *Folies Bourgeoises* (UK: *The Twist*); *Family Plot; Black Sunday*
1978 *Coming Home\*; The Driver*
1979 *Middle Age Crazy*
1980 *Tattoo*
1981 *Harry Tracy — Desperado*
1982 *That Championship Season*
1984 *On The Edge*
1985 *Space* (TV); *Toughlove* (TV)
1987 *The Big Town; World Gone Wild; Uncle Tom's Cabin* (TV); *Roses Are For The Rich* (TV)
1988 *1969*
1989 *The 'burbs\*; Trenchcoat In Paradise* (TV)
1990 *After Dark, My Sweet; The Court Martial Of Jackie Robinson* (TV)
1991 *Carolina Skeletons* (TV)
1992 *Diggstown* (UK: *Midnight Sting*)
1993 *It's Nothing Personal* (TV)

## DE VITO, Danny
real name: Daniel Michael De Vito
(1944– ) USA

1971 *La Mortadella* (UK: *Lady Liberty*)
1073 *Scalawag; Hurry Up Or I'll Be Thirty*
1975 *One Flew Over The Cuckoo's Nest\*; Minestrone* (short, also director)
1976 *The Van; Car Wash*
1977 *The Sound Sleeper* (short, also director); *The World's Greatest Lover*
1978 *Goin' South*
1979 *Valentine* (TV)
1981 *Going Ape*
1983 *Terms of Endearment\**
1984 *Romancing The Stone\*; The Ratings Game* (TV) (also director); *Johnny Dangerously*
1985 *Jewel Of The Nile\*; Head Office*
1986 *Ruthless People; Wise Guys; My Little Pony* (voice only)
1987 *Tin Men\*; Throw Momma From The Train\** (also director)
1988 *Twins\**

1989 *The War Of The Roses\** (also director)
1991 *Other People's Money*
1992 *Jack The Bear; Batman Returns\*; Hoffa\** (also director)

See also directors listing

## DICKINSON, Angie
real name: Angeline Brown
(1931– ) USA

1954 *Lucky Me*
1955 *The Man With The Gun* (UK:*The Trouble Shooter*); *The Return Of Jack Slade* (UK: *Texas Rose*); *Tennessee's Partner; Hidden Guns*
1956 *Gun The Man Down; The Black Whip; Tension At Table Rock; The Unfinished Task; Down Liberty Road*
1957 *Calypso Joe; I Married A Woman; Shoot-Out At Medicine Bend; Run Of The Arrow* (voice only)
1958 *China Gate; Cry Terror!; Frontier Rangers*
1959 *Rio Bravo\*; The Bramble Bush*
1960 *A Fever In The Blood; Ocean's Eleven\**
1961 *The Sins Of Rachel Cade; I'll Give My Life; Jessica*
1962 *Rome Adventure* (UK: *Lovers Must Learn*)
1963 *Captain Newman MD*
1964 *The Killers*
1965 *The Art Of Love*
1966 *The Chase; Cast A Giant Shadow; The Poppy Is Also A Flower* (UK: *Danger Grows Wild*)
1967 *Point Blank\*; The Last Challenge* (UK: *The Pistolero Of Red River*)
1968 *A Case Of Libel* (TV)
1969 *Sam Whiskey; The Love War* (TV); *Young Billy Young*
1970 *Some Kind Of Nut*
1971 *The Resurrection Of Zachary Wheeler* (TV); *Thief* (TV); *See The Man Run* (TV); *Pretty Maids All In A Row*

**DICKINSON, Angie** (cont.)

1972 *Un Homme Est Mort* (UK: *The Outside Man*); *The Scorpio Scarab*

1973 *The Norliss Tapes* (TV)

1974 *Pray For The Wildcats* (TV); *Big Bad Mama*

1977 *A Sensitive Passionate Man* (TV)

1978 *Le Labyrinthe; Overboard* (TV)

1979 *L'Homme En Colère; Klondike Fever; The Suicide's Wife* (TV)

1980 *Dressed To Kill*

1981 *Death Hunt; Charlie Chan And The Curse Of The Dragon Queen; Dial M For Murder* (TV)

1982 *One Shoe Makes It Murder* (TV)

1983 *Jealousy* (TV)

1984 *A Touch Of Scandal* (TV)

1987 *Still Watch* (TV); *Big Bad Mama II; Police Story: The Freeway Killings* (TV)

1988 *Once Upon A Texas Train* (TV)

1989 *Prime Target* (TV)

1990 *Fire And Rain* (TV)

1992 *Treacherous Crossing* (TV)

**DIETRICH, Marlene**
real name: Maria Magdalene Dietrich
(1901–92) Germany

1922 *So Sind Die Männer/Der Kleine Napoleon*

1923 *Tragödie Der Liebe; Der Sprung Ins Leben; Der Mensch Am Wege*

1925 *Die Freudlose Gasse* (UK: *Joyless Street*); *Manon Lescaut*

1926 *Eine DuBarry Von Heute* (UK: *A Modern DuBarry*); *Madame Wunscht Keine Kinder; Kopf Hoch; Charly!; Der Juxbaron*

1927 *Seine Grosster Bluff; Cafe Electric*

1928 *Prinzessin Olala; Die Glückliche Mutter* (short)

1929 *Die Frau, Der Nach Der Man Sich Sehnt; Ich Küsse Ihre Hand, Madame; Liebesnachte; Das Schiff Der Verlorenen Menschen*

1930 *Der Blaue Engel** (UK: *The Blue Angel*); *Morocco*

1931 *Dishonored*

1932 *Shanghai Express; Blonde Venus*

1933 *The Song Of Songs*

1934 *The Scarlet Empress*

1935 *The Devil Is A Woman*

1936 *Desire; The Garden Of Allah*

1937 *Knight Without Armour; Angel*

1939 *Destry Rides Again*

1940 *Seven Sinners*

1941 *Manpower; The Flame Of New Orleans*

1942 *The Lady Is Willing; The Spoilers; Pittsburgh*

1943 *Screen Snapshots No 103; Showbusiness At War* (both documentaries)

1944 *Follow The Boys; Kismet*

1946 *Martin Roumagnac*

1947 *Golden Earrings*

1948 *A Foreign Affair*

1949 *Jigsaw*

1950 *Stage Fright*

1951 *No Highway* (UK: *No Highway In The Sky*)

1952 *Rancho Notorious*

1956 *Around The World In 80 Days**; *The Monte Carlo Story*

1957 *Witness For The Prosecution**

1958 *Touch Of Evil**

1961 *Judgement At Nuremberg**

1962 *The Black Fox* (narrator only)

1964 *Paris When It Sizzles*

1978 *Just A Gigolo*

1984 *Marlene* (documentary)

**DILLON, Matt**
(1964– ) USA

1979 *Over The Edge*

1980 *Little Darlings; My Bodyguard*

1981 *Fallen Angel* (TV); *Liar's Moon*

1982 *The Great American Fourth Of July And Other Disasters* (TV); *The Outsiders**; *Tex*

1983 *Rumblefish*

1984 *The Flamingo Kid*

1985 *Rebel; Target*

1986 *Native Son*

1987 *The Big Town; Dear America* (voice only)

1988 *Kansas*

1989 *Bloodhounds Of Broadway; Drugstore Cowboy*

1991  *A Kiss Before Dying; Women And Men: In Love There Are No Rules* (TV)
1992  *Singles*
1993  *Mr Wonderful; Golden Gate*

## DONAT, Robert
(1905–58) UK

1932  *Men Of Tomorrow; That Night In London*
1933  *Cash; The Private Life Of Henry VIII\**
1934  *The Count Of Monte Cristo*
1935  *The 39 Steps\**
1936  *The Ghost Goes West*
1937  *Knight Without Armour*
1938  *The Citadel\**
1939  *Goodbye Mr Chips\**
1941  *Cavalcade Of The Academy Awards* (documentary)
1942  *The Young Mr Pitt*
1943  *The Adventures Of Tartu*
1945  *Perfect Strangers*
1947  *Captain Boycott; The British— Are They Artistic?* (documentary)
1948  *The Winslow Boy*
1949  *The Cure For Love* (also director)
1951  *The Magic Box*
1953  *Royal Heritage* (narrator only)
1954  *Lease Of Life*
1956  *The Stained Glass At Fairford* (short)
1958  *Inn Of The Sixth Happiness*

## DOUGLAS, Kirk
real name: Issur Danielovich
(1916–  ) USA

1946  *The Strange Love Of Martha Ivers*
1947  *I Walk Alone; Out Of The Past* (UK: *Build My Gallows High*); *Mourning Becomes Electra*
1948  *My Dear Secretary; The Walls Of Jericho*
1949  *A Letter To Three Wives\*; Champion*
1950  *Young Man With A Horn* (UK: *Young Man Of Music*); *The Glass Menagerie*

1951  *Along The Great Divide; Detective Story; The Big Carnival* (UK: *Ace In The Hole*)
1952  *The Big Sky; The Big Trees; The Bad And The Beautiful\**
1953  *The Story Of Three Loves; The Juggler; Act Of Love*
1954  *20,000 Leagues Under The Sea\*; Ulysses*
1955  *Man Without A Star; The Racers* (UK: *Such Men Are Dangerous*); *The Indian Fighter*
1956  *Lust For Life\**
1957  *Gunfight At The OK Corral; Paths Of Glory\*; Top Secret Affair* (UK: *Their Secret Affair*)
1958  *The Vikings\*; Last Train From Gun Hill*
1959  *The Devil's Disciple*
1960  *Spartacus\*; Strangers When We Meet*
1961  *The Last Sunset; Town Without Pity*
1962  *Lonely Are The Brave; Two Weeks In Another Town*
1963  *The List Of Adrian Messenger; For Love Or Money; The Hook; Seven Days In May\**
1965  *In Harm's Way; The Heroes Of Telemark*
1966  *Paris Brûle T'Il?* (UK: *Is Paris Burning?*); *Cast A Giant Shadow*
1967  *The War Wagon; The Way West*
1968  *A Lovely Way To Die* (UK: *A Lovely Way To Go*); *The Brotherhood; French Lunch* (short)
1969  *The Arrangement*
1970  *There Was A Crooked Man; A Gunfight*
1971  *The Light At The Edge Of The World; Catch Me A Spy*
1972  *A Man To Respect* (UK: *The Master Touch*)
1973  *Mousey* (TV) (UK: *Cat And Mouse*); *Scalawag* (also director)
1974  *Once Is Not Enough*
1975  *Posse* (also director)
1976  *Victory At Entebbe*
1977  *Holocaust 2000*
1978  *The Fury*

**DOUGLAS, Kirk** (cont.)
1979 *The Villain* (UK: *Cactus Jack*)
1980 *Home Movies; Saturn 3; The Final Countdown*
1982 *Remembrance Of Love* (TV); *The Man From Snowy River*
1983 *Eddie Macon's Run*
1984 *Draw!* (TV)
1985 *Amos* (TV)
1986 *Tough Guys*
1988 *Inherit The Wind* (TV)
1991 *Oscar; Welcome To Veraz*


## DOUGLAS, Melvyn

real name: Michael Hesselberg
(1901–81) USA

1931 *Tonight Or Never*
1932 *Prestige; The Wiser Sex; Broken Wing; The Old Dark House; As You Desire Me*
1933 *Nagana; The Vampire Bat*
1934 *Counsellor At Law; Dangerous Corner; Woman In The Dark*
1935 *Mary Burns — Fugitive; She Married Her Boss; Annie Oakley; People's Enemy*
1936 *The Lone Wolf Returns; The Gorgeous Hussy; And So They Were Married; Theodora Goes Wild*
1937 *Angel; Captains Courageous\*; Women Of Glamour; I Met Him In Paris*
1938 *Arsene Lupin Returns; The Toy Wife* (UK: *Frou Frou*); *Fast Company; The Shining Hour; There's Always A Woman; There's That Woman Again; That Certain Age*
1939 *Good Girls Go To Paris; Tell No Tales; Ninotchka\*; The Amazing Mr Williams*
1940 *Too Many Husbands* (UK: *My Two Husbands*); *Third Finger, Left Hand; He Stayed For Breakfast*
1941 *Our Wife; Two-Faced Woman; That Uncertain Feeling; A Woman's Face; This Thing Called Love* (UK: *Married But Single*)

1942 *They All Kissed The Bride; We Were Dancing*
1943 *Three Hearts For Julia*
1947 *The Guilt Of Janet Ames; Sea Of Grass; Make Way For Youth* (narrator only)
1948 *Mr Blandings Builds His Dream House; My Own True Love*
1949 *A Woman's Secret; The Great Sinner*
1950 *My Forbidden Past*
1951 *On The Loose*
1954 *You Can Win Elections* (narrator only)
1961 *The Highest Commandment* (narrator only)
1962 *Billy Budd*
1963 *Hud\**
1964 *Advance To The Rear* (UK: *Company Of Cowards*); *The Americanization Of Emily*
1965 *Rapture; The Fast I Have Chosen* (narrator only)
1967 *Hotel; Companions In Nightmare* (TV)
1970 *I Never Sang For My Father; Hunters Are For Killing* (TV)
1971 *Death Takes A Holiday* (TV); *The Going Up Of David Lev* (TV)
1972 *The Candidate; One Is A Lonely Number*
1973 *Death Squad* (TV)
1974 *Murder Or Mercy* (TV)
1975 *Benjamin Franklin: The Statesman* (TV)
1976 *Le Locataire* (UK: *The Tenant*)
1977 *Twilight's Last Gleaming; Intimate Strangers* (TV)
1978 *Battered!* (TV)
1979 *The Changeling; The Seduction Of Joe Tynan; Being There*
1980 *Tell Me A Riddle*
1981 *The Hot Touch; Ghost Story*


## DOUGLAS, Michael Kirk

(1944–   ) USA

1968 *The Experiment* (TV)
1969 *Hail, Hero!*
1970 *Adam at 6AM*

1971 *Summertree; When Michael Calls* (TV)
1972 *Napoleon And Samantha; The Streets Of San Francisco* (TV)
1975 *One Flew Over The Cuckoo's Nest** (co-producer only)
1977 *Minestrone* (short)
1978 *Coma*
1979 *The China Syndrome*; Running*
1980 *It's My Turn; Three Mile Island* (documentary)
1983 *The Star Chamber*
1984 *Romancing The Stone*; Starman* (producer only)
1985 *A Chorus Line; The Jewel Of The Nile**
1987 *Fatal Attraction*; Wall Street**
1989 *The War Of The Roses*; Black Rain*
1990 *Flatliners* (producer only)
1991 *Shining Through*
1992 *Basic Instinct**
1993 *Falling Down; Made In America* (co-producer only)


## DREYFUSS, Richard
(1947–  ) USA

1967 *The Graduate*; Valley Of The Dolls*
1968 *Hello Down There; The Young Runaways*
1971 *Two For The Money* (TV)
1973 *American Graffiti*; Dillinger*
1974 *The Second Coming Of Suzanne; The Apprenticeship Of Duddy Kravitz*
1975 *Jaws*; Inserts*
1976 *Victory At Entebbe; The Sentinel*
1977 *The Goodbye Girl*; Close Encounters Of The Third Kind*
1978 *The Big Fix*
1980 *The Competition*
1981 *Whose Life Is It Anyway?*
1983 *The Buddy System*
1986 *Down And Out In Beverly Hills*
1987 *Stand By Me; Tin Men*; Nuts*; Stakeout*
1988 *Moon Over Parador*
1989 *Let It Ride; Always*

1990 *Postcards From The Edge*; Rosencrantz And Guildenstern Are Dead; Once Around*
1991 *What About Bob?; Prisoners Of Honor* (TV)
1993 *Lost In Yonkers; Stakeout 2*


## DUNAWAY, Dorothy Faye
(1941–  ) USA

1966 *The Happening; Hurry Sundown*
1967 *Bonnie And Clyde**
1968 *The Extraordinary Seaman; The Thomas Crown Affair*; Amanti* (UK: *A Place For Lovers*)
1969 *The Arrangement*
1970 *Little Big Man*; Puzzle Of A Downfall Child*
1971 *Doc; La Maison Sous Les Arbres* (UK: *The Deadly Trap*)
1972 *The Woman I Love* (TV)
1973 *Oklahoma Crude; The Three Musketeers**
1974 *After The Fall* (TV); *The Four Musketeers; Chinatown*; The Towering Inferno**
1975 *Three Days Of The Condor**
1976 *Network*; Voyage Of The Damned; The Disappearance Of Aimee* (TV)
1978 *Eyes Of Laura Mars*
1979 *The Champ; Arthur Miller — On Home Ground* (documentary)
1980 *The First Deadly Sin*
1981 *Mommie Dearest; Evita Peron* (TV)
1983 *The Wicked Lady*
1984 *Supergirl; Ordeal By Innocence; Ellis Island* (TV)
1985 *13 For Dinner(TV)*
1986 *Beverly Hills Madam(TV)*
1987 *Barfly; Casanova* (TV); *Raspberry Ripple* (TV)
1988 *Midnight Crossing; Burning Secret; The Match*
1989 *Helmut Newton: Frames From The Edge* (documentary); *Wait Until Spring, Bandini; On A Moonlit Night; The Cold Sassy Tree* (TV)

**DUNAWAY, Dorothy Faye** (cont.)

1990 *The Handmaid's Tale; The Two Jakes* (voice only)
1991 *Scorchers; Silhouette* (TV); *Three Weeks In Jerusalem*
1992 *Arizona Dream; The Temp*
1993 *Even Cowgirls Get The Blues*

## DUNNE, Irene
real name: Irene Dunn
(1898–1990) USA

1930 *Leathernecking* (UK: *Present Arms*)
1931 *Consolation Marriage* (UK: *Married In Haste*); *Cimarron\*; Bachelor Apartment; The Great Lover*
1932 *Symphony Of Six Million* (UK: *Melody Of Love*); *Thirteen Women; Back Street; The Stolen Jools* (UK: *The Slippery Pearls*) (short)
1933 *The Secret Of Madame Blanche; No Other Women; The Silver Chord; Ann Vickers; If I Were Free* (UK: *Behold We Live*)
1934 *This Man Is Mine; Stingaree; The Age Of Innocence*
1935 *Magnificent Obsession; Sweet Adeline; Roberta*
1936 *Show Boat; Theodora Goes Wild*
1937 *High Wide And Handsome; The Awful Truth\**
1938 *Joy Of Living*
1939 *Invitation To Happiness; Love Affair\*; When Tomorrow Comes*
1940 *My Favorite Wife*
1941 *Penny Serenade; Unfinished Business*
1942 *Lady In A Jam*
1943 *Showbusiness At War* (documentary); *A Guy Named Joe*
1944 *Together Again; The White Cliffs Of Dover*
1945 *Over 21*
1946 *Anna And The King Of Siam*
1947 *Life With Father\**
1948 *I Remember Mama*
1950 *Never A Dull Moment; The Mudlark*
1952 *It Grows On Trees*

## DURBIN, Deanna
real name: Edna Mae Durbin
(1921– ) Canada

1936 *Every Sunday; Three Smart Girls\**
1937 *One Hundred Men And A Girl\**
1938 *Mad About Music; That Certain Age*
1939 *Three Smart Girls Grow Up; First Love*
1940 *It's A Date; Spring Parade*
1941 *Nice Girl?; It Started With Eve*
1943 *The Amazing Mrs Holliday; Hers To Hold; His Butler's Sister*
1944 *The Shining Future* (short); *Christmas Holiday; Can't Help Singing*
1945 *Lady On A Train*
1946 *Because Of Him*
1947 *I'll Be Yours; Something In The Wind*
1948 *Up In Central Park; For The Love Of Mary*

## DUVALL, Robert
(1931– ) USA

1962 *To Kill A Mockingbird\**
1963 *Captain Newman MD; Nightmare In The Sun*
1966 *The Chase; Fame Is The Name Of The Game* (TV)
1967 *Cosa Nostra: An Arch Enemy Of The FBI* (TV)
1968 *Countdown; Bullitt\*; The Detective*
1969 *True Grit\*; The Rain People*
1970 *M\*A\*S\*H\*; Lawman*
1971 *The Revolutionary; THX 1138; Tomorrow*
1972 *The Godfather\*; The Great Northfield Minnesota Raid; Joe Kidd*
1973 *Badge 373; Lady Ice*
1974 *The Outfit; The Godfather Part II\*; The Conversation\*; We're Not The Jet Set* (director only)
1975 *Breakout; The Killer Elite*
1976 *Network\*; The Seven Per Cent Solution; The Eagle Has Landed*
1977 *The Greatest*

1978 *Invasion Of The Bodysnatchers; The Betsy; Ike: The War Years* (TV)
1979 *The Great Santini; Apocalypse Now\**
1981 *True Confessions; The Pursuit Of DB Cooper*
1983 *Tender Mercies\*; The Terry Fox Story* (TV); *Angelo My Love* (director only)
1984 *The Natural; The Stone Boy*
1985 *The Lightship; Belizaire The Cajun*
1986 *Let's Get Harry; Hotel Colonial*
1988 *Colors\*; The White Crow*
1990 *The Handmaid's Tale; A Show Of Force; Days Of Thunder\*; Convicts*
1991 *Rambling Rose*
1992 *Newsies; Stalin* (TV)
1993 *Falling Down; Wrestling Ernest Hemingway*

# E

## EASTWOOD, Clint
real name: Clinton Eastwood Junior
(1930– ) USA

1955 *Revenge Of The Creature; Francis In The Navy; Lady Godiva* (UK: *Lady Godiva Of Coventry*); *Tarantula!*
1956 *Never Say Goodbye; Star In The Dust; The First Travelling Saleslady*
1957 *Escapade In Japan; Lafayette Escadrille* (UK: *Hell Bent For Glory*)
1958 *Ambush At Cimarron Pass*
1964 *Per Un Pugno Di Dollari\** (UK: *A Fistful Of Dollars*)
1965 *Per Qualche Dollari In Piu\** (UK: *For A Few Dollars More*)
1966 *Il Buono, Il Brutto, Il Cattivo\** (UK: *The Good, The Bad And The Ugly*; *Le Streghe* (UK: *The Witches*)
1967 *Hang'Em High*

1968 *Coogan's Bluff; Where Eagles Dare\**
1969 *Paint Your Wagon\*; Two Mules For Sister Sara*
1970 *Kelly's Heroes; The Beguiled*
1971 *Dirty Harry\*; Play Misty For Me\**
1972 *Joe Kidd; High Plains Drifter*
1973 *Magnum Force*
1974 *Thunderbolt And Lightfoot*
1975 *The Eiger Sanction*
1976 *The Outlaw Josey Wales\*; The Enforcer*
1977 *The Gauntlet*
1978 *Every Which Way But Loose\**
1979 *Escape From Alcatraz*
1980 *Bronco Billy; Any Which Way You Can*
1982 *Firefox; Honkytonk Man*
1983 *Sudden Impact*
1984 *City Heat; Tightrope*
1985 *Pale Rider\**
1986 *Heartbreak Ridge*
1987 *The Dead Pool*
1988 *Thelonius Monk: Straight No Chaser* (executive producer only)
1989 *Pink Cadillac*
1990 *White Hunter, Black Heart; The Rookie*
1992 *Unforgiven\**
1993 *In The Line Of Fire; Perfect World*

See also directors listing

## EDDY, Nelson
(1901–67) USA

1933 *Broadway To Hollywood* (UK: *Ring Up The Curtain*); *Dancing Lady*
1934 *Student Tour*
1935 *Naughty Marietta*
1936 *Rose Marie\**
1937 *Maytime; Rosalie*
1938 *Girl Of The Golden West; Sweethearts*
1939 *Let Freedom Ring; Balalaika*
1940 *New Moon; Bitter Sweet*
1941 *The Chocolate Soldier*
1942 *I Married An Angel*
1943 *The Phantom Of The Opera*
1944 *Knickerbocker Holiday*

**EDDY, Nelson** (cont.)
1946  *Make Mine Music* (voice only)
1947  *Northwest Outpost* (UK: *End Of The Rainbow*)

**EKLAND, Britt**
real name: Britt-Marie Eklund
(1942–   ) Sweden

1962  *Kort Ar Sommaren*
1963  *Det Är Hos Mig Han Her Varit; Il Commandante; Il Diavolo*
1964  *Carol For Another Christmas* (TV)
1965  *Too Many Thieves* (TV)
1966  *After The Fox*
1967  *The Double Man; The Bobo*
1968  *The Night They Raided Minsky's*
1969  *Stiletto; Nell'Anno Del Signore; Machine Gun McCain*
1970  *Percy; Il Cannibali/The Cannibals; Tinto Mara*
1971  *Get Carter; Endless Night; Night Hair Child; A Time For Loving*
1972  *Asylum; Baxter!*
1973  *The Wicker Man*
1974  *The Man With The Golden Gun\*; The Ultimate Thrill*
1975  *Royal Flash*
1976  *High Velocity*
1977  *Casanova And Co* (UK: *The Rise And Rise Of Casanova*); *Slavers*
1978  *King Solomon's Treasure; Ring Of Passion* (TV); *The Great Wallendas* (TV)
1980  *The Monster Club; The Hostage Tower*
1981  *Satan's Mistress; Dead Wrong* (TV); *Greed*
1983  *Erotic Images*
1984  *Hellhole*
1985  *Fraternity Vacation; Marbella; Love Scenes*
1987  *Moon In Scorpio*
1989  *Scandal\*; Beverly Hills Vamp*
1990  *The Children*

**ELLIOTT, Denholm**
(1922–92) UK

1949  *Dear Mr Prohack*

1952  *The Sound Barrier; The Ringer; The Holly And The Ivy*
1953  *The Cruel Sea; The Heart Of The Matter*
1954  *They Who Dare; Lease Of Life; The Man Who Loved Redheads*
1955  *The Night My Number Came Up*
1956  *Pacific Destiny*
1960  *Scent Of Mystery* (UK: *Holiday In Spain*)
1962  *Station Six Sahara*
1964  *Nothing But The Best; The High Bright Sun*
1965  *You Must Be Joking!; King Rat*
1966  *Alfie\*; The Spy With A Cold Nose; Maroc 7*
1967  *Here We Go Round The Mulberry Bush*
1968  *The Night They Raided Minsky's*
1969  *The Sea Gull; Too Late The Hero*
1970  *The Rise And Rise Of Michael Rimmer; The House That Dripped Blood; Percy*
1971  *Quest For Love*
1972  *Madame Sin* (TV)
1973  *A Doll's House; Vault Of Horror; The Last Chapter* (short)
1974  *Percy's Progress; The Apprenticeship Of Duddy Kravitz*
1975  *Russian Roulette; To The Devil A Daughter*
1976  *Partners; Robin And Marian; Voyage Of The Damned*
1977  *A Bridge Too Far; The Hound Of The Baskervilles*
1978  *Sweeney 2; The Little Girl In Blue Velvet; The Boys From Brazil; Watership Down* (voice only)
1979  *Games For Vultures; Saint Jack; Zulu Dawn; Cuba*
1980  *Rising Damp; Sunday Lovers; Bad Timing\**
1981  *Raiders Of The Lost Ark\**
1982  *Brimstone And Treacle; The Missionary*
1983  *The Wicked Lady; Trading Places\**
1984  *A Private Function; Camille* (TV); *The Razor's Edge*
1985  *Underworld; Defence Of The Realm; A Room With A View\*; Hotel Du Lac* (TV)

1986 *The Whoopee Boys; Mrs Delafield Wants To Marry* (TV); *The Happy Valley* (TV)
1987 *Maurice\*; September*
1988 *Hanna's War; Stealing Heaven*
1989 *Killing Dad; The Return From The River Kwai; Indiana Jones And The Last Crusade\**
1990 *The Love She Sought* (TV)
1991 *Scorchers; A Murder of Quality* (TV); *Toy Soldiers; One Against The World* (TV)
1992 *Noises Off*


## ENGLUND, Robert
(1947–  ) USA
1974 *Buster And Billie*
1975 *Hustle*
1976 *A Star Is Born\*; St Ives; Stay Hungry; Eaten Alive* (UK: *Death Trap*)
1977 *Last Of The Cowboys/The Great Smokey Roadblock; Young Joe, The Forgotten Kennedy* (TV)
1978 *Big Wednesday; Blood Brothers*
1980 *The Fifth Floor*
1981 *Dead And Buried; Galaxy Of Terror; Don't Cry, It's Only Thunder*
1982 *Thou Shalt Not Kill* (TV); *Starflight One* (TV)
1983 *Hobson's Choice* (TV); *I Want To Live!; The Fighter* (TV)
1984 *A Nightmare On Elm Street\**
1985 *A Nightmare On Elm Street 2: Freddy's Revenge*
1986 *A Nightmare On Elm Street 3: Dream Warriors; Downtown* (TV); *Never Too Young To Die*
1987 *Infidelity* (TV)
1988 *976-EVIL* (also director); *A Nightmare On Elm Street 4: The Dream Master*
1989 *A Nightmare On Elm Street 5: The Dream Child; Phantom Of The Opera*
1990 *The Adventures Of Ford Fairlane*
1991 *Freddy's Dead: A Nightmare On Elm Street 6; Terror Of Manhattan*

## ESTEVEZ, Emilio
(1962–  ) USA
1980 *Seventeen Going Nowhere* (TV)
1981 *To Climb A Mountain* (TV)
1982 *The Outsiders\*; In The Custody Of Strangers* (TV); *Tex*
1983 *Nightmares*
1984 *Repo Man; The Breakfast Club*
1985 *St Elmo's Fire; That Was Then, This Is Now*
1986 *Maximum Overdrive; Wisdom* (also director)
1987 *Never On Tuesday; Stakeout\**
1988 *Young Guns\**
1989 *Nightbreaker* (TV)
1990 *Men At Work* (also director); *Young Guns II*
1992 *Freejack; The Mighty Ducks* (UK: *Champions*)
1993 *National Lampoon's Loaded Weapon; Judgment Night; Stakeout 2*


## EVANS, Edith
(1888–1976) UK
1915 *A Honeymoon For Three; A Welsh Singer*
1916 *East Is East*
1948 *The Queen Of Spades*
1949 *The Last Days Of Dolwyn*
1952 *The Importance Of Being Earnest*
1959 *The Nun's Story\*; Look Back In Anger*
1963 *Tom Jones\**
1964 *The Chalk Garden; Young Cassidy*
1966 *The Whisperers*
1967 *Fitzwilly* (UK: *Fitzwilly Strikes Back*)
1968 *Prudence And The Pill; Crooks And Coronets*
1969 *The Madwoman Of Chaillot; David Copperfield* (TV)
1970 *Scrooge; Upon This Rock*
1973 *A Doll's House; Craze*
1974 *QB VII* (TV)
1976 *The Slipper And The Rose; Nasty Habits*

# F

## FARROW, Mia
real name: Maria Farrow
(1945–   ) USA

1959 *John Paul Jones*
1963 *The Age Of Curiosity* (short)
1964 *Guns At Batasi*
1968 *A Dandy In Aspic; Rosemary's Baby\**
1969 *Secret Ceremony; John And Mary*
1971 *Blind Terror; Goodbye Raggedy Ann* (TV); *Follow Me*
1972 *Docteur Popaul* (UK: *Scoundrel In White*)
1974 *The Great Gatsby*
1975 *Peter Pan* (TV)
1976 *Full Circle*
1978 *Death On The Nile; A Wedding; Avalanche*
1979 *Hurricane*
1981 *The Last Unicorn* (voice only); *Sarah/The Seventh Match*
1982 *A Midsummer Night's Sex Comedy*
1983 *Zelig\**
1984 *Supergirl; Broadway Danny Rose\**
1985 *The Purple Rose Of Cairo\**
1986 *Hannah And Her Sisters\**
1987 *Radio Days; September*
1988 *Another Woman\**
1989 *New York Stories; Crimes And Misdemeanours\**
1990 *Alice*
1992 *Shadows And Fog; Husbands And Wives*


## FAYE, Alice
real name: Alice Leppert
(1912–   ) USA

1934 *George White's Scandals; She Learned About Sailors; Now I'll Tell* (UK: *When New York Sleeps*); *365 Nights In Hollywood*
1935 *George White's 1935 Scandals; Music Is Magic; Every Night At Eight*
1936 *Poor Little Rich Girl; Sing, Baby, Sing; King Of Burlesque; Stowaway*
1937 *On The Avenue; Wake Up And Live; You Can't Have Everything; You're A Sweetheart*
1938 *In Old Chicago\*; Sally, Irene And Mary; Alexander's Ragtime Band\*; Tail Spin*
1939 *Hollywood Cavalcade; Barricade; Rose Of Washington Square*
1940 *Lillian Russell; Little Old New York; Tin Pan Alley*
1941 *That Night In Rio; The Great American Broadcast; Weekend In Havana*
1943 *Hello Frisco Hello; The Gang's All Here* (UK: *The Girl He Left Behind*)
1944 *Four Jills In A Jeep*
1945 *Fallen Angel*
1962 *State Fair*
1975 *Won Ton Ton — The Dog Who Saved Hollywood*
1978 *The Magic Of Lassie*


## FIELD, Sally
(1946–   ) USA

1967 *The Way West*
1970 *Marriage Year One* (TV); *Maybe I'll Come Home In The Spring* (TV)
1971 *Hitched* (TV) (UK: *Westward The Wagon*); *Mongo's Back In Town* (TV)
1972 *Home For The Holidays* (TV)
1976 *Stay Hungry; Sybil* (TV)
1977 *Smokey And The Bandit\*; Heroes*
1978 *Hooper; The End*
1979 *Norma Rae\*; Beyond The Poseidon Adventure*
1980 *Smokey And The Bandit II* (UK: *Smokey And The Bandit Ride Again*)
1981 *Back Roads; Absence Of Malice\**
1982 *Kiss Me Goodbye*
1984 *Places In The Heart\**
1986 *Murphy's Romance*
1987 *Surrender*
1988 *Punchline\**

1989 *Steel Magnolias\**
1991 *Not Without My Daughter;
Soapdish*
1993 *Homeward Bound* (voice only);
*Mrs Doubtfire*

## FIELDS, W C
real name: William Claude Dukenfield
(1879–1946) USA

1915 *Pool Sharks; His Lordship's
Dilemma*
1924 *Janice Meredith* (UK: *The
Beautiful Rebel*)
1925 *Sally Of The Sawdust; That Royle
Girl*
1926 *So's Your Old Man; It's The Old
Army Game*
1927 *The Potters; Running Wild; Two
Flaming Youths* (UK: *The Side
Show*)
1928 *Fools For Luck; Tillie's Punctured
Romance* (UK: *Marie's Millions*)
1930 *The Golf Specialist* (short)
1931 *Her Majesty Love*
1932 *The Dentist* (short); *If I Had A
Million; Million Dollar Legs*
1933 *The Fatal Glass Of Beer; The
Pharmacist; Hip Action;
Hollywood On Parade; The
Barber Shop* (all shorts);
*International House; Tillie And
Gus; Alice In Wonderland*
1934 *Six Of A Kind; You're Telling Me!;
The Old Fashioned Way; It's A
Gift; Mrs Wiggs Of The Cabbage
Patch*
1935 *David Copperfield\*; Mississippi;
The Man On The Flying Trapeze*
(UK: *The Memory Expert*)
1936 *Poppy*
1938 *The Big Broadcast Of 1938*
1939 *You Can't Cheat An Honest Man*
1940 *My Little Chickadee; The Bank
Dick\** (UK: *The Bank Detective*)
1941 *Never Give A Sucker An Even
Break* (UK: *What A Man!*)
1942 *Tales Of Manhattan*
1944 *Follow The Boys; Songs Of
The Open Road; Sensations Of
1945*

## FINCH, Peter
real name: William Mitchell
(1916–77) UK

1935 *Magic Shoes*
1938 *Dad And Dave Come To Town;
Mr Chedworth Steps Out*
1939 *Ants In His Pants*
1940 *The Power And The Glory*
1942 *Another Threshold; While There's
Still Time*
1943 *South-West Pacific; Red Sky At
Morning*
1944 *Rats Of Tobruk; Jungle Patrol*
(narrator only)
1945 *Indonesia Calling* (short)
1946 *A Son Is Born; Native Earth*
(narrator only)
1947 *The Nomads* (narrator only)
1948 *Eureka Stockade; The Hunt*
(narrator only)
1949 *Train Of Events; The Corroboree*
(narrator only)
1950 *The Wooden Horse; The Miniver
Story*
1952 *The Story Of Robin Hood And His
Merrie Men*
1953 *The Story Of Gilbert And Sullivan;
The Heart Of The Matter*
1954 *Father Brown; Elephant Walk;
Make Me An Offer*
1955 *Passage Home; The Dark
Avenger; Simon And Laura;
Josephine And Men*
1956 *The Queen In Australia;
Melbourne — Olympic City; The
Royal Tour Of New South Wales*
(all narrator only); *A Town Like
Alice; The Battle Of The River
Plate*
1957 *The Shiralee; Robbery Under
Arms; Windom's Way*
1958 *Operation Amsterdam; A Far Cry*
(narrator only)
1959 *The Nun's Story\**
1960 *The Trials Of Oscar Wilde;
Kidnapped; No Love For Johnnie*
1961 *The Sins Of Rachel Cade*
1962 *I Thank A Fool; The Day* (short,
also director)
1963 *In The Cool Of The Day*

**FINCH, Peter** (cont.)

1964 *The Girl With Green Eyes; The First Men In The Moon; The Pumpkin Eater*
1965 *Judith; The Flight Of The Phoenix*
1966 *10.30pm Summer*
1967 *Far From The Madding Crowd*
1968 *The Legend Of Lylah Clare*
1969 *The Red Tent; The Greatest Mother Of Them All* (short)
1971 *Sunday, Bloody Sunday\**
1972 *Something To Hide; England Made Me*
1973 *Lost Horizon; Bequest To The Nation*
1974 *The Abdication*
1976 *Raid On Entebbe; Network\**

**FINNEY, Albert**
(1936–   ) UK

1960 *The Entertainer\*; Saturday Night And Sunday Morning\**
1963 *Tom Jones\*; The Victors*
1964 *Night Must Fall*
1967 *Two For The Road; Charlie Bubbles* (also director)
1969 *The Picasso Summer*
1970 *Scrooge*
1971 *Gumshoe*
1972 *Alpha Beta*
1974 *Murder On The Orient Express\**
1975 *The Adventures Of Sherlock Holmes Smarter Brother*
1977 *The Duellists*
1980 *Loophole*
1981 *Wolfen; Looker; Shoot The Moon*
1982 *Annie\**
1983 *The Dresser\**
1984 *Under The Volcano; Pope John Paul II* (TV)
1987 *Orphans*
1989 *The Image* (TV)
1990 *Miller's Crossing*
1992 *The Playboys; Rich In Love*

**FLYNN, Errol**
(1909–59) Tasmania

1932 *Dr H Erben's New Guinea Expedition*

1933 *In The Wake Of The Bounty*
1934 *Murder At Monte Carlo*
1935 *The Case Of The Curious Bride; Don't Bet On Blondes; Captain Blood\**
1936 *The Charge Of The Light Brigade; Pirate Party On Catalina Island* (documentary)
1937 *The Green Light; The Prince And The Pauper; Another Dawn; The Perfect Specimen*
1938 *The Adventures Of Robin Hood\*; The Sisters; Four's A Crowd; The Dawn Patrol*
1939 *Dodge City; The Private Lives Of Elizabeth And Essex\**
1940 *Virginia City; Santa Fe Trail; The Sea Hawk\**
1941 *Footsteps In The Dark; Dive Bomber; They Died With Their Boots On*
1942 *Desperate Journey; Gentleman Jim*
1943 *Edge Of Darkness; Northern Pursuit; Thank Your Lucky Stars*
1944 *Uncertain Glory*
1945 *Objective Burma; San Antonio; Peeks At Hollywood* (short)
1946 *Never Say Goodbye*
1947 *Cry Wolf; Escape Me Never; Always Together*
1948 *Silver River; The Adventures Of Don Juan* (UK: *The New Adventures Of Don Juan*)
1949 *That Forsyte Woman* (UK: *The Fosyte Saga*); *It's A Great Feeling*
1950 *Montana; Rocky Mountain; Kim*
1951 *Hello God; The Adventures Of Captain Fabian*
1952 *Cruise Of The Zacca; Deep Sea Fishing* (both documentaries); *Mara, Maru; Against All Flags*
1953 *The Master Of Ballantrae; Crossed Swords*
1954 *Lilacs In The Spring*
1955 *The Dark Avenger; King's Rhapsody*
1957 *Istanbul; The Sword Of Villon* (TV); *The Big Boodle* (UK: *Night In Havana*); *The Sun Also Rises; Without Incident* (TV)

1958 *The Roots Of Heaven; Too Much, Too Soon*
1959 *Cuban Rebel Girls*

## FONDA, Bridget
(1964–   ) USA

1987 *Aria*
1988 *Light Years; Shag; You Can't Hurry Love*
1989 *Scandal\*; Strapless*
1990 *The Godfather Part III\*; Iron Maze; Roger Corman's Frankenstein Unbound*
1991 *'Doc' Hollywood*
1992 *Single White Female; Singles; Army Of Darkness: The Medieval Dead*
1993 *Bodies, Rest And Motion; The Little Buddha; Point Of No Return*

## FONDA, Henry Jaynes
(1905–82) USA

1935 *The Farmer Takes A Wife; Way Down East; I Dream Too Much*
1936 *The Trail Of The Lonesome Pine; Spendthrift; The Moon's Our Home*
1937 *Slim; Wings Of The Morning; That Certain Woman; You Only Live Once*
1938 *Blockade; I Met My Love Again; The Mad Miss Manton; Jezebel\*; Spawn Of The North*
1939 *Jesse James\*; The Story Of Alexander Graham Bell (UK: The Modern Miracle); Let Us Live; Drums Along The Mohawk; Young Mr Lincoln*
1940 *The Grapes Of Wrath\*; The Return Of Frank James; Lillian Russell; Chad Hanna*
1941 *The Lady Eve\*; Wild Geese Calling; You Belong To Me (UK: Good Morning Doctor)*
1942 *Rings On Her Fingers; The Male Animal; The Magnificent Dope; The Big Street; Tales Of Manhattan; The Battle Of Midway (narrator only)*

1943 *The Immortal Sergeant; The Ox-Bow Incident\* (UK: Strange Incident); It's Everybody's War (narrator only)*
1946 *My Darling Clementine\**
1947 *The Fugitive; Daisy Kenyon; The Long Night*
1948 *Fort Apache; A Miracle Can Happen (UK: On Our Merry Way)*
1949 *Jigsaw*
1950 *Home Of The Hopeless (narrator only)*
1951 *Grant Wood; Benjy; The Growing Years (all narrator only)*
1952 *The Impressionable Years*
1953 *Main Street To Broadway*
1955 *Mister Roberts\**
1956 *The Wrong Man; War And Peace\**
1957 *12 Angry Men\*; The Tin Star*
1958 *Stagestruck; Fabulous Hollywood (documentary); Reach For Tomorrow (narrator only)*
1959 *Warlock; The Man Who Understood Women*
1962 *Advise And Consent; The Longest Day\*; How The West Was Won\**
1963 *Spencer's Mountain; Rangers Of Yellowstone (narrator)*
1964 *The Best Man; Failsafe; Sex And The Single Girl*
1965 *The Rounders; In Harm's Way; Battle Of The Bulge; La Guerre Secrète (UK: The Dirty Game)*
1966 *A Big Hand For A Little Lady (UK: Big Deal At Dodge City); Welcome To Hard Times (UK: Killer On A Horse)*
1967 *Firecreek; Stranger On The Run (TV); All About People; The Golden Flame (narrator only)*
1968 *Yours, Mine And Ours; Madigan; The Boston Strangler; C'Era Una Volta Il West\* (UK: Once Upon A Time In The West); Born To Buck (narrator)*
1969 *Too Late The Hero; An Impression Of John Steinbeck— Writer (narrator)*
1970 *There Was A Crooked Man; The Cheyenne Social Club*

**FONDA, Henry Jaynes** (cont.)

1971  *Sometimes A Great Notion* (UK: *Never Give An Inch*); *Directed By John Ford* (documentary)

1972  *Le Serpent* (UK: *The Serpent*)

1973  *Ash Wednesday; The Alpha Caper* (TV); *The Red Pony* (TV); *Il Mio Nome E Nessurno* (UK: *My Name Is Nobody*); *Filmmaking Techniques: Acting* (documentary)

1974  *Mussolini: Ultimo Atto* (UK: *Mussolini: The Last Four Days*); *Valley Forge* (narrator only)

1976  *Midway* (UK: *Battle Of Midway*); *Collision Course; Tentacoli* (UK: *Tentacles*)

1977  *Rollercoaster; The Last Of The Cowboys; Il Grande Attacca* (UK: *The Biggest Battle*); *Alcohol Abuse — The Early Warning Signs* (narrator)

1978  *The Swarm; Fedora; City On Fire; Home To Stay* (TV); *Big Yellow Schooner To Byzantium* (narrator); *America's Sweetheart — The Mary Pickford Story* (narrator)

1979  *Meteor; Wanda Nevada; The Man Who Loved Bears* (narrator)

1980  *Gideon's Trumpet* (TV); *The Oldest Living Graduate* (TV)

1981  *On Golden Pond\*; Summer Solstice* (TV)

**FONDA, Jane Seymour**
(1937–  ) USA

1960  *Tall Story*

1961  *A String Of Beads* (TV)

1962  *The Chapman Report; Walk On The Wild Side; Period Of Adjustment*

1963  *In The Cool Of The Day; Jane; Sunday In New York*

1964  *Les Félins* (UK: *The Love Cage*); *La Ronde*

1965  *Cat Ballou\**

1966  *The Chase; La Curée* (UK: *The Game Is Over*); *Any Wednesday; Hurry Sundown*

1967  *Barefoot In The Park\*; Histoires Extraordinaires* (UK: *Tales Of Mystery*)

1968  *Barbarella\**

1969  *They Shoot Horses Don't They?\**

1971  *Klute\**

1972  *Steelyard Blues; Tout Va Bien; FTA*

1973  *A Doll's House; Jane Fonda On Vietnam* (documentary)

1974  *Vietnam Journey*

1976  *The Bluebird; Fun With Dick And Jane*

1977  *Julia\**

1978  *Coming Home\*; Comes A Horseman; California Suite\**

1979  *The China Syndrome\*; The Electric Horseman\**

1980  *Nine To Five\*; No Nukes* (documentary)

1981  *Rollover; On Golden Pond\*; Lee Strasberg And The Actors' Studio* (documentary)

1984  *The Dollmaker* (TV)

1985  *Agnes Of God\**

1986  *The Morning After*

1987  *Leonard Part VI*

1989  *Old Gringo\*; Stanley And Iris*

**FONDA, Peter**
(1939–  ) USA

1963  *Tammy And The Doctor; The Victors*

1964  *Carol For Another Christmas* (TV); *The Young Lovers; Lilith*

1965  *The Rounders*

1966  *The Wild Angels*

1967  *The Trip; Histoires Extraordinaires* (UK: *Tales Of Mystery*)

1969  *Easy Rider\**

1971  *The Hired Hand* (also director); *The Last Movie*

1973  *Not So Easy* (short); *Motorcycle Safety; Two People; Idaho Transfer* (director only)

1974  *Open Season; Dirty Mary, Crazy Larry*

1975  *92 In The Shade; Race With The Devil; The Diamond Mercenaries*

1976  *Fighting Mad; Futureworld*

1977 *Outlaw Blues; Highballin'*
1978 *Roger Corman: Hollywood's Wild Angel* (documentary)
1979 *Wanda Nevada* (also director)
1980 *The Hostage Tower*
1981 *The Cannonball Run\*; Spasms*
1982 *Split Image; Dance Of The Dwarfs*
1984 *Peppermint Freedom; A Reason To Live* (TV)
1985 *Certain Fury; Come The Day*
1986 *Hawker*
1987 *Freedom Fighters; Time Of Indifference* (TV); *Hawken's Breed; The Long Voyage*
1988 *Sound; Fatal Mission*
1989 *The Rose Garden*
1990 *American Express; Fatal Mission*
1992 *Nightcaller*
1993 *Molly & Gina; Bodies, Rest And Motion*

## FONTAINE, Joan

real name: Joan De Havilland
(1917–   ) UK

1935 *No More Ladies*
1937 *Quality Street; Music For Madame; A Damsel In Distress; You Can't Beat Love*
1938 *The Man Who Found Himself; Sky Giant; Blonde Cheat; Maid's Night Out*
1939 *The Duke Of West Point; Gunga Din; Man Of Conquest; The Women\**
1940 *Rebecca\**
1941 *Suspicion\**
1943 *The Constant Nymph*
1944 *Jane Eyre; Frenchman's Creek*
1945 *The Affairs Of Susan*
1946 *From This Day Forward*
1947 *Ivy*
1948 *Letter From An Unknown Woman; Kiss The Blood Off My Hands* (UK: *Blood On My Hands*); *The Emperor Waltz*
1949 *You Gotta Stay Happy*
1950 *Born To Be Bad; September Affair*
1951 *Darling, How Could You?* (UK: *Rendezvous*); *Something To Live For*

1952 *Ivanhoe\*; Decameron Nights*
1953 *Flight To Tangier; The Bigamist*
1954 *Casanova's Big Night*
1956 *Serenade; Beyond A Reasonable Doubt*
1957 *Island In The Sun; Until They Sail*
1958 *A Certain Smile*
1961 *Voyage To The Bottom Of The Sea; Tender Is The Night*
1966 *The Witches* (UK: *The Devil's Own*)
1978 *The Users* (TV)
1986 *Crossings* (TV); *Dark Mansions* (TV)

## FORD, Glenn

real name: Gwyllyn Newton
(1916–   ) Canada

1937 *Night In Manhattan* (short)
1939 *Heaven With A Barbed Wire Fence; My Son Is Guilty* (UK: *Crime's End*)
1040 *Convicted Woman; Babies For Sale; Men Without Souls; Blondie Plays Cupid; The Lady In Question*
1941 *Texas, So Ends Our Night; Go West, Young Lady*
1942 *The Adventures Of Martin Eden; Flight Lieutenant*
1943 *Destroyer; Desperadoes; Hollywood In Uniform* (documentary)
1946 *Gilda\*; A Stolen Life*
1947 *Gallant Journey; Framed* (UK: *Paula*)
1948 *The Mating Of Millie; The Loves Of Carmen; The Return Of October* (UK: *Date With Destiny*); *The Man From Colorado*
1949 *The Undercover Man; Lust For Gold; Mr Soft Touch* (UK: *House Of Settlement*); *The Doctor And The Girl; Hollywood Goes To Church* (short)
1950 *The White Tower; Convicted; The Flying Missile; The Redhead And the Cowboy*

171

**FORD, Glenn** (cont.)
1951 *Follow The Sun; The Secret Of Convict Lake; Young Man With Ideas; The Green Glove*
1952 *Affair In Trinidad*
1953 *The Man From The Alamo; Time Bomb* (UK: *Terror On A Train*); *Plunder Of The Sun; The Big Heat\*; Appointment In Honduras*
1954 *Human Desire; The Americano; City Story* (narrator only)
1955 *The Violent Men* (UK: *Rough Company*); *Interrupted Melody; Hollywood Fathers* (short); *Blackboard Jungle\*; Trial; Ransom!*
1956 *Jubal; The Fastest Gun Alive; The Teahouse Of The August Moon\*; Hollywood Goes A-Fishing* (short)
1957 *3:10 To Yuma; Don't Go Near The Water*
1958 *The Sheepman; Cowboy; Torpedo Run; Imitation General*
1959 *It Started With A Kiss; The Gazebo*
1960 *Cimarron*
1961 *Cry For Happy; Pocketful Of Miracles; The Four Horsemen Of The Apocalypse*
1962 *Experiment In Terror* (UK: *The Grip Of Fear*)
1963 *The Courtship Of Eddie's Father; Love Is A Ball* (UK: *All This And Money Too*)
1964 *Advance To The Rear* (UK: *Company Of Cowards*); *Fate Is The Hunter; Dear Heart*
1965 *The Money Trap; The Rounders; Seapower* (narrator only)
1966 *Paris Brûle T'Il?* (UK: *Is Paris Burning?*); *Rage*
1967 *A Time For Killing* (UK: *The Long Ride Home*); *The Last Challenge* (UK: *The Pistolero Of Red River*)
1968 *Day Of The Evil Gun*
1969 *Smith!; Heaven With A Gun*
1970 *The Brotherhood Of The Bell* (TV)
1971 *Slayride* (TV)
1972 *The Gold Diggers* (TV); *Santee*
1973 *Jarrett* (TV)

1974 *Punch And Jody* (TV); *The Greatest Gift* (TV); *The Disappearance Of Flight 412* (TV)
1975 *Long Way Home* (TV)
1976 *Midway* (UK: *The Battle Of Midway*)
1977 *Goodbye E Amen; The 3,000 Mile Chase* (TV)
1979 *The Visitor; The Sacketts* (TV); *The Gift* (TV); *The Family Holvack* (TV)
1980 *Virus*
1981 *Happy Birthday To Me; Day Of The Assassins*
1989 *Casablanca Express*
1990 *Border Shootout*

## FORD, Harrison
(1942–  ) USA

1966 *Dead Heat On A Merry-Go-Round*
1967 *Luv; A Time For Killing* (UK: *The Long Ride Home*)
1968 *Journey To Shiloh*
1969 *Zabriskie Point*
1970 *The Intruders(TV); Getting Straight*
1973 *American Graffiti\**
1974 *The Conversation\**
1976 *Dynasty*
1977 *The Trial Of Lt Calley* (TV); *Star Wars\*; Heroes; The Possessed* (TV)
1978 *Force Ten From Navarone; Hanover Street*
1979 *Apocalypse Now\*; The Frisco Kid*
1980 *The Empire Strikes Back\**
1981 *Raiders Of The Lost Ark\**
1982 *Blade Runner\**
1983 *Return Of The Jedi\**
1984 *Indiana Jones And The Temple Of Doom\**
1985 *Witness*
1986 *The Mosquito Coast*
1988 *Frantic\*; Working Girl\**
1989 *Indiana Jones And The Last Crusade*
1990 *Presumed Innocent\**
1991 *Regarding Henry\**
1992 *Patriot Games*
1993 *The Fugitive*

## FOSTER, Jodie
real name: Alicia Christian Foster
(1962–   ) USA

1972 *Napoleon And Samantha; Kansas City Bomber; Menace On The Mountain* (TV)
1973 *Rookie Of The Year* (TV); *Tom Sawyer*
1974 *One Little Indian; Smile Jenny, You're Dead* (TV); *Alice Doesn't Live Here Anymore*\*
1975 *Echoes Of A Summer*
1976 *Freaky Friday; The Little Girl Who Lives Down The Lane; Bugsy Malone*\*; *Taxi Driver*\*; *Il Cassotto* (UK: *The Beach Hut*)
1977 *Candleshoe; Fleur Bleue*
1978 *Movies Are My Life*
1979 *Foxes*
1980 *Carny*
1981 *O'Hara's Wife*
1983 *Svengali* (TV); *Le Sang Des Autres*
1984 *The Hotel New Hampshire; Mesmerized*
1987 *Siesta; Five Corners*
1988 *The Accused*\*; *Stealing Home*
1980 *Backtrack* (UK: *Catchfire*)
1991 *The Silence Of The Lambs*\*; *Little Man Tate* (also director)
1992 *Shadows And Fog; Sommersby*


## FOX, Michael J
real name: Michael Andrew Fox
(1961–   ) USA

1979 *Letters From Frank* (TV)
1980 *Midnight Madness; Palmerstown USA* (UK: *Palmerstown*)
1982 *Class Of 1984*
1983 *High School USA* (TV)
1984 *Poison Ivy* (TV)
1985 *Teen Wolf; Back To The Future*\*
1986 *Family Ties Vacation* (TV)
1987 *Light Of Day; The Secret Of My Success; Dear America* (voice only)
1988 *Bright Lights, Big City*

1989 *Casualties Of War; Back To The Future Part II*
1990 *Back To The Future Part III*
1991 *The Hard Way; 'Doc' Hollywood*
1993 *The Concierge; Life With Mikey; Homeward Bound* (voice only)


## FREEMAN, Morgan
(1937–   ) USA

1971 *Who Says I Can't Ride A Rainbow*
1979 *Hollow Image* (TV)
1980 *Attica* (TV); *Brubaker*
1981 *Eyewitness* (UK: *The Janitor*); *The Marva Collins Story* (TV)
1984 *Harry And Son; Teachers*
1985 *The Atlanta Child Murders* (TV); *Marie; That Was Then, This Is Now*
1986 *Resting Place* (TV)
1987 *Fight For Life* (TV); *Street Smart*
1988 *Clean And Sober*
1989 *Driving Miss Daisy*\*; *Glory*\*; *Johnny Handsome; Lean On Me*
1990 *Bonfire Of The Vanities*\*
1991 *Robin Hood — Prince Of Thieves*\*
1992 *The Power Of One; Unforgiven*\*
1993 *Bopha* (director only)


# G

## GABIN, Jean
real name: Jean Alexis Gabin Moncourge
(1904–76) France

1930 *Chacun Sa Chance; Mephisto*
1931 *Paris–Béguin; Tout Ça Ne Vaut Pas L'Amour; Gloria*
1932 *Les Gaietés De L'Escadron; La Belle Marinière; La Foule Hurle; Coeur De Lilas*
1933 *L'Etoile De Valencia; Adieu Les Beaux Jours; Le Tunnel; Du Haut En Bas; Au Bout Du Monde*
1934 *Zouzou; Maria Chapdelaine*
1935 *Golgotha; La Banddéra; Variétés*
1936 *La Belle Equipe; Les Bas Fonds; Pépé Le Moko*

**GABIN, Jean** (cont.)

1937 *Le Messager; La Grande Illusion\*;
Gueule D'Amour*
1938 *Quai Des Brumes; La Bête
Humaine* (UK: *Judas Was A
Woman*)
1939 *Le Jour Se Lève\** (UK: *Daybreak*);
*La Récif De Corail; Rémorques*
1942 *Moontide*
1943 *The Imposter*
1946 *Martin Roumagnac* (UK: *The Man
Upstairs*)
1947 *Le Miroir*
1948 *Au Delà Des Grilles*
1949 *La Marie Du Port*
1950 *E Piu Facile Che Un Camelo*
1951 *Victor; La Nuit Est Mon Royaume;
Le Plaisir; La Vérité Sur Bébé
Donge* (UK: *The Truth About
Marriage*)
1952 *La Minute De Vérité* (UK: *The
Moment Of Truth*); *Bufere; Echos
De Plateau* (short)
1953 *Leur Dernière Nuit; La Vierge Du
Rhin; Touchez Pas Au Grisbi* (UK:
*Honor Among Thieves*)
1954 *L'Air De Paris; Napoléon; Le Port
Du Désir*
1955 *French Can-Can; Razzia Sur La
Chnouf* (UK: *Chnouf*); *Chiens
Perdus Sans Collier; Gas—Oil*
1956 *Des Gens Sans Importance; Voici
Le Temps Des Assassins* (UK:
*Twelve Hours To Live*); *La
Traversée De Paris* (UK: *Pig
Across Paris*); *Le Sang A La Tête;
Crime Et Châtiment* (UK: *Crime
And Punishment*)
1957 *Le Cas Du Docteur Laurent* (UK:
*The Case Of Dr Laurent*); *Le
Rouge Est Mis; Maigret Tend Un
Piège* (UK: *Maigret Sets A Trap*);
*Les Misérables; Le Désordre Et
La Nuit*
1958 *En Cas De Malheur* (UK: *Love Is
My Profession*); *Les Grandes
Familles; Archimède Le Clochard*
1959 *Maigret Et L'Affaire Saint-Fiacre;
Rue Des Prairies*
1960 *Le Baron De L'Ecluse; Les Vieux
De La Vieille* (UK: *The Old Guard*)

1961 *Le President; Le Cave Se
Rebiffe*
1962 *Un Singe En Hiver* (UK: *It's Hot In
Hell*); *Le Gentleman D'Epsom;
Mélodie En Sous-Sol* (UK: *The
Big Snatch*)
1963 *Maigret Voit Rouge*
1964 *Monsieur; L'Age Ingrat*
1965 *Le Tonnerre De Dieu; Du Rififi A
Paname*
1966 *Le Jardinier D'Argenteuil*
1967 *Le Soleil Des Voyous* (UK: *Action
Man*); *Le Pacha*
1968 *Sous La Signe Du Taureau; Le
Tatou*
1969 *Le Clan Des Siciliens* (UK: *The
Sicilian Clan*); *Fin De Journée*
1970 *La Horse*
1971 *Le Chat; Le Drapeau Noir Flotte
Sur La Marmite*
1972 *Le Tueur*
1973 *L'Affaire Dominici; Deux Hommes
Dans La Ville*
1974 *Verdict*
1976 *L'Année Sainte* (UK: *Holy Year*)

**GABLE, William Clark**
(1901–60) USA

1924 *Forbidden Paradise; White Man*
1925 *The Merry Widow; Déclassé;
Ben-Hur; The Pacemakers; The
Plastic Age*
1926 *Fighting Blood; The Johnstown
Flood* (UK: *The Flood*); *North
Star; The Plastic Age*
1930 *The Painted Desert*
1931 *The Easiest Way; Dance, Fools,
Dance; The Finger Points;
Laughing Sinners; The Secret Six;
Night Nurse; A Free Soul;
Sporting Blood; Possessed;
Susan Lenox—Her Fall And Rise*
(UK: *The Rise of Helga*);
*Possessed*
1932 *Hell Divers; Polly Of The Circus;
Strange Interlude* (UK: *Strange

*Interval*); *Red Dust; No Man Of Her Own; Jackie Cooper's Christmas* (UK: *The Christmas Party*) (short)
1933 *Hold Your Man; The White Sister; Night Flight; Dancing Lady*
1934 *Men in White; It Happened One Night\*; Manhattan Melodrama; Chained; Forsaking All Others; Hollywood On Parade No 13* (short)
1935 *After Office Hours; Call Of The Wild; China Seas; Mutiny On the Bounty\**
1936 *Wife Vs Secretary; San Francisco\*; Cain And Mabel; Love On The Run*
1937 *Parnell; Saratoga*
1938 *Too Hot To Handle; Test Pilot\**
1939 *Idiot's Delight; Gone With The Wind\**
1940 *Strange Cargo; Boom Town; Comrade X*
1941 *They Met In Bombay; Honky Tonk*
1942 *Somewhere I'll Find You; Wings Up* (narrator only); *Aerial Gunner* (documentary); *Hollywood In Uniform* (documentary)
1944 *Combat America* (documentary); *Be Careful* (narrator only)
1945 *Adventure*
1947 *The Hucksters\**
1948 *Command Decision; Homecoming*
1949 *Any Number Can Play*
1950 *Key To The City; To Please A Lady; The Screen Actor* (documentary)
1951 *Across The Wide Missouri; Callaway Went Thataway* (UK: *The Star Said No!*)
1952 *Lone Star*
1953 *Never Let Me Go; Memories In Uniform* (documentary); *Mogambo*
1954 *Betrayed*
1955 *Soldier Of Fortune; The Tall Men*
1956 *The King And Four Queens*
1957 *Band Of Angels*
1958 *Teacher's Pet; Run Silent, Run Deep*
1959 *But Not For Me*
1960 *It Started In Naples; The Misfits\**

## GARBO, Greta

real name: Greta Lovisa Gustafsson
(1905–90) Sweden

1921 *En Lyckoriddare* (UK: *A Fortune Hunter*); *Herr Och Fru Stockholm* (UK: *How Not To Dress*) (short)
1922 *Our Daily Bread; Luffar-Peter* (UK: *Peter The Tramp*)
1924 *Gösta Berlings Saga* (UK: *The Atonement Of Gosta Berling*)
1925 *Die Freudlose Gasse* (UK: *Street Of Sorrow*)
1926 *The Torrent; The Temptress*
1927 *Flesh And The Devil; Love* (UK: *Anna Karenina*)
1928 *The Mysterious Lady; The Divine Woman; A Woman Of Affairs*
1929 *Wild Orchids; The Single Standard; The Kiss; A Man's Man*
1930 *Anna Christie\*; Romance*
1931 *Susan Lenox — Her Fall And Rise* (UK: *The Rise Of Helga*); *Inspiration*
1932 *Mata Hari; Grand Hotel\*; As You Desire Me*
1933 *Queen Christina\**
1934 *The Painted Veil*
1935 *Anna Karenina\**
1936 *Camille\**
1937 *Conquest* (UK: *Marie Walewska*)
1939 *Ninotchka\**
1941 *Two-Faced Woman*

## GARCIA, Andy

(1956–  ) Cuba

1983 *Blue Skies Again*
1984 *The Mean Season*
1985 *8 Million Ways To Die*
1987 *The Untouchables\**
1988 *Stand And Deliver; Clinton And Nadine; American Roulette*
1989 *The Sixth Family; Black Rain; Internal Affairs*
1990 *A Show Of Force; The Godfather Part III\**
1991 *Dead Again*
1992 *Jennifer Eight; Hero* (UK: *Accidental Hero*)

## GARDNER, Ava Lavinia
real name: Lucy Johnson
(1922–90) USA

1941 *Fancy Answers* (short); *HM Pulham Esq*
1942 *Joe Smith — American* (UK: *Highway To Freedom*); *We Were Dancing; This Time For Keeps; Kid Glove Killer; Sunday Punch; Calling Dr Gillespie; Mighty Lak A Goat* (short); *Reunion In France* (UK: *Mademoiselle France*)
1943 *Pilot No 5; Du Barry Was A Lady; Ghosts On The Loose* (UK: *Ghosts In The Night*); *Hitler's Madman; Young Ideas; The Lost Angel; Swing Fever*
1944 *Three Men In White; Two Girls And A Sailor; Maisie Goes To Reno* (UK: *You Can't Do That To Me*); *Music For Millions; Blonde Fever*
1945 *She Went To The Races*
1946 *Whistle Stop; The Killers**
1947 *The Hucksters*; Singapore*
1948 *One Touch Of Venus*
1949 *The Great Sinner; The Bribe; East Side, West Side*
1950 *My Forbidden Past*
1951 *Showboat*; Pandora And The Flying Dutchman*
1952 *Lone Star; The Snows Of Kilimanjaro**
1953 *Ride, Vaquero!; The Bandwagon*; Mogambo*
1954 *The Knights Of The Round Table; The Barefoot Contessa**
1956 *Bhowani Junction*
1957 *The Little Hut; The Sun Also Rises*
1959 *The Naked Maja; On The Beach*
1960 *The Angel Wore Red*
1962 *55 Days At Peking*
1963 *Seven Days In May**
1964 *The Night Of The Iguana**
1966 *The Bible...In The Beginning**
1968 *Mayerling*
1971 *Tam Lin* (UK: *The Devil's Widow*)
1972 *The Life And Times Of Judge Roy Bean*
1974 *Earthquake**
1975 *Permission To Kill*

1976 *The Bluebird; Cassandra Crossing; The Sentinel*
1979 *City On Fire*
1980 *The Kidnapping Of The President; Priest Of Love*
1982 *Regina*
1985 *The Long Hot Summer* (TV)
1986 *Harem* (TV)

## GARFIELD, John
real name: Julius Garfinkle
(1912–52) USA

1938 *Secrets Of An Actress; Four Daughters; Blackwell's Island*
1939 *Juarez; They Made Me A Criminal; Daughters Courageous; Dust Be My Destiny*
1940 *Saturday's Children; Flowing Gold; East Of The River; Castle On The Hudson* (UK: *Years Without Days*)
1941 *The Sea Wolf; Out Of The Fog*
1942 *Tortilla Flat; Dangerously They Live*
1943 *Air Force; Destination Tokyo; Thank Your Lucky Stars; The Fallen Sparrow*
1944 *Between Two Worlds; Hollywood Canteen*
1945 *Pride Of The Marines* (UK: *Forever In Love*)
1946 *The Postman Always Rings Twice*; Nobody Lives Forever; Humoresque*
1947 *Daisy Kenyon; Body And Soul; Gentleman's Agreement**
1948 *Force Of Evil*
1949 *We Were Strangers; Jigsaw*
1950 *Under My Skin; The Breaking Point; Difficult Years* (narrator)
1951 *He Ran All The Way*

## GARLAND, Judy
real name: Frances Ethel Gumm
(1922–69) USA

1929 *The Meglin Kiddie Revue* (short)
1930 *A Holiday In Storyland; The Wedding Of Jack And Jill* (both shorts)

1931 *The Old Lady In The Shoe* (short)
1936 *La Fiesta De Santa Barbara*
(short); *Every Sunday* (short);
*Pigskin Parade* (UK: *The
Harmony Parade*)
1937 *Broadway Melody Of 1938;
Thoroughbreds Don't Cry*
1938 *Everybody Sing; Love Finds Andy
Hardy; Listen, Darling*
1939 *The Wizard Of Oz\*; Babes In
Arms\**
1940 *Andy Hardy Meets Debutante;
Strike Up The Band; Little Nellie
Kelly*
1941 *Life Begins For Andy Hardy;
Ziegfeld Girl; Babes On
Broadway; Meet The Stars No 4*
(short); *Cavalcade Of The
Academy Awards* (short)
1942 *For Me And My Gal* (UK: *For Me
And My Girl*); *We Must Have
Music* (short)
1943 *Presenting Lily Mars; Girl Crazy;
Thousands Cheer*
1944 *Ziegfeld Follies\*; Meet Me In St
Louis\**
1945 *The Clock* (UK: *Under The Clock*)
1946 *The Harvey Girls\*; Till The Clouds
Roll By\**
1948 *The Pirate; Words And Music;
Easter Parade\**
1949 *In The Good Old Summertime*
1950 *Summer Stock* (UK: *If You Feel
Like Singing*)
1954 *A Star Is Born\**
1960 *Pepe* (voice only)
1961 *Judgement At Nuremberg*
1962 *A Child Is Waiting; Gay Purr-ee*
(voice only)
1963 *I Could Go On Singing*

1958 *Darby's Rangers* (UK: *The Young
Invaders*)
1959 *Up Periscope; Alias Jesse James;
Cash McCall*
1962 *The Children's Hour* (UK: *The
Loudest Whisper*); *Boys' Night
Out*
1963 *The Thrill Of It All; Move Over,
Darling; The Great Escape\*; The
Wheeler Dealers* (UK: *Separate
Beds*)
1964 *The Americanization Of Emily; 36
Hours*
1965 *The Art Of Love; Mister Buddwing*
(UK: *Woman Without A Face*)
1966 *A Man Could Get Killed; Duel At
Diablo; Grand Prix*
1967 *Hour Of The Gun*
1968 *The Pink Jungle; How Sweet It Is!*
1969 *Support Your Local Sheriff;
Marlowe*
1971 *The Skin Game; Support Your
Local Gunfighter*
1972 *They Only Kill Their Masters; Just
To Prove It* (narrator)
1973 *One Little Indian*
1974 *The Castaway Cowboy*
1978 *The New Maverick* (TV)
1980 *Health*
1981 *The Fan*
1982 *The Long Summer Of George
Adams* (TV); *Victor/Victoria*
1984 *Tank; The Glitter Dome* (TV);
*Heartsounds* (TV)
1985 *Murphy's Romance*
1986 *Promise* (TV)
1988 *Sunset*
1989 *My Name Is Bill W* (TV)
1990 *Decoration Day* (TV)
1992 *Distinguished Gentleman*
1993 *Fire In The Sky; Barbarians At
The Gate*

## GARNER, James
real name: James Baumgarner
(1928–   ) USA

1956 *Toward The Unknown* (UK:
*Brink Of Hell*); *The Girl He
Left Behind*
1957 *Sayonara\*; Shoot-Out At
Medicine Bend*

## GARSON, Greer
(1908–   ) USA

1939 *Goodbye Mr Chips\*; Remember?*
1940 *Pride And Prejudice*
1941 *Blossoms In The Dust; When
Ladies Meet*
1942 *Mrs Miniver\*; Random Harvest\**

**GARSON, Greer** (cont.)

1943  *The Youngest Profession; Madame Curie\*; A Report From Miss Greer Garson* (short)
1944  *Mrs Parkington; The Miracle Of Hickory* (short)
1945  *The Valley Of Decision; Adventure*
1947  *Desire Me*
1948  *Julia Misbehaves*
1949  *That Forsyte Woman* (UK: *The Forsyte Saga*)
1950  *The Miniver Story*
1951  *The Law And The Lady*
1952  *Scandal At Scourie*
1953  *Julius Caesar\**
1954  *Her Twelve Men*
1955  *Strange Lady In Town*
1960  *Sunrise At Campobello; Pepe*
1966  *The Singing Nun*
1967  *The Happiest Millionaire*
1978  *Little Women* (TV); *The Little Drummer Boy* (voice only)
1986  *Directed By William Wyler* (documentary)

## GAZZARA, Ben
real name: Biago Gazzara
(1930–   ) USA

1957  *The Strange One* (UK: *End As A Man*)
1959  *Anatomy Of A Murder\**
1960  *Risate Di Gioia* (UK: *The Passionate Thief*)
1961  *The Young Doctors*
1962  *Convicts Four* (UK: *Reprieve!*); *La Citta Prigoniera* (UK: *The Captive City*)
1964  *Carol For Another Christmas* (TV)
1965  *A Rage To Live*
1966  *Celebration* (short, narrator only)
1968  *The Bridge At Remagen; If It's Tuesday This Must Be Belgium*
1970  *Husbands; King: A Filmed Record, Montgomery To Memphis* (documentary)
1971  *When Michael Calls* (TV)
1972  *Afyon–Opium; Fireball Forward* (TV); *The Family Rico* (TV); *Pursuit* (TV)

1973  *The Neptune Factor; Maneater* (TV)
1974  *QB VII* (TV)
1975  *Capone; A Friend In Deed* (TV) (director only)
1976  *The Death Of Ritchie* (TV); *High Velocity; Voyage Of The Damned; The Killing Of A Chinese Bookie*
1977  *Opening Night; The Trial Of Lee Harvey Oswald* (TV)
1979  *Bloodline; Saint Jack*
1980  *Inchon!*
1981  *They All Laughed; Tales Of Ordinary Madness; A Question Of Honor* (TV)
1982  *La Ragazza Di Trieste*
1983  *Boogie Woogie; Uno Scandalo Perbene* (UK: *Only For Love*)
1984  *Richie* (TV); *Il Camorrista* (UK: *The Professor*); *The Woman Of Wonders*
1985  *Figlio Mio Infinimente Caro; An Early Frost* (TV)
1986  *A Letter To Three Wives* (TV); *La Memoire Tatouée*
1987  *The Day Before* (TV); *Downpayment On Murder* (TV); *Fatale; Police Story: The Freeway Killings* (TV)
1988  *Don Bosco; Quicker Than Eye; Road House; God's Peasant Forever*
1990  *Beyond The Ocean* (also director)
1991  *Lies Before Kisses* (TV)
1993  *And Quiet Flows The Don*

## GERE, Richard
(1949–   ) USA

1975  *Report To The Commissioner* (UK: *Operation Undercover*); *Strike Force* (TV)
1976  *Baby Blue Marine*
1977  *Looking Mr Goodbar*
1978  *Bloodbrothers; Days Of Heaven\**
1979  *Yanks*
1980  *American Gigolo\**
1982  *An Officer And An Gentleman\**
1983  *Breathless; The Honorary Consul*
1984  *The Cotton Club*
1985  *King David; Power*

1986 *No Mercy*
1988 *Miles From Home*
1989 *Internal Affairs*
1990 *Pretty Woman**
1991 *Rhapsody In August*
1992 *Final Analysis; Mr North;
   Sommersby*
1993 *And The Band Played On* (TV);
   *Intersection*

## GIBSON, Mel
(1956–   ) USA

1977 *Summer City*
1978 *Tim*
1979 *Chain Reaction; Mad Max**
1980 *Attack Force Z*
1981 *Gallipoli*; Mad Max 2: The Road
   Warrior**
1982 *The Year Of Living Dangerously**
1984 *The Bounty*; Mrs Soffel; The
   River*
1985 *Mad Max — Beyond
   Thunderdome**
1987 *Lethal Weapon**
1988 *Tequila Sunrise**
1989 *Lethal Weapon 2*
1990 *Air America; Bird On A Wire*;
   Hamlet**
1992 *Lethal Weapon 3; Forever Young;
   Earth And The American Dream*
   (voice only)
1993 *The Man Without A Face* (also
   director)

## GIELGUD, Sir Arthur John
(1904–   ) UK

1924 *Who Is The Man?*
1929 *The Clue Of The New Pin*
1932 *Insult*
1933 *The Good Companions*
1936 *The Secret Agent*
1937 *Full Fathom Five* (voice only)
1939 *Hamlet*
1942 *The Prime Minister; An Airman's
   Letter To His Mother* (voice only)
1944 *Unfinished Journey;
   Shakespeare's Country* (both
   voice only)
1945 *A Diary For Timothy*

1953 *Julius Caesar**
1954 *Romeo And Juliet*
1955 *Richard III**
1956 *Around The World In 80 Days**
1957 *The Barretts Of Wimpole Street;
   Saint Joan*
1958 *The Immortal Land* (narrator only)
1962 *To Die In Madrid* (narrator only)
1963 *Hamlet*
1964 *Becket**
1965 *The Loved One*
1966 *Chimes At Midnight*
1967 *Assignment To Kill; October
   Revolution* (narrator only)
1968 *Shoes Of The Fisherman;
   Sebastian; The Charge Of The
   Light Brigade*
1969 *Oh! What A Lovely War*
1970 *Julius Caesar; Eagle In A Cage*
1972 *Probe* (TV)
1973 *Lost Horizon; Frankenstein: The
   True Story* (TV); *Luther*
1974 *QB VII* (TV); *11 Harrowhouse;
   Gold; Murder On The Orient
   Express*; Galileo*
1976 *Aces High; Joseph Andrews*
1977 *A Portrait Of The Artist As A
   Young Man; Providence*
1978 *Les Misérables* (TV); *Caligula;
   Murder By Decree*
1979 *Omar Mukhtar: Lion Of The
   Desert; The Human Factor*
1980 *Dyrygent* (UK: *The Conductor*);
   *Sphinx; Priest Of Love; The
   Elephant Man*
1981 *Arthur*; Chariots Of Fire**
1982 *The Hunchback Of Notre Dame*
   (TV); *Wagner* (TV); *Gandhi**
1983 *The Wicked Lady; The Scarlet
   And The Black* (TV); *Invitation To
   The Wedding; Scandalous!*
1984 *The Shooting Party; Camille* (TV);
   *The Master Of Ballantrae* (TV)
1985 *Plenty; Romance On The
   Orient Express* (TV); *Leave All
   Fair*
1986 *The Whistle Blower; Time After
   Time* (TV)
1987 *Quartermaine's Terms* (TV);
   *Bluebeard, Bluebeard;
   Appointment With Death*

**GIELGUD, Sir Arthur John** (cont.)
1988  *A Man For All Seasons* (TV);
      *Arthur 2: On The Rocks*
1989  *Getting It Right; Strike It Rich*
1991  *Prospero's Books; Shining
      Through*
1992  *The Power Of One*

**GISH, Lillian**
real name: Lillian de Guiche
(1893–1993) USA

1912  *An Unseen Enemy; Oil And
      Water; The New York Hat; The
      Musketeers Of Pig Alley; Gold
      And Glitter; My Baby; A Cry For
      Help; Two Daughters Of Eve; In
      The Aisles Of The Wild; The
      Burglar's Dilemma; The
      Unwelcome Guest*
1913  *The Stolen Bride; Just Gold; The
      Lady And The Mouse; A
      Misunderstood Boy; House Of
      Darkness; The Left-Handed Man;
      During The Round-Up; The
      Mothering Heart; An Indian's
      Loyalty; The Madonna Of The
      Storm; A Woman In The Ultimate;
      A Timely Interception; A Modest
      Hero; The Battle Of Elderbrush
      Gulch; Just Kids; So Runs The
      Way; The Blue Or The Gray; The
      Conscience Of Hassan Bey*
1914  *Judith Of Bethulia; Home Sweet
      Home; The Green-Eyed Devil;
      The Escape; Silent Sandy; The
      Tear That Burned; The
      Quicksands; The Sisters; The
      Battle Of The Sexes; Lord
      Chumley; The Hunchback; Man's
      Enemy; His Lesson; The
      Rebellion Of Kitty Belle; The Folly
      Of Anne; The Wife; The Angel Of
      Contention*
1915  *Enoch Arden* (UK: *As Fate
      Ordained*); *Birth Of A Nation;
      Captain Macklin; The Lost House;
      The Lily And The Rose*
1916  *Intolerance; Sold For Marriage;
      Flirting With Fate; Daphne And
      The Pirate; An Innocent*

*Magdalene; Diane Of The Follies;
Pathways Of Life; The Children
Pay*
1917  *Souls Triumphant; The House
      Built Upon Sand*
1918  *Hearts Of The World; Buy Liberty
      Bonds; The Great Love; The
      Greatest Things In Life*
1919  *Broken Blossoms; True Heart
      Susie; The Greatest Question;
      The Romance Of Happy Valley*
1920  *Way Down East; Remodelling Her
      Husband* (director)
1922  *Orphans Of The Storm*
1923  *The White Sister*
1924  *Romola*
1926  *La Bohème; The Scarlet Letter*
1927  *Annie Laurie*
1928  *The Enemy; The Wind*
1930  *One Romantic Night*
1933  *His Double Life*
1942  *Commandos Strike At Dawn*
1943  *Top Man*
1946  *Miss Susie Slagle's; Duel In The
      Sun**
1948  *Portrait Of Jennie* (UK: *Jennie*)
1955  *The Cobweb; Salute To The
      Theatres* (documentary); *Night Of
      The Hunter**
1958  *Orders To Kill*
1960  *The Unforgiven*
1966  *Follow Me Boys!; Warning Shot*
1967  *The Comedians; Arsenic And Old
      Lace* (TV); *The Comedians In
      Africa* (documentary)
1970  *Henri Langlois* (documentary)
1976  *Twin Detectives* (TV)
1977  *Sparrow*
1978  *A Wedding*
1981  *Thin Ice* (TV)
1984  *Hobson's Choice* (TV); *Hambone
      And Hillie* (UK: *The Adventures Of
      Hambone*)
1986  *Sweet Liberty*
1987  *The Whales Of August*

**GLEASON, Jackie**
real name: Herbert John Gleason
(1916–87) USA

1941  *Navy Blues*

1942 *Larceny Inc; All Through The Night; Lady Gangster; Escape From Crime; Orchestra Wives; Springtime In The Rockies*
1950 *The Desert Hawk*
1961 *The Hustler\**
1962 *Gigot; Requiem For A Heavyweight* (UK: *Blood Money*
1963 *Papa's Delicate Condition; Soldier In The Rain*
1968 *Skidoo*
1969 *Don't Drink The Water; How To Commit Marriage*
1970 *How Do I Love Thee?*
1977 *Mr Billion; Smokey And The Bandit\**
1980 *Smokey And The Bandit II* (UK: *Smokey And The Bandit Ride Again*)
1982 *The Toy*
1983 *The Sting II; Smokey And The Bandit Part 3*
1984 *Fools Die*
1985 *Izzy And Mo* (TV)
1986 *Nothing In Common*

## GLOVER, Danny
(1947– ) USA

1979 *Escape From Alcatraz*
1981 *Chu Chu And The Philly Flash; Keeping On* (TV)
1982 *Out*
1984 *Iceman; Places In The Heart\*; The Stand-In*
1985 *The Color Purple\*; Silverado\*; Witness*
1987 *Lethal Weapon\*; Mandela* (TV)
1988 *Bat 21*
1989 *Dead Man Out* (TV); *Lethal Weapon 2*
1990 *Predator 2; To Sleep With Anger* (also co-executive producer)
1991 *Flight Of The Intruder; A Rage In Harlem; Pure Luck; Grand Canyon*
1992 *Lethal Weapon 2*
1993 *Bopha*

## GOLDBERG, Whoopi
real name: Caryn Johnson
(1949– ) USA

1985 *The Color Purple\**
1986 *Jumpin' Jack Flash*
1987 *Burglar; The Telephone; Fatal Beauty*
1988 *Clara's Heart*
1989 *Homer And Eddie; Beverly Hills Brat; Kiss Shot* (TV)
1990 *The Long Walk Home; Ghost\**
1991 *Soapdish*
1992 *The Player\*; Sister Act; Sarafina!*
1993 *Change Of Heart; Made In America; Sister Act 2; Naked In New York; The Page Master* (voice only)

## GOLDBLUM, Jeff
(1952– ) USA

1974 *Death Wish\*; California Split*
1975 *Nashville\**
1976 *Next Stop Greenwich Village; Special Delivery; The Sentinel; St Ives*
1977 *Between The Lines; Annie Hall\**
1978 *Thank God It's Friday; Remember My Name; Invasion Of The Bodysnatchers*
1979 *The Legend Of Sleepy Hollow* (TV)
1980 *Tenspeed And Brownshoe* (TV)
1981 *Threshold*
1982 *Rehearsal For Murder* (TV)
1983 *The Big Chill\*; The Right Stuff\**
1984 *Ernie Kovacs: Between The Laughter* (TV); *The Adventures Of Buckaroo Banzai: Across The Eighth Dimension*
1985 *Silverado\*; Into The Night; Transylvania 6-5000*
1986 *The Fly\*; Beyond Therapy*
1988 *Vibes*
1989 *Earth Girls Are Easy; The Tall Guy; The Mad Monkey*
1990 *Mister Frost; Framed* (TV)
1991 *The Favor, The Watch And The Very Big Fish; Fathers And Sons*
1992 *The Player\*; Deep Cover*
1993 *Jurassic Park*

## GOODMAN, John
(c1952–   ) USA

1984 *Revenge Of The Nerds; Maria's Lovers*
1985 *Sweet Dreams\**
1986 *True Stories*
1987 *The Big Easy\*; Burglar; Raising Arizona\**
1988 *Everybody's All-American* (UK: *When I Fall In Love*); *The Wrong Guys; Punchline\**
1989 *Always; Sea Of Love\**
1990 *Arachnophobia; Stella*
1991 *King Ralph; Barton Fink\**
1992 *The Babe; Matinee*
1993 *Born Yesterday; We're Back* (voice only)

## GOULD, Elliott
real name: Elliott Goldstein
(1938–   ) USA

1964 *The Confession*
1968 *The Night They Raided Minsky's*
1969 *Bob & Carol & Ted & Alice\**
1970 *M\*A\*S\*H; Getting Straight; I Love My Wife; Move; The Touch*
1971 *Little Murders*
1973 *The Long Goodbye; Busting*
1974 *SPYS; California Split; Who?*
1975 *Nashville\*; Whiffs* (UK: *C\*A\*S\*H*); *I Will, I Will...For Now; Mean Johnny Barrows*
1976 *Harry And Walter Go To New York*
1977 *A Bridge Too Far; Capricorn One*
1978 *The Silent Partner; Matilda; Escape To Athena*
1979 *The Muppet Movie\*; The Lady Vanishes*
1980 *The Last Flight Of Noah's Ark; Falling In Love Again; Dirty Tricks; The Devil And Max Devlin; A New Life*
1981 *The Rules Of Marriage* (TV)
1983 *Over The Brooklyn Bridge*
1984 *The Naked Face; The Muppets Take Manhattan*
1985 *Inside Out*
1986 *The Myth; Boogie Woogie; Vanishing Act* (TV)

1987 *Joker; Conspiracy: The Trial Of The Chicago 8* (TV); *My First 40 Years/Story Of A Woman*
1988 *Dangerous Love; The Big Picture*
1989 *The Wounded King; Never Cry Devil; Judgment; The Lemon Sisters; Dead Men Don't Die; Secret Scandal*
1990 *Human Portrait; Stolen: One Husband* (TV)
1991 *Bugsy*
1992 *The Player\**

## GRABLE, Betty
real name: Elizabeth Grasle
(1916–73) USA

1929 *Happy Days; Let's Go Places* (UK: *Mirth And Melody*)
1930 *Fox Movietone Follies Of 1930; Whoopee!*
1931 *Ex-Sweeties; Crashing Hollywood* (both shorts); *Kiki; Palmy Days*
1932 *Hollywood Luck; Hollywood Lights; Lady, Please; Over The Counter; The Flirty Sleepwalker* (all shorts); *The Greeks Had A Word For Them; Child Of Manhattan; The Kid From Spain; Hold'Em Jail; Probation* (UK: *Second Chance*)
1933 *Air Tonic* (short); *Cavalcade; The Sweethearts Of Sigma Chi* (UK: *Girl Of My Dreams*); *Melody Cruise; What Price Innocence* (UK: *Shall The Children Pay?*)
1934 *Love Detectives; Business Is A Pleasure; Elmer Steps Out; Susie's Affairs* (all shorts); *Student Tour; Hips, Hips, Hooray!; By Your Leave; The Gay Divorcee\** (UK: *The Gay Divorce*)
1935 *A Quiet Fourth; A Night At The Biltmore Bowl; Drawing Rumors; The Spirit Of 1776* (all shorts); *The Nitwits; Old Man Rythmn*
1936 *Follow The Fleet; Don't Turn'Em Loose; Pigskin Parade* (UK: *The Harmony Parade*); *Collegiate* (UK: *The Charm School*)

1937 *This Way Please; Thrill Of A Lifetime*
1938 *Give Me A Sailor; College Swing* (UK: *Swing Teacher Swing*); *Campus Confessions* (UK: *Fast Play*)
1939 *Man About Town; Million Dollar Legs; The Day The Bookies Wept*
1940 *Down Argentine Way; Tin Pan Alley*
1941 *A Yank In The RAF; Moon Over Miami; I Wake Up Screaming* (UK: *Hot Spot*)
1942 *Footlight Serenade; Song Of The Islands; Springtime In The Rockies*
1943 *Coney Island; Sweet Rosie O'Grady*
1944 *Four Jills In A Jeep; Pin-Up Girl*
1945 *Billy Rose's Diamond Horseshoe* (UK: *Diamond Horseshoe*); *The Dolly Sisters; All Star Bond Rally* (short)
1946 *Do You Love Me?; The Shocking Miss Pilgrim; Hollywood Park* (short)
1947 *Mother Wore Tights*
1948 *That Lady In Ermine; When My Baby Smiles At Me*
1949 *The Beautiful Blonde From Bashful Bend*
1950 *Wabash Avenue; My Blue Heaven*
1951 *Call Me Mister; Meet Me After The Show*
1953 *The Farmer Takes A Wife; How To Marry A Millionaire**
1954 *Three For The Show*
1955 *How To Be Very Very Popular*

## GRAHAME, Gloria
real name: Gloria Grahame Hallward
(1924–81) USA

1943 *Cry Havoc*
1944 *Blonde Fever*
1945 *Without Love*
1946 *It's A Wonderful Life**
1947 *It Happened In Brooklyn; Merton Of The Movies; Song Of The Thin Man; Crossfire*
1949 *A Woman's Secret; Roughshod*

1950 *In A Lonely Place*
1952 *Macao; Sudden Fear; The Greatest Show On Earth*; The Bad And The Beautiful**
1953 *Man On A Tightrope; The Glass Wall; The Big Heat*; Prisoners Of The Casbah*
1954 *The Good Die Young; Human Desire; Naked Alibi*
1955 *Oklahoma!*; The Cobweb; Not As A Stranger**
1956 *The Man Who Never Was*
1957 *Ride Out For Revenge*
1959 *Odds Against Tomorrow*
1966 *Ride Beyond Vengeance*
1971 *Blood And Lace; Chandler; The Todd Killings; Black Noon; Escape* (TV)
1972 *The Loners; Julio And Stein*
1973 *Tarot*
1974 *Mama's Dirty Girls; The Girl On The Late, Late Show* (TV)
1975 *Mansion Of The Doomed* (UK: *The Terror Of Dr Chaney*)
1979 *Chilly Scenes Of Winter; The Nesting*
1980 *Melvin And Howard; The Biggest Bank Robbery* (TV)

## GRANGER, Stewart
real name: James Stewart
(1913–  ) UK

1933 *I Spy* (stand-in only); *A Southern Maid*
1934 *Give Her A Ring; Over The Garden Wall*
1937 *Mademoiselle Docteur*
1939 *So This Is London*
1940 *Convoy*
1942 *Secret Mission*
1943 *Thursday's Child; The Lamp Still Burns; The Man In Grey*
1944 *Love Story; Fanny By Gaslight; Madonna Of The Seven Moons; Waterloo Road*
1945 *Caesar And Cleopatra*
1946 *Caravan; The Magic Bow*
1947 *Captain Boycott; Blanche Fury*
1948 *Saraband For Dead Lovers; Woman Hater*

**GRANGER, Stewart** (cont.)

1949 *Adam And Evelyne*
1950 *King Solomon's Mines**
1951 *Soldiers Three; The Light Touch*
1952 *Scaramouche; The Prisoner Of Zenda*; The Wild North*
1953 *Young Bess; All The Brothers Were Valiant; Salome*
1954 *Beau Brummell; Green Fire*
1955 *Moonfleet; Footsteps In The Fog*
1956 *The Last Hunt; Bhowani Junction*
1957 *The Little Hut; Gun Glory*
1958 *The Whole Truth; Harry Black*
1960 *North To Alaska*
1961 *The Secret Partner*
1962 *Swordsman Of Siena; La Congiura Dei Dieci; Sodom And Gomorrah*
1963 *Il Giorno Piu Corto Commedia Umaristica* (UK: *The Shortest Day*); *March Or Die* (UK: *The Legion's Last Patrol*)
1964 *The Secret Invasion; The Crooked Road; Among Vultures*
1965 *Der Ölprinz* (UK: *Rampage At Apache Wells*); *Old Surehand Erste Teil* (UK: *Flaming Frontier*)
1966 *Das Geheimnis Der Drei Dschunken; Das Geheimnis Der Gelben Mönche; Der Chef Schickt Seinen Besten Mann; Gern Hab' Ich Die Frauen Gekillt*
1967 *The Last Safari; The Trygon Factor*
1969 *Any Second Now* (TV)
1972 *The Hound Of The Baskervilles* (TV)
1978 *The Wild Geese*
1982 *The Royal Romance Of Charles And Diana* (TV)
1986 *Hell Hunters*
1987 *A Hazard Of Hearts* (TV)
1988 *Oro Fino/Fine Gold*
1990 *Strange Bedfellows* (TV)

## GRANT, Cary

real name: Archibald Leach
(1904–86) UK

1932 *Singapore Sue* (short); *This Is The Night; Merrily We Go To Hell*

(UK: *Merrily We Go To—*));
*Sinners In The Sun; Hot Saturday; The Devil And The Deep; Blonde Venus; Madame Butterfly*
1933 *The Woman Accused; I'm No Angel*; She Done Him Wrong*; The Eagle And The Hawk; Gambling Ship; Alice In Wonderland*
1934 *Thirty-Day Princess; Born To Be Bad; Ladies Should Listen; Kiss And Make Up; Enter Madame*
1935 *Wings In The Dark; The Last Outpost; Sylvia Scarlett*
1936 *The Amazing Quest Of Ernest Bliss; Wedding Present; Big Brown Eyes; Suzy; Pirate Party On Catalina Isle* (short)
1937 *The Toast Of New York; Topper; The Awful Truth*; When You're In Love* (UK: *For You Alone*)
1938 *Holiday; Bringing Up Baby**
1939 *Only Angels Have Wings; Gunga Din; In Name Only*
1940 *His Girl Friday*; My Favorite Wife; The Philadelphia Story*; The Howards Of Virginia* (UK: *Tree Of Liberty*)
1941 *Penny Serenade; Suspicion**
1942 *Talk Of The Town; Once Upon A Honeymoon*
1943 *Mr Lucky; Destination Tokyo*
1944 *Arsenic And Old Lace*; Once Upon A Time; The Road To Victory* (short); *The Shining Future; None But The Lonely Heart*
1946 *Night And Day*; Without Reservations; Notorious**
1947 *The Bachelor And The Bobbysoxer* (UK: *Bachelor Knight*)
1948 *The Bishop's Wife*; Mr Blandings Builds His Dream House; Every Girl Should Be Married*
1949 *I Was A Male War Bride** (UK: *You Can't Sleep Here*)
1950 *Crisis*
1951 *People Will Talk*
1952 *Room For One More; Monkey Business*
1953 *Dream Wife*

1955  *To Catch A Thief\**
1957  *The Pride And The Passion; An Affair To Remember; Kiss Them For Me*
1958  *Indiscreet; Houseboat*
1959  *North By Northwest\*; Operation Petticoat\**
1960  *The Grass Is Greener*
1961  *Captive Island* (short)
1962  *That Touch Of Mink*
1963  *Charade\**
1964  *Father Goose*
1966  *Walk Don't Run*
1970  *Elvis — That's The Way It Is*
1977  *Once Upon A Time Is Now* (voice only)

## GREENWOOD, Joan
(1921–87) UK

1940  *John Smith Wakes Up*
1941  *My Wife's Family; He Found A Star*
1943  *The Gentle Sex*
1945  *They Knew Mr Knight; Latin Quarter*
1946  *A Girl In A Million*
1947  *The Man Within; The October Man; The White Unicorn*
1948  *Saraband For Dead Lovers; Whisky Galore\**
1949  *The Bad Lord Byron; Kind Hearts And Coronets\**
1951  *Flesh And Blood; Young Wives' Tale; The Man In The White Suit\*; Monsieur Ripos*
1952  *The Importance Of Being Earnest*
1954  *Knave Of Hearts; Father Brown*
1955  *Moonfleet*
1958  *Stagestruck*
1962  *Mysterious Island; The Amorous Prawn*
1963  *Tom Jones\*; The Moon-Spinners*
1971  *Girl Stroke Boy*
1977  *The Uncanny; The Hound Of The Baskervilles*
1978  *The Water Babies*
1979  *The Flame Is Love* (TV)
1984  *Ellis Island* (TV)
1987  *Little Dorrit*

## GRENFELL, Joyce
real name: Joyce Phipps
(1910–79) UK

1943  *The Demi-Paradise; The Lamp Still Burns*
1946  *While The Sun Shines*
1948  *Designing Woman* (short); *Alice In Wonderland* (voice only)
1949  *Poet's Pub; Scrapbook For 1933* (voice only); *A Run For Your Money*
1950  *The Happiest Days Of Your Life; Stage Fright*
1951  *Laughter In Paradise; The Galloping Major; The Magic Box*
1952  *The Pickwick Papers*
1953  *Genevieve\*; The Million Pound Note*
1954  *Forbidden Cargo; The Belles Of St Trinians\**
1957  *The Good Companions; Happy Is The Bride*
1958  *Blue Murder At St Trinian's*
1961  *The Pure Hell Of St Trinian's*
1962  *The Old Dark House*
1964  *The Americanization Of Emily; The Yellow Rolls-Royce*

## GRIFFITH, Melanie
(1957–  ) USA

1969  *Smith!*
1973  *The Harrad Experiment* (extra only)
1975  *Smile; The Drowning Pool; Night Moves*
1977  *Joyride; One On One*
1978  *Steel Cowboy* (TV); *Daddy I Don't Like It Like This* (TV)
1981  *Golden Gate* (TV); *Underground Aces; She's In The Army Now* (TV); *Roar; The Star Maker* (TV)
1984  *Fear City; Body Double*
1985  *Alfred Hitchcock Presents* (TV)
1986  *Something Wild; Cherry 2000*
1987  *The Milagro Beanfield War; Stormy Monday*
1988  *Working Girl\**
1989  *In The Spirit*

**GRIFFITH, Melanie** (cont.)

1990 *Pacific Heights; Bonfire Of The Vanities\*; Men And Women: Stories Of Seduction* (TV)
1991 *Paradise; Shining Through*
1992 *A Stranger Among Us*
1993 *Born Yesterday*

## GUINNESS, Sir Alec
(1914– ) UK

1933 *Evensong*
1946 *Great Expectations\**
1948 *Oliver Twist\**
1949 *Kind Hearts And Coronets\*; A Run For Your Money*
1950 *Last Holiday; The Mudlark*
1951 *The Lavender Hill Mob\*; The Man In The White Suit\**
1952 *The Card*
1953 *The Malta Story; The Captain's Paradise*
1954 *Father Brown; To Paris With Love; The Stratford Adventure* (documentary)
1955 *The Prisoner; The Ladykillers\**
1956 *The Swan; Rowlandson's England* (narrator only)
1957 *Bridge On The River Kwai\*; Barnacle Bill*
1958 *The Horse's Mouth*
1959 *The Scapegoat*
1960 *Our Man In Havana; Tunes Of Glory\**
1961 *A Majority Of One*
1962 *HMS Defiant; Lawrence Of Arabia\**
1963 *The Fall Of The Roman Empire*
1965 *Situation Hopeless, But Not Serious; Doctor Zhivago\**
1966 *Hotel Paradiso; The Quiller Memorandum*
1967 *The Comedians; The Comedians In Africa* (documentary)
1970 *Cromwell; Scrooge*
1972 *Hitler: The Last Ten Days; Brother Sun, Sister Moon*
1976 *Murder By Decree*
1977 *Star Wars\**
1980 *The Empire Strikes Back\*; Raise The Titanic; Little Lord Fauntleroy*

1983 *Lovesick; Return Of The Jedi\**
1984 *A Passage To India\**
1987 *Little Dorrit*
1988 *A Handful Of Dust*
1991 *Kafka*
1993 *A Foreign Field* (TV)

# H

## HACKMAN, Gene
real name: Eugene Alden Hackman
(1930– ) USA

1961 *Mad Dog Coll*
1964 *Lilith*
1966 *Hawaii; First To Fight; Covenant With Death*
1967 *Banning; Bonnie And Clyde\**
1968 *Shadow On The Land* (TV); *The Split; Riot*
1969 *The Gypsy Moths; Marooned; Downhill Racer*
1970 *Confrontation* (short); *I Never Sang For My Father; Doctors' Wives*
1971 *The Hunting Party; Cisco Pike; The French Connection\**
1972 *Prime Cut; The Poseidon Adventure\**
1973 *Scarecrow*
1974 *The Conversation\*; Zandy's Bride; Young Frankenstein\**
1975 *Night Moves; Bite The Bullet; French Connection II; Lucky Lady*
1976 *The Domino Principle* (UK: *The Domino Killings*)
1977 *A Look At Liv Ullmann's Norway* (documentary); *March Or Die!; A Bridge Too Far*
1978 *Superman\*; Speed Fever* (documentary)
1979 *The Making Of Superman — The Movie* (documentary)
1980 *Superman II*
1981 *All Night Long; Reds\**
1982 *Eureka*
1983 *Misunderstood; Under Fire\*; Uncommon Valor; Two Of A Kind* (voice only)

1985 *Twice In A Lifetime; Target; Power*
1986 *Hoosiers* (UK: *Best Shot*)
1987 *No Way Out\*; Superman IV; Split Decisions*
1988 *Full Moon In Blue Water; Bat 21; Mississippi Burning\*; Another Woman\**
1989 *The Package*
1990 *Loose Cannons; Narrow Margin; Class Action; Postcards From The Edge\**
1991 *Company Business*
1992 *Unforgiven\**
1993 *The Firm*

## HANKS, Tom
(1956– ) USA

1980 *He Knows You're Alone*
1982 *Mazes And Monsters* (TV)
1984 *Bachelor Party; Splash\**
1985 *Volunteers; The Man With One Red Shoe; The Money Pit*
1986 *Nothing In Common; Every Time We Say Goodbye*
1987 *Dragnet*
1988 *Punchline\*; Big\**
1989 *The 'burbs\*; Turner And Hooch\**
1990 *Joe Versus The Volcano; Bonfire Of The Vanities\**
1992 *Radio Flyer; A League Of Their Own*
1993 *Sleepless In Seattle; Philadelphia*

## HANNAH, Daryl
(1960– ) USA

1978 *The Fury*
1981 *The Final Terror; Hard Country*
1982 *Summer Lovers; Paper Dolls* (TV); *Blade Runner\**
1984 *Splash\*; Reckless; The Pope Of Greenwich Village*
1986 *The Clan Of The Cave Bear; Legal Eagles*
1987 *Roxanne\*; Wall Street\**
1988 *High Spirits*
1989 *Crimes And Misdemeanours\*; Steel Magnolias\**
1990 *Crazy People*

1991 *At Play In The Fields Of The Lord*
1992 *Memoirs Of An Invisible Man*
1993 *Grumpy Old Men*

## HARLOW, Jean
real name: Harlean Carpentier
(1911–37) USA

1928 *Moran Of The Movies*
1929 *Why Is A Plumber?; Thundering Toupees; Double Whoopee; Bacon Grabbers; Liberty; The Unkissed Man; Weak But Willing* (all shorts); *Fugitives; Close Harmony; The Love Parade\*; The Saturday Night Kid; New York Nights; This Thing Called Love*
1930 *Hell's Angels*
1931 *City Lights\*; Iron Man; Goldie; The Public Enemy\** (UK: *Enemies Of The Public*); *Platinum Blonde; The Secret Six*
1932 *Three Wise Girls; The Beast Of The City; Red-Headed Woman; Red Dust*
1933 *Hold Your Man; Dinner At Eight; Bombshell* (UK: *Blonde Bombshell*)
1934 *The Girl From Missouri* (UK: *100 Per Cent Pure*)
1935 *Reckless; China Seas; Riffraff*
1936 *Wife Versus Secretary; Suzy; Libelled Lady*
1937 *Personal Property* (UK: *The Man In Possession*); *Saratoga*

## HARRIS, Richard
(1930– ) Ireland

1958 *Alive And Kicking*
1959 *Shake Hands With The Devil; The Wreck Of The Mary Deare*
1960 *A Terrible Beauty; The Long And The Short And The Tall*
1961 *The Guns Of Navarone\**
1962 *Mutiny On The Bounty\**
1963 *This Sporting Life*
1964 *The Red Desert; Carol For Another Christmas* (TV); *I Tre Volti* (UK: *Three Faces Of Love*)

**HARRIS, Richard** (cont.)
1965 *Major Dundee; The Heroes Of Telemark*
1966 *The Bible...In The Beginning\*; Hawaii*
1967 *Camelot\*; Caprice*
1969 *Bloomfield* (also director)*; The Molly Maguires*
1970 *A Man Called Horse; Cromwell*
1971 *Man In The Wilderness; The Snow Goose* (TV)
1972 *Today Mexico, Tomorrow The World* (short)
1973 *The Deadly Trackers*
1974 *99 And 44/100 Per Cent Dead* (UK: *Call Harry Crown*)*; Juggernaut*
1975 *Echoes Of A Summer*
1976 *Robin And Marian; The Return Of A Man Called Horse; Gulliver's Travels; The Cassandra Crossing*
1977 *Orca — Killer Whale; Golden Rendezvous*
1978 *The Wild Geese; Ravagers*
1979 *The Last Word; Game For Vultures; Highpoint*
1980 *Your Ticket Is No Longer Valid*
1981 *Tarzan The Apeman*
1982 *Triumphs Of A Man Called Horse*
1984 *Martin's Day*
1988 *The Return; Maigret* (TV)
1989 *Mack The Knife; King Of The Wind*
1990 *The Field*
1992 *Unforgiven\*; Patriot Games; Silent Tongue*
1993 *Wrestling Ernest Hemingway*

**HARRISON, Sir Rex**
real name: Reginald Harrison
(1908–90) UK

1930 *The Great Game; The School For Scandal*
1934 *Get Your Man; Leave It To Blanche*
1935 *All At Sea*
1936 *Men Are Not Gods*
1937 *Storm In A Teacup; School For Husbands; Over The Moon*
1938 *St Martin's Lane; The Citadel\**

1939 *The Silent Battle; Ten Days In Paris*
1940 *Night Train To Munich; Major Barbara*
1945 *I Live In Grosvenor Square; Blithe Spirit\*; Journey Together; The Rake's Progress*
1946 *Anna And The King Of Siam*
1947 *The Ghost And Mrs Muir; The Foxes Of Harrow*
1948 *Escape; Unfaithfully Yours*
1949 *On Stage* (short)
1951 *The Long Dark Hall*
1952 *The Four-Poster*
1953 *Main Street To Broadway*
1954 *King Richard And The Crusaders*
1955 *The Constant Husband*
1958 *The Reluctant Debutante*
1960 *Midnight Lace*
1962 *The Happy Thieves*
1963 *Cleopatra\**
1964 *My Fair Lady\*; The Yellow Rolls-Royce*
1965 *The Agony And The Ecstasy*
1967 *The Honey Pot; Dr Dolittle*
1968 *A Flea In Her Ear*
1969 *Staircase*
1972 *Don Quixote* (TV)
1974 *Three Faces Of Love* (TV)
1977 *The Prince And The Pauper; Behind The Iron Mask* (UK: *The Fifth Musketeer*)
1978 *Shalimar*
1979 *Ashanti*
1980 *Seven Graves For Rogan*

**HARVEY, Laurence**
real name: Larushka Mischa Skikne
(1928–73)

1948 *House Of Darkness; Man On The Run*
1949 *The Man From Yesterday; Landfall*
1950 *The Dancing Years; Cairo Road; The Black Rose*
1951 *There Is Another Sun; Scarlet Thread*
1952 *A Killer Walks; Women Of Twilight; I Believe In You; Decameron Nights*

1953 *Innocents In Paris*
1954 *The Good Die Young; Romeo And Juliet; King Richard And The Crusaders*
1955 *I Am A Camera; Storm Over The Nile*
1956 *Three Men In A Boat*
1957 *After The Ball*
1958 *The Truth About Women; The Silent Enemy; Power Among Men* (narrator only)
1959 *Room At The Top\*; Expresso Bongo*
1960 *Butterfield 8\*; The Alamo\*; The Long And The Short And The Tall*
1961 *Summer And Smoke; Two Loves* (UK: *Spinster*)
1962 *The Wonderful World Of The Brothers Grimm; The Manchurian Candidate\*; A Walk On The Wild Side; A Girl Named Tamiko*
1963 *The Running Man; The Ceremony* (also director)
1964 *The Outrage; Of Human Bondage*
1965 *Darling\*; Life At The Top*
1966 *The Spy With A Cold Nose; The Winter's Tale*
1968 *A Dandy In Aspic* (also co-director); *Heisses Spiel Für Harte Männer; Kampf Um Rom I*
1969 *She And He* (also director); *The Magic Christian; Kampf Um Rom II*
1970 *WUSA*
1972 *Escape To The Sun*
1973 *Welcome To Arrow Beach* (also director); *Night Watch; F For Fake*
1974 *The Yellow-Headed Submarine*

## HAUER, Rutger
(1944– ) Holland

1973 *Repelsweltje; Turks Fruit* (UK: *Turkish Delight*)
1974 *The Wilby Conspiracy; Pusteblume* (UK: *Hard To Remember*)
1975 *Le Vent De La Violence; Keetje Tippel; La Donneuse* (UK: *Naked And Lustful*)

1976 *Max Havelaar; Het Jaar Van De Kreeft; Griechische Feigen*
1977 *Soldier Of Orange*
1978 *Femme Entre Chien Et Loup; Jewel In The Deep; Mysteries; Pastorale 1943*
1980 *Spetters*
1981 *Nighthawks; Chanel Solitaire*
1982 *Blade Runner\*; Eureka; Grijpstra And De Gier* (UK: *Outsider In Amsterdam*); *Inside The Third Reich* (TV)
1983 *The Osterman Weekend*
1984 *A Breed Apart*
1985 *Ladyhawke; Flesh And Blood*
1986 *The Hitcher; Wanted — Dead Or Alive*
1987 *Escape From Sobibor* (TV)
1988 *The Legend Of The Holy Drinker*
1989 *Bloodhounds Of Broadway; The Salute Of The Jugger; On A Moonlit Night; The Edge* (TV)
1990 *Blind Fury*
1991 *Deadlock*
1992 *Split Second*

## HAWKINS, Jack
(1910–73) UK

1930 *Birds Of Prey*
1932 *The Lodger*
1933 *The Lost Chord; The Good Companions; I Lived With You; The Jewel; A Shot In The Dark*
1934 *Lorna Doone; Autumn Crocus; Death At Broadcasting House*
1935 *Peg Of Old Drury*
1937 *Beauty And The Barge; The Frog*
1938 *Who Goes Next?; A Royal Divorce*
1939 *Murder Will Out*
1940 *The Flying Squad*
1942 *The Next Of Kin*
1948 *The Fallen Idol; Bonnie Prince Charlie; The Small Back Room*
1950 *The Black Rose; The Elusive Pimpernel; State Secret; The Adventurers*
1951 *No Highway* (UK: *No Highway In The Sky*); *Home At Seven*

**HAWKINS, Jack** (cont.)
1952 *Mandy; The Planter's Wife; Angels One Five*
1953 *The Cruel Sea; Twice Upon A Time; Malta Story; The Intruder; Front Page Story; Prince Philip* (narrator only); *Pathway Into Light* (narrator only)
1954 *The Seekers*
1955 *Land Of The Pharaohs; The Prisoner; Touch And Go*
1956 *The Long Arm; The Man In The Sky; Fortune Is A Woman*
1957 *The Battle For Britain* (narrator only); *The Bridge On The River Kwai\**
1958 *Gideon's Day; The Two-Headed Spy*
1959 *Ben-Hur\**
1960 *The League Of Gentlemen*
1961 *La Fayette; Two Loves*
1962 *Lawrence Of Arabia\*; Five Finger Exercise; Rampage*
1963 *Zulu\**
1964 *The Third Secret; Guns At Batasi; Masquerade*
1965 *Lord Jim; Judith*
1966 *The Poppy Is Also A Flower* (UK: *Danger Grows Wild*)
1968 *Great Catherine; Shalako*
1969 *Oh, What A Lovely War; Monte Carlo Or Bust; Twinky*
1970 *The Adventures Of Gerard; The Beloved, Jane Eyre* (TV); *Waterloo*
1971 *When Eight Bells Toll; Kidnapped; Nicholas And Alexandra*
1972 *Young Winston; Escape To The Sun*
1973 *Theatre Of Blood; Tales That Witness Madness; The Last Lion*
1974 *QB VII* (TV)

**HAWN, Goldie Jeanne**
(1945–  ) USA

1968 *The One And Only Genuine Original Family Band*
1969 *Cactus Flower\**
1970 *There's A Girl In My Soup*
1971 *$* (UK: *The Heist*)

1972 *Butterflies Are Free*
1974 *Sugarland Express; The Girl From Petrovka*
1975 *Shampoo\**
1976 *The Duchess And The Dirtwater Fox*
1978 *Foul Play\**
1979 *Travels With Anita*
1980 *Private Benjamin\*: Seems Like Old Times*
1982 *Best Friends*
1984 *Swing Shift; Protocol*
1986 *Wildcats*
1987 *Overboard*
1989 *Bird On A Wire\*; My Blue Heaven* (co-executive producer only)
1991 *Criss Cross; Deceived*
1992 *Housesitter; Death Becomes Her\**

**HAY, Will**
(1888–1949) UK

1933 *Know Your Apples* (short)
1934 *Those Were The Days; Radio Parade Of 1935*
1935 *Dandy Dick; Boys Will Be Boys*
1936 *Where There's A Will; Windbag The Sailor*
1937 *Good Morning, Boys; Oh, Mr Porter\**
1938 *Convict 99; Hey! Hey! USA; Old Bones Of The River*
1939 *Ask A Policeman; Where's That Fire?*
1941 *The Ghost Of St Michael's; The Black Sheep Of Whitehall* (also co-director); *The Big Blockade*
1942 *Go To Blazes!* (short); *The Goose Steps Out* (also co-director)
1943 *My Learned Friend* (also co-director)

**HAYDEN, Sterling**
real name: Christian Walter
(1916–86)

1941 *Virginia; Bahama Passage*
1947 *Variety Girl; Blaze Of Noon*
1949 *El Paso; Manhandled*
1950 *The Asphalt Jungle\**

1951 *Journey Into Light; Flaming Feather*
1952 *Denver And Rio Grande; The Golden Hawk; Hellgate; Flat Top* (UK: *Eagles Of The Fleet*); *The Star*
1953 *Take Me To Town; Kansas Pacific; Fighter Attack; So Big; Crime Wave* (UK: *The City Is Dark*)
1954 *Arrow In The Dust; Johnny Guitar; Naked Alibi; Suddenly!; Prince Valiant; Battle Taxi*
1955 *Timberjack; The Eternal Sea; Shotgun; The Last Command; Top Gun*
1956 *The Come-On; The Killing**
1957 *Five Steps To Danger; Crime Of Passion; The Iron Sheriff; Valerie; Zero Hour; Gun Battle At Monterey*
1958 *Terror In A Texas Town; Ten Days To Tulara*
1964 *Dr Strangelove Or How I Learned To Stop Worrying And Love The Bomb*; Carol For Another Christmas* (TV)
1960 *Sweet Hunters; Hard Contract*
1970 *Loving*
1971 *Le Saut De L'Ange/Cobra*
1972 *The Godfather*; Le Grand Départ*
1973 *The Long Goodbye; The Final Programme*
1974 *Deadly Strangers*
1975 *Cry Onion*
1976 *Novecento** (UK: *1900*)
1977 *Winter Kills*
1978 *King Of The Gypsies*
1980 *Gas; 9 to 5**
1981 *Possession; Charlie Chan And The Curse Of The Dragon Queen; Venom*
1983 *Leuchtturm Des Chaos*

## HAYES, Helen
real name: Helen Hayes Brown
(1900–93) USA

1910 *Jean And The Calico Doll* (short)
1917 *The Weavers Of Life*
1920 *Babs*

1931 *The Sin Of Madelon Claudet* (UK: *The Lullaby*); *Arrowsmith**
1932 *A Farewell To Arms*; The Son-Daughter*
1933 *The White Sister; Another Language; Night Flight*
1934 *What Every Woman Knows; Crime Without Passion*
1935 *Vanessa, Her Love Story*
1943 *Stage Door Canteen*
1952 *My Son John*
1953 *Main Street To Broadway*
1956 *Anastasia*
1959 *Third Man On The Mountain*
1969 *Airport**
1971 *Do Not Fold, Spindle Or Mutilate* (TV)
1972 *The Snoop Sisters* (TV)
1974 *Herbie Rides Again*
1975 *One Of Our Dinosaurs Is Missing*
1976 *Victory At Entebbe*
1977 *Candleshoe*
1979 *A Family Upside Down* (TV)
1981 *Hopper's Silence* (voice only); *Murder Is Easy* (TV)
1983 *A Caribbean Mystery* (TV)
1984 *Highway To Heaven* (TV)
1985 *Murder With Mirrors* (TV)

## HAYWARD, Susan
real name: Edythe Marrenner
(1917–75) USA

1937 *Hollywood Hotel*
1938 *I Am The Law; Campus Cinderella; The Sisters; Girls On Probation; The Amazing Dr Clitterhouse; Comet Over Broadway*
1939 *Our Leading Citizen; $1,000 A Touchdown; Beau Geste**
1941 *Adam Had Four Sons; Sis Hopkins; Among The Living*
1942 *Reap The Wild Wind*; I Married A Witch; Star Spangled Rythmn; Forest Rangers; A Letter From Bataan* (short)
1943 *Hit Parade Of 1943; Young And Willing; Jack London*

**HAYWARD, Susan** (cont.)

1944 *The Fighting Seabees; The Hairy Ape; Skirmish On The Home Front* (short); *And Now Tomorrow*
1946 *Deadline At Dawn; Canyon Passage*
1947 *Smash-Up: The Story Of A Woman* (UK: *A Woman Destroyed*); *The Lost Moment; They Won't Believe Me*
1948 *Tap Roots; The Saxon Charm*
1949 *Tulsa; House Of Strangers; My Foolish Heart*
1950 *Rawhide*
1951 *I Can Get It For You Wholesale* (UK: *This Is My Affair*); *I'd Climb The Highest Mountain; David And Bathsheba*
1952 *With A Song In My Heart; The Snows Of Kilimanjaro\*; The Lusty Men*
1953 *The President's Lady; White Witch Doctor*
1954 *Demetrius And The Gladiators; Garden Of Evil*
1955 *Untamed; Soldier Of Fortune; I'll Cry Tomorrow\**
1956 *The Conqueror*
1957 *Top Secret Affair* (UK: *Their Secret Affair*)
1958 *I Want To Live!\**
1959 *Woman Obsessed; Thunder In The Sun*
1960 *The Marriage Go-Round*
1961 *Ada; Back Street*
1962 *I Thank A Fool*
1963 *Stolen Hours*
1964 *Where Love Has Gone*
1967 *The Honey Pot; Valley Of The Dolls; Think* (short)
1971 *Heat Of Anger* (TV)
1972 *The Revengers; Say Goodbye Maggie Cole* (TV)

**HAYWORTH, Rita**
real name: Margarita Carmen Cansino
(1918–87) USA

1926 *La Fiesta* (short)
1934 *Cruz Diablo* (short)
1935 *Rose De Francia* (short); *Under The Pampas Moon; Dante's Inferno; Charlie Chan In Egypt; In Caliente; Silk Legs; Paddy O'Day*
1936 *Human Cargo; A Message To Garcia; Rebellion; Meet Nero Wolfe*
1937 *Hit The Saddle; Trouble In Texas; Old Louisiana* (UK: *Treason*); *Criminals Of The Air; The Game That Kills; Paid To Dance; Girls Can Play; The Shadow* (UK: *The Circus Shadow*)
1938 *There's Always A Woman; Who Killed Gail Preston?; Juvenile Court; Convicted; Homicide Bureau; Renegade Ranger*
1939 *The Lone Wolf Spy Hunt* (UK: *The Lone Wolf's Daughter*); *Only Angels Have Wings; Special Inspector* (UK: *Across The Border*)
1940 *Music In My Heart; Blondie On A Budget; Susan And God* (UK: *The Gay Mrs Trexel*); *The Lady In Question; Angels Over Broadway*
1941 *The Strawberry Blonde; Affectionately Yours; Blood And Sand; You'll Never Get Rich*
1942 *My Gal Sal; Tales Of Manhattan; You Were Never Lovelier*
1943 *Showbusiness At War* (short)
1944 *Cover Girl*
1945 *Tonight And Every Night*
1946 *Gilda\**
1947 *Down To Earth*
1948 *The Lady From Shanghai\*; The Loves Of Carmen*
1951 *Champagne Safari* (documentary)
1952 *Affair In Trinidad*
1953 *Salome; Miss Sadie Thompson*
1954 *Screen Snapshots No 225* (short)
1957 *Fire Down Below; Pal Joey*
1958 *Separate Tables\**
1959 *They Came To Cordura; The Story On Page One*
1962 *The Happy Thieves*
1964 *Circus World* (UK: *The Magnificent Showman*)
1965 *The Money Trap*

1966 *The Poppy Is Also A Flower* (UK: *Danger Grows Wild*); *L'Avventriero*
1968 *I Bastardi* (UK: *Sons Of Satan*)
1970 *The Road To Salina*
1971 *The Naked Zoo*
1972 *The Wrath Of God*
1976 *Circle*


## HEMMINGS, David
(1941– ) UK

1950 *Night And The City*
1954 *The Rainbow Jacket*
1957 *Five Clues To Fortune; Saint Joan; The Heart Within*
1959 *In The Wake Of A Stranger; No Trees In The Street; Men Of Tomorrow*
1961 *The Wind Of Change; The Painted Smile*
1962 *Some People; Play It Cool; Two Left Feet*
1963 *West II; Live It Up*
1964 *The System; Be My Guest*
1965 *Dateline Diamonds*
1966 *Eye Of The Devil; Blow-Up\**
1967 *Camelot\**
1968 *Barbarella\*; The Charge Of The Light Brigade; Only When I Larf; The Long Day's Dying*
1969 *The Best House In London; Alfred The Great*
1970 *The Walking Stick; Fragments Of Fear; Simon, Simon* (short)
1971 *Unman, Wittering And Zigo; The Love Machine*
1972 *Autobiography; Today Mexico, Tomorrow The World* (short); *Running Scared* (director only)
1973 *Voices; The 14* (also director)
1974 *Juggernaut; Mister Quilp; No Es Naada, Mama, Solo Un Juego*
1975 *Profundo Rosso/Deep Red*
1976 *Islands In The Stream*
1977 *Squadra Antitruffa; Blood Relatives; The Squeeze; The Prince And The Pauper; The Heroin Busters*

1978 *Power Play; Murder By Decree; The Disappearance; Just A Gigolo* (also director)
1979 *Thirst; Charlie Muffin* (TV); *Harlequin*
1980 *Beyond Reasonable Doubt; Dr Jekyll And Mr Hyde* (TV)
1981 *The Survivor; Race For The Yankee Zephyr* (both director only)
1982 *Man, Woman And Child*
1983 *Airwolf* (TV)
1984 *Calamity Jane* (TV)
1985 *Come The Day* (director only); *Beverly Hills Cowboy Blues* (TV) (UK: *Beverly Hills Connection*)
1986 *Harry's Hong Kong* (TV); *3 On A Match* (TV)
1987 *Werewolf* (TV) (director only)
1988 *Davy Crockett: Rainbow In The Thunder* (TV) (also director)
1989 *Quantum Leap* (TV); *Hardball* (TV) (both director only); *The Rainbow*


## HEPBURN, Audrey
real name: Edda Van Heemstra Hepburn-Ruston
(1929–93) Belgium

1948 *Nederland In 7 Lessen*
1951 *Nous Irons A Monte Carlo* (UK: *Monte Carlo Baby*); *Laughter In Paradise; One Wild Oat; Young Wives' Tail; The Lavender Hill Mob\**
1952 *Secret People*
1953 *Introducing Audrey Hepburn* (short); *Roman Holiday\**
1954 *Sabrina* (UK: *Sabrina Fair*)
1956 *War And Peace\*; Funny Face\**
1957 *Love In The Afternoon*
1958 *Mayerling* (TV)
1959 *The Nun's Story\*; Green Mansions*
1960 *The Unforgiven*
1961 *Breakfast At Tiffany's\**
1962 *The Children's Hour* (UK: *The Loudest Whisper*)
1963 *Charade\*; Paris When It Sizzles*
1964 *My Fair Lady\**

**HEPBURN, Audrey** (cont.)
1966 *How To Steal A Million*
1967 *Two For The Road; Wait Until Dark*
1976 *Robin And Marian*
1979 *Bloodline*
1981 *They All Laughed*
1986 *Directed By William Wyler* (documentary)
1987 *Love Among Thieves* (TV)
1989 *Always*

**HEPBURN, Katharine Houghton**
(1907– ) USA

1932 *A Bill Of Divorcement\**
1933 *Christopher Strong; Morning Glory; Little Women\**
1934 *Spitfire; Break Of Hearts; The Little Minister*
1935 *Alice Adams; Sylvia Scarlett*
1936 *Mary Of Scotland; A Woman Rebels*
1937 *Quality Street; Stage Door\**
1938 *Bringing Up Baby\*; Holiday*
1940 *The Philadelphia Story\**
1942 *Woman Of The Year\*; Keeper Of The Flame*
1943 *Stage Door Canteen; Women In Defense* (narrator only)
1944 *Dragon Seed*
1945 *Without Love*
1946 *Undercurrent*
1947 *Song Of Love; Sea Of Grass*
1948 *State Of The Union* (UK: *The World And His Wife*)
1949 *Adam's Rib\**
1951 *The African Queen\**
1952 *Pat And Mike\**
1955 *Summer Madness*
1956 *The Rainmaker; The Iron Petticoat*
1957 *Desk Set* (UK: *His Other Woman*)
1959 *Suddenly Last Summer\**
1962 *Long Day's Journey Into Night\**
1967 *Guess Who's Coming To Dinner?\**
1968 *The Lion In Winter\**
1969 *The Madwoman Of Chaillot*
1971 *The Trojan Women*

1973 *The Glass Menagerie; A Delicate Balance*
1975 *Love Among The Ruins* (TV); *Rooster Cogburn*
1978 *Olly Olly Oxen Free*
1979 *The Corn Is Green* (TV)
1981 *On Golden Pond\**
1984 *The Ultimate Solution Of Grace Quigley* (UK: *Grace Quigley*)
1986 *Mrs Delafield Wants To Marry* (TV)
1988 *Laura Lansing Slept Here* (TV)
1992 *The Man Upstairs* (TV)

**HERSHEY, Barbara**
real name: Barbara Herzstein
(1947– ) USA

1968 *With Six You Get Egg Roll; Heaven With A Gun*
1969 *Last Summer*
1970 *The Liberation Of LB Jones; The Babymaker*
1971 *The Pursuit Of Happiness*
1972 *Boxcar Bertha; Dealing: Or The Berkeley-To-Boston-Forty-Bricks-Lost-Bag Blues*
1973 *Time To Run*
1974 *Vrooder's Hooch; You And Me*
1975 *Diamonds; Love Comes Quietly*
1976 *Trial By Combat; The Last Hard Men; Flood* (TV)
1977 *In The Glitter Palace* (TV); *Sunshine Christmas* (TV)
1978 *Just A Little Inconvenience* (TV)
1979 *A Man Called Intrepid* (TV)
1980 *Angel On My Shoulder* (TV); *The Stunt Man*
1981 *Take This Job And Shove It; Americana*
1982 *The Entity*
1983 *The Right Stuff\**
1984 *The Natural*
1985 *My Wicked, Wicked Ways — The Legend Of Errol Flynn* (TV)
1986 *Hannah And Her Sisters\*; Passion Flower* (TV); *Hoosiers* (UK: *Best Shot*)
1987 *Shy People; Tin Men\**
1988 *A World Apart; The Last Temptation Of Christ\*; Beaches*

1990 *Aunt Julia And The Scriptwriter; A Killing In A Small Town* (TV)
1991 *Defenseless; Paris Trout* (TV)
1992 *Swing Kids*
1993 *Falling Down; Splitting Heirs*

## HESTON, Charlton
real name: John Charlton Carter
(1923– ) USA

1941 *Peer Gynt*
1949 *Julius Caesar*
1950 *Dark City*
1952 *The Greatest Show On Earth\*; The Savage; Ruby Gentry*
1953 *Pony Express; The President's Lady; Arrowhead; Bad For Each Other; Three Lives* (short)
1954 *The Secret Of The Incas; The Naked Jungle; The Far Horizons*
1955 *The Private War Of Major Benson; Lucy Gallant*
1956 *Three Violent People; Forbidden Area* (TV); *The Ten Commandments\*; Many Voices* (narrator only)
1958 *Touch Of Evil\*; Point Of No Return* (TV); *The Buccaneer; The Big Country\**
1959 *The Wreck Of The Mary Deare; Ben-Hur\**
1961 *El Cid\**
1962 *Five Cities Of June* (narrator only); *The Pigeon That Took Rome; 55 Days At Peking; Diamond Head*
1964 *Major Dundee*
1965 *The Greatest Story Ever Told; The Agony And The Ecstasy; The War Lord; The Egyptologists* (narrator only)
1966 *Khartoum; While I Run This Race* (narrator only)
1967 *Counterpoint; All About People; Planet Of The Apes\*; Will Penny; Think 20th*
1969 *Rowan And Martin At The Movies; Number One; Beneath The Planet Of The Apes; The Heart Of Variety; The Festival Game; Rod Laver's Wimbledon* (narrator only)

1970 *Julius Caesar; King: A Filmed Record...Montgomery To Memphis; The Hawaiians* (UK: *Master Of The Islands*)
1971 *The Omega Man; Antony And Cleopatra* (also director)
1972 *Skyjacked; Call Of The Wild; Our Active Earth* (narrator only)
1973 *Soylent Green; The Three Musketeers\*; Lincoln's Gettysburg Address* (narrator only)
1974 *Earthquake\*; The Four Musketeers; Airport'75*
1975 *The Fun Of Your Life* (narrator only)
1976 *The Last Hard Men; Two Minute Warning; Midway* (UK: *Battle Of Midway*); *America At The Movies* (narrator only)
1977 *The Prince And The Pauper; Gray Lady Down*
1979 *Mountain Men*
1980 *The Awakening*
1982 *Mother Lode* (also director)
1984 *Nairobi Affair* (TV)
1986 *Directed By William Wyler* (documentary)
1987 *Proud Men* (TV)
1988 *A Man For All Seasons* (TV) (also director)
1989 *Original Sin* (TV); *Treasure Island* (TV)
1990 *Starfire; The Little Kidnappers* (TV); *Almost An Angel*
1991 *Crucifer Of Blood* (TV)

## HILLER, Dame Wendy
(1912– ) UK

1937 *Lancashire Luck*
1938 *Pygmalion\**
1940 *Major Barbara*
1945 *I Know Where I'm Going*
1951 *To Be A Woman* (narrator only); *Outcast Of The Islands*
1953 *Single-Handed*
1957 *How To Murder A Rich Uncle; Something Of Value; Bernard Shaw* (short)
1958 *Separate Tables\**
1960 *Sons And Lovers\**

**HILLER, Dame Wendy** (cont.)
1963 *Toys In The Attic*
1966 *A Man For All Seasons\**
1969 *David Copperfield* (TV)
1974 *Murder On The Orient Express\**
1976 *Voyage Of The Damned*
1978 *The Cat And The Canary*
1980 *The Elephant Man\**
1982 *Making Love; Witness For The Prosecution* (TV)
1983 *Attracta* (TV)
1985 *The Importance Of Being Earnest* (TV)
1986 *The Death Of The Heart*
1987 *The Lonely Passion Of Judith Hearne*


**HOFFMAN, Dustin**
(1937–   ) USA

1966 *Un Dollaro Per Sette Vigliacci* (UK: *Madigan's Millions*)
1967 *The Tiger Makes Out; The Graduate\**
1969 *John And Mary; Midnight Cowboy\**
1970 *Little Big Man\*; Arthur Penn, 1922: Themes And Variations* (documentary); *Arthur Penn: The Director* (documentary)
1971 *The Point* (TV) (narrator only); *Who Is Harry Kellerman And Why Is He Saying These Terrible Things About Me?; Alfredo, Alfredo; Straw Dogs*
1973 *Sunday Father* (short); *Papillon\**
1974 *Lenny\**
1976 *All The President's Men\*; Marathon Man*
1977 *Straight Time*
1978 *Agatha*
1979 *Kramer Vs Kramer\**
1982 *Tootsie\**
1985 *Death Of A Salesman* (TV)
1987 *Ishtar*
1988 *Rain Man\**
1989 *Family Business\*; Common Threads* (narrator only)
1990 *Dick Tracy\**
1991 *Billy Bathgate; Hook\**

1992 *Hero* (UK: *Accidental Hero); Earth And The American Dream* (voice only)


**HOGAN, Paul**
(1942–   ) Australia

1985 *Anzacs*
1986 *'Crocodile' Dundee\**
1988 *'Crocodile' Dundee 2*
1989 *The Humpty Dumpty Man* (director only)
1990 *Almost An Angel*


**HOLDEN, William**
real name: William Franklin Beedle Junior
(1918–81) USA

1938 *Prison Farm*
1939 *Each Dawn I Die; Million Dollar Legs; Golden Boy; Invisible Stripes*
1940 *Those Were The Days* (UK: *Good Old School Days); Our Town\*; Arizona*
1941 *I Wanted Wings; Texas*
1942 *The Remarkable Andrew; Meet The Stewarts; The Fleet's In*
1943 *Young And Willing; Wings Up* (short)
1947 *Variety Girl; Blaze Of Noon; Dear Ruth*
1948 *Apartment For Peggy; The Man From Colorado; Rachel And The Stranger*
1949 *Hollywood Goes To Church* (short); *Miss Grant Takes Richmond* (UK: *Innocence Is Bliss); Dear Wife; The Dark Past; Streets Of Laredo*
1950 *Father Is A Bachelor; Born Yesterday\*; You Can Change The World; Sunset Boulevard\*; Union Station*
1951 *Submarine Command; Force Of Arms; Boots Malone*
1952 *The Turning Point*
1953 *The Moon Is Blue; Stalag 17\*; Forever Female; Escape From Fort Bravo*

1954 *Executive Suite; The Bridges At Toko-Ri; Sabrina* (UK: *Sabrina Fair*); *The Country Girl**
1955 *Love Is A Many Splendored Thing; Picnic**
1956 *Toward The Unknown* (UK: *Brink Of Hell*); *The Proud And The Profane*
1957 *Bridge On The River Kwai**
1958 *The Key*
1959 *The Horse Soldiers*
1960 *The World Of Suzie Wong*
1961 *The Counterfeit Traitor*
1962 *Satan Never Sleeps* (UK: *The Devil Never Sleeps*); *The Lion*
1963 *Paris When It Sizzles*
1964 *The Seventh Dawn*
1966 *Alvarez Kelly*
1967 *Casino Royale*
1968 *The Devil's Brigade*
1969 *The Christmas Tree; The Wild Bunch**
1971 *The Wild Rovers*
1972 *The Revengers*
1973 *The Blue Knight* (TV); *Breezy*
1974 *The Towering Inferno*; Open Season*
1976 *21 Hours At Munich* (TV); *Network**
1978 *Damien—Omen II; Fedora; Escape To Athena*
1979 *Ashanti*
1980 *When Time Ran Out...; The Earthling*
1981 *SOB; Mysteries Of The Sea* (TV) (narrator only)

## HOLLIDAY, Judy
real name: Judith Tuvim
(1922–65) USA

1938 *Too Much Johnson*
1944 *Winged Victory; Greenwich Village; Something For The Boys*
1949 *Adam's Rib**
1950 *Born Yesterday**
1952 *The Marrying Kind*
1954 *It Should Happen To You; Phffft; Extra Dollars* (short)

1956 *The Solid Gold Cadillac; Full Of Life*
1960 *Bells Are Ringing*

## HOLM, Celeste
(1919– ) USA

1946 *Three Little Girls In Blue*
1947 *Carnival In Costa Rica; Gentleman's Agreement**
1948 *Road House; The Snake Pit*; Chicken Every Sunday*
1949 *Come To The Stable; Everybody Does It; A Letter To Three Wives** (voice only)
1950 *Champagne For Caesar; All About Eve**
1955 *The Tender Trap*
1956 *High Society**
1961 *Bachelor Flat*
1967 *Cosa Nostra–An Arch Enemy Of The FBI* (TV); *Doctor, You've Got To Be Kidding*
1972 *The Delphi Bureau* (TV)
1973 *Tom Sawyer*
1974 *The Underground Man* (TV); *Death Cruise* (TV)
1976 *Bittersweet Love*
1977 *The Private Files Of J Edgar Hoover; The Love Boat 2* (TV)
1981 *Midnight Lace* (TV)
1983 *This Girl For Hire* (TV)
1985 *Jessie* (TV)
1987 *Three Men And A Baby*; Marilyn Monroe: Beyond The Legend; Murder By The Book* (TV)
1989 *Polly* (TV); *Christine Cromwell: Things That Go Bump In The Night* (TV)
1990 *Polly Comin' Home* (TV)

## HOPE, Bob
real name: Leslie Townes Hope
(1903– ) UK

1934 *Going Spanish; Paree, Paree; Soup For Nuts* (all shorts)
1935 *Watch The Birdie; The Old Grey Mayor; Double Exposure* (all shorts)
1936 *Shop Talk* (short); *Calling All Tars*

**HOPE, Bob** (cont.)
1938 *The Big Broadcast Of 1938;
College Swing* (UK: *Swing,
Teacher, Swing*); *Give Me A
Sailor; Thanks For The Memory;
Don't Hook Now*
1939 *Never Say Die; The Cat And The
Canary; Some Like It Hot\**
1940 *Road To Singapore\*; The Ghost
Breakers*
1941 *Caught In The Draft; Cavalcade
Of The Academy Awards* (short)
*Road To Zanzibar; Louisiana
Purchase; Nothing But The Truth*
1942 *Road To Morocco; My Favourite
Blonde; Star Spangled Rythmn;
They Got Me Covered*
1943 *Welcome To Britain;
Showbusiness At War* (both
shorts); *Let's Face It*
1944 *The Princess And The Pirate*
1945 *All Star Bond Rally; Hollyood
Victory Caravan* (both shorts);
*Duffy's Tavern; Road To Utopia*
1946 *Monsieur Beaucaire*
1947 *Variety Girl; My Favourite
Brunette; Where There's Life;
Road To Rio*
1948 *Radio Broadcasting Today* (short);
*The Paleface\*; Screen Snapshots
No 166* (short); *Rough But
Hopeful*
1949 *Honor Caddie* (short); *Sorrowful
Jones; The Great Lover*
1950 *Fancy Pants; On Stage
Everybody* (short)
1951 *The Lemon Drop Kid; My
Favourite Spy*
1952 *The Greatest Show On Earth\*;
Son Of Paleface: Road To Bali; A
Sporting Oasis* (short)
1953 *Off Limits* (UK: *Military
Policeman*); *Scared Stiff; Here
Come The Girls*
1954 *Casanova's Big Night; Screen
Snapshots No 224* (voice only)
1955 *The Seven Little Foys*
1956 *That Certain Feeling; The Iron
Petticoat*
1957 *Beau James; The Heart Of
Showbusiness*

1958 *Paris Holiday; Showdown At Ulcer
Gulch* (short)
1959 *The Five Pennies; Alias Jesse
James*
1960 *The Facts Of Life*
1961 *Bachelor In Paradise; Road To
Hong Kong; Kitty Caddy* (voice
only)
1962 *Critic's Choice*
1963 *A Global Affair; Call Me Bwana*
1965 *I'll Take Sweden*
1966 *The Oscar; Boy Did I Get A
Wrong Number; Not With My Wife
You Don't; Hollywood Star-
Spangled Revue* (short)
1967 *Eight On The Lam* (UK: *Eight On
The Run*); *The Movie Maker* (TV)
1968 *The Private Navy Of Sergeant
O'Farrell*
1969 *How To Commit Marriage*
1972 *Cancel My Reservation*
1979 *The Muppet Movie\*; Ken Murray's
Shooting Stars*
1985 *Spies Like Us*
1986 *A Masterpiece Of Murder* (TV)

**HOPKINS, Sir Anthony**
(1937–   ) UK

1967 *The White Bus*
1968 *The Lion In Winter\**
1969 *Hamlet; The Looking Glass War*
1970 *When Eight Bells Toll*
1972 *Young Winston*
1973 *A Doll's House*
1974 *QB VII* (TV); *Juggernaut; The Girl
From Petrovka; All Creatures
Great And Small*
1975 *Dark Victory*
1976 *The Lindbergh Kidnapping Case*
(TV); *Victory At Entebbe*
1977 *Audrey Rose; A Bridge Too Far*
1978 *International Velvet; Magic*
1979 *Mayflower: The Pilgrims
Adventure* (TV)
1980 *A Change Of Seasons; The
Elephant Man\**
1981 *The Bunker* (TV); *Peter And Paul*
(TV)
1982 *The Hunchback Of Notre Dame*
(TV)

1984 *Io E Il Duce; Arch Of Triumph*
(TV); *The Bounty**
1985 *Guilty Conscience* (TV);
*Hollywood Wives* (TV)
1986 *The Good Father; 84 Charing
Cross Road; Blunt* (TV)
1988 *Across The Lake* (TV); *The Tenth
Man* (TV); *The Dawning*
1989 *A Chorus Of Disapproval; Face Of
The Earth* (TV); *Great
Expectations* (TV)
1990 *The Desperate Hours; One Man's
War*
1991 *The Silence Of The Lambs*;
Spotswood*
1992 *Freejack; Howard's End*; Bram
Stoker's Dracula*; Chaplin; The
Innocent* (TV); *The Trial* (TV);
*Earth And The American Dream*
(voice only)
1993 *Remains Of The Day;
Shadowlands*

## HOPKINS, Miriam
real name: Ellen Miriam Hopkins
(1902–72) USA

1928 *The Home Girl* (short)
1930 *Fast And Loose*
1931 *The Smiling Lieutenant; Dr Jekyll
And Mr Hyde*; Twenty-Four
Hours* (UK: *The Hours Between*)
1932 *The World And The Flesh; Two
Kinds Of Women; Trouble In
Paradise; Dancers In The Dark*
1933 *The Story Of Temple Dark;
Design For Living; The Stranger's
Return*
1934 *All Of Me; She Loves Me Not; The
Richest Girl In The World*
1935 *Barbary Coast; Becky Sharp*;
Splendor*
1936 *These Three; Men Are Not Gods*
1937 *Woman Chases Man; The
Woman I Love* (UK: *The Woman
Between*)
1938 *Wise Girl*
1939 *The Old Maid**
1940 *Virginia City; The Lady With Red
Hair*
1942 *A Gentleman After Dark*

1943 *Old Acquaintance*
1944 *Skirmish On The Home Front*
(short)
1949 *The Heiress**
1951 *The Mating Season*
1952 *Carrie; The Outcasts Of Poker
Flat*
1962 *The Children's Hour* (UK: *The
Loudest Whisper*)
1965 *Fanny Hill*
1966 *The Chase*
1970 *Comeback* (aka *Savage Intruder*)

## HOPPER, Dennis
(1936–   ) USA

1954 *Johnny Guitar*
1955 *I Died A Thousand Times; Rebel
Without A Cause**
1956 *The Steel Jungle; Giant**
1957 *Gunfight At The OK Corral; No
Man's Road* (TV); *A Question Of
Loyalty* (TV); *Sayonara** (voice
only); *The Story Of Mankind*
1958 *From Hell To Texas* (UK:
*Manhunt*)
1959 *The Young Land*
1960 *Key Witness*
1963 *Night Tide; Tarzan And Jane
Regained . . . Sort Of*
1965 *The Sons Of Katie Elder*
1966 *Planet Of Blood*
1967 *The Glory Stompers; Cool Hand
Luke*; Panic In The City; Hang
'Em High; The Trip*
1968 *Head*
1969 *True Grit*; The Festival Game;
Easy Rider**
1970 *The American Dreamer*
1971 *The Last Movie; Crush Proof*
1973 *Kid Blue; Hex*
1975 *James Dean: The First American
Teenager* (documentary); *The Sky
Is Falling*
1976 *Tracks; Mad Dog Moran* (UK: *Mad
Dog*)
1977 *Der Amerikanische Freund* (UK:
*The American Friend*); *Les
Apprentis Sorciers*

**HOPPER, Dennis** (cont.)
1978 *L'Ordre Et La Sécurité Du Monde; Couleur Chair; The Human Highway*
1979 *Apocalypse Now\**
1980 *Out Of The Blue* (also director); *Wild Times* (TV)
1981 *King Of The Mountain; Reborn*
1982 *Human Highway*
1983 *White Star; Jungle Warriors; The Osterman Weekend; Rumble Fish*
1984 *OC And Stiggs; The Inside Man*
1985 *My Science Project; Running Out Of Luck; Stark* (TV)
1986 *The American Way; Stark: Mirror Image* (TV); *Blue Velvet\*; The Texas Chainsaw Massacre 2; River's Edge\*; Hoosiers* (UK: *Best Shot*)
1987 *Black Widow; Straight To Hell; Blood Red; The Pick-Up Artist*
1989 *Backtrack* (UK: *Catchfire*) (also director)
1990 *Chattahoochee; Flashback; The Life And Times Of Andy Warhol* (documentary)
1991 *Paris Trout* (TV); *The Indian Runner*
1992 *Money Men; Red Rock West; Nails* (TV); *The Heart Of Justice* (TV)
1993 *The Super Mario Brothers; True Romance; Short Cuts*

See also directors listing

**HOSKINS, Bob**
full name: Robert William Hoskins
(1942–   ) UK

1973 *The National Health*
1975 *Royal Flash; Inserts*
1979 *Zulu Dawn*
1980 *The Long Good Friday\**
1982 *Pink Floyd — The Wall*
1983 *The Act; The Honorary Consul; Lassiter*
1984 *Io E Il Duce; The Cotton Club*
1985 *Brazil\**

1986 *Sweet Liberty; Mona Lisa\*; The Woman Who Married Clark Gable* (short)
1987 *A Prayer For The Dying; The Secret Policeman's Third Ball* (voice only); *The Lonely Passion Of Judith Hearne*
1988 *The Raggedy Rawney* (also director); *Who Framed Roger Rabbit\**
1990 *Heart Condition; Mermaids*
1991 *Shattered; Hook\*; The Favour, The Watch And The Very Big Fish*
1992 *The Inner Circle; Passed Away; Blue Ice*
1993 *The Super Mario Brothers*

**HOWARD, Leslie**
real name: Leslie Howard Stainer
(1893–1943) UK

1914 *The Heroine Of Mons* (short)
1917 *The Happy Warrior*
1918 *The Lackey And The Lady*
1920 *Five Pounds Reward; Bookworms* (both shorts)
1930 *Outward Bound*
1931 *Never The Twain Shall Meet; A Free Soul; Devotion; Service For Ladies; Five And Ten* (UK: *Daughter Of Luxury*)
1932 *Smilin' Through; The Animal Kingdom* (UK: *The Woman In His House*)
1933 *The Lady Is Willing; Secrets; Berkeley Square; Captured*
1934 *British Agent; Of Human Bondage; The Scarlet Pimpernel; Hollywood On Parade No 13* (short)
1936 *The Petrified Forest\*; Romeo And Juliet*
1937 *It's Love I'm After; Stand-In*
1938 *Pygmalion\** (also co-director)
1939 *Gone With The Wind\*; Intermezzo: A Love Story* (UK: *Escape To Happiness*)
1940 *Common Heritage* (narrator only)
1941 *Pimpernel Smith* (also director); *From The Four Corners* (short); *49th Parallel\*; The White Eagle* (short)

1942 *The First Of The Few* (also
director)
1943 *The Gentle Sex* (co-director)

See also directors listing

## HOWARD, Trevor
(1916–88) UK

1944 *The Way Ahead*
1945 *The Way To The Stars; Brief
Encounter\**
1946 *I See A Dark Stranger; Green For
Danger*
1947 *So Well Remembered; They
Made Me A Fugitive*
1948 *The Passionate Friends*
1949 *The Third Man\*; Golden
Salamander*
1950 *Odette; The Clouded Yellow*
1951 *Lady Godiva Rides Again;
Outcast Of The Islands*
1952 *Gift Horse*
1953 *The Heart Of The Matter*
1954 *April In Portugal* (voice only); *The
Stranger's Hand; Les Amants Du
Tage* (UK: *The Lovers Of Lisbon*)
1955 *Cockleshell Heroes*
1956 *Deception; Around The World In
80 Days\*; Run For The Sun*
1957 *Interpol; Manuela*
1958 *The Roots Of Heaven; The Key*
1960 *Moment Of Danger; The Hiding
Place* (TV); *Sons And Lovers\**
1962 *Mutiny On The Bounty\*; The Lion*
1963 *Man In The Middle*
1964 *Father Goose*
1965 *Operation Crossbow; The
Liquidator; Morituri* (UK: *The
Saboteur—Code Name Morituri*);
*Von Ryan's Express*
1966 *The Poppy Is Also A Flower* (UK:
*Danger Grows Wild*); *Triple Cross*
1967 *The Long Duel; Pretty Polly*
1968 *The Charge Of The Light Brigade*
1969 *The Battle Of Britain; Twinky*
1970 *Ryan's Daughter\**
1971 *The Night Visitor; Mary, Queen Of
Scots; Catch Me A Spy;
Kidnapped*
1972 *Ludwig; Pope Joan; The Offence*

1973 *A Doll's House; Catholics* (TV);
*Craze*
1974 *Il Harrowhouse; Persecution; The
Count Of Monte Cristo* (TV);
*Who?*
1975 *Hennessy; Death In The Sun; The
Bawdy Adventures Of Tom Jones;
Conduct Unbecoming*
1976 *Aces High*
1977 *The Last Remake Of Beau Geste;
Eliza Fraser; Slavers*
1978 *Die Rebellen* (UK: *Flashpoint
Africa*); *Superman\*; Stevie; How
To Score . . . A Movie*
(documentary)
1979 *Meteor; Hurricane; The
Shillingbury Blowers* (TV); *Night
Flight* (short)
1980 *Sir Henry At Rawlinson End; The
Sea Wolves; Windwalker*
1981 *Les Années Lumières* (UK: *Light
Years Away*)
1982 *Gandhi\*; Inside The Third Reich*
(TV); *The Deadly Game* (TV); *The
Missionary*
1983 *Sword Of The Valiant; The Devil
Impostor*
1985 *Dust; Time After Time* (TV)
1986 *Foreign Body; Rumpelstiltskin;
Christmas Eve* (TV); *Peter The
Great* (TV)
1988 *White Mischief; The Dawning; The
Unholy*

## HUDSON, Rock
real name: Roy Scherer
(1925–85) USA

1948 *Fighter Squadron*
1949 *Undertow*
1950 *I Was A Shoplifter; Winchester
'73; One Way Street; Peggy; The
Desert Heart; Shakedown; Double
Crossbones; Tomahawk* (UK: *The
Battle Of Powder River*); *Bright
Victory* (UK: *Lights Out*)
1951 *Iron Man; The Fat Man; Air Cadet*
(UK: *Jet Men Of The Air*)
1952 *Has Anybody Seen My Gal?;
Scarlet Angel; Here Come The
Nelsons; Horizons West; The*

**HUDSON, Rock** (cont.)
*Lawless Breed; Bend Of The River*
(UK: *Where The River Bends*)
1953 *Gun Fury; Seminole; The Golden*
*Blade; Back To God's Country,*
*Sea Devils*
1954 *Taza, Son Of Cochise; Bengal*
*Brigade* (UK: *Bengal Rifles*);
*Captain Lightfoot; Magnificent*
*Obsession\**
1955 *All That Heaven Allows; One*
*Desire*
1956 *Never Say Goodbye; Written On*
*The Wind; Four Girls In Town;*
*Giant\**
1957 *Battle Hymn; The Tarnished*
*Angels; A Farewell To Arms;*
*Something Of Value*
1958 *Twilight For The Gods*
1959 *This Earth Is Mine; Pillow Talk\**
1961 *The Last Sunset; Lover Come*
*Back; Come September*
1962 *The Spiral Road*
1963 *A Gathering Of Eagles; Marilyn*
(narrator only)
1964 *Send Me No Flowers; Man's*
*Favourite Sport?*
1965 *Strange Bedfellows; A Very*
*Special Favor; The Nurse* (short,
narrator only)
1966 *Blindfold; Seconds*
1967 *Tobruk*
1968 *Ice Station Zebra*
1969 *A Fine Pair; The Undefeated*
1970 *Darling Lili; Hornet's Nest*
1971 *Pretty Maids All In A Row*
1972 *Showdown*
1975 *Embryo*
1978 *Avalanche*
1979 *The Martian Chronicles* (TV)
1980 *The Mirror Crack'd*
1981 *The Star Maker* (TV); *The Patricia*
*Neal Story* (TV)
1982 *World War III* (TV)
1984 *The Vegas Strip War* (TV); *The*
*Ambassador*

**HUPPERT, Isabelle**
(1955– ) France

1971 *Faustine Et Le Bel Eté* (UK: *Faustine*)

1972 *César Et Rosalie* (UK: *Cesar And*
*Rosalie); Le Bar De La Fourche*
1973 *L'Ampélopède; Les Valseuses*
(UK: *Making It*)
1974 *Glissements Progressifs Du*
*Plaisir; Dupont Lajoie; Sérieux*
*Comme Le Plaisir; Rosebud; Le*
*Grand Délire; Aloise*
1975 *Docteur Françoise Gailland; Le*
*Juge Et L'Assassin; Je Suis*
*Pierre Rivière; Flash Back; Le*
*Petit Marcel*
1977 *La Dentillière* (UK: *The*
*Lacemaker*); *Des Enfants Gâtés;*
*Les Indiens Sont Encore Loin*
1978 *Violete Nozière; Retour La Bien-*
*Aimée; The Brontë Sisters*
1979 *La Couleur Du Temps; Loulou*
1980 *Heaven's Gate\*; Sauve Qui Peut*
*La Vie* (UK: *Slow Motion*); *Le Vera*
*Storia Della Signora Delle*
*Camelie; Orökseg*
1981 *Les Ailes De La Colombe; Coup*
*De Torchon* (UK: *Clean Slate*);
*Eaux Profonds*
1982 *Passion; Le Truite* (UK: *The*
*Trout*)
1983 *Coup De Foudre* (UK: *At First*
*Sight*); *Storia Di Piera; La Femme*
*De Ma Pote* (UK: *My Best*
*Friend's Girl*)
1984 *Violence; La Garce* (UK: *The*
*Bitch*)
1985 *Signé Charlotte; Sac De Noeuds;*
*Partage De Minuit*
1986 *Cactus*
1987 *The Possessed; The Bedroom*
*Window; Chatov Et Les Demons;*
*Milan Noir*
1988 *Migrations; Une Affaire De*
*Femmes*
1989 *Vengeance D'Une Femme*
1990 *Malina*
1991 *Madame Bovary*
1992 *Après L'Amour*

**HURT, John**
(1940– ) UK

1962 *The Wild And The Willing*
1963 *This Is My Street*

1966 *A Man For All Seasons**
1967 *The Sailor From Gibraltar*
1968 *In Search Of Gregory*
1969 *Sinful Davey; Before Winter Comes*
1970 *10 Rillington Place*
1971 *Mr Forbush And The Penguins*
1972 *The Pied Piper*
1974 *The Ghoul; Little Malcolm And His Struggle Against The Eunuchs*
1975 *The Naked Civil Servant* (TV)
1976 *East Of Elephant Rock; Stream Line*
1977 *Spectre* (TV); *The Shout*
1978 *Watership Down; The Lord Of The Rings* (both voice only); *Midnight Express**; *The Disappearance*
1979 *Alien**
1980 *Heaven's Gate**; *The Elephant Man**
1981 *The History Of The World Part I; Partners*
1982 *Night Crossing; The Plague Dogs* (voice only)
1983 *The Osterman Weekend; Champions*
1984 *The Hit; 1984; Success Is The Best Revenge*
1985 *The Black Cauldron* (voice only); *After Darkness*
1986 *Jake Speed*
1987 *Rocinante; From The Hip; Aria; Hem; Vincent — The Life And Death Of Vincent Van Gogh* (voice only)
1988 *White Mischief; Poison Candy* (TV)
1989 *Scandal**; *The Bengali Night*
1990 *Frankenstein Unbound; The Field; Windprints*
1991 *King Ralph; Resident Alien; Lapse Of Memory; I Dreamt I Woke Up* (documentary)
1992 *L'Oeil Qui Ment*
1993 *Great Moments In Aviation; Monolith*

## HURT, William
(1950– ) USA

1978 *Verna, The USO Girl* (TV)

1980 *Altered States*
1981 *Body Heat**; *Eyewitness* (UK: *The Janitor*)
1983 *Gorky Park; The Big Chill**
1985 *Kiss Of The Spiderwoman**
1986 *Children Of A Lesser God**
1987 *Broadcast News**
1988 *A Time Of Destiny; The Accidental Tourist**
1990 *I Love You To Death; Alice*
1991 *The Doctor; Until The End Of The World*
1992 *The Plague*
1993 *Mr Wonderful*

## HUSTON, Anjelica
(1951– ) USA

1969 *A Walk With Love And Death; Sinful Davey; Hamlet*
1976 *The Last Tycoon; Swashbuckler* (UK: *The Scarlet Buccaneer*)
1981 *The Postman Always Rings Twice**
1982 *Frances**
1984 *This Is Spinal Tap; The Ice Pirates; The Cowboy And The Ballerina* (TV)
1985 *Prizzi's Honor**
1987 *Gardens Of Stone; The Dead**; *John Huston And The Dubliners* (documentary)
1988 *A Handful Of Dust; Mr North*
1989 *The Witches; Crimes And Misdemeanours**; *Enemies: A Love Story**
1990 *The Grifters**
1991 *The Addams Family**
1992 *The Player**
1993 *And The Band Played On* (TV); *Addams Family Values*

## HUSTON, Walter
real name: Walter Houghston
(1884–1950) USA

1929 *The Bishop's Candlesticks; Two Americans; The Carnival Man* (all shorts); *Gentlemen Of The Press; The Lady Lies; The Virginian*

**HUSTON, Walter** (cont.)

1930 *Abraham Lincoln; The Bad Man; The Virtuous Sin* (UK: *Cat Iron*)
1931 *The Criminal Code; The Star Witness; The Ruling Voice*
1932 *Night Court* (UK: *Justice For Sale*); *Kongo; A Woman From Monte Carlo; A House Divided; Law And Order; Beast Of The City; American Madness; Rain; The Wet Parade*
1933 *Hell Below; Ann Vickers; The Prizefighter And The Lady* (UK: *Every Woman's Man*); *The Spoon* (short); *Storm At Daybreak; Gabriel Over The White House*
1934 *Keep'Em Rolling!*
1935 *The Tunnel*
1936 *Dodsworth\*; Rhodes Of Africa* (UK: *Rhodes*)
1938 *Of Human Hearts*
1939 *The Light That Failed*
1941 *Our Russian Front* (narrator only); *The Maltese Falcon\*; The Shanghai Gesture; All That Money Can Buy; Swamp Water* (UK: *The Man Who Came Back*)
1942 *Prelude To War; America Can Give It* (both narrator only); *Always In My Heart; Yankee Doodle Dandy\*; In This Our Life*
1943 *The Nazis Strike; Divide And Conquer; The Battle Of Britain; December 7th; For God And Country* (all narrator only); *The Outlaw\*; Edge Of Darkness; Mission To Moscow; North Star; Safeguarding Military Information* (short)
1944 *The Battle Of China; Know Your Enemy: Japan; Suicide Battalion* (all narrator only); *Dragon Seed*
1945 *War Comes To America; Let There Be Light* (both narrator only); *And Then There Were None* (UK: *Ten Little Niggers*)
1946 *Dragonwyck; Duel In The Sun\**
1948 *Summer Holiday; The Treasure Of The Sierra Madre\**
1949 *The Great Sinner*
1950 *The Furies*

**HUTTON, Betty**
real name: Betty Thornburg
(1921–   ) USA

1939 *Vincent Lopez And His Orchestra; One For The Book; Headline Bands; Public Jitterbug Number One* (all shorts)
1942 *The Fleet's In; Star-Spangled Rythmn*
1943 *Happy Go Lucky; Let's Face It*
1944 *Skirmish On The Home Front* (short); *The Miracle Of Morgan's Creek; Here Come The Waves; And The Angels Sing*
1945 *Incendiary Blonde; Duffy's Tavern; The Stork Club; Hollywood Victory Caravan* (short)
1946 *Cross My Heart*
1947 *The Perils Of Pauline; Dream Girl*
1949 *Red Hot And Blue*
1950 *Annie Get Your Gun\*; Let's Dance*
1951 *Sailor Beware*
1952 *The Greatest Show On Earth\*; Somebody Loves Me*
1957 *Spring Reunion*
1990 *Preston Sturges: The Rise And Fall Of An American Dreamer* (documentary)

**HUTTON, Timothy**
(1960–   ) USA

1965 *Never Too Late*
1978 *Zuma Beach* (TV)
1979 *An Innocent Love* (TV); *And Baby Makes Six* (TV); *Friendly Fire* (TV); *The Best Place To Be* (TV); *Young Love, First Love* (TV)
1980 *Father Figure* (TV); *Ordinary People\**
1981 *A Long Way Home* (TV); *Taps*
1983 *Daniel; Iceman*
1984 *The Falcon And Snowman*
1985 *Turk 182!*
1987 *Made In Heaven*
1988 *A Time Of Destiny; Everybody's All-American* (UK: *When I Fall In Love*)
1989 *The Torrents Of Spring*
1990 *Q & A*
1991 *The Dark Half*
1992 *The Temp*

# I

## IRONS, Jeremy
(1948–   ) UK

1980 *Nijinsky*
1981 *The French Lieutenant's Woman\**
1982 *Moonlighting; The Masterbuilders* (narrator only); *The Captain's Doll* (TV)
1983 *Betrayal; The Wild Duck; Un Amour De Swann* (UK: *Swann In Love*)
1984 *The Lie*
1985 *The Statue Of Liberty* (narrator only)
1986 *The Mission*
1988 *Dead Ringers\**
1989 *A Chorus Of Disapproval; Danny The Champion Of The World; Australia*
1990 *Reversal Of Fortune\**
1991 *Kafka*
1992 *Waterland; Damage; Earth And The American Dream* (voice only)
1993 *M Butterfly; The House Of The Spirits*

# J

## JACKSON, Glenda
(1936–   ) UK

1963 *This Sporting Life*
1966 *The Persecution And Assassination Of Jean Paul Marat; Benefit Of The Doubt*
1967 *Tell Me Lies*
1968 *Negatives*
1969 *Women In Love\**
1970 *The Music Lovers*
1971 *Sunday, Bloody Sunday\*; The Boyfriend; Mary, Queen Of Scots*
1972 *The Triple Echo*
1973 *Bequest To The Nation; Il Sorriso Del Grande Tentatore* (UK: *The Tempter*); *A Touch Of Class*
1974 *The Maids*
1975 *The Romantic Englishwoman; Hedda*

1976 *Nasty Habits; The Incredible Sarah*
1978 *House Calls; The Class Of Miss MacMichael; Stevie*
1979 *Lost And Found; Build Me A World* (narrator only)
1980 *Health; Hopscotch*
1981 *Stop Polio* (short); *The Patricia Neal Story* (TV)
1982 *The Return Of The Soldier* (TV); *Giro City* (TV)
1984 *Sakharov* (TV)
1985 *Turtle Diary*
1987 *Beyond Therapy; Business As Usual*
1988 *Salome's Last Dance; Imago* (narrator only)
1989 *The Rainbow; King Of The Wind*
1990 *Doombeach*
1991 *A Murder Of Quality* (TV)

## JOHNSON, Dame Celia
(1908–82) UK

1934 *Dirty Work*
1941 *We Serve; A Letter From Home* (both shorts)
1942 *In Which We Serve\**
1943 *Dear Octopus*
1944 *This Happy Breed*
1945 *Brief Encounter\**
1950 *The Astonished Heart*
1952 *I Believe In You; The Holly And The Ivy*
1953 *The Captain's Paradise*
1955 *A Kid For Two Farthings*
1957 *The Good Companions*
1969 *The Prime Of Miss Jean Brodie\**
1978 *Les Misérables* (TV)
1980 *The Hostage Tower*

## JOLSON, Al
real name: Asa Yoelson
(1885–1950) USA

1926 *April Showers* (short)
1927 *The Jazz Singer\**
1928 *The Singing Fool*
1929 *Sonny Boy; New York Nights; Say It With Songs*

**JOLSON, Al** (cont.)
1930 *Mammy; Big Boy; Showgirl In Hollywood*
1933 *Hallelujah, I'm A Bum* (UK: *Hallelujah I'm A Tramp*)
1934 *Wonder Bar*
1935 *Go Into Your Dance* (UK: *Casino De Paree*); *Kings Of The Turf* (short)
1936 *The Singing Kid*
1939 *Rose Of Washington Square; Hollywood Cavalcade; Swanee River*
1941 *Cavalcade Of The Academy Awards* (short)
1945 *Rhapsody In Blue*
1946 *The Jolson Story**
1948 *Screen Snapshots No 166* (short)
1949 *Jolson Sings Again* (voice only)

**JONES, Dean**
(1933– ) USA

1956 *Gaby; These Wilder Years; The Opposite Sex; The Great American Pastime; The Rack; Somebody Up There Likes Me; Tea And Sympathy*
1957 *Ten Thousand Bedrooms; Designing Woman; Until They Sail; Jailhouse Rock*
1958 *Handle With Care; Imitation General; Torpedo Run*
1959 *Night Of The Quarter Moon; Never So Few*
1963 *Under The Yum Yum Tree; The New Interns*
1964 *Two On A Guillotine*
1965 *That Darn Cat!*
1966 *The Ugly Daschund; Any Wednesday* (UK: *Bachelor Girl Apartment*)
1967 *Monkeys Go Home; Blackbeard's Ghost*
1968 *The Horse In The Grey Flannel Suit; The Mickey Mouse Anniversary Show* (narrator only)
1969 *The Love Bug**
1970 *Mr Superinvisible*

1971 *Million Dollar Duck; The Great Man's Whiskers* (TV)
1972 *Snowball Express*
1973 *Guess Who's Sleeping In My Bed* (TV)
1976 *The Shaggy DA*
1977 *Herbie Goes To Monte Carlo; Once Upon A Brothers Grimm* (TV)
1978 *When Every Day Was The Fourth Of July* (TV); *Born Again*
1980 *The Long Days Of Summer* (TV)
1990 *Fire And Money* (TV)
1991 *Other People's Money*
1992 *Beethoven*

**JONES, James Earl**
(1931– ) USA

1964 *Dr Strangelove Or How I Learned To Stop Worrying And Love The Bomb**
1967 *The Comedians*
1970 *The Great White Hope; End Of The Road; King: A Filmed Record...Montgomery To Memphis* (documentary)
1972 *The Man; Malcolm X* (documentary)
1974 *Claudine*
1975 *The UFO Incident* (TV)
1976 *Deadly Hero; The River Niger; The Bingo Long Traveling All-Stars And Motor Kings; Swashbuckler* (UK: *The Scarlett Buccaneer*)
1977 *The Greatest; The Last Remake Of Beau Geste; Exorcist II: The Heretic; A Piece Of The Action; The Greatest Thing That Almost Happened* (TV); *Star Wars** (voice only)
1979 *The Bushido Blade*
1980 *Guyana Tragedy: The Story Of Jim Jones* (TV); *The Empire Strikes Back** (voice only)
1982 *Conan The Barbarian; Blood Tide*
1983 *Return Of The Jedi** (voice only)
1984 *The Vegas Strip Wars* (TV)

1985 *City Limits; The Atlanta Child Murders* (TV)
1986 *Soul Man; My Little Girl*
1987 *Gardens Of Stone; Allan Quatermain And The Lost City Of Gold; Matewan; Pinocchio And The Emperor Of The Night* (voice only)
1988 *Coming To America\*; Teach 109* (short)
1989 *Three Fugitives; Field Of Dreams\*; Best Of The Best*
1990 *The Hunt For Red October\*; Grim Prairie Tales; Dy Dawn's Early Light* (TV); *Last Flight Out* (TV); *Heat Wave* (TV); *The Last Elephant* (TV); *The Ambulance*
1991 *True Identity*
1992 *Patriot Games; Sneakers; Sommersby; Excessive Force*

## JONES, Jennifer
real name: Phylis Isley
(1919– ) USA

1939 *Dick Tracy's G-Men; The New Frontier*
1940 *The Ranger Rides Again*
1943 *The Song Of Bernadette\**
1944 *Since You Went Away\**
1945 *Love Letters*
1946 *Cluny Brown; Duel In The Sun\*; The American Creed* (short)
1948 *Portrait Of Jennie* (UK: *Jennie*)
1949 *We Were Strangers; Madame Bovary*
1950 *Gone To Earth*
1952 *Carrie; Ruby Gentry*
1953 *Beat The Devil*
1954 *Stazione Termini* (UK: *Indiscretion*)
1955 *Love Is A Many Splendored Thing\*; Good Morning, Miss Dove*
1956 *The Man In The Grey Flannel Suit*
1957 *The Barretts Of Wimpole Street; A Farewell To Arms*
1961 *Tender Is The Night*
1966 *The Idol*
1969 *Angel, Angel, Down You Go*
1974 *The Towering Inferno\**

## JOURDAN, Louis
real name: Louis Gendre
(1919– ) France

1939 *Le Corsaire; Félicie Nanteuil*
1940 *Untel Père Et Fils; Le Comédie De Bonheur*
1941 *Premier Rendez-Vous* (UK: *First Appointment*); *Nous Les Jeunes; Parade En Sept Nuits*
1942 *L'Arlesienne; La Belle Aventure; La Vie De Bohème*
1943 *Les Petites Du Quai Aux Fleurs*
1947 *The Paradine Case*
1948 *Letter From An Unknown Woman; No Minor Vices*
1949 *Madame Bovary*
1951 *Bird Of Paradise; Anne Of The Indies*
1952 *The Happy Time; Decameron Nights*
1953 *Rue De L'Etrapade* (UK: *Françoise Steps Out*)
1954 *Three Coins In The Fountain\**
1956 *The Swan; Julie; La Mariée Est Trop Belle* (UK: *The Bride Is Too Beautiful*)
1957 *Escapade; Dangerous Exile*
1958 *Gigi\**
1959 *The Best Of Everything*
1960 *Les Vierges De Rome* (UK: *The Virgins Of Rome*)
1961 *Dark Journey; Léviathan; Le Compte De Monte Cristo* (UK: *The Story Of The Count Of Monte Cristo*)
1962 *Le Désordre* (UK: *Disorder*); *Mathia Sandorf*
1963 *The VIPs*
1965 *Made In Paris; Les Sultans*
1966 *Cervantes*
1967 *Peau D'Espion* (UK: *To Commit A Murder*)
1968 *To Die In Paris* (TV); *A Flea In Her Ear*
1969 *Fear No Evil* (TV); *Run A Crooked Mile* (TV); *Ritual Of Evil* (TV)
1972 *The Great American Beauty Contest* (TV)
1974 *The Count Of Monte Cristo* (TV)
1976 *The Man In The Iron Mask* (TV)

**JOURDAN, Louis** (cont.)
1977   *The Silver Bears*
1981   *Double Deal*
1982   *Swamp Thing*
1983   *Octopussy\**
1986   *Beverly Hills Madam* (TV)
1987   *Counterforce*
1988   *Grand Larceny(TV)*
1989   *The Return Of Swamp Thing;
         Speed Zone*
1992   *The Year Of The Comet*


**JULIA, Raul**
(1940–   ) Puerto Rico

1971   *Been Down So Long It Looks Like
         Up To Me; Panic In Needle Park*
1976   *The Gumball Rally*
1978   *Eyes Of Laura Mars*
1982   *The Escape Artist; One From The
         Heart; Tempest*
1985   *Compromising Positions; Kiss Of
         The Spiderwoman\**
1986   *The Morning After*
1987   *La Gran Fiesta*
1988   *Moon Over Parador; The
         Penitent; Tango Bar; Tequila
         Sunrise; Trading Hearts; Onassis:
         The Richest Man In The World*
         (TV)
1989   *Mack The Knife; Romero*
1990   *Presumed Innocent\*; Havana;
         The Rookie; Roger Corman's
         Frankenstein Unbound; A Life Of
         Sin*
1991   *The Addams Family\**
1993   *Addams Family Values*


# K

**KARLOFF, Boris**
real name: William Henry Pratt
(1887–1969) UK

1916   *The Young Girl Of Portici*
1917   *Wild And Woolly*

1919   *Ashes Of Desire; His Majesty,
         The American* (UK: *One Of The
         Blood*); *The Prince And Betty; The
         Lightning Raider; The Masked
         Raider*
1920   *The Deadlier Sex; The Courage
         Of Marge O'Doone; The Last Of
         The Mohicans; The Notorious
         Miss Lisle*
1921   *The Hope Diamond Mystery* (UK:
         *The Romance Of The Hope
         Diamond*); *Without Benefit Of
         Clergy; Cheated Hearts; The
         Cave Girl*
1922   *The Man From Downing Street*
         (UK: *The Jade*); *The Altar Stairs;
         Omar, The Tentmaker, The
         Infidel; Nan Of The North*
1923   *The Woman Conquers; The
         Prisoner; The Love Brand; The
         Gentleman From America*
1924   *The Hellion; Dynamite Dan;
         Raiders Of The Plains; Parisian
         Nights*
1925   *Lady Robin Hood; Perils Of
         The Wild; Forbidden Cargo* (UK:
         *The Dangerous Cargo*); *The
         Prairie Wife; Never The Twain
         Shall Meet*
1926   *The Greater Glory; The Eagle Of
         The Sea; Her Honor, The
         Governor* (UK: *The Second Mrs
         Fenway*); *The Nickel Hopper*
         (short); *The Golden Web; Flames;
         Old Ironsides* (UK: *Sons Of The
         Sea*); *The Man In The Saddle;
         Phantoms Of The Bat; Flaming
         Fury; The Bells; Valencia* (UK:
         *The Love Song*)
1927   *The Meddlin' Stranger; Tarzan
         And The Golden Lion; Let It Rain;
         The Princess From Hoboken;
         Phantom Buster; Two Arabian
         Nights; Soft Cushions; The Love
         Mart*
1928   *Burning The Wind; Vultures Of
         The Sea; The Vanishing Rider;
         The Little Wild Girl*
1929   *Phantom Of The North; Behind
         That Curtain; King Of The Kongo;
         The Fatal Warning; Two Sisters;*

The Devil's Chaplain; The Unholy Night; Anne Against The World
1930 The Bad One; The Utah Kid; Mother's Cry; The Sea Bat; King Of The Wild; The Criminal Code
1931 Cracked Nuts; Sous Les Verrous; I Like Your Nerve; The Public Defender; Young Donovan's Kid (UK: Donovan's Kid); Smart Money; Business And Pleasure; Graft; The Guilty Generation; The Mad Genius; Dirigible; The Yellow Ticket (UK: The Yellow Passport); The Last Parade; Frankenstein*; Tonight Or Never; Five Star Final*
1932 Behind The Mask; Scarface*; Alias The Doctor; The Cohens And The Kellys In Hollywood; The Miracle Man; Night World; The Old Dark House; The Mask Of Fu Manchu; The Mummy
1933 The Man Who Dared; The Ghoul; The House Of Rothschild
1934 The Lost Patrol; The Black Cat (UK: The House Of Doom); Gift Of Gab; Screen Snapshots No 11 (short)
1935 Bride Of Frankenstein*; The Black Room; The Raven; Charlie Chan At The Opera; Hollywood Hobbies (short)
1936 The Invisible Ray; The Man Who Changed His Mind; Juggernaut; The Walking Dead
1937 Night Key; West Of Shanghai; Cinema Circus (short)
1938 The Invisible Menace; Mr Wong, Detective
1939 Son Of Frankenstein; The Mystery Of Mr Wong; The Man They Could Not Hang; Mr Wong In Chinatown; Tower Of London; Devil's Island
1940 The Fatal Hour (UK: Mr Wong At Headquarters); British Intelligence (UK: Enemy Agent); Black Friday; The Man With Nine Lives (UK: Behind The Door); Doomed To Die (UK: The Mystery Of The Wentworth Castle); Before I Hang; The Ape; You'll Find Out

1941 Information Please No 8; Information Please No 12 (both shorts); The Devil Commands
1942 The Boogie Man Will Get You
1944 The Climax; House Of Frankenstein
1945 The Body Snatcher; Isle Of The Dead
1946 Bedlam
1947 Unconquered; The Secret Life Of Walter Mitty; Lured (UK: Personal Column); Dick Tracy Meets Gruesome (UK: Dick Tracy's Amazing Adventure)
1948 Tap Roots
1949 Abbott And Costello Meet The Killer, Boris Karloff
1951 The Strange Door; The Emperor's Nightingale (short)
1952 The Black Castle
1953 Colonel March Investigates; Abbott And Costello Meet Dr Jekyll And Mr Hyde; The Hindu (UK: Sabaka); Il Monstro Dell'Isola (UK: Monster Of The Island)
1957 Voodoo Island; The Juggler Of Our Lady (short, narrator only)
1958 Frankenstein 1970; Grip Of The Strangler; Corridors Of Blood
1963 The Raven; The Terror; Black Sabbath; Comedy Of Terrors; Today's Teens (narrator only)
1964 Bikini Beach
1965 Monster Of Terror; Mondo Balordo (UK: Strange World) (narrator only)
1966 The Ghost In The Invisible Bikini; The Venetian Affair; The Sorcerers; The Daydreamer (voice only)
1967 Mad Monster Party (voice only); El Coleccionista De Cadaveras (UK: Cauldron Of Blood)
1968 Targets; Curse Of The Crimson Altar
1969 Isle Of The Snake People; The Incredible Invasion; The Fear Chamber; House Of Evil

## KAYE, Danny
real name: David Daniel Kaminski
(1913–87) USA

1937 *Dime A Dance; Cupid Takes A Holiday* (both shorts)
1938 *Money On Your Life; Getting An Eyeful* (both shorts)
1942 *Night Shift* (short)
1944 *Up In Arms*
1945 *Wonder Man*
1946 *The Kid From Brooklyn*
1947 *The Secret Life of Walter Mitty*
1948 *A Song Is Born*
1949 *The Inspector General; It's A Great Feeling*
1951 *On The Riviera*
1952 *Hans Christian Andersen\**
1953 *Knock On Wood*
1954 *Assignment Children; Hula From Hollywood* (both shorts); *White Christmas\**
1956 *The Court Jester*
1958 *Merry Andrew; Me And The Colonel*
1959 *The Five Pennies*
1961 *On The Double*
1963 *The Man From The Diner's Club*
1969 *The Madwoman Of Chaillot*
1975 *Peter Pan* (TV)
1977 *Pinocchio* (TV)
1981 *Skokie* (TV) (UK: *Once They Marched Through A Thousand Towns*)

## KEATON, Buster
Joseph Francis Keaton
(1895–1966) USA

1917 *The Butcher Boy; A Reckless Romeo; The Rough House; His Wedding Night; A Country Hero; Coney Island; Oh, Doctor!*
1918 *Out West; The Bell Boy; Moonshine; Good Night Nurse; The Cook*
1919 *Love; A Desert Hero; Back Stage; The Hayseed; The Garage*
1920 *One Week; The High Sign; The Scarecrow; Neighbours; Convict 13* (all also co-director); *The Round-Up; The Saphead*

1921 *Hard Luck; The Goat; The Boat; The Paleface; The Playhouse; The Haunted House* (all also co-director)
1922 *The Electric House; The Frozen North; My Wife's Relations; The Blacksmith; Daydreams; Cops* (all also co-director); *Screen Snapshots No 3*
1923 *The Balloonatic; The Love Nest; The Three Ages; Our Hospitality* (all also co-director)
1924 *Sherlock Junior; The Navigator* (both also director)
1925 *Seven Chances; Go West* (both also co-director)
1926 *The General* (also co-director); *Battling Butler* (also director)
1927 *College*
1928 *Steamboat Bill Junior; The Cameraman*
1929 *Spite Marriage; Hollywood Revue Of 1929*
1930 *Free And Easy; Doughboys* (UK: *Forward March*)
1931 *Parlor, Bedroom And Bath* (UK: *Romeo In Pyjamas*); *Sidewalks Of New York*
1932 *Speak Easily; The Passionate Plumber*
1933 *What! No Beer?*
1934 *Le Roi Des Champs-Elysées*
1935 *L'Horloger Amoureux; The Invader; La Fiesta De Santa Barbara; Allez-Oop; The Serenade; The Gold Ghost; Palooka From Paducah; Hayseed Romance; Tars And Stripes; The E Flat Man; One Run Elmer*
1936 *The Timid Young Man; Three On A Limb; Grand Slam Opera; Blue Blazes; The Chemist; Three Men On A Horse; Mixed Magic*
1937 *Jail Bait; Ditto; Love Nest On Wheels*
1938 *Hollywood Handicap; Life In Sometown USA; Streamlined Swing* (all director only)
1939 *Pest From The West; Mooching Through Georgia; The Jones Family In Hollywood* (co-writer

only); *Hollywood Cavalcade; Nothing But Pleasure; The Jones Family In Quick Millions* (co-writer only)
1940 *Li'l Abner* (UK: *Trouble Chaser*); *The Villain Still Pursued Her; Pardon My Berth Marks; The Spook Speaks; The Taming Of The Snood*
1941 *His Ex Marks The Spot; General Nuisance; She's Oil Mine; So You Won't Squawk*
1943 *Forever And A Day*
1944 *San Diego, I Love You; Two Girls And A Sailor*
1945 *That Night With You; That's The Spirit*
1946 *God's Country; El Moderno Barba Azul* (UK: *Boom In The Moon*)
1948 *Un Duel A Mort*
1949 *In The Good Old Summertime; The Loveable Cheat; You're My Everything*
1950 *Sunset Boulevard\**
1952 *Limelight\*; Paradise For Buster*
1953 *L'Incantevole Nemica*
1955 *The Misadventures Of Buster Keaton*
1956 *Around The World In 80 Days\**
1960 *The Adventures Of Huckleberry Finn*
1963 *It's A Mad, Mad, Mad, Mad World\*; The Triumph Of Lester Snapwell*
1964 *Pajama Party*
1965 *The Railrodder; Sergeant Deadhead; Buster Keaton Rides Again; Beach Blanket Bingo* (UK: *Malibu Beach*); *Film* (short); *How To Stuff A Wild Bikini; Due Marines E Uno Generale*
1966 *A Funny Thing Happened On The Way To The Forum; The Scribe* (short)

## KEATON, Diane

real name: Diane Hall
(1946–  ) USA

1970 *Lovers And Other Strangers*
1972 *The Godfather\*; Play It Again, Sam\**

1973 *Sleeper\**
1974 *The Godfather Part II\**
1975 *Love And Death; I Will, I Will...For Now*
1976 *Harry And Walter Go To New York*
1977 *Annie Hall\*; Looking For Mr Goodbar*
1978 *Interiors*
1979 *Manhattan\**
1981 *Shoot The Moon; Reds\**
1982 *What Does Dorrie Want* (short, director only)
1984 *Mrs Soffel; The Little Drummer Girl*
1986 *Crimes Of The Heart*
1987 *Radio Days; Baby Boom; Heaven* (director only)
1988 *The Good Mother*
1989 *The Lemon Sisters*
1990 *The Godfather Part III\**
1991 *Father Of The Bride; Wildflower* (TV) (director only)
1992 *Running Mates* (TV)
1993 *Manhattan Murder Mystery*

## KEATON, Michael

real name: Michael Douglas
(1951–  ) USA

1982 *Night Shift*
1983 *Mr Mom*
1984 *Johnny Dangerously*
1986 *Gung Ho; Touch And Go*
1987 *The Squeeze*
1988 *Beetlejuice\*; Clean And Sober*
1989 *Batman\*; The Dream Team*
1990 *Pacific Heights*
1991 *One Good Cop*
1992 *Batman Returns\**
1993 *Much Ado About Nothing; My Life*

## KEEL, Howard

real name: Harold Leek
(1917–  ) USA

1948 *The Small Voice*
1950 *Annie Get Your Gun\*; Pagan Love Song*

**KEEL, Howard** (cont.)
1951 *Three Guys Named Mike; Texas Carnival; Show Boat\*; Across The Wide Missouri* (narrator only); *Callaway Went Thataway* (UK: *The Star Said No!*)
1952 *Lovely To Look At; Desperate Search; I Love Melvin*
1953 *Fast Company; Ride Vaquero!; Calamity Jane\*; Kiss Me Kate*
1954 *Rose Marie; Seven Brides For Seven Brothers\*; Deep In My Heart*
1955 *Jupiter's Darling; Kismet*
1958 *Floods Of Fear*
1959 *The Big Fisherman*
1961 *Armored Command*
1963 *The Day Of The Triffids*
1964 *The Man From Button Willow* (voice only)
1966 *Waco*
1967 *Red Tomahawk; The War Wagon*
1968 *Arizona Bushwackers*

**KEELER, Ruby**
real name: Ethel Keeler
(1909–93) USA

1928 *Ruby Keeler* (short)
1933 *42nd Street\*; Gold Diggers Of 1933\*; Footlight Parade\**
1934 *Dames; Flirtation Walk*
1935 *Go Into Your Dance* (UK: *Casino De Paree*); *Shipmates Forever*
1936 *Colleen*
1937 *Ready Willing And Able*
1938 *Mother Carey's Chickens*
1941 *Sweetheart Of The Campus* (UK: *Broadway Ahead*)
1970 *The Phynx*
1989 *Beverly Hills Brats*

**KEITEL, Harvey**
(1947–  ) USA

1968 *Who's That Knocking At My Door?*
1970 *Street Scene*
1973 *Mean Streets*
1974 *Alice Doesn't Live Here Anymore\*; The Virginia Hill Story* (TV)

1975 *That's The Way Of The World*
1976 *Buffalo Bill And The Indians; Welcome To LA; Mother Jugs And Speed; Taxi Driver\**
1977 *Fingers; The Duellists*
1978 *Blue Collar*
1979 *The Eagle's Wing*
1980 *Saturn 3; Bad Timing\*; Mort En Direct* (UK: *Deathwatch*)
1981 *The Border*
1982 *La Nuit De Varennes* (UK: *That Night In Varennes*)
1983 *Order Of Death; Une Pierre Dans La Bouche* (UK: *A Stone In The Mouth*)
1984 *Falling In Love; Dream One*
1985 *El Caballero Del Dragon; Un Complicato Intrigo Di Donne; Vicoli E Delitti* (UK: *The Naples Connection*)
1986 *The Men's Club; Off-Beat; Wise Guys; The American; La Sposa Americana* (UK: *The American Bride*)
1987 *Blindside; The Pick-Up Artist; L'Inchiesta* (UK: *The Inquiry*)
1988 *The Last Temptation Of Christ\*; Caro Gorbaciov* (UK: *Dear Gorbachev*); *Down Where The Buffalo Go* (TV)
1989 *The January Man; Tambores De Fuego* (UK: *Drums Of Fire*)
1990 *The Two Jakes\*; Due Occhi Diabolici* (UK: *Two Evil Eyes*); *Il Grande Cacciatore* (UK: *The Great Hunter*)
1991 *Thelma And Louise\*; Bugsy; Mortal Thoughts*
1992 *Reservoir Dogs; Sister Act; The Bad Lieutenant*
1993 *Point Of No Return; The Piano; Rising Sun; The Young Americans*

**KELLY, Gene**
real name: Eugene Curran Kelly
(1912–  ) USA

1942 *For Me And My Gal* (UK: *For Me And My Girl*)

1943 *Dubarry Was A Lady; Pilot No 5; Thousands Cheer; The Cross Of Lorraine*
1944 *Cover Girl; Christmas Holiday; The Ziegfeld Follies\**
1945 *Anchors Aweigh\**
1947 *Living In A Big Way*
1948 *Words And Music; The Pirate; The Three Musketeers\**
1949 *On The Town\*; Take Me Out To The Ballgame* (UK: *Everybody's Cheering*)
1950 *Summer Stock* (UK: *If You Feel Like Singing*); *The Black Hand*
1951 *An American In Paris\*; It's A Big Country*
1952 *Singin' In The Rain\*; The Devil Makes Three; Love Is Better Than Ever*
1954 *Seagulls Over Sorrento; Brigadoon; Deep In My Heart*
1955 *It's Always Fair Weather*
1956 *Invitation To The Dance*
1957 *Les Girls*
1958 *Marjorie Morningstar*
1960 *Inherit The Wind; Let's Make Love*
1964 *What A Way To Go!*
1967 *Les Demoiselles De Rochefort* (UK: *The Young Girls Of Rochefort*)
1973 *Forty Carats*
1974 *That's Entertainment*
1976 *That's Entertainment Part II*
1977 *Viva Knievel!*
1978 *America's Sweetheart: The Mary Pickford Story* (narrator only)
1980 *Xanadu*
1985 *That's Dancing*
1987 *Sins* (TV); *North And South, Book Two* (TV)

See also directors listing

## KELLY, Grace Patricia
(1929–82) USA

1951 *Fourteen Hours*
1952 *High Noon\**
1953 *Mogambo*
1954 *Rear Window\*; Dial M For Murder; The Country Girl\*; Green Fire; The Bridges At Toko-Ri*

1955 *To Catch A Thief\**
1956 *High Society\*; The Swan; The Wedding In Monaco* (documentary)
1959 *Invitation To Monte Carlo* (documentary)
1964 *Mediterranean Holiday* (documentary)
1977 *The Children Of Theatre Street* (narrator only)
1982 *The Nativity* (narrator only)

## KENDALL, Kay
real name: Justine Kendall McCarthy
(1926–1959) UK

1944 *Fiddlers Three; Champagne Charlie; Dreaming*
1945 *Waltz Time; Caesar And Cleopatra*
1946 *Spring Song; London Town*
1950 *Night And The City; Dance Hall; Happy Go Lovely*
1951 *Lady Godiva Rides Again*
1952 *Wings Of Danger; Curtain Up; It Started In Paradise*
1953 *Mantrap; Street Of Shadows; Genevieve\*; The Square Ring; Meet Mr Lucifer*
1954 *Fast And Loose; Doctor In The House\*; Abdullah's Harem*
1955 *The Constant Husband; Simon And Laura; The Adventures Of Quentin Durward*
1957 *Les Girls*
1958 *The Reluctant Debutante*
1959 *Once More With Feeling*

## KENNEDY, Arthur
(1914–90) USA

1940 *City For Conquest; Santa Fe Trail*
1941 *High Sierra\*; Knockout; Highway West; Strange Alibi; They Died With Their Boots On; Bad Men Of Missouri*
1942 *Desperate Journey*
1943 *Air Force*
1946 *Devotion*
1947 *Boomerang; Cheyenne*

**KENNEDY, Arthur** (cont.)
1949 *The Window; Champion; Too Late For Tears; The Walking Hills; Chicago Deadline*
1950 *The Glass Menagerie; Bright Victory* (UK: *Lights Out*)
1951 *Red Mountain*
1952 *Rancho Notorious; The Girl In White* (UK: *So Bright The Flame*); *Bend Of The River* (UK: *Where The River Bends*); *The Lusty Men*
1954 *Impulse*
1955 *Crashout; The Man From Laramie; The Naked Dawn; Trial; The Desperate Hours*
1956 *The Rawhide Years*
1957 *Peyton Place\**
1958 *Twilight For The Gods; Some Came Running*
1959 *A Summer Place; Home Is The Hero*
1960 *Elmer Gantry\**
1961 *Claudelle Inglish* (UK: *Young And Eager*)
1962 *Murder She Said; Barabbas; Hemingway's Adventures Of A Young Man; Lawrence Of Arabia\**
1964 *Cheyenne Autumn; Italiano Bravo Gente* (UK: *Attack And Retreat*)
1965 *Murieta* (UK: *Vendetta*); *Joy In The Morning*
1966 *Nevada Smith; Fantastic Voyage; The Brave Rifles* (narrator only)
1967 *Il Chica Del Lunes* (UK: *Monday's Child*)
1968 *Anzio; A Minute To Pray, A Second To Die* (UK: *Dead Or Alive*); *Day Of The Evil Gun; The Prodigal Gun*
1969 *Shark!; Hail Hero*
1970 *The Movie Murderer* (TV)
1971 *The President's Plane Is Missing* (TV); *A Death Of Innocence* (TV); *Glory Boy* (UK: *My Old Man's Place*)
1972 *Crawlspace* (TV)
1973 *Ricco/The Dirty Mob; Baciamo Le Mane* (UK: *Family Killer*)
1974 *Nakia* (TV); *The Living Dead At The Machester Morgue; The Antichrist*

1975 *Killer Cop/The Police Can't Move*
1976 *The Sentinel; Roma A Mano Armata; Nove Ospiti Per Un Delitto*
1977 *Porco Mondo; Cyclone; The Last Angels; Emmanuelle On Taboo Island*
1978 *La Cueva De Los Triburones* (UK: *The Shark's Cave*); *Ab Morgen Sind Wir Reich Und Ehrlich; Covert Action*
1979 *The Humanoid*
1980 *Due Nelle Stelle*
1989 *Signs Of Life*
1990 *Grandpa*

## KERR, Deborah
real name: Deborah Jane Kerr-Trimmer (1921–   ) UK

1939 *Contraband* (extra)
1940 *Major Barbara*
1941 *Love On The Dole; Hatter's Castle*
1942 *Penn Of Pennsylvania; The Day Will Dawn*
1943 *The Life And Death Of Colonel Blimp\**
1945 *Perfect Strangers*
1946 *I See A Dark Stranger; Black Narcissus\**
1947 *The Hucksters\**
1948 *If Winter Comes*
1949 *Edward My Son; Please Believe Me*
1950 *King Solomon's Mines\**
1951 *Quo Vadis?\*; Thunder In The East*
1952 *The Prisoner Of Zenda*
1953 *Julius Caesar\*; Young Bess; Dream Wife; From Here To Eternity\**
1955 *The End Of The Affair*
1956 *The King And I\*; The Proud And The Profane; Tea And Sympathy*
1957 *Heaven Knows Mr Allison; An Affair To Remember*
1958 *Bonjour Tristesse; Separate Tables\*; The Journey*
1959 *Count Your Blessings; Beloved Infidel*

1960 *The Sundowners\*; The Grass Is Greener*
1961 *The Naked Edge; The Innocents*
1964 *The Chalk Garden; The Night Of The Iguana\**
1965 *Marriage On The Rocks*
1966 *Eye Of The Devil*
1967 *Casino Royale*
1968 *Prudence And The Pill*
1969 *The Gypsy Moths; The Arrangement*
1982 *Witness For The Prosecution* (TV)
1985 *The Assam Garden; Reunion At Fairborough* (TV)

## KINGSLEY, Ben
real name: Krishna Banji
(1944–  ) UK

1972 *Fear Is The Key*
1982 *Gandhi\**
1983 *Betrayal*
1984 *Camille* (TV)
1985 *Turtle Diary*
1986 *Harem*
1987 *The Sahara Secret; Maurice; Testimony; The Sealed Train*
1988 *Pascali's Island; Without A Clue*
1989 *Slipstream; The 5th Monkey; Cellini: A Violent Life*
1990 *The Children; Romeo–Juliet* (voice only)
1991 *The Necessary Love; Bugsy*
1992 *Freddie As FRO7* (voice only); *Sneakers*
1993 *Searching For Bobby Fischer; Dave*

## KINSKI, Nastassja
real name: Nastassja Nakszynski
(1959–  ) Germany

1975 *Falsche Bewegung* (UK: *Wrong Movement*)
1976 *To The Devil A Daughter; Reifezeugnis* (UK: *For You Love Only*)
1978 *Leidenschaftliche Blumchen* (UK: *Passion Flower Hotel*); *Cosi Come Sei* (UK: *Stay As You Are*)
1979 *Tess\**

1982 *One From The Heart; Cat People*
1983 *Frühlingssinfonie; Exposed; La Lune Dans Le Caniveau* (UK: *The Moon In The Gutter*)
1984 *Unfaithfully Yours; The Hotel New Hampshire; Paris, Texas\*; Maria's Lovers*
1985 *Revolution*
1986 *Harem*
1987 *Intervista; Maladie D'Amour*
1988 *Paganini; Torrents Of Spring*
1989 *13; Magdalene; On A Moonlit Night; The Secret*
1990 *Il Sole Anche Di Notte*
1991 *The Insulted And The Injured*
1993 *In Weiter Ferne, So Nah* (UK: *Far Away So Close*)

## KLINE, Kevin
(1947–  ) USA

1982 *The Pirates Of Penzance; Sophie's Choice\**
1983 *The Big Chill\**
1985 *Silverado\**
1986 *Violets Are Blue*
1987 *Cry Freedom\**
1988 *A Fish Called Wanda\**
1989 *The January Man*
1990 *I Love You To Death*
1991 *Soapdish; Grand Canyon*
1992 *Consenting Adults; Chaplin*
1993 *Dave*

## KRISTOFFERSON, Kris
(1936–  ) USA

1971 *The Last Movie*
1972 *Cisco Pike*
1973 *The Gospel Road; Blume In Love; Pat Garrett And Billy The Kid*
1974 *Bring Me The Head Of Alfredo Garcia; Alice Doesn't Live Here Anymore\**
1975 *Vigilante Force*
1976 *The Sailor Who Fell From Grace With The Sea; A Star Is Born\**
1977 *Semi-Tough*
1978 *Convoy*
1979 *Freedom Road*
1980 *Heaven's Gate\**

**KRISTOFFERSON, Kris** (cont.)

1981 *Roll-Over; The Million Dollar Face* (TV)

1983 *The Lost Honor Of Kathryn Beck* (TV) (UK: *Acts Of Passion*)

1984 *Flashpoint*

1985 *Songwriter; Trouble In Mind*

1986 *Stagecoach* (TV); *The Last Days Of Frank And Jesse James* (TV)

1988 *Dead Or Alive; Big Top Pee-Wee; The Tracker* (TV)

1989 *Millenium; Welcome Home; Ryder*

1990 *Original Intent; Night Of The Cyclone; Pair Of Aces* (TV); *Sandino*

1991 *Tipperary; No Place To Hide; Another Pair Of Aces: Three Of A Kind* (TV); *Miracle In The Wilderness* (TV)

1992 *Paper Hearts*


# L

**LADD, Alan**
(1913–64) USA

1932 *Once In A Lifetime; Island Of Lost Souls; Tom Brown Of Culver*

1933 *Saturday's Millions; No Man Of Her Own*

1936 *Anything Goes; Pigskin Parade* (UK: *The Harmony Parade*)

1937 *Last Train From Madrid; All Over Town; Rustlers' Valley; Souls At Sea; Hold'Em Navy* (UK: *That Navy Spirit*)

1938 *The Goldwyn Follies; Come On Leathernecks; Born To The West; Freshman Year; The Texans*

1939 *Rulers Of The Sea; The Green Hornet; Rita Rio And Her Orchestra* (short); *Goose Step* (UK: *Hitler—Beast Of Berlin*)

1940 *Gangs Of Chicago; Brother Rat And A Baby* (UK: *Baby Be Good*); *Light Of Western Stars; The Howards Of Virginia* (UK: *The Tree Of Liberty*); *Her First Romance; In Old Missouri; Meet The Missus; Captain Caution;*

*Wildcat Bus; Cross Country Romance; Those Were The Days* (UK: *Good Old School Days*)

1941 *Great Guns; The Parson Of Panamint; Paper Bullets; Petticoat Politics; The Reluctant Dragon; They Met In Bombay; The Black Cat; Cadet Girl; Citizen Kane\*; I Look At You* (short)

1942 *Joan Of Paris; This Gun For Hire; The Glass Key; Star Spangled Rythmn; Lucky Jordan*

1943 *Hollywood In Uniform; Letter From A Friend* (both shorts): *China*

1944 *Skirmish On The Home Front* (short); *And Now Tomorrow*

1945 *Duffy's Tavern; Salty O'Rourke; Calcutta; Hollywood Victory Caravan* (short)

1946 *Two Years Before The Mast; The Blue Dahlia; OSS*

1947 *Variety Girl; My Favourite Brunette; Wild Harvest*

1948 *Saigon; Beyond Glory; Whispering Smith*

1949 *Eyes Of Hollywood; Variety Club Hospital* (both shorts); *Chicago Deadline; The Great Gatsby; Captain Carey USA* (UK: *After Midnight*)

1950 *Branded; The Road To Hope* (short)

1951 *Appointment With Danger; Red Mountain*

1952 *Thunder In The East; The Iron Mistress; The Sporting Oasis* (short)

1953 *Shane\*; Botany Bay; Desert Legion; Hell Below Zero; The Red Beret*

1954 *The Black Knight; Drum Beat; Saskatchewan* (UK: *O'Rourke Of The Royal Mounted*)

1955 *Hell On Frisco Bay; The McConnell Story* (UK: *Tiger In The Sky*)

1956 *Santiago* (UK: *The Gun Runner*); *A Cry In The Night* (narrator only)

1957 *Boy On A Dolphin; The Big Land* (UK: *Stampeded!*)

1958 *The Deep Six; The Proud Rebel; The Badlanders*

1959 *The Man In The Net; Guns Of The Timberland*
1960 *All The Young Men; One Foot In Hell*
1961 *Orazi E Curiazi* (UK: *Duel Of Champions*)
1962 *13 West Street*
1964 *The Carpetbaggers**

## LAMARR, Hedy
real name: Hedwig Kiesler
(1913– ) Austria

1930 *Geld Auf Der Strasse*
1931 *Sturm Im Wasserglas; Wir Brauchen Kein Geld; Die Koffer Des Hern OF; Die Blumenfrau Von Lindenau*
1936 *Extase* (UK: *Ecstasy*)
1938 *Algiers*
1939 *Lady Of The Tropics; I Take This Woman; Screen Snapshots No 10*
1940 *Comrade X; Boom Town*
1941 *Come Live With Me; HM Pulham Esq; Ziegfeld Girl*
1942 *Tortilla Flat; Crossroads; White Cargo*
1943 *The Heavenly Body; The Conspirators; Showbusiness At War*
1944 *Experiment Perilous*
1945 *Her Highness And The Bellboy*
1946 *The Strange Woman*
1947 *Dishonoured Lady*
1948 *Let's Live A Little*
1949 *Samson And Delilah**
1950 *A Lady Without Passport; Copper Canyon*
1951 *My Favourite Spy*
1953 *The Loves Of Three Queens*
1954 *L'Amante Di Paride* (UK: *The Face That Launched A Thousand Ships*)
1957 *The Story Of Mankind; The Female Animal; Slaughter On 10th Avenue*

## LAMBERT, Christopher
real name: Christophe Lambert
(1957– ) USA

1981 *Le Bar Du Telephone*

1983 *Legitime Violence*
1984 *Greystoke — The Legend Of Tarzan, Lord Of The Apes*; Paroles Et Musique*
1985 *Subway**
1986 *Highlander*; I Love You*
1987 *The Sicilian; Priceless Beauty*
1988 *The Yellow Jersey; Love Dream; To Kill A Priest*
1989 *Why Me?*
1991 *Highlander II — The Quickening; Knight Moves*
1992 *Max Et Jeremie; Fortress*
1993 *The Gunman*

## LAMOUR, Dorothy
real name: Mary Dorothy Slaton
(1914– ) USA

1936 *The Stars Can't Be Wrong* (short); *College Holiday; The Jungle Princess*
1937 *Swing High, Swing Low; High, Wide And Handsome; Last Train From Madrid; The Hurricane*; Thrill Of A Lifetime*
1938 *Her Jungle Love; The Big Broadcast Of 1938; Tropic Holiday; Spawn Of The North*
1939 *St Louis Blues; Man About Town; Disputed Passage*
1940 *Typhoon; Johnny Apollo; Moon Over Burma; Road To Singapore*; Chad Hanna*
1941 *Aloma Of The South Seas; Road To Zanzibar; Caught In The Draft*
1942 *Beyond The Blue Horizon; Road To Morocco; The Fleet's In; Star-Spangled Rythmn; They Got Me Covered*
1943 *Dixie; Riding High* (UK: *Melody Inn*)
1944 *Rainbow Island; And The Angels Sing*
1945 *Road To Utopia; Duffy's Tavern; A Medal For Benny; Masquerade In Mexico*
1947 *My Favourite Brunette; Variety Girl; Road To Rio; Wild Harvest*
1948 *A Miracle Can Happen; Lulu Belle; The Girl From Manhattan*

**LAMOUR, Dorothy** (cont.)

1949 *Slightly French; Manhandled; The Lucky Stiff*
1951 *Here Comes The Groom*
1952 *The Greatest Show On Earth*; Road To Bali; Screen Snapshots No 205* (short)
1961 *Road To Hong Kong*
1963 *Donovan's Reef*
1964 *Pajama Party*
1970 *The Phynx*
1975 *Won Ton Ton — The Dog Who Saved Hollywood*
1976 *Death At Love House* (TV)
1987 *Creepshow 2*

**LANCASTER, Burt**
real name: Stephen Burton Lancaster
(1913–  ) USA

1946 *The Killers**
1947 *Desert Fury; Brute Force; I Walk Alone; Variety Girl*
1948 *All My Sons; Sorry, Wrong Number; Kiss The Blood Off My Hands* (UK: *Blood On My Hands*)
1949 *Criss Cross; Rope Of Sand*
1950 *The Flame And The Arrow; Mister 880*
1951 *Vengeance Valley; Jim Thorpe — All American* (UK: *Man Of Bronze*); *Ten Tall Men*
1952 *The Crimson Pirate; Come Back Little Sheba*
1953 *South Sea Woman; From Here To Eternity*; His Majesty O'Keefe; Three Girls And A Sailor*
1954 *Apache; Vera Cruz*
1955 *The Kentuckian* (also director); *The Rose Tattoo**
1956 *Trapeze*; The Rainmaker*
1957 *Gunfight At The OK Corral*; Sweet Smell Of Success*; Playtime In Hollywood*
1958 *Run Silent, Run Deep; Separate Tables**
1959 *The Devil's Disciple*
1960 *The Unforgiven; Elmer Gantry**

1961 *The Young Savages; Judgment At Nuremberg**
1962 *Birdman Of Alcatraz*; A Child Is Waiting; Il Gattopardo** (UK: *The Leopard*)
1963 *Seven Days In May*; The List Of Adrian Messenger*
1964 *The Train*
1965 *The Hallelujah Trail*
1966 *The Professionals**
1968 *The Swimmer; The Scalphunters*
1969 *Castle Keep; The Gypsy Moths; Airport*; King: A Filmed Record...Montgomery To Memphis* (documentary)
1970 *Valdez Is Coming; Lawman*
1972 *Ulzana's Raid; Scorpio*
1974 *The Midnight Man* (also co-director); *Gruppo Di Famiglia In Un Interno* (UK: *The Conversation Piece*)
1975 *Moses* (TV)
1976 *Novecento** (UK: *1900*); *Buffalo Bill And The Indians; The Cassandra Crossing; Victory At Entebbe; The Cinema According To Bertolucci* (documentary)
1977 *Twilight's Last Gleaming; The Island Of Dr Moreau*
1978 *Go Tell The Spartans*
1979 *Zulu Dawn*
1980 *Cattle Annie And Little Britches; Atlantic City USA** (UK: *Atlantic City*)
1981 *La Pelle* (UK: *The Skin*)
1983 *Local Hero*; The Osterman Weekend*
1985 *Little Treasure; Scandal Sheet* (TV)
1986 *Tough Guys; Barnum* (TV); *On Wings Of Eagles* (TV); *Sins Of The Fathers* (TV)
1987 *The Day Before* (TV); *The Suspect; The Goldsmith's Shop*
1988 *Rocket Gibraltar*
1989 *The Betrothed; Field Of Dreams*; Voyage Of Terror: The Achille Lauro Affair* (TV)
1990 *The Phantom Of The Opera* (TV)
1991 *Separate But Equal* (TV)

## LANGE, Jessica
(1949–  ) USA

1976  *King Kong\**
1979  *All That Jazz\**
1980  *How To Beat The High Cost Of Living*
1981  *The Postman Always Rings Twice\**
1982  *Frances\*; Tootsie\**
1984  *Country*
1985  *Sweet Dreams\**
1986  *Crimes Of The Heart*
1988  *Made In Germany; Far North; Everybody's All-American* (UK: *When I Fall In Love*)
1989  *The Music Box*
1990  *Men Don't Leave*
1991  *Blue Sky; Cape Fear\**
1992  *O Pioneers!* (TV); *Night And The City*

## LANSBURY, Angela
(1925–  ) UK

1944  *Gaslight\** (UK: *The Murder In Thornton Square*); *National Velvet\**
1945  *The Picture Of Dorian Gray; The Harvey Girls\**
1946  *Till The Clouds Roll By\*; The Hoodlum Saint*
1947  *Tenth Avenue Girl; The Private Affairs Of Bel Ami; If Winter Comes*
1948  *State Of The Union* (UK: *The World And His Wife*); *The Three Musketeers\**
1949  *The Red Danube; Samson And Delilah\**
1951  *Kind Lady*
1952  *Mutiny*
1953  *Remains To Be Seen*
1955  *The Purple Mask; A Lawless Street; The Key Man* (UK: *A Life At Stake*)
1956  *The Court Jester; Please Murder Me*
1958  *The Reluctant Debutante; The Long Hot Summer*

1960  *A Breath Of Scandal; The Dark At The Top Of The Stairs; Summer Of The 17th Doll* (UK: *Season Of Passion*)
1961  *Blue Hawaii*
1962  *The Manchurian Candidate\*; All Fall Down; The Four Horsemen Of The Apocalypse* (voice only)
1963  *In The Cool Of The Day*
1964  *The World Of Henry Orient; Dear Heart*
1965  *Harlow; The Greatest Story Ever Told; The Amorous Adventures Of Moll Flanders*
1966  *Mister Buddwing* (UK: *Woman Without A Face*)
1970  *Something For Everyone* (UK: *Black Flowers For The Bride*)
1971  *Bedknobs And Broomsticks*
1978  *Death On The Nile*
1979  *The Lady Vanishes*
1980  *The Mirror Crack'd*
1981  *The Last Unicorn* (voice only)
1982  *Little Gloria — Happy At Last* (TV); *The Pirates Of Penzance*
1983  *The Gift Of Love: A Christmas Story* (TV)
1984  *Lace* (TV); *The Company Of Wolves*
1986  *Rage Of Angels: The Story Continues* (TV); *A Talent For Murder* (TV)
1988  *Shootdown* (TV)
1989  *The Shell-Seekers*(TV)
1990  *The Love She Sought*(TV)
1991  *Beauty And The Beast\** (voice only)
1992  *Mrs 'Arris Goes To Paris* (TV)

## LAUGHTON, Charles
(1899–1962) UK

1928  *Bluebottles; Daydreams* (both shorts)
1929  *Piccadilly; Comets*
1930  *Wolves*
1931  *Down River*
1932  *The Old Dark House; Payment Deferred; The Devil And The Deep; The Sign Of The Cross; If I*

**LAUGHTON, Charles** (cont.)

*Had A Million; Island Of Lost Souls*

1933 *The Private Life Of Henry VIII\*: White Woman*

1934 *The Barretts Of Wimpole Street\**

1935 *Ruggles Of Red Gap\*; Mutiny On The Bounty\*; Les Misérables\*; Frankie And Johnny* (short)

1936 *Rembrandt*

1938 *Vessel Of Wrath; St Martin's Lane*

1939 *Jamaica Inn; The Hunchback Of Notre Dame\**

1940 *They Knew What They Wanted*

1941 *It Started With Eve*

1942 *The Tuttles Of Tahiti; Tales Of Manhattan; Stand By For Action* (UK: *Cargo Of Innocents*)

1943 *This Land Is Mine; The Man From Down Under; Forever And A Day*

1944 *The Canterville Ghost*

1945 *The Suspect; Captain Kidd*

1946 *Because Of Him*

1947 *The Queen's Necklace* (short)

1948 *The Paradine Case; Arch Of Triumph; The Girl From Manhattan; The Big Clock; On Our Merry Way* (UK: *A Miracle Can Happen*)

1949 *The Bribe; The Man On The Eiffel Tower*

1951 *The Blue Veil; The Strange Door*

1952 *O'Henry's Full House; Abbott And Costello Meet Captain Kidd*

1953 *Young Bess; Salome*

1954 *Hobson's Choice*

1955 *Night Of The Hunter\** (director only)

1957 *Witness For The Prosecution\**

1958 *Fabulous Hollywood* (documentary)

1960 *Sotto Dieci Bandiere* (UK: *Under Ten Flags*); *Spartacus\**

1962 *Advise And Consent*

**LAUREL, Stan**

real name: Arthur Stanley Jefferson (1890–1965) UK

**HARDY, Oliver**

real name: Norvell Hardy Junior (1892–1957) USA

1917 *Lucky Dog*

1926 *Forty-Five Minutes From Hollywood*

1927 *Duck Soup; Slipping Wives; Love 'Em And Weep; Why Girls Love Sailors; With Love And Hisses; Sailors Beware!; Do Detectives Think?* (UK: *The Bodyguard*); *Flying Elephants; Sugar Daddies; The Call Of The Cuckoo; The Second Hundred Years; Hats Off; Putting Pants On Philip; The Battle Of The Century*

1928 *Leave 'Em Laughing; The Finishing Touch; From Soup To Nuts; You're Darn Tootin'* (UK: *The Music Blasters*); *Their Purple Moment; Should Married Men Go Home?; Early To Bed; Two Tars; Habeus Corpus; We Faw Down* (UK: *We Slip Up*)

1929 *Liberty; Wrong Again; That's My Wife; Big Business; Double Whoopee; Unaccustomed As We Are; Berth Marks; Men O'War; The Perfect Day; They Go Boom; Bacon Grabbers; The Hoosegow; The Hollywood Revue Of 1929; Angora Love*

1930 *Night Owls; The Rogue Song; Blotto; Brats; Below Zero; Hog Wild* (UK: *Aerial Antics*); *The Laurel–Hardy Murder Case; Another Fine Mess; Be Big*

1931 *Chickens Come Home; Laughing Gravy; Our Wife; Pardon Us* (UK: *Jailbirds*); *Come Clean; One Good Turn; Helpmates; Beau Hunks* (UK: *Beau Chumps*)

1932 *Any Old Port; The Music Box; The Chimp; County Hospital; Scram; Pack Up Your Troubles; Their First Mistake; Towed In A Hole; The Stolen Jools* (UK: *The Slippery Pearls*)

1933 *Twice Two; Me And My Pal;*
*The Devil's Brother* (UK: *Fra*
*Diavolo*); *The Midnight Patrol;*
*Busy Bodies; Wild Poses; Dirty*
*Work; Sons Of The Desert* (UK:
*Fraternally Yours*)
1934 *Oliver The Eighth* (UK: *The*
*Private Life Of Oliver The Eighth*);
*Hollywood Party; Going Bye Bye;*
*Them Thar Hills; Babes In*
*Toyland; The Live Ghost*
1935 *Tit For Tat; The Fixer-Uppers;*
*Thicker Than Water; Bonnie*
*Scotland*
1936 *The Bohemian Girl; On The*
*Wrong Trek; Our Relations*
1937 *Way Out West\*; Pick A Star*
1938 *Swiss Miss; Block Heads*
1939 *The Flying Deuces*
1940 *A Chum At Oxford; Saps At Sea*
1941 *Great Guns*
1942 *A Haunting We Will Go*
1943 *Air Raid Wardens; Tree In A Test*
*Tube; Jitterbugs; The Dancing*
*Masters*
1944 *The Big Noise; Nothing But Trouble*
1045 *The Bullfighters*
1951 *Atoll K* (UK: *Robinson Crusoeland*)

## LAURIE, Piper
real name: Rosetta Jacobs
(1932–   ) USA

1950 *Louisa; The Milkman; The Prince*
*Who Was A Thief*
1951 *Francis Goes To The Races*
1952 *Has Anybody Seen My Gal?; No*
*Room For The Groom; Son Of Ali*
*Baba*
1953 *Mississippi Gambler; The Golden*
*Blade*
1954 *Dangerous Mission; Johnny Dark;*
*Dawn At Socorro; Queens Of*
*Beauty* (short)
1955 *Smoke Signal; Ain't Misbehavin'*
1957 *Kelly And Me; Until They Sail*
1961 *The Hustler\**
1976 *Carrie\**
1977 *Ruby; In The Matter Of Karen Ann*
*Quinlan* (TV)
1978 *The Boss's Son; Tim; Rainbow* (TV)

1980 *Skag* (TV)
1981 *The Bunker* (TV)
1982 *Mae West* (TV)
1985 *Return To Oz; Toughlove* (TV);
*Love, Mary* (TV)
1986 *Promise* (TV); *Children Of A*
*Lesser God\**
1987 *Distortions; Tiger Warsaw*
1988 *Appointment With Death; Go*
*Toward The Light* (TV)
1989 *Dream A Little Dream; Twin*
*Peaks* (TV)
1990 *Rising Son* (TV)
1991 *Other People's Money*
1992 *Storyville; Rich In Love*
1993 *Wrestling Ernest Hemingway*

## LEE, Christopher
(1922–   )

1948 *Corridor Of Mirrors; One Night*
*With You; Hamlet\*; A Song For*
*Tomorrow; Saraband For Dead*
*Lovers; My Brother's Keeper;*
*Penny And The Pownall Case;*
*The Luck Of The Irish; Scott Of*
*The Antarctic*
1949 *Trottie True*
1950 *Prelude To Fame; They Were Not*
*Divided*
1951 *Captain Horatio Hornblower RN;*
*The Valley Of Eagles*
1952 *Top Secret; Babes In Bagdad;*
*Paul Temple Returns; The*
*Crimson Pirate; Moulin Rouge\**
1953 *Innocents In Paris; The Triangle;*
*The Mirror And Markheim* (short)
1954 *Destination Milan; The Death Of*
*Michael Turbin*
1955 *The Dark Avenger; That Lady;*
*The Final Column; Storm Over*
*The Nile; Man In Demand; Police*
*Dog; Stranglehold; Cockleshell*
*Heroes; Crossroads* (short)
1956 *Private's Progress; Port Afrique;*
*The Battle Of The River Plate;*
*Beyond Mombasa; Ill Met By*
*Moonlight; Alias John Preston;*
*The Curse Of Frankenstein*
1957 *Fortune Is A Woman; The Traitor;*
*Bitter Victory*

**LEE, Christopher** (cont.)

1958 *A Tale Of Two Cities; The Truth About Women; Battle Of The V-1; Dracula\*; Corridors Of Blood*

1959 *The Mummy; The Hound Of The Baskervilles; The Man Who Could Cheat Death; The Treasure Of San Teresa; 'Beat' Girl*

1960 *City Of The Dead; The Two Faces Of Dr Jekyll; Too Hot To Handle; The Hands Of Orlac*

1961 *Hard Times For Vampires; The Terror Of The Tongs; Taste Of Fear; Hercules In The Centre Of The Earth; Mystery Of The Red Orchid; The Pirates Of Blood River*

1962 *The Devil's Daffodil; The Longest Day\*; In Namen Des Teufels* (UK: *The Devil's Agent*)

1963 *La Cripta E L'Incubo* (UK: *Crypt Of Horror*); *La Vergina Di Norimberga* (UK: *Castle Of Terror*); *The Devil Ship Pirates; La Frustra E Il Corpo* (UK: *Night Is The Phantom*); *Catharsis; Sherlock Holmes Und Das Halsband Des Todes* (UK: *Sherlock Holmes And The Deadly Necklace*)

1964 *The Gorgon; Dr Terror's House Of Horrors; Castle Of The Living Dead; The Masque Of The Red Death* (voice only)

1965 *The Face Of Fu Manchu; She; Rasputin, The Mad Monk; Theatre Of Death; Circus Of Fear; Dracula, Prince Of Darkness; The Skull*

1966 *The Brides Of Fu Manchu*

1967 *Victims Of Terror* (short, narrator only); *Five Golden Dragons; The Vengeance Of Fu Manchu; Night Of The Big Heat; Die Schlangengrube Und Das Pendel* (UK: *The Blood Demon*)

1968 *The Devil Rides Out; Dracula Has Risen From The Grave; The Castle Of Fu Manchu; The Face Of Eve; Blood Of Fu Manchu; The Curse Of The Crimson Altar*

1969 *The Oblong Box; Philosophy In The Boudoir; The Magic Christian; Scream And Scream Again; One More Time*

1970 *Taste The Blood Of Dracula; The Private Life Of Sherlock Holmes; Julius Caesar; The House That Dripped Blood; Der Hexentöter Von Blackmoor; Il Trono Di Fuoco* (UK: *Throne Of Fire*); *Bram Stoker's Count Dracula; El Umbraculo; Scars Of Dracula*

1971 *I, Monster; Hannie Caulder*

1972 *Poor Devil* (TV); *Dracula AD 1972; Panico En El Transiberio* (UK: *Horror Express*); *The Creeping Flesh; Death Line; Nothing But The Night*

1973 *Dark Places; The Satanic Rites Of Dracula; The Wicker Man; The Three Musketeers\*; Eulalie Quitte Les Champs*

1974 *The Four Musketeers; The Man With The Golden Gun\*; Diagnosis: Murder*

1975 *To The Devil A Daughter; The Diamond Mercenaries; The Keeper; Death In The Sun; Revenge Of The Dead* (narrator only)

1976 *Dracula, Father And Son*

1977 *Airport'77; End Of The World; Meat Cleaver Massacre; Starship Invasion/Alien Encounter*

1978 *Jaguar Lives; The Passage; Caravans; The Pirate* (TV); *Return From Witch Mountain; The Silent Flute*

1979 *Arabian Adventure; Bear Island; 1941\*; Captain America II* (TV); *Nutcracker Fantasy* (voice only)

1980 *Once Upon A Spy* (TV); *Serial; Sunday Games* (TV); *Rollerboy*

1981 *The Salamander; The Last Unicorn* (voice only); *Rally; An Eye For An Eye; Goliath Awaits* (TV)

1982 *The Return Of Captain Invincible; House Of The Long Shadows; Charles And Diana: A Royal Love Story* (TV)

1983 *Massarati And The Brain* (TV); *The Keeper*
1985 *Mask Of Murder; The Howling II...Your Sister Is A Werewolf; The Rosebud Beach Hotel; Road Trip*
1986 *Mio In The Land Of Faraway; The Girl; Jocks; Desperate Moves*
1987 *Dark Mission: Flowers Of Evil*
1988 *The Avalon Awakening; Murder Story*
1989 *Treasure Island* (TV); *Return Of The Musketeers*
1990 *The French Revolution; Gremlins 2: The New Batch; Honeymoon Academy; The Cave Of Time; The Rainbow Thief; L'Avaro; The Monastery; Shogun Mayeda; Curse III: Blood Sacrifice*
1991 *Sherlock Holmes And The Incident At Victoria Falls*

## LEIGH, Janet
real name: Jeanette Morrison
(1927– ) USA

1947 *The Romance Of Rosy Ridge; If Winter Comes*
1948 *Words And Music; Act Of Violence; Hills Of Home* (UK: *Master Of Lassie*)
1949 *That Forsyte Woman\** (UK: *The Forsyte Saga*); *The Red Danube; Little Women; The Doctor And The Girl; Holiday Affair*
1950 *Jet Pilot*
1951 *Strictly Dishonourable; Two Tickets To Broadway; It's A Big Country; Angels In The Outfield* (UK: *Angels And The Pirates*)
1952 *Just This Once; Scaramouche; Fearless Fagan*
1953 *The Naked Spur; Confidentially Connie; Houdini; Walking My Baby Back Home; Hollywood Laugh Parade* (short)
1954 *Prince Valiant; Living It Up; The Black Shield Of Falworth; Rogue Cop*
1955 *My Sister Eileen; Pete Kelly's Blues*
1956 *Safari*

1958 *The Vikings\*; Touch Of Evil\*; The Perfect Furlough* (UK: *Strictly For Pleasure*)
1959 *Who Was That Lady?*
1960 *Pepe; Psycho\**
1962 *The Manchurian Candidate\**
1963 *Bye Bye Birdie; Wives And Lovers*
1965 *Kid Rodelo*
1966 *Three On A Couch; Harper* (UK: *The Moving Target*); *An American Dream* (UK: *See You In Hell, Darling*)
1967 *Grand Slam*
1968 *Hello Down There*
1969 *The Monk* (TV); *Honeymoon With A Stranger* (TV)
1970 *The House On Greenapple Street* (TV)
1971 *The Deadly Dream* (TV)
1972 *One Is A Lonely Number; Night Of The Lepus*
1973 *Murdock's Gang* (TV)
1976 *Murder At The World Series* (TV)
1977 *Telethon* (TV)
1979 *Boardwalk*
1980 *The Fog; The Fall Guy* (TV); *Mirror, Mirror* (TV)

## LEIGH, Vivien
real name: Vivian Hartley
(1913–67) UK

1934 *Things Are Looking Up*
1935 *The Village Squire; Gentleman's Agreement; Look Up And Laugh*
1936 *Fire Over England*
1937 *Dark Journey; Storm In A Teacup*
1938 *21 Days; St Martin's Lane; A Yank At Oxford; Guide Dogs For The Blind* (short)
1939 *Gone With The Wind\**
1940 *Waterloo Bridge*
1941 *That Hamilton Woman* (UK: *Lady Hamilton*); *Cavalcade Of The Academy Awards* (short)
1945 *Caesar And Cleopatra*
1948 *Anna Karenina*
1951 *A Streetcar Named Desire\**
1955 *The Deep Blue Sea*
1961 *The Roman Spring Of Mrs Stone*
1965 *Ship Of Fools\**

## LEMMON, Jack
real name: John Uhler Lemmon
(1925–  ) USA

1954 *It Should Happen To You; Phffft; Three For The Show*
1955 *Mister Roberts\*; My Sister Eileen*
1956 *Hollywood Bronco Busters* (short); *You Can't Run Away From It*
1957 *Fire Down Below; Operation Mad Ball; The Mystery Of 13* (TV)
1958 *Cowboy; Bell, Book And Candle*
1959 *It Happened To Jane; Some Like It Hot\**
1960 *The Wackiest Ship In The Army; The Apartment\*; Stowaway In The Sky* (narrator only); *Pepe*
1962 *The Notorious Landlady; Days Of Wine And Roses\**
1963 *Irma La Douce\*; Under The Yum Yum Tree*
1964 *Good Neighbour Sam*
1965 *How To Murder Your Wife; The Great Race\**
1966 *The Fortune Cookie* (UK: *Meet Whiplash Willie*)
1967 *Luv; The Odd Couple\**
1969 *The April Fools*
1970 *The Out-Of-Towners*
1971 *Kotch* (director only)
1972 *The War Between Men And Women; Avanti!*
1973 *Wednesday* (short); *Save The Tiger*
1974 *The Front Page*
1975 *The Prisoner Of Second Avenue*
1976 *The Entertainer* (TV); *Alex And The Gypsy*
1977 *Airport '77*
1979 *The China Syndrome\*; Ken Murray's Shooting Stars* (documentary)
1980 *Tribute; Portrait Of A 60% Perfect Man* (documentary)
1981 *Buddy, Buddy; Missing\**
1984 *Mass Appeal*
1985 *Macaroni*
1986 *That's Life*
1987 *The Murder Of Mary Phagan* (TV)
1989 *Dad*
1991 *JFK\**
1992 *For Richer, For Poorer* (TV) (aka *Father, Son And The Mistress*); *The Player\*; Glengarry Glen Ross*
1993 *Shortcuts; Grumpy Old Men*

## LEWIS, Jerry
real name: Joseph Levitch
(1926–  ) USA

1949 *My Friend Irma*
1950 *My Friend Irma Goes West*
1951 *At War With The Army; That's My Boy; Screen Snapshots No 197* (short); *Sailor Beware*
1952 *Screen Snapshots No 207; Hollywood Fun Festival* (both shorts); *The Stooge; Jumping Jacks; Road To Bali*
1953 *Scared Stiff; The Caddy*
1954 *Money From Home; Living It Up; Three Ring Circus; Paramount Presents Vistavision* (short)
1955 *You're Never Too Young; Artists And Models*
1956 *Pardners; Hollywood Or Bust; Hollywood Premiere* (short)
1957 *The Delicate Delinquent; The Sad Sack*
1958 *Rock-A-Bye Baby; The Geisha Boy*
1959 *Don't Give Up The Ship; L'il Abner*
1960 *Visit To A Small Planet; Cinderfella; The Bellboy* (also director)
1961 *The Ladies' Man; The Errand Boy* (both director also)
1962 *It's Only Money*
1963 *It's A Mad, Mad, Mad, Mad World\*; Who's Minding The Store?; The Nutty Professor* (also director)
1964 *The Disorderly Orderly; The Patsy* (also director)
1965 *The Family Jewels* (also director); *Boeing, Boeing*
1966 *Three On A Couch* (also director); *Way...Way Out!*
1967 *The Big Mouth* (also director)

1968 *Don't Raise The Bridge, Lower The River*
1969 *Hook Line And Sinker*
1970 *One More Time* (director only); *Which Way To The Front?* (UK: *Ja! Ja! Mein General, But Which Way To The Front?*) (also director)
1979 *Rascal Dazzle* (narrator only)
1980 *Hardly Working* (also director)
1982 *Slapstick; The King Of Comedy**
1983 *Smorgasbord* (also director)
1984 *Par Ou T'Es Rentre, On T'A Pas Vue Sortir?*
1987 *Fight For Life* (TV)
1989 *Cookie*
1992 *Arizona Dream; Mr Saturday Night*

## LIOTTA, Ray
(1955–   ) USA

1980 *Hardhat And Legs* (TV)
1983 *The Lonely Lady*
1986 *Something Wild*
1988 *Dominick And Eugene* (UK: *Nicky And Gino*)
1989 *Field Of Dreams**
1990 *Goodfellas**
1991 *Women & Men: In Love There Are No Rules* (TV)
1992 *Article 99; Unlawful Entry*

## LOCKWOOD, Margaret
(1911–90) UK

1934 *Lorna Doone*
1935 *The Case Of Gabriel Perry/Wild Justice; Some Day; Honours Easy; Man Of The Moment; Midshipman Easy*
1936 *The Beloved Vagabond; Irish For Luck*
1937 *The Street Singer; Who's Your Lady Friend?; Dr Syn; Melody And Romance; Owd Bob; Bank Holiday*
1938 *The Lady Vanishes**
1939 *Rulers Of The Sea; Susannah Of The Mounties; A Girl Must Live; The Stars Look Down*

1940 *Night Train To Munich; The Girl In The News*
1941 *Quiet Wedding*
1942 *Alibi*
1943 *Dear Octopus; The Man In Grey*
1944 *Give Us The Moon; Love Story*
1945 *A Place Of One's Own; I'll Be Your Sweetheart; The Wicked Lady*
1946 *Bedelia; Hungry Hill*
1947 *Jassy; The White Unicorn*
1948 *Look Before You Love*
1949 *Cardboard Cavalier; Madness Of The Heart*
1950 *Highly Dangerous*
1952 *Trent's Last Case*
1953 *Laughing Anne*
1954 *Trouble In The Glen*
1955 *Cast A Dark Shadow*
1976 *The Slipper And The Rose*

## LOMBARD, Carole
real name: Jane Peters
(1908–42) USA

1921 *A Perfect Crime*
1925 *Marriage In Transit; Hearts And Spurs; Durand Of The Badlands; Gold And The Girl*
1926 *The Road To Glory*
1927 *Smith's Pony; The Girl From Everywhere; Hold That Pose; The Campus Vamp; The Campus Carmen; A Gold Digger Of Weepah* (all shorts); *The Fighting Eagle*
1928 *Run Girl Run; The Beach Club; The Best Man; Matchmaking Mammas; The Swim Princess; The Bicycle Flirt; The Girl From Nowhere; His Unlucky Night* (all shorts); *The Divine Sinner; Power; Show Folks; Me, Gangster; Ned McCobb's Daughter*
1929 *Big News; High Voltage* (UK: *Wanted*); *The Racketeer* (UK: *Love's Conquest*)
1930 *The Arizona Kid; Safety In Numbers; Fast And Loose*

**LOMBARD, Carole** (cont.)
1931 *It Pays To Advertise; Ladies' Man; Take This Woman; Up Pops The Devil; Man Of The Wild*
1932 *Sinners In The Sun; No One Man; No Man Of Her Own; No More Orchids; Virtue*
1933 *Supernatural; From Hell To Heaven; The Eagle And The Hawk; White Woman; Brief Moment*
1934 *Twentieth Century; Bolero; We're Not Dressing; Now And Forever; The Gay Bride; Lady By Chance*
1935 *Rumba; Hands Across The Table*
1936 *My Man Godfrey; The Princess Comes Across; Love Before Breakfast*
1937 *Swing High, Swing Low; True Confession; Nothing Sacred*
1938 *Fools For Scandal*
1939 *In Name Only; Made For Each Other*
1940 *Vigil In The Night; They Knew What They Wanted; Picture People No 4* (short)
1941 *Mr And Mrs Smith*
1942 *To Be Or Not To Be**

**LOREN, Sophia**
real name: Sofio Scicolone
(1934– ) Italy

1950 *Cuori Su Mare; Luci Del Varieta; Toto Tarzan; Il Voto; Il Sono Il Capatza; Anna; Le Sei Mogli Di Barbalu* (UK: *Bluebeard's Seven Wives*)
1951 *Lebra Bianca; Milano Miliardi; Il Mago Per Forza* (UK: *The Magician In Spite Of Himself*); *Il Sogno Di Zorro* (UK: *The Dream Of Zorro*); *Quo Vadis?**; *E'Arrivato L'Accordatore; Era Lui...Si,Si*
1952 *La Favorita; Il Tratta Della Bianche* (UK: *Girls Marked Danger*); *Africo Sotto I Mari* (UK: *Woman Of The Red Sea*)
1953 *Carosello Napoletano; Aida; Ci Troviamo In Galleria; Tempi Nostri* (UK: *Anatomy Of Love*); *Il Paese*

*Dei Campanelli; La Domenica Della Buona Gente; Un Girono In Pretura; Two Nights With Cleopatra; Attila The Hun*
1954 *Peccato Che Sia Una Canaglia* (UK: *Too Bad She's Bad*); *L'Oro Di Napoli* (UK: *Gold Of Naples*); *La Donna Del Fiume* (UK: *Woman Of The River*); *Miseria E Nobilita*
1955 *Pellegrini D'Amore; Il Segno Di Venere* (UK: *The Sign Of Venus*); *La Bella Mugnaia; La Fortuna Di Essera Donna* (UK: *Lucky To Be A Woman*); *Pane, Amore, E...* (UK: *Scandal In Sorrento*)
1957 *The Pride And The Passion; Boy On A Dolphin; Legend Of The Lost*
1958 *Desire Under The Elms; Houseboat; The Key*
1959 *Black Orchid; That Kind Of Woman*
1960 *Heller In Pink Tights; It Started In Naples; A Breath Of Scandal*
1961 *The Millionairess; Madame; El Cid**; *La Ciociara** (UK: *Two Women*); *Captive Island*
1962 *Five Miles To Midnight; Boccaccio 70; The Condemned Of Altona*
1963 *Ieri, Oggi E Domani* (UK: *Yesterday, Today And Tomorrow*); *The Fall Of The Roman Empire*
1964 *Matrimonio All'Italiana* (UK: *Marriage—Italian Style*)
1965 *Operation Crossbow; Judith; Lady L*
1966 *Arabesque; A Countess From Hong Kong*
1967 *C'Era Una Volta* (UK: *Cinderella—Italian Style*)
1968 *Questi Fantasmi* (UK: *Ghosts—Italian Style*)
1969 *Il Girasoli* (UK: *Sunflower*)
1970 *La Moglia Del Prete* (UK: *The Priest's Wife*)
1971 *La Mortadella* (UK: *Lady Liberty*); *Bianco, Rosso E...* (UK: *White Sister*)
1972 *Man Of La Mancha*
1974 *Il Viaggio* (UK: *The Voyage*); *Verdict; La Pupa Del Gangster*

1975 *Brief Encounter* (TV)
1976 *The Cassandra Crossing*
1977 *Una Giornata Particolare* (UK: *A Special Day*); *Angela*
1978 *Vengeance; Brass Target*
1979 *Firepower; Blood Feud; Shimmy Lugano E Tarantelle E Tarallucci E Vino*
1980 *Sophia Loren: Her Own Story* (TV)
1984 *Aurora*
1986 *Courage* (TV)
1988 *The Fortunate Pilgrim* (TV)
1989 *Two Women* (TV)
1990 *Saturday, Sunday And Monday*

## LORRE, Peter
real name: Laszlo Löwenstein
(1904–64)

1931 *Bomben Auf Monte Carlo; M\*; Die Koffer Des Hern OF*
1932 *Der Weisse Dämon; FPI Antwortet Nicht; Fünf Von Der Jazzband; Schuss Im Morgengrauen*
1933 *Was Frauen Träumen; Unsichtbare Gegner; Du Haut En Bas*
1934 *The Man Who Knew Too Much*
1935 *Mad Love* (UK: *Hands Of Orlac*); *Crime And Punishment*
1936 *Secret Agent; Crack-Up*
1937 *Lancer Spy; Nancy Steele Is Missing; Think Fast Mr Moto; Thank You, Mr Moto*
1938 *Mysterious Mr Moto; I'll Give A Million; Mr Moto's Gamble; Mr Moto Takes A Chance*
1939 *Mr Moto Takes A Vacation; Mr Moto's Last Warning; Mr Moto In Danger Island* (UK: *Mr Moto On Danger Island*)
1940 *Island Of Doomed Men; I Was An Adventuress; Strange Cargo; You'll Find Out; Stranger On The Third Floor*
1941 *Mister District Attorney; The Maltese Falcon\*; The Face Behind The Mask; They Met In Bombay*

1942 *Invisible Agent; All Through The Night; The Boogie Man Will Get You; Casablanca\*; In This Our Life*
1943 *Background To Danger; The Constant Nymph; The Cross Of Lorraine*
1944 *Arsenic And Old Lace\*; Passage To Marseille; Hollywood Canteen; The Mask Of Dimitrios; The Conspirators*
1945 *Hotel Berlin; Confidential Agent*
1946 *Three Strangers; The Chase; Black Angel; The Verdict; The Beast With Five Fingers*
1947 *My Favourite Brunette*
1948 *Casbah*
1949 *Rope Of Sand*
1950 *Double Confession; Quicksand*
1951 *Die Verlorene* (also director)
1953 *Beat The Devil*
1954 *20,000 Leagues Under The Sea\**
1956 *Congo Crossing; Around The World In 80 Days\*; Meet Me In Las Vegas* (UK: *Viva Las Vegas!*)
1957 *The Story Of Mankind; The Buster Keaton Story; Silk Stockings; Hell Ship Mutiny; The Sad Sack*
1959 *The Big Circus*
1960 *Scent Of Mystery* (UK: *Holiday In Spain*)
1961 *Voyage To The Bottom Of The Sea*
1962 *Tales Of Terror; The Raven; Five Weeks In A Balloon*
1963 *The Comedy Of Terrors*
1964 *The Patsy; Muscle Beach Party*

## LOWE, Rob
(1964– ) USA

1982 *The Outsiders\**
1983 *Thursday's Child* (TV)
1984 *The Hotel New Hampshire; Oxford Blues*
1985 *St Elmo's Fire*
1986 *About Last Night; Square Dance*
1987 *Illegally Yours*
1988 *Masquerade*
1990 *Bad Influence*

**LOWE, Rob** (cont.)
1991 *Desert Shield; The Dark Backward*
1992 *Wayne's World\**
1993 *L'Arbre Metallique*

**LOY, Myrna**
real name: Myrna Williams
(1905–  ) USA

1925 *Ben-Hur; Satan In Sables; Pretty Ladies; Sporting Life*
1926 *The Wanderer; When A Man Loves* (UK: *His Lady*); *Cave Man; The Gilded Highway; Across The Pacific; Don Juan; Why Girls Go Back Home; The Love Toy; The Third Degree; Millionairess; The Exquisite Sinner; So This Is Paris; Finger Prints*
1927 *Ham And Eggs At The Front* (UK: *Ham And Eggs*); *Bitter Apples; The Heart Of Maryland; The Jazz Singer\*; If I Were Single; The Climbers; The Girl From Chicago; Simple Sis; A Sailor's Sweetheart*
1928 *A Girl In Every Port; What Price Beauty?; Turn Back The Hours; Crimson City; State Secret; Sadie* (UK: *The Girl From State Street*); *Beware Of Married Men; Midnight Taxi; Pay As You Enter*
1929 *Noah's Ark; The Desert Song; Fancy Baggage; The Black Watch* (UK: *King Of The Khyber Rifles*); *Hardboiled Rose; Evidence; The Show Of Shows; The Squall*
1930 *Jazz Cinderella* (UK: *Love Is Like That*); *Cameo Kirby; Isle Of Escape; The Bad Man; The Great Divide; Cock O' The Walk; Bride Of The Regiment* (UK: *Lady Of The Rose*); *Last Of The Duanes; Under A Texas Moon; Rogue Of The Rio Grande; The Truth About Youth; Renegades; The Devil To Pay*
1931 *A Connecticut Yankee* (UK: *The Yankee At King Arthur's Court*); *Naughty Flirt; Arrowsmith\*; Consolation Marriage* (UK:

*Married In Haste*); *Skyline; Rebound; Transatlantic; Hush Money; Body And Soul*
1932 *The Wet Parade; The Woman In Room 13; Emma; Love Me Tonight; Thirteen Women; The Animal Kingdom* (UK: *The Woman In His House*); *The Mask Of Fu Manchu; Vanity Fair; New Morals For Old*
1933 *Topaze; Penthouse* (UK: *A Night In Cairo*); *The Prizefighter And The Lady* (UK: *Everywoman's Man*); *Night Flight; Scarlet River; When Ladies Meet*
1934 *Men In White; Stamboul Quest; Manhattan Melodrama; The Thin Man\*; Evelyn Prentice; Broadway Bill* (UK: *Strictly Confidential*)
1935 *Wings In The Dark; Whipsaw*
1936 *Wife Vs Secretary; Libeled Lady; After The Thin Man; The Great Ziegfeld\*; Petticoat Fever; To Mary — With Love*
1937 *Parnell; Double Wedding; Man-Proof*
1938 *Test Pilot\*; Too Hot To Handle*
1939 *Lucky Night; Another Thin Man; The Rains Came*
1940 *Third Finger, Left Hand; I Love You Again*
1941 *Shadow Of The Thin Man; Love Crazy*
1943 *Showbusiness At War*
1944 *The Thin Man Goes Home*
1946 *The Best Years Of Our Lives\*; So Goes My Love* (UK: *A Genius In The Family*)
1947 *The Senator Was Indiscreet* (UK: *Mr Ashton Was Indiscreet*); *Song Of The Thin Man; The Bachelor And The Bobby Soxer* (UK: *Bachelor Knight*)
1948 *Mr Blandings Builds His Dream House*
1949 *The Red Pony; That Dangerous Age* (UK: *If This Be Sin*)
1950 *Cheaper By The Dozen\**
1952 *Belles On Their Toes*
1956 *The Ambassador's Daughter*
1958 *Lonelyhearts*

1960 *From The Terrace\*; Midnight Lace*
1969 *The April Fools*
1971 *Death Takes A Holiday* (TV); *Do Not Fold, Spindle Or Mutilate* (TV)
1972 *The Couple Takes A Wife* (TV)
1974 *Indict And Convict* (TV); *Airport '75*
1975 *The Elevator* (TV)
1977 *It Happened At Lakewood Manor* (TV) (UK: *Panic At Lakewood Manor*)
1978 *The End*
1980 *Just Tell Me What You Want*
1981 *Summer Solstice* (TV)

## LUGOSI, Bela
real name: Bela Blasko
(1882–1956) Transylvania

1917 *Alarscobal; Az Elet Kiralya; The Leopard; A Naszdal; Tavaszi Vihar; Az Ezredes*
1918 *Casanova; Lulu; 99; Kuzdelem A Létért*
1919 *Sklaven Fremden Willens*
1920 *Der Fluch Der Menschen; The Head Of Janus* (UK: *Dr Jekyll And Mr Hyde*); *Die Frau Im Delphin; Die Todeskarawane; Nat Pinkerton Im Kampf; Lederstrumpf; Die Teufelsanbeter*
1921 *Johann Hopkins III; Der Tanz Auf Dem Vulkan*
1922 *The Last Of The Mohicans*
1923 *The Silent Command*
1924 *The Rejected Woman*
1925 *The Midnight Girl; Daughters Who Pay*
1926 *Punchinello* (short)
1928 *How To Handle Women; The Veiled Woman*
1929 *Prisoners; The Thirteenth Chair; The Last Performance; Such Men Are Dangerous*
1930 *Wild Company; Renegades; Viennese Nights; Oh, For A Man; Dracula\**
1931 *Fifty Million Frenchmen; Women Of All Nations; The Black Camel; Broadminded*
1932 *The Murders In The Rue Morgue; White Zombie; Chandu, The Magician; The Death Kiss; Island Of Lost Souls*
1933 *Whispering Shadows; International House; Night Of Terror; The Devil's In Love*
1934 *The Black Cat* (UK: *The House Of Doom*); *Gift Of Gab; The Return Of Chandu; The Best Man Wins; Chandu On The Magic Isle; Screen Snapshots No 11* (short)
1935 *The Mysterious Mr Wong; Murder By Television; Mark Of The Vampire; The Raven; The Mystery Of The Marie Celeste; The Invisible Ray*
1936 *Shadow Of Chinatown* (UK: *The Yellow Phantom*); *Postal Inspector*
1937 *SOS Coastguard*
1939 *The Dark Eyes Of London; The Phantom Creeps; Son Of Frankenstein; Ninotchka\*; The Gorilla*
1940 *The Saint's Double Trouble; Black Friday; You'll Find Out, The Devil Bat*
1041 *The Invisible Ghost; The Black Cat; Spooks Run Wild; The Wolf Man*
1942 *The Ghost Of Frankenstein; Black Dragons; The Corpse Vanishes* (UK: *The Case Of The Missing Brides*); *Night Monster* (UK: *House Of Mystery*); *Bowery At Midnight*
1943 *Frankenstein Meets The Wolf Man; The Ape Man; Ghosts On The Loose; The Return Of The Vampire*
1944 *Voodoo Man; Return Of The Ape Man* (UK: *Lock Your Doors*); *One Body Too Many*
1945 *The Body Snatcher; Zombies On Broadway* (UK: *Loonies On Broadway*)
1946 *Genius At Work; Devil Bat's Daughter*
1947 *Scared To Death*
1948 *Abbott And Costello Meet Frankenstein* (UK: *Abbott And Costello Meet The Ghosts*)

**LUGOSI, Bela** (cont.)

1952 *Mother Riley Meets The Vampire; Bela Lugosi Meets A Brookyln Gorilla* (UK: *Monster Meets The Gorilla*); *Meet Bela Lugosi And Oliver Hardy* (short)
1953 *Glen Or Glenda?*
1954 *Bride Of The Monster*
1956 *The Black Sleep; Plan 9 From Outer Space*

**LUPINO, Ida**
(1914– ) USA

1932 *The Love Race; Her First Affaire*
1933 *Money For Speed; High Finance; I Lived With You; Prince Of Arcadia; The Ghost Camera*
1934 *Search For Beauty; Ready For Love; Come On Marines!*
1935 *Paris In Spring* (UK: *Paris Love Song*); *Peter Ibbetson; Smart Girl; La Fiesta De Santa Barbara* (short)
1936 *Anything Goes; The Gay Desperado; One Rainy Afternoon; Yours For The Asking*
1937 *Sea Devils; Artists And Models; Let's Get Married; Fight For Your Lady*
1939 *The Lone Wolf Spy Hunt* (UK: *The Lone Wolf's Daughter*); *The Adventures Of Sherlock Holmes* (UK: *Sherlock Holmes*); *The Lady And The Mob; The Light That Failed*
1940 *They Drive By Night* (UK: *The Road To Frisco*)
1941 *The Sea Wolf; High Sierra*; *Out Of The Fog; Ladies In Retirement*
1942 *Moontide; Life Begins At 8.30* (UK: *The Light Of Heart*); *The Hard Way*
1943 *Forever And A Day; Thank Your Lucky Stars*
1944 *Hollywood Canteen; In Our Time*
1945 *Pillow To Post*
1946 *Devotion; The Man I Love*
1947 *Deep Valley; Escape Me Never*
1948 *Road House*

1949 *Lust For Gold; Not Wanted* (co-director only)
1950 *Outrage; Never Fear* (director only); *Woman In Hiding*
1951 *On Dangerous Ground; Hard, Fast And Beautiful* (director only)
1952 *Beware My Lovely*
1953 *Jennifer; The Bigamist* (also director); *The Hitchhiker* (director only)
1954 *Private Hell 36*
1955 *The Big Knife; Women's Prison*
1956 *While The City Sleeps; Strange Intruder*
1966 *The Trouble With Angels* (director only)
1967 *I Love A Mystery* (TV)
1968 *Backtrack* (TV)
1971 *Women In Chains* (TV)
1972 *Female Artillery* (TV); *Deadhead Miles; Junior Bonner; My Boys Are Good Boys; The Strangers In 7A* (TV)
1973 *The Letters* (TV)
1975 *The Devil's Rain*
1976 *The Food Of The Gods*

# M

**MACCHIO, Ralph**
(1961– ) USA

1980 *Up The Academy*
1982 *Dangerous Company* (TV); *The Outsiders**
1984 *The Karate Kid*; *The Three Wishes Of Billy Grier* (TV); *Teachers*
1986 *Crossroads; The Karate Kid Part II*
1988 *Distant Thunder*
1989 *The Karate Kid Part III*
1990 *Too Much Sun*
1992 *My Cousin Vinny*
1993 *Naked In New York*

**MACDONALD, Jeanette**
(1901–65) USA

1929 *The Love Parade**

1930 *The Vagabond King; Let's Go Native; Oh, For A Man; Monte Carlo; The Lottery Bride*
1931 *Annabelle's Affairs; Don't Bet On Women* (UK: *More Than A Kiss*)
1932 *One Hour With You; Love Me Tonight*
1933 *Hollywood On Parade No 7* (short)
1934 *The Cat And The Fiddle; The Merry Widow*
1935 *Naughty Marietta*
1936 *Rose Marie\*; San Francisco\**
1937 *Maytime; The Firefly*
1938 *The Girl Of The Golden West; Sweethearts*
1939 *Broadway Serenade*
1940 *New Moon; Bitter Sweet*
1941 *Smilin' Through*
1942 *I Married An Angel; Cairo*
1944 *Follow The Boys*
1948 *Three Daring Daughters* (UK: *The Birds And The Bees*); *The Sun Comes Up*

## MACGRAW, Ali
full name: Alice MacGraw
(1938– ) USA

1968 *A Lovely Way To Die* (UK: *A Lovely Way To Go*)
1969 *Goodbye Columbus\**
1970 *Love Story\**
1972 *The Getaway*
1978 *Convoy*
1979 *Players*
1980 *Just Tell Me What You Want*
1983 *China Rose* (TV)
1985 *Murder Elite*

## MACLAINE, Shirley
Real name: Shirley McLean Beaty
(1934– ) USA

1955 *The Trouble With Harry; Artists And Models*
1956 *Around The World In 80 Days\**
1958 *Hot Spell; The Sheepman; The Matchmaker; Some Came Running*
1959 *Ask Any Girl; Career*

1960 *Can-Can; Oceans Eleven\*; The Apartment\**
1961 *All In A Night's Work; Two Loves* (UK: *The Spinster*)
1962 *The Children's Hour* (UK: *The Loudest Whisper*); *My Geisha; Two For The Seesaw*
1963 *Irma La Douce\**
1964 *What A Way To Go!; John Goldfarb, Please Come Home; The Yellow Rolls-Royce*
1966 *Gambit*
1967 *Woman Times Seven*
1968 *The Bliss Of Mrs Blossom; Sweet Charity\**
1969 *Two Mules For Sister Sara*
1971 *Desperate Characters*
1972 *The Possession Of Joel Delaney*
1974 *The Other Half Of The Sky: A China Memoir* (also director)
1977 *The Turning Point\*; Sois Belle Et Tais-Toi*
1979 *Being There*
1980 *Loving Couples; A Change Of Seasons*
1983 *Terms Of Endearment\*; Cannonball Run II*
1987 *Out On A Limb* (TV)
1988 *Madame Sousatzka*
1989 *Steel Magnolias\*; Waiting For The Light*
1990 *Postcards From The Edge\**
1991 *Defending Your Life*
1992 *Used People*
1993 *Wrestling Ernest Hemingway*

## MACMURRAY, Fred
(1907–91) USA

1929 *Girls Gone Wild; Tiger Rose; Glad Rag Doll*
1934 *Friends Of Mr Sweeney*
1935 *Grand Old Girl; Car 99; Alice Adams; Men Without Names; Hands Across The Table; The Bride Comes Home; The Gilded Lily*
1936 *The Trail Of The Lonesome Pine; The Princess Comes Across; The Texas Rangers; Thirteen Hours By Air*

**MACMURRAY, Fred** (cont.)
1937 *Swing High, Swing Low; Maid Of Salem; True Confession; Exclusive; Champagne Waltz*
1938 *Cocoanut Grove; Men With Wings; Sing, You Sinners*
1939 *Cafe Society; Honeymoon In Bali* (UK: *Husbands Or Lovers*); *Invitation To Happiness; Remember The Night*
1940 *Little Old New York; Rangers Of Fortune; Too Many Husbands* (UK: *My Two Husbands*)
1941 *Virginia; New York Town; Dive Bomber; One Night In Lisbon*
1942 *Star Spangled Rythmn; The Lady Is Waiting; The Forest Rangers; Take A Letter Darling* (UK: *The Green-Eyed Woman*)
1943 *The Last Will And Testament Of Tom Smith; Showbusiness At War* (both shorts); *Above Suspicion; Flight For Freedom*
1944 *Skirmish On The Home Front* (short); *Standing Room Only; Double Indemnity*; *And The Angels Sing*
1945 *Murder, He Says; Where Do We Go From Here?; Practically Yours; Captain Eddie*
1946 *Smoky*
1947 *Singapore; Suddenly It's Spring; The Egg And I*
1948 *On Our Merry Way; The Miracle Of The Bells; Family Honeymoon; Don't Trust Your Husband*
1949 *Father Was A Fullback; Borderline*
1950 *Never A Dull Moment*
1951 *Callaway Went Thataway* (UK: *The Star Said No!*); *A Millionaire For Christy*
1953 *Fair Wind To Java; The Moonlighter*
1954 *The Caine Mutiny*; *Woman's World; Pushover; The Far Horizons*
1955 *There's Always Tomorrow; The Rains Of Ranchipur; At Gunpoint* (UK: *Gunpoint!*)
1956 *Gun For A Coward*
1957 *Quantez; Day Of The Bad Man*

1958 *Good Day For A Hanging*
1959 *The Shaggy Dog; Face Of A Fugitive; The Oregon Trail*
1960 *The Apartment*
1961 *The Absent-Minded Professor*
1962 *Bon Voyage!; How To Get There When You Want To Go* (short)
1963 *Son Of Flubber*
1964 *Kisses For My President*
1966 *Follow Me, Boys!*
1967 *The Happiest Millionaire*
1973 *Charley And The Angel*
1974 *The Chadwick Family* (TV)
1975 *Beyond The Bermuda Triangle* (TV)
1978 *The Swarm*

## MADONNA
full name: Madonna Ciccone
(1958– ) USA

1978 *A Certain Sacrifice*
1984 *Vision Quest* (aka *Crazy For You*)
1985 *Desperately Seeking Susan*
1986 *Shanghai Surprise*
1987 *Who's That Girl?*
1989 *Bloodhounds Of Broadway*
1990 *Dick Tracy*
1991 *Truth Or Dare* (UK: *In Bed With Madonna*)
1992 *Shadows And Fog; A League Of Their Own; Body Of Evidence*
1993 *Snake Eyes*

## MAGNANI, Anna
(1907–73) Italy

1928 *Scampolo*
1934 *La Cieca Di Sorrento*
1936 *Tempo Massimo; Cavalleria; Trenta Secondi D'Amore*
1937 *La Principessa Tarakanova*
1939 *Una Lampada Alla Finestra*
1940 *Finalmenti Soli*
1941 *La Fuggitiva; Teresa Venerdi*
1942 *La Fortuna Viena Dal Cielo*
1943 *L'Ultima Carrozzella; Campo De Fiori; T'Amero Sempre; La Vita E Bella; Abbasso La Miseria*
1944 *Il Fiore Sotto Gli Occhi*

1945 *Roma—Citta Aperta\** (UK: *Rome—Open City*); *Quartetto Pazzo*
1946 *Un Uomo Ritorna; Il Bandito; Abbasso La Ricchezza!; Damanti A Lui Tremava Tutta Roma* (aka *Tosca*)
1947 *La Sconosciuto Di San Marino; L'Onorevole Angelina*
1948 *Assunto Spina; Molti Sogni Per Le Strade* (UK: *Woman Trouble*); *Amore* (UK: *Ways Of Love*)
1949 *Volcano*
1951 *Bellissima*
1952 *Camicie Rosse* (aka *Anita Garibaldi*); *La Carrozza D'Oro* (UK: *The Golden Coach*)
1953 *Siamo Donne* (UK: *We The Women*)
1955 *The Rose Tattoo\**
1956 *Suor Letizia*
1957 *Wild Is The Wind*
1958 *Nella Città L'Inferno* (UK: *Caged*)
1959 *The Fugitive Kind*
1960 *Risate Di Gioia* (UK: *The Passionate Thief*)
1962 *Mamma Roma*
1963 *La Magot De Joséfa*
1964 *Volles Herz Und Leere Taschen*
1965 *Made In Italy*
1969 *The Secret Of Santa Vittoria*
1972 *1870* (TV); *Fellini's Roma*

**MALDEN, Karl**
real name: Karl Mladen Sekulovich
(1913– ) USA

1940 *They Knew What They Wanted*
1944 *Winged Victory*
1946 *13 Rue Madeleine*
1947 *Boomerang!; Kiss Of Death*
1950 *Where The Sidewalk Ends; The Gunfighter; Halls Of Montezuma*
1951 *The Sellout; A Streetcar Named Desire\**
1952 *Diplomatic Courier; Ruby Gentry; Operation Secret*
1953 *Take The High Ground; I Confess*
1954 *Phantom Of The Rue Morgue; On The Waterfront\**
1956 *Baby Doll*

1957 *Fear Strikes Out; Bombers B-52)* (UK: *No Sleep Till Dawn*)
1958 *The Hanging Tree*
1960 *Pollyanna*
1961 *One-Eyed Jacks\*; The Great Imposter; Parrish; All Fall Down*
1962 *Birdman Of Alcatraz\*; Gypsy\*; How The West Was Won\*; Come Fly With Me*
1964 *Cheyenne Autumn; Dead Ringer* (UK: *Dead Image*)
1965 *The Cincinnati Kid\*; The Adventures Of Bullwhip Griffin*
1966 *Nevada Smith; Murderers' Row*
1967 *Hotel; Billion Dollar Brain*
1968 *Blue; Hot Millions*
1970 *Patton\*; Cat O' Nine Tails*
1971 *Wild Rovers; The Summertime Killer*
1972 *The Streets Of San Francisco* (TV)
1977 *Captains Courageous* (TV)
1979 *Beyond The Poseidon Adventure; Meteor*
1980 *Skag* (TV)
1981 *Word Of Honor* (TV); *Miracle On Ice* (TV)
1982 *Twilight Time*
1983 *Sting II*
1984 *Intent To Kill* (TV)
1986 *Billy Galvin*
1987 *Nuts\**
1988 *My Father, My Son* (TV)
1989 *The Hijacking Of The Achille Lauro* (TV)
1990 *Call Me Anna* (TV)
1991 *Absolute Strangers* (TV)

**MALKOVICH, John**
(1954– ) USA

1981 *Word Of Honor* (TV); *American Dream* (TV)
1984 *The Killing Fields\*; Places In The Heart\**
1985 *Eleni; Death Of A Salesman* (TV)
1987 *The Glass Menagerie; Making Mr Right; Empire Of The Sun*
1988 *Dangerous Liaisons\*; Miles From Home; The Accidental Tourist\** (executive producer only)

**MALKOVICH, John** (cont.)
1990 *The Sheltering Sky; Queen's Logic*
1991 *The Object Of Beauty*
1992 *Shadows And Fog; Of Mice And Men; Alive; Jennifer Eight*
1993 *In The Line Of Fire*

## MALONE, Dorothy
real name: Dorothy Maloney
(1925– ) USA

1943 *The Falcon And The Co-Eds; Gildersleeve On Broadway; Higher And Higher*
1944 *Step Lively; Youth Runs Wild; Show Business; One Mysterious Night* (UK: *Behind Closed Doors*); *Hollywood Canteen; Seven Days Ashore*
1945 *Frontier Days; Too Young To Know*
1946 *Janie Gets Married; Night And Day*\*; *The Big Sleep*\*
1948 *Two Guys From Texas* (UK: *Two Texas Nights*); *To The Victor; One Sunday Afternoon*
1949 *Flaxy Martin; South Of St Louis; Colorado Territory*
1950 *The Nevadan* (UK: *The Man From Nevada*); *Mrs O'Malley And Mr Malone; Convicted; The Killer That Stalked New York* (UK: *Frightened City*)
1951 *Saddle Legion; The Bushwhackers* (UK: *The Rebel*)
1952 *Torpedo Alley*
1953 *Scared Stiff; Law And Order; Jack Slade* (UK: *Slade*)
1954 *Pushover; Loophole; Security Risk; The Lone Gun; Private Hell 36; The Fast And The Furious; Five Guns West; Tall Man Riding; Battle Cry*
1955 *Sincerely Yours; Artists And Models; At Gunpoint* (UK: *Gunpoint!*)
1956 *Pillars Of The Sky* (UK: *The Tomahawk And The Cross*); *Tension At Table Rock; Written In The Wind*

1957 *Quantez; Man Of A Thousand Faces; The Tarnished Angels; Tip On A Dead Jockey* (UK: *Time For Action*)
1958 *Too Much, Too Soon*
1959 *Warlock*
1960 *The Last Voyage*
1961 *The Last Sunset*
1963 *Beach Party*
1964 *Fate Is The Hunter*
1969 *The Pigeon* (TV); *Femmine Insaziabili* (UK: *The Insatiables*)
1970 *Exzess*
1975 *The Man Who Would Not Die; Abduction*
1976 *The November Plan* (TV)
1977 *Golden Rendezvous; Winter Kills; Little Ladies Of The Night* (TV)
1978 *Murder In Peyton Place* (TV); *Katie: Portrait Of A Centrefold* (TV)
1979 *Good Luck Miss Wycoff; The Day Time Ended*
1980 *Easter Sunday; Off Your Rocker*
1983 *The Being*
1984 *He's Not Your Son!* (TV)
1985 *Peyton Place: The Next Generation* (TV)
1986 *Rest In Pieces*
1992 *Basic Instinct*\*

## MARCH, Fredric
real name: Ernest Fredrick Bikel
(1897–1975) USA

1920 *The Devil*
1921 *The Glorious Adventure; Paying The Piper*
1929 *Footlights And Fools; The Dummy; The Studio Murder Mystery; Jealousy; The Wild Party; Paris Bound; The Marriage Playground*
1930 *Paramount On Parade; Sarah And Son; Manslaughter; The Royal Family Of Broadway; Ladies Love Brutes; True To The Navy; Laughter*
1931 *My Sin; Honor Among Lovers; The Night Angel; Dr Jekyll And Mr Hyde*\*

1932 *Hollywood On Parade* (short);
*Strangers In Love; Merrily We Go
To Hell* (UK: *Merrily We Go To*—);
*Make Me A Star; Smilin' Through;
The Sign Of The Cross*
1933 *The Eagle And The Hawk;
Tonight Is Ours; Design For Living*
1934 *Good Dame* (UK: *Good Girl*); *All
Of Me; The Barretts Of Wimpole
Street\*; We Live Again; Death
Takes A Holiday; The Affairs Of
Cellini*
1935 *Les Misérables\*; Anna Karenina\*;
The Dark Angel*
1936 *Mary Of Scotland; The Road To
Glory; Anthony Adverse*
1937 *Nothing Sacred; A Star Is Born\**
1938 *The Buccaneer; Trade Winds;
There Goes My Heart*
1939 *The 400 Million* (narrator only)
1940 *Victory; Susan And God* (UK: *The
Gay Mrs Trexel*); *Lights Out In
Europe* (short)
1941 *So Ends Our Night; One Foot In
Heaven; Bedtime Story;
Cavalcade Of The Academy
Awards* (short)
1942 *I Married A Witch; Lake Carrier*
(short)
1944 *Tomorrow The World; The
Adventures Of Mark Twain; Salute
To France* (short)
1946 *The Best Years Of Our Lives\**
1948 *An Act Of Murder; Another Part Of
The Forest*
1949 *Christopher Columbus*
1950 *The Titan—The Story Of
Michelangelo* (also narrator)
1951 *It's A Big Country*
1952 *Death Of A Salesman*
1953 *Man On A Tightrope*
1954 *Executive Suite; The Bridges At
Toko-Ri*
1955 *The Desperate Hours*
1956 *Alexander The Great; The Man In
The Grey Flannel Suit*
1957 *Albert Schweitzer* (narrator only)
1959 *The Middle Of The Night*
1960 *Inherit The Wind*
1962 *The Condemned Of Altona*
1963 *Seven Days In May\**

1967 *Hombre*
1970 *...tick...tick...tick*
1973 *The Iceman Cometh*

## MARTIN, Dean
real name: Dino Crocetti
(1917–  ) USA

1949 *My Friend Irma*
1950 *My Friend Irma Goes West; At
War With The Army*
1951 *That's My Boy; Sailor Beware;
Screen Snapshots No 197* (short)
1952 *Screen Snapshots No 207;
Hollywood Fun Festival* (both
shorts); *The Stooge; Jumping
Jacks; Road To Bali*
1953 *Scared Stiff; The Caddy*
1954 *Money From Home; Living It Up;
Three Ring Circus*
1955 *You're Never Too Young; Artists
And Models*
1956 *Pardners; Hollywood Or Bust;
Hollywood Premiere* (short)
1957 *Ten Thousand Bedrooms*
1958 *The Young Lions; Some Came
Running*
1959 *Career; Rio Bravo\*; Who Was
That Lady?*
1960 *Bells Are Ringing; Pepe; Oceans
Eleven\**
1961 *All In A Night's Work; Ada; The
Road To Hong Kong*
1962 *Sergeants Three; Who's Got The
Action?; Canzoni Nel Mondo*
1963 *Toys In The Attic; Come Blow
Your Horn; Who's Been Sleeping
In My Bed?; Four For Texas*
1964 *What A Way To Go!; Robin And
The Seven Hoods; Kiss Me Stupid*
1965 *The Sons Of Katie Elder;
Marriage On The Rocks*
1966 *The Silencers; Texas Across The
River; Murderers' Row*
1967 *Rough Night In Jericho; The
Ambushers*
1968 *Bandolero!; Five Card Stud; How
To Save A Marriage—And Ruin
Your Life*
1969 *The Wrecking Crew; Airport\**
1971 *Something Big*

**MARTIN, Dean** (cont.)
1972  *Showdown*
1975  *Mr Ricco*
1978  *Angels In Vegas* (TV)
1981  *The Cannonball Run**
1983  *The Cannonball Run II*
1985  *Half-Nelson* (TV)


**MARTIN, Steve**
(1945–   ) USA

1977  *The Absent-Minded Waiter* (short)
1978  *Sgt Pepper's Lonely Hearts Club Band; The Kids Are Alright*
1979  *The Muppet Movie*; The Jerk**
1981  *Pennies From Heaven*
1982  *Dead Men Don't Wear Plaid*
1983  *The Man With Two Brains*
1984  *The Lonely Guy; All Of Me**
1985  *Movers And Shakers*
1986  *The Three Amigos; Little Shop Of Horrors*
1987  *Roxanne*; Planes, Trains And Automobiles*
1988  *Dirty Rotten Scoundrels*
1989  *Parenthood**
1990  *My Blue Heaven*
1991  *LA Story; Grand Canyon; Father Of The Bride*
1992  *Housesitter; Leap Of Faith*
1993  *And The Band Played On* (TV)


**MARVIN, Lee**
(1924–87) USA

1951  *Teresa; You're In The Navy Now; Hong Kong*
1952  *We're Not Married; Diplomatic Courier; Duel At Silver Creek; Eight Iron Men; Hangman's Knot*
1953  *Gun Fury; The Stranger Wore A Gun; The Wild One*; The Big Heat*; The Glory Brigade; Seminole; Down Among The Sheltering Palms*
1954  *The Caine Mutiny*; The Raid; Gorilla At Large; Bad Day At Black Rock**

1955  *Not As A Stranger*; A Life In The Balance; Violent Saturday; Pete Kelly's Blues; Shack Out On 101; I Died A Thousand Times; Attack!*
1956  *Pillars Of The Sky* (UK: *The Tomahawk And The Cross*); *Seven Men From Now; The Rack*
1957  *Raintree County*
1958  *The Missouri Traveller*
1961  *The Commancheros*
1962  *The Man Who Shot Liberty Valance**
1963  *Donovan's Reef*
1964  *The Killers*
1965  *Cat Ballou*; Ship Of Fools**
1966  *The Professionals**
1967  *Tonite Let's All Make Love In London* (documentary); *Our Time In Hell* (narrator only); *The Dirty Dozen**
1968  *Hell In The Pacific; Sergeant Ryker*
1969  *Paint Your Wagon**
1970  *Monte Walsh*
1972  *Pocket Money; Prime Cut*
1973  *The Iceman Cometh; The Emperor Of The North Pole*
1974  *The Spikes Gang; The Klansman*
1976  *Shout At The Devil; The Great Scout And Cathouse Thursday*
1979  *Samuel Fuller And The Big Red One* (documentary); *Avalanche Express*
1980  *Death Hunt; The Big Red One*
1983  *Gorky Park*
1984  *Dog Day*
1985  *The Dirty Dozen: Next Mission* (TV)
1986  *The Delta Force*


**The MARX BROTHERS**
Chico (Leonard) (1886–1961)
Harpo (Adolph) (1888–1964)
Groucho (Julius Henry) (1890–1977)
Zeppo (Herbert) (1901–79)

1926  *Humorisk*
1929  *The Cocoanuts*
1930  *Animal Crackers**
1931  *Monkey Business*
1932  *Horse Feathers*

1933 Duck Soup*; Screen Snapshots No 36 (short)
1935 A Night At The Opera*
1937 A Day At The Races
1938 Room Service
1939 At The Circus
1940 Go West
1941 The Big Store
1943 Screen Snapshots No 110 (short)
1946 A Night In Casablanca
1949 Love Happy
1957 The Story Of Mankind
1958 Showdown At Ulcer Gulch
1959 The Incredible Jewel Robbery (TV)

## MASON, James
(1909–84) UK

1935 Late Extra
1936 Troubled Waters; Twice Branded; Blind Man's Bluff; Prison Breaker; The Secret Of Stamboul; Fire Over England; The Mill On The Floss
1937 The High Command; Catch As Catch Can; The Return Of The Scarlet Pimpernel
1939 I Met A Murderer
1941 The Patient Vanishes; Hatter's Castle
1942 The Night Has Eyes; Alibi; Secret Mission; Thunder Rock
1943 The Bells Go Down; The Man In Grey; They Met In The Dark; Candlelight In Algeria
1944 Fanny By Gaslight; Hotel Reserve
1945 A Place Of One's Own; They Were Sisters; The Seventh Veil; The Wicked Lady
1946 Odd Man Out*
1947 The Upturned Glass
1949 Caught; Madame Bovary; The Reckless Moment; East Side, West Side
1950 One Way Street
1951 Pandora And The Flying Dutchman; The Desert Fox (UK: Rommel, Desert Fox)

1952 Lady Possessed; Five Fingers; The Prisoner Of Zenda; Face To Face
1953 The Man Between; Charade; The Story Of Three Loves; Julius Caesar*; The Desert Rats; Botany Bay
1954 Prince Valiant; A Star Is Born*; 20,000 Leagues Under The Sea
1956 Forever Darling; Bigger Than Life
1957 Island In The Sun; The Thundering Wave (TV)
1958 Not The Glory (TV); Cry Terror!; The Decks Ran Red
1959 North By Northwest*; Journey To The Center Of The Earth; The Second Man (TV); A Touch Of Larceny; Big Ben
1960 The Trials Of Oscar Wilde; John Brown's Raid (TV)
1961 The Marriage Go-Round
1962 Escape From Zahrain; Lolita*; Hero's Island; Tiara Tahiti; Torpedo Bay
1963 The Fall Of The Roman Empire
1964 The Pumpkin Eater
1965 Lord Jim; Genghis Khan; Les Pianos Mécaniques
1966 The Blue Max; Georgy Girl*; The Deadly Affair
1967 The London Nobody Knows; Stranger In The House
1968 Duffy; The Legend Of Silent Night (TV); Mayerling
1969 Age Of Consent; The Seagull; Spring And Port Wine
1970 The Yin And The Yang Of Dr Go
1971 L'Uomo Dalle Due Ombre (UK: Cold Sweat); Bad Man's River
1972 Kill; Child's Play; The Wind In The Wires (narrator only)
1973 The Last Of Sheila; The Mackintosh Man; Frankenstein: The True Story (TV)
1974 11 Harrowhouse; The Marseille Contract; Trikimia; Nostro Nero In Casa Nichols
1975 Mandingo; Inside Out; Autobiography Of A Princess; Great Expectations (TV); Gente Di Respetto; The Schoolmistress

**MASON, James** (cont.)
And The Devil; La Polizi
Interviene — Ordine Di Uccidere
(UK: *The Left Hand Of The Law*);
*The Deal*
1976 *People Of The Wind; Homage To*
*Chaghall* (both narrator only);
*Voyage Of The Damned; Kidnap*
*Syndicate*
1977 *Cross Of Iron; Paura In Citta*
1978 *Heaven Can Wait\*; Murder By*
*Decree; The Boys From Brazil;*
*The Water Babies; The Passage*
1979 *Bloodline; North Sea Hijack;*
*Salem's Lot* (TV)
1981 *Evil Under The Sun*
1982 *Ivanhoe* (TV); *The Verdict\*; A*
*Dangerous Summer*
1983 *Yellowbeard; Alexandre*
1984 *The Assissi Underground; The*
*Shooting Party; Dr Fischer Of*
*Geneva* (TV)

## MASSEY, Raymond
(1896–1983) Canada

1929 *The Crooked Billet*
(aka *International Spy*); *High*
*Treason*
1931 *The Speckled Band*
1932 *The Face At The Window; The*
*Old Dark House*
1934 *The Scarlet Pimpernel*
1936 *Things To Come; Fire Over*
*England*
1937 *Dreaming Lips; Under The Red*
*Robe; The Prisoner Of Zenda\*;*
*The Hurricane\**
1938 *Black Limelight; The Drum*
1940 *Abe Lincoln In Illinois* (UK: *Spirit*
*Of The People*); *Santa Fe Trail*
1941 *49th Parallel\*; Dangerously They*
*Live*
1942 *Desperate Journey; Reap The*
*Wild Wind\**
1943 *Action In The North Atlantic*
1944 *Arsenic And Old Lace\*; The*
*Woman In The Window*
1945 *Hotel Berlin; God Is My Co-Pilot*
1946 *A Matter Of Life And Death\**

1947 *Possessed; Mourning Becomes*
*Electra*
1949 *The Fountainhead; Roseanna*
*McCoy; Chain Lightning*
1950 *Barricade; Dallas*
1951 *Sugarfoot; Come Fill The Cup*
1952 *David And Bathsheba; Carson*
*City*
1953 *The Desert Song*
1954 *East Of Eden\**
1955 *Prince Of Players; Battle Cry;*
*Seven Angry Men*
1957 *Omar Khayyam*
1958 *The Naked And The Dead*
1960 *The Great Imposter*
1961 *The Fiercest Heart; The Queen's*
*Guards*
1962 *How The West Was Won\**
1963 *Report On China* (narrator only)
1968 *McKenna's Gold*
1971 *The President's Plane Is Missing*
(TV)
1972 *All My Darling Daughters* (TV)
1973 *My Darling Daughters'*
*Anniversary* (TV)

## MASTROIANNI, Marcello
(1934– ) Italy

1938 *Marionette*
1940 *La Colonna Di Ferro*
1942 *Una Storie D'Amore; I Bambini Ci*
*Guardaro*
1947 *I Miserabili*
1949 *Vent'Anni; Domenica D'Agosto*
(UK: *Sunday In August*)
1950 *Cuori Sul Mare; Vita Da Cane*
1951 *Atto Di Accusa; A Tale Of Five*
*Cities; Contro La Legge; Parigi*
*E'Sempre Parigi; Sensualita; La*
*Ragazze Di Piazza Di Spagna*
(UK: *Girls Of The Spanish Steps*)
1952 *L'Eterna Catena; Tragico Ritorno;*
*Lulu; Gli Eroi Della Domenica;*
*Penne Nere*
1953 *Il Viale Della Speranza; La Valigia*
*Dei Sogni; Non E'Mai Troppo*
*Tradi; Siamo Donne* (UK: *We Are*
*The Women*); *Cronache Di Poveri*
*Amanti; Tempi Nostri* (UK:
*Anatomy Of Love*)

1954 *Casa Ricordi; Peccato Che Sia Una Canaglia* (UK: *Too Bad She's Bad*); *Tam-Tam Mayumba; Giorni D'Amore; La Schiava Del Peccato; Febbre Di Vivere*

1955 *La Fortuna Di Essere Donna* (UK: *Lucky To Be A Woman*); *La Bella Mugnaia* (UK: *The Miller's Wife*); *La Principessa Della Canarie*

1956 *Mädchen Und Männer; Il Bigamo* (UK: *The Bigamist*)

1957 *Un Ettaro Di Cielo; Padre E Figli; La Ragazza Della Salina; Il Momento Più Bello; Le Notti Bianche* (UK: *White Nights*); *Il Medico E Lo Stregone*

1958 *La Loi* (UK: *Where The Hot Wind Blows*); *Racconti D'Estate* (UK: *Girls For The Summer*); *I Soliti Ignoti*

1959 *Tutti Innamorati; Il Nemico Di Mia Moglie; Ferdinand Of Naples*

1960 *La Dolce Vita\*; La Notte; Fantasmi A Roma* (UK: *Phantom Lovers*); *Il Bell'Antonio; Adua E La Compagne*

1961 *L'Assassino; Vie Privée* (UK: *A Very Private Affair*); *Divorzio All'Italiana* (UK: *Divorce — Italian Style*)

1962 *Cronaca Familiare* (UK: *Family Diary*)

1963 *Otto E Mezzo\** (UK: *8½*); *I Compagni; Il Giorno Più Corto; Ieri, Oggi E Domani* (UK: *Yesterday, Today And Tomorrow*)

1964 *Matrimonio All'Italiana* (UK: *Marriage — Italian Style*)

1965 *Io, Io, Io...E Gli Altri; Paranoia; La Decima Vittima* (UK: *The Tenth Victim*); *Casanova 70; The Organizer*

1966 *The Poppy Is Also A Flower* (UK: *Danger Grows Wild*); *Spara Forte, Più Forte...Non Capisco* (UK: *Shoot Loud, Louder, I Don't Understand*)

1967 *Lo Straniero* (UK: *The Stranger*)

1968 *Diamonds For Breakfast; Gli Amanti* (UK: *A Place For Lovers*); *Questi Fantasmi* (UK: *Ghosts — Italian Style*)

1969 *Il Girasoli* (UK: *Sunflower*)

1970 *Giochi Particolari* (UK: *The Voyeur*); *Dramma Della Gelosia; Leo The Last; Scipione, Detto Anche 'L'Africano'; La Moglia Del Prete* (UK: *The Priest's Wife*)

1971 *Permette?; Rocco Papaleo*

1972 *Liza; Mordi E Fuggi; What?; Ça N'Arrive Qu'Aux Autres; 1870; Melampo; Fellini's Roma*

1973 *La Grande Bouffe* (UK: *Blow-Out*); *Rappresaglia* (UK: *Massacre In Rome*); *Salut L'Artiste* (UK: *The Bit Player*); *L'Evènement Le Plus Important Depuis Que L'Homme A Marché Sur La Lune* (UK: *The Slightly Pregnant Man*)

1974 *Touchez Pas La Femme Blanche; C'Eravamo Tanto Amati* (UK: *We All Loved Each Other So Much*); *Allosanfan*

1975 *Cilastrisce, Nobile Veneziano; Par Le Antiche* (UK: *Down The Ancient Stairs*); *La Divine Creatura; La Donna Nelle Domenica* (UK: *The Sunday Woman*)

1976 *La Fantasie Amorose Di Luca Maria Nobile Veneto; Signore E Signori, Buonanotte*

1977 *Una Giornata Particolare* (UK: *A Special Day*); *Mogliamanate* (UK: *Wifemistress*); *Ciao Male* (UK: *Bye By Monkey*); *Doppo Delitto* (UK: *Double Murders*)

1978 *L'Ingorgo; Vengeance*

1979 *Shimmy Lugano E Tarantelle E Tarallucci E Vino; Blood Feud; La Città Delle Donne* (UK: *City Of Women*); *Cosi Come Sei; L'Embouteillage; Giallo Napoletano*

1980 *Atti Atrocissimi Di Amore E Di Vendetta; Todo Mondo; La Terrazza*

1981 *La Pelle* (UK: *Skin*); *Fantôme D'Amour*

1982 *Revolution; Oltre La Porta* (UK: *Beyond The Door*); *La Nuit De Varennes*

1983 *Il Generale Dell'Amata Morta; Gabriela; Enrico IV*

**MASTROIANNI, Marcello** (cont.)

1984 *Il Fu Mattia Pascal*
1985 *Ginger And Fred; Macaroni; I Soliti Ignoti 20 Anni Doppo*
1986 *The Good Ship Ulysses; O Melissokomos* (UK: *The Beekeeper*)
1987 *Oci Ciornie* (UK: *Dark Eyes*); *I Picari; Intervista* (UK: *The Interview*); *Miss Arizona*
1988 *Beyond Obsesssion; Splendor*
1989 *Che Ore E?* (UK: *What Time Is It?*)
1990 *Stanno Tutti Bene* (UK: *Everybody's Fine*); *Tchin Tchin*
1991 *Le Pas Suspendu De La Cigogne* (UK: *The Suspended Step Of The Stork*); *Verso Sera* (UK: *Towards Evening*)
1992 *Used People*
1993 *Un Deux Trois Soleil*

## MATTHAU, Walter
real name: Walter Matuschanskayasky
(1920–   ) USA

1955 *The Kentuckian; The Indian Fighter*
1956 *Bigger Than Life*
1957 *Slaughter On 10th Avenue; Voice In The Mirror; A Face In The Crowd*
1958 *Onionhead; King Creole; Ride A Crooked Trail*
1960 *The Gangster Story* (also director); *Strangers When We Meet*
1962 *Lonely Are The Brave; Who's Got The Action?*
1963 *Island Of Love; Charade**
1964 *Ensign Pulver; Goodbye Charlie; Failsafe*
1965 *Mirage*
1966 *The Fortune Cookie* (UK: *Meet Whiplash Willie*)
1967 *A Guide For The Married Man; The Odd Couple**
1968 *The Secret Life Of An American Wife; Candy*
1969 *Hello! Dolly*; Cactus Flower**
1970 *A New Leaf*

1971 *Plaza Suite; Kotch*
1972 *Pete'n' Tillie*
1973 *Charley Varrick; The Laughing Policeman* (UK: *Investigation Of A Murder*)
1974 *Earthquake*; The Taking Of Pelham 123; The Front Page*
1975 *The Sunshine Boys; The Gentleman Tramp* (narrator only)
1976 *The Bad News Bears**
1977 *Casey's Shadow*
1978 *House Calls; California Suite**
1979 *Funny Business* (narrator only); *Little Miss Marker*
1980 *Hopscotch; Portrait Of A 60% Perfect Man* (documentary)
1981 *A Change Of Heart* (short); *Buddy Buddy; First Monday In October*
1982 *I Ought To Be In Pictures*
1983 *The Survivors*
1985 *Movers And Shakers*
1986 *Pirates*
1988 *The Couch Trip*
1989 *Il Piccolo Diavolo* (UK: *The Little Devil*)
1990 *The Incident* (TV)
1991 *Mrs Lambert Remembers Love* (TV); *JFK**
1992 *Against Her Will: An Incident In Baltimore* (TV)
1993 *Dennis; Grumpy Old Men*

## MATURE, Victor
(1915–   ) USA

1939 *The Housekeeper's Daughter*
1940 *One Million BC* (UK: *Man And His Mate*); *Captain Caution; No, No Nanette*
1941 *The Shanghai Gesture; I Wake Up Screaming* (UK: *Hot Spot*)
1942 *Song Of The Islands; My Gal Sal; Footlight Serenade; Seven Days' Leave*
1946 *My Darling Clementine**
1947 *Kiss Of Death; Moss Rose*
1948 *Fury At Furnace Creek; Cry Of The City*
1949 *Samson And Delilah*; Easy Living; Red Hot And Blue*

1950 *Wabash Avenue; I'll Get By; Gambling House; Stella*
1952 *The Las Vegas Story; Androcles And The Lion; Something For The Birds; Million Dollar Mermaid* (UK: *The One Piece Bathing Suit*)
1953 *The Glory Brigade; Affair With A Stranger; The Robe*; Veils Of Bagdad*
1954 *Demetrius And The Gladiators; Betrayed; Dangerous Mission; The Egyptian*
1955 *Violent Saturday; The Last Frontier; Chief Crazy Horse* (UK: *Valley Of Fury*)
1956 *Zarak; Safari; The Sharkfighters*
1957 *The Long Haul; Interpol*
1958 *No Time To Die!; China Doll*
1959 *The Bandit Of Zhobe; Escort West; Timbuktu; The Big Circus*
1960 *Hannibal; The Tartars*
1966 *After The Fox*
1968 *Head*
1972 *Every Little Crook And Nanny*
1975 *Won Ton Ton — The Dog Who Saved Hollywood*
1979 *Firepower*
1984 *Samson And Delilah* (TV)

## MAURA, Carmen
(1946– ) Spain

1970 *El Hombre Oculto*
1972 *El Love Feroz*
1976 *La Peticion*
1977 *Tigres De Papel*
1978 *Los Ojos Vendados; Que Hace Una Chica Como Tu En Un Sitio Como Este?*
1980 *Aquella Casa En Las Afueras; La Mano Negra; Pepi, Luci, Bom Y Otras Chicas Del Montón* (UK: *Pepi, Luci, Bom And The Other Girls*)
1981 *Gary Cooper Que Estas En Los Cielos* (UK: *Gary Cooper Who Art In Heaven*)
1983 *El Cid Cabreador; Entre Tinieblas* (UK: *Dark Habits*)
1984 *Qué He Hecho Yo Para Merecer Esto?* (UK: *What Have I Done To Deserve This?*)

1985 *Extramuros; Se Infiel Y No Mires Con Quien*
1986 *Matador; Tata Mia*
1987 *La Ley Del Deseo* (UK: *Law Of Desire*)
1988 *Mujeres Al Borde De Un Ataque De Nervios** (UK: *Women On The Verge Of A Nervous Breakdown*); *Baton Rouge*
1989 *Mieux Vaut Courir*
1990 *Ay Carmela!*
1991 *Como Ser Mujer Y No Morir En El Intento* (UK: *How To Be A Woman And Not Die In The Attempt*)
1992 *Sur La Terre Comme Au Ciel* (UK: *On Earth As In Heaven*)

## MCCREA, Joel
(1905–90) USA

1927 *The Fair Co-Ed* (UK: *The Varsity Girl*)
1928 *Freedom Of The Press; The Jazz Age; The Enemy*
1929 *So This Is College; The Five O'Clock Girl; The Single Standard; Dynamite*
1930 *The Silver Horde; Lightnin'; Once A Sinner*
1931 *Born To Love; Kept Husbands; Girls About Town*
1932 *Business And Pleasure; Bird Of Paradise; Rockabye; The Lost Squadron; The Sport Parade; The Most Dangerous Game* (UK: *The Hounds Of Zaroff*)
1933 *The Silver Cord; One Man's Journey; Bed Of Roses; Chance At Heaven; Scarlet River*
1934 *Half A Sinner; Gambling Lady; The Richest Girl In The World*
1935 *Splendor; Barbary Coast; Woman Wanted*
1936 *Come And Get It; Banjo On My Knee; These Three; Two In A Crowd; Adventure In Manhattan* (UK: *Manhattan Madness*)
1937 *Internes Can't Take Money* (UK: *You Can't Take Money*); *Woman Chases Man; Wells Fargo; Dead End**

**MCCREA, Joel** (cont.)
1938 *Three Blind Mice; Youth Takes A Fling*
1939 *They Shall Have Music; He Married His Wife; Espionage Agent; Union Pacific*
1940 *The Primrose Path; Foreign Correspondent\**
1941 *Sullivan's Travels\*; Reaching For The Sun*
1942 *The Palm Beach Story\*; The Great Man's Lady*
1943 *The More The Merrier; Stars On Horseback* (short)
1944 *The Great Moment; Buffalo Bill*
1945 *The Unseen*
1946 *The Virginian*
1947 *Ramrod*
1948 *Four Faces West* (UK: *They Passed This Way*)
1949 *Colorado Territory; South Of St Louis*
1950 *Saddle Tramp; The Outriders; Stars In My Crown; Frenchie*
1951 *The Hollywood Story; Cattle Drive*
1952 *The San Francisco Story*
1953 *Lone Hand; Rough Shoot*
1954 *Border River; Black Horse Canyon*
1955 *Wichita; Stranger On Horseback*
1956 *The First Texan*
1957 *The Oklahoman; Trooper Hook; Gunsight Ridge; The Tall Stranger*
1958 *Fort Massacre; Cattle Empire*
1959 *The Gunfight At Dodge City*
1962 *Ride The High Country* (UK: *Guns In The Afternoon*)
1971 *Cry Blood, Apache*
1974 *The Great American Cowboy* (narrator only)
1976 *Mustang Country*
1990 *Preston Sturges: The Rise And Fall Of An American Dreamer* (documentary)

## MCDOWALL, Roddy

real name: Andrew Roderick McDowall
(1928–  ) USA

1938 *Murder In The Family; Scruffy; Hey! Hey! USA!; I See Ice;*
*Convict 99; Yellow Sands; John Halifax, Gentleman*
1939 *Just William; Dead Men's Shoes; Poison Pen; Murder Will Out; His Brother's Keeper; The Outsider*
1940 *You Will Remember; Saloon Bar*
1941 *This England; Man Hunt; How Green Was My Valley\*; Confirm Or Deny*
1942 *The Pied Piper; Son Of Fury; On The Sunny Side*
1943 *My Friend Flicka; Lassie Come Home*
1944 *The Keys Of The Kingdom; The White Cliffs Of Dover*
1945 *Thunderhead, Son Of Flicka; Molly And Me; Hangover Square* (voice only)
1946 *Holiday In Mexico*
1948 *Macbeth; Rocky; Kidnapped*
1949 *Tuna Clipper; Black Midnight*
1950 *Killer Shark; Big Timber; Everybody's Dancin'*
1951 *Hill Number One*
1952 *The Steel Fist*
1960 *The Subterraneans; Midnight Lace*
1962 *The Longest Day\**
1963 *Cleopatra\**
1964 *Shock Treatment*
1965 *The Adventures Of Bullwhip Griffin; The Greatest Story Ever Told; The Third Day; That Darn Cat!; The Loved One; Inside Daisy Clover*
1966 *Paris, Brûle T'Il?* (UK: *Is Paris Burning?*); *L'Espion* (UK: *The Defector*); *Lord Love A Duck; It*
1967 *The Cool Ones; Planet Of The Apes\**
1968 *The Fatal Mistake* (TV); *Five Card Stud; Hello Down There*
1969 *Night Gallery* (TV); *Midas Run* (UK: *A Run On Gold*); *Angel, Angel, Down We Go*
1971 *Escape From The Planet Of The Apes; Terror In The Sky* (TV); *A Taste Of Evil* (TV); *Corky; Bedknobs And Broomsticks; Pretty Maids All In A Row; Tam Lin* (director only)

1972 *The Poseidon Adventure\*; The Life And Times Of Judge Roy Bean; Conquest Of The Planet Of The Apes; What's A Nice Girl Like You?* (TV)
1973 *Battle For The Planet Of The Apes; Arnold; The Legend Of Hell House*
1974 *Dirty Mary, Crazy Larry; The Elevator* (TV); *Miracle On 34th Street* (TV)
1975 *Funny Lady; Mean Johnny Barrows; Embryo*
1976 *Flood!* (TV)
1977 *Sixth And Main; Laser Blast; Circle Of Iron*
1978 *Rabbit Test; The Cat From Outer Space*
1979 *The Thief Of Bagdad; The Martian Chronicles* (TV); *Hart To Hart* (TV); *Scavenger Hunt; Nutcracker Fantasy* (voice only)
1980 *Charlie Chan And The Curse Of The Dragon Queen; The Memory Of Eva Ryker*
1981 *Kiss Of Gold; The Million Dollar Face* (TV); *Evil Under The Sun*
1982 *Class Of 1984; Mae West* (TV)
1983 *The Zany Adventures Of Robin Hood* (TV); *This Girl For Hire* (TV)
1985 *Deceptions* (TV); *Fright Night*
1986 *GoBots: Battle Of The Rock Lords* (voice only)
1987 *Dead Of Night; Overboard; Shadow Of Death; The Edison Effect*
1988 *Fright Night, Part 2; The Big Picture*
1989 *Cutting Class; Camilla* (TV)
1990 *Dive*
1991 *The Color Of Evening; Prodigy; Under The Gun; Earth Angel* (TV); *An Inconvenient Woman* (TV)

## MCDOWELL, Malcolm
(1943– ) UK

1967 *Poor Cow; If*
1970 *Figures In A Landscape; The Raging Moon*
1971 *A Clockwork Orange\**

1973 *O Lucky Man!*
1975 *Royal Flash*
1976 *Aces High; Voyage Of The Damned*
1977 *Caligula*
1978 *She Fell Among Thieves* (TV); *The Passage*
1979 *Time After Time; Tigers Are Better Looking* (short)
1982 *Cat People; Britannia Hospital; Blue Thunder*
1983 *Flip Out; Arthur The King* (TV); *Get Crazy; Cross Creek*
1985 *Gulag*
1986 *Monte Carlo* (TV)
1987 *The Caller; Buy And Cell*
1988 *Sunset*
1989 *The Hateful Dead; Class Of 1999; Musical May; Moon 44; The Maestro*
1990 *Schweitzer; Snake Eyes; Jezebel's Kiss; Happily Ever After* (voice only)
1991 *Disturbed; The Assassin Of The Tsar*
1992 *Chain Of Desire*
1993 *Bopha*

## MCGUIRE, Dorothy
(1918– ) USA

1943 *Claudia*
1944 *A Tree Grows In Brooklyn*
1945 *The Enchanted Cottage; The Spiral Staircase*
1946 *Claudia And David; Till The End Of Time*
1947 *Gentleman's Agreement\**
1950 *Mother Didn't Tell Me; Mister 880*
1951 *Callaway Went Thataway* (UK: *The Star Said No*); *I Want You*
1952 *Invitation*
1954 *Make Haste To Live; Three Coins In The Fountain\**
1955 *Trial*
1956 *Friendly Persuasion\**
1957 *Old Yeller*
1959 *This Earth Is Mine; The Remarkable Mr Pennypacker; A Summer Place*

**MCGUIRE, Dorothy** (cont.)

1960  The Dark At The Top Of The
      Stairs; Swiss Family Robinson*
1961  Susan Slade
1962  Summer Magic
1965  The Greatest Story Ever Told
1971  Flight Of The Doves; She Waits
      (TV)
1975  The Runaways (TV)
1978  Little Women (TV)
1979  The Incredible Journey Of Dr Meg
      Laurel (TV)
1983  Ghost Dancing (TV)
1985  Amos (TV)
1986  American Geisha (TV)
1987  I Never Sang For My Father (TV)
1990  Caroline? (TV)

**MCQUEEN, Terence Steve**
(1930–80) USA

1956  Somebody Up There Likes Me;
      Beyond A Reasonable Doubt
1958  Never Love A Stranger; The Blob
1959  The Great St Louis Bank
      Robbery; Never So Few
1960  The Magnificent Seven*
1961  The Honeymoon Machine
1962  Hell Is For Heroes!; The War
      Lover
1963  The Great Escape*; Soldier In
      The Rain
1964  Love With The Proper Stranger
1965  Baby, The Rain Must Fall; The
      Cincinnatic Kid*
1966  Nevada Smith; The Sand Pebbles*
1968  The Thomas Crown Affair*; Bullitt*
1969  The Reivers
1971  Le Mans; On Any Sunday
1972  The Getaway; Junior Bonner
1973  Papillon*
1974  The Towering Inferno*
1976  Dixie Dynamite
1977  An Enemy Of The People
1980  Tom Horn; The Hunter

**MEREDITH, Burgess**
full name: Oliver Burgess Meredith
(1908–  ) USA

1936  Winterset

1937  There Goes The Groom
1938  Spring Madness
1939  Idiot's Delight; Of Mice And Men*
1940  San Francisco Docks; Castle On
      The Hudson (UK: Years Without
      Days); Second Chorus
1941  That Uncertain Feeling; Tom, Dick
      And Harry; The Forgotten Village
      (narrator only)
1942  Street Of Chance
1943  Welcome To Britain (short, also
      director)
1944  Salute To France (short, also
      director)
1945  The Story Of GI Joe
1946  Magnificent Doll; The Diary Of A
      Chambermaid
1947  Mine Own Executioner; A Yank
      Comes Back (short)
1948  On Our Merry Way
1949  The Man On The Eiffel Tower
      (also director); Jigsaw; Golden
      Arrow
1954  Screen Snapshots No 224 (short)
1957  Joe Butterfly
1961  Universe (narrator only)
1962  Advise And Consent
1963  The Cardinal
1964  Man On The Run
1965  In Harm's Way
1966  Batman; Hurry Sundown;
      Madame X; Crazy Quilt (narrator
      only); Big Hand For A Little Lady
      (UK: Big Deal At Dodge City)
1967  Torture Garden
1968  McKenna's Gold; Stay Away Joe;
      Skidoo; Hard Contract
1969  The Reivers (narrator only)
1970  There Was A Crooked Man; Lock,
      Stock And Barrel (TV); The Yin
      And The Yang Of Mr Go (also
      director)
1971  Getting Away From It All (TV); Clay
      Pigeon (UK: Trip To Kill); The
      Strange Monster Of Strawberry
      Cove (TV); Such Good Friends
1972  The New Healers (TV); Probe
      (TV); The Man; A Fan's Notes
1973  'B' Must Die
1974  Of Men And Women (TV); The
      Day Of The Locust; Golden

244

Needles; Beware! The Blob (UK:
Son Of The Blob)
1975 *92 In The Shade; The
Hindenburg; The Master
Gunfighter* (narrator only)
1976 *The Sentinel; Burnt Offerings;
Rocky\**
1977 *Tail Gunner Joe* (TV); *SST Death
Flight* (TV); *The Wandering Muse
Of Artemus Flagg; Golden
Rendezvous; Remember Those
Poker-Playing Monkeys?; The
Manitou; Johnny, We Hardly
Knew Ye* (TV)
1978 *The Amazing Captain Nemo; The
Great Georgia Bank Hoax; Foul
Play\*; Magic; Kate Bliss And The
Ticker Tape Kid* (TV); *The Last
Hurrah* (TV)
1979 *Puff The Magic Dragon* (short,
voice only); *Rocky II*
1980 *When Time Ran Out; The Last
Chase; The Final Assignment*
1981 *Clash Of The Titans; True
Confessions*
1982 *Rocky III*
1983 *The Twilight Zone — The Movie*
(narrator only)
1984 *Wet Gold* (TV); *Santa Claus*
1986 *Outrage!* (TV); *Mr Corbett's Ghost*
(TV)
1987 *King Lear; GI Joe* (voice only)
1988 *John Huston* (documentary); *Full
Moon In Blue Water*
1990 *Odd Ball Hall; State Of Grace;
Rocky V*
1991 *Night Of The Hunter* (TV)
1993 *Grumpy Old Men*

## MERMAN, Ethel
real name: Ethel Zimmerman
(1908–84)

1930 *Follow The Leader*
1931 *Devil Sea; Roaming* (both shorts)
1932 *Ireno* (short); *Time On My Hands*
(short, voice only); *The Big
Broadcast*
1933 *Be Like Me* (short)
1934 *We're Not Dressing; Kid Millions;
Shoot The Works*

1935 *The Big Broadcast Of 1936*
1936 *Strike Me Pink; Anything Goes*
1938 *Happy Landing; Alexander's
Ragtime Band\*; Straight, Place
And Show* (UK: *They're Off*)
1943 *Stage Door Canteen*
1953 *Call Me Madam*
1954 *There's No Business Like Show
Business*
1963 *It's A Mad, Mad, Mad, Mad
World\**
1965 *The Art Of Love*
1971 *Journey Back To Oz* (voice only)
1975 *Won Ton Ton — The Dog That
Saved Hollywood*
1979 *Rudolph And Frosty's Christmas
In July* (TV) (voice only)
1980 *Airplane!\**

## MIDLER, Bette
(1945– ) USA

1966 *Hawaii*
1968 *The Detective*
1969 *Goodbye Columbus\**
1974 *The Divine Mr J*
1979 *The Rose\**
1980 *Divine Madness*
1982 *Jinxed!*
1986 *Down And Out In Beverly Hills;
Ruthless People*
1987 *Outrageous Fortune*
1988 *Big Business; Oliver And
Company* (voice only); *Beaches\**
1990 *Stella*
1991 *Scenes From The Mall; For The
Boys*
1992 *Earth And The American Dream*
(voice only)
1993 *Hocus Pocus*

## MILES, Sarah
(1941– ) UK

1962 *Term Of Trial*
1963 *The Servant\*; The Ceremony;
The Six-Sided Triangle* (short)
1965 *Those Magnificent Men In Their
Flying Machines; I Was Happy
Here*
1966 *Blow-Up\**

**MILES, Sarah** (cont.)
1970 *Ryan's Daughter\**
1972 *Lady Caroline Lamb*
1973 *The Hireling; The Man Who Loved Cat Dancing*
1975 *Great Expectations* (TV); *Pepita Jimenez* (aka *Bride To Be*)
1976 *The Sailor Who Fell From Grace With The Sea; Dynasty* (TV)
1978 *The Big Sleep*
1980 *Priest Of Love*
1981 *Venom*
1984 *Ordeal By Innocence; Steaming*
1986 *Eat The Peach*
1987 *Hope And Glory\**
1988 *White Mischief*
1990 *A Ghost In Monte Carlo* (TV)
1992 *The Silent Touch*

**MILLAND, Ray**
real name: Reginald Truscott-Jones
(1905–86) UK

1929 *The Plaything; Piccadilly; The Informer; The Flying Scotsman; The Lady From The Sea*
1930 *Way For A Sailor; Passion Flower*
1931 *Strangers May Kiss; Bachelor Father; Just A Gigolo* (UK: *The Dancing Partner*); *Ambassador Bill; Bought; Blonde Crazy* (UK: *Larceny Lane*)
1932 *Payment Deferred; Polly Of The Circus; The Man Who Played God* (UK: *The Silent Voice*)
1933 *Orders Is Orders; This Is The Life*
1934 *Many Happy Returns; Bolero; Charlie Chan In London; We're Not Dressing; Menace*
1935 *Four Hours To Kill; The Gilded Lily; Alias Mary Dow; One Hour Late; The Glass Key*
1936 *The Return Of Sophie Lang; The Jungle Princess; The Big Broadcast Of 1937; Next Time We Love* (UK: *Next Time We Live*); *Three Smart Girls\**
1937 *Easy Living; Wise Girl; Ebb Tide; Wings Over Honolulu; Bulldog Drummond Escapes*

1938 *Her Jungle Love; Say It In French; Men With Wings*
1939 *Hotel Imperial; Everything Happens At Night; Beau Geste\*; French Without Tears*
1940 *Untamed; The Doctor Takes A Wife; Irene; Arise, My Love*
1941 *Skylark; I Wanted Wings*
1942 *Are Husbands Really Necessary?; Reap The Wild Wind\*; The Major And The Minor; The Lady Has Plans; Star Spangled Rythmn*
1943 *The Crystal Ball; Forever And A Day*
1944 *Ministry Of Fear; Till We Meet Again; The Uninvited; Lady In The Dark*
1945 *The Lost Weekend\*; Kitty; The Trouble With Women*
1946 *The Well-Groomed Bride; California; The Imperfect Lady* (UK: *Mrs Loring's Secret*)
1947 *Variety Girl; Golden Earrings*
1948 *So Evil My Love; Sealed Verdict; The Big Clock; Miss Tatlock's Millions; Alias Nick Beal* (UK: *The Contact Man*)
1949 *It Happens Every Spring*
1950 *A Woman Of Distinction; Copper Canyon; A Life Of Her Own*
1951 *Circle Of Danger; Night Into Morning; Close To My Heart; Rhubarb*
1952 *Something To Live For; The Thief; Bugles In The Afternoon*
1953 *Jamaica Run; Let's Do It Again*
1954 *Dial M For Murder*
1955 *A Man Alone* (also director); *The Girl In The Red Velvet Swing*
1956 *Lisbon* (also director)
1957 *The River's Edge; Three Brave Men*
1958 *High Flight; The Safecracker* (also director)
1962 *The Premature Burial; Panic In Year Zero* (also director)
1963 *X* (UK: *The Man With The X-Ray Eyes*)
1964 *The Confession*
1967 *Rose Rosse Per Il Führer*
1968 *Hostile Witness* (also director)

1969 *Daughter Of The Mind* (TV)
1970 *Love Story\*; River Of Gold* (TV); *Company Of Killers*
1971 *Black Noon* (TV)
1972 *The Thing With Two Heads; Embassy; Frogs; The Big Game*
1973 *The House In Nightmare Park; Terror In The Wax Museum*
1974 *The Student Connection; Gold; Escape To Witch Mountain*
1975 *The Dead Don't Die* (TV); *Oil: The Billion Dollar Fire; Ellery Queen: Don't Look Behind You* (TV); *The Swiss Conspiracy*
1976 *The Last Tycoon; Aces High; Mayday At 40,000 Feet* (TV); *Look What's Happened To Rosemary's Baby* (TV)
1977 *Slavers; The Uncanny; I Gabiani Volano Bassi*
1978 *Spree; Oliver's Story; Battlestar Galactica; The Darker Side Of Terror* (TV); *Cruise Of Terror* (TV); *Blackout*
1979 *The Concorde Affair; Game For Vultures; Cave In!* (TV); *La Ragazza In Pigiamo Giallo*
1980 *The Attic; Survival Run*
1981 *Our Family Business* (TV)
1982 *Starflight One* (TV)
1983 *Cocaine: One Man's Seduction* (TV)
1984 *The Masks Of Death* (TV)
1985 *The Sea Serpent; The Gold Key*

## MILLS, Sir John
real name: Lewis 'Johnny' Mills
(1908– ) UK

1932 *Words And Music; The Midshipman*
1933 *Britannia Of Billingsgate; The Ghost Camera; The River Wolves; A Political Party*
1934 *The Lash; Those Were The Days; Blind Justice; Doctors' Orders*
1935 *Royal Cavalcade; Brown On Resolution* (aka *For Ever England*); *Car Of Dreams; Charing Cross Road*
1936 *First Offence; Tudor Rose; OHMS*

1937 *The Green Cockatoo*
1939 *Goodbye Mr Chips!\*; Happy Families* (short)
1940 *Old Bill And Son; All Hands* (short)
1941 *Cottage To Let; The Black Sheep Of Whitehall; The Big Blockade*
1942 *The Young Mr Pitt; In Which We Serve\**
1943 *We Dive At Dawn*
1944 *This Happy Breed; Waterloo Road; Victory Wedding* (short)
1945 *The Sky's The Limit* (short); *Total War In Britain* (narrator only); *The Way To The Stars*
1946 *Great Expectations\*; Land Of Promise* (voice only)
1947 *So Well Remembered; The October Man*
1948 *Scott Of The Antarctic*
1949 *Friend Of The Family; The Flying Skyscraper* (both narrator only); *The History Of Mr Polly; The Rocking Horse Winner*
1950 *Morning Departure*
1951 *Mr Denning Drives North*
1952 *The Gentle Gunman; The Long Memory*
1954 *Hobson's Choice; The Colditz Story*
1955 *The End Of The Affair; Above Us The Waves; Escapade*
1956 *War And Peace\*; It's Great To Be Young; The Baby And The Battleship; Around The World In 80 Days\*; Town On Trial!*
1957 *The Vicious Circle*
1958 *Dunkirk; Ice Cold In Alex; I Was Monty's Double*
1959 *Tiger Bay; Summer Of The Seventeenth Doll*
1960 *Tunes Of Glory\*; Swiss Family Robinson\*; The Singer Not The Song*
1961 *Flame In The Streets; The Valiant*
1962 *Tiara Tahiti*
1964 *The Chalk Garden; The Truth About Spring*
1965 *King Rat; Operation Crossbow*
1966 *Sky West And Crooked* (director only); *The Wrong Box; The Family Way*

**MILLS, Sir John** (cont.)
1967 *Chuka; Africa—Texas Style*
1968 *Lady Hamilton—Zwischen Smach Und Liebe* (UK: *Emma Hamilton*); *La Morte Non Ha Sesso* (UK: *A Black Veil For Lisa*)
1969 *Oh! What A Lovely War; Run Wild, Run Free; Adam's Woman*
1970 *Ryan's Daughter\**
1971 *Dulcima*
1972 *Young Winston; Lady Caroline Lamb*
1973 *Oklahoma Crude*
1975 *The Human Factor*
1976 *Trial By Combat*
1977 *The Devil's Advocate*
1978 *The Big Sleep; The Thirty-Nine Steps; Dr Strange* (TV)
1979 *Zulu Dawn; Quatermass* (TV)
1982 *Gandhi\**
1983 *Sahara*
1984 *The Masks Of Death* (TV)
1985 *Murder With Mirrors* (TV); *The Adventures Of Little Lord Fauntleroy* (TV)
1986 *When The Wind Blows* (voice only)
1987 *Who's That Girl?*
1989 *The Lady And The Highwayman* (TV)

**MINNELLI, Liza**
(1946– ) USA

1949 *In The Good Old Summertime*
1967 *Charlie Bubbles*
1969 *The Sterile Cuckoo* (UK: *Pookie*)
1970 *Tell Me That You Love Me, Junie Moon*
1971 *Journey Back To Oz* (voice only)
1972 *Cabaret\**
1974 *That's Entertainment*
1975 *Lucky Lady*
1976 *A Matter Of Time; Silent Movie*
1977 *New York, New York\**
1979 *Movies Are My Life* (documentary)
1981 *Arthur\**
1984 *The Muppets Take Manhattan*
1985 *That's Dancing; A Time To Live* (TV)
1986 *Intensive Care* (TV)

1987 *Rent-A-Cop*
1988 *Arthur 2: On The Rocks*
1991 *Stepping Out*

**MIRREN, Helen**
real name: Ilyena Mironoff
(1945– ) UK

1967 *Herostratus*
1968 *A Midsummer Night's Dream*
1969 *Age Of Consent*
1972 *Savage Messiah*
1973 *O Lucky Man!*
1976 *Hamlet*
1977 *Caligula*
1979 *SOS Titanic* (TV); *Hussy*
1980 *The Long Good Friday\*; The Fiendish Plot Of Dr Fu Manchu*
1981 *Excalibur\**
1984 *Cal; 2010*
1985 *White Nights*
1986 *Heavenly Pursuits; The Mosquito Coast*
1988 *When The Whales Came; Pascali's Island; Cause Celèbre* (TV); *People Of The Forest* (narrator only)
1989 *The Cook, The Thief, His Wife And Her Lover\*; Red King, White Knight* (TV)
1990 *The Comfort Of Strangers; Bethune: The Making Of A Hero*
1991 *Where Angels Fear To Tread*
1993 *The Hawk; Blue Room*

**MITCHUM, Robert**
(1917– ) USA

1943 *Border Patrol; Follow The Band; Bar 20; Hoppy Serves A Writ; Colt Comrades; We've Never Been Licked* (UK: *Texas To Tokyo*); *The Lone Star Trail; False Colors; Corvette K-225* (UK: *The Nelson Touch*); *Riders Of The Deadline; Gung Ho!; The Leather Burners; The Human Comedy; Beyond The Last Frontier; Doughboys In Ireland; Aerial Gunner; The Dancing Masters; Cry Havoc; Minesweeper*

1944 *Mr Winkle Goes To War* (UK: *Arms And The Woman*); *When Strangers Marry; Girl Rush; Johnny Doesn't Live Here Anymore; Thirty Seconds Over Tokyo; Nevada*

1945 *West Of The Pecos; The Story Of GI Joe*

1946 *Till The End Of Time; The Locket; Undercurrent*

1947 *Pursued; Desire Me; Crossfire\*; Out Of The Past* (UK: *Build My Gallows High*)

1948 *Blood On The Moon; Rachel And The Stranger*

1949 *Holiday Affair; The Red Pony; The Big Steal*

1950 *Where Danger Lives*

1951 *My Forbidden Past; The Racket; His Kind Of Woman*

1952 *The Lusty Men; One Minute To Zero; Macao; Angel Face*

1953 *Second Chance; White Witch Doctor; She Couldn't Say No* (UK: *Beautiful But Dangerous*)

1954 *Track Of The Cat; River Of No Return*

1955 *The Man With The Gun* (UK: *The Trouble Shooter*); *Not As A Stranger\*; Night Of The Hunter\**

1956 *Foreign Intrigue; Bandido!*

1957 *Heaven Knows Mr Allison; The Enemy Below; Fire Down Below*

1958 *Thunder Road; The Hunters*

1959 *The Angry Hills; The Wonderful Country*

1960 *A Terrible Beauty; The Sundowners\*; Home From The Hill; The Grass Is Greener*

1961 *The Last Time I Saw Archie*

1962 *Cape Fear\*; Two For The Seesaw; The Longest Day\*; Rampage!*

1963 *The List Of Adrian Messenger*

1964 *What A Way To Go!; Man In The Middle*

1965 *Mr Moses*

1967 *The Way West; El Dorado*

1968 *Villa Rides!; Five Card Stud; Secret Ceremony*

1969 *Young Billy Young; The Good Guys And The Bad Guys*

1970 *Ryan's Daughter\**

1971 *Going Home*

1972 *The Wrath Of God*

1973 *The Friends Of Eddie Coyle*

1974 *The Yakuza*

1975 *Farewell My Lovely*

1976 *The Last Tycoon; Midway* (UK: *The Battle Of Midway*)

1977 *The Amsterdam Kill*

1978 *The Big Sleep*

1979 *Breakthrough*

1980 *Agency; Night Kill*

1982 *That Championship Season; One Shoe Makes It Murder* (TV)

1983 *A Killer In The Family* (TV)

1984 *Maria's Lovers; The Ambassador*

1985 *Reunion At Fairborough* (TV); *The Hearst And Davies Affair* (TV)

1986 *Thompson's Last Run* (TV); *Promises To Keep* (TV); *The Conspiracy*

1987 *Marilyn Monroe: Beyond The Legend* (documentary)

1988 *Mr North; Scrooged; John Huston* (documentary)

1989 *Jake Spanner — Private Eye* (TV); *Believed Violent*

1990 *A Family For Joe* (TV)

1991 *Midnight Ride; Cape Fear\**

## MODINE, Matthew
(1960– ) USA

1981 *Amy And The Angel* (TV)

1982 *Baby, It's You*

1983 *Private School; Streamers*

1984 *Vision Quest* (aka *Crazy For You*); *The Hotel New Hampshire; Birdy; Mrs Soffel*

1987 *Full Metal Jacket\*; Orphans*

1988 *Married To The Mob*

1989 *The Gamble; Gross Anatomy*

1990 *Memphis Belle\*; Pacific Heights*

1992 *Wind; Equinox*

1993 *And The Band Played On* (TV)

## MONROE, Marilyn
real name: Norma Jean Baker
(1926–62) USA

1947 *The Shocking Miss Pilgrim;
Dangerous Years*
1948 *Scudda-Hoo! Scudda-Hay!* (UK:
*Summer Lightning*); *Ladies Of
The Chorus*
1949 *Love Happy*
1950 *The Fireball; Right Cross; A Ticket
To Tomahawk; The Asphalt
Jungle\*; All About Eve\**
1951 *The Hometown Story; Love Nest;
Let's Make It Legal; As Young As
You Feel*
1952 *We're Not Married; Clash By
Night; O Henry's Full House;
Monkey Business; Don't Bother
To Knock*
1953 *Niagara; Gentlemen Prefer
Blondes\*; How To Marry A
Millionaire\**
1954 *River Of No Return; There's No
Business Like Showbusiness*
1955 *The Seven Year Itch\**
1956 *Bus Stop\**
1957 *The Prince And The Showgirl\**
1959 *Some Like It Hot\**
1960 *Let's Make Love; The Misfits\**
1962 *Something's Gotta Give*
(unfinished)

## MONTAND, Yves
real name: Ivo Livi
(1921–91) Italy

1945 *Silence...Antenne* (short)
1946 *Etoile Sans Lumière; Les Portes
De La Nuit*
1947 *L'Idole*
1950 *Souvenirs Perdus* (UK: *Lost
Property*)
1951 *Paris Chante Toujours*
1953 *Tempi Nostri; Le Salaire De La
Peur* (UK: *Wages Of Fear*)
1954 *Napoléon; Une Tranche De La
Vie*
1955 *Les Héros Sont Fatigués* (UK:
*The Heroes Are Tired*);
*Marguerite De La Nuit*

1956 *Uomini E Lupi* (UK: *Men And
Wolves*); *Der Vind Rose*
1957 *Les Sorcières De Salem* (UK: *The
Witches Of Salem*); *Premier Mai;
La Grande Strada Azzurra*
1958 *La Loi* (UK: *Where The Hot Wind
Blows*)
1959 *Yves Montand Chante; Le Père Et
L'Enfant*
1960 *Let's Make Love*
1961 *Sanctuary; Aimez-Vous Brahms*
(UK: *Goodbye Again*)
1962 *My Geisha*
1965 *Compartiment Tueurs* (UK: *The
Sleeping Car Murders*)
1966 *Paris, Brûle-T-Il?* (UK: *Is Paris
Burning?*); *Grand Prix; La Guerre
Est Finie*
1967 *Vivre Pour Vivre*
1968 *Z\*; Mr Freedom; Un Soir...Un
Train; Le Diable Par La Queue*
1969 *Le Deuxième Procès D'Artur
London* (documentary); *Jour Du
Tournage; Le Joli Mai* (narrator
only)
1970 *Le Cercle Rouge* (UK: *The Red
Circle*); *L'Aveu* (UK: *The
Confession*); *On A Clear Day You
Can See Forever*
1971 *La Folie Des Grandeurs*
1972 *Tout Va Bien; Le Fils; César Et
Rosalie; Die Dummen Streiche
Der Reichen*
1973 *Etat De Siège* (UK: *State Of
Siege*)
1974 *Le Hasard Et Le Violence* (UK:
*The Scarlet Room*); *Vincent,
François, Paul Et Les Autres; Le
Sauvage; La Solitude Du
Chanteur De Fond* (documentary)
1975 *Police Python 357*
1977 *Le Grand Escogriffe; Flashback;
La Menace*
1978 *Les Routes Du Sud*
1979 *Clair De Femme*
1980 *I Comme Icare*
1981 *Le Choix Des Armes*
1982 *Tout Feu, Tout Flamée*
1983 *Garçon!*
1986 *Jean De Florette\*; Manon Des
Sources\**

1988 *Trois Places Pour Le Vingt-Six*
1989 *Netchaiev Est De Retour*
1992 *IP5*

## MOORE, Demi
real name: Demi Guynes
(1962– ) USA

1981 *Choices*
1982 *Young Doctors In Love; Parasite*
1983 *Blame It On Rio*
1984 *No Small Affair*
1985 *St Elmo's Fire*
1986 *One Crazy Summer; About Last Night; Wisdom*
1988 *The Seventh Sign*
1989 *We're No Angels*
1990 *Ghost\*; Tales From The Crypt* (TV)
1991 *The Butcher's Wife; Nothing But Trouble; Mortal Thoughts*
1992 *A Few Good Men\**
1993 *Indecent Proposal*

## MOORE, Dudley
(1935– ) UK

1964 *The Hat* (narrator only)
1966 *The Wrong Box*
1967 *30 Is A Dangerous Age Cynthia; Bedazzled*
1969 *The Bed Sitting Room; Monte Carlo Or Bust*
1972 *Alice's Adventures In Wonderland*
1977 *The Hound Of The Baskervilles*
1978 *Foul Play\**
1979 *10\*; To Russia With Elton* (narrator only)
1980 *Wholly Moses!*
1981 *Arthur\**
1982 *Derek And Clive Get The Horn; Six Weeks*
1983 *Lovesick; Unfaithfully Yours; Romantic Comedy*
1984 *Best Defense; Micki And Maude*
1985 *Santa Claus*
1986 *The Adventures Of Milo And Otis* (narrator only)
1987 *Like Father, Like Son*
1988 *Arthur 2: On The Rocks*
1990 *Crazy People*
1992 *Blame It On The Bellboy*

## MOORE, Roger
(1927– ) UK

1945 *Caesar And Cleopatra; Perfect Strangers*
1946 *Gaiety George; Piccadilly Incident*
1949 *Paper Orchid; Trottie True*
1954 *The Last Time I Saw Paris*
1955 *Interrupted Melody; The King's Thief; Diane*
1959 *The Miracle*
1960 *The Sins Of Rachel Cade*
1961 *Gold Of The Seven Saints; Il Ratto Delle Sabine* (UK: *Rape Of The Sabines*)
1962 *Un Branco Di Vigliacchi* (UK: *No Man's Land*)
1969 *Crossplot*
1970 *The Man Who Haunted Himself*
1973 *Live And Let Die\**
1974 *Gold; The Man With The Golden Gun\**
1975 *That Lucky Touch*
1976 *Shout At The Devil; Sicilian Cross; Sherlock Holmes In New York* (IV)
1977 *The Spy Who Loved Me\**
1978 *The Wild Geese; Escape To Athena*
1979 *Moonraker\*; North Sea Hijack*
1980 *The Sea Wolves; Sunday Lovers*
1981 *For Your Eyes Only\*; The Cannonball Run\**
1983 *Octopussy\*; Curse Of The Pink Panther*
1984 *The Naked Face*
1985 *A View To A Kill\**
1987 *The Magic Snowman* (voice only)
1989 *Bed And Breakfast*
1990 *Bullseye; Fire, Ice And Dynamite*

## MOOREHEAD, Agnes
(1906–74) USA

1941 *Citizen Kane\**
1942 *The Magnificent Ambersons\*; The Big Street; Journey Into Fear*
1943 *Government Girl; The Youngest Profession; Jane Eyre*
1944 *Since You Went Away\*; The Seventh Cross; Dragon Seed;*

**MOOREHEAD, Agnes** (cont.)
*Tomorrow The World; Mrs Parkington*
1945 *Keep Your Powder Dry; Her Highness And The Bellboy; Our Vines Have Tender Grapes*
1946 *Summer Holiday*
1947 *The Beginning Or The End?; The Lost Moment; Dark Passage*
1948 *The Woman In White; Johnny Belinda*; Station West*
1949 *Without Honor; The Great Sinner; The Stratton Story*
1950 *Caged; Blackjack; The Adventures Of Captian Fabian*
1951 *The Blue Veil; Show Boat*; Fourteen Hours*
1952 *The Blazing Forest*
1953 *The Story Of Three Loves; Main Street To Broadway; Scandal At Scourie; Those Redheads From Seattle*
1954 *Magnificent Obsession**
1955 *Untamed; The Left Hand Of God*
1956 *All That Heaven Allows; Meet Me In Las Vegas* (UK: *Viva Las Vegas!*); *The Revolt Of Mamie Stover; The Swan; The Conqueror; Pardners; The Opposite Sex*
1957 *The True Story Of Jesse James* (UK: *The James Brothers*); *Raintree County; Jeanne Eagels*
1958 *Tempest*
1959 *The Bat; Night Of The Quarter Moon*
1960 *Pollyanna*
1961 *Bachelor In Paradise; Jessica; Twenty Plus Two* (UK: *It Started In Tokyo*)
1962 *How The West Was Won**
1963 *Who's Minding The Store?*
1964 *Hush, Hush...Sweet Charlotte*
1966 *The Singing Nun*
1969 *The Ballad Of Andy Crocker* (TV)
1970 *Marriage: Year One* (TV)
1971 *Suddenly Single* (TV); *What's The Matter With Helen?*
1972 *Rolling Man* (TV); *Night Of Terror* (TV); *Dear Dead Delilah; Charlotte's Web* (voice only)

1973 *Frankenstein: The True Story* (TV)
1974 *Three Faces Of Love* (TV)

**MORANIS, Rick**
(1954– ) Canada

1983 *Strange Brew* (also director)
1984 *Ghostbusters*; Streets Of Fire; The Wild Life*
1985 *Brewster's Millions*
1986 *Club Paradise; Little Shop Of Horrors; Head Office*
1987 *Spaceballs*
1989 *Parenthood*; Honey I Shrunk The Kids*; Ghostbusters II*
1990 *My Blue Heaven*
1991 *LA Story*
1992 *Honey, I Blew Up The Baby*
1993 *Splitting Heirs*

**MORE, Kenneth**
(1914–82) UK

1935 *Look Up And Laugh*
1936 *Carry On London; Windmill Revels; Not Wanted On Voyage*
1946 *School For Secrets*
1948 *Scott Of The Antarctic; For Them That Trespass*
1949 *Man On The Run; Now Barabbas...Was A Robber; Stop Press Girl*
1950 *Morning Departure; The Clouded Yellow; Chance Of A Lifetime*
1951 *No Highway; The Franchise Affair; Appointment With Venus; Brandy For The Parson*
1952 *The Yellow Balloon*
1953 *Never Let Me Go; Genevieve*; Our Girl Friday*
1954 *Doctor In The House*
1955 *Raising A Riot; The Deep Blue Sea*
1956 *Reach For The Sky*
1957 *The Admirable Crichton*
1958 *A Night To Remember; Next To No Time!; The Sheriff Of Fractured Jaw*
1959 *The 39 Steps; Northwest Frontier*
1960 *Sink The Bismarck!; Man In The Moon*

1961  *The Greengage Summer*
1962  *Some People; We Joined The Navy; The Longest Day\**
1963  *The Comedy Man*
1967  *The Mercenaries*
1968  *Fraulein Doktor*
1969  *Oh! What A Lovely War; Battle Of Britain*
1970  *Scrooge*
1976  *The Slipper And The Rose; Where Time Began*
1977  *Leopard In The Snow*
1978  *The Silent Witness* (narrator only)
1979  *The Spaceman And King Arthur*
1981  *A Tale Of Two Cities* (TV)

## MOREAU, Jeanne
(1928– ) France

1948  *Dernier Amour*
1950  *Pigalle-Saint-Germain-De Prés; Meurtres*
1951  *L'Homme De Ma Vie*
1952  *Docteur Schweitzer; Il Est Minuit*
1953  *Julietta; Dortoir Des Grandes; Secrets D'Alcove* (UK: *The Bed*); *Touchez Pas Au Grisbi* (UK: *Grisbi*)
1954  *Les Intrigantes; La Reine Margot*
1955  *Les Hommes En Blanc; M'sieur La Caille* (UK: *Parasites*); *Gas-Oil*
1956  *La Salaire Du Péché; Les Louves* (UK: *The She-Wolves*)
1957  *Jusqu'Au Dernier; L'Etrange Monsieur Stève; Trois Jours A Vivre*
1958  *Ascenseur Pour L'Echaufaud* (UK: *Lift To The Scaffold*); *Le Dos Au Mur* (UK: *Evidence In Concrete*); *Echec Au Porteur; Les Amants*
1959  *Les Quatres Cents Coups\** (UK: *The Four Hundred Blows*); *Les Liaisons Dangereuses; Five Branded Women*
1960  *Les Carmelites; Moderato Cantabile*
1961  *Une Femme Est Une Femme; La Notte; Jules Et Jim\**
1962  *Eva; La Baie Des Anges*

1963  *Le Feu Follet* (UK: *A Time To Live And A Time To Die*); *The Trial; The Victors; Peau De Banane* (UK: *Banana Peel*)
1964  *Le Journal D'Une Femme De Chambre* (UK: *Diary Of A Chambermaid*); *Mata Hari Agent H 21* (UK: *Mata Hari*); *The Yellow Rolls-Royce; La Peau Douce* (UK: *Silken Skin*) (voice only); *The Train*
1965  *Viva Maria!*
1966  *Chimes At Midnight; Mademoiselle; Sailor From Gibraltar*
1967  *The Oldest Profession*
1968  *La Mariée Etait En Noir* (UK: *The Bride Wore Black*); *Great Catherine; The Immortal Story*
1969  *Le Corps De Diane; Le Petit Théatre De Jean Renoir*
1970  *Monte Walsh; Compte A Rebours*
1971  *Alex In Wonderland; Cannibales En Sicile; Dead Reckoning; L'Humeur Vagabonde; Mille Baisers De Florence*
1972  *Chère Louise; Nathalie Granger*
1973  *Les Valseuses* (UK: *Making It*)
1974  *La Race Des Seigneurs; Je T'Aime; Hu-Man*
1975  *Le Jardin Qui Bascule; Souvenirs D'En France*
1976  *Mr Klein; The Last Tycoon; Lumière* (director only)
1979  *L'Adolescente* (director only)
1980  *Your Ticket Is No Longer Valid*
1981  *La DéBandade; Plein Sud; Mille Milliards De Dollars*
1982  *La Truite* (UK: *The Trout*); *Querelle*
1983  *Der Bauer Von Babylon* (UK: *The Wizard Of Babylon*) (documentary)
1984  *Lillian Gish* (documentary, director only)
1986  *Le Paltoquet; Sauve-Toi Lola*
1987  *Le Stimulateur; Le Miraculé; La Nuit De L'Ocean*
1990  *Nikita*
1991  *Until The End Of The World; Le Pas Suspendu De La Cigogne*

**MOREAU, Jeanne** (cont.)
(UK: *The Suspended Step Of The Stork*); *Anna Karamazova; La Vieille Qui Marchait Dans La Mer*
1992 *Clothes In The Wardrobe* (TV); *A Demain*
1993 *A Foreign Field* (TV); *Je M'Appelle Victor*


**MUNI, Paul**
real name: Muni Weisenfreund
(1895–1967)

1929 *The Valiant; Seven Faces*
1932 *I Am A Fugitive From A Chain Gang\*; Scarface\**
1933 *The World Changes*
1934 *Hi Nellie*
1935 *Bordertown; Dr Socrates; Black Fury*
1936 *The Story Of Louis Pasteur\**
1937 *The Good Earth\*; The Life Of Emile Zola\*; The Woman I Love*
1938 *For Auld Lang Syne* (short)
1939 *Juarez; We're Not Alone*
1940 *Hudson's Bay*
1942 *Commmandos Strike At Dawn*
1943 *Stage Door Canteen*
1945 *Counter Attack* (UK: *One Against Seven*); *A Song To Remember*
1946 *Angel On My Shoulder*
1953 *Stranger On The Prowl*
1959 *The Last Angry Man*


**MURPHY, Audie**
(1924–71) USA

1948 *Beyond Glory; Texas, Brooklyn And Heaven* (UK: *The Girl From Texas*)
1949 *The Bad Boy; The Kid From Texas* (UK: *Texas Kid—Outlaw*)
1950 *Sierra; Kansas Raiders*
1951 *The Red Badge Of Courage\*; The Cimarron Kid*
1952 *The Duel At Silver Creek*
1953 *Gunsmoke!; Column South; Tumbleweed*

1954 *Ride Clear Of Diablo; Drums Across The River; Destry; Queens Of Beauty* (short)
1955 *To Hell And Back\**
1956 *Walk The Proud Land; World In My Corner*
1957 *Joe Butterly; Night Passage; Rock'Em Cowboy* (short); *The Guns Of Fort Petticoat*
1958 *The Quiet American; The Gun Runners; Ride A Crooked Trail*
1959 *No Name On The Bullet; The Wild And The Innocent; Cast A Long Shadow*
1960 *The Unforgiven; Hell Bent For Leather; Seven Ways From Sundown*
1961 *Battle At Blood Beach* (UK: *Battle On The Beach*); *Posse Hell*
1962 *Six Black Horses*
1963 *Showdown; Gunfight At Commanche Creek*
1964 *Bullet For A Badman; The Quick Gun; Apache Rifles*
1965 *Arizona Raiders*
1966 *Gunpoint; The Texan; Trunk To Cairo*
1967 *40 Guns To Apache Pass*
1969 *A Time For Dying*


**MURPHY, Eddie**
full name: Edward Regan Murphy
(1961– ) USA

1982 *48 Hrs\**
1983 *Trading Places\**
1984 *Best Defense; Beverly Hills Cop\**
1986 *The Golden Child*
1987 *Beverly Hills Cop 2; Eddie Murphy—Raw*
1988 *Coming To America\**
1989 *Harlem Nights* (also director)
1990 *Another 48 Hrs; The Kid Who Loved Christmas* (TV) (producer only)
1992 *Boomerang; Distinguished Gentleman*

## MURRAY, Bill
real name: William Doyle-Murray
(1950–   )

1975 *Jungle Burger* (voice only)
1979 *Meatballs*
1980 *Where The Buffalo Roam;
Caddyshack*
1981 *Stripes\*; Loose Shoes*
1982 *Tootsie\**
1984 *The Razor's Edge; Ghostbusters\*;
Nothing Lasts Forever*
1986 *Little Shop Of Horrors*
1987 *Rolling In The Aisles*
1988 *Scrooged*
1989 *Ghostbusters II*
1990 *Quick Change* (also co-director)
1991 *What About Bob?*
1992 *Mad Dog And Glory*
1993 *Groundhog Day*


# N

## NEAL, Patricia
real name: Patsy Neal
(1925–   ) USA

1949 *John Loves Mary; The
Fountainhead; It's A Great
Feeling; The Hasty Heart*
1950 *Bright Leaf; Three Secrets; The
Breaking Point; Raton Pass* (UK:
*Canyon Pass*)
1951 *Operation Pacific; The Day The
Earth Stood Still; Weekend With
Father*
1952 *Diplomatic Courier; Something
For The Birds; Washington Story*
(UK: *Target For Scandal*)
1954 *Stranger From Venus; La Tua
Donna*
1957 *A Face In The Crowd*
1961 *Breakfast At Tiffany's\**
1963 *Hud\**
1964 *Psyche 59*
1965 *In Harm's Way*
1968 *The Subject Was Roses*
1971 *The Homecoming; The Night
Digger* (TV)
1972 *Baxter!*

1973 *Happy Mother's Day...Love
George*
1974 *'B' Must Die; Things In Their
Season* (TV)
1975 *Eric* (TV)
1977 *Tail Gunner Joe* (TV); *A Love
Affair—The Eleanor And Lou
Gehrig Story* (TV); *Widows' Nest*
1978 *The Passage*
1979 *All Quiet On The Western Front*
(TV)
1981 *Ghost Story; The Patricia Neal
Story* (TV)
1984 *Shattered Vows* (TV); *Love Leads
The Way*
1989 *Taking Chances: An
Unremarkable Life*
1990 *Caroline?* (TV)


## NEILL, Sam
real name: Nigel Neill
(1947–   ) Ireland

1975 *Ashes; Landfall*
1977 *Sleeping Dogs*
1979 *The Journalist; Out Of Reach; My
Brilliant Career*
1980 *Attack Force Z*
1981 *From A Far Country: Pope John
Paul II; The Final Conflict;
Possession*
1982 *Ivanhoe* (TV); *Enigma*
1983 *The Country Girls* (TV)
1984 *Le Sang Des Autres*
1985 *Plenty; Robbery Under Arms*
1986 *The Good Wife; For Love Alone*
1987 *Leap Of Faith* (TV)
1988 *A Cry In The Dark\*; Dead Calm*
1989 *The French Revolution*
1990 *The Hunt For Red October\**
1991 *Until The End Of The World;
Death In Brunswick; One Against
The Wind* (TV)
1992 *Memoirs Of An Invisible Man*
1993 *The Piano; Jurassic Park*


## NEWMAN, Paul
(1925–   ) USA

1954 *The Silver Chalice*

**NEWMAN, Paul** (cont.)
1956 *The Rack; Somebody Up There Likes Me*
1957 *Until They Sail; The Helen Morgan Story* (UK: *Both Ends Of The Candle*)
1958 *The 80 Yard Run* (TV); *Cat On A Hot Tin Roof\*; The Long Hot Summer; The Left-Handed Gun*
1959 *Rally Round The Flag Boys!; The Young Philadelphians* (UK: *The City Jungle*); *On The Harmfulness Of Tobacco* (also director)
1960 *From The Terrace\*; Exodus\**
1961 *Paris Blues; The Hustler\**
1962 *Hemingway's Adventures Of A Young Man; Sweet Bird Of Youth\**
1963 *Hud\*; A New Kind Of Love; The Prize*
1964 *What A Way To Go!; The Outrage*
1965 *Lady L*
1966 *Harper* (UK: *The Moving Target*); *Torn Curtain*
1967 *Hombre; Cool Hand Luke\**
1968 *The Secret War Of Harry Frigg*
1969 *Butch Cassidy And The Sundance Kid\*; Winning*
1970 *WUSA; King: A Filmed Record...Montgomery To Memphis*
1971 *Sometimes A Great Notion* (UK: *Never Give An Inch*) (also director)
1972 *Pocket Money; The Life And Times Of Judge Roy Bean*
1973 *The Sting\*; The Mackintosh Man*
1974 *The Towering Inferno\**
1975 *The Drowning Pool*
1976 *Silent Movie; Buffalo Bill And The Indians*
1977 *Slap Shot*
1979 *Angel Death* (narrator only); *Quintet*
1980 *When Time Ran Out...*
1981 *Fort Apache The Bronx; Absence Of Malice\**
1982 *The Verdict\**
1984 *Harry And Son* (also director)
1986 *The Color Of Money\**
1987 *Hello Actors Studio* (documentary)
1988 *John Huston* (documentary)
1989 *Fat Man And Little Boy* (UK: *The Shadowmakers*); *Blaze*
1990 *Mr And Mrs Bridge*
1993 *The Hudsucker Proxy*

See also directors listing

**NEWTON, Robert**
(1905–56) UK

1932 *Reunion*
1936 *Fire Over England*
1937 *Dark Journey; Farewell Again; The Squeaker; The Green Cockatoo; 21 Days*
1938 *Vessel Of Wrath; Yellow Sands*
1939 *Poison Pen; Dead Men Are Dangerous; Jamaica Inn; Hell's Cargo*
1940 *Bulldog Sees It Through; Busman's Honeymoon; Gaslight; Channel Incident* (short)
1941 *Major Barbara; Hatter's Castle*
1942 *They Flew Alone*
1944 *This Happy Breed; Henry V\**
1945 *Night Boat To Dublin*
1946 *Odd Man Out\**
1947 *Temptation Harbour*
1948 *Snowbound; Oliver Twist\*; Kiss The Blood Off My Hands* (UK: *Blood On My Hands*); *Obsession*
1950 *Treasure Island; Waterfront*
1951 *Tom Brown's Schooldays; Soldiers Three*
1952 *Blackbeard The Pirate; Les Misérables*
1953 *Androcles And The Lion; The Desert Rats*
1954 *Long John Silver; The High And The Mighty\*; The Beachcomber*
1955 *Under The Black Flag*
1956 *Around The World In 80 Days\**

**NICHOLSON, Jack**
(1937– ) USA

1958 *Cry Baby Killer*
1959 *Too Soon To Love* (UK: *Teenage Lovers*)
1960 *Studs Lonigan; The Wild Ride; The Little Shop Of Horrors*

1961 *The Broken Land*
1963 *The Raven; The Terror*
1964 *Back Door To Hell; Ensign Pulver*
1966 *The Shooting*
1967 *Ride The Whirlwind; The St Valentine's Day Massacre; Hell's Angels On Wheels*
1968 *Head; Psych-Out*
1969 *Rebel Rousers; Easy Rider\**
1970 *On A Clear Day You Can See Forever; Five Easy Pieces\**
1971 *A Safe Place; Carnal Knowledge*
1972 *The King Of Marvin Gardens*
1973 *The Last Detail*
1974 *The Fortune; Chinatown\*; Tommy*
1975 *Professione: Reporter* (UK: *The Passenger*); *One Flew Over The Cuckoo's Nest\**
1976 *The Last Tycoon; The Missouri Breaks*
1978 *Goin' South* (also director)
1980 *The Shining\**
1981 *The Border; The Postman Always Rings Twice\*; Reds\**
1983 *Terms Of Endearment\**
1985 *Prizzi's Honor\**
1986 *Heartburn*
1987 *The Witches Of Eastwick\*; Broadcast News\*; Ironweed\**
1989 *Batman\**
1990 *The Two Jakes\** (also director)
1992 *Man Trouble; A Few Good Men\*; Hoffa\**
1993 *Wolf*

See also directors listing

## NIELSEN, Leslie
(1925– ) Canada

1955 *The Vagabond King*
1956 *Forbidden Planet; Ransom!; The Opposite Sex*
1957 *Hot Summer Night; Tammy And The Bachelor* (UK: *Tammy*)
1958 *The Sheepman*
1964 *Night Train To Paris*
1965 *Harlow; Dark Intruder*
1966 *Beau Geste; The Plainsman*
1967 *Gunfight In Abilene; Rosie!; The Reluctant Astronaut;*

*Counterpoint; Code Name: Heraclitus* (TV); *Companions In Nightmare* (TV)
1968 *Dayton's Devils; Shadow Over Elveron* (TV)
1969 *Four Rode Out; How To Commit Marriage; Deadlock* (TV); *Trial Run* (TV)
1970 *The Aquarians* (TV); *Hauser's Memory; Incident In San Francisco; Night Slaves* (TV)
1971 *They Call It Murder* (TV)
1972 *The Poseidon Adventure\*; Snatched* (TV)
1973 *The Letters* (TV); *And Millions Will Die; The Resurection Of Zachary Wheeler*
1974 *Can Ellen Be Saved?* (TV); *Guadalcanal Odyssey* (narrator only)
1975 *King Of The Underwater World* (narrator only)
1976 *Day Of The Animals; Project: Kill; Brink's: The Great Robbery* (TV); *The Siege* (TV)
1977 *Viva Knievel!; The Amsterdam Kill; Sixth And Main; Grand Jury* (TV)
1978 *Institute For Revenge* (TV); *Little Mo* (TV); *City On Fire*
1979 *The Mad Trapper; RIEL; Cave In!* (TV)
1980 *Prom Night; Airplane!\**
1981 *The Creature Wasn't Nice; A Choice Of Two*
1982 *Creepshow; Wrong Is Right* (UK: *The Man With The Deadly Lens*)
1985 *Reckless Disregard* (TV); *Blade In Hong Kong* (TV); *Striker's Mountain* (TV); *The Homefront* (narrator only)
1986 *Foxfire Light; The Patriot; Soul Man; Home Is Where The Hart Is*
1987 *Nuts\*; Fatal Confession* (TV); *Calhoun* (aka *Night Stick*)
1988 *Dangerous Curves* (TV); *The Naked Gun: From The Files Of Police Squad\**
1990 *Repossessed*
1991 *The Naked Gun 2½: The Smell Of Fear; All I Want For Christmas*

**NIELSEN, Leslie** (cont.)
1993  Surf Samurai Of The Seven Seas;
      Digger; The Naked Gun 33⅓


## NIMOY, Leonard

(1931–  ) USA

1951  Queen For A Day; Rhubarb
1952  Francis Goes To West Point; Kid
      Monk Baroni; Zombies Of The
      Stratosphere
1953  Old Overland Trail
1958  The Brain Eaters
1963  The Balcony
1966  Deathwatch
1971  Catlow
1973  The Alpha Caper (TV)
1978  Invasion Of The Bodysnatchers
1979  Star Trek—The Motion Picture*
1981  A Woman Called Golda (TV)
1982  Star Trek II—The Wrath Of Khan
1984  Star Trek III—The Search For
      Spock (also director)
1986  Transformers—The Movie (voice
      only); Star Trek IV—The Voyage
      Home (also director)
1988  Just One Step: The Great Peace
      March
1989  Star Trek V—The Final Frontier
1991  Star Trek VI—The Undiscovered
      Country; Never Forget (TV)
1993  The Pagemaster (voice only)

See also directors listing


## NIVEN, David

real name: James David Graham Nevins
(1910–83) UK

1932  There Goes The Bride
1935  Mutiny On The Bounty*; Splendor;
      Without Regret; A Feather In Her
      Hat; Barbary Coast
1936  Palm Springs (UK: Palm Springs
      Affair); Rose Marie*; Dodsworth*;
      Thank You, Jeeves; The Charge
      Of The Light Brigade; Beloved
      Enemy

1937  Dinner At The Ritz; We Have Our
      Moments; The Prisoner Of Zenda*
1938  The Cowboy And The Lady;
      Three Blind Mice; Four Men And
      A Prayer; The Dawn Patrol;
      Bluebeard's Eighth Wife
1939  The Real Glory; Wuthering
      Heights*; Bachelor Mother;
      Eternally Yours
1940  Raffles
1942  The First Of The Few
1944  The Way Ahead
1946  A Matter Of Life And Death*;
      Magnificent Doll; The Perfect
      Marriage
1947  The Other Love; The Bishop's
      Wife*
1948  Bonnie Prince Charlie;
      Enchantment
1949  A Kiss For Corliss; A Kiss In The
      Dark
1950  The Elusive Pimpernel; The Toast
      Of New Orleans
1951  Happy-Go-Lovely; Appointment
      With Venus; Soldiers Three; The
      Lady Says No
1953  The Moon Is Blue; The Love
      Lottery
1954  Carrington VC; Happy Ever After
1955  The King's Thief
1956  The Silken Affair; The Birds And
      The Bees; Around The World In
      80 Days*
1957  Oh Men! Oh Women!; The Little
      Hut; My Man Godfrey
1958  Bonjour Tristesse; Glamorous
      Hollywood (documentary);
      Separate Tables*
1959  Happy Anniversary; Ask Any Girl
1960  Please Don't Eat The Daisies
1961  The Guns Of Navarone*; The
      Best Of Enemies; Road To Hong
      Kong
1962  Guns Of Darkness; La Città
      Prigioniera (UK: The Captive
      City); 55 Days At Peking
1963  The Pink Panther*
1964  Bedtime Story
1965  Where The Spies Are; Lady L
1966  Eye Of The Devil
1967  Casino Royale

1968 *Prudence And The Pill; The Extraordinary Seaman; The Impossible Years*
1969 *Before Winter Comes; The Brain*
1970 *The Statue*
1972 *King, Queen, Knave*
1974 *Paper Tiger; Vampira*
1976 *No Deposit, No Return; Murder By Death*
1977 *Candleshoe*
1978 *Escape To Athena; Death On The Nile; The Billion Dollar Movies* (narrator only)
1979 *A Man Called Intrepid* (TV)
1980 *Rough Cut; The Sea Wolves; The Biggest Bank Robbery* (TV)
1982 *Better Late Than Never; Trail Of The Pink Panther*
1983 *Curse Of The Pink Panther*

## NOIRET, Philippe
(1930– ) France

1948 *Gigi*
1951 *Olivia; Agence Matrimoniale*
1955 *La Pointe Courte*
1960 *Ravissante; Zazie Dans Le Métro*
1961 *Le Capitaine Fracasse; Le Rendezvous; Les Amours Célèbres; Tout L'Or Du Monde*
1962 *Comme Un Poisson Dans L'Eau; Le Crime Ne Paie Pas; Thérèse Desqueyroux; Ballade Pour Un Voyou*
1963 *Clémentine Chérie; Cyrano Et D'Artagnan; Le Massagiatrici; La Porteuse De Pain*
1964 *Mort, Où Est Ta Victoire?; Monsieur*
1965 *Les Copains; Lady L*
1966 *La Vie De Château; Qui Etes-Vous, Polly Magoo?; Les Sultans; Le Voyage Du Père; Tendre Voyou; Night Of The Generals*
1967 *L'Une Et L'Autre; Woman Times Seven; Alexandre Le Bienheureux; Adolphe, Ou L'Age Tendre*
1968 *Mister Freedom; The Assassination Bureau*
1969 *Topaze; Justine; Clerambard*

1970 *Les Caprices De Marie; Murphy's War*
1971 *Les Aveux Les Plus Doux*
1972 *A Time For Loving; La Vieille Fille; Le Trèfle A Cinq Feuilles; La Mandarine; Siamo Tutti In Libertà Provvisoria; L'Attentat*
1973 *La Grand Bouffe* (UK: *Blow-Out*); *L'Horloger De Saint-Paul* (UK: *The Watchmaker Of St Paul*); *Les Gaspards; Un Nuage Entre Les Dents; Le Secret*
1975 *Le Jeu Avec Le Feu; Que La Fête Comence* (UK: *Let Joy Reign*); *Le Vieux Fusil; Amici Miei*
1976 *Le Juge Et L'Assasin* (UK: *The Judge And The Assassin*); *Monsieur Albert; Il Commune Senso Del Pudore; Une Femme A Sa Fenêtre; Il Deserto Dei Tartari*
1977 *Taxi Mauve* (UK: *Purple Taxi*); *Tendre Poulet* (UK: *Dear Inspector*)
1978 *La Barricade Du Point Du Jour; Le Témoin; Who Is Killing The Great Chefs Of Europe?*
1979 *Due Pezzi Di Pane; Rue Du Pied-De-Grue*
1980 *On A Volé La Cuisse De Jupiter; Une Semaine De Vacances; Pile Ou Face*
1981 *Tre Fratelli* (UK: *Three Brothers*); *Coup De Torchon* (UK: *Clean Slate*); *Il Faut Tuer Birgitt Haas*
1982 *L'Étoile Du Nord* (UK: *The Northern Star*)
1983 *Amici Miei Atto II; L'Africain; L'Ami De Vincent; Le Grand Carnaval*
1984 *Fort Saganne; Aurora; Les Ripoux* (UK: *Le Cop*); *Souvenirs, Souvenirs*
1985 *L'Eté Prochain; Speriamo Che Sia Femmina* (UK: *Let's Hope It's A Girl*)
1987 *Masques; Gli Occhiali D'Oro; Noyade Interdite*
1988 *Il Giovane Toscanini* (UK: *Young Toscanini*)
1989 *Nuovo Cinema Paradiso\** (UK: *Cinema Paradiso*); *Il Frullo Del*

**NOIRET, Philippe** (cont.)
Passero; Return Of The
Musketeers; La Vie Est Rien
D'Autre (UK: Life And Nothing
But)
1990 Dimenticare Palermo; Les Ripoux
Contre Les Ripoux (UK: Le Cop
2); Momsieur Albert; Faux Et
Usage De Faux; Uranus
1991 J'Embrasse Pas; Zuppa Di Pesce;
La Domenica Specialmente
1992 Max Et Jeremie
1993 Le Roi De Paris; Tango


## NOLTE, Nick
(1940– ) USA

1974 The California Kid (TV); Winter Kill
(TV); Death Sentence (TV)
1975 Adam Of Eagle Lake (TV); The
Runaway Barge (TV); Return To
Macon County (UK: Highway Girl)
1977 The Deep*
1978 Who'll Stop The Rain (UK: Dog
Soldiers)
1979 Heart Beat; North Dallas Forty
1982 48 Hrs*; Cannery Row
1984 Teachers; The Ultimate Solution
Of Grace Quigley (UK: Grace
Quigley)
1986 Down And Out In Beverly Hills
1987 Extreme Prejudice; Weeds
1988 Farewell To The King; Three
Fugitives
1989 New York Stories
1990 Everybody Wins; Q & A; Another
48 Hrs
1991 Cape Fear*; Prince Of Tides*
1992 The Player*; Lorenzo's Oil*
1993 I'll Do Anything


## NOVAK, Kim
real name: Marilyn Novak
(1933– ) USA

1953 The Veils Of Bagdad
1954 Son Of Sinbad; The French Line;
Pushover; Phffft

1955 Five Against The House; Picnic*;
The Man With The Golden Arm
1956 The Eddy Duchin Story
1957 Jeanne Eagels; Pal Joey
1958 Bell, Book And Candle; Vertigo*
1959 Middle Of The Night
1960 Strangers When We Meet; Pepe
1962 The Notorious Landlady; Boys'
Night Out
1964 Kiss Me Stupid; Of Human
Bondage
1965 The Amorous Adventures Of Moll
Flanders
1968 The Legend Of Lylah Clare
1969 The Great Bank Robbery
1973 Third Girl From The Left (TV);
Tales That Witness Madness
1975 Satan's Triangle (TV)
1976 Massacre At Blood Bath Drive-In
1977 The White Buffalo
1978 Just A Gigolo
1980 The Mirror Crack'd
1983 Malibu (TV)
1990 The Children
1991 Liebestraum


# O

## OBERON, Merle
full name: Estelle Merle O'Brien
Thompson
(1911–79) UK

1929 The Three Passions
1930 A Warm Corner; Alf's Button
1931 Fascination; Never Trouble
Trouble; Service For Ladies
1932 Ebbtide; For The Love Of Mike;
Aren't We All?; Wedding
Rehearsal; Strange Evidence;
Men Of Tomorrow
1933 The Private Life Of Henry VIII*
1934 The Battle; The Broken Melody;
The Private Life Of Don Juan; The
Scarlet Pimpernel

1935 The Dark Angel; Folies Bergère
1936 These Three; Beloved Enemy
1937 Over The Moon; The Divorce Of Lady X
1938 The Cowboy And The Lady
1939 Wuthering Heights*; The Lion Has Wings
1940 Till We Meet Again
1941 Lydia; Affectionately Yours; That Uncertain Feeling
1943 Forever And A Day; Stage Door Canteen; First Comes Courage
1944 The Lodger; Dark Waters
1945 A Song To Remember; This Love Of Ours
1946 A Night In Paradise; Temptation
1947 Night Song
1948 Berlin Express
1949 Dans La Vie Tout S'Arrange
1951 Pardon My French (UK: The Lady From Boston)
1952 24 Hours Of A Woman's Life
1954 Todo Es Possible En Grenada; Desiree; Deep In My Heart
1955 Cavalcade
1956 The Price Of Fear
1963 Of Love And Desire
1966 The Oscar
1967 Hotel
1973 Interval

## O'BRIEN, Edmond
(1915–85) USA

1938 Prison Break
1939 The Hunchback Of Notre Dame*
1941 The Obliging Young Lady; A Girl, A Guy And A Gob (UK: The Navy Steps Out); Parachute Battalion
1942 Powder Town
1943 The Amazing Mrs Holliday
1944 Winged Victory
1946 The Killers*
1947 The Web; A Double Life
1948 Another Part Of The Forest; An Act Of Murder; Fighter Squadron; For The Love Of Mary
1949 DOA; White Heat*
1950 Backfire; 711 Ocean Drive; Between Midnight And Dawn; The

Admiral Was A Lady; The Redhead And The Cowboy
1951 Two Of A Kind; Warpath; Silver City (UK: High Vermilion)
1952 Denver And The Rio Grande; The Greatest Show On Earth*; The Turning Point
1953 Cow Country; China Venture; Man In The Dark; Julius Caesar*; The Hitch-Hiker; The Bigamist
1954 The Shanghai Story; Shield For Murder (also co-director); The Barefoot Contessa*
1955 Pete Kelly's Blues; 1984
1956 A Cry In The Night; D-Day The Sixth Of June; The Rack; The Girl Can't Help It
1957 Stopover Tokyo; The Big Land (UK: Stampeded!)
1958 The World Was His Jury; Sing, Boy, Sing; Up Periscope!
1959 The Third Voice; The Restless And The Damned (UK: The Climbers)
1960 The Last Voyage
1961 The Great Imposter; Man-Trap (director only)
1962 The Man Who Shot Liberty Valance*; Moon Pilot; Birdman Of Alcatraz*; The Longest Day*
1963 Seven Days In May*
1964 Rio Conchos; The Hanged Man (TV)
1965 Sylvia; Synanon (UK: Get Off My Back)
1966 Fantastic Voyage
1967 Peau D'Espion (UK: To Commit A Murder); The Viscount; The Doomsday Flight (TV); The Outsider (TV)
1969 The Wild Bunch*; The Love God?
1970 The Intruders (TV); River Of Mystery (TV)
1971 What's A Nice Girl Like You? (TV)
1972 They Only Kill Their Masters; Jigsaw (TV); The Other Side Of The Wind (unreleased)
1973 Isn't It Shocking; Lucky Luciano
1974 99 And 44/100% Dead (UK: Call Harry Crown)

## O'CONNOR, Donald
(1925– ) USA

1937 *Melody For Two*
1938 *Men With Wings; Sing, You Sinners; Tom Sawyer— Detective; Sons Of The Legion*
1939 *Million Dollar Legs; Unmarried (UK: Night Club Hostess); Boy Trouble; Death Of A Champion; Night Work; On Your Toes; Beau Geste**
1941 *What's Cookin' (UK: Wake Up And Dream)*
1942 *Get Hep To Love (UK: She's My Lovely); Give Out Sisters; It Comes Up Love (UK: A Date With An Angel); When Johnny Comes Marching Home; Private Buckaroo*
1943 *Strictly In The Groove; Mister Big; Top Man*
1944 *Follow The Boys; This Is The Life; The Merry Monahans; Chip Off The Old Block; Bowery To Broadway*
1945 *Patrick The Great*
1947 *Something In The Wind*
1948 *Feudin', Fussin' And A Fightin'; Are You With It?*
1949 *Yes Sir, That's My Baby; Curtain Call At Cactus Creek (UK: Take The Stage)*
1950 *Francis; The Milkman; Double Crossbones*
1951 *Francis Goes To The Races*
1952 *Singin' In The Rain*; Francis Goes To West Point; I Love Melvin*
1953 *Call Me Madam; Walking My Baby Back Home; Francis Covers The Big Town*
1954 *There's No Business Like Showbusiness; Francis Joins The WACs*
1955 *Francis In The Navy*
1956 *Anything Goes*
1957 *The Buster Keaton Story*
1961 *The Wonders Of Aladdin; Cry For Happy*
1965 *That Funny Feeling*
1974 *That's Entertainment*

1981 *Ragtime; Thursday The 12th*
1984 *Miracle In A Manger*
1992 *Toys*

## O'HARA, Maureen
real name: Maureen Fitzsimmons
(1920– ) Ireland

1938 *Kicking The Moon Around; My Irish Molly*
1939 *Jamaica Inn; The Hunchback Of Notre Dame**
1940 *Bill Of Divorcement; Dance, Girl, Dance*
1941 *They Met In Argentina; How Green Was My Valley**
1942 *Ten Gentlemen From West Point; The Black Swan; To The Shores Of Tripoli*
1943 *The Immortal Sergeant; The Fallen Sparrow; This Land Is Mine*
1944 *Buffalo Bill*
1945 *The Spanish Main*
1946 *Sentimental Journey; Do You Love Me?*
1947 *Sinbad The Sailor; Miracle On 34th Street* (UK: The Big Heart); The Foxes Of Harrow; The Homestretch*
1948 *Sitting Pretty*
1949 *Britannia Mews; Father Was A Fullback; A Woman's Secret; Bagdad*
1950 *Comanche Territory; Rio Grande; Tripoli*
1951 *Flame Of Araby; At Sword's Point (UK: Sons Of The Musketeers); Australian Diary 144/145 (short)*
1952 *Kangaroo; The Quiet Man*; Against All Flags; The Redhead From Wyoming*
1953 *War Arrow*
1954 *Malaga; The Long Grey Line*
1955 *Lady Godiva (UK: Lady Godiva Of Coventry); The Magnificent Matador (UK: The Brave And The Beautiful)*
1956 *Everything But The Truth; Lisbon*
1957 *The Wings Of Eagles*
1960 *Our Man In Havana*

1961 *The Deadly Companions; The
Parent Trap*
1962 *Mr Hobbs Takes A Vacation*
1963 *Spencer's Mountain*
1964 *McLintock!*
1965 *The Battle Of The Villa Fiorita*
1966 *The Rare Breed*
1970 *How Do I Love Thee?*
1971 *Big Jake*
1973 *The Red Pony* (TV)
1991 *Only The Lonely*

## OLDMAN, Gary
(1959–  ) UK

1982 *Remembrance*
1983 *Meantime* (TV)
1985 *Honest, Decent And True* (TV)
1986 *Sid And Nancy*
1987 *Prick Up Your Ears**
1988 *Track 29; Criminal Law*
1989 *We Think The World Of You;
Chattahoochee*
1990 *State Of Grace; Rosencrantz And
Guildenstern Are Dead*
1991 *JFK**; *Heading Home*
1992 *Bram Stoker's Dracula**
1993 *Romeo Is Bleeding*

## OLIVIER, Lord Laurence
(1907–89)

1930 *Hocus Pocus; Too Many Crooks;
The Temporary Widow*
1931 *Potiphar's Wife; The Yellow Ticket*
(UK: *The Yellow Passport*);
*Friends And Lovers*
1932 *Westward Passage; Perfect
Understanding*
1933 *No Funny Business*
1935 *Moscow Nights; Conquest Of The
Air*
1936 *As You Like It; Fire Over England*
1937 *21 Days*
1938 *The Divorce Of Lady X*
1939 *Q Planes; Wuthering Heights**
1940 *Rebecca**; *Pride And Prejudice*
1941 *That Hamilton Woman* (UK: *Lady
Hamilton*); *49th Parallel**; *Words
For Battle* (narrator only)

1942 *George Cross Island* (narrator
only)
1943 *The Demi-Paradise; Malta GC*
(narrator only); *The Volunteer*
1944 *Henry V** (also director); *This
Happy Breed* (narrator only)
1945 *Fighting Pilgrims* (narrator
only)
1948 *Hamlet** (also director)
1951 *The Magic Box*
1952 *Carrie*
1953 *The Beggar's Opera; A Queen Is
Crowned* (narrator only)
1955 *Richard III** (also director)
1957 *The Prince And The Showgirl**
(also director)
1959 *The Devil's Disciple*
1960 *Spartacus**; *The Entertainer**
1961 *The Power And The Glory* (TV)
1962 *Term Of Trial*
1963 *Uncle Vanya*
1965 *Bunny Lake Is Missing; Othello*
1966 *Khartoum*
1968 *The Shoes Of The Fisherman;
Romeo And Juliet* (narrator
only)
1969 *Oh! What A Lovely War; The
Battle Of Britain; The Dance Of
Death; David Copperfield*
1970 *Three Sisters* (also director)
1971 *Nicholas And Alexandra*
1972 *Lady Caroline Lamb; Sleuth**
1975 *Love Among The Ruins* (TV); *The
Gentleman Tramp* (narrator only)
1976 *Marathon Man; The Seven-
Percent Solution*
1977 *A Bridge Too Far; The Betsy*
1978 *The Boys From Brazil*
1979 *Dracula; A Little Romance*
1980 *Inchon!; The Jazz Singer*
1981 *Clash Of The Titans*
1982 *The Jigsaw Man*
1984 *The Bounty**; *The Last Days Of
Pompeii* (TV)
1985 *Wild Geese II*
1986 *Directed By William Wyler*
(documentary); *A Talent For
Murder* (TV)
1988 *War Requiem*

See also directors listing

## O'NEAL, Patrick Ryan
(1941– ) USA

1962 *This Rugged Land*
1968 *The Games; The Big Bounce*
1970 *Love Story\*; Love Hate Love* (TV)
1971 *The Wild Rovers*
1972 *What's Up Doc?\**
1973 *The Thief Who Came To Dinner; Paper Moon\**
1975 *Barry Lyndon\**
1976 *Nickelodeon*
1977 *A Bridge Too Far*
1978 *Oliver's Story; The Driver*
1979 *The Main Event*
1980 *Circle Of Two*
1981 *Green Ice; Partners; So Fine*
1984 *Irreconcilable Differences*
1985 *Fever Pitch*
1987 *Tough Guys Don't Dance*
1989 *Chances Are; Small Sacrifices* (TV)
1992 *The Man Upstairs* (TV)

## O'TOOLE, Peter Seamus
(1932– ) Ireland

1959 *The Savage Innocents*
1960 *Kidnapped; The Day They Robbed The Bank Of England*
1962 *Lawrence Of Arabia\**
1964 *Becket\**
1965 *Lord Jim; What's New Pussycat?*
1966 *The Bible...In The Beginning\*; How To Steal A Million; The Night Of The Generals*
1967 *Casino Royale*
1968 *Great Catherine; The Lion In Winter\**
1969 *Goodbye Mr Chips; Country Dance*
1970 *Murphy's War*
1971 *Under Milk Wood*
1972 *The Ruling Class; Man Of La Mancha*
1974 *Rosebud*
1975 *Man Friday; Foxtrot*
1976 *Rogue Male* (TV)
1977 *Caligula*
1978 *Power Play*
1980 *Masada* (TV); *The Stunt Man*

1982 *My Favourite Year*
1983 *Svengali* (TV); *The World Of James Joyce* (TV)
1984 *Kim* (TV); *Supergirl*
1985 *Creator*
1986 *Club Paradise*
1987 *The Last Emperor\**
1988 *High Spirits*
1989 *Wings Of Fame; On A Moonlit Night; The Pied Piper* (TV)
1990 *Isabelle Eberhardt; The Rainbow Thief*
1991 *King Ralph*
1992 *Rebecca's Daughters* (TV)

# P

## PACINO, Al
full name: Alfred James Pacino
(1940– ) USA

1969 *Me Natalie*
1971 *The Panic In Needle Park*
1972 *The Godfather\**
1973 *Scarecrow; Serpico*
1974 *The Godfather Part II\**
1975 *Dog Day Afternoon\**
1977 *Bobby Deerfield*
1979 *...And Justice For All*
1980 *Cruising*
1982 *Author! Author!*
1983 *Scarface*
1985 *Revolution\**
1989 *The Local Stigmatic; Sea Of Love\**
1990 *Dick Tracy\*; The Godfather Part III\**
1991 *Frankie And Johnny*
1992 *Glengarry Glen Ross; Scent Of A Woman\**
1993 *Carlito's Way*

## PALANCE, Jack
real name: Vladimir Palanuik
(1920– ) USA

1950 *Panic In The Streets; The Halls Of Montezuma*
1952 *Sudden Fear*

1953 Shane*; Second Chance; Flight To Tangier; Arrowhead; Man In The Attic
1954 Sign Of The Pagan; The Silver Chalice
1955 Kiss Of Fire; The Big Knife; I Died A Thousand Times
1956 Attack!
1957 The Lonely Man; House Of Numbers; Flor De Mayo (UK: A Mexican Affair)
1958 The Man Inside; Ten Seconds To Hell
1959 Austerlitz (UK: The Battle Of Austerlitz)
1960 Revak The Rebel; Treno Di Natale
1961 Il Giudizio Universale; Rosmundo E Alboino; The Mongols; La Dernière Attaque; Warriors Five
1962 Barabbas
1963 Le Mépris (UK: Contempt); Il Criminale
1965 Once A Thief; Night Train To Milan
1966 The Spy In The Green Hat; The Professionals*
1967 Torture Garden; To Kill A Dragon
1968 Dr Jekyll And Mr Hyde (TV); Il Mercenario (UK: A Professional Gun); They Came To Rob Las Vegas; L'Urlo Dei Giganti (UK: A Bullet For Rommel)
1969 Ché!; The Desperados; Marquis De Sade; Justine; Una Ragazza Di Eraga; La Legione Di Dannati; The McMasters
1970 Companeros!; Monte Walsh; The Horsemen
1971 Si Puo Fare...Amigo
1972 Chato's Land; Operation: Catastrophe
1973 The Blue Gang; Dracula (TV); Oklahoma Crude; Crazy; Te Deum (UK: The Con Men)
1974 The Godchild (TV)
1975 Bronk (TV); Il Richiamo Del Lupo; L'Infermiera (UK: I Will If You Will); The Hatfields And The McCoys (TV); The Four Deuces

1976 Africa Express; Godzilla Versus The Cosmic Monster (UK: Gozilla Vs The Bionic Monster); Eva Nera (UK: Erotic Eva); Squadra Antiscippo (UK: The Cop In Blue Jeans); God's Gun; The Great Adventure
1977 Sangue Di Sbirro; Il Padrone Della Città; Jimbuck
1978 Seven From Heaven; Dead On Arrival
1979 Unknown Powers; The Shape Of Things To Come; Cocaine Cowboys; The Ivory Ape; The Last Ride Of The Dalton Gang (TV)
1980 Hawk The Slayer; One Man Jury; Ladyfingers; Without Warning (UK: The Warning)
1982 Alone In The Dark
1983 Evil Stalks The House (TV); The Golden Moment (TV)
1986 Deadly Sanctuary
1987 Gor; Outlaw Of Gor; Bagdad Cafe
1988 Young Guns*
1989 Batman*; Tango & Cash
1990 Solar Crisis
1991 City Slickers*
1993 Cops And Robbersons

## PALIN, Michael
(1943– ) UK

1970 And Now For Something Completely Different
1974 Monty Python And The Holy Grail
1976 Jabberwocky; Pleasure At Her Majesty's
1979 Monty Python's Life Of Brian; The Secret Policeman's Ball
1980 Time Bandits*
1981 The Secret Policeman's Other Ball
1982 The Missionary; Monty Python Live At The Hollywood Bowl
1983 Monty Python's Meaning Of Life
1984 A Private Function
1985 Brazil*
1988 A Fish Called Wanda*
1991 American Friends

## PARTON, Dolly
(1945–   ) USA

1970  *The Nashville Sound*
1980  *Nine To Five\**
1982  *The Best Little Whorehouse In Texas\**
1984  *Rhinestone*
1986  *A Smoky Mountain Christmas* (TV)
1989  *Steel Magnolias\**
1992  *Straight Talk*


## PECK, Eldred Gregory
(1916–   ) USA

1943  *Days Of Glory*
1944  *The Keys Of The Kingdom*
1945  *The Valley Of Decision; Spellbound\**
1946  *Duel In The Sun\*; The Yearling\**
1947  *Gentleman's Agreement\*; The Macomber Affair; The Paradine Case*
1948  *Yellow Sky*
1949  *The Great Sinner; Twelve O'Clock High\**
1950  *The Gunfighter*
1951  *Captain Horatio Hornblower RN; Only The Valiant*
1952  *David And Bathsheba; The Snows Of Kilimanjaro; The World In His Arms*
1953  *Roman Holiday\*; The Million Pound Note*
1954  *Night People; The Purple Plain*
1956  *The Man In The Grey Flannel Suit; Moby Dick*
1957  *Designing Woman*
1958  *The Bravados; The Big Country\**
1959  *Beloved Infidel; On The Beach; Pork Chop Hill*
1961  *The Guns Of Navarone\**
1962  *Cape Fear\*; How The West Was Won\*; To Kill A Mockingbird\**
1963  *Captain Newman MD*
1964  *Behold A Pale Horse*
1965  *Mirage*
1966  *Arabesque; John F Kennedy: Years Of Lightning, Days Of Drums* (narrator only)
1968  *McKenna's Gold; The Stalking Moon*
1969  *Marooned; The Chairman* (UK: *The Most Dangerous Man In The World*)
1970  *I Walk The Line*
1971  *Shootout*
1972  *The Trial Of The Catsonville Nine* (producer only)
1973  *Billy Two Hats*
1974  *The Dove* (producer only)
1976  *The Omen\**
1977  *MacArthur*
1978  *The Boys From Brazil*
1979  *Ken Murray's Shooting Stars*
1980  *The Sea Wolves*
1982  *The Blue And The Gray* (TV)
1983  *The Scarlet And The Black* (TV)
1986  *Directed By William Wyler* (documentary)
1987  *Amazing Grace And Chuck* (UK: *Silent Voice*)
1989  *Old Gringo\**
1991  *Other People's Money; Cape Fear\**
1992  *The Painting* (TV)


## PENN, Sean
(1960–   ) USA

1980  *The Killing Of Randy Webster* (TV)
1981  *Hellinger's Law* (TV); *Taps*
1982  *Fast Times At Ridgemont High* (UK: *Fast Times*)
1983  *Bad Boys; Crackers*
1984  *Racing With The Moon; The Falcon And The Snowman*
1985  *At Close Range*
1986  *Shanghai Surprise*
1987  *Dear America* (voice only)
1988  *Colors\*; Judgement In Berlin*
1989  *Casualties Of War; We're No Angels*
1990  *Cool Blue; State Of Grace*
1991  *The Indian Runner* (director only)
1993  *Carlito's Way*

## PEPPARD, George
(1928– ) USA

1957 The Strange One (UK: End As A Man)
1959 Pork Chop Hill
1960 Home From The Hill; The Subterraneans
1961 Breakfast At Tiffany's*
1962 How The West Was Won*
1963 The Victors
1964 The Carpetbaggers*
1965 Operation Crossbow; The Third Day
1966 The Blue Max
1967 Rough Night In Jericho; Tobruk
1968 House Of Cards; What's So Bad About Feeling Good?; PJ (UK: New Face In Hell)
1969 Pendulum
1970 The Executioner; Cannon For Cordoba
1971 One More Train To Rob; The Bravos (TV)
1972 The Groundstar Conspiracy
1974 Newman's Law
1975 Guilty Or Innocent: The Sam Sheppard Case; One Of Our Own (TV); Doctors' Secrets (TV)
1977 Damnation Alley
1978 Five Days From Home (also director)
1979 Crisis In Mid-Air (TV); Torn Between Two Lovers (TV); Da Dunkerque Alla Vittoria (UK: From Hell To Victory)
1980 Battle Beyond The Stars; Your Ticket Is No Longer Valid
1981 Helicopter; Race For The Yankee Zephyr
1982 Target Eagle
1983 The A-Team (TV)
1988 Man Against The Mob (TV) (UK: Murder In The City Of Angels)
1989 Silence Like A Glass; Man Against The Mob: The Chinatown Murders (TV)
1990 Night Of The Fox (TV)

## PERKINS, Anthony
(1932–92) USA

1953 The Actress

1956 Friendly Persuasion*
1957 The Lonely Man; Fear Strikes Out; The Tin Star
1958 Desire Under The Elms; The Matchmaker; This Angry Age (UK: The Sea Wall)
1959 Green Mansions; On The Beach
1960 Tall Story; Psycho*
1961 Phaedra; Aimez-Vous Brahms (UK: Goodbye Again)
1962 Five Miles To Midnight; The Trial; Le Glaive Et La Balance (UK: Two Are Guilty)
1963 Une Ravissante Idiote (UK: A Ravishing Idiot)
1965 The Fool Killer
1966 Paris Brûle-T-Il? (UK: Is Paris Burning?)
1967 Le Scandale (UK: The Champagne Murders)
1968 Pretty Poison
1970 How Awful About Allan (TV); WUSA; Catch 22*
1971 La Decade Prodisieuse (UK: Ten Days Wonder); Quelqu'un Derrière La Porte (UK: Two Minds For Murder)
1972 The Life And Times Of Judge Roy Bean; Play It As It Lays
1973 Lovin' Molly
1974 Murder On The Orient Express*
1975 Mahogany
1977 Winter Kills
1978 First, You Cry (TV); Remember My Name; Les Misérables (TV)
1979 North Sea Hijack; Double Negative; The Horror Show; The Black Hole*; Twee Vruowen (UK: Twice A Woman)
1982 For The Term Of His Natural Life (TV); The Sins Of Dorian Gray (TV)
1983 Psycho II
1984 Crimes Of Passion
1986 Psycho III (also director)
1988 Lucky Stiff (director only); Destroyer
1989 Dr Jekyll And Mr Hyde (aka Edge Of Sanity)
1990 Daughter Of Darkness (TV); I'm Dangerous Tonight (TV); Psycho IV (TV)
1991 A Demon In My View

## PESCI, Joe
(1943– ) USA

1961 Hey, Let's Twist (extra)
1975 Death Collector (aka Family Enforcer)
1980 Raging Bull*
1982 I'm Dancing As Fast As I Can; Dear Mr Wonderful; Eureka
1983 Easy Money; Once Upon A Time In America*
1987 Man On Fire
1989 Lethal Weapon 2; Backtrack (UK: Catchfire)
1990 Betsy's Wedding; Goodfellas*; Home Alone*
1991 The Super; JFK*
1992 Lethal Weapon 3; My Cousin Vinny; The Public Eye; Home Alone 2: Lost In New York

## PFEIFFER, Michelle
(1958– ) USA

1979 The Solitary Man (TV)
1980 Falling In Love Again; Hollywood Knights
1981 Charlie Chan And The Curse Of The Dragon Queen; Splendor In The Grass (TV); The Children Nobody Wanted (TV); Callie And Son (TV)
1982 Grease 2
1983 Scarface*
1985 Ladyhawke; Into The Night
1986 Sweet Liberty
1987 Amazon Women On The Moon; The Witches Of Eastwick*
1988 Married To The Mob; Tequila Sunrise*; Dangerous Liaisons*
1989 The Fabulous Baker Boys*
1990 The Russia House
1991 Frankie And Johnny; Love Field
1992 Batman Returns*
1993 Age Of Innocence; Wolf

## PHOENIX, River
(1970– ) USA

1985 Surviving (TV); Explorers
1986 The Mosquito Coast; Circle Of Violence: A Family Drama (TV)

1987 Stand By Me; A Night In The Life Of Jimmy Reardon (UK: Jimmy Reardon)
1988 Little Nikita; Running On Empty
1989 Indiana Jones And The Last Crusade*
1990 I Love You To Death
1991 Dogfight; My Own Private Idaho*
1992 Sneakers; Silent Tongue
1993 The Thing Called Love

## PIDGEON, Walter
(1897–1984) Canada

1925 Mannequin
1926 Old Loves And New; The Outsider; Miss Nobody; Marriage License
1927 The Gorilla; Heart Of Salome; Thirteenth Juror; The Girl From Rio (UK: Lola)
1928 Turn Back The Hours; The Gateway Of The Moon; Woman Wise; Melody Of Love; Clothes Make The Woman
1929 A Most Immoral Lady; Her Private Life
1930 Sweet Kitty Bellairs; Viennese Nights; Show Girl In Hollywood; Bride Of The Regiment (UK: Lady Of The Rose)
1931 Hot Heiress; Going Wild; The Gorilla (remake); Kiss Me Again (UK: The Toast Of The Legion)
1932 Rockabye
1933 The Kiss Before The Mirror
1934 Journal Of A Crime
1935 Good Badminton (short)
1936 Big Brown Eyes; Fatal Lady
1937 As Good As Married; Girl Overboard; A Girl With Ideas; She's Dangerous; Saratoga; My Dear Miss Aldrich
1938 The Shopworn Angel; Man Proof; Listen Darling; Girl Of The Golden West; Too Hot To Handle
1939 Society Lawyer; Stronger Than Desire; 6,000 Enemies; Nick Carter, Master Detective

1940 *Sky Murder; The Dark Command; It's A Date; The House Across The Bay; Phantom Raiders*

1941 *How Green Was My Valley\*; Man Hunt; Blossoms In The Dust; Flight Command; Design For Scandal*

1942 *Mrs Miniver\*; White Cargo*

1943 *The Youngest Profession; Madame Curie\**

1944 *Mrs Parkington*

1945 *Weekend At The Waldorf*

1946 *Holiday In Mexico; The Secret Heart*

1947 *If Winter Comes; Cass Timberlane*

1948 *Julia Misbehaves; Command Decision*

1949 *The Red Danube; That Forsyte Woman* (UK: *The Forsyte Saga*)

1950 *The Miniver Story*

1951 *Soldiers Three; The Unknown Man; Calling Bulldog Drummond; Quo Vadis?\** (narrator only)

1952 *The Sellout; The Bad And The Beautiful\*; Million Dollar Mermaid* (UK: *The One Piece Bathing Suit*)

1953 *Scandal At Scourie*

1954 *The Last Time I Saw Paris; Men Of The Fighting Lady; Executive Suite*

1955 *Hit The Deck; The Glass Slipper* (narrator only)

1956 *Forbidden Planet; The Rack; These Wilder Years*

1961 *Voyage To The Bottom Of The Sea*

1962 *Advise And Consent; Big Red; The Two Colonels*

1963 *Il Giorno Piu Corto Commedia Umaristica*

1966 *How I Spent My Summer Vacation* (UK: *Deadly Roulette*)

1967 *Cosa Nostra: An Arch Enemy Of The FBI* (TV); *Warning Shot*

1968 *Funny Girl\**

1969 *The Vatican Affair; Rascal* (narrator only)

1970 *The House On Greenapple Road* (TV); *The Mask Of Sheba* (TV)

1972 *The Screaming Woman* (TV); *Skyjacked*

1973 *The Neptune Factor; Harry Never Holds* (UK: *Harry In Your Pocket*)

1974 *The Girl On The Late, Late Show* (TV); *The Yellow Headed Summer; Live Again, Die Again* (TV)

1975 *You Lie So Deep, My Love* (TV); *Murder On Flight 502* (TV); *Won Ton Ton — The Dog Who Saved Hollywood*

1976 *The Lindbergh Kidnapping Case* (TV); *Mayday At 40,000 Feet* (TV)

1977 *Sextette*

## PITT, Brad
(1964– ) USA

1990 *Too Young To Die* (TV)

1991 *Thelma And Louise\*; Johnny Suede*

1992 *Cool World; A River Runs Through It*

1993 *Kalifornia; True Romance*

## PLUMMER, Christopher
(1927– ) Canada

1958 *Wind Across The Everglades; Stage Struck; Trans-Canada Journey* (narrator only)

1965 *The Sound Of Music\*; Inside Daisy Clover*

1966 *The Night Of The Generals; Triple Cross*

1967 *Oedipus The King*

1968 *Nobody Runs Forever*

1969 *Lock Up Your Daughters!; Battle Of Britain; The Royal Hunt Of The Sun*

1970 *Waterloo*

1973 *The Pyx*

1974 *The Return Of The Pink Panther*

1975 *Conduct Unbecoming; The Man Who Would Be King\*; The Spiral Staircase*

1976 *Aces High; Assassination!* (UK: *The Day That Shook The World*)

1977 *Uppdragget* (UK: *The Assignment*)

**PLUMMER, Christopher** (cont.)

1978 *The Silent Partner; Murder By Decree; International Velvet; The Disappearance*

1979 *Hanover Street; Star Crash; RIEL; Arthur Miller — On Home Ground* (documentary)

1980 *Highpoint; Somewhere In Time; The Shadow Box* (TV); *Desperate Voyage; Eyewitness* (UK: *The Janitor*)

1981 *Dial M For Murder* (TV); *When The Circus Came To Town* (TV); *Being Different* (narrator only)

1982 *The Amateur; Little Gloria — Happy At Last* (TV)

1983 *The Scarlet And The Black* (TV); *Prototype* (TV); *Játszani Kell* (UK: *Lily In Love*)

1984 *Dreamscape; Ordeal By Innocence*

1985 *The Boy In Blue*

1986 *The Boss's Wife; Vampires In Venice; An American Tail* (voice only)

1987 *Dragnet; Spearfield's Daughter; I Love New York; Souvenir; A Hazard Of Hearts* (TV)

1988 *Stage Fright; Shadow Dancing; Light Years* (voice only)

1989 *Mindfield; Kingsgate*

1990 *Where The Heart Is; The Dispossessed; Firehead; Red-Blooded American Girl; A Ghost In Monte Carlo* (TV)

1991 *Star Trek VI: The Undiscovered Country; Young Catherine* (TV)

1992 *Rock-A-Doodle* (voice only); *Malcolm X*

## POITIER, Sidney
(1924– ) USA

1949 *From Whence Cometh My Help* (documentary)

1950 *No Way Out*

1952 *Cry The Beloved Country; Red Ball Express*

1954 *Go Man Go!*

1955 *The Blackboard Jungle\**

1956 *Goodbye My Lady*

1957 *Edge Of The City* (UK: *A Man Is Ten Feet Tall*); *Something Of Value; Band Of Angels; The Mark Of The Hawk*

1958 *The Defiant Ones\*; Virgin Island*

1959 *Porgy And Bess*

1960 *All The Young Men*

1961 *A Raisin' In The Sun; Paris Blues*

1962 *Pressure Point*

1963 *Lilies Of The Field\*; The Long Ships*

1965 *The Greatest Story Ever Told; The Bedford Incident; The Slender Thread; A Patch Of Blue*

1966 *Duel At Diablo*

1967 *To Sir With Love; In The Heat Of The Night\*; Guess Who's Coming To Dinner\**

1968 *For Love Of Ivy*

1969 *The Lost Man*

1970 *Brother John; They Call Me Mister Tibbs; King: A Filmed Record...Montgomery To Memphis*

1971 *The Organization*

1972 *Buck And The Preacher* (also director)

1973 *A Warm December* (also director)

1974 *Uptown Saturday Night* (also director); *The Wilby Conspiracy*

1975 *Let's Do It Again* (also director)

1977 *A Piece Of The Action* (also director)

1988 *Little Nikita; Shoot To Kill* (UK: *Deadly Pursuit*)

1991 *Separate But Equal* (TV)

1992 *Sneakers*

See also directors listing

## POWELL, Dick
(1904–63) USA

1931 *Street Scene*

1932 *Big City Blues* (voice only); *Too Busy To Work; Blessed Event*

1933 *The King's Vacation; Convention City; 42nd Street\*; Gold Diggers Of 1933\*; Footlight Parade\*; College Coach* (UK: *Football Coach*)

1934 *Twenty Million Sweethearts;*
*Dames; Flirtation Walk;*
*Happiness Ahead; Wonder Bar*
1935 *Gold Diggers Of 1935; Broadway*
*Gondolier; Shipmates Forever;*
*Page Miss Glory; A Midsummer*
*Night's Dream\*; Thanks A Million*
1936 *Stage Struck; Colleen; Hearts*
*Divided; Gold Diggers Of 1937*
1937 *On The Avenue; Varsity Show; The*
*Singing Marine; Hollywood Hotel*
1938 *Cowboy From Brooklyn* (UK:
*Romance And Rythmn*); *Going*
*Places; Hard To Get; For Auld*
*Lang Syne* (short)
1939 *Naughty But Nice*
1940 *Christmas In July; I Want A*
*Divorce*
1941 *In The Navy; Model Wife*
1942 *Star Spangled Rythmn; Happy Go*
*Lucky*
1943 *True To Life; Riding High* (UK:
*Melody Inn*)
1944 *It Happened Tomorrow; Meet The*
*People*
1945 *Murder, My Sweet* (UK: *Farewell*
*My Lovely*); *Cornered*
1947 *Johnny O'Clock*
1948 *Pitfall; To The Ends Of The Earth;*
*Station West; Rogues' Regiment*
1949 *Mrs Mike*
1950 *The Reformer And The Redhead;*
*Right Cross; Cry Danger*
1951 *The Tall Target; Callaway Went*
*Thataway* (UK: *The Star Said*
*No!*); *You Never Can Tell* (UK:
*You Never Know*)
1952 *The Bad And The Beautiful\**
1953 *Split Second* (director only)
1954 *Susan Slept Here*
1956 *The Conqueror; You Can't Run*
*Away From It* (both director only)
1957 *The Enemy Below* (director only)
1958 *The Hunters* (director only)

## POWELL, William

(1892–1984) USA

1922 *When Knighthood Was In Flower;*
*Outcast; Sherlock Holmes* (UK:
*Moriarty*)

1923 *The Bright Shawl*
1924 *Romola; Under The Red Robe;*
*Dangerous Money*
1925 *White Mice; Too Many Kisses;*
*The Beautiful City; Faint Perfume;*
*My Lady's Lips*
1926 *The Runaway; Sea Horses; Beau*
*Geste; The Great Gatsby; Desert*
*Gold; Aloma Of The South Seas;*
*Tin Gods*
1927 *Special Delivery; New York; Paid*
*To Love; Nevada; She's A Sheik;*
*Time For Love; Senorita; Love's*
*Greatest Mistake*
1928 *Partners In Crime; Beau Sabreur;*
*The Dragnet; Forgotten Faces;*
*The Last Command; Feel My*
*Pulse; The Vanishing Pioneer*
1929 *The Greene Murder Case;*
*Interference; The Four Feathers;*
*The Canary Murder Case;*
*Charming Sinners; Pointed Heels*
1930 *Shadow Of The Law; The Benson*
*Murder Case; Street Of Chance;*
*Paramount On Parade; Behind*
*The Makeup; For The Defense*
1931 *The Road To Singapore; Man Of*
*The World; Ladies' Man*
1932 *Jewel Robbery; Lawyer Man; High*
*Pressure; One Way Passage*
1933 *Private Detective 62; The Kennel*
*Murder Case; Double Harness*
1934 *The Key; Manhattan Melodrama;*
*The Thin Man\*; Evelyn Prentice;*
*Fashions Of 1934* (UK: *Fashion*
*Follies Of 1934*)
1935 *Escapade; Star Of Midnight;*
*Reckless; Rendezvous*
1936 *My Man Godfrey; The Great*
*Ziegfeld\*; The Ex-Mrs Bradford;*
*After The Thin Man; Libeled Lady*
1937 *Double Wedding; The Last Of Mrs*
*Cheyney; The Emperor's*
*Candlesticks*
1938 *The Baroness And The Butler*
1939 *Another Thin Man*
1940 *I Love You Again*
1941 *Shadow Of The Thin Man; Love*
*Crazy*
1942 *Crossroads*
1943 *The Youngest Profession*

**POWELL, William** (cont.)
1944 *The Thin Man Goes Home; Ziegfeld Follies\**
1946 *The Hoodlum Saint*
1947 *Song Of The Thin Man; Life With Father\**
1948 *Mr Peabody And The Mermaid; The Senator Was Indiscreet* (UK: *Mr Ashton Was Indiscreet*)
1949 *Take One False Step; Dancing In The Dark*
1951 *It's A Big Country*
1952 *The Treasure Of Lost Canyon*
1953 *The Girl Who Had Everything; How To Marry A Millionaire\**
1955 *Mister Roberts\**

## POWER, Tyrone
(1913–58) USA

1932 *Tom Brown Of Culver*
1934 *Flirtation Walk*
1935 *Northern Frontier*
1936 *Girl's Dormitory; Ladies In Love; Lloyds Of London*
1937 *Thin Ice* (UK: *Lovely To Look At*); *Love Is News; Café Metropole; Second Honeymoon; Ali Baba Goes To Town*
1938 *Marie Antoinette; In Old Chicago\*; Alexander's Ragtime Band; Suez*
1939 *Jesse James\*; The Rains Came; Rose Of Washington Square; Daytime Wife; Second Fiddle*
1940 *Brigham Young; The Mark Of Zorro; Johnny Apollo*
1941 *Blood And Sand; A Yank In The RAF*
1942 *This Above All; Son Of Fury; The Black Swan*
1943 *Crash Dive; Screen Snapshots No 108* (short)
1946 *Razor's Edge\**
1947 *Nightmare Alley; Captain From Castile*
1948 *That Wonderful Urge; The Luck Of The Irish*
1949 *Prince Of Foxes*
1950 *The Black Rose; An American Guerrilla In The Philippines* (UK: *I Shall Return*)

1951 *Rawhide; The House In The Square* (UK: *I'll Never Forget You*)
1952 *Diplomatic Courier; Pony Soldier* (UK: *McDonald Of The Canadian Mounties*)
1953 *King Of The Kyber Rifles; Mississippi Gambler; Memories In Uniform* (short)
1954 *The Long Gray Line*
1955 *Untamed*
1956 *The Eddy Duchin Story*
1957 *Seven Waves Away; The Rising Of The Moon* (narrator only); *Witness For The Prosecution\*; The Sun Also Rises*

## PRESTON, Robert
real name: Robert Preston Meservey
(1917–87) USA

1938 *King Of Alcatraz; Illegal Traffic*
1939 *Union Pacific; Disbarred; Beau Geste\**
1940 *North West Mounted Police; Moon Over Burma; Typhoon*
1941 *The Lady From Cheyenne; New York Town; The Night Of January 16th; Parachute Battalion*
1942 *Wake Island; This Gun For Hire; Pacific Blackout; Star Spangled Rythmn; Reap The Wild Wind\**
1943 *Night Plane From Chungking*
1947 *Variety Girl; The Macomber Affair; Wild Harvest*
1948 *Blood On The Moon; Big City*
1949 *Whispering Smith; The Lady Gambles; Tulsa*
1950 *The Sundowners* (UK: *Thunder In The Dust*)
1951 *My Outlaw Brother; When I Grow Up; Cloudburst; Best Of The Badmen*
1952 *Face To Face*
1955 *The Last Frontier*
1956 *Sentinels In The Air* (narrator only)
1960 *The Dark At The Top Of The Stairs*
1962 *The Music Man\*; How The West Was Won\**

1963 *Island Of Love; All The Way Home*
1972 *Junior Bonner; Child's Play*
1974 *Mame*
1975 *My Father's House* (TV)
1977 *Semi-Tough*
1979 *The Chisholms* (TV)
1981 *SOB*
1982 *Victor/Victoria; Rehearsal For Murder* (TV)
1983 *September Gun* (TV)
1984 *Finnegan Begin Again* (TV); *The Last Starfighter*
1986 *Outrage!* (TV)

## PRICE, Dennis
real name: Dennistoun Rose-Price
(1915–73) UK

1938 *No Parking* (extra)
1944 *A Canterbury Tale*
1945 *A Place Of One's Own; The Echo Murders*
1946 *Caravan; Hungry Hill; The Magic Bow*
1947 *Jassy; Holiday Camp; Master Of Bankdown; Dear Murderer; Easy Money; The White Unicorn*
1948 *Snowbound; Good Time Girl; The Bad Lord Byron*
1949 *Kind Hearts And Coronets*; Helter Skelter; The Lost People*
1950 *The Dancing Years; Murder Without Crime; The Adventurers*
1951 *The Magic Box; The House In The Square; Lady Godiva Rides Again*
1952 *Song Of Paris; Tall Headlines*
1953 *Noose For A Lady; Murder At 3am; The Intruder*
1954 *Eight Witnesses; Time Is My Enemy; For Better, For Worse*
1955 *The Price Of Greed; That Lady; Oh Rosalinda!; Account Closed* (short)
1956 *Private's Progress; Charley Moon; Port Afrique; A Touch Of The Sun*
1957 *The Tommy Steele Story; Fortune Is A Woman; The Naked Truth*
1958 *Hello London*
1959 *Dark At The Night; Danger Within; Don't Panic Chaps; I'm All Right, Jack**

1960 *Piccadilly Third Stop; The Millionairess; Double Bunk; The Rebel; School For Scoundrels; Oscar Wilde; Tunes Of Glory*; No Love For Johnnie*
1961 *The Pure Hell Of St Trinian's; Victim*; Five Golden Hours; Watch It Sailor!; What A Carve Up!*
1962 *The Amorous Prawn; Go To Blazes; Play It Cool; The Pot Carriers; Kill Or Cure; The Cool Mikado; Behave Yourself* (short)
1963 *Doctor In Distress; Tamahine; The Comedy Man; The VIPs; A Jolly Bad Fellow; The Horror Of It All; The Cracksman*
1964 *The Earth Dies Screaming; Murder Most Foul; Curse Of Simba*
1965 *Ten Little Indians; A High Wind In Jamaica*
1966 *Just Like A Woman*
1967 *Rocket To The Moon*
1969 *The Magic Christian; The Haunted House Of Horror*
1970 *Some Will, Some Won't; Count Downe; Venus In Furs; The Horror Of Frankenstein; The Rise And Rise Of Michael Rimmer*
1971 *Vampyros Lesbos; Twins Of Evil*
1972 *Pulp; Tower Of Evil; Alice's Adventures In Wonderland; That's Your Funeral; Go For A Take; The Adventures Of Barry McKenzie; Dracula Contro El Doctor Frankenstein* (UK: *Dracula, Prisoner Of Frankenstein*)
1973 *Horror Hospital; Theatre Of Blood*

## PRICE, Vincent
(1911– ) USA

1938 *Service De Luxe*
1939 *The Private Lives Of Elizabeth And Essex*; Tower Of London; The Invisible Man Returns*
1940 *The House Of Seven Gables; Green Hell; Brigham Young; Hudson's Bay*

**PRICE, Vincent** (cont.)

1943 *The Song Of Bernadette\**
1944 *Wilson\*; The Eve Of St Mark; Laura\*; The Keys Of The Kingdom*
1945 *Leave Her To Heaven; A Royal Scandal* (UK: *Czarina*)
1946 *Dragonwyck; Shock*
1947 *Moss Rose; The Long Night; The Web*
1948 *Abbott And Costello Meet Frankenstein* (UK: *Abbott And Costello Meet The Ghosts*) (voice only); *Up In Central Park; Rogues' Regiment; The Three Musketeers\**
1949 *Bagdad; The Bribe*
1950 *Curtain Call At Cactus Creek* (UK: *Take The Stage*); *Baron Of Arizona; Champagne For Caesar; The Adventures Of Captain Fabian*
1951 *His Kind Of Woman; Pictura: An Adventure In Art*
1952 *The Las Vegas Story*
1953 *House Of Wax*
1954 *Casanova's Big Night; The Mad Magician; Dangerous Mission*
1955 *Son Of Sinbad; The Story Of Colonel Drake* (short)
1956 *Serenade; The Ten Commandments\*; While The City Sleeps*
1957 *The Story Of Mankind*
1958 *The Fly; The House On Haunted Hill*
1959 *The Bat; The Big Circus; The Tingler; Return Of The Fly*
1960 *The Fall Of The House Of Usher*
1961 *Master Of The World; The Pit And The Pendulum; Nefertite, Regina Del Nile* (UK: *Queen Of The Nile*); *Gordon Il Pirata Nero* (UK: *The Black Buccaneer*); *The Last Man On Earth; Naked Terror* (narrator only)
1962 *Tales Of Terror; Tower Of London; Confessions Of An Opium Eater* (UK: *Evils Of Chinatown*); *Convicts Four* (UK: *Reprieve!*)

1963 *Chagall; Taboos Of The World* (both narrator only); *The Raven; Comedy Of Terrors; Twice Told Tales; Diary Of A Madman; Beach Party; The Haunted Palace*
1964 *The Masque Of The Red Death*
1965 *The Tomb Of Ligeia; City Under The Sea; Dr Goldfoot And The Bikini Machine* (UK: *Dr G And The Bikini Machine*)
1966 *Dr Goldfoot And The Girl Bombs* (UK: *Dr G And The Love Bomb*)
1967 *House Of 1,000 Dolls; The Jackals*
1968 *Witchfinder General; More Dead Than Alive*
1969 *The Oblong Box; The Trouble With Girls...And How To Get Into It*
1970 *Scream And Scream Again; Cry Banshee*
1971 *The Abominable Dr Phibes; What's A Nice Girl Like You?* (TV)
1972 *The Aries Computer; Dr Phibes Rises Again*
1973 *Theatre Of Blood*
1974 *Percy's Progress; Madhouse*
1976 *Journey Into Fear; The Butterfly Ball* (narrator only)
1978 *Days Of Fury* (narrator only)
1979 *Scavenger Hunt*
1980 *The Monster Club*
1982 *House Of The Long Shadows; Vincent* (short, voice only)
1983 *Blood Bath At The House Of Death*
1985 *Escapes*
1986 *The Offspring* (aka *From A Whisper To A Scream*); *Basil, The Great Mouse Detective* (voice only)
1987 *The Little Troll Prince* (TV) (voice only); *The Whales Of August*
1988 *Dead Heat*
1989 *Backtrack* (UK: *Catchfire*)
1990 *Edward Scissorhands\**

**PRYOR, Richard**
(1940–   ) USA

1967 *The Busy Body*
1968 *Wild In The Streets; The Green Berets*

1969 *The Young Lawyers* (TV)
1970 *The Phynx; Carter's Army* (TV)
1971 *You've Got To Walk It Like You Talk It Or You'll Lose That Beat; Dynamite Chicken; Richard Pryor — Live And Smokin'*
1972 *Lady Sings The Blues*
1973 *Wattstax; The Mack; Hit!; Some Call It Loving*
1974 *Uptown Saturday Night; Blazing Saddles\** (co-writer only)
1975 *Adios Amigo*
1976 *The Bingo Long Travelling All-Stars And Motor Kings; Car Wash; Silver Streak\**
1977 *Greased Lightning; Which Way Is Up?*
1978 *Blue Collar; The Wiz; California Suite\**
1979 *The Muppet Movie\*; Richard Pryor Live In Concert; Richard Pryor Is Back Live In Concert*
1980 *In God We Trust; Wholly Moses!; Stir Crazy\**
1981 *Bustin' Loose*
1982 *Richard Pryor Live On The Sunset Strip; Some Kind Of A Hero; The Toy*
1983 *Richard Pryor Here And Now; Superman III*
1985 *Brewster's Millions*
1986 *Jo, Jo Dancer Your Life Is Calling* (also director)
1987 *Critical Condition*
1988 *Moving*
1989 *See No Evil, Hear No Evil; Harlem Nights*
1990 *Look Who's Talking Too* (voice only)
1991 *Another You*

# Q

## QUAID, Dennis
(1954–   ) USA

1975 *Crazy Mama*
1977 *9/30/55; I Never Promised You A Rose Garden*

1978 *Are You In The House Alone?* (TV); *Seniors* (TV); *Our Winning Season*
1979 *Amateur Night At The Dixie Bar And Grill* (TV); *Breaking Away\**
1980 *The Long Riders; Gorp*
1981 *All Night Long; Caveman; The Night The Lights Went Out In Georgia; Bill* (TV)
1982 *Johnny Belinda* (TV); *Tough Enough*
1983 *Jaws 3-D; The Right Stuff\*; Bill: On His Own* (TV)
1984 *Dreamscape*
1985 *Enemy Mine*
1987 *The Big Easy\*; Innerspace; Suspect\**
1988 *DOA; Everybody's All-American* (UK: *When I Fall In Love*)
1989 *Great Balls Of Fire*
1990 *Come See The Paradise; Postcards From The Edge\**
1993 *Wilder Napalm; Undercover Blues; Flesh And Bone*

## QUAYLE, Anthony
(1913–89) UK

1935 *Moscow Nights*
1938 *Pygmalion\**
1948 *Hamlet\*; Saraband For Dead Lovers*
1955 *Oh, Rosalinda!*
1956 *The Battle Of The River Plate; The Wrong Man*
1957 *Woman In A Dressing Gown; No Time For Tears*
1958 *The Man Who Wouldn't Talk; Ice Cold In Alex*
1959 *Tarzan's Greatest Adventure; Serious Charge*
1960 *The Challenge*
1961 *The Guns Of Navarone\*; Drums For A Queen* (narrator only)
1962 *HMS Defiant; Lawrence Of Arabia\*; This Is Lloyd's* (narrator only)
1963 *The Fall Of The Roman Empire*
1964 *East Of Sudan*

**QUAYLE, Anthony** (cont.)

1965 *Operation Crossbow; A Study In Terror*

1966 *The Poppy Is Also A Flower* (UK: *Danger Grows Wild*)

1967 *Incompreso* (UK: *Misunderstood*)

1968 *McKenna's Gold*

1969 *Island Unknown* (narrator only); *Destiny Of A Spy* (TV); *Before Winter Comes; Anne Of The Thousand Days**

1972 *Everything You Always Wanted To Know About Sex But Were Afraid To Ask*

1973 *Bequest To The Nation; Jarrett* (TV)

1974 *The Tamarind Seed; QB VII* (TV)

1975 *Moses* (TV); *Great Expectations* (TV)

1976 *The Eagle Has Landed; 21 Hours At Munich* (TV)

1977 *Holocaust 2000*

1978 *Murder By Decree*

1980 *Masada* (TV)

1981 *Dial M For Murder* (TV); *The Manions Of America* (TV)

1984 *The Last Days Of Pompeii* (TV)

1988 *Buster; The Bourne Identity* (TV); *The Legend Of The Holy Drinker*

1989 *The Confessional* (TV); *King Of The Wind*


**QUINN, Anthony**
(1915–   )

1936 *The Milky Way; Parole!; Sworn Enemy; Night Waitress; The Plainsman*

1937 *Swing High, Swing Low; Waikiki Wedding; Last Train From Madrid; Partners In Crime; Daughter Of Shanghai* (UK: *Daughter Of The Orient*)

1938 *The Buccaneer; Tip-Off Girls; Dangerous To Know; Bulldog Drummond In Africa; Hunted Men; King Of Alcatraz*

1939 *Island Of Lost Men; King Of Chinatown; Union Pacific; Television Spy*

1940 *Road To Singapore; Parole Fixer; Emergency Squad; City For Conquest; The Ghost Breakers*

1941 *Thieves Fall Out; Kockout; Texas Rangers Ride Again; Blood And Sand; Bullets For O'Hara; They Died With Their Boots On; The Perfect Snob*

1942 *The Black Swan; Road To Morocco; Larceny Inc*

1943 *The Ox-Bow Incident** (UK: *Strange Incident*); *Guadalcanal Diary*

1944 *Buffalo Bill; Roger Touhy, Gangster* (UK: *The Last Gangster*); *Ladies Of Washington; Irish Eyes Are Smiling*

1945 *Where Do We Go From Here?; China Sky; Back To Bataan*

1946 *California; The Imperfect Lady* (UK: *Mrs Loring's Secret*)

1947 *Sinbad The Sailor; Black Gold; Tycoon*

1951 *The Brave Bulls; Mask Of The Avenger*

1952 *Viva Zapata!; The World In His Arms; The Brigand; Against All Flags*

1953 *City Beneath The Sea; Seminole; Ride, Vaquero!; East Of Sumatra; Blowing Wild; Donne Proibite* (UK: *Forbidden Women*); *Cavallerla Rusticana*

1954 *Ulysses; Attila The Hun; The Long Wait; La Strada**

1955 *The Naked Street; Seven Cities Of Gold; The Magnificent Matador* (UK: *The Brave And The Beautiful*)

1956 *The Man From Del Rio; Lust For Life**; *The Wild Party*

1957 *The River's Edge; The Ride Back; The Hunchback Of Notre Dame; Wild Is The Wind*

1958 *Hot Spell; Last Train From Gun Hill; The Buccaneer* (director only)

1959 *The Black Orchid; Warlock; The Savage Innocents*

1960 *Heller In Pink Tights; Portrait In Black*

1961 *The Guns Of Navarone**

1962 *Barabbas; Lawrence Of Arabia\*;*
*Requiem For A Heavyweight* (UK:
*Blood Money*)
1964 *Behold A Pale Horse; The Visit;*
*Zorba The Greek\*; The Fabulous*
*Adventures Of Marco Polo* (UK:
*Marco The Magnificent*)
1965 *A High Wind In Jamaica*
1966 *The Lost Command; The*
*Happening*
1967 *The Rover; The 25th Hour*
1968 *Guns For San Sebastian; The*
*Shoes Of The Fisherman; The*
*Magus*
1969 *The Secret Of Santa Vittoria; A*
*Dream Of Kings*
1970 *A Walk In The Spring Rain; RPM;*
*Flap* (UK: *The Last Warrior*); *King:*
*A Filmed Record...Montgomery*
*To Memphis*
1971 *The City* (TV); *Forbidden*
*Knowledge* (TV); *Arruza* (narrator
only)
1972 *Across 110th Street; The Voice Of*
*La Raza*
1973 *Los Amigos* (UK: *Deaf Smith And*
*Johnny Ears*); *The Don Is Dead*
1974 *The Marseilles Contract*
1975 *Bluff: Storia De Truffe E Di*
*Imbroglioni; L'Eredità Ferramonti*
(UK: *The Inheritance*)
1976 *Tigers Don't Cry; Al-Risalah* (UK:
*The Message*)
1977 *Jesus Of Nazareth* (TV)
1978 *The Greek Tycoon; Caravans;*
*The Children Of Sanchez; The*
*Passage*
1980 *Omar Mukhtar — Lion Of The*
*Desert; The Contender*
1981 *High Risk; The Salamander;*
*Bon Appetit; The Dream Of*
*Tangier*
1982 *Regina; Valentina*
1983 *1919 — Crónica Del Alba*
1984 *The Last Days Of Pompeii* (TV)
1987 *L'Isola Del Tesoro* (TV) (UK:
*Treasure Island*)
1988 *Stradivarius; Tough Guys In*
*Marseilles; A Man Of Passion;*
*Onassis: The Richest Man In The*
*World* (TV)

1990 *The Old Man And The Sea* (TV);
*Revenge; A Star For Two; Ghosts*
*Can't Do It*
1991 *Jungle Fever\*; Mobsters; Only*
*The Lonely*
1993 *The Last Action Hero*

# R

## RAFT, George
real name: George Rauft
(1895–1980) USA

1929 *Queen Of The Night Clubs*
1931 *Goldie; Quick Millions; Hush*
*Money; Palmy Days*
1932 *Night World; Dancers In The*
*Dark; Night After Night; Scarface\*;*
*If I Had A Million; Undercover*
*Man; Taxi; Love Is A Racket;*
*Madame Racketeer* (UK: *The*
*Sporting Widow*)
1933 *The Bowery; Pick-Up; Midnight*
*Club*
1934 *The Trumpet Blows; All Of Me;*
*Bolero; Limehouse Blues*
1935 *Rumba; The Glass Key; She*
*Couldn't Take It; Every Night At*
*Eight; Stolen Harmony*
1936 *It Had To Happen; Yours For The*
*Asking*
1937 *Souls At Sea*
1938 *You And Me; Spawn Of The*
*North; The Lady's From Kentucky*
1939 *Each Dawn I Die; I Stole A Million;*
*Invisible Stripes*
1940 *The House Across The Bay; They*
*Drive By Night* (UK: *The Road To*
*Frisco*)
1941 *Manpower*
1942 *Broadway*
1943 *Background To Danger; Stage*
*Door Canteen*
1944 *Follow The Boys*
1945 *Nob Hill; Johnny Angel*
1946 *Whistle Stop; Mr Ace; Nocturne*
1947 *Christmas Eve; Intrigue*
1948 *Race Street*
1949 *Outpost In Morocco; Johnny*
*Allegro* (UK: *Hounded*); *Nous*

**RAFT, George** (cont.)
Irons A Paris (UK: Let's Go To Paris); A Dangerous Profession; Red Light
1951 Lucky Nick Cain (UK: I'll Get You For This)
1952 Loan Shark; Adventures In Algiers (aka Secret Of The Casbah); Escape Route
1953 Man From Cairo (UK: Crime Squad)
1954 Rogue Cop; Black Widow
1955 A Bullet For Joey
1956 Around The World In 80 Days*
1959 Jet Over The Atlantic; Some Like It Hot*
1960 Oceans' Eleven*
1961 The Ladies' Man
1964 The Patsy; For Those Who Think Young
1965 Du Rififi A Paname (UK: Rififi In Paris)
1967 Five Golden Dragons; Casino Royale
1968 Skidoo
1972 Hammersmith Is Out; Deadhead Miles
1977 Sextette
1979 The Man With Bogart's Face


**RAINER, Luise**
(1909–   ) Austria

1930 Ja, Der Himmel Über Wien
1931 Sehnsucht 202
1933 Heut'Kommt's Drauf An
1935 Escapade
1936 The Great Ziegfeld*
1937 The Good Earth*; The Big City; The Emperor's Candlesticks
1938 The Great Waltz; The Toy Wife (UK: Frou Frou); Dramatic School
1943 Hostages


**RAINS, Claude**
full name: William Claude Rains
(1889–1967) UK

1920 Build Thy House

1933 The Invisible Man
1934 Crime Without Passion
1935 The Man Who Reclaimed His Head; The Mystery Of Edwin Drood; The Clairvoyant; The Last Outpost
1936 Hearts Divided; Anthony Adverse; Stolen Holiday
1937 The Prince And The Pauper; They Won't Forget
1938 The Adventures Of Robin Hood*; Gold Is Where You Find It; Four Daughters; White Banners
1939 Daughters Courageous; They Made Me A Criminal; Juarez; Four Wives; Mr Smith Goes To Washington*; Sons Of Liberty (short)
1940 The Sea Hawk*; Lady With Red Hair; Saturday's Children
1941 Four Mothers; The Wolf Man; Here Comes Mr Jordan*
1942 King's Row*; Now Voyager*; Moontide; Casablanca*
1943 Forever And A Day; Phantom Of The Opera
1944 Passage To Marseilles; Mr Skeffington
1945 Caesar And Cleopatra; This Love Of Ours; Strange Holiday (UK: The Day After Tomorrow)
1946 Angel On My Shoulder; Notorious*; Deception
1947 The Unsuspected
1948 Rope Of Sand; Song Of Surrender; The Passionate Friends
1950 The White Tower; Where Danger Lives
1951 Sealed Cargo
1952 The Man Who Watched Trains Go By
1956 Lisbon
1959 This Earth Is Mine
1960 The Lost World
1961 Battle Of The Worlds
1962 Lawrence Of Arabia*
1963 Twilight Of Honor (UK: The Charge Murder)
1965 The Greatest Story Ever Told

## RAMPLING, Charlotte
(1945–   ) UK

1965 *The Knack...And How To Get It; Rotten To The Core*
1966 *Georgy Girl\**
1967 *The Long Duel*
1968 *Sequestro Di Persona* (UK: *Island Of Crime*)
1969 *La Caduta Degli Dei\** (UK: *The Damned*); *How To Make It* (UK: *Target: Harry*); *Three*
1970 *Zabriskie Point*
1971 *The Ski Bum;'Tis Pity She's A Whore; Corky*
1972 *Henry VIII And His Six Wives; Asylum*
1973 *Zardoz; Revolt Of The City*
1974 *The Night Porter; Caravan To Vacarres; La Chair De L'Orchidée*
1975 *Farewell My Lovely; Foxtrot; Yuppi-Du*
1976 *Sherlock Holmes In New York* (TV)
1977 *Taxi Mauve; Orca — Killer Whale*
1979 *Bugsy*
1980 *Stardust Memories*
1982 *The Verdict\**
1984 *Vive La Vie*
1985 *Tristesse Et Beauté; On Ne Meurt Que Deux Fois* (UK: *He Died With His Eyes Open*)
1987 *Angel Heart; Mascara*
1988 *DOA; Rebus; Paris By Night*
1989 *Helmut Newton: Frames From The Edge* (documentary); *Tre Colonne In Cronaca*
1992 *Hammers Over The Anvil; Une Femme Abandonée* (TV)
1993 *Time Is Money*


## RATHBONE, Philip Basil
(1892–1967) USA

1921 *Innocent; The Fruitful Vine*
1923 *The Loves Of Mary, Queen Of Scots; The School For Scandal*
1924 *Trouping With Ellen*
1925 *The Masked Bride*
1926 *The Great Deception*
1929 *The Last Of Mrs Cheyney; Barnum Was Right*
1930 *The Bishop Murder Case; A Notorious Affair; This Mad World; The Flirting Widow; A Lady Surrenders* (UK: *Blind Wives*); *The Lady Of Scandal* (UK: *High Road*); *Sin Takes A Holiday*
1931 *Once A Lady*
1932 *A Woman Commands; After The Ball*
1933 *One Precious Year; Loyalties*
1935 *David Copperfield\*; Anna Karenina\*; The Last Days Of Pompeii; A Feather In Her Hat; Captain Blood\*; A Tale Of Two Cities\**
1936 *Kind Lady* (UK: *House Of Menace*); *Private Number* (UK: *Secret Interlude*); *Romeo And Juliet; The Garden Of Allah*
1937 *Confession; Love From A Stranger; Make A Wish; Tovarich*
1938 *The Adventures Of Marco Polo; The Adventures Of Robin Hood\*; If I Were King; The Dawn Patrol*
1939 *Son Of Frankenstein; The Hound Of The Baskervilles; The Sun Never Sets; The Adventures Of Sherlock Holmes* (UK: *Sherlock Holmes*); *Rio; Tower Of London*
1940 *Rhythmn On The River; The Mark Of Zorro; The Mad Doctor* (UK: *A Date With Destiny*)
1941 *The Black Cat; International Lady; Paris Calling; Screen Snapshots No 87* (short)
1942 *Fingers At The Window; Crossroads; Sherlock Holmes And The Voice Of Terror; Sherlock Holmes And The Secret Weapon*
1943 *Sherlock Holmes In Washington; Crazy House; Above Suspicion; Sherlock Holmes Faces Death; Sherlock Holmes And The Spiderwoman* (UK: *Spiderwoman*)
1944 *The Scarlet Claw; Bathing Beauty; The Pearl Of Death; Frenchman's Creek*

**RATHBONE, Philip Basil** (cont.)

1945 *The House Of Fear; The Woman In Green; Pursuit To Algiers*

1946 *Terror By Night; Heartbeat; Dressed To Kill* (UK: *Sherlock Holmes And The Secret Code*)

1949 *The Adventures Of Ichabod And Mr Toad* (narrator only)

1954 *Casanova's Big Night*

1955 *We're No Angels*

1956 *The Court Jester; The Black Sleep*

1958 *The Last Hurrah*

1961 *The Magic Sword; Pontius Pilate*

1962 *Red Hell; Tales Of Terror; Two Before Zero* (narrator only)

1963 *The Comedy Of Terrors*

1966 *Ghost In The Invisible Bikini; Planet Of Blood*

1967 *Voyage To A Prehistoric Planet* (UK: *Prehistoric Planet Women*); *Dr Rock And Mr Roll; Autopsy Of A Ghost; Hillbillys In A Haunted House*

## REAGAN, Ronald
(1911–　) USA

1937 *Love Is In The Air* (UK: *The Radio Murder Mystery*); *Submarine D-I; Hollywood Hotel; Swing Your Lady*

1938 *Cowboy From Brooklyn; Sergeant Murphy; Brother Rat; Girls On Probation; Boy Meets Girl; Going Places; Accidents Will Happen*

1939 *Code Of The Secret Service ; Dark Victory*; Hell's Kitchen; Smashing The Money Ring; Angels Wash Their Faces; Naughty But Nice; Secret Service Of The Air*

1940 *Brother Rat And A Baby* (UK: *Baby Be Good*); *Murder In The Air; Tugboat Annie Sails Again; Knute Rockne — All American* (UK: *A Modern Hero*); *Santa Fé Trail; Angel From Texas*

1941 *Nine Lives Are Not Enough; International Squadron; Million Dollar Baby; The Bad Man* (UK:

*Two Gun Cupid*); *How To Improve Your Golf* (short)

1942 *King's Row*; Juke Girl; Desperate Journey; Mr Gardenia Jones* (short)

1943 *Rear Gunner; Hollywood In Uniform* (both shorts); *This Is The Army*

1944 *For God And Country* (short)

1947 *That Hagen Girl; Stallion Road; The Voice Of The Turtle; So You Want To Be In Pictures* (short)

1948 *Studio Tour; OK For Pictures* (both shorts)

1949 *Night Unto Night; John Loves Mary; The Girl From Jones Beach; It's A Great Feeling; The Hasty Heart*

1950 *Louisa; Storm Warning*

1951 *The Last Outpost; Bedtime For Bonzo; Hong Kong*

1952 *The Winning Team; She's Working Her Way Through College*

1953 *Law And Order; Tropic Zone*

1954 *Prisoner Of War; Cattle Queen Of Montana*

1955 *Tennessee's Partner*

1957 *Hellcats Of The Navy*

1961 *The Young Doctors* (narrator only)

1963 *The Truth About Communism* (narrator only)

1964 *The Killers*

## REDFORD, Charles Robert
(1937–　) USA

1960 *In The Presence Of Mine Enemies* (TV)

1962 *War Hunt*

1965 *Situation Hopeless But Not Serious; Inside Daisy Clover*

1966 *The Chase; This Property Is Condemned*

1967 *Barefoot In The Park**

1969 *Tell Them Willie Boy Is Here; Butch Cassidy And The Sundance Kid*; Downhill Racer; The Making Of Butch Cassidy And The Sundance Kid* (documentary)

1970 *Little Fauss And Big Halsy*

1972 *Jeremiah Johnson; The Candidate; The Hot Rock* (UK: *How To Steal A Diamond In Four Uneasy Lessons*)
1973 *The Way We Were\*; The Sting\**
1974 *The Great Gatsby*
1975 *The Great Waldo Pepper; Three Days Of The Condor\**
1976 *All The President's Men\**
1977 *A Bridge Too Far*
1979 *The Electric Horseman\**
1980 *Brubaker*
1984 *The Natural*
1985 *Out Of Africa\**
1986 *Legal Eagles*
1990 *Havana*
1991 *Incident At Oglala* (narrator only)
1992 *Sneakers*
1993 *Indecent Proposal*

See also directors listing


## REDGRAVE, Lynn
(1943–   ) UK

1963 *Tom Jones\**
1964 *The Girl With Green Eyes*
1966 *The Deadly Affair; Georgy Girl\**
1967 *Smashing Time*
1969 *The Virgin Soldiers; Last Of The Mobile Hot Shots* (aka *Blood Kin*)
1971 *Los Guerilleros*
1972 *Viva La Muerta-Tua!; Everything You Always Wanted To Know About Sex But Were Afraid To Ask; Every Little Crook And Nanny*
1973 *The National Health*
1975 *The Happy Hooker; Don't Turn The Other Cheek*
1976 *The Big Bus*
1978 *Sooner Or Later* (TV)
1980 *Gauguin — The Savage* (TV); *The Seduction Of Miss Leona* (TV); *Sunday Lovers*
1982 *The Bad Seed* (TV); *Rehearsal For Murder* (TV)
1986 *My Two Loves* (TV)
1987 *Morgan Stewart's Coming Home*
1988 *Death Of A Son* (TV)

1989 *Midnight; Getting It Right; Jury Duty; The Comedy* (TV)
1991 *What Ever Happened To Baby Jane?* (TV)


## REDGRAVE, Sir Michael
(1908–85) UK

1936 *Secret Agent*
1938 *The Lady Vanishes\*; Stolen Life; Climbing High*
1939 *A Window In London; The Stars Look Down*
1941 *Kipps; Jeannie; Atlantic Ferry; The Big Blockade*
1942 *Thunder Rock*
1945 *The Way To The Stars; Dead Of Night; A Diary For Timothy* (narrator only)
1946 *The Captive Heart; The Years Between*
1947 *The Man Within; Fame Is The Spur; Mourning Becomes Electra*
1948 *Secret Beyond The Door*
1949 *Her Fighting Chance* (short, narrator only)
1951 *Painter And Poet; Winter Garden* (both shorts, both narrator only); *The Browning Version; The Magic Box*
1952 *The Importance Of Being Earnest*
1954 *The Sea Shall Not Have Them; The Green Scarf; The Dam Busters*
1955 *Oh Rosalinda!; The Night My Number Came Up; 1984; Confidential Report; The Lake District* (short, narrator only)
1956 *The Happy Road; Kings And Queens* (short, narrator only)
1957 *Time Without Pity*
1958 *The Quiet American; Law And Disorder; Behind The Mask; The Immortal Land* (short, narrator only)
1959 *Shake Hands With The Devil; The Wreck Of The Mary Deare*
1960 *May Wedding; The Questioning City* (both shorts, both narrator only)

**REDGRAVE, Sir Michael** (cont.)
1961 *No, My Darling Daughter; The Innocents*
1962 *The Loneliness Of The Long Distance Runner*
1963 *Uncle Vanya*
1964 *Young Cassidy*
1965 *The Hill; The Heroes Of Telemark*
1966 *Palaces Of A Queen* (narrator only)
1967 *The 25th Hour; Assignment K; October Revolution* (narrator only)
1968 *Heidi Comes Home* (TV)
1969 *Oh! What A Lovely War; Goodbye Mr Chips; Connecting Rooms; David Copperfield* (TV); *Battle Of Britain*
1970 *Goodbye Gemini*
1971 *The Go-Between; Nicholas And Alexandra*


**REDGRAVE, Vanessa**
(1937–   ) UK

1958 *Behind The Mask*
1961 *The Circus At Clopton Hall* (narrator only)
1966 *Morgan — A Suitable Case For Treatment; A Man For All Seasons\*; Blow-Up*
1967 *Tonite Let's All Make Love In London* (documentary); *Red And Blue; Sailor From Gibraltar; Camelot\**
1968 *The Charge Of The Light Brigade; Isadora; The Seagull*
1969 *Un Tranquillo Posto Di Campagna* (UK: *A Quiet Place In The Country*); *Oh! What A Lovely War*
1970 *La Vacanza* (UK: *Drop Out!*); *The Body* (narrator only)
1971 *The Devils; The Trojan Women; Mary Queen Of Scots*
1974 *Murder On The Orient Express\**
1975 *Out Of Season*
1976 *The Seven Percent Solution*
1977 *Julia\**
1978 *Agatha; The Palestinian*
1979 *Yanks; Bear Island*
1980 *Playing For Time* (TV)

1982 *Wagner* (TV); *My Body, My Child* (TV)
1983 *Sing Sing*
1984 *The Bostonians; Steaming*
1985 *Wetherby; Three Sovereigns For Sarah* (TV)
1986 *Second Serve* (TV)
1987 *Prick Up Your Ears\**
1988 *Consuming Passions; A Man For All Seasons* (TV)
1990 *Diceria Dell'Untore; Orpheus Descending* (TV); *Romeo–Juliet* (voice only)
1991 *The Ballad Of The Sad Café; What Ever Happened To Baby Jane?* (TV); *Young Catherine* (TV)
1992 *Howard's End\**
1993 *Le Maître Savane; Mother's Boys; Great Moments In Aviation; The House Of The Spirits*


**REED, Donna**
real name: Donna Mullenger
(1921–86) USA

1941 *Babes On Broadway; The Get-Away; The Bugle Sounds; Shadow Of The Thin Man*
1942 *Mokey; Calling Dr Gillespie; Apache Trail; The Courtship Of Andy Hardy; Eyes In The Night*
1943 *Thousands Cheer; The Human Comedy; Dr Gillespie's Criminal Case* (UK: *Crazy To Kill*); *The Man From Down Under*
1944 *Gentle Annie; See Here, Private Hargrove; Mrs Parkington*
1945 *The Picture Of Dorian Gray; They Were Expendable*
1946 *Faithful In My Fashion; It's A Wonderful Life\**
1947 *Green Dolphin Street*
1948 *Beyond Glory*
1949 *Chicago Deadline*
1951 *Scandal Sheet* (UK: *The Dark Page*); *Saturday's Hero* (UK: *Idols In The Dust*)
1952 *Hangman's Knot*
1953 *Hollywood Laugh Parade* (short); *Raiders Of The Seven Seas; Trouble Along The Way; The*

Caddy; From Here To Eternity*;
Gun Fury
1954 Three Hours To Kill; The Last
Time I Saw Paris; They Rode
West
1955 The Far Horizons
1956 Ransom!; The Benny Goodman
Story; Backlash; Beyond Mombasa
1958 The Whole Truth
1960 Pepe
1974 The Yellow Headed Summer
1979 The Best Place To Be (TV)
1983 Deadly Lessons
1987 Arriva Frank Capra (documentary)

## REED, Oliver
(1937– ) UK

1955 Value For Money
1958 Hello London; The Square Peg;
The Captain's Table
1959 'Beat' Girl; The Angry Silence
1960 The League Of Gentlemen; The
Two Faces Of Dr Jekyll; Sword Of
Sherwood Forest; His And Hers;
No Love For Johnnie; The Rebel;
The Bulldog Breed
1961 The Curse Of The Werewolf; The
Pirates Of Blood River
1962 Captain Clegg; The Damned;
Paranoiac; The Party's Over
1963 The Scarlet Blade
1964 The System
1965 The Brigand Of Kandahar
1966 The Trap
1967 The Shuttered Room; The Jokers;
I'll Never Forget What's 'Is Name
1968 Oliver!*; Hannibal Brooks; The
Assassination Bureau
1969 Women In Love*; Take A Girl Like
You
1970 The Lady In The Car With
Glasses And A Gun
1971 The Devils; The Hunting Party
1972 Sitting Target; ZPG (UK: Zero
Population Growth); The Age Of
Pisces; The Triple Echo
1973 Mordi E Fuggi (UK: Bite And
Run); Un Uomo (UK: Fury); The
Three Musketeers*; Blue Blood;
Revolver

1974 And Then There Were None; The
Four Musketeers; Tommy
1975 Lisztomania; Royal Flash; The
Sellout; Blood In The Streets
1976 The Great Scout And Cathouse
Thursday; Burnt Offerings
1977 The Prince And The Pauper;
Tomorrow Never Comes; Assault
On Paradise (UK: Ransom)
1978 The Big Sleep; The Class Of Miss
MacMichael; Touch Of The Sun
1979 The Brood
1980 Omar Mukhtar—Lion Of The
Desert; Dr Heckyl And Mr Hype;
Condorman
1981 Spasms; Venom
1982 The Great Question; Clash Of
Loyalties; Masquerade (TV)
1983 The Sting II; 99 Women; Frank
And I; Fanny Hill; Two Of A Kind
1984 The Black Arrow (TV)
1986 Captive; Last Of The Templars
1987 Castaway; Wheels Of Terror; Gor;
Dragonard; Skeleton Coast; Rage
To Kill
1988 Damnation Express; Captive
Rage; Hold My Hand, I'm Dying;
The Adventures Of Baron
Munchausen*
1989 The Return Of The Musketeers;
The Lady And The Highwayman
(TV); Treasure Island (TV); The
Revenger (TV)
1990 A Ghost In Monte Carlo (TV); The
House Of Usher; Panama Sugar
1991 Army; The Pit And The Pendulum;
Prisoners Of Honor (TV)

## REEVE, Christopher
(1952– ) USA

1977 Gray Lady Down
1978 Superman*
1980 Somewhere In Time; Superman II
1982 Deathtrap; Monsignor
1983 Superman III
1984 The Bostonians
1985 The Aviator; Anna Karenina (TV)
1987 Street Smart; Superman IV: The
Quest For Peace; Switching
Channels

**REEVE, Christopher** (cont.)
1988 *The Great Escape: The Untold Story* (TV)
1990 *Midnight Spy; The Rose And The Jackal* (TV)
1991 *The Horror Of Charles Dexter Ward*
1992 *Noises Off; Nightmare In The Daylight* (TV)
1993 *The Remains Of The Day*

## REEVES, Keanu
(1964– ) USA

1985 *Act Of Vengeance* (TV)
1986 *Under The Influence* (TV); *Youngblood; Brotherhood Of Justice* (TV); *Babes In Toyland* (TV)
1987 *I Wish I Were Eighteen Again* (TV); *River's Edge**
1988 *Permanent Record; The Prince Of Pennsylvania; Dangerous Liaisons**
1989 *Bill And Ted's Excellent Adventure*; Parenthood**
1990 *I Love You To Death; Aunt Julia And The Scriptwriter*
1991 *Point Break*; Bill And Ted's Bogus Journey; My Own Private Idaho**
1992 *Bram Stoker's Dracula**
1993 *Freakz; Much Ado About Nothing; The Little Buddha; Even Cowgirls Get The Blues*

## REMICK, Lee
(1935–91) USA

1957 *A Face In The Crowd*
1958 *The Long Hot Summer*
1959 *These Thousand Hills; Anatomy Of A Murder**
1960 *Wild River*
1961 *Sanctuary*
1962 *Experiment In Terror* (UK: *Grip Of Fear*); *Days Of Wine And Roses**
1963 *The Running Man; The Wheeler Dealers* (UK: *Separate Beds*)
1965 *Baby, The Rain Must Fall; The Hallelujah Trail*

1968 *No Way To Treat A Lady; The Detective*
1969 *Hard Contract*
1970 *A Severed Head; Loot*
1971 *Sometimes A Great Notion* (UK: *Never Give An Inch*)
1972 *Of Men And Women* (TV); *And No One Could Save Her* (TV)
1973 *The Blue Knight* (TV); *A Delicate Balance*
1974 *A Girl Named Sooner* (TV); *QB VII* (TV)
1975 *Hustling* (TV); *Hennessy*
1976 *Touch Me Not* (aka *The Hunted*); *The Omen**
1977 *Telefon*
1978 *The Medusa Touch; Breaking Up* (TV)
1979 *The Europeans; Ike* (TV); *Torn Between Two Lovers* (TV)
1980 *Tribute; The Women's Room* (TV); *The Competition*
1981 *The Letter* (TV); *Haywire* (TV)
1983 *A Gift Of Love: A Christmas Story* (TV)
1984 *Mistral's Daughter* (TV); *Rearview Murder* (TV); *A Good Sport* (TV)
1985 *Toughlove* (TV)
1986 *Emma's War; Of Pure Blood* (TV)
1987 *The Vision* (TV)
1988 *Jesse* (TV)
1989 *Bridge To Silence* (TV); *Dark Holiday* (TV)

## REYNOLDS, Burt
full name: Burton Reynolds
(1936– ) USA

1960 *Angel Baby*
1961 *Armored Command*
1965 *Last Message From Saigon* (UK: *Operation CIA*)
1966 *Un Dollaro A Testa* (UK: *Navajo Joe*)
1968 *Impasse; Fade-In*
1969 *Shark!; 100 Rifles; Sam Whiskey*
1970 *Skullduggery; Run Simon Run* (TV); *Hunters Are For Killing* (TV)
1972 *Everything You Always Wanted To Know About Sex But Were Afraid To Ask; Deliverance*; Fuzz*

1973 *Shamus; White Lightning; The Man Who Loved Cat Dancing*
1974 *The Longest Yard\** (UK: *The Mean Machine*)
1975 *WW And The Dixie Dancekings; At Long Last Love; Hustle; Lucky Lady*
1976 *Gator* (also director); *Nickelodeon; Silent Movie*
1977 *Smokey And The Bandit; Semi-Tough*
1978 *Hooper; The End* (also director)
1979 *Starting Over*
1980 *Smokey And The Bandit II* (UK: *Smokey And The Bandit Ride Again*); *Rough Cut*
1981 *The Cannonball Run\*; Paternity; Sharky's Machine* (also director)
1982 *The Best Little Whorehouse In Texas\*; Best Friends*
1983 *Stroker Ace; Cannonball Run II; The Man Who Loved Women; Smokey And The Bandit 3*
1984 *City Heat*
1985 *Stick* (also director); *Uphill All The Way; Sherman's March*
1987 *Heat; Malone; Rent-A-Cop*
1988 *Switching Channels*
1989 *Physical Evidence; Breaking In; All Dogs Go To Heaven* (voice only)
1990 *Modern Love*
1992 *The Player\**
1993 *Cop And A Half*

## REYNOLDS, Debbie
real name: Mary Reynolds
(1932– ) USA

1948 *June Bride*
1950 *The Daughter Of Rosie O'Grady; Mr Imperium* (UK: *You Belong To Me*); *Three Little Words; Two Weeks With Love*
1952 *Skirts Ahoy; Singin' In The Rain\*; I Love Melvin*
1953 *The Affairs Of Dobie Gillis; Give A Girl A Break*
1954 *Athena; Susan Slept Here*
1955 *The Tender Trap; Hit The Deck*

1956 *Bundle Of Joy; The Catered Affair* (UK: *Wedding Breakfast*); *Meet Me In Las Vegas* (UK: *Viva Las Vegas!*)
1957 *Tammy And The Bachelor* (UK: *Tammy*)
1958 *This Happy Feeling*
1959 *The Mating Game; Say One For Me; The Gazebo*
1960 *Pepe; The Rat Race*
1961 *The Second Time Around; The Pleasure Of His Company*
1962 *How The West Was Won\**
1963 *My Six Loves; Mary, Mary*
1964 *Goodbye Charlie; The Unsinkable Molly Brown*
1966 *The Singing Nun*
1967 *Divorce—American Style*
1968 *How Sweet It Is!*
1971 *What's The Matter With Helen?*
1972 *Charlotte's Web* (voice only)
1974 *That's Entertainment*
1987 *Sadie And Son* (TV)
1989 *Perry Mason: The Case Of The Musical Murder* (TV)
1992 *The Bodyguard*
1993 *Heaven And Earth*

## RICHARDSON, Miranda
(1958– ) UK

1984 *The Innocent*
1985 *Dance With A Stranger*
1986 *After Pilkington* (TV); *The Death Of The Heart; Underworld*
1987 *Eat The Rich; Empire Of The Sun\**
1989 *El Mono Loco* (UK: *The Mad Monkey*)
1990 *The Bachelor; The Fool*
1992 *Enchanted April; The Crying Game; Damage*

## RICHARDSON, Sir Ralph
(1902–83)

1933 *The Ghoul; Friday The Thirteenth*
1934 *The King Of Paris; Thunder In The Air; The Return Of Bulldog Drummond; Java Head*
1935 *Bulldog Jack*

**RICHARDSON, Sir Ralph** (cont.)
1936  *Things To Come; The Man Who Could Work Miracles; Thunder In The City; The Amazing Quest Of Ernest Bliss*
1937  *South Riding; The Divorce Of Lady X*
1938  *The Citadel\*; Smith* (short)
1939  *Q Planes; The Four Feathers; The Lion Has Wings; On The Night Of The Fire*
1940  *Health For The Nation; Forty Million People* (both shorts, both narrator only)
1942  *The Day Will Dawn*
1943  *The Silver Fleet; The Volunteer; The Biter Bit* (narrator only)
1946  *School For Secrets*
1948  *Anna Karenina; The Fallen Idol*
1949  *Faster Than Sound; Come Saturday; Rome And Vatican City* (all narrator only); *The Heiress\**
1950  *Eagles Of The Fleet* (short, narrator only)
1951  *Cricket* (short, narrator only)
1952  *Home At Seven* (also director); *The Sound Barrier; The Holly And The Ivy*
1955  *Richard III\**
1956  *Smiley*
1957  *The Passionate Stranger*
1960  *Our Man In Havana; Exodus\*; Oscar Wilde*
1962  *The 300 Spartans; Long Day's Journey Into Night\**
1964  *Woman Of Straw*
1965  *Doctor Zhivago\**
1966  *The Wrong Box; Khartoum*
1969  *Oh! What A Lovely War; Battle Of Britain; The Looking Glass War; David Copperfield* (TV); *The Bed-Sitting Room; Midas Run* (UK: *A Run On Gold*)
1970  *Eagle In A Cage*
1971  *Whoever Slew Auntie Roo?*
1972  *Tales From The Crypt; Alice's Adventures In Wonderland; Lady Caroline Lamb*
1973  *A Doll's House; O Lucky Man!; Frankenstein — The True Story* (TV)

1975  *Rollerball*
1976  *The Man In The Iron Mask* (TV)
1977  *Jesus Of Nazareth* (TV)
1978  *Watership Down* (voice only)
1979  *Charlie Muffin* (TV)
1980  *Time Bandits\**
1981  *Dragonslayer*
1982  *Wagner* (TV); *Witness For The Prosecution* (TV)
1983  *Invitation To The Wedding*
1984  *Greystoke: The Legend Of Tarzan, Lord Of The Apes\*; Give My Regards To Broad Street*
1986  *Directed By William Wyler* (documentary)

**RICKMAN, Alan**
(19?–  ) UK

1988  *Die Hard\**
1989  *The January Man*
1990  *Quigley Down Under*
1991  *Truly, Madly, Deeply; Closet Land; Close My Eyes; Robin Hood: Prince Of Thieves\**
1992  *Bob Roberts\**
1993  *Blue Room*

**ROBARDS, Jason (Jnr)**
(1920–  ) USA

1958  *The Journey*
1961  *By Love Possessed; Tender Is The Night*
1962  *Long Day's Journey Into Night\**
1963  *Act One*
1965  *A Thousand Clowns*
1966  *Any Wednesday; A Big Hand For The Little Lady* (UK: *Big Deal At Dodge City*)
1967  *Divorce — American Style; Hour Of The Gun; The St Valentine's Day Massacre*
1968  *Isadora; The Night They Raided Minsky's; Cera Una Volta Il West\** (UK: *Once Upon A Time In The West*)
1969  *Rosolino Paternò, Soldato*
1970  *Tora! Tora! Tora!; Julius Caesar; The Ballad Of Cable Hogue; Fools*

1971 *Murders In The Rue Morgue; Johnny Got His Gun*
1972 *The House Without A Christmas* (TV); *The War Between Men And Women; Tod Eines Fremden* (UK: *The Execution*)
1973 *Play It As It Lays; Pat Garrett And Billy The Kid*
1974 *A Boy And His Dog*
1975 *Mr Sycamore*
1976 *All The President's Men**
1977 *Julia*; L'Imprécateur*
1978 *Comes A Horseman; A Christmas To Remember* (TV)
1979 *Hurricane; Cabo Blanco*
1980 *Haywire* (TV); *Raise The Titanic!; Melvin And Howard; Ghosts Of Cape Horn* (narrator only)
1981 *The Legend Of The Lone Ranger; FDR: The Last Year* (TV)
1982 *Burden Of Dreams* (documentary); *Something Wicked This Way Comes*
1983 *Max Dugan Returns; The Day After* (TV)
1984 *Sakharov* (TV); *America And Lewis Hine* (voice only)
1985 *The Atlanta Child Murders* (TV); *The Long Hot Summer* (TV)
1986 *Square Dance; Johnny Bull* (TV); *The Last Frontier* (TV)
1987 *Breaking Home Ties* (TV); *Laguna Heat* (TV)
1988 *Bright Lights, Big City; The Good Mother; Inherit The Wind* (TV); *The Christmas Wife* (TV)
1989 *Dream A Little Dream; Reunion; Parenthood*; Black Rainbow; Thomas Hart Benton* (narrator only)
1990 *Quick Change*
1991 *The Perfect Tribute* (TV); *Chernobyl: The Final Warning* (TV); *An Inconvenient Woman* (TV); *Mark Twain And Me* (TV)
1992 *Storyville*

## ROBBINS, Tim
(1958– ) USA

1984 *No Small Affair*

1985 *Fraternity Vacation; The Sure Thing*
1986 *Howard The Duck; Top Gun**
1987 *The Five Corners*
1988 *Bull Durham*; Tapeheads*
1989 *Erik The Viking; Miss Firecracker*
1990 *Cadillac Man; Jacob's Ladder*
1991 *Jungle Fever**
1992 *Bob Roberts** (also director); *The Player**
1993 *The Hudsucker Proxy*

## ROBERTS, Julia
(1967– ) USA

1987 *Blood Red*
1988 *Baja Oklahoma* (TV); *Mystic Pizza; Satisfaction*
1989 *Steel Magnolias**
1990 *Pretty Woman*; Flatliners*
1991 *Sleeping With The Enemy*; Dying Young; Hook**
1992 *The Player**

## ROBERTS, Rachel
(1927–80) UK

1953 *Valley Of Song; The Limping Man; The Weak And The Wicked*
1954 *The Crowded Day*
1957 *The Good Companions; Davy*
1960 *Our Man In Havana; Saturday Night And Sunday Morning**
1962 *Girl On Approval*
1963 *This Sporting Life*
1968 *A Flea In Her Ear*
1969 *Destiny Of A Spy* (TV); *The Reckoning*
1970 *Doctors' Wives*
1971 *Wild Rovers; Baffled!*
1973 *O Lucky Man!; The Belstone Fox; Alpha Beta*
1974 *Murder On The Orient Express**
1975 *Great Expectations* (TV); *Picnic At Hanging Rock**
1977 *A Circle Of Children* (TV)
1978 *Foul Play**
1979 *Yanks*; A Man Called Intrepid* (TV); *When A Stranger Calls*

**ROBERTS, Rachel** (cont.)
1980  *Charlie Chan And The Curse Of
       The Dragon Queen; The Hostage
       Tower*
1981  *The Wall* (TV)

**ROBERTSON, Cliff**
(1925–  ) USA

1943  *Corvette K-225* (UK: *The Nelson
       Touch*); *We've Been Licked* (UK:
       *Texas To Tokyo*)
1955  *Picnic\**
1956  *Autumn Leaves*
1957  *The Girl Most Likely*
1958  *The Naked And The Dead*
1959  *Gidget; Battle Of The Coral Sea;
       As The Sea Rages*
1961  *Underworld USA; All In A Night's
       Work; The Big Show*
1962  *The Interns; PT 109*
1963  *My Six Loves; Sunday In New
       York*
1964  *633 Squadron; The Best Man;
       Love Has Many Faces*
1965  *Masquerade; Up From The Beach*
1967  *The Honey Pot*
1968  *The Devil's Brigade; Charly\*; The
       Sunshine Patriot* (TV)
1969  *Too Late The Hero*
1972  *J W Coop* (also director); *The
       Great Northfield Minnesota Raid*
1973  *Ace Eli And Rodger Of The Skies;
       The Man Without A Country* (TV)
1974  *A Tree Grows In Brooklyn* (TV):
       *Man On A Swing*
1975  *My Father's House; Three Days
       Of The Condor\*; Out Of Season;
       Obsession*
1976  *Midway* (UK: *The Battle Of
       Midway*); *Return To Earth* (TV);
       *Shoot*
1977  *Fraternity Row* (narrator only)
1978  *Overboard* (TV); *Dominique*
1979  *The Pilot* (also director)
1982  *Two Of A Kind* (TV)
1983  *Brainstorm; Class; Star 80*
1985  *Shaker Run*
1986  *Dreams Of Gold: The Mel Fisher
       Story* (TV)
1987  *Malone*

1990  *Dead Reckoning* (TV)
1991  *Wild Hearts Can't Be Broken*
1992  *Wind*

**ROBINSON, Edward G**
real name: Emmanuel Goldenberg
(1899–1973) USA

1916  *Arms And The Woman*
1923  *The Bright Shawl*
1929  *The Hole In The Wall*
1930  *Outside The Law; Night Ride; The
       Widow From Chicago; A Lady To
       Love; East Is West; Little Caesar\**
1931  *Five Star Final\*; Smart Money*
1932  *Tiger Shark; Silver Dollar; Two
       Seconds; The Hatchet Man* (UK:
       *The Honourable Mr Wong*); *The
       Stolen Jools* (UK: *The Slippery
       Pearls*) (short)
1933  *Little Giant; I Loved A Woman*
1934  *The Man With Two Faces; Dark
       Hazard; The Whole Town's
       Talking* (UK: *Passport To Fame*)
1935  *Barbary Coast*
1936  *Bullets Or Ballots; Thunder In The
       City; A Day At Santa Anita* (short)
1937  *The Last Gangster; Kid Galahad*
1938  *I Am The Law; The Amazing Dr
       Clitterhouse; A Slight Case Of
       Murder*
1939  *Confessions Of A Nazi Spy;
       Blackmail*
1940  *Brother Orchid; Dr Ehrlich's Magic
       Bullet* (UK: *The Story Of Dr
       Ehrlich's Magic Bullet*); *A
       Dispatch From Reuter's* (UK: *This
       Man Reuters*)
1941  *Manpower; The Sea Wolf; Unholy
       Partners*
1942  *Larceny Inc; Tales Of Manhattan*
1943  *Flesh And Fantasy; Destroyer*
1944  *Tampico; The Woman In The
       Window; Double Indemnity\*; Mr
       Winkle Goes To War* (UK: *Arms
       And The Woman*)
1945  *Scarlet Street; Our Vines Have
       Tender Grapes; Journey Together*
1946  *The Stranger*
1947  *The Red House*

1948 *All My Sons; Night Has A Thousand Eyes; Key Largo\**
1949 *House Of Strangers; It's A Great Feeling*
1950 *My Daughter Joy*
1951 *Hollywood Memories* (short, narrator only)
1952 *Actors And Sin*
1953 *The Big Leaguer; The Glass Web; Vice Squad* (UK: *The Girl In Room 17)*
1954 *Black Tuesday; The Violent Men* (UK: *Rough Company)*
1955 *A Bullet For Joey; Illegal; Hell On Frisco Bay; Tight Spot*
1956 *Nightmare; The Ten Commandments\**
1959 *A Hole In The Head; Israeli* (narrator)
1960 *Seven Thieves; Pepe*
1962 *My Geisha; Two Weeks In Another Town; Sammy Going South*
1963 *The Prize*
1964 *The Outrage; Good Neighbour Sam; Robin And The Seven Hoods; Cheyenne Autumn*
1965 *The Cincinnati Kid\*; Who Has Seen The Wind?* (TV)
1966 *The Biggest Bundle Of Them All*
1967 *La Blonde De Pékin; Never A Dull Moment; Grand Slam; Operation St Peter's*
1968 *Uno Scacco Tutto Matto* (UK: *It's Your Move); McKenna's Gold*
1969 *UMC* (TV) (UK: *Operation Heartbeat)*
1970 *Song Of Norway; The Old Man Who Cried Wolf* (TV)
1972 *Neither By Day Or By Night*
1973 *Soylent Green*

## ROBSON, Flora
(1902–84) UK

1931 *Gentleman Of Paris*
1932 *Dance Pretty Lady*
1933 *One Precious Year*
1934 *Catherine The Great*
1936 *Fire Over England*
1937 *Farewell Again*

1939 *Poison Pen; Wuthering Heights\*; Invisible Strips; We Are Not Alone; Smith* (short)
1940 *The Sea Hawk\**
1941 *Bahama Passage*
1944 *2,000 Women*
1945 *Saratoga Trunk; Great Day; Caesar And Cleopatra*
1946 *The Years Between; Black Narcissus\**
1947 *Frieda; Holiday Camp*
1948 *Good Time Girl; Saraband For Dead Lovers*
1953 *Tall Headlines*
1953 *Malta Story; She Shall Be Called Woman* (short, narrator only)
1954 *Romeo And Juliet*
1957 *High Tide At Noon; The Gypsy And The Gentleman; No Time For Tears*
1958 *Innocent Sinners*
1962 *55 Days At Peking*
1963 *Murder At The Gallop*
1964 *Guns At Batasi; Young Cassidy*
1965 *Those Magnificent Men In Their Flying Machines; Seven Women; A King's Story* (voice only)
1966 *Eye Of The Devil; Cry In The Wind*
1967 *The Shuttered Room*
1970 *The Beast In The Cellar; The Beloved; Fragment Of Fear*
1972 *Alice's Adventures In Wonderland*
1978 *Les Misérables* (TV); *Dominique*
1979 *A Man Called Intrepid* (TV)
1980 *Gauguin — The Savage* (TV)
1981 *A Tale Of Two Cities* (TV); *Clash Of The Titans*

## ROGERS, Ginger
real name: Virginia McMath
(1911– ) USA

1929 *Campus Sweethearts; A Night In A Dormitory; A Day Of A Man Of Affairs* (all shorts)
1930 *Office Blues* (short); *Queen High; Young Man Of Manhattan; Follow The Leader; The Sap From Syracuse* (UK: *The Sap Abroad)*

**ROGERS, Ginger** (cont.)
1931 *Honor Among Lovers; Suicide Fleet; The Tip-Off* (UK: *Looking For Trouble*)
1932 *Hollywood On Parade No 1; Screen Snapshots No 12* (both shorts); *The Tenderfoot; Carnival Boat; You Said A Mouthful; The Thirteenth Guest; Hat Check Girl* (UK: *Embassy Girl*)
1933 *Hollywood On Parade No 3* (short); *Broadway Bad* (UK: *Her Reputation*); *Professional Sweetheart* (UK: *Imaginary Sweetheart*); *A Shriek In The Night; 42nd Street\*; Gold Diggers Of 1933\*; Don't Bet On Love; Sitting Pretty; Flying Down To Rio; Chance At Heaven*
1934 *Hollywood On Parade No 13* (short); *Rafter Romance; Finishing School; Change Of Heart; 20 Million Sweethearts; Upperworld; Romance In Manhattan; The Gay Divorcee\** (UK: *The Gay Divorce*)
1935 *Star Of Midnight; Top Hat\*; In Person; Roberta*
1936 *Follow The Fleet; Swing Time\**
1937 *Shall We Dance?; Stage Door\*; Holiday Greetings* (short)
1938 *Vivacious Lady; Having Wonderful Time; Carefree*
1939 *Bachelor Mother; The Story Of Vernon And Irene Castle*
1940 *Lucky Partners; The Primrose Path; Kitty Foyle\**
1941 *Tom, Dick And Harry*
1942 *Tales Of Manhattan; Once Upon A Honeymoon; Roxie Hart; The Major And The Minor*
1943 *Showbusiness At War; Safeguarding Military Information* (both shorts); *Tender Comrade*
1944 *Battle Stations* (short, narrator only); *Lady In The Dark; I'll Be Seeing You; Ginger Rogers Finds A Bargain* (short)
1945 *Weekend At The Waldorf*
1946 *Heartbeat; Magnificent Doll*
1947 *It Had To Be You*

1949 *The Barkleys Of Broadway*
1950 *Storm Warning; Perfect Strangers* (UK: *Too Dangerous To Love*)
1951 *The Groom Wore Spurs*
1952 *We're Not Married; Dreamboat; Monkey Business*
1953 *Forever Female; Hollywood's Great Entertainers* (short)
1954 *Black Widow; Beautiful Stranger*
1955 *Tight Spot*
1956 *The First Traveling Saleslady; Teenage Rebel*
1957 *Oh, Men! Oh!, Women!*
1964 *The Confession* (UK: *Quick, Let's Get Married*)
1965 *Harlow* (TV)

**ROONEY, Mickey**
real name: Ninian Joseph Yule
(1920– ) USA

1926 *Not To Be Trusted* (short)
1927 *Mickey's Pals; Mickey's Circus; Mickey's Eleven; Mickey's Battle* (all shorts); *Orchids And Ermine*
1928 *Mickey's Parade; Mickey's Little Eva; Mickey's Nine; Fillum Frolics; Mickey's Athletes; Mickey's Rivals; Mickey's Triumph; Mickey's Movies; Mickey's Big Game Hunt; Mickey The Detective; Mickey's Babies* (UK: *Baby Show*); *Mickey's Wild West* (all shorts)
1929 *Rattling Racers; Mickey's Surprise; Mickey's Big Moment; Mickey's Brown Derby; Mickey's Explorers; Mickey's Great Idea; Mickey's Initiation; Mickey's Last Chance; Mickey's Menagerie; Mickey's Northwest Mounted; Mickey's Mix-Up; Birthday Squeakings; Mickey's Midnight Follies* (all shorts)
1930 *Mickey's Strategy; Mickey's Champs; Mickey's Luck; Mickey's Master Mind; Mickey's Musketeers; Mickey's Whirlwinds; Mickey's Winners; Mickey's Warriors; Mickey The Romeo;*

*Mickey's Merry Men; Mickey's Bargain* (all shorts)

1931 *Mickey's Rebellion; Mickey's Diplomacy; Mickey's Thrill Hunters; Mickey's Helping Hand; Mickey's Stampede; Mickey's Crusaders; Mickey's Sideline; Mickey's Big Business; Mickey's Wildcats* (all shorts)

1932 *Mickey's Travels; Mickey's Holiday; Mickey's Golden Rule; Mickey's Busy Day; Mickey's Charity* (all shorts); *My Pal The King; Sin's Pay Day; Beast Of The City; Information Kid* (aka *Fast Companions*)

1933 *Mickey's Ape Man; Mickey's Race; Mickey's Big Broadcast; Mickey's Covered Wagon; Mickey's Disguises; Mickey's Touchdown; Mickey's Tent Show* (all shorts); *Broadway To Hollywood* (UK: *Ring Up The Curtain*); *The Big Cage; The Chief* (UK: *My Old Man's A Fireman*); *The World Changes; The Life Of Jimmy Dolan* (UK: *The Kid's Last Fight*); *The Big Chance*

1934 *Mickey's Minstrels; Mickey's Rescue; Mickey's Medicine Man* (all shorts); *The Lost Jungle; Love Birds; Beloved; I Like It That Way; Manhattan Melodrama; Hide-Out; Half A Sinner; Death On The Diamond; Chained; Upper World; Blind Date*

1935 *The County Chairman; A Midsummer Night's Dream\*; The Healer; Reckless; Riff Raff; Ah, Wilderness!*

1936 *Pirate Party On Catalina Isle* (short); *Down The Stretch; Little Lord Fauntleroy; The Devil Is A Sissy* (UK: *The Devil Takes The Count*)

1937 *The Hoosier Schoolboy* (UK: *Yesterday's Hero*); *Thoroughbreds Don't Cry; Captains Courageous\*; A Family Affair; Slave Ship; Live, Love And Learn; You're Only Young Once*

1938 *Judge Hardy's Children; Hold That Kiss; Love Is A Headache; Lord Jeff* (UK: *The Boy From Barnardo's*); *Love Finds Andy Hardy; Boys' Town\*; Out West With The Hardys; Stablemates*

1939 *The Adventures Of Huckleberry Finn; The Hardys Ride High; Babes In Arms\*; Judge Hardy And Son; Andy Hardy Gets Spring Fever*

1940 *Rodeo Dough* (short); *Men Of Boys' Town; Andy Hardy Meets Debutante; Young Tom Edison; Strike Up The Band; Andy Hardy's Private Secretary*

1941 *Meet The Stars No 4; Cavalcade Of The Academy Awards* (both shorts); *Life Begins For Andy Hardy; Babes On Broadway*

1942 *The Courtship Of Andy Hardy; A Yank At Eton; Andy Hardy's Double Life*

1943 *Girl Crazy; Thousands Cheer; The Human Comedy*

1944 *National Velvet\*; Andy Hardy's Blonde Trouble*

1946 *Love Laughs At Andy Hardy*

1947 *Killer McCoy*

1948 *Summer Holiday; Words And Music; Rough But Hopeful* (short)

1949 *The Big Wheel*

1950 *He's A Cockeyed Wonder; The Fireball*

1951 *My Outlaw Brother; The Strip*

1952 *Sound Off; Screen Snapshots No 205* (short)

1953 *A Slight Case Of Larceny; Mickey Rooney — Then And Now* (short); *Off-Limits* (UK: *Military Policeman*)

1954 *Drive A Crooked Road; The Bridges At Toko-Ri; The Atomic Kid*

1955 *The Twinkle In God's Eye*

1956 *The Bold And The Brave; Magnificent Roughnecks; Francis In The Haunted House*

1957 *Operation Mad Ball; Baby Face Nelson; Playtime In Hollywood* (short)

291

**ROONEY, Mickey** (cont.)
1958 *Andy Hardy Comes Home;
Glamorous Hollywood* (short)
1959 *A Nice Little Bank That Should Be
Robbed; The Last Mile; The Big
Operator*
1960 *The Private Lives Of Adam And
Eve; Platinum High School* (UK:
*Rich, Young And Deadly*)
1961 *Everything's Ducky; Breakfast At
Tiffany's\*; King Of The Roaring
Twenties* (UK: *The Big Bankroll*)
1962 *Requiem For A Heavyweight* (UK:
*Blood Money*)
1963 *It's A Mad, Mad, Mad, Mad
World\**
1964 *The Secret Invasion*
1965 *How To Stuff A Wild Bikini; The
Devil In Love; 24 Hours To Kill*
1966 *Ambush Bay*
1968 *The Extraordinary Seaman;
Skidoo*
1969 *80 Steps To Jonah; The Comic;
The Cockeyed Cowboys Of Calico
County* (UK: *A Woman For Charlie*)
1970 *Hollywood Blue*
1971 *Evil Roy Slade* (TV); *Journey
Back To Oz* (TV) (voice only); *B J
Lang Presents*
1972 *Pulp; Richard*
1974 *That's Entertainment; Ace Of
Hearts; Bon Baisers De Hong
Kong*
1975 *Rachel's Man*
1976 *The Domino Principle* (UK: *The
Domino Killings*); *Find The Lady*
1977 *Pete's Dragon*
1978 *The Magic Of Lassie; Donovan's
Kid* (TV)
1979 *Arabian Adventure; The Black
Stallion; Rudolph And Frosty's
Christmas In July* (TV) (voice
only)
1980 *My Kidnapper, My Love* (TV);
*Odyssey Of The Pacific*
1981 *Leave 'Em Laughing* (TV); *Bill*
(TV); *Senior Trip* (TV); *The Fox
And The Hound* (voice only)
1983 *Bill: On His Own* (TV)
1984 *It Came Upon The Midnight Clear*
(TV)

1985 *The Care Bears Movie* (voice
only)
1986 *The White Stallion; The Return Of
Mike Hammer* (TV); *Little Spies*
(TV)
1988 *Bluegrass* (TV)
1989 *Erik The Viking*
1991 *My Heroes Have Always Been
Cowboys; The Gambler Returns:
The Luck Of The Draw* (TV); *The
Christmas Without Santa Claus*
(TV) (voice only)
1992 *Silent Night, Deadly Night 5: The
Toy Maker; The Legend Of Wolf
Mountain; Sweet Justice;
Maximum Force; La Vida Lactea*

**ROURKE, Mickey**
real name: Philip Rourke
(1955– ) USA

1979 *1941\**
1980 *City In Fear* (TV); *Act Of Love*
(TV); *Heaven's Gate\*; Fade To
Black; Rape And Marriage: The
Rideout Case* (TV)
1981 *Body Heat\**
1982 *Eureka; Diner*
1983 *Rumble Fish*
1984 *The Pope Of Greenwich Village*
1985 *Year Of The Dragon*
1986 *9½ Weeks*
1987 *Angel Heart; Barfly; A Prayer For
The Dying*
1988 *Homeboy*
1989 *Francesco; Johnny Handsome*
1990 *Wild Orchid; The Desperate
Hours*
1991 *Harley Davidson And The
Marlboro Man*
1992 *White Sands*

**ROWLANDS, Gena**
real name: Virginia Rowlands
(1934– ) USA

1958 *The High Cost Of Loving*
1962 *A Child Is Waiting; Lonely Are The
Brave; The Spiral Road*
1967 *Tony Rome*

1968 *Faces; Gli Intoccabili* (UK: *Machine Gun McCain*)
1969 *The Happy Ending*
1971 *Minnie And Moskowitz*
1974 *A Woman Under The Influence*
1976 *Two-Minute Warning*
1977 *Opening Night*
1978 *The Brink's Job; A Question Of Love* (TV)
1979 *Strangers: The Story Of A Mother And Daughter* (TV)
1980 *Gloria*
1982 *Tempest*
1983 *Thursday's Child* (TV); *Love Streams*
1984 *I'm Almost Not Crazy*
1985 *An Early Frost* (TV)
1986 *The Third Day Comes*
1987 *Light Of Day; The Betty Ford Story* (TV); *Hem*
1988 *Another Woman**
1989 *Montana(TV)*
1990 *Once Around*
1991 *Night On Earth; Face Of A Stranger* (TV)
1992 *Crazy In Love* (TV)

## RUSSELL, Jane
full name: Ernestine Jane Russell
(1921– ) USA

1943 *The Outlaw**
1946 *Young Widow*
1948 *The Paleface*; Montana Belle*
1950 *Double Dynamite; Hollywood Goes To Bat* (short)
1951 *His Kind Of Woman*
1952 *Road To Bali; Macao; Son Of Paleface; The Las Vegas Story; Screen Snapshots No 205* (short)
1953 *Gentlemen Prefer Blondes**
1954 *The French Line; Hollywood Cowboy Stars* (short)
1955 *Gentlemen Marry Brunettes; Foxfire; Underwater; The Tall Men*
1956 *Hot Blood; The Revolt Of Mamie Stover*
1957 *The Fuzzy Pink Nightgown; Playtime In Hollywood* (short)
1964 *Fate Is The Hunter*
1966 *Johnny Reno; Waco*

1967 *Born Losers*
1970 *Darker Than Amber*

## RUSSELL, Kurt
(1951– ) USA

1962 *It Happened At The World's Fair*
1965 *Guns Of Diablo* (TV)
1966 *Follow Me Boys!; Mosby's Maurauders*
1968 *The One And Only Genuine Original Family Band; The Horse In The Gray Flannel Suit; Guns In The Heather*
1969 *The Computer Wore Tennis Shoes*
1970 *Dad, Can I Borrow The Car?* (short, narrator only)
1971 *Fool's Parade* (UK: *Dynamite Man From Glory Jail*)
1972 *Now You See Him, Now You Don't*
1973 *Charley And The Angel*
1974 *Superdad*
1975 *The Strongest Man In The World; Search For The Gods* (TV); *The Deadly Tower* (TV)
1976 *The Quest* (TV)
1977 *Christmas Miracle In Caulfield USA* (TV) (UK: *The Christmas Coal Mine Miracle*)
1979 *Elvis — The Movie*
1980 *Amber Waves* (TV); *Used Cars*
1981 *The Fox And The Hound* (voice only); *Escape From New York*
1982 *The Thing*
1983 *Silkwood**
1984 *Swing Shift*
1985 *The Mean Season*
1986 *The Best Of Times; Big Trouble In Little China*
1987 *Overboard*
1988 *Tequila Sunrise*; Winter People*
1989 *Tango & Cash*
1991 *Backdraft**
1992 *Unlawful Entry; Captain Ron*

## RUSSELL, Rosalind
(1908–76) USA

1934 *Forsaking All Others; Evelyn Prentice*

**RUSSELL, Rosalind** (cont.)
1935  *West Point Of The Air; The
      President Vanishes* (UK:
      *Strange Conspiracy*); *The Casino
      Murder Case; China Seas; The
      Night Is Young; Reckless;
      Rendezvous*
1936  *Trouble For Two* (UK: *The Suicide
      Club*); *It Had To Happen; Under
      Two Flags; Craig's Wife*
1937  *Live, Love And Learn; Night Must
      Fall*
1938  *Man-Proof; The Citadel\*; Four's A
      Crowd*
1939  *The Women\*; Fast And Loose*
1940  *His Girl Friday\*; Hired Wife; No
      Time For Comedy*
1941  *Design For Scandal; They Met In
      Bombay; The Feminine Touch;
      This Thing Called Love* (UK:
      *Married But Single*)
1942  *My Sister Eileen; Take A Letter,
      Darling* (UK: *The Green-Eyed
      Woman*)
1943  *Flight For Freedom; What A
      Woman* (UK: *The Beautiful
      Cheat*)
1945  *Roughly Speaking; She Wouldn't
      Say Yes*
1946  *Sister Kenny*
1947  *The Guilt Of Janet Ames;
      Mourning Becomes Electra*
1948  *The Velvet Touch*
1949  *Tell It To The Judge*
1950  *A Woman Of Distinction*
1952  *Never Wave At A WAC* (UK:
      *The Private Wore Skirts*)
1954  *Screen Snapshots No 222*
      (short)
1955  *The Girl Rush; Picnic\**
1958  *Auntie Mame\**
1961  *A Majority Of One*
1962  *Five Finger Exercise; Gypsy\**
1966  *The Trouble With Angels*
1967  *Oh Dad, Poor Dad, Mama's Hung
      You In The Closet And I'm
      Feeling So Sad; Rosie!*
1968  *Where Angels Go...Trouble
      Follows!*
1971  *Mrs Pollifax — Spy*
1972  *The Crooked Hearts* (TV)

**RUSSELL, Theresa**
(1957–  ) USA

1976  *The Last Tycoon*
1977  *Straight Time*
1979  *Blind Ambition* (TV)
1980  *Bad Timing\**
1982  *Eureka*
1984  *The Razor's Edge*
1985  *Insignificance*
1987  *Aria; Black Widow*
1988  *Track 29*
1989  *Physical Evidence*
1990  *Impulse; Cold Heaven*
1991  *Whore; Kafka*

**RUTHERFORD, Dame Margaret**
(1892–1972) UK

1936  *Dusty Ermine; Troubled Waters;
      Talk Of The Devil*
1937  *Missing, Believed Married; Beauty
      And The Barge; Big Fella; Catch
      As Catch Can*
1940  *Spring Meeting*
1941  *Quiet Wedding*
1943  *The Yellow Canary; The Demi-
      Paradise*
1944  *English Without Tears*
1945  *Blithe Spirit\**
1946  *While The Sun Shines*
1947  *Meet Me At Dawn*
1948  *Miranda; Passport To Pimlico*
1950  *The Happiest Days Of Your Life;
      Her Favourite Husband*
1951  *The Magic Box*
1952  *Curtain Up; The Importance Of
      Being Earnest; Castle In The Air;
      Miss Robin Hood*
1953  *Innocents In Paris; Trouble In
      Store*
1954  *Aunt Clara; The Runaway Bus;
      Mad About Men*
1955  *An Alligator Named Daisy*
1957  *Just My Luck*
1958  *The Smallest Show On Earth*
1959  *I'm All Right Jack\**
1961  *On The Double; Murder She Said*
1963  *The Mouse On The Moon; Murder
      At The Gallop; The VIPs*
1964  *Murder Most Foul*

1965 *The Alphabet Murders; Murder Ahoy*
1966 *Chimes At Midnight; A Countess From Hong Kong; The Wacky World Of Mother Goose* (voice only)
1967 *Arabella*

## RYAN, Robert
(1909–73) USA

1940 *The Ghost Breakers; Queen Of The Mob; Golden Gloves; Northwest Mounted Police; Texas Rangers Ride Again*
1941 *The Feminine Touch*
1943 *Gangway For Tomorrow; The Sky's The Limit; Behind The Rising Sun; Bombardier; The Iron Major; Tender Comrade*
1944 *Marine Raiders*
1947 *Johnny O'Clock; The Woman On The Beach; Trail Steet; Crossfire\**
1948 *Return Of The Bad Men; Berlin Express; The Boy With Green Hair; Act Of Violence*
1949 *Caught; The Set-Up; I Married A Communist* (UK: *The Woman On Pier 13*)
1950 *The Secret Fury; Born To Be Bad*
1951 *The Racket; Best Of The Bad Men; The Flying Leathernecks; On Dangerous Ground*
1952 *Clash By Night; Horizons West; Beware My Lovely*
1953 *The Naked Spur; City Beneath The Sea; Inferno*
1954 *Alaska Seas; About Mrs Leslie; Her Twelve Men; Bad Day At Black Rock\**
1955 *Escape To Burma; House Of Bamboo; The Tall Men*
1956 *The Proud Ones; Back From Eternity*
1957 *Men In War*
1958 *God's Little Acre; Lonelyhearts*
1959 *Day Of The Outlaw; Odds Against Tomorrow*
1960 *Ice Palace*
1961 *The Canadians; King Of Kings*
1962 *Billy Budd; The Longest Day\**

1964 *The Inheritance* (narrator only); *The Crooked Road*
1965 *La Guerre Secrète* (UK: *The Dirty Game*); *The Battle Of The Bulge*
1966 *The Professionals\**
1967 *The Busy Body\*; Custer Of The West; Hour Of The Gun; The Dirty Dozen\**
1968 *Anzio* (UK: *The Battle For Anzio*); *A Minute To Pray, A Second To Die* (UK: *Dead Or Alive*)
1969 *Captain Nemo And The Underwater City; The Wild Bunch\**
1970 *Lawman*
1971 *The Love Machine*
1972 *And Hope To Die; La Course Du Lièvre A Travers Les Champs*
1973 *The Iceman Cometh; Executive Action; Man Without A Country* (TV); *Lolly Madonna XXX* (UK: *The Lolly Madonna War*)
1974 *The Outfit*

## RYDER, Winona
real name: Winona Laura Horowitz
(1971–   ) USA

1986 *Lucas*
1987 *Square Dance*
1988 *Beetlejuice\*; 1969*
1989 *Heathers\*; Great Balls Of Fire*
1990 *Welcome Home Roxy Carmichael; Mermaids; Edward Scissorhands\**
1991 *Night On Earth*
1992 *Bram Stoker's Dracula\**
1993 *The House Of The Spirits; Company Of Angels*

# S

## SANDERS, George
(1906–72) Russia

1934 *Love, Life And Laughter*
1936 *Find The Lady; Strange Cargo; The Man Who Could Work Miracles; Dishonour Bright; Things To Come; My Second Wife; Lloyd's Of London*

**SANDERS, George** (cont.)
1937 *The Lady Escapes; Love Is News;
Slave Ship; Lancer Spy*
1938 *International Settlement; Four
Men And A Prayer*
1939 *Mr Moto's Last Warning; So This
Is London; The Saint Strikes
Back; The Outsider; Nurse Edith
Cavell; The Saint In London;
Confessions Of A Nazi Spy;
Allegheny Uprising* (UK: *The First
Rebel)*
1940 *The Saint Takes Over; Green
Hell; Bitter Sweet; Foreign
Correspondent\*; Son Of Monte
Cristo; The Saint's Double
Trouble; Rebecca\*; The House Of
Seven Gables*
1941 *Man Hunt; The Saint In Palm
Springs; Rage In Heaven; A Date
With The Falcon; Sundown; The
Gay Falcon*
1942 *Her Cardboard Lover; The Black
Swan; The Falcon Takes Over;
Quiet Please, Murder; The Moon
And Sixpence; Tales Of
Manhattan; Son Of Fury; The
Falcon's Brother*
1943 *Appointment In Berlin; This Land
Is Mino; Paris After Dark; They
Came To Blow Up America*
1944 *Action In Arabia; The Lodger;
Summer Storm*
1945 *Hangover Square; The Picture Of
Dorian Gray; The Strange Affair
Of Uncle Harry*
1946 *A Scandal In Paris; The Strange
Woman*
1947 *The Private Affairs Of Bel Ami;
The Ghost And Mrs Muir; Forever
Amber; Lured* (UK: *Personal
Column)*
1949 *Samson And Delilah\*; The Fan*
(UK: *Lady Windermere's Fan)*
1950 *All About Eve\*; Blackjack*
1951 *I Can Get It For You Wholesale*
(UK: *This Is My Affair); The Light
Touch*
1952 *Ivanhoe\*; Assignment — Paris;
Screen Snapshots No 205*
(short)

1953 *Call Me Madam; Viaggio In Italia*
(UK: *Voyage To Italy)*
1954 *Witness To Murder; King Richard
And The Crusaders*
1955 *Jupiter's Darling; Moonfleet; The
Scarlet Coat; The King's Thief*
1956 *Death Of A Scoundrel; While The
City Sleeps; Never Say Goodbye;
That Certain Feeling*
1957 *The Seventh Sin*
1958 *Rock-A-Bye Baby; The Whole
Truth; From The Earth To The
Moon*
1959 *A Touch Of Larceny; Solomon
And Sheba; That Kind Of Woman*
1960 *Bluebeard's 10 Honeymoons;
Cone Of Silence; Village Of The
Damned; The Last Voyage; The
Rebel*
1961 *Five Golden Hours*
1962 *Le Rendez-Vous; Operation
Snatch; In Search Of The
Castaways*
1963 *Cairo; The Cracksman; Un Aereo
Per Baalbeck; Dark Purpose*
1964 *A Shot In The Dark; The Golden
Head*
1965 *The Amorous Adventures Of Moll
Flanders; Trunk To Cairo; World
By Night* (narrator only)
1966 *The Quiller Memorandum*
1967 *Warning Shot; Good Times; The
Jungle Book\** (voice only); *Laura*
(TV); *One Step To Hell*
1968 *The Best House In London; The
Candy Man*
1969 *The Body Stealers; The Seven
Men Of Sumuru; The Kremlin
Letter*
1971 *Endless Night; The Night Of The
Assassin*
1972 *Doomwatch; Psychomania*


**SARANDON, Susan**
real name: Susan Tomaling
(1946–   ) USA

1970 *Joe*
1971 *La Mortadella* (UK: *Lady Liberty)*
1972 *Walk Away; Madden*

1973 *The Haunting Of Rosalind* (TV); *Lovin' Molly*
1974 *The Satan Murders* (TV); *The Front Page; F Scott Fitzgerald And The Last Of The Belles* (TV)
1975 *The Great Waldo Pepper; The Rocky Horror Picture Show*
1976 *Crash; Dragonfly* (aka *One Summer's Love*)
1977 *The Other Side Of Midnight; The Last Of The Cowboys* (aka *The Great Smokey Roadblock*)
1978 *Pretty Baby; King Of The Gypsies*
1979 *Something Short Of Paradise*
1980 *Loving Couples; Atlantic City USA** (UK: *Atlantic City*)
1981 *Who Am I This Time?* (TV)
1982 *Tempest*
1983 *The Hunger; The Buddy System*
1984 *Eyes; Io E Il Duce*
1985 *Compromising Positions; Women Of Valor* (TV)
1987 *The Witches Of Eastwick**
1988 *Sweethearts Dance; Bull Durham**
1980 *The January Man, A Dry White Season*
1990 *White Palace; Through The Wire* (narrator only)
1991 *Thelma And Louise*; Light Sleeper*
1992 *The Player*; Bob Roberts*; Lorenzo's Oil**

## SCHEIDER, Roy
(1934–   ) USA

1963 *The Curse Of The Living Corpse*
1968 *Paper Lion*
1969 *Stiletto*
1970 *Puzzle Of A Downfall Child; Loving*
1971 *Klute*; The French Connection**
1972 *L'Attentat* (UK: *Plot*); *Un Homme Est Mort* (UK: *The Outside Man*); *Assignment Munich* (TV)
1973 *The Seven-Ups*
1975 *Jaws*; Sheila Levine Is Dead And Living In New York*
1976 *Marathon Man*
1977 *Sorcerer* (UK: *Wages Of Fear*)
1978 *Jaws 2*

1979 *The Last Embrace; All That Jazz**
1982 *Still Of The Night; Blue Thunder*
1983 *Tiger Town; Jacobo Timmerman/ Prisoner Without A Name, Cell Without A Number* (TV)
1984 *2010; In Our Hands* (documentary)
1985 *Mishima* (narrator only)
1986 *The Men's Club; 52 Pick-Up*
1988 *Cohen & Tate*
1989 *Night Game; Listen To Me*
1990 *The Fourth War; The Russia House; Somebody Has To Shoot The Picture* (TV)
1991 *Naked Lunch*
1993 *Romeo Is Bleeding*

## SCHELL, Maximilian
(1930–   ) Austria

1955 *Kinder, Mütter Und Ein General; Ein Mädchen Aus Flandern*
1956 *Der 20 Juli; Reifende Jügend; Fin Herz Kehrt Heim*
1957 *Taxi–Chauffeur Bartz; Die Letzten Werden Die Ersten Sein*
1958 *Ein Wunderbaren Sommer; The Young Lions*
1961 *Judgement At Nuremberg**
1962 *Five Finger Exercise; The Reluctant Saint; The Condemned Of Altona*
1964 *Topkapi*
1965 *Return From The Ashes*
1966 *The Deadly Affair*
1967 *Counterpoint*
1968 *The Desperate Ones; Krakatoa — East Of Java; Heidi Comes Home* (TV)
1969 *The Castle* (also director); *Simon Bolivár*
1970 *First Love* (also director)
1971 *Trotta*
1972 *Pope Joan*
1973 *Paulina 1880; Der Fussgänger* (also director)
1974 *The Odessa File*
1975 *The Man In The Glass Booth*
1976 *St Ives; Assassination!; End Of The Game* (director only)

**SCHELL, Maximilian** (cont.)

1977 *Julia\*; Cross Of Iron; A Bridge Too Far*

1979 *Avalanche Express; Tales From The Vienna Woods* (director only); *The Black Hole\*; I Love You, I Love You Not; Players*

1980 *Diary Of Anne Frank* (TV) (also director)

1981 *The Chosen; Les Iles*

1983 *Phantom Of The Opera* (TV)

1984 *Morgen In Alabama; The Assissi Underground; Marlene* (documentary, also director)

1989 *The Rose Garden*

1990 *The Freshman; Labyrinth; An American Place* (also director)

1991 *Young Catherine* (TV)

1992 *Stalin* (TV); *Miss Rose White*

1993 *A Far Off Place*

**SCHWARZENEGGER, Arnold**
(1947–   ) USA

1969 *Hercules Goes Bananas* (aka *Hercules In New York*)

1973 *The Long Goodbye*

1976 *Stay Hungry*

1977 *Pumping Iron* (documentary)

1979 *Scavenger Hunt; The Villain* (UK: *Cactus Jack*)

1980 *The Jayne Mansfield Story* (TV)

1981 *Conan The Barbarian*

1984 *Conan The Destroyer; The Terminator\**

1985 *Red Sonja; Commando*

1986 *Raw Deal*

1987 *The Running Man; Predator*

1988 *Red Heat; Twins\**

1990 *Total Recall\*; Kindergarten Cop\*; Tales From The Crypt* (TV) (co-director only)

1991 *Terminator 2: Judgment Day\**

1992 *Christmas In Connecticut* (TV) (director only)

1993 *The Last Action Hero*

**SCOFIELD, Paul**
full name: David Paul Scofield
(1922–   ) UK

1955 *That Lady*

1958 *Carve Her Name With Pride*

1964 *The Train*

1966 *A Man For All Seasons\*; The Other World Of Winston Churchill* (narrator only)

1967 *Tell Me Lies*

1970 *King Lear; Bartleby*

1973 *Scorpio; A Delicate Balance*

1984 *1919*

1985 *Summer Lightning* (TV)

1986 *The Conspiracy; Mr Corbett's Ghost*

1989 *When The Whales Came; Henry V\**

1990 *Hamlet\**

**SCOTT, George C**
(1926–   ) USA

1958 *The Hanging Tree*

1959 *Anatomy Of A Murder\**

1961 *The Hustler\**

1963 *The List Of Adrian Messenger*

1964 *Dr Strangelove Or How I Stopped Worrying And Learned To Love The Bomb\*; The Yellow Rolls-Royce*

1966 *The Bible, In The Beginning\*; Not With My Wife You Don't*

1967 *Shadow On The Land* (TV); *The Flim Flam Man* (UK: *One Born Every Minute*)

1968 *Petulia*

1970 *Patton\**

1971 *Jane Eyre* (TV); *They Might Be Giants; The Last Run; The Hospital*

1972 *Rage* (also director); *The New Centurions* (UK: *Precinct 45: Los Angeles Police*)

1973 *Oklahoma Crude; The Day Of The Dolphins*

1974 *Bank Shot; The Savage Is Loose* (also director)

1975 *The Hindenburg; Fear On Trial* (TV)

1976 *Beauty And The Beast*
1977 *Islands In The Stream; The Prince And The Pauper*
1978 *Movie, Movie*
1979 *The Changeling; Hardcore* (UK: *The Hardcore Life*); *Arthur Miller — On Home Ground* (documentary)
1980 *The Formula*
1981 *Taps*
1982 *Oliver Twist* (TV)
1983 *China Rose* (TV)
1984 *Firestarter; A Christmas Carol* (TV)
1985 *The Indomitable Teddy Roosevelt* (narrator only)
1986 *The Last Days Of Patton* (TV); *Choices* (TV); *Murders In The Rue Morgue* (TV)
1987 *Pals* (TV)
1989 *The Ryan White Story* (TV)
1990 *The Descending Angel* (TV); *Exorcist III; The Rescuers Down Under* (voice only)
1991 *Finding The Way Home* (TV)
1993 *Damages*

## SCOTT, Randolph
full name: George Randolph Crane Scott
(1898–1987) USA

1928 *Sharp Shooters*
1929 *The Far Call; The Black Watch; The Virginian; Dynamite*
1931 *The Women Men Marry; Sky Bride*
1932 *Hot Saturday; Island Of Lost Souls; Heritage Of The Desert; A Successful Calamity*
1933 *Supernatural; When The West Was Young; Murders In The Zoo; Wild Horse Mesa; Cocktail Hour; To The Last Man; The Thundering Herd; Hello, Everybody!; Sunset Pass; Man Of The Forest; Broken Dreams*
1934 *Wagon Wheels; The Last Round-Up; The Lone Cowboy*
1935 *Home On The Range; The Rocky Mountain Mystery; She; Roberta; Village Tale; So Red The Rose*

1936 *And Sudden Death; Follow The Fleet; The Last Of The Mohicans; Go West, Young Man; Pirate Party On Catalina Island* (short)
1937 *High, Wide And Handsome*
1938 *The Texans; Rebecca Of Sunnybrook Farm; Road To Reno*
1939 *Jesse James\*; Susannah Of The Mounties; Frontier Marshal; 20,000 Men A Year; Coast Guard*
1940 *When The Daltons Rode; Virginia City; My Favorite Wife*
1941 *Paris Calling; Western Union; Belle Starr*
1942 *Pittsburgh; To The Shores Of Tripoli; The Spoilers*
1943 *Bombardier; Gung Ho!; The Desperadoes; Corvette K-225* (UK: *The Nelson Touch*)
1944 *Follow The Boys; Belle Of The Yukon*
1945 *China Sky; Captain Kidd*
1946 *Home Sweet Homicide; Abilene Town; Badman's Territory*
1947 *Christmas Eve; Trail Street; Gunfighters* (UK: *The Assassins*)
1948 *Coroner Creek; Return Of The Bad Men; Albuquerque* (UK: *Silver City*)
1949 *The Walking Hills; Canadian Pacific; Fighting Man Of The Plains; The Doolins Of Oklahoma* (UK: *The Great Manhunt*)
1950 *The Cariboo Trail; Colt 45; The Nevadan* (UK: *The Man From Nevada*)
1951 *Sugarfoot; Santa Fé; Starlift; Fort Worth; Man In The Saddle* (UK: *The Outcast*)
1952 *Carson City; Hangman's Knot; The Man Behind The Gun*
1953 *Thunder Over The Plains; The Stranger Wore A Gun*
1954 *Riding Shotgun; The Bounty Hunter*
1955 *Ten Wanted Men; Tall Man Riding; Rage At Dawn; A Lawless Street*
1956 *Seventh Cavalry; Seven Men From Now*

**SCOTT, Randolph** (cont.)
1957 *The Tall T; Shoot Out At Medicine Bend; Decision At Sundown*
1958 *Buchanan Rides Alone*
1959 *Ride Lonesome; Westbound*
1960 *Comanche Station*
1962 *Ride The High Country* (UK: *Guns In The Afternoon*)


**SEGAL, George**
(1934–   ) USA

1961 *The Young Doctors*
1962 *The Longest Day\**
1963 *Act One*
1964 *Invitation To A Gunfighter; The New Interns*
1965 *King Rat; Ship Of Fools*
1966 *Lost Command; Who's Afraid Of Virgina Woolf?\*; The Quiller Memorandum*
1967 *The St Valentine's Day Massacre*
1968 *No Way To Treat A Lady; Bye Bye Braverman; The Girl Who Couldn't Say No*
1969 *The Southern Star; The Bridge At Remagen*
1970 *Loving; Where's Poppa?; The Owl And The Pussycat\**
1971 *Born To Win*
1972 *The Hot Rock* (UK: *How To Steal A Diamond In Four Uneasy Lessons*)
1973 *A Touch Of Class; Blume In Love*
1974 *The Terminal Man; California Split*
1975 *The Black Bird; Russian Roulette*
1976 *The Duchess And The Dirtwater Fox; Fun With Dick And Jane*
1977 *Rollercoaster*
1978 *Who Is Killing The Great Chefs Of Europe?* (UK: *Too Many Chefs*)
1979 *Lost And Found; Arthur Miller On Home Ground* (documentary)
1980 *The Last Married Couple In America*
1981 *Carbon Copy*
1983 *The Cold Room; The Zany Adventures Of Robin Hood* (TV); *Trackdown: Finding The Goodbar Killer* (TV)

1985 *Stick; Not My Kid; Who's In The Closet?; Killing'Em Softly*
1986 *Many Happy Returns*
1987 *Marathon*
1988 *All's Fair; Skirmish*
1989 *Look Who's Talking\**
1990 *The Endless Game*
1991 *For The Boys*
1993 *The Joshua Tree*


**SELLECK, Tom**
(1945–   )

1969 *Judd For The Defense: The Holy Ground Murder* (TV)
1970 *Myra Breckinridge; The Movie Murderer* (TV)
1971 *The Seven Minutes*
1972 *Daughters Of Satan*
1973 *Terminal Island* (UK: *Knuckle-Men*)
1974 *A Case Of Rape* (TV)
1975 *Returning Home* (TV)
1976 *Midway* (UK: *Battle Of Midway*); *Most Wanted* (TV)
1977 *Washington Affair*
1978 *Coma; Superdome* (TV)
1979 *The Sacketts* (TV); *Concrete Cowboys* (TV)
1982 *Divorce Wars: A Love Story* (TV); *The Shadow Riders* (TV); *The Chinese Typewriter* (TV)
1983 *High Road To China*
1984 *Lassiter; Runaway*
1986 *Sullivan's Travels* (TV)
1987 *Three Men And A Baby\**
1989 *Her Alibi; An Innocent Man*
1990 *Three Men And A Little Lady; Quigley Down Under*
1992 *Folks!; Christopher Columbus — The Discovery; Mr Baseball*


**SELLERS, Peter**
full name: Peter Richard Henry Sellers
(1925–80) UK

1951 *Penny Points To Paradise; Let's Go Crazy; London Entertains; Burlesque On Carmen*
1952 *Down Among The Z Men*

1953 *The Super Secret Service* (short);
*Our Girl Friday* (voice only)
1954 *Orders Are Orders*
1955 *John And Julie; The Ladykillers\*;
The Case Of The Mukkinese
Battlehorn* (short)
1956 *The Man Who Never Was* (voice
only)
1957 *Insomnia Is Good For You; Cold
Comfort; Dearth Of A Salesman*
(all shorts); *The Smallest Show
On Earth*
1958 *The Naked Truth; Up The Creek;
tom thumb*
1959 *Carlton Browne Of The FO; I'm All
Right Jack\*; The Mouse That
Roared; The Battle Of The Sexes*
1960 *Two-Way Stretch; Climb Up The
Wall; Never Let Go; The
Millionairess*
1961 *The Running, Jumping, Standing
Still Film* (short); *Only Two Can
Play; The Road To Hong Kong;
Mr Topaze* (also director)
1962 *Lolita\*; The Waltz Of The
Toreadors; The Dock Brief; The
Wrong Arm Of The Law*
1963 *Heavens Above; The Pink
Panther\**
1964 *Dr Strangelove Or How I Learned
To Stop Worrying And Love The
Bomb\*; A Shot In The Dark; A
Carol For Another Christmas* (TV);
*The World Of Henry Orient*
1965 *What's New Pussycat?*
1966 *After The Fox; The Wrong Box;
Birds, Bees And Storks* (narrator
only)
1967 *Woman Times Seven; The Bobo;
Casino Royale*
1968 *The Party; I Love You, Alice B
Toklas*
1969 *The Magic Christian*
1970 *Hoffman; Simon, Simon* (short);
*There's A Girl In My Soup; A Day
At The Beach*
1972 *Where Does It Hurt?; Alice's
Adventures In Wonderland*
1973 *Soft Beds, Hard Battles; The
Optimists Of Nine Elms; The
Blockhouse*

1974 *The Return Of The Pink Panther;
Ghost In The Noonday Sun; The
Great McGonagall*
1976 *Murder By Death; The Pink
Panther Strikes Again*
1978 *Revenge Of The Pink Panther;
The Great Pram Race* (voice only)
1979 *Being There; The Prisoner Of
Zenda*
1980 *The Fiendish Plot Of Dr Fu
Manchu*
1982 *The Trail Of The Pink Panther*

## SHARIF, Omar
real name: Michel Shalhoub
(1932–   ) Egypt

1954 *The Blazing Sun; Our Happy
Days; Devil Of The Sahara*
1955 *Struggle On The Pier; Land Of
Peace*
1956 *No Sleep; La Chatelaine Du Liban*
1957 *Shore Of Secrets; My Lover's
Mistake; Goha*
1958 *For The Sake Of A Woman; The
Lady Of The Castle; Rendezvous
With A Stranger; Scandal At
Zamalek*
1959 *We The Students; Struggle On
The Nile*
1960 *Love Rumour; The Beginning And
The End; The Agony Of Love;
River Of Love; I Love My Boss;
My Only Love; The Mamelukes*
(UK: *Revolt Of The Mamelukes*)
1961 *A Man In Our House*
1962 *Lawrence Of Arabia\**
1963 *The Fall Of The Roman Empire*
1964 *Behold A Pale Horse; The
Fabulous Adventures Of Marco
Polo* (UK: *Marco The
Magnificent*); *The Yellow Rolls-
Royce*
1965 *Genghis Khan; Doctor Zhivago\**
1966 *The Night Of The Generals; The
Poppy Is Also A Flower* (UK:
*Danger Grows Wild*)
1967 *C'Era Una Volta* (UK:
*Cinderella — Italian Style*)
1968 *Funny Girl\*; Mayerling;
McKenna's Gold*

**SHARIF, Omar** (cont.)
1969 *The Appointment; Che!*
1970 *The Horsemen; The Last Valley; Simon, Simon* (short)
1971 *Le Casse* (UK: *The Burglars*)
1972 *Elle Lui Chrait Dans L'Ile* (UK: *Brainwashed*)
1973 *The Mysterious Island Of Captain Nemo*
1974 *Juggernaut; The Tamarind Seed*
1975 *Funny Lady; Crime And Passion*
1976 *The Pink Panther Strikes Again*
1979 *Ashanti; Bloodline; S\*H\*E; The Baltimore Bullet*
1980 *Oh Heavenly Dog; Pleasure Palace* (TV)
1981 *Chanel Solitaire; Green Ice*
1984 *Ayoub* (TV); *Top Secret!*
1987 *La Novice; Chatov Et Les Démons; The Possessed*
1988 *Grand Larceny* (TV); *Les Pyramides Bleues*
1989 *Keys To Freedom; Michelangelo And Me*
1990 *The Rainbow Thief; Viaggio D'Amore*
1991 *Mayrig*

**SHATNER, William**
(1931– ) Canada

1958 *The Brothers Karamazov*
1961 *Judgement At Nuremberg\*; The Explosive Generation; The Intruder* (UK: *The Stranger*)
1964 *The Outrage*
1965 *Incubus*
1968 *Hour Of Vengeance*
1969 *Sole Survivor*
1971 *Vanished* (TV); *Owen Marshall, Counsellor At Law* (TV)
1972 *The People* (TV); *The Hound Of The Baskervilles* (TV)
1973 *Incident* (TV)
1974 *Dead Of Night; Big Bad Mama; Indict And Convict* (TV); *Pray For The Wildcats* (TV)
1975 *Impulse; The Devil's Rain; Barbary Coast* (TV)
1976 *Perilous Voyage* (TV); *A Whale Of A Tale*

1977 *Kingdom Of The Spiders*
1978 *Land Of No Return; Little Women* (TV); *The Third Walker; Crash* (TV)
1979 *Star Trek — The Motion Picture\*; RIEL; The Kidnapping Of The President*
1980 *The Babysitter* (TV)
1981 *Visiting Hours*
1982 *Star Trek II — The Wrath Of Khan; Airplane II — The Sequel*
1984 *Secrets Of A Married Man* (TV); *Star Trek III — The Search For Spock*
1985 *North Beach And Rawhide* (TV)
1986 *Star Trek IV — The Voyage Home; Blood Sport* (TV)
1988 *Broken Angel* (TV)
1989 *Star Trek V — The Final Frontier* (also director)
1990 *Kingdom Of The Spiders II*
1991 *Star Trek VI — The Undiscovered Country*
1993 *National Lampoon's Loaded Weapon*

**SHAW, Robert**
(1927–78) UK

1951 *The Lavender Hill Mob\**
1954 *The Dam Busters*
1956 *Doublecross; A Hill In Korea*
1958 *Sea Fury*
1959 *Libel*
1961 *The Valiant*
1962 *Tomorrow At Ten*
1963 *North To The Dales* (narrator only); *The Cracksman; The Caretaker; From Russia With Love\**
1964 *The Luck Of Ginger Coffey; Carol For Another Christmas* (TV)
1965 *Battle Of The Bulge*
1966 *A Man For All Seasons\**
1967 *Custer Of The West*
1969 *Battle Of Britain; The Royal Hunt Of The Sun; The Birthday Party*
1970 *Figures In A Landscape*
1971 *A Town Called Bastard*
1972 *Young Winston*

1973 *A Reflection Of Fear; The Hireling; The Sting\**
1974 *The Taking Of Pelham 1-2-3*
1975 *Jaws\*; Diamonds; The Judge And His Hangman*
1976 *Robin And Marian; Black Sunday; Swashbuckler* (UK: *The Scarlet Buccaneer*)
1977 *The Deep\**
1978 *Force Ten From Navarone*
1979 *Avalanche Express*

## SHEARER, Norma
real name: Edith Norma Fisher
(1900-83) Canada

1920 *Way Down East; The Flapper; The Stealers; The Restless Sex*
1921 *The Sign On The Door; Torch's Millions*
1922 *The Bootleggers; The Devil's Partner; Channing Of The Northwest; The Man Who Paid; The Leather Pushers*
1923 *Pleasure Mad; A Clouded Name; Man And Wife; The Wanters; Lucretia Lombard*
1924 *Blue Waters; Broadway After Dark; Empty Hands; He Who Gets Slapped; Married Flirts; Trail Of The Law; The Wolf Man; Broken Barriers; The Snob*
1925 *Pretty Ladies; Lady Of The Night; The Tower Of Lies; His Secretary; A Slave Of Fashion; Excuse Me; Waking Up The Town*
1926 *The Devil's Circus; The Waning Sex; Upstage* (UK: *The Mask Of Comedy*)
1927 *The Student Prince; The Demi-Bride; After Midnight*
1928 *Lady Of Chance; The Latest From Paris; The Actress* (UK: *Trelawny Of The Wells*)
1929 *Hollywood Revue Of 1929; The Trial Of Mary Dugan; The Last Of Mrs Cheyney*
1930 *Let Us Be Gay; The Divorcee; Their Own Desire*
1931 *Private Lives; Strangers May Kiss; A Free Soul; Jackie Cooper's*

*Christmas* (UK: *The Christmas Party*) (short)
1932 *Smilin' Through; Strange Interlude* (UK: *Strange Interval*); *The Stolen Jools* (UK: *The Slippery Pearls*) (short)
1934 *Riptide; The Barretts Of Wimpole Street\*; Hollywood On Parade No 13*
1936 *Romeo And Juliet*
1938 *Marie Antoinette*
1939 *The Women\*; Idiot's Delight*
1940 *Escape*
1941 *Cavalcade Of The Academy Awards* (short)
1942 *We Were Dancing; Her Cardboard Lover*

## SHEEN, Charlie
real name: Carlos Estevez
(1965–   ) USA

1974 *The Execution Of Private Slovik* (TV)
1977 *Grizzly II. The Predator*
1984 *Red Dawn; Silence Of The Heart* (TV); *The Boys Next Door*
1985 *Three For The Road*
1986 *Lucas; The Wraith; Ferris Bueller's Day Off; Platoon\*; Wisdom*
1987 *Wall Street\*; No Man's Land*
1988 *Eight Men Out; Young Guns\*; Never On A Tuesday*
1989 *Beverly Hills Brats; Major League; Courage Mountain; Backtrack* (UK: *Catchfire*); *A Tale Of Two Sisters* (narrator only)
1990 *Men At Work; Cadence* (UK: *Stockade*); *Navy SEALS; The Rookie*
1991 *Hot Shots*
1993 *Hot Shots 2*

## SHEEN, Martin
real name: Ramon Estevez
(1940–   ) USA

1967 *The Incident*
1968 *The Subject Was Roses*
1969 *Then Came Bronson* (TV)

**SHEEN, Martin** (cont.)

1970 *When The Line Goes Through; Catch 22\**
1971 *The Forests Are Nearly All Gone; Welcome Home, Johnny Bristol* (TV); *Mongo's Back In Town* (TV); *Goodbye, Raggedy Ann* (TV); *No Drums, No Bugles*
1972 *Rage; Crime Club* (TV); *Pursuit* (TV); *That Certain Summer* (TV); Pick-Up On 101 (UK: *Echoes Of The Road*)
1973 *Message To My Daughter* (TV); *Letters From Three Lovers* (TV); *Catholics* (TV); *Harry O* (TV); *A Prowler In The Heart* (TV); *Badlands\**
1974 *The Execution Of Private Slovik* (TV); *Pretty Boy Floyd* (TV); *The Missiles Of October* (TV); *The California Kid* (TV)
1975 *The Legend Of Earl Durand; Roman Gray* (TV) (UK: *The Art of Crime*); *Sweet Hostage* (TV); *The Last Survivors* (TV)
1976 *The Cassandra Crossing; The Little Girl Who Lives Down The Lane*
1978 *Eagle's Wing*
1979 *Apocalypse Now\*; Blind Ambition* (TV)
1980 *The Final Countdown; Loophole*
1982 *Gandhi\*; In The Custody Of Strangers* (TV); *Engima; That Championship Season; in The King Of Prussia; Man, Woman, Child; No Place To Hide* (narrator only)
1983 *Kennedy* (TV); *The Dead Zone; Choices Of The Heart* (TV)
1984 *Firestarter; The Atlanta Child Murders* (TV); *The Guardian* (TV)
1985 *Consenting Adults* (TV); *Shattered Spirits* (TV); *Out Of The Darkness* (TV); *A State Of Emergency; In The Name Of The People* (narrator only)
1986 *News At Eleven* (TV); Samaritan: The Mitch Snyder Story (TV); *Broken Rainbow* (voice only)

1987 *The Believers; Wall Street\*; Judgment In Berlin; Conspiracy: The Trial Of The Chiacgo 8* (TV); *Siesta; Dear America* (voice only)
1988 *Da*
1989 *Beverly Hills Brats; Walking After Midnight; Cold Front; Nightbreaker* (TV); *Marked For Murder; Beyond The Stars*
1990 *Cadence* (UK: *Stockade*) (also director); *Original Intent; The Maid*
1991 *Limited Time; Another Time, Another Place; Secret Society; Hearts Of Darkness* (documentary)
1993 *Finnegan's Wake*

**SHEPARD, Sam**
full name: Sam Shepard Rogers
(1943– ) USA

1969 *Easy Rider\** (voice only)
1978 *Renaldo And Clara; Days Of Heaven\**
1980 *Resurrection*
1981 *Raggedy Man*
1982 *Frances\**
1983 *The Right Stuff\**
1984 *Country*
1985 *Fool For Love*
1986 *Crimes Of The Heart*
1987 *Baby Boom*
1988 *Far North* (director only)
1989 *Steel Magnolias\**
1990 *Defenseless; Bright Angels*
1991 *Voyager*
1992 *Silent Tongue* (director only)

**SIDNEY, Sylvia**
real name: Sophia Kosow
(1910– ) USA

1927 *Broadway Nights*
1929 *Thru Different Eyes*
1930 *Five Minutes From The Station* (short)

1931 *Street Scene; City Streets; Ladies Of The Big House; An American Tragedy; Confessions Of A Co-Ed* (UK: *Her Dilemma*)
1932 *The Miracle Man; Madame Butterfly; Make Me A Star; Merrily We Go To Hell* (UK: *Merrily We Go To—*)
1933 *Jennie Gerhardt; Pick-Up*
1934 *Behold My Wife; Thirty Day Princess; Good Dame* (UK: *Good Girl*)
1935 *Accent On Youth; Mary Burns, Fugitive*
1936 *Fury; Trail Of The Lonesome Pine; Sabotage*
1937 *Dead End\*; You Only Live Once*
1938 *You And Me*
1939 *One Third Of A Nation*
1941 *The Wagons Roll At Night*
1945 *Blood On The Sun*
1946 *The Searching Wind; Mr Ace*
1947 *Love From A Stranger* (UK: *A Stranger Walked In*)
1952 *Les Misérables*
1955 *Man On The Lodge; Violent Saturday*
1956 *Behind The High Wall*
1971 *Do Not Fold, Spindle Or Mutilate* (TV)
1973 *Summer Wishes, Winter Dreams*
1975 *Winner Takes All* (TV); *The Secret Night Caller* (TV)
1976 *Raid On Entebbe; Demon; Death At Love House* (TV)
1977 *I Never Promised You A Rose Garden; Snowbeast* (TV)
1978 *Damien—Omen II; Siege* (TV)
1979 *The Gossip Columnist* (TV)
1980 *The Shadow Box* (TV)
1981 *A Small Killing* (TV); *FDR: The Last Year* (TV)
1982 *Having It All; Hammett*
1983 *Order Of Death*
1984 *Finnegan Begin Again* (TV)
1985 *An Early Frost* (TV)
1987 *Pals* (TV)
1988 *Beetlejuice\**
1990 *The Exorcist III*
1992 *Used People*

## SIGNORET, Simone
real name: Simone Henriette Charlotte Kaminker
(1921–85) Germany

1942 *Le Prince Charmant; Boléro; Les Visiteurs Du Soir* (UK: *The Devil's Envoy*)
1943 *La Boîte Aux Rêves; Adieu Léonard; L'Ange De La Nuit*
1944 *Béatrice Devant Le Désir*
1945 *Les Démons De L'Aube; Le Couple Idéal*
1946 *Macadam*
1947 *Dédée D'Anvers* (UK: *Dédée*); *Fantomas*
1948 *Against The Wind; L'Impasse Aux Deux Anges*
1949 *Manèges* (UK: *The Wanton*)
1950 *Four Days' Leave; Le Traqué; La Ronde*
1951 *Ombre Et Lumière*
1952 *Casque D'Or* (UK: *Golden Marie*)
1953 *Thérèse Raquin*
1954 *Les Diaboliques* (UK: *The Fiends*)
1956 *La Muerte En Este Jardin* (UK: *Evil Eden*); *Die Wind Rose*
1957 *Les Sorcières De Salem* (UK: *The Witches Of Salem*)
1959 *Room At The Top\*; Yves Montand Chante*
1960 *Les Mauvais Coups; Adua E La Compagne* (UK: *Hungry For Love*)
1961 *Les Amours Célèbres*
1962 *Le Jour Et L'Heure; Term Of Trial*
1963 *Dragées Au Poivre* (UK: *Sweet And Sour*); *Il Giomo Piu Corto Commedia Umaristica*
1965 *Ship Of Fools\*; Compartiment Tueurs* (UK: *The Sleeping Car Murders*)
1966 *Paris, Brûle-T-Il?* (UK: *Is Paris Burning?*)
1967 *Games*
1968 *The Seagull; Mr Freedom*
1969 *Le Joli Mai* (narrator only); *L'Américain; L'Armée Des Ombres*
1970 *Le Rose Et Le Noir; L'Aveu* (UK: *The Confession*); *Compte A Rebours*

**SIGNORET, Simone** (cont,)

1971 *La Veuve Couderc; Le Chat* (UK: *The Cat*)

1973 *Les Granges Brûlées* (UK: *The Investigation*); *Rude Journée Pour La Reine*

1974 *La Chair De L'Orchidée; Defense De Savoir*

1975 *Madame Le Juge* (TV); *Police Python 357*

1977 *La Vie Devant Soi* (UK: *Madame Rosa*)

1978 *Une Femme Dangereuse*

1979 *L'Adolescente* (UK: *The Adolescent*); *Judith Therpauve; Je T'Ai Ecrit Une Lettre D'Amour* (aka *Chère Inconnue*)

1981 *Gina*

1982 *L'Etoile Du Nord* (UK: *The Northern Star*); *Guy De Maupassant*

1983 *Des 'Terroristes' A La Retraite* (narrator only)


**SIM, Alistair**
(1900–76) UK

1935 *The Case Of Gabriel Perry; The Riverside Murder; A Fire Has Been Arranged; The Private Secretary; Late Extra*

1936 *Wedding Group; Troubled Waters; Keep Your Seats Please; The Mysterious Mr Davis; The Big Noise; The Man In The Mirror; She Knew What She Wanted; Strange Experiment*

1937 *The Squeaker; Clothes And The Woman; Melody And Romance; Gangway; A Romance In Flanders*

1938 *Alf's Button Afloat; Sailing Along; The Terror; Climbing High; This Man Is News; Inspector Hornleigh*

1939 *This Man Is News; Inspector Hornleigh On Holiday*

1940 *Law And Disorder; Her Father's Daughter* (short)

1941 *Cottage To Let; Inspector Hornleigh Goes To It*

1942 *Let The People Sing*

1943 *Fiddling Fuel* (short)

1944 *Waterloo Road*

1945 *Journey Together*

1946 *Green For Danger; Hue And Cry*

1947 *Captain Boycott*

1948 *London Belongs To Me*

1950 *The Happiest Days Of Your Life; Stage Fright*

1951 *Laughter In Paradise; Lady Godiva Rides Again; Scrooge*

1952 *Folly To Be Wise*

1953 *Innocents In Paris*

1954 *The Belles Of St Trinian's\*; An Inspector Calls*

1955 *Escapade; Festival In Edinburgh* (short, narrator only)

1956 *Geordie; The Green Man*

1958 *Blue Murder At St Trinian's*

1959 *The Doctor's Dilemma; Left, Right And Centre*

1960 *The Millionairess; School For Scoundrels*

1961 *The Anatomist*

1972 *The Ruling Class*

1975 *Royal Flash*

1976 *Rogue Male* (TV); *Escape From The Dark*


**SIMMONS, Jean**
(1929– ) USA

1944 *Give Us The Moon; Mr Emmanuel; Kiss The Bride Goodbye; Meet Sexton Blake*

1945 *The Way To The Stars; Caesar And Cleopatra; Sports Day* (short)

1946 *Great Expectations\*; Hungry Hill; Black Narcissus\**

1947 *Uncle Silas; The Woman In The Hall*

1948 *Hamlet\*; The Blue Lagoon*

1949 *Adam And Evelyne*

1950 *Trio; So Long At The Fair; Cage Of Gold; The Clouded Yellow*

1952 *Androcles And The Lion; Angel Face*

1953 *Young Bess; The Actress; Affair With A Stranger; She Couldn't Say No* (UK: *Beautiful But Dangerous*)

1954 *The Egyptian; Desirée; A Bullet Is Waiting*
1955 *Footsteps In The Fog; Guys And Dolls\**
1956 *Hilda Crane*
1957 *This Could Be The Night; Until They Sail*
1958 *Home Before Dark; The Big Country\**
1959 *This Earth Is Mine*
1960 *Elmer Gantry\*; Spartacus\**
1961 *The Grass Is Greener*
1963 *All The Way Home*
1965 *Life At The Top; Mr Buddwing* (UK: *Woman Without A Face*)
1967 *Rough Night In Jericho; Divorce—American Style*
1968 *Heidi Comes Home* (TV)
1969 *The Happy Ending*
1970 *Decisions! Decisions!* (TV); *Say Hello To Yesterday*
1975 *Mr Sycamore; The Easter Promise* (TV)
1978 *The Dain Curse* (TV); *Dominique*
1981 *A Small Killing* (TV); *Golden Gate* (TV)
1983 *Robin Hood* (TV)
1984 *Midas Valley* (TV)
1987 *Perry Mason: The Case Of The Lost Love* (TV)
1988 *The Dawning; Going Undercover; Inherit The Wind* (TV)
1989 *Great Expectations* (TV)
1990 *People Like Us* (TV); *Sense And Sensibility* (TV); *Laker Girls* (TV); *Dark Shadows* (TV)

## SINATRA, Frank
full name: Francis Albert Sinatra
(1915–   ) USA

1935 *Major Bowes Amateur Theatre Of The Air* (short)
1941 *Las Vegas Nights*
1942 *Ship Ahoy*
1943 *Reveille With Beverly; Higher And Higher; Showbusiness At War* (documentary)
1944 *Step Lively; The Shining Future* (documentary)

1945 *Anchors Aweigh\*; All Star Bond Rally* (short); *The House I Live In*
1946 *Till The Clouds Roll By\**
1947 *It Happened In Brooklyn*
1948 *The Miracle Of The Bells; The Kissing Bandit*
1949 *Take Me Out To The Ball Game* (UK: *Everybody's Cheering*); *On The Town\**
1951 *Double Dynamite; Meet Danny Wilson*
1952 *Screen Snapshots No 206* (short)
1953 *From Here To Eternity\**
1954 *Suddenly; Young At Heart*
1955 *Not As A Stranger\*; The Tender Trap; Guys And Dolls\*; The Man With The Golden Arm*
1956 *Meet Me In Las Vegas* (UK: *Viva Las Vegas!*); *Johnny Concho; High Society\*; Around The World In 80 Days\**
1957 *The Pride And The Passion; The Joker Is Wild; Pal Joey*
1958 *Kings Go Forth; Some Came Running*
1959 *A Hole In The Head; Never So Few; Invitation To Monte Carlo* (short)
1960 *Can-Can; Ocean's Eleven\*; Pepe*
1961 *The Devil At Four O'Clock; Road To Hong Kong*
1962 *Sergeants Three; The Manchurian Candidate\*; Sinatra In Israel* (short)
1963 *The List Of Adrian Messenger; Come Blow Your Horn; Four For Texas*
1964 *Robin And The Seven Hoods*
1965 *None But The Brave* (also director); *Von Ryan's Express; Marriage On The Rocks*
1966 *The Oscar; Cast A Giant Shadow; Assault On A Queen*
1967 *Tony Rome; The Naked Runner*
1968 *Lady In Cement; The Detective*
1970 *Dirty Dingus Magee*
1974 *That's Entertainment*
1977 *Contract On Cherry Street* (TV)
1980 *The First Deadly Sin*
1983 *Cannonball Run II*
1988 *Who Framed Roger Rabbit\** (voice only)
1990 *Listen Up* (documentary)

## SLATER, Christian
(1965–   ) USA

1983  *Living Proof: The Hank Williams Jnr Story* (TV)
1985  *The Legend Of Billie Jean*
1986  *The Name Of The Rose; Twisted* (released 1992)
1988  *Tucker: The Man And His Dream\*; Gleaming The Cube*
1989  *Beyond The Stars; Heathers\*; The Wizard*
1990  *Tales From The Darkside: The Movie; Young Guns II; Pump Up The Volume*
1991  *Robin Hood: Prince Of Thieves\*; Mobsters; Star Trek VI — The Undiscovered Country*
1992  *Kuffs; Fern Gully: The Last Rain Forest* (voice only)
1993  *Untamed Heart; True Romance*

## SMITH, Dame Maggie
(1934–   ) UK

1958  *Nowhere To Go*
1962  *Go To Blazes*
1963  *The VIPs*
1964  *Young Cassidy; The Pumpkin Eater*
1965  *Othello*
1967  *The Honey Pot*
1968  *Hot Millions*
1969  *The Prime Of Miss Jean Brodie\*; Oh! What A Lovely War*
1972  *Love And Pain And The Whole Damned Thing; Travels With My Aunt*
1976  *Murder By Death*
1978  *Death On The Nile; California Suite\**
1981  *Clash Of The Titans; Quartet*
1982  *Evil Under The Sun; Ménage A Trois* (UK: *Better Late Than Never*); *The Missionary*
1983  *Jatsani Kell* (UK: *Lily In Love*)
1984  *A Private Function*
1985  *A Room With A View\**
1987  *The Lonely Passion Of Judith Hearne*

1990  *Romeo–Juliet* (voice only)
1991  *Hook\**
1992  *Sister Act; Momento Mori*
1993  *The Secret Garden; Suddenly Last Summer* (TV)

## SNIPES, Wesley
(1963–   ) USA

1986  *Streets Of Gold; Wildcats*
1987  *Critical Condition*
1989  *Major League*
1990  *King Of New York; Mo' Better Blues*
1991  *Jungle Fever\*; New Jack City; The Waterdance*
1992  *White Men Can't Jump; Passenger 57*
1993  *Money Men; The Rising Sun*

## SPACEK, Sissy
real name: Mary Elizabeth Spacek
(1949–   ) USA

1970  *Trash* (extra)
1972  *Prime Cut*
1973  *Badlands\*; Ginger In The Morning* (TV); *The Girls Of Huntingdon House* (TV)
1974  *Phantom Of The Paradise* (set decorator only); *The Migrants* (TV)
1975  *Katherine* (TV)
1976  *Carrie; Welcome To LA*
1977  *Three Women*
1979  *Heart Beat*
1980  *Coal Miner's Daughter\**
1981  *Raggedy Man; Missing\**
1983  *The Man With Two Brains\** (voice only)
1984  *The River*
1985  *Violets Are Blue; Marie*
1986  *'Night Mother; Crimes Of The Heart*
1990  *The Long Walk Home*
1991  *JFK\*; Hard Promises*
1992  *Private Matter* (TV)
1993  *The Mommy Market*

## SPADER, James
(1961–  ) USA

1978 *Team-Mates*
1981 *Endless Love*
1983 *Killer In The Family* (TV);
*Cocaine: One Man's War* (TV)
1984 *Family Secrets* (TV)
1985 *The New Kids; Star Crossed* (TV);
*Tuff Turf*
1986 *Pretty In Pink*
1987 *Mannequin; Baby Boom; Less
Than Zero; Wall Street\**
1988 *Jack's Back*
1989 *sex, lies and videotape\*; The
Rachel Papers*
1990 *Bad Influence; White Palace*
1991 *True Colors*
1992 *Storyville; The Music Of Chance*
1993 *Wolf*

## STALLONE, Sylvester
(1946–  ) USA

1970 *Party At Kitty And Stud's* (aka *The
Italian Stallion*)
1071 *Bananas*
1972 *The Rebel* (aka *A Man Called
Rainbo*)
1974 *No Place To Hide; The Lords Of
Flatbush*
1975 *The Prisoner Of Second Avenue;
Farewell, My Lovely; Capone;
Death Race 2000*
1976 *Rocky\*; Cannonball* (UK:
*Carquake*)
1978 *F\*I\*S\*T; Paradise Alley* (also
director)
1979 *Rocky II* (also director)
1981 *Nighthawks; Escape To Victory*
1982 *First Blood\*; Rocky III* (also
director)
1984 *Rhinestone*
1985 *Rambo: First Blood Part II; Rocky
IV* (also director)
1986 *Cobra*
1987 *Over The Top*
1988 *Rambo III*
1989 *Lock-Up; Tango & Cash*
1990 *Rocky V*
1991 *Oscar*

1992 *Stop Or My Mom Will Shoot*
1993 *Bartholemew Vs Neff; Cliffhanger*

See also directors listing

## STANLEY, Kim
real name: Patricia Reid
(1921–  ) USA

1958 *The Goddess*
1964 *Seance On A Wet Afternoon*
1966 *Three Sisters*
1982 *Frances\**
1983 *The Right Stuff\**

## STANWYCK, Barbara
real name: Ruby Stevens
(1907–90) USA

1927 *Broadway Nights*
1929 *The Locked Door; Mexicali Rose;
The Voice Of Hollywood*
(documentary)
1930 *Ladies Of Leisure*
1931 *Illicit; Ten Cents A Dance; Miracle
Woman; Night Nurse; Screen
Snapshots No 4* (documentary)
1932 *Forbidden; Shopworn; So Big;
The Purchase Price*
1933 *Baby Face; The Bitter Tea Of
General Yen; Ladies They Talk
About; Ever In My Heart*
1934 *Gambling Lady; The Secret Bride*
(UK: *Concealment*); *A Lost Lady*
(UK: *Courageous*)
1935 *The Woman In Red; Annie
Oakley; Red Salute* (UK: *Arms
And The Girl*)
1936 *The Bride Walks Out; A Message
To Garcia; The Plough And The
Stars; His Brother's Wife; Banjo
On My Knee*
1937 *Stella Dallas\*; Breakfast For Two;
Internes Can't Take Money* (UK:
*You Can't Take Money*); *This Is
My Affair* (UK: *His Affair*)
1938 *The Mad Miss Manton; Always
Goodbye*
1939 *Union Pacific; Golden Boy;
Remember The Night*
1941 *You Belong To Me; Ball Of Fire\*;
Meet John Doe; The Lady Eve\**

**STANWYCK, Barbara** (cont.)

1942 *The Gay Sisters; The Great Man's Lady*
1943 *Flesh And Fantasy; Lady Of Burlesque* (UK: *Striptease Lady*)
1944 *Hollywood Canteen; Double Indemnity\**
1945 *Hollywood Victory Caravan* (short); *Christmas In Connecticut* (UK: *Indiscretion*)
1946 *My Reputation; The Bride Wore Boots; California; The Strange Love Of Martha Ivers*
1947 *The Two Mrs Carrolls; Variety Girl; The Other Love; Cry Wolf*
1948 *Sorry, Wrong Number; BF's Daughter* (UK: *Polly Fulton*)
1949 *The Lady Gambles; Eyes Of Hollywood; Thelma Jordan* (UK: *The File On Thelma Jordan*)
1950 *East Side, West Side; To Please A Lady; The Furies; No Man Of Her Own*
1951 *The Man With A Cloak*
1952 *Clash By Night*
1953 *All I Desire; Titanic; Jeopardy; The Moonlighter; Blowing Wild*
1954 *Witness To Murder; Executive Suite; Cattle Queen Of Montana*
1955 *The Violent Men* (UK: *Rough Company*); *Escape To Burma*
1956 *The Maverick Queen; The Wilder Years; There's Always Tomorrow; Crime Of Passion*
1957 *Forty Guns; Trooper Hook*
1962 *Walk On The Wild Side*
1964 *Roustabout*
1965 *The Night Walker*
1970 *The House That Wouldn't Die* (TV)
1971 *A Taste Of Evil* (TV)
1973 *The Letters* (TV)

**STEIGER, Rod**
(1925–   ) USA

1951 *Teresa*
1954 *On The Waterfront\**
1955 *The Big Knife; The Court Martial Of Billy Mitchell* (UK: *One Man Mutiny*)

1956 *Oklahoma!\*; The Harder They Fall; Back From Eternity; Jubal*
1957 *The Unholy Wife; Run Of The Arrow; Across The Bridge*
1958 *Cry Terror!*
1959 *Al Capone*
1960 *Seven Thieves*
1961 *The Mark; On Friday At 11*
1962 *Convicts Four* (UK: *Reprieve!*); *13 West Street; The Longest Day\**
1963 *Hands Across The City; Gli Indifferenti* (UK: *Time Of Indifference*)
1964 *E Venne Un Uomo* (UK: *A Man Named John*)
1965 *The Pawnbroker; The Loved One; Doctor Zhivago\**
1967 *In The Heat Of The Night\*; The Girl And The General; The Movie Maker* (TV)
1968 *No Way To Treat A Lady; The Sergeant*
1969 *The Illustrated Man; Three Into Two Won't Go*
1970 *Waterloo*
1971 *Duck You Sucker; Happy Birthday Wanda June*
1972 *The Heroes*
1973 *Lucky Luciano; Lolly Madonna XXX* (UK: *Lolly Madonna War*)
1974 *Innocents With Dirty Hands*
1975 *Hennessy; Mussolini: The Last Four Days*
1976 *W C Fields And Me*
1977 *Jimbuck* (aka *Portrait Of A Hitman*)
1978 *Love And Bullets; Wolf Lake; F\*I\*S\*T*
1979 *Breakthrough; The Amityville Horror\**
1980 *Klondike Fever; Cattle Annie And Little Britches; Omar Mukhtar: Lion Of The Desert; The Lucky Star*
1981 *The Chosen*
1982 *Der Zauerberg*
1983 *Mafia Kingpin; Cook And Peary: The Race To The Pole* (TV)
1984 *The Naked Face*
1986 *Feel The Heat; The Kindred; Sword Of Gideon* (TV)

1987 *American Gothic; Hello Actors Studio* (documentary)
1988 *Desperado: Avalanche At Devil's Ridge* (TV); *Ice Runner; Celluloid*
1989 *The January Man; That Summer Of White Roses; Tennessee Nights; Passion And Paradise* (TV)
1990 *Men Of Respect; The Exiles*
1991 *In The Line Of Duty: Manhunt In The Dakotas* (TV); *The Ballad Of The Sad Café*
1992 *Guilty As Charged; The Player\**
1993 *The Neighbor*

## STEWART, James Maitland
(1908– ) USA

1935 *Important News* (short); *Murder Man*
1936 *Next Time We Love* (UK: *Next Time We Live*); *Rose Marie\*; Wife Vs Secretary; Small Town Girl; Speed; Born To Dance; The Gorgeous Hussy; After The Thin Man*
1937 *The Last Gangster; Seventh Heaven; Navy Blue And Gold*
1938 *Of Human Hearts; The Shopworn Angel; Vivacious Lady; You Can't Take It With You\**
1939 *Ice Follies Of 1939; It's A Wonderful World; Made For Each Other; Destry Rides Again; Mr Smith Goes To Washington\**
1940 *No Time For Comedy; The Shop Around The Corner\*; The Mortal Storm; The Philadelphia Story\**
1941 *Ziegfeld Girl; Come Live With Me; Pot O' Gold* (UK: *The Golden Hour*)
1942 *Screen Snapshots No 103; Fellow Americans; Winning Your Wings* (all documentaries)
1946 *American Brotherhood Week* (documentary); *It's A Wonderful Life\**
1947 *Thunderbolt* (documentary); *Magic Town; Call Northside 777*
1948 *A Miracle Can Happen* (aka *On Our Merry Way*); *Rope; You Gotta Stay Happy; 10,000 Kids And A Cop* (short)
1949 *The Stratton Story; Malaya* (UK: *East Of The Rising Sun*)
1950 *And Then There Were None* (narrator only); *The Jackpot; Winchester'73; Broken Arrow; Harvey\**
1951 *No Highway* (UK: *No Highway In The Sky*)
1952 *The Greatest Show On Earth\*; Carbine Williams; Bend Of The River* (UK: *Where The River Bends*)
1953 *Thunder Bay; The Naked Spur; The Glenn Miller Story\*; Hollywood Laugh Parade* (documentary)
1954 *Rear Window; The Far Country*
1955 *Strategic Air Command; The Man From Laramie*
1956 *The Man Who Knew Too Much*
1957 *Night Passage; The Spirit Of St Louis*
1958 *Bell, Book And Candle; Vertigo\**
1959 *The FBI Story; Anatomy Of A Murder\**
1960 *The Mountain Road*
1961 *Two Rode Together; X-15* (narrator only)
1962 *The Man Who Shot Liberty Valance\*; How The West Was Won\*; Mr Hobbs Takes A Vacation*
1963 *Take Her She's Mine*
1964 *Cheyenne Autumn*
1965 *Dear Brigitte; The Flight Of The Phoenix; Shenandoah*
1966 *The Rare Breed; Hollywood Star Spangled Revue* (documentary)
1967 *Firecreek*
1968 *Bandolero*
1970 *The Cheyenne Social Club*
1971 *Fool's Parade* (UK: *Dynamite Man From Glory Jail*); *Directed By John Ford* (documentary)
1973 *Hawkins On Murder* (TV)
1974 *That's Entertainment*
1976 *The Shootist\**
1978 *The Big Sleep; The Magic Of Lassie*

**STEWART, James Maitland** (cont.)
1980 *Mr Krueger's Christmas* (TV)
(short)
1981 *A Tale Of Africa*
1983 *Right Of Way* (TV)
1987 *North And South Book II* (TV)
1991 *An American Tail 2: Fievel Goes West* (voice only)

## STONE, Sharon
(19?–   ) USA

1980 *Stardust Memories*
1981 *Deadly Blessing*
1984 *Irreconcilable Differences*
1985 *King Solomon's Mines*
1986 *Allan Quatermain And The Lost City Of Gold*
1987 *Police Academy 4: Citizens On Patrol; Cold Steel*
1988 *Action Jackson; Above The Law* (UK: *Nico*); *Personal Choice*
1989 *Blood And Sand*
1990 *Total Recall*; *Let Sleeping Dogs Lie*
1991 *He Said, She Said; Scissors; Year Of The Gun*
1992 *Diary Of A Hitman; Basic Instinct*
1993 *Sliver; The Lady Takes An Ace; The Last Action Hero; Intersection*

## STREEP, Meryl
real name: Mary Louise Streep
(1949–   ) USA

1976 *Everybody Rides A Carousel* (voice only)
1977 *Julia*; *The Deadliest Season* (TV)
1978 *The Deer Hunter**
1979 *Manhattan*; *The Seduction Of Joe Tynan; Kramer Vs Kramer**
1981 *The French Lieutenant's Woman**
1982 *Still Of The Night; Sophie's Choice**
1983 *Silkwood**
1984 *In Our Hands* (documentary); *Falling In Love*
1985 *Out Of Africa*; *Plenty*
1986 *Heartburn*
1987 *Ironweed**

1988 *A Cry In The Dark**
1989 *She-Devil*
1990 *Postcards From The Edge**
1991 *Defending Your Life*
1992 *Death Becomes Her**
1993 *The House Of The Spirits*

## STREISAND, Barbra
real name: Barbara Joan Streisand
(1942–   ) USA

1968 *Funny Girl**
1969 *Hello, Dolly!**
1970 *On A Clear Day You Can See Forever; The Owl And The Pussycat**
1972 *Up The Sandbox; What's Up Doc?**
1973 *The Way We Were**
1974 *For Pete's Sake*
1975 *Funny Lady*
1976 *A Star Is Born**
1979 *The Main Event*
1981 *All Night Long*
1983 *Yentl* (also director)
1987 *Nuts**
1990 *Listen Up: The Lives Of Quincy Jones* (documentary)
1991 *Prince Of Tides**

See also directors listing

## SULLAVAN, Margaret
real name: Margaret Brooke
(1911–60) USA

1933 *Only Yesterday*
1934 *Little Man, What Now?*
1935 *The Good Fairy, So Red The Rose*
1936 *The Moon's Our Home; Next Time We Love* (UK: *Next Time We Live*)
1938 *The Shining Hour; Three Comrades; The Shopworn Angel*
1940 *The Shop Around The Corner*; *The Mortal Storm*
1941 *Appointment For Love; Backstreet; So Ends Our Night*
1943 *Cry Havoc*
1950 *No Sad Songs For Me*

## SUTHERLAND, Donald
(1934– ) Canada

1963 *The World Ten Times Over*
1964 *Castle Of The Living Dead*
1965 *Dr Terror's House Of Horrors; The Bedford Incident; Promise Her Anything; Fanatic*
1966 *Morgan—A Suitable Case For Treatment* (voice only)
1967 *The Dirty Dozen\*; Billion Dollar Brain; Oedipus The King*
1968 *Interlude; Sebastian; The Sunshine Patriot* (TV); *Joanna; The Split*
1969 *Start The Revolution Without Me*
1970 *M\*A\*S\*H; Kelly's Heroes; Act Of The Heart*
1971 *Little Murders; Alex In Wonderland; Johnny Got His Gun; Klute\**
1972 *Steelyard Blues*
1973 *Don't Look Now; Lady Ice; FTA; Dan Candy's Law*
1974 *3\*P\*Y\*S, The Day Of The Locust*
1975 *The Judge And His Hangman; Murder On The Bridge; La Spirale* (narrator only)
1976 *The Eagle Has Landed; Novecento\** (UK: *1900*); *Fellini's Casanova*
1977 *Blood Relatives; Kentucky Fried Movie; The Disappearance*
1978 *National Lampoon's Animal House\*; Bethune* (TV); *The First Great Train Robbery; Invasion Of The Bodysnatchers; Murder By Decree*
1979 *Bear Island; Nothing Personal; A Man, A Woman And A Bank*
1980 *Gas; Ordinary People\**
1981 *Eye Of The Needle; Threshold*
1982 *A War Story* (narrator only)
1983 *Max Dugan Returns; The Winter Of Our Discontent* (TV); *Crackers; Hotel De La Paix*
1984 *Ordeal By Innocence*
1985 *Revolution\*; The Trouble With Spies; Heaven Help Us* (UK: *Catholic Boys*)
1986 *Gauguin; Oviri; The Rosary Murders*

1987 *Apprentice To Murder; The Long-Lost Friends; Orn*
1988 *Lunatics; Bethune*
1989 *A Dry White Season; Lock-Up; Lost Angels* (UK: *The Road Home*)
1990 *Eminent Domain; Buster's Bedroom*
1991 *Backdraft\*; JFK\*; Schrei Aus Stein* (UK:*Scream Of Stone*); *The Railway Station Man*
1992 *Buffy, The Vampire Slayer; Quicksand: No Escape* (TV)
1993 *Younger And Younger; Six Degrees Of Separation*

## SUTHERLAND, Kiefer
(1967– ) Canada

1983 *Max Dugan Returns*
1984 *The Bay Boy*
1985 *At Close Range*
1986 *Trapped In Silence* (TV); *Brotherhood Of Justice* (TV); *Crazy Moon*
1987 *Stand By Me; The Killing Time; The Lost Boys; Amazing Stories* (TV)
1988 *Bright Lights, Big City; Young Guns\*; 1969; The Promised Land*
1989 *Renegades*
1990 *Flashback; The Nutcracker* (voice only); *Chicago Joe And The Showgirl; Flatliners; Young Guns II*
1992 *Article 99; A Few Good Men\**
1993 *The Vanishing*

## SWANSON, Gloria
real name: Gloria Swenson
(1897–1983) USA

1915 *The Romance Of An American Duchess; At The End Of A Perfect Day; Broken Pledge; The Ambition Of The Baron; The Fable Of Elvira And Farina And The Meal Ticket; His New Job* (all shorts)
1916 *Sweedie Goes To College; A Dash Of Courage; Girls'*

**SWANSON, Gloria** (cont.)
*Dormitory; Hearts And Sparks; A Social Club; Haystacks And Steeples; Danger Girl; The Nick-Of-Time Baby; Teddy At The Throttle* (all shorts)
1917 *Baseball Madness; The Pullman Bride; The Sultan's Wife; Dangers Of A Bride* (all shorts)
1918 *Her Decision; You Can't Believe Everything; Society For Sale; Station Content; Shifting Sands; The Secret Code; Everywoman's Husband; Wife Or Country*
1919 *Don't Change Your Husband; Male And Female* (UK: *The Admirable Crichton*); *For Better, For Worse*
1920 *Why Change Your Wife?; Something To Think About*
1921 *Don't Tell Everything; The Affairs Of Anatol* (UK: *A Prodigal Night*); *The Great Moment; Under The Lash* (UK: *The Shulamite*)
1922 *Her Husband's Trademark; Beyond The Rock; The Gilded Cage; The Impossible Mrs Bellew; My American Wife*
1923 *Bluebeard's Eighth Wife; Prodigal Daughters; Hollywood; Zaza*
1924 *Manhandled; The Humming Bird; The Wages Of Virtue; A Society Scandal; Her Love Story*
1925 *Madame Sans Gêne; The Coast Of Folly; Stage Struck*
1926 *The Untamed Lady; Fine Manners*
1927 *The Loves Of Sunya*
1928 *Queen Kelly; Sadie Thompson*
1929 *The Trespasser*
1930 *What A Widow!*
1931 *Indiscreet; Tonight Or Never; Screen Snapshots No 4* (short)
1932 *Perfect Understanding*
1934 *Music In The Air*
1941 *Father Takes A Wife*
1950 *Sunset Boulevard**
1952 *Three For Bedroom C*
1956 *Mio Figlio Nerone* (UK: *Nero's Weekend*)
1974 *The Killer Bees* (TV); *Airport 1975*

**SWAYZE, Patrick Wayne**
(1952–   ) USA

1979 *Skatetown USA*
1980 *The Comeback Kid* (TV)
1981 *Return Of The Rebels* (TV)
1982 *The Renegades* (TV); *The Outsiders**
1983 *The New Season* (TV); *Uncommon Valor*
1984 *Pigs Vs Freaks* (TV) (aka *Off Sides*); *Grandview USA; Red Dawn*
1986 *Youngblood*
1987 *In Love And War* (TV); *Steel Dawn; Dirty Dancing*; Tiger Warsaw*
1988 *Road House*
1989 *Next Of Kin*
1990 *Ghost**
1991 *Point Break**
1992 *City Of Joy*

# T

**TANDY, Jessica**
(1909–   ) USA

1932 *The Indiscretion Of Eve*
1938 *Murder In The Family*
1994 *The Seventh Cross*
1945 *The Valley Of Decision*
1946 *The Green Years; Dragonwyck*
1947 *Forever Amber; A Woman's Vengeance*
1950 *September Affair*
1951 *The Desert Fox* (UK: *Rommel— Desert Fox*)
1958 *The Light In The Forest*
1962 *Hemingway's Adventures Of A Young Man*
1963 *The Birds**
1973 *Butley*
1981 *Honky Tonk Freeway*
1982 *Still Of The Night; Best Friends; The World According To Garp*
1984 *The Bostonians*
1985 *Cocoon**
1987 *batteries not included; Foxfire* (TV)

1988 *The House On Carroll Street;*
     *Cocoon: The Return*
1989 *Driving Miss Daisy**
1991 *Fried Green Tomatoes At The*
     *Whistle Stop Café; The Story*
     *Lady* (TV)
1992 *Used People*

## TATI, Jacques
real name: Jacques Tatischeff
(1908–82) France

1932 *Oscar, Champion De Tennis*
1934 *On Demande Une Brute*
1935 *Gai Dimanche*
1936 *Soigne Ton Gauche*
1938 *Retour A La Terre*
1945 *Sylvie Et Le Fantôme*
1946 *Le Diable Au Corps*
1947 *L'Ecole Des Facteurs*
1949 *Le Jour De Fête*
1952 *Les Vacances De Monsieur Hulot*
     (UK: *Monsieur Hulot's Holiday*)
1958 *Mon Oncle*
1967 *Playtime*
1971 *Traffic*
1973 *Parade*

See also directors listing

## TAYLOR, Elizabeth Rosemond
(1932–   ) USA

1942 *Man Or Mouse* (short); *There's*
     *One Born Every Minute*
1943 *Lassie Come Home; Jane Eyre*
1944 *The White Cliffs Of Dover;*
     *National Velvet**
1946 *The Courage Of Lassie*
1947 *Cynthia* (UK: *The Rich Full Life*);
     *Life With Father**
1948 *A Date With Judy; Julia*
     *Misbehaves*
1949 *Little Women; Conspirator*
1950 *The Big Hangover; Father Of The*
     *Bride*
1951 *Love Is Better Than Ever* (UK:
     *The Light Fantastic*); *A Place In*
     *The Sun*; Quo Vadis?*; Father's*
     *Little Dividend; Callaway Went*
     *Thataway* (UK: *The Star Said No*)

1952 *Ivanhoe**
1953 *The Girl Who Had Everything*
1954 *The Last Time I Saw Paris;*
     *Rhapsody; Beau Brummell;*
     *Elephant Walk*
1956 *Giant**
1957 *Raintree County*
1958 *Cat On A Hot Tin Roof**
1959 *Suddenly Last Summer**
1960 *Butterfield 8*; Scent Of Mystery*
     (UK: *Holiday In Spain*)
1963 *Cleopatra*; The VIPs*
1965 *The Sandpiper; What's New*
     *Pussycat?*
1966 *Who's Afraid Of Virginia Woolf?**
1967 *The Taming Of The Shrew; The*
     *Comedians; Reflections In A*
     *Golden Eye; Dr Faustus*
1968 *Boom; Secret Ceremony*
1969 *Anne Of The Thousand Days*;*
     *The Only Game In Town*
1971 *Zee And Co; Under Milk Wood*
1972 *Hammersmith Is Out*
1973 *Night Watch; Ash Wednesday;*
     *Divorce His, Divorce Hers* (TV)
1974 *That's Entertainment*
1976 *Victory At Entebbe* (TV); *The Blue*
     *Bird*
1977 *A Little Night Music; Winter Kills*
1978 *Return Engagement* (TV)
1980 *The Mirror Crack'd*
1981 *Genocide* (narrator only)
1983 *Between Friends* (TV)
1985 *Malice In Wonderland* (TV)
1986 *There Must Be A Pony* (TV)
1987 *Poker Alice* (TV)
1988 *Il Giovane Toscanini* (UK: *Young*
     *Toscanini*)
1989 *Sweet Bird Of Youth* (TV)

## TAYLOR, Robert
real name: Spangler Brugh
(1911–69) USA

1934 *Handy Andy; A Wicked Woman;*
     *There's Always Tomorrow; Buried*
     *Loot* (short)
1935 *Society Doctor; Lest We Forget;*
     *Murder In The Fleet; West Point*
     *Of The Air; Times Square Lady;*

**TAYLOR, Robert** (cont.)
*Magnificent Obsession; Broadway Melody Of 1936; Only Eight Hours*
1936 *La Fiesta De Santa Barbara* (short); *His Brother's Wife; Small Town Girl; Private Number* (UK: *Secret Interlude*); *The Gorgeous Hussy; Camille\**
1937 *Personal Property* (UK: *The Man In Possession*); *This Is My Affair* (UK: *The Man In Possession*); *Broadway Melody Of 1938; Lest We Forget* (short)
1938 *A Yank At Oxford; The Crowd Roars; Three Comrades*
1939 *Lady Of The Tropics; Remember?; Stand Up And Fight; Lucky Night*
1940 *Escape; Waterloo Bridge; Flight Command*
1941 *Billy The Kid; When Ladies Meet; Johnny Eager*
1942 *Her Cardboard Lover; Stand By For Action!* (UK: *Cargo Of Innocents*)
1943 *The Youngest Profession; Bataan; Song Of Russia*
1945 *The Fighting Lady* (narrator only)
1946 *Undercurrent*
1947 *The High Wall*
1948 *The Secret Land* (narrator only)
1949 *The Bribe; Ambush; Conspirator*
1950 *Devil's Doorway*
1951 *Quo Vadis?\*; Westward The Women; Challenge In The Wilderness* (short)
1952 *Above And Beyond; Ivanhoe\*; I Love Melvin*
1953 *All The Brothers Were Valiant; Ride, Vaquero!*
1954 *Knights Of The Round Table; Rogue Cop; Valley Of The Kings*
1955 *Many Rivers To Cross; The Adventures Of Quentin Durward*
1956 *The Last Hunt; The Power And The Prize; D-Day Sixth Of June*
1957 *Tip On A Dead Jockey* (UK: *Time For Action*)
1958 *Party Girl; Saddle The Wind; The Law And Jake Wade*
1959 *The House Of The Seven Hawks;*

*The Hangman; Killers Of Kilimanjaro*
1962 *Miracle Of The White Stallions* (UK: *Flight Of The White Stallions*)
1963 *Cattle King* (UK: *Guns Of Wyoming*)
1964 *A House Is Not A Home*
1965 *The Night Walker*
1966 *Savage Pampas; Johnny Tiger; Hondo And The Apaches* (TV)
1967 *Return Of The Gunfighter* (TV); *The Glass Sphinx*
1968 *Where Angels Go...Trouble Follows*
1969 *The Day The Hot Line Got Hot; Devil May Care*


**TAYLOR, Rod**
real name: Robert Taylor
(1929–   ) Australia

1951 *The Stuart Expedition*
1954 *Long John Silver; King Of The Coral Sea*
1955 *The Virgin Queen; Hell On Frisco Bay; Top Gun*
1956 *The Rack; Giant\*; World Without End; The Catered Affair* (UK: *Wedding Breakfast*)
1957 *Raintree County*
1958 *Separate Tables\*; Step Down To Terror* (UK: *The Silent Stranger*)
1959 *Ask Any Girl; Queen Of The Amazons* (UK: *Colossus And The Amazon Queen*)
1960 *The Time Machine*
1961 *Seven Seas To Calais; One Hundred And One Dalmatians* (voice only)
1963 *Sunday In New York; A Gathering Of Eagles; The Birds\*; The VIPs*
1964 *Fate Is The Hunter; Thirty-Six Hours; Young Cassidy*
1965 *Do Not Disturb; The Liquidator*
1966 *The Glass Bottom Boat*
1967 *Hotel; Chuka; The Mercenaries*
1968 *The Hell With Heroes; Nobody Runs Forever*
1969 *Zabriskie Point*

1970 *The Man Who Had Power Over Women; Darker Than Amber*
1971 *Powderkeg*
1972 *Family Flight* (TV); *The Heroes*
1973 *The Train Robbers; Trader Horn; The Deadly Trackers*
1974 *Partizan*
1975 *Blondy; Shamus* (TV) (UK: *A Matter Of Wife And Death*)
1976 *The Oregon Trail* (TV)
1977 *The Picture Show Man; Treasure Seekers*
1978 *Cry Of The Innocent* (TV); *An Eye For An Eye*
1979 *Seven Graves For Rogan*
1980 *Hellinger's Law* (TV)
1981 *Jacqueline Bouvier Kennedy* (TV)
1982 *Charles And Diana — A Royal Love Story* (TV); *On The Run*
1983 *Masquerade* (TV)
1985 *Marbella; Half Nelson* (TV); *Mask Of Murder*
1986 *Outlaws* (TV)

## TEMPLE, Shirley Jane
(1928– ) USA

1932 *War Babies; Glad Rags To Riches; Pie Covered Wagon; The Runt Page* (all shorts); *Red-Haired Alibi*
1933 *Polly-Tix In Washington; Kid'n' Hollywood; Kid'n' Africa; Kid's Last Fight; Merrily Yours; Dora's Dunkin' Donuts* (all shorts); *To The Last Man; Out All Night*
1934 *Pardon My Pups; Managed Money; Hollywood Cavalcade* (all shorts); *Mandalay; New Deal Rythmn; Carolina* (UK: *The House Of Connelly*); *Stand Up And Cheer; Now I'll Tell* (UK: *When New York Sleeps*); *Change Of Heart; Baby Takes A Bow; Now And Forever; Bright Eyes; Little Miss Marker* (UK: *Girl In Pawn*)
1935 *Curly Top; The Little Colonel; Our Little Girl; The Littlest Rebel*
1936 *Captain January; Dimples; Poor Little Rich Girl; Stowaway*

1937 *Wee Willie Winkie; Heidi; Ali Baba Goes To Town*
1938 *Rebecca Of Sunnybrook Farm; Little Miss Broadway; Just Around The Corner*
1939 *The Little Princess; Susannah Of The Mounties*
1940 *The Blue Bird; Young People*
1941 *Kathleen*
1942 *Miss Annie Rooney*
1944 *Since You Went Away*; I'll Be Seeing You*
1945 *Kiss And Tell*
1947 *Honeymoon* (UK: *Two Men And A Girl*); *The Bachelor And The Bobbysoxer* (UK: *Bachelor Knight*); *That Hagen Girl*
1948 *Fort Apache*
1949 *Mr Belvedere Goes To College; Adventure In Baltimore* (UK: *Bachelor Bait*); *The Story Of Seabiscuit* (UK: *Pride And Kentucky*); *A Kiss For Corliss*

## TERRY-THOMAS
real name: Thomas Terry Hoar-Stevens
(1911–90) UK

1936 *It's Love Again; Rhythmn In The Air; This'll Make You Whistle*
1937 *Rhythmn Racketeer*
1940 *For Freedom; Under Your Heat*
1947 *The Brass Monkey*
1948 *A Date With A Dream*
1949 *Helter Skelter; Melody Club*
1950 *Cookery Nook; The Queen Steps Out* (both shorts)
1956 *Private's Progress; The Green Man*
1957 *Brothers In Law; Lucky Jim; The Naked Truth*
1958 *Blue Murder At St Trinian's; Happy Is The Bride; tom thumb*
1959 *Too Many Crooks; Carlton Browne Of The FO; I'm All Right Jack*
1960 *School For Scoundrels; Make Mine Mink; His And Hers*
1961 *A Matter Of WHO*
1962 *Operation Snatch; Bachelor Flat; Kill Or Cure; The Wonderful World Of The Brothers Grimm*

**TERRY-THOMAS** (cont.)
1963 *It's A Mad, Mad, Mad, Mad World\*; Mouse On The Moon*
1964 *The Wild Affair*
1965 *Strange Bedfellows; Those Magnificent Men In Their Flying Machines; How To Murder Your Wife; You Must Be Joking*
1966 *The Daydreamer* (voice only); *Our Man In Marrakesh; Operation Paradise; The Sandwich Man; Munster Go Home; Kiss The Girls And Make Them Die; La Grande Vadrouille* (UK: *Don't Look Now, We're Being Shot At*)
1967 *Rocket To The Moon; Arabella; Bandidos; I Love A Mystery* (TV); *The Karate Killers* (TV); *The Perils Of Pauline; A Guide For The Married Man; Top Crack; Danger: Diabolik*
1968 *How Sweet It Is; Where Were You When The Lights Went Out?; Don't Raise The Bridge, Lower The River; Uno Scacco Tutto Matto; Sette Volte Sette* (UK: *Seven Times Seven*)
1969 *2,000 Years Later; Monte Carlo Or Bust!; Una Su Zradici* (UK: *Twelve Plus One*)
1970 *Le Mur De L'Atlantique*
1971 *The Abominable Dr Phibes*
1972 *The Cherrypicker; The Heroes; Dr Phibes Rises Again*
1973 *Vault Of Horror; Robin Hood* (voice only)
1974 *Who Stole The Shah's Jewels?*
1975 *Side By Side; The Bawdy Adventures Of Tom Jones; Spanish Fly*
1977 *The Hound Of The Baskervilles; The Last Remake Of Beau Geste*
1981 *Happy Birthday Harry!*

**TOMLIN, Lily**
(1939– ) USA

1975 *Nashville\**
1976 *The Late Show*
1979 *Moment By Moment*

1980 *Nine To Five\**
1981 *The Incredible Shrinking Woman*
1984 *All Of Me\**
1986 *Lily Tomlin* (documentary)
1988 *Big Business*
1991 *The Search For Signs Of Intelligent Life In The Universe*
1992 *Shadows And Fog*
1993 *Short Cuts; And The Band Played On* (TV)

**TRACY, Spencer**
(1900–67) USA

1930 *Taxi Talks; The Strong Arm; The Hard Guy* (all shorts); *Up The River*
1931 *Quick Millions; Six Cylinder Love; Goldie*
1932 *She Wanted A Millionaire; Sky Devils; Disorderly Conduct; Young America* (UK: *We Humans*); *Society Girl; The Painted Woman; Me And My Gal* (UK: *Pier 13*); *20,000 Years In Sing Sing*
1933 *The Face In The Sky; Shanghai Madness; The Power And The Glory; The Mad Game; Man's Castle*
1934 *Bottoms Up!; The Show-Off; Looking For Trouble; Now I'll Tell* (UK: *When New York Sleeps*); *Marie Galante*
1935 *It's A Small World; Dante's Inferno; The Murder Man; Whipsaw; Riff Raff*
1936 *San Francisco\*; Libeled Lady; Fury*
1937 *They Gave Him A Gun; Captains Courageous\*; The Big City; Mannequin*
1938 *Boys' Town\*; Test Pilot\**
1939 *Stanley And Livingstone; I Take This Woman*
1940 *Edison The Man; Northwest Passage; Boom Town*
1941 *Men Of Boys' Town; Dr Jekyll And Mr Hyde*
1942 *Woman Of The Year\*; Keeper Of The Flame; Tortilla Flat; Ring Of Steel* (narrator only)

1943 *A Guy Named Joe; US War Bonds Trailer* (short)
1944 *The Seventh Cross; Thirty Seconds Over Tokyo; Battle Stations* (narrator only)
1945 *Without Love*
1947 *The Sea Of Grass; Cass Timberlane*
1948 *State Of The Union* (UK: *The World And His Wife*)
1949 *Adam's Rib\*; Edward My Son; Malaya* (UK: *East Of The Rising Sun*)
1950 *Father Of The Bride\**
1951 *The People Against O'Hara; Father's Little Dividend*
1952 *Pat And Mike\*; Plymouth Adventure*
1953 *The Actress*
1954 *Broken Lance*
1955 *Bad Day At Black Rock\**
1956 *The Mountain*
1957 *Desk Set* (UK: *His Other Women*)
1958 *The Old Man And The Sea; The Last Hurrah*
1960 *Inherit The Wind*
1961 *The Devil At Four O'Clock; Judgment At Nuremberg\**
1962 *How The West Was Won\** (narrator only)
1963 *It's A Mad, Mad, Mad, Mad World\**
1967 *Guess Who's Coming To Dinner\**

## TRAVOLTA, John
(1954– ) USA

1975 *The Devil's Rain*
1976 *The Boy In The Bubble* (TV); *Carrie*
1977 *Saturday Night Fever\**
1978 *Grease\**
1979 *Moment By Moment*
1980 *Urban Cowboy*
1981 *Blow Out*
1983 *Staying Alive; Three Of A Kind*
1985 *Perfect*
1989 *The Experts; Look Who's Talking\**
1990 *The Tender; Chains Of Gold; Look Who's Talking Too*

1991 *Shout*
1992 *Boris And Natasha*

## TURNER, Kathleen
(1954– ) USA

1981 *Body Heat\**
1983 *The Man With Two Brains\**
1984 *Romancing The Stone\*; A Breed Apart; Crimes Of Passion*
1985 *Prizzi's Honor\*; The Jewel Of The Nile\**
1986 *Peggy Sue Got Married\**
1987 *Julia And Julia; Switching Channels; Dear America* (voice only)
1988 *Who Framed Roger Rabbit\** (voice only); *The Accidental Tourist\**
1989 *War Of The Roses\*; Tummy Trouble* (short, voice only)
1990 *Roller Coaster Rabbit* (short, voice only)
1991 *V I Warshawski*
1992 *House Of Cards*
1993 *Undercover Blues; Naked In New York; Serial Mom*

## TURNER, Lana
real name: Julia 'Judy' Turner
(1920– ) USA

1937 *A Star Is Born\*; Topper; The Great Garrick; They Won't Forget*
1938 *The Chaser; Four's A Crowd; The Adventures Of Marco Polo; Dramatic School; Love Finds Andy Hardy; Rich Man, Poor Girl*
1939 *Calling Dr Kildare; These Glamour Girls; Dancing Co-Ed* (UK: *Every Other Inch A Lady*)
1940 *We Who Are Young; Two Girls On Broadway* (UK: *Change Your Partners*)
1941 *Dr Jekyll And Mr Hyde; Ziegfeld Girl; Johnny Eager; Honky Tonk*
1942 *Somewhere I'll Find You*
1943 *Slightly Dangerous; Du Barry Was A Lady; The Youngest Profession; Showbusiness At War* (short)

**TURNER, Lana** (cont.)
1944 *Marriage Is A Private Affair*
1945 *Weekend At The Waldorf; Keep Your Powder Dry*
1946 *The Postman Always Rings Twice\**
1947 *Green Dolphin Street; Cass Timberlane*
1948 *Homecoming; The Three Musketeers\**
1950 *A Life Of Her Own; Mr Imperium (UK: You Belong To My Heart)*
1952 *The Bad And The Beautiful\*; The Merry Widow*
1953 *Latin Lovers*
1954 *Flame And The Flesh; Betrayed*
1955 *The Prodigal; The Sea Chase; Diane; The Rains Of Ranchipur*
1957 *Peyton Place\**
1958 *The Lady Takes A Flyer; Another Time, Another Place*
1959 *Imitation Of Life\**
1960 *Portrait In Black*
1961 *Bachelor In Paradise; By Love Possessed*
1962 *Who's Got The Action?*
1964 *Love Has Many Faces*
1966 *Madame X*
1969 *The Big Cube*
1974 *Persecution*
1976 *Bittersweet Love*
1978 *Witches' Brew*


**TURTURRO, John**
(1957– ) USA

1980 *Raging Bull\**
1984 *Exterminator 2; The Flamingo Kid*
1985 *Desperately Seeking Susan*
1986 *Hannah And Her Sisters\*; The Color Of Money\*; Gung Ho; Off Beat*
1987 *Five Corners; The Sicilian*
1989 *Do The Right Thing\**
1990 *Backtrack (UK: Crossfire); Miller's Crossing\*; Mo' Better Blues; State Of Grace; Men Of Respect*
1991 *Barton Fink\*; Jungle Fever\**
1992 *Mac (also director)*
1993 *Fearless; Being Human*


# U

**ULLMANN, Liv**
(1939– ) Sweden

1957 *Fjols Til Fjells (UK: Fools In The Mountains)*
1959 *Ung Flukt (UK: The Wayward Girl)*
1962 *Tonny; Kort Är Sommaren*
1965 *De Kalte Ham Skarven*
1966 *Persona\**
1968 *Skammen (UK: The Shame); Vargtimmen (UK: Hour Of The Wolf)*
1969 *An-Magritt; En Passion (UK: A Passion)*
1970 *Cold Sweat*
1971 *The Night Visitor; Utvandrarna\* (UK: The Emigrants)*
1972 *Pope Joan; Nybyggama (UK: The New Land); Viskningar Och Rop\* (UK: Cries And Whispers)*
1973 *Foto: Sven Nykvist (documentary); Lost Horizon; Forty Carats*
1974 *Scener Ur Ett Äktenskap (UK: Scenes From A Marriage); The Abdication; Zandy's Bride*
1975 *Ansikte Mot Ansikte (UK: Face To Face)*
1976 *Leonor*
1977 *Das Schlangenei (UK: The Serpent's Egg); A Bridge Too Far*
1978 *Hostsonaten (UK: Autumn Sonata); Couleur Chair*
1979 *A Look At Liv (documentary); Players*
1980 *The Gates Of The Forest*
1981 *Richard's Things (TV)*
1983 *The Wild Duck; Prisoner Without A Name, Cell Without A Number (TV)*
1984 *The Bay Boy*
1985 *La Diagonale Du Fou (UK: Dangerous Moves); Speriamo Che Sia Femmina (UK: Let's Hope It's A Girl)*
1987 *Moscow Goodbye; Moon Circus; Time Of Indifference (TV); Gaby—A True Story*
1988 *La Amiga*
1989 *The Rose Garden*

1990 *Mindwalk*
1991 *The Long Shadow; The Ox*
1992 *Sofie* (also director)

## USTINOV, Sir Peter
(1921– ) UK

1940 *Hullo Fame!; Mein Kampf, My Crimes*
1941 *One Of Our Aircraft Is Missing*
1942 *The Goose Steps Out*
1944 *The Way Ahead*
1946 *School For Secrets* (director only)
1947 *Vice Versa* (director only)
1949 *Private Angelo* (also co-director)
1950 *Odette*
1951 *Hotel Sahara; The Magic Box; Quo Vadis?\**
1954 *Beau Brummell; The Egyptian*
1955 *We're No Angels; Lola Montes; I Girovaghi* (UK: *The Wanderers*)
1957 *Les Espions; Un Angelo E Sceso A Brooklyn* (UK: *The Man Who Wagged His Tail*)
1959 *Adventures Of Mr Wonderbird* (voice only)
1960 *Spartacus\*; The Sundowners\**
1961 *Romanoff And Juliet* (also director)
1962 *Billy Budd* (also director)
1964 *The Peaches* (short, narrator only); *Topkapi; John Goldfarb, Please Come Home*
1965 *Lady L* (also director)
1967 *The Comedians; Blackbeard's Ghost*
1968 *Hot Millions*
1969 *Viva Max!; A Storm In Summer* (TV)
1972 *Hammersmith Is Out* (also director); *Big Mack And Poor Clare*
1973 *Robin Hood* (voice only)
1975 *One Of Our Dinosaurs Is Missing*
1976 *Logan's Run; Treasure Of Matecumbe*
1977 *The Last Remake Of Beau Geste; The Mouse And His Child* (voice only); *Taxi Mauve* (UK: *Purple Taxi*); *Doppio Delitto* (UK: *Double Murders*)

1978 *Death On The Nile; The Thief Of Bagdad; Tarka The Otter* (narrator only)
1979 *Ashanti; Players; Winds Of Change* (narrator only)
1980 *Charlie Chan And The Curse Of The Dragon Queen; Short Cut To Haifa*
1981 *Grendel Grendel Grendel* (voice only); *The Great Muppet Caper; Evil Under The Sun*
1984 *Memed My Hawk* (also director)
1985 *Thirteen At Dinner* (TV)
1986 *Dead Man's Folly* (TV); *Three Act Tragedy* (TV)
1988 *Appointment With Death*
1989 *The French Revolution; The Grandpa* (voice only)
1992 *Lorenzo's Oil\**

# V

## VITTI, Monica
real name: Monica Ceciarelli
(1933– ) Italy

1955 *Ridere, Ridere, Ridere*
1956 *Una Pelliccia Di Visone*
1957 *Il Grido* (UK: *The City*) (voice only)
1958 *Le Dritte*
1960 *L'Avventura\**
1961 *La Notte*
1962 *L'Eclisse* (UK: *Eclipse*)
1963 *Les Quatres Vérités* (UK: *Three Fables Of Love*); *Château En Suède; Dragées Au Poivre* (UK: *Sweet And Sour*)
1964 *Deserto Rosso* (UK: *Red Desert*); *Alta Infedeltà* (UK: *High Infidelity*); *Il Disco Volante; Le Bambole* (UK: *Four Kinds Of Love*)
1966 *Le Fate* (UK: *Sex Quartet*); *Modesty Blaise; Fai In Fretta Ad Uccidermi...Ho Freddo!*
1967 *The Chastity Belt*
1968 *La Femme Ecarlate; Le Ragazza Con La Pistola*
1969 *Amore Mio, Aiutami; Vedo Nudo*

**VITTI, Monica** (cont.)

1970 *Le Coppie* (UK: *Couples*); *Nini Tirabuscio, La Donna Che Inventò La Mossa; Dramma Della Gelosia* (UK: *Jealousy Italian Style*)

1971 *La Pacifista; Lei; La Supertestimone; Noi Donne Siamo Fatte Cosi*

1972 *Gli Ordini Sonto Ordini*

1973 *Teresa La Ladra; Tosca*

1974 *Le Fântome De La Liberté* (UK: *The Phantom Of Liberty*); *Polvere Di Stelle*

1975 *A Mezzanotte Va La Ronda Del Piacere* (UK: *Midnight Pleasures*); *Canard A L'Orange*

1976 *Qui Comincia L'Avventura; L'Anitra All'Arancia; Mimi Bluette; La Goduria; Basta Che Non Si Sappia In Giro*

1977 *L'Altra Meta Del Cielo*

1978 *La Raison D'Etat; Amori Mei; Per Vivere Meglio*

1979 *The Mystery Of Krantz; An Almost Perfect Affair; Take Two; Letti Selvaggi*

1980 *Il Mistero Di Oberwald* (UK: *The Mystery Of Oberwald*); *Camera D'Albergo*

1981 *Appuntamento D'Amore; Tango Della Gelosia*

1982 *Io So Che Tu Sai, Che Io So*

1983 *Infidelmente Tua; Quando Suona Veronica*

1989 *Scandalo Secreto* (UK: *Secret Scandal*) (also director)

**VOIGHT, Jon**
(1938–   ) USA

1967 *The Hour Of The Gun*

1968 *Fearless Frank*

1969 *Out Of It; Midnight Cowboy\**

1970 *Catch 22\*; The Revolutionary*

1972 *The All-American Boy; Deliverance\**

1974 *The Odessa File; Conrack*

1976 *The Judge And His Hangman*

1978 *Coming Home\**

1979 *The Champ*

1982 *Lookin' To Get Out*

1983 *Table For Five*

1985 *Runaway Train*

1986 *Desert Bloom*

1990 *Eternity*

1991 *Chernobyl: The Final Warning* (TV)

1992 *The Last Of His Tribe* (TV)

**VON STROHEIM, Erich Von Stroheim**
real name: Hans Erich Stroheim Von Nordenwall
(1885–1957) Austria

1914 *Captain McLean*

1915 *The Birth Of A Nation; Old Heidelberg; A Bold Impersonation; The Failure; Ghosts*

1916 *Intolerance; His Picture In The Papers; Macbeth; The Social Secretary; Less Than Dust*

1917 *For France; Reaching For The Moon; In Again, Out Again; Sylvia Of The Secret Service; Panthea*

1918 *Hearts Of The World; Hearts Of Humanity; The Unbeliever; The Hun Within*

1919 *Blind Husbands* (also director)

1920 *The Devil's Pass Key* (director only)

1921 *Foolish Wives* (also director)

1923 *Merry-Go-Round* (director only)

1924 *Greed* (director only)

1925 *The Merry Widow* (director only)

1928 *The Wedding March* (also director); *Mariage Du Prince; Queen Kelly* (both director only)

1929 *The Great Gabbo*

1930 *Three Faces East*

1931 *Friends And Lovers*

1932 *The Lost Squadron; As You Desire Me*

1933 *Hello Sister* (aka *Walking Down Broadway*) (director only)

1934 *Crimson Romance; House Of Strangers; The Fugitive Road*

1935 *The Crime Of Dr Crepsi*

1936 *Marthe Richard Au Service De La France*

1937 *Mademoiselle Docteur; Between Two Women; La Grande Illusion\*; Les Pirates Du Rail; L'Alibi*
1938 *L'Affaire Lafarge; Les Disparus De Saint-Agil; Gibraltar*
1939 *Tempête Sur Paris* (UK: *Thunder Over Paris*); *Derrière La Façade; Rappel Immédiat* (UK: *Instant Recall*); *Macao—L'Enfer Du Jeu* (UK: *Gambling Hell*); *Paris–New York; Pièges; Le Monde Tremblera*
1940 *I Was An Adventuress; Ultimatum*
1941 *So Ends Our Night*
1943 *Storm Over Lisbon; Five Graves To Cairo; North Star*
1944 *Armored Attack; The Lady And The Monster* (UK: *The Lady And The Doctor*); *32 Rue De Montmartre*
1945 *Scotland Yard Investigator; The Great Flamarion*
1946 *The Mask Of Dijon; La Foire Aux Chimères* (UK: *The Fair Angel*); *On Ne Meurt Pas Comme Ça; La Danse De Mort*
1948 *Le Signal Rouge*
1949 *Portrait D'Un Assassin; Le Diable Et L'Ange*
1950 *Sunset Boulevard\**
1952 *La Maison Du Crime; Alraune*
1953 *Alert Au Sud; L'Envers Du Paradis; Minuit-Quai De Bercy*
1954 *Napoléon; Série Noire*
1955 *La Modone Des Sleepings*
1956 *L'Homme Aux Cent Visages* (UK: *Man Of 100 Faces*)

## VON SYDOW, Max
full name: Max Carl Adolf Von Sydow
(1929–   ) Sweden

1949 *Bara En Mor*
1951 *Froken Julie* (UK: *Miss Julie*)
1953 *Ingen Mans Kvinna*
1956 *Rätten Att Älska*
1957 *Der Sjunde Inseglet\** (UK: *The Seventh Seal*); *Prästen I Uddarbo; Smultronstället\** (UK: *Wild Strawberries*)

1958 *Nära Livet* (UK: *So Close To Life*); *Spion 503; Ansiktet* (UK: *The Face*)
1960 *Jungfrukällen* (UK: *The Virgin Spring*); *Bröllopsdagen*
1961 *Sasom I En Spegel* (UK: *Through A Glass Darkly*)
1962 *Nils Holgerssons Underbara Resa; Älskarinnen; Nattvardsgästerna* (UK: *Winter Light*)
1965 *Uppehall I Myrlandet* (UK: *4 x 4*); *The Greatest Story Ever Told; Reward*
1966 *Hawaii; The Quiller Memorandum*
1967 *Svarta Pälmkroner* (UK: *The Black Palm Trees*)
1968 *Vargtimmen* (UK: *Hour Of The Wolf*); *Här, Här Du Ditt Liv* (UK: *Here Is Your Life*); *Skammen* (UK: *The Shame*)
1969 *Made In Sweden; En Passion* (UK: *A Passion*); *The Kremlin Letter*
1971 *The Night Visitor; The Touch; Utvandrana\** (UK: *The Emigrants*); *Äppelkriegt; I Havsbandet*
1972 *Embassy; Nybyggarna* (UK: *The New Land*)
1973 *The Exorcist\**
1974 *Steppenwolf; Ägget Är Löst* (UK: *Egg! Egg! A Hardboiled Story*)
1975 *Foxtrot; Cadaveri Eccellenti* (UK: *Illustrious Corpses*); *Three Days Of The Condor\*; The Ultimate Warrior; Cuore Di Cane*
1976 *Voyage Of The Damned*
1977 *Le Désert Des Tartares; Exorcist II: The Heretic; March Or Die; La Signora Della Orrori*
1978 *Brass Target; Gran Bolitto*
1979 *Hurricane; Le Mort En Direct* (UK: *Deathwatch*); *Footloose* (aka *Venetian Lies*); *A Look At Liv* (documentary)
1980 *Flash Gordon*
1981 *Ingenjör Andrees Luftfard* (UK: *Flight Of The Eagle*); *Escape To Victory; Conan The Barbarian*
1982 *Target Eagle; She Dances Alone*
1983 *Strange Brew; Never Say Never Again\**

**VON SYDOW, Max** (cont.)
1984 *Dreamscape; Dune; Samson And Delilah* (TV)
1985 *Kojak: The Belarus File* (TV); *Il Pentito; Code Name: Emerald*
1986 *Hannah And Her Sisters\*; Duet For One; The Second Victory; Oviri*
1987 *Pelle Erobreren* (UK: *Pelle The Conqueror*)
1988 *Katinka* (director only)
1989 *Cellini: A Violent Life; Red King, White Knight* (TV)
1990 *Dra Grassler; The Father*
1991 *Until The End Of The World; A Kiss Before Dying; Hiroshima: Out Of The Ashes* (TV); *The Ox*
1992 *The Magic Touch; Den Goda Viljan* (UK: *The Best Intentions*)
1993 *Needful Things; Time Is Money*

# W

**WALKEN, Christopher**
real name: Ronald Walken
(1943– ) USA

1968 *Me And My Brother*
1971 *The Anderson Tapes*
1972 *The Happiness Cage*
1976 *Next Stop Greenwich Village; The Sentinel*
1977 *Annie Hall\*; Roseland*
1978 *The Deer Hunter\**
1979 *The Last Embrace*
1980 *Heaven's Gate\*; The Dogs Of War; Shoot The Sun Down*
1981 *Pennies From Heaven; Who Am I This Time?* (TV)
1983 *The Dead Zone; Brainstorm*
1985 *A View To A Kill\*; At Close Range*
1986 *The Conspiracy; River Of Death; War Zone*
1987 *Puss In Boots; The Milagro Beanfield War*
1988 *Biloxi Blues; In From The Cold; Communion; Homeboy*
1989 *The Mind Snatchers*
1990 *The King Of New York; The Comfort Of Strangers*

1991 *McBain; Sarah Plain And Tall* (TV)
1992 *Batman Returns\**
1993 *Snake Eyes; A Business Affair*

**WALLACH, Eli**
(1915– ) USA

1956 *Baby Doll*
1958 *The Line-Up*
1959 *Seven Thieves*
1960 *A Death Of Princes; The Magnificent Seven\*; The Misfits\**
1962 *Hemingway's Adventures Of A Young Man; How The West Was Won\**
1963 *Act One; The Victors; The Moon-Spinners*
1964 *Kisses For My President*
1965 *Lord Jim; Genghis Khan*
1966 *The Poppy Is Also A Flower* (UK: *Danger Grows Wild*); *How To Steal A Million; Il Buono, Il Brutto, Il Cattivo\** (UK: *The Good, The Bad And The Ugly*)
1967 *The Tiger Makes Out; How To Save A Marriage And Ruin Your Life*
1968 *McKenna's Gold; A Lovely Way To Go; I Quattro Dell'Ave Maria* (UK: *Revenge In El Paso*)
1969 *Tho Brain; Ace High*
1970 *Zigzag* (UK: *False Witness*); *The Angel Levine; The People Next Door; The Adventures Of Gérard*
1971 *Romance Of A Horsethief; Los Guerilleros*
1973 *A Cold Night's Death* (TV); *The Last Chance*
1974 *Indict And Convict* (TV); *Crazy Joe; Cinderella Liberty; Samurai*
1975 *Don't Turn The Other Cheek*
1976 *The Domino Principle* (UK: *The Domino Killings*); *Nasty Habits; The Sentinel; Twenty Shades Of Pink*(TV)
1977 *The Deep\*; Winter Kills*
1978 *The Silent Flute* (aka *Circle Of Iron*); *Girl Friends; Movie, Movie; Squadra Antimafia*
1979 *Firepower*
1980 *The Hunter; Fugitive Family* (TV)

1981 *The Salamander; The Wall* (TV);
*The Pride Of Jesse Hallam* (TV);
*Skokie* (TV) (UK: *Once They
Marched Through A Thousand
Towns*)
1982 *The Executioner's Song* (TV);
*Alby And Elizabeth*
1984 *Anatomy Of An Illness* (TV);
*Sam's Son*
1985 *Our Family Honor* (TV)
1986 *Murder: By Reason Of Insanity*
(TV); *Tough Guys; Something In
Common* (TV)
1987 *Nuts\*; The Impossible Spy* (TV);
*Hello Actors Studio* (documentary)
1990 *The Two Jakes\*; The Godfather
Part III\**
1992 *Article 99; Mistress; Night And
The City*

## WALTERS, Julie
(1950–  ) UK

1976 *Occupy*
1983 *Educating Rita\**
1984 *She'll Be Wearing Pink Pyjamas*
(TV)
1985 *Car Trouble; Dreamchild* (voice
only)
1987 *Personal Services\*; Prick Up Your
Ears\**
1988 *Buster*
1989 *Mack The Knife; Killing Dad*
1991 *Stepping Out*
1992 *Just Like A Woman; The Clothes
In The Wardrobe* (TV)

## WASHINGTON, Denzel
(1954–  ) USA

1977 *Wilma* (TV)
1979 *Flesh And Blood* (TV)
1981 *Carbon Copy*
1983 *Licence To Kill* (TV)
1984 *A Soldier's Story*
1985 *Power*
1986 *The George McKenna Story* (TV)
1987 *Cry Freedom\**
1988 *For Queen And Country*
1989 *The Mighty Quinn; Glory\**

1990 *Heart Condition; Mo' Better Blues*
1991 *Mississippi Masala; Ricochet*
1992 *Malcolm X\**
1993 *Much Ado About Nothing;
Philadelphia*

## WAYNE, John
Marion Michael Morrison
(1907–79) USA

1926 *Brown Of Harvard*
1927 *The Drop Kick* (UK: *Glitter*);
*Mother Machree*
1928 *Hangman's House; Four Sons*
1929 *Salute; Words And Music*
1930 *Cheer Up And Smile; Men
Without Women; The Big Trail;
Born Reckless; Rough Romance*
1931 *Arizona* (UK: *The Virtuous Wife*);
*Men Are Like That; Girls Demand
Excitement; Range Feud; Three
Girls Lost*
1932 *The Hurricane Express; Maker Of
Men; The Hollywood Handicap*
(documentary); *Texas Cyclone;
Ride Him Cowboy* (UK: *The
Hawk*); *Big Stampede; Shadow Of
The Eagle; Two-Fisted Law; Lady
And The Gent* (aka *The
Challenger*); *Station STAR* (short);
*Haunted Gold*
1933 *The Telegraph Trail; The Three
Musketeers; Central Airport; The
Sagebrush Trail; The Life Of
Jimmy Dolan* (UK: *The Kid's Last
Fight*); *The Man From Monterey;
College Coach* (UK: *Football
Coach*); *His Private Secretary;
Baby Face; Somewhere In
Sonora; Riders Of Destiny*
1934 *Lucky Texan; West Of The Divide;
Randy Rides Alone; The Trail
Beyond; Blue Steel; The Man
From Utah; The Star Packer;
'Neath Arizona Skies*
1935 *Lawless Range; Texas Terror;
Paradise Canyon; Westward Ho!;
The Lawless Frontier; Rainbow
Valley; The Dawn Rider; Desert
Trail; New Frontier*

**WAYNE, John** (cont.)

1936 *The Lawless Nineties; King Of The Pecos; The Oregon Trail; Winds Of The Wasteland; The Sea Spoilers; The Lonely Trail; Conflict*

1937 *California Straight Ahead; I Cover The War; Idol Of The Crowds; Adventure's End; Born To The West* (aka *Hell Town*)

1938 *Pals Of The Saddle; Overland Stage Raiders; Red River Range; Santa Fe Stampede*

1939 *The Night Riders; Three Texas Steers* (UK: *Danger Rides The Range*); *Wyoming Outlaw; Stagecoach\*; The New Frontier* (aka *Frontier Horizon*); *Allegheny Uprising* (UK: *The First Rebel*)

1940 *Dark Command; Three Faces West; Seven Sinners; The Long Voyage Home*

1941 *Lady For A Night; The Shepherd Of The Hills; The Lady From Louisiana; A Man Betrayed* (UK: *Citadel Of Crime*)

1942 *Reunion In France; In Old California; Pittsburgh; Reap The Wild Wind; The Spoilers; Flying Tigers*

1943 *In Old Oklahoma* (UK: *War Of The Wildcats*); *A Lady Takes A Chance*

1944 *The Fighting Seabees; Tall In The Saddle*

1945 *Flame Of The Barbary Coast; They Were Expendable; Back To Bataan; Dakota*

1946 *Without Reservations*

1947 *Angel And The Bandman; Tycoon*

1948 *Wake Of The Red Witch; Three Godfathers; Red River\*; Fort Apache*

1949 *Hollywood Rodeo* (documentary); *Sands Of Iwo Jima\*; She Wore A Yellow Ribbon; The Fighting Kentuckian*

1950 *Rio Grande; Jet Pilot; Reno's Silver Spurs Award* (documentary)

1951 *Flying Leathernecks; Operation Pacific*

1952 *The Quiet Man\*; Big Jim McLain*

1953 *Island In The Sky; Trouble Along The Way; Hondo*

1954 *The High And The Mighty; Hollywood Cowboy Stars* (documentary)

1955 *Blood Alley; The Sea Chase; Rookie Of The Year* (TV)

1956 *The Searchers\*; The Conqueror*

1957 *The Wings Of Eagles; Legend Of The Lost; I Married A Woman*

1958 *The Barbarian And The Geisha*

1959 *Rio Bravo\*; The Horse Soldiers*

1960 *North To Alaska; The Alamo\**

1961 *The Comancheros*

1962 *The Man Who Shot Liberty Valance\*; Hatari!; How The West Was Won\*; Flashing Spikes* (TV)

1963 *Donovan's Reef; McLintock!*

1964 *Circus World* (UK: *The Magnificent Showman*)

1965 *In Harm's Way; The Sons Of Katie Elder; The Greatest Story Ever Told*

1966 *Cast A Giant Shadow; The Artist And The American West* (documentary)

1967 *El Dorado\*; The War Wagon*

1968 *The Green Berets* (also co-director); *Hellfighters*

1969 *The Undefeated; True Grit\**

1970 *Rio Lobo; Chisum; Chesty: A Tribute To A Legend* (narrator only)

1971 *Big Jake; No Substitute For Victory* (narrator only); *Directed By John Ford* (documentary)

1972 *The Cowboys; Cancel My Reservation*

1973 *The Train Robbers; Cahill: United States Marshal* (UK: *Cahill*)

1974 *McQ; Brannigan*

1975 *Rooster Cogburn*

1976 *The Shootist\**

## WEAVER, Sigourney
real name: Susan Weaver
(1949–   ) USA

1977 *Annie Hall\*; Tribute To A Madman*

1978 *Camp 708*

1979 *Alien\**
1981 *Eyewitness* (UK: *The Janitor*)
1982 *The Year Of Living Dangerously\**
1983 *Deal Of The Century*
1984 *Ghostbusters\**
1985 *Une Femme Ou Deux*
1986 *Half-Moon Street; Aliens\**
1988 *Gorillas In The Mist\*; Working Girl\**
1989 *Ghostbusters II; Helmut Newton: Frames From The Edge* (documentary)
1992 *Aliens 3; 1492: The Conquest Of Paradise*
1993 *Dave*

## WEBB, Clifton
real name: Webb Hollenbeck
(c1893–1966) USA

1920 *Polly With A Past*
1924 *Let Not Man Put Asunder; New Toys*
1925 *The Heart Of A Siren*
1926 *Still Alarm* (short)
1944 *Laura\**
1946 *The Razor's Edge\*; The Dark Corner*
1948 *Sitting Pretty*
1949 *Mr Belvedere Goes To College*
1950 *Cheaper By The Dozen\*; For Heaven's Sake*
1951 *Mr Belvedere Rings The Bell; Elopement*
1952 *Dreamboat; Stars And Stripes Forever* (UK: *Marching Along*)
1953 *Titanic; Mr Scoutmaster*
1954 *Woman's World; Three Coins In The Fountain\**
1956 *The Man Who Never Was*
1957 *Boy On A Dolphin*
1959 *The Remarkable Mr Pennypacker; Holiday For Lovers*
1962 *Satan Never Sleeps* (UK: *The Devil Never Sleeps*)

## WEISSMULLER, Peter Johnny
(1904–84) USA

1929 *Glorifying The American Girl*
1930 *Grantland Rice's Swim Shorts* (series of shorts)

1932 *Tarzan The Apeman\**
1934 *Tarzan And His Mate; Hollywood Party*
1936 *Tarzan Escapes!*
1939 *Tarzan Finds A Son*
1940 *Rodeo Dough* (short)
1941 *Tarzan's Secret Treasure*
1942 *Tarzan's New York Adventure*
1943 *Stage Door Canteen; Tarzan Triumphs; Tarzan's Desert Mystery*
1945 *Tarzan And The Amazons*
1946 *Swamp Fire; Tarzan And The Leopard Woman*
1947 *Tarzan And The Huntress*
1948 *Tarzan And The Mermaids; Jungle Jim*
1949 *Sports Serenade* (short); *The Lost Tribe*
1950 *Captive Girl; Mark Of The Gorilla; Pigmy Island*
1951 *Fury Of The Congo; Jungle Manhunt*
1952 *Voodoo Tiger; Jungle Jim In The Forbidden Land*
1953 *Savage Mutiny; Valley Of The Headhunters; Killer Ape*
1954 *Jungle Man-Eaters; Cannibal Attack*
1955 *Jungle Moon Men; Devil Goddess*
1970 *The Phynx*
1975 *Won Ton Ton — The Dog Who Saved Hollywood*

## WELD, Tuesday
real name: Susan Weld
(1943–   ) USA

1956 *The Wrong Man; Rock, Rock, Rock*
1959 *Rally Round The Flag, Boys!; The Five Pennies*
1960 *Because They're Young; High Time; Sex Kittens Go To College; The Private Lives Of Adam And Eve*
1961 *Return To Peyton Place; Wild In The Country*
1962 *Bachelor Flat*
1963 *Soldier In The Rain*

**WELD, Tuesday** (cont.)

1965 *I'll Take Sweden; The Cincinnati Kid\**
1966 *Lord Love A Duck*
1968 *Pretty Poison*
1970 *I Walk The Line*
1971 *A Safe Place*
1973 *Play It As It Lays*
1974 *Reflections Of Murder* (TV)
1976 *F Scott Fitzgerald In Hollywood* (TV)
1977 *Looking For Mr Goodbar*
1978 *Who'll Stop The Rain?* (UK: *Dog Soldiers*); *A Question Of Guilt* (TV)
1980 *Serial; Madame X* (TV)
1981 *Thief* (UK: *Violent Streets*)
1982 *Author! Author!*
1983 *Once Upon A Time In America\*; The Winter Of Our Discontent* (TV)
1984 *Scorned And Swindled* (TV)
1986 *Circle Of Violence: A Family Drama* (TV); *Something In Common* (TV)
1988 *Heartbreak Hotel*
1993 *Falling Down*

**WELLER, Peter**
(1947– ) USA

1979 *Butch And Sundance — The Early Days; TED*
1980 *Just Tell Me What You Want*
1981 *Shoot The Moon*
1983 *Two Kinds Of Love* (TV); *Kentucky Women* (TV); *Of Unknown Origin*
1984 *Firstborn; The Adventures Of Buckaroo Banzai Across The Eighth Dimension*
1985 *A Killing Affair* (aka *My Sister's Keeper*)
1986 *Apology — For Murder* (TV)
1987 *The Tunnel; Robocop\**
1988 *Shakedown* (UK: *Blue Jean Cop*); *Cat Chaser*
1989 *Leviathan*
1990 *Rainbow Drive; Robocop 2; Women And Men: Stories Of Seduction* (TV)
1991 *Naked Lunch*

**WELLES, George Orson**
(1915–85) USA

1934 *The Hearts Of Age* (short, also co-director)
1938 *Too Much Johnson* (also director)
1940 *Swiss Family Robinson* (narrator only)
1941 *Citizen Kane\** (also director)
1942 *The Magnificent Ambersons\** (director and narrator only); *Journey Into Fear* (also co-director)
1943 *Showbusiness At War* (short); *Jane Eyre*
1944 *Follow The Boys*
1945 *Tomorrow Is Forever*
1946 *Duel In The Sun\** (narrator only); *The Stranger* (also director)
1948 *The Lady From Shangai\*; Macbeth* (both also director)
1949 *The Third Man\*; Black Magic; Prince Of Foxes*
1950 *Désordre* (short); *The Black Rose*
1951 *Return To Glennauscaul* (short)
1952 *Othello\** (also director); *Trent's Last Case; Man, Beast And Virtue*
1953 *Si Versailles M'Etait Conté*
1954 *Napoléon; Trouble In The Glen*
1955 *Three Cases Of Murder; Confidential Report* (also director)
1956 *Moby Dick*
1957 *Man In The Shadow* (UK: *Pay The Devil*)
1958 *The Vikings\*; South Seas Adventure; Lords Of The Forest* (all narrator only); *The Long Hot Summer; The Roots Of Heaven; Touch Of Evil\** (also director)
1959 *High Journey* (narrator only); *Ferry To Hong Kong; Compulsion; Crack In The Mirror; Austerlitz* (UK: *The Battle Of Austerlitz*)
1960 *The Mongols; The Tartars; David And Goliath; Masters Of The Congo Jungle* (narrator only)
1961 *La Fayette; King Of Kings* (narrator only)
1962 *The Trial* (also director); *RoGoPaG; River Of The Ocean* (narrator only)

1963 *The VIPs*
1964 *The Fabulous Adventures Of Marco Polo* (UK: *Marco The Magnificent*); *The Finest Hours* (narrator only)
1966 *Paris, Brûle T'II?* (UK: *Is Paris Burning?*); *A Man For All Seasons\**; *Chimes At Midnight* (also director)
1967 *Casino Royale; Sailor From Gibraltar; I'll Never Forget What's 'Is Name; Oedipus The King*
1968 *House Of Cards; Kampf Um Rom; Immortal Story* (also director)
1969 *Twelve Plus One; The Southern Star; Kampf Um Rom II; The Battle Of Neretva; Start The Revolution Without Me; The Kremlin Letter; Barbed Water* (narrator only)
1970 *Get To Know Your Rabbit; Waterloo; Catch 22\**
1971 *La Décade Prodigieuse* (UK: *Ten Days' Wonder*); *Malpertuis; Happiness In 20 Years* (narrator only); *A Safe Place*
1972 *Treasure Island; Necromancy; Kelly Country* (narrator only)
1973 *F For Fake* (also director)
1974 *And Then There Were None* (voice only)
1975 *Bugs Bunny, Superstar* (narrator only)
1976 *Voyage Of The Damned*
1977 *It Happened One Christmas* (TV)
1978 *A Woman Called Moses* (TV) (narrator only); *Filming Othello* (documentary)
1979 *The Muppet Movie\*; The Late, Great Planet Earth; Future Shock* (TV); *The Double McGuffin* (voice only)
1980 *Never Trust An Honest Thief; The Secret Of Nikola Tesla; The Man Who Saw Tomorrow; Shogun* (narrator only)
1981 *Butterfly; History Of The World Part I; Genocide* (narrator only)
1982 *Slapstick* (voice only)
1984 *In Our Hands* (documentary); *Where Is Parsifal?; Almonds And Raisins* (voice only)

1985 *Hot Money*
1986 *Transformers* (voice only)
1987 *Someone To Love*

See also directors listing

## WEST, Mae
real name: Mary Jane West
(c1892–1980) USA

1932 *Night After Night*
1933 *She Done Him Wrong\*; I'm No Angel\**
1934 *Belle Of The Nineties*
1935 *Goin' To Town*
1936 *Klondike Annie; Go West, Young Man*
1938 *Every Day's A Holiday*
1940 *My Little Chickadee*
1943 *The Heat's On* (UK: *Tropicana*)
1970 *Myra Breckinridge*
1977 *Sextette*

## WHITAKER, Forest
(1961– ) USA

1982 *Fast Times At Ridgemont High* (UK: *Fast Times*)
1985 *Vision Quest*
1986 *The Color Of Money\*; Platoon\**
1987 *Good Morning Vietnam\*; Stakeout*
1988 *Bird\*; Bloodsport*
1989 *Johnny Handsome*
1990 *Downtown*
1991 *A Rage In Harlem*
1992 *Diary Of A Hit Man; Consenting Adults; The Crying Game\**
1993 *Body Snatchers*

## WIDMARK, Richard
(1914– ) USA

1947 *Kiss Of Death*
1948 *Road House; The Street With No Name; Yellow Sky*
1949 *Down To The Sea In Ships; Slattery's Hurricane*
1950 *Night And The City; Panic In The Streets; Halls Of Montezuma*
1951 *The Frogmen*

**WIDMARK, Richard** (cont.)

1952 *Red Skies Of Montana; Don't Bother To Knock; O Henry's Full House; My Pal Gus; Screen Snapshots No 206*

1953 *Take The High Ground; Destination Gobi; Pickup On South Street*

1954 *Hell And High Water; Garden Of Evil; Broken Lance*

1955 *A Prize Of Gold; The Cobweb*

1956 *Backlash; Run For The Sun; The Last Wagon*

1957 *Saint Joan; Time Limit*

1958 *The Law And Jake Wade; The Tunnel Of Love; The Trap* (UK: *The Baited Trap*)

1959 *Warlock*

1960 *The Alamo\**

1961 *The Secret Ways; Two Rode Together; Judgment At Nuremberg\**

1962 *How The West Was Won\**

1963 *The Long Ships*

1964 *Flight From Ashiya; Cheyenne Autumn*

1965 *The Bedford Incident*

1966 *Alvarez Kelly*

1967 *The Way West*

1968 *Madigan; A Talent For Loving*

1969 *Death Of A Gunfighter*

1970 *The Moonshine War*

1971 *Vanished* (TV)

1972 *When The Legends Die*

1973 *Brock's Last Case* (TV)

1974 *Murder On The Orient Express\**

1975 *The Sellout; The Last Day* (TV)

1976 *To The Devil A Daughter; The Domino Principle* (UK: *The Domino Killings*)

1977 *Twilight's Last Gleaming; Rollercoaster*

1978 *Coma; The Swarm*

1979 *Mr Horn* (TV); *Bear Island*

1980 *All God's Children* (TV)

1981 *A Whale For The Killing* (TV); *National Lampoon's Movie Madness*

1982 *Hanky Panky; Who Dares Wins*

1984 *Against All Odds*

1985 *Blackout* (TV)

1987 *A Gathering Of Old Men* (TV)

1988 *Once Upon A Texas Train* (TV)

1989 *Cold Sassy Tree* (TV)

1991 *True Colors*

**WILDE, Cornel**
real name: Cornelius Louis Wilde
(1915–89) USA

1940 *The Lady With Red Hair*

1941 *Right To The Heart* (UK: *Knockout*); *Kisses For Breakfast; The Perfect Snob; High Sierra\**

1942 *Manila Calling; Life Begins At 8.30* (UK: *The Light Of Heart*)

1943 *Wintertime*

1944 *Guest In The House*

1945 *A Song To Remember; A Thousand And One Nights; Leave Her To Heaven*

1946 *Centennial Summer; The Bandit Of Sherwood Forest*

1947 *Forever Amber; The Homestretch; It Had To Be You*

1948 *Road House; The Walls Of Jericho*

1949 *Shockproof; Four Days' Leave*

1950 *Two Flags West*

1951 *At Sword's Point* (UK: *Sons Of The Musketeers*)

1952 *The Greatest Show On Earth\*; California Conquest; Operation Secret*

1953 *Treasure Of The Golden Condor; Main Street To Broadway; Saadia; Star Of India*

1954 *Passion; Woman's World; The Big Combo*

1955 *The Scarlet Coat; Storm Fear* (also director)

1956 *Hot Blood; Beyond Mombasa*

1957 *The Devil's Hairpin; Omar Khayyam*

1958 *Maracaibo* (also director)

1959 *Edge Of Eternity*

1960 *Constantine The Great*

1963 *Lancelot And Guinevere* (UK: *Sword Of Lancelot*) (also director)

1966 *The Naked Prey* (also director)

1967 *Beach Red* (also director)

1969 *The Comic*

1970 *No Blade Of Grass* (director only)
1972 *Gargoyles* (TV)
1975 *Shark's Treasure* (also director)
1977 *Behind The Iron Mask* (UK: *The Fifth Musketeer*)
1978 *The Norseman*
1983 *Flesh And Bullets* (also director)
1987 *My Very Wild Life*

## WILDER, Gene
real name: Jerry Silberman
(1934– ) USA

1967 *Bonnie And Clyde\**
1968 *The Producers*
1969 *Start The Revolution Without Me*
1970 *Quackser Fortune Has A Cousin In The Bronx*
1971 *Willy Wonka And The Chocolate Factory*
1972 *The Scarecrow; The Trouble With People* (TV); *Everything You Always Wanted To Know About Sex But Were Afraid To Ask*
1973 *Rhinoceros*
1974 *The Little Prince; Thursday's Game* (TV); *Blazing Saddles\*; Young Frankenstein\**
1975 *The Adventures Of Sherlock Holmes' Smarter Brother* (also director)
1976 *Silver Streak\**
1977 *The World's Greatest Lover* (also director)
1979 *The Frisco Kid*
1980 *Stir Crazy\*; Sunday Lovers*
1982 *Hanky Panky*
1984 *The Woman In Red* (also director)
1986 *Haunted Honeymoon* (also director)
1987 *Grandpère; Hello Actors Studio* (documentary)
1989 *See No Evil, Hear No Evil*
1990 *Funny About Love*
1991 *Another You*

## WILLIAMS, Robin
(1952– ) USA

1977 *Can I Do It 'Til I Need Glasses?*
1980 *Popeye\**

1982 *The World According To Garp*
1983 *The Survivors*
1984 *Moscow On The Hudson*
1985 *The Best Of Times*
1986 *Club Paradise; Seize The Day* (TV)
1987 *Dear America* (voice only); *Good Morning Vietnam\**
1988 *The Adventures Of Baron Munchausen\**
1989 *Dead Poets Society\**
1990 *Cadillac Man; Awakenings\**
1991 *Dead Again; The Fisher King\*; Hook\**
1992 *Shakes The Clown; Ferngully: The Last Rainforest* (voice only); *Toys; Aladdin* (voice only)
1993 *Being Human; Mrs Doubtfire*

## WILLIS, Bruce
(1955– ) USA

1978 *Ziegfeld — The Man And His Women* (TV)
1980 *The First Deadly Sin* (TV)
1981 *Prince Of The City*
1982 *The Verdict\**
1985 *Moonlighting* (TV)
1986 *That's Adequate*
1987 *Blind Date*
1988 *Sunset; Die Hard\**
1989 *In Country; Look Who's Talking* (voice only)
1990 *Die Hard 2; The Bonfire Of The Vanities\*; Look Who's Talking Too* (voice only)
1991 *Mortal Thoughts; Hudson Hawk; Billy Bathgate; The Last Boy Scout*
1992 *Death Becomes Her\**
1993 *Striking Distance*

## WINGER, Debra
(1955– ) USA

1977 *Slumber Party '57*
1978 *Special Olympics* (TV); *Thank God It's Friday*
1979 *French Postcards*
1980 *Urban Cowboy*

**WINGER, Debra** (cont.)

1982 *An Officer And A Gentleman\*; Cannery Row; Mike's Murder; ET\** (voice only)
1983 *Terms Of Endearment\**
1986 *Legal Eagles*
1987 *Black Widow; Made In Heaven*
1988 *Betrayed*
1990 *Everybody Wins; The Sheltering Sky*
1992 *Leap Of Faith*
1993 *Wilder Napalm; Shadowlands*

**WINTERS, Shelley**
real name: Shirley Schrift
(1922– ) USA

1943 *What A Woman!* (UK: *The Beautiful Cheat*); *The Racket Man*
1944 *Two-Man Submarine; Sailor's Holiday; She's A Soldier Too; Nine Girls; Cover Girl; Knickerbocker Holiday; Together Again*
1945 *Tonight And Every Night; A Thousand And One Nights; Dancing In Manhattan; Escape In The Fog*
1946 *Suspense*
1947 *New Orleans; Killer McCoy; Living In A Big Way; Tho Gangster; A Double Life*
1948 *Larceny; Cry Of The City; Red River\**
1949 *The Great Gatsby; Johnny Stool Pigeon; Take One False Step; South Sea Sinner* (UK: *East of Java*)
1950 *Winchester '73; Frenchie*
1951 *The Raging Tide; A Place In The Sun\*; Meet Danny Wilson; He Ran All The Way; Behave Yourself!*
1952 *Phone Call From A Stranger; My Man And I; Untamed Frontier*
1954 *Playgirl; Saskatchewan* (UK: *O'Rourke Of The Royal Mounted*); *To Dorothy A Son; Tennessee Champ; Executive Suite*
1955 *I Am A Camera; Mambo; Night Of The Hunter\*; I Died A Thousand*

*Times; The Treasure Of Pancho Villa; The Big Knife*
1959 *Odds Against Tomorrow; The Diary Of Anne Frank\**
1960 *Let No Man Write My Epitaph*
1961 *The Young Savages*
1962 *The Chapman Report; Lolita\**
1963 *The Balcony; Wives And Lovers; Gli Indifferenti* (UK: *Time Of Indifference*)
1964 *A House Is Not A Home*
1965 *The Greatest Story Ever Told; A Patch Of Blue*
1966 *Alfie\*; Harper* (UK: *The Moving Target*)
1967 *Enter Laughing*
1968 *The Scalphunters; Wild In The Streets; The Mad Room; Buona Sera, Mrs Campbell*
1969 *The Greatest Mother Of Them All* (short)
1970 *Bloody Mama; How Do I Love Thee*
1971 *What's The Matter With Helen?; Whoever Slew Auntie Roo?; Revenge* (TV); *A Death Of Innocence* (TV)
1972 *The Poseidon Adventure\*; Something To Hide; The Devil's Daughter* (TV); *The Adventures Of Nick Carter* (TV)
1973 *Blume In Love; Cleopatra Jones*
1974 *Big Rose* (TV); *Poor Pretty Eddie; The Sex Symbol* (TV)
1975 *Diamonds; That Lucky Touch*
1976 *Next Stop Greenwich Village; The Tenant; The Scarlet Dahlia; Mimi Bluette; The Three Sisters; Journey Into Fear*
1977 *Tentacles; The Initiation Of Sarah* (TV); *Pete's Dragon; La Signora Degli Orrori*
1978 *City On Fire; King Of The Gypsies*
1979 *The Visitor; Elvis — The Movie; The Magician Of Lublin; Redneck County Rape; Rudolph And Frosty's Christmas In July* (voice only)
1981 *SOB; My Mother, My Daughter; Looping*
1983 *Fanny Hill; Over The Brooklyn Bridge; Ellie*

1985 *Deja Vu; Witchfire*
1986 *The Delta Force; Very Close Quarters*
1987 *Hello Actors Studio; Marilyn Monroe: Beyond The Legend* (both documentaries)
1988 *The Order Of Things; Purple People Eater*
1989 *Taking Chances; An Unremarkable Life*
1990 *Touch Of A Stranger*
1991 *Stepping Out*
1992 *The Pickle*

## WOOD, Natalie
real name: Natasha Gurdin
(1938–81) USA

1943 *Happy Land*
1946 *Tomorrow Is Forever; The Bride Wore Boots*
1947 *Driftwood; Miracle On 34th Street\** (UK: *The Big Heart*); *The Ghost And Mrs Muir*
1948 *Scudda-Hoo, Scudda-Hay!* (UK: *Summer Lightning*); *Chicken Every Sunday*
1949 *Father Was A Fullback; The Green Promise* (UK: *Raging Waters*)
1950 *The Jackpot; Our Very Own; Never A Dull Moment; No Sad Songs For Me*
1951 *Dear Brat; The Blue Veil*
1952 *The Star; Just For You; The Rose Bowl Story*
1954 *The Silver Chalice*
1955 *One Desire; Rebel Without A Cause\**
1956 *The Searchers\*; The Burning Hills; The Girl He Left Behind; A Cry In The Night*
1957 *Bombers B-52* (UK: *No Sleep Till Dawn*)
1958 *Marjorie Morningstar; Girl On The Subway* (TV); *Kings Go Forth*
1959 *Cash McCall*
1960 *All The Fine Young Cannibals*
1961 *Splendor In The Grass; West Side Story\**
1962 *Gypsy\**

1963 *Love With The Proper Stranger*
1964 *Sex And The Single Girl*
1965 *The Great Race; Inside Daisy Clover*
1966 *This Property Is Condemned; Penelope*
1969 *Bob & Carol & Ted & Alice\**
1972 *The Candidate*
1973 *The Affair* (TV); *I'm A Stranger Here Myself* (documentary)
1975 *James Dean, The First American Teenager* (documentary); *Peeper*
1979 *The Cracker Factory* (TV); *Meteor; Hart To Hart* (TV)
1980 *The Last Married Couple In America; The Memory Of Eva Ryker* (TV); *Willie And Phil*
1983 *Brainstorm*

## WOODS, James
(1947– ) USA

1972 *The Visitors; Hickey And Boggs; Footsteps* (TV); *A Great American Tragedy* (TV) (UK: *Man At The Crossroads*)
1973 *The Way We Were\**
1974 *The Gambler*
1975 *Night Moves; Foster And Laurie* (TV); *Distance*
1976 *The Disappearance Of Aimee* (TV); *Raid On Entebbe; Alex And The Gypsy; F Scott Fitzgerald In Hollywood* (TV)
1977 *The Choirboys*
1978 *The New Maverick* (TV); *The Gift Of Love* (TV)
1979 *The Incredible Journey Of Dr Meg Laurel* (TV); *And Your Name Is Jonah* (TV); *The Onion Field*
1980 *The Black Marble*
1981 *Fast-Walking; Eyewitness* (UK: *Janitor*)
1982 *Split Image; Videodrome*
1983 *Once Upon A Time In America\**
1984 *Against All Odds*
1985 *Cat's Eye; Joshua Then And Now; Badge Of The Assassin* (TV)
1986 *Salvador\*; Promise* (TV)

**WOODS, James** (cont.)

1987 *Best Seller; In Love And War* (TV); *Cop*
1988 *The Boost*
1989 *True Believer; Immediate Family; My Name Is Bill W* (TV)
1990 *Women And Men: Stories Of Seduction* (TV)
1991 *The Hard Way; The Boys* (TV)
1992 *Citizen Cohn* (TV); *Straight Talk; Chaplin; Diggstown* (UK: *Midnight Sting*)

## WOODWARD, Joanne
(1930– ) USA

1955 *Count Three And Pray; The Late George Apley* (TV)
1956 *A Kiss Before Dying*
1957 *The Three Faces Of Eve; No Down Payment*
1958 *The Long Hot Summer; The 80 Yard Run* (TV)
1959 *Rally Round The Flag Boys; The Sound And The Fury; The Fugitive Kind*
1960 *From The Terrace\**
1961 *Paris Blues*
1963 *The Stripper* (UK: *Woman Of Summer*); *A New Kind Of Love*
1964 *Signpost To Murder*
1966 *Big Hand For A Little Lady* (UK: *Big Deal At Dodge City*); *A Fine Madness*
1968 *Rachel, Rachel\**
1969 *Winning*
1970 *WUSA; King: A Filmed Record...Montgomery To Memphis* (documentary)
1971 *They Might Be Giants*
1972 *The Effect Of Gamma Rays On Man-In-The-Moon Marigolds*
1973 *Summer Wishes, Winter Dreams*
1975 *The Drowning Pool*
1976 *Sybil* (TV)
1978 *The End; See How She Runs* (TV); *The Melodeon* (TV); *A Christmas To Remember* (TV)
1979 *Angel Death* (TV) (narrator only); *Streets Of LA* (TV)

1980 *Crisis At Central High* (TV); *The Shadow Box* (TV)
1984 *Harry And Son; Passions* (TV)
1985 *Do You Remember Love?* (TV)
1987 *The Glass Menagerie*
1990 *Mr And Mrs Bridge*
1992 *Foreign Affairs* (TV)
1993 *Philadelphia*

## WYMAN, Jane
real name: Sarah J Fulks
(1914– ) USA

1932 *The Kid From Spain*
1933 *Elmer The Great*
1934 *College Rhythm*
1935 *Rhumba; All The King's Horses; Stolen Harmony; King Of Burlesque*
1936 *Polo Joe; Anything Goes; Cain And Mabel; Gold Diggers Of 1937; My Man Godfrey; Smart Blonde*
1937 *Stage Struck; Slim; Public Wedding; Ready, Willing And Able; The Singing Marine; Mr Dodd Takes The Air; The King And The Chorus Girl* (UK: *Romance Is Sacred*)
1938 *Wide Open Spaces; The Spy Ring; Brother Rat; The Crowd Roars; He Couldn't Say No; Fools For Scandal; Tailspin*
1939 *The Kid From Kokomo* (UK: *Orphans Of The Ring*); *Private Detective; Torchy Plays With Dynamite; Kid Nightingale*
1940 *Brother Rat And A Baby* (UK: *Baby Be Good*); *The Sunday Round-Up* (short); *Flight Angels; Tugboat Annie Sails Again; An Angel From Texas; My Love Came Back; Gambling On The High Seas*
1941 *The Body Disappears; Bad Men Of Missouri; You're In The Army Now*
1942 *Footlight Serenade; Larceny Inc; My Favorite Spy*
1943 *Princess O'Rourke*

1944 *The Doughgirls; Make Your Own Bed; Hollywood Canteen; Crime By Night*
1945 *The Lost Weekend\**
1946 *One More Tomorrow; Night And Day\*; The Yearling\**
1947 *Magic Town; Cheyenne*
1948 *Johnny Belinda\**
1949 *The Lady Takes A Sailor; A Kiss In The Dark; It's A Great Feeling*
1950 *Stage Fright; The Glass Menagerie*
1951 *The Blue Veil; Three Guys Named Mike; Starlift; Here Comes The Groom*
1952 *Just For You; The Will Rogers Story* (UK: *The Story Of Will Rogers*)
1953 *Let's Do It Again; So Big*
1954 *Magnificent Obsession\**
1955 *All That Heaven Allows; Lucy Gallant*
1956 *Miracle In The Rain*
1959 *Holiday For Lovers*
1960 *Pollyanna*
1962 *Bon Voyage!*
1969 *How To Commit Marriage*
1071 *The Failing Of Raymond* (TV)
1979 *The Incredible Journey Of Dr Meg Laurel* (TV)

# Y

## YORK, Michael
(1942– ) UK

1963 *The Mind Benders*
1967 *The Taming Of The Shrew\*; Smashing Time; Accident; Red And Blue; Confessions Of A Loving Couple*
1968 *The Guru; Romeo And Juliet; The Strange Affair*
1969 *Justine; Alfred The Great*
1970 *Something For Everyone* (UK: *Black Flowers For The Bride*)
1971 *Zeppelin*
1972 *Cabaret\*; England Made Me*
1973 *Lost Horizon; The Three Musketeers\**

1974 *Murder On The Orient Express\*; The Four Musketeers*
1975 *Great Expectations* (TV); *Conduct Unbecoming; Touch And Go*
1976 *Seven Nights In Japan; Logan's Run*
1977 *The Island Of Dr Moreau; The Last Remake Of Beau Geste*
1978 *Fedora*
1979 *The Riddle Of The Sands; A Man Called Intrepid* (TV)
1980 *The Final Assignment*
1982 *The Phantom Of The Opera* (TV)
1983 *The White Lions; For Those I Loved; Le Sang Des Autres*
1984 *Success Is The Best Revenge; The Master Of Ballantrae* (TV)
1985 *L'Aube*
1986 *Dark Mansions* (TV); *Sword Of Gideon* (TV)
1987 *Joker*
1988 *Phantom Of Death; City Blue*
1989 *A Proposito Di Quelle Strana Ragazza; The Return Of The Musketeers; The Lady And The Highwayman* (TV); *Midnight Cop*
1990 *Duel Of Hearts*
1992 *Mindwalk*

## YORK, Susannah
real name: Susannah Fletcher
(1939– ) UK

1960 *Tunes Of Glory\*; There Was A Crooked Man*
1961 *The Greengage Summer*
1962 *Freud* (UK: *Freud — The Secret Passion*)
1963 *Tom Jones\**
1964 *The Seventh Dawn; Scene Nun, Take One* (short)
1965 *Sands Of The Kalahari; Scruggs* (short)
1966 *Kaleidoscope; A Man For All Seasons\**
1968 *Sebastian; Duffy; The Killing Of Sister George*
1969 *They Shoot Horses Don't They?\*; Lock Up Your Daughters!; Oh! What A Lovely War; Battle Of Britain; Country Dance*

**YORK, Susannah** (cont.)
1970  *Jane Eyre* (TV)
1971  *Zee And Co; Happy Birthday, Wanda June*
1972  *Images*
1974  *Gold; The Maids*
1975  *Conduct Unbecoming; That Lucky Touch*
1976  *Skyriders*
1977  *The Rollicking Adventures Of Eliza Fraser; The Shout*
1978  *Long Shot; The Silent Partner; Superman\**
1979  *The Golden Gate Murders* (TV)
1980  *Falling In Love Again; The Awakening; Alice; Superman II; Late Flowering Love* (short); *Loophole*
1983  *Yellowbeard; 99 Women; Nelly's Version*
1984  *A Christmas Carol* (TV)
1986  *Daemon*
1987  *Mio Min Mio; Pretty Kill; Barbablu, Barbablu* (UK: *Bluebeard, Bluebeard*); *Superman IV: The Quest For Peace* (voice only)
1988  *Just Ask For Diamond; A Summer Story; American Roulette*
1989  *Melancholia; En Handfull Tid* (UK: *A Handful of Time*)
1991  *Fate*

**YOUNG, Loretta**
real name: Gretchen Belzer
(1913–   ) USA

1917  *The Only Way*
1921  *The Sheik*
1927  *Naughty But Nice*
1928  *The Magnificent Flirt; Whip Woman; Scarlet Seas; Laugh, Clown, Laugh; The Head Man*
1929  *The Fast Life; The Squall; The Show Of Shows; The Girl In The Glass Cage; The Careless Age; The Forward Pass*
1930  *Show Girl In Hollywood; The Man from Blankley's; The Second Floor Mystery; Loose Ankles; Kismet; The Devil To Pay; Road To Paradise; The Truth About Youth*

1931  *Three Girls Lost; Beau Ideal; Platinum Blonde; The Right Of Way; Too Young To Marry; I Like Your Nerve; The Ruling Voice*
1932  *Play Girl; Taxi; Life Begins* (UK: *The Dawn Of Life*); *The Hatchet Man* (UK: *The Honourable Mr Wong*); *They Call It Sin* (UK: *The Way Of Life*); *Weekend Marriage* (UK: *Working Wives*)
1933  *The Life Of Jimmy Dolan* (UK: *The Kid's Last Fight*); *Employees' Entrance; Grand Slam; Zoo In Budapest; Midnight Mary; The Devil's In Love; Man's Castle; Heroes For Sale; She Had To Say Yes*
1934  *The House Of Rothschild; Bulldog Drummond Strikes Back; The White Parade; Born To Be Bad; Caravan*
1935  *Call Of The Wild; Clive Of India; Shanghai; The Crusades*
1936  *Ramona; The Unguarded Hour; Ladies In Love; Private Number* (UK: *Secret Interlude*)
1937  *Love Under Fire; Love Is News; Second Honeymoon; Café Metropole; Wife, Doctor And Nurse*
1938  *Suez; Four Men And A Prayer; Kentucky; Three Blind Mice*
1939  *Eternally Yours; Wife, Husband And Friend; The Story Of Alexander Graham Bell* (UK: *The Modern Miracle*)
1940  *The Doctor Takes A Wife; He Stayed For Breakfast*
1941  *Bedtime Story; The Lady From Cheyenne; The Men In Her Life*
1942  *A Night To Remember*
1943  *China*
1944  *And Now Tomorrow; Ladies Courageous*
1945  *Along Came Jones*
1946  *The Stranger; The Perfect Marriage*
1947  *The Bishop's Wife\*; The Farmer's Daughter*
1948  *Rachel And The Stranger; The Accused*

1949 *Mother Is A Freshman* (UK: *Mother Knows Best*); *Come To The Stable*
1950 *Key To The City*
1951 *Half Angel; Cause For Alarm*
1952 *Paula* (UK: *The Silent Voice*); *Because Of You*
1953 *It Happens Every Thursday*
1986 *Christmas Eve* (TV)
1989 *Lady In The Corner* (TV)


## YOUNG, Robert
(1907– ) USA

1931 *The Sin Of Madelon Claudet* (UK: *The Lullaby*); *The Black Camel; Hell Divers; Guilty Generation*
1932 *New Morals For Old; The Wet Parade; The Kid From Spain; Unashamed; Strange Interlude* (UK: *Strange Interval*)
1933 *Men Must Fight; Today We Live; Saturday's Millions; Tugboat Annie\*; Right To Romance; Hell Below*
1934 *The House Of Rothschild; Cardboard City; Spitfire; Hollywood Party; Paris Interlude; The Band Plays On; Lazy River; Whom The Gods Destroy; Death On The Diamond; Carolina* (UK: *The House Of Connelly*)
1935 *Calm Yourself; West Point Of The Air; The Bride Comes Home; Vagabond Lady; Remember Last Night?; Red Salute* (UK: *Arms And The Girl*)
1936 *It's Love Again; Secret Agent; Sworn Enemy; The Longest Night; Three Wise Guys; The Bride Walks Out; Stowaway*
1937 *The Emperor's Candlesticks; Dangerous Number; The Bride Wore Red; I Met Him In Paris; Married Before Breakfast*

1938 *The Toy Wife* (UK: *Frou-Frou*); *Paradise For Three* (UK: *Romance For Three*); *Rich Man, Poor Girl; Josette; Three Comrades: The Shining Hour*
1939 *Maisie; Honolulu; Miracles For Sale; Bridal Suite*
1940 *The Mortal Storm; Florian; Sporting Blood; Dr Kildare's Crisis; Northwest Passage*
1941 *Lady Be Good; The Trial Of Mary Dugan; Married Bachelor; Western Union; H M Pulham Esq*
1942 *Cairo; Journey For Margaret; Joe Smith, American* (UK: *Highway To Freedom*)
1943 *Sweet Rosie O'Grady; Slightly Dangerous; Claudia*
1944 *The Canterville Ghost*
1945 *Those Endearing Young Charms; The Enchanted Cottage*
1946 *Lady Luck; Claudia And David; The Searching Wind*
1947 *Crossfire\*; They Won't Believe Me*
1948 *Relentless; Sitting Pretty*
1949 *Bride For Sale; Adventure In Baltimore* (UK: *Bachelor Bait*); *That Forsyte Woman* (UK: *The Forsyte Saga*)
1950 *And Baby Makes Three; The Second Woman* (UK: *Ellen*)
1951 *Goodbye, My Fancy*
1952 *The Half-Breed*
1954 *Secret Of The Incas*
1969 *Marcus Welby MD* (TV)
1971 *Vanished* (TV)
1972 *All My Darling Daughters* (TV)
1973 *My Darling Daughters' Anniversary* (TV)
1978 *Little Women* (TV)
1984 *The Return Of Marcus Welby MD* (TV)
1987 *Murder Or Mercy?* (TV)
1988 *Marcus Welby MD: A Holiday Affair* (TV)

# Directors

## A

### ABRAHAMS, Jim
(1944–   )

1977 *Kentucky Fried Movie* (co-writer and performer only)
1980 *Airplane!** (co-writer and director)
1984 *Top Secret!* (co-writer and director)
1986 *Ruthless People*
1988 *Big Business; Naked Gun — From The Files Of Police Squad!** (co-writer only)
1990 *Welcome Home Roxy Carmichael; Cry Baby* (executive producer only)
1991 *Hot Shots!*; Naked Gun 2½: The Smell Of Fear* (executive producer only)
1993 *Hot Shots 2*

### ALDRICH, Robert
(1918–83) USA

1945 *Pardon My Past; The Southerner; The Story Of G I Joe* (all assistant director)
1946 *The Strange Love Of Martha Ivers* (assistant director)
1947 *Body And Soul; The Private Affairs Of Bel Ami* (both assistant director)
1948 *Arch Of Triumph; So This Is New York; No Minor Vices* (all assistant director)
1949 *Force Of Evil; Caught; The Red Pony; A Kiss For Corliss* (all assistant director)
1950 *The White Tower* (assistant director)
1951 *M; Of Men And Music; The Prowler* (all assistant director); *The Big Night* (actor only); *Ten Tall Men* (associate producer); *When I Grow Up* (production manager only)

1952 *Abbott And Costello Meet Captain Kid; Limelight** (both assistant director); *The First Time* (associate producer only)
1953 *The Big Leaguer*
1954 *World For Ransom; Apache; Vera Cruz*
1955 *Kiss Me Deadly; The Big Knife*
1956 *Autumn Leaves; Attack!*
1957 *The Garment Jungle* (uncredited); *The Ride Back* (producer only)
1959 *The Angry Hills; Ten Seconds To Hell*
1961 *The Last Sunset*
1962 *Sodom And Gomorrah; Whatever Happened To Baby Jane?**
1963 *Four For Texas*
1964 *Hush...Hush, Sweet Charlotte*
1966 *Flight Of The Phoenix*
1967 *The Dirty Dozen**
1968 *The Legend Of Lylah Clare; The Killing Of Sister George*
1969 *Whatever Happened To Aunt Alice?* (producer only)
1970 *Too Late The Hero*
1971 *The Grissom Gang*
1972 *Ulzana's Raid*
1973 *Emperor Of The North*
1974 *The Longest Yard** (UK: *The Mean Machine*)
1975 *Hustle*
1977 *Twilight's Last Gleaming; The Choirboys*
1979 *The Frisco Kid*
1981 *All the Marbles* (UK: *The California Dolls*)

### ALLEN, Irwin
(1916–91) USA

1952 *A Girl In Every Port* (producer only); *The Sea Around Us* (documentary)
1954 *Dangerous Mission* (producer only)

1956 *The Animal World* (documentary)
1957 *The Story Of Mankind*
1959 *The Big Circus* (producer only)
1960 *The Lost World*
1961 *Voyage To The Bottom Of The Sea*
1962 *Five Weeks In A Balloon*
1972 *The Poseidon Adventure\**
(producer only)
1974 *The Towering Inferno\** (co-director)
1976 *The Time Travellers* (TV)
1978 *The Swarm*
1979 *Hanging By A Thread* (TV);
*Beyond The Poseidon Adventure*
1980 *When Time Ran Out* (producer only)

## ALLEN, Woody
real name: Allen Stewart Konigsberg
(1935– ) USA

1966 *What's Up Tiger Lily?*
1969 *Take The Money And Run* (also actor); *Don't Drink The Water* (original author only)
1971 *Bananas* (also actor)
1972 *Everything You Always Wanted To Know About Sex (But Were Afraid To Ask)* (also actor)
1973 *Sleeper\** (also actor)
1975 *Love And Death* (also actor)
1977 *Annie Hall\** (also actor)
1978 *Interiors*
1979 *Manhattan\** (also actor)
1980 *Stardust Memories* (also actor)
1982 *A Midsummer Night's Sex Comedy* (also actor)
1983 *Zelig\** (also actor)
1984 *Broadway Danny Rose\** (also actor)
1985 *The Purple Rose Of Cairo\**
1986 *Hannah And Her Sisters\** (also actor)
1987 *Radio Days; September*
1988 *Another Woman\**
1989 *New York Stories* (co-director, also actor); *Crimes And Misdemeanours\** (also actor)
1990 *Alice*
1992 *Shadows And Fog* (also actor); *Husbands And Wives* (also actor)

1993 *Manhattan Murder Mystery* (also actor)

See also actors listing

## ALMODÓVAR, Pedro
(1951– ) Spain

1974 *Dos Putas, Or, Historia De Amor Que Termina En Boda* (UK: *Two Whores, Or, A Love Story That Ends In Marriage*) (short); *Film Politico* (UK: *Political Film*) (short)
1975 *La Caida De Sodoma* (UK: *The Fall Of Sodom*) (short); *Homenaje* (UK: *Tribute*) (short); *La Estrella* (UK: *The Star*) (short); *Blancor* (UK: *Whiteness*) (short)
1976 *Trailer Of Who's Afraid Of Virgina Woolf?* (short); *Sea Caritativo* (UK: *Be Charitable*) (short)
1977 *Las Tres Ventajas De Ponte* (UK: *Ponte's Three Advantages*) (short); *Sexo Va, Sexo Vienne* (UK: *Sex Comes, Sex Goes*) (short); *Complementos*
1978 *Folle, Folle, Folleme, Tim* (UK: *Fuck, Fuck, Fuck Me, Tim*); *Salome*
1980 *Pepi, Luci, Bom Y Otras Chicas Del Montón* (UK: *Pepi, Luci, Bom And Lots Of Other Girls*)
1982 *Laberinto De Pasiones* (UK: *Labyrinth Of Passions*)
1983 *Entre Tinieblas* (UK: *Dark Habits*)
1984 *Qué He Hecho Yo Para Merecer Esto?* (UK: *What Have I Done To Deserve This?*)
1985 *Trailer Para Amantes De Lo Prohibido* (UK: *Trailer For Lovers Of The Forbidden* (TV))
1986 *Matador*
1987 *La Ley Del Deseo* (UK: *Law Of Desire*)
1988 *Mujeres Al Borde De Un Ataque De Nervios\** (UK: *Women On The Verge Of A Nervous Breakdown*)
1990 *Atame!\** (UK: *Tie Me Up, Tie Me Down!*)
1991 *Tacones Lejanos* (UK: *High Heels*)

## ALTMAN, Robert
(1925–   ) USA

1954 *The Builders*
1955 *The Delinquents*
1957 *The James Dean Story*
1964 *The Party* (short)
1965 *Pot Au Feu* (short); *The Katherine Reed Story* (short)
1967 *Countdown*
1969 *That Cold Day In The Park*
1970 *M\*A\*S\*H\*; Brewster McCloud*
1971 *McCabe And Mrs Miller*
1972 *Images*
1973 *The Long Goodbye*
1974 *Thieves Like Us; California Split*
1975 *Nashville\**
1976 *Buffalo Bill And The Indians, Or Sitting Bull's History Lesson; Welcome To L A* (producer only)
1977 *The Late Show* (producer only); *Three Women*
1978 *A Wedding; Remember My Name* (producer only)
1979 *Quintet; A Perfect Couple; Rich Kids* (producer only)
1980 *Health; Popeye*
1982 *Come Back To The Five And Dime, Jimmy Dean, Jimmy Dean*
1983 *Streamers*
1984 *Secret Honor*
1985 *Fool For Love; O C And Stiggs; Jatszani Kid* (associate producer only)
1986 *Beyond Therapy*
1987 *Aria* (co-director)
1988 *The Caine Mutiny Court-Martial* (TV); *Tanner 88* (TV)
1989 *The Room; The Dumb Waiter*
1990 *Vincent And Theo*
1992 *The Player\**
1993 *Short Cuts*


## ANDERSON, Michael
(1920–   )

1949 *Private Angelo* (co-director)
1950 *Waterfront* (US: *Waterfront Women*)
1951 *Hell Is Sold Out; Night Was Our Friend*
1952 *Dial 17* (documentary)
1953 *Will Any Gentleman...?; The House Of The Arrow*
1954 *The Dambusters*
1955 *1984*
1956 *Around The World In 80 Days\**
1957 *Yangtse Incident* (US: *Battle Hell*)
1958 *Chase A Crooked Shadow*
1959 *Shake Hands With The Devil; The Wreck Of The Mary Deare*
1960 *All The Fine Young Cannibals*
1961 *The Naked Edge*
1963 *Wild And Wonderful*
1964 *Flight From Ashiya*
1965 *Operation Crossbow* (US: *The Great Spy Mission*)
1966 *The Quiller Memorandum; Eye of The Devil* (uncredited)
1968 *The Shoes Of The Fisherman*
1972 *Pope Joan*
1975 *Doc Savage — Man Of Bronze; Conduct Unbecoming*
1976 *Logan's Run*
1977 *Orca — Killer Whale*
1978 *Dominique*
1979 *The Martian Chronicles* (TV)
1981 *Bells* (aka *Murder By Phone*)
1984 *Second Time Lucky*
1985 *Troupers* (executive producer)
1986 *Separate Vacations*
1989 *La Boutique De L'Orfèvre; Millenium*
1991 *Young Catherine* (TV)


## ANNAKIN, Ken
(1914–   ) UK

1942 *Cooks* (documentary); *London — 1942* (documentary)
1943 *A Ride With Uncle Joe* (documentary)
1944 *Black Diamonds* (documentary); *The New Crop* (documentary); *Combined Cadets* (documentary)
1945 *A Farm In The Fens* (documentary); *Make Fruitful the*

Land (documentary); Pacific
Thrust (documentary); Three
Cadets (documentary)
1946 The West Riding (documentary); It
Began On The Clyde
(documentary); English Criminal
Justice (documentary)
1947 Turn It Out (documentary);
Holiday Camp; Broken Journey
1948 Here Come The Huggetts;
Miranda; Quartet (co-director)
1949 Vote For Huggett; Landfall; The
Huggetts Abroad
1950 Trio (co-director); Double
Confession
1951 Hotel Sahara
1952 The Planter's Wife; The Story Of
Robin Hood And His Merrie Men
1953 The Sword And The Rose
1954 The Seekers; You Know What
Sailors Are
1955 Value For Money
1956 Loser Takes All; Three Men In A
Boat
1957 Across the Bridge
1958 Nor The Moon By Night
1959 Third Man On The Mountain
1960 Swiss Family Robinson*
1961 Very Important Person; The
Hellions
1962 Crooks Anonymous; The Fast
Lady; The Longest Day* (co-
director)
1963 The Informers
1965 Those Magnificent Men In Their
Flying Machines; The Battle Of
The Bulge
1967 The Long Duel
1968 The Biggest Bundle Of Them All
1969 Monte Carlo Or Bust!
1972 Call Of The Wild
1975 Paper Tiger
1977 The Fifth Musketeer
1978 Murder At The Mardi Gras (TV);
The Pirate (TV)
1979 Institute For Revenge
1980 Cheaper To Keep Her
1982 The Pirate Movie
1988 The New Adventures Of Pippi
Longstocking
1992 Gengis Khan

## ANTONIONI, Michelangelo
(1912–   ) Italy

1947 Gente Del Po (documentary)
1948 N U (Nettezza Urbana); Oltre
L'Oblio; Roma–Montevideo (all
documentaries)
1949 Bomarzo; L'Amorosa Menzogna;
Superstizione; Ragazze In Bianco
(all documentaries)
1950 La Villa Dei Mostri; La Funivia Del
Faloria; Sette Canne E Un Vestito
(all documentaries); Cronaca Di
Un Amore (UK: Story Of A Love
Affair)
1952 I Vinti/I Nostri Figli
1953 Amore In Città (UK: Love In The
City) (co-director); La Signora
Senza Camelie (UK: The Lady
Without Camellias)
1955 Le Amiche
1957 Il Grido (UK: The Cry)
1958 Nel Segno Di Roma (co-director)
1960 L'Avventura*
1961 La Notte (UK: The Night)
1962 L'Eclisse (UK: The Eclipse)
1964 Deserto Rosso (UK: Red Desert)
1965 I Tre Volti (co-director)
1966 Blow-Up*
1970 Zabriskie Point
1972 La Cina (documentary)
1975 Professione: Reporter (UK: The
Passenger)
1979 Il Mistero Di Oberwald (UK: The
Oberwald Mystery)
1982 Identificazione Di Una Donna (UK:
Identification Of A Woman)
1992 Noto Mandorli Volcano Stromboli
Carnivale (short documentary)

## APTED, Michael
(1941–   ) UK

1973 The Triple Echo
1974 Stardust
1976 Trick Or Treat (uncompleted)
1977 The Squeeze; Stronger Than The
Sun (TV)
1978 Agatha
1980 Coal Miner's Daughter*
1981 Continental Divide

**APTED, Michael** (cont.)

1982 *P'Tang, Yang, Kipperbang* (TV)
1983 *Gorky Park*
1984 *First Born; The River Rat*
(executive producer only)
1985 *28 Up* (TV); *Bring On The Night*
(both documentaries); *Spies Like
Us* (actor only)
1987 *Critical Condition*
1988 *Gorillas In The Mist**
1989 *The Long Way Home*
(documentary)
1991 *35 Up* (TV) (documentary); *Class
Action; Incident At Oglala*
(documentary)
1992 *Thunderheart*

## ARCAND, Denys
(1939–   ) Canada

1962 *Seul Ou Avec D'Autres* (short)
1970 *On Est Au Coton* (documentary)
1972 *Une Maudite Galette; Québec:
Duplessis Et Après...*
(documentary)
1973 *Rejeanne Padovanni*
1975 *Gina*
1984 *Le Crime D'Ovide Plouffe*
1986 *Le Déclin De L'Empire Américain*
(UK: *The Decline Of The
American Empire*)
1987 *Un Zoo La Nuit* (UK: *Night Zoo*)
1989 *Jésus De Montréal** (UK: *Jesus of
Montreal*)
1991 *Montréal Vu Par...*(co-director)
1993 *Unidentified Human Remains And
The True Nature Of Love*

## ASHBY, Hal
(c.1929–88) USA

1958 *The Big Country** (assistant editor
only)
1959 *The Diary Of Anne Frank**
(assistant editor only)
1961 *The Young Doctors* (assistant
editor only)
1962 *The Children's Hour* (assistant
editor only)
1964 *The Best Man* (assistant editor
only)

1965 *The Greatest Story Ever Told;
The Loved One; The Cincinnati
Kid** (all editor only)
1966 *The Russians Are Coming, The
Russians Are Coming** (editor only)
1967 *In The Heat Of The Night** (editor
only)
1968 *The Thomas Crown Affair**
(associate producer only)
1969 *Gaily, Gaily* (associate producer
only)
1970 *The Landlord*
1971 *Harold And Maude*
1973 *The Last Detail*
1975 *Shampoo**
1976 *Bound For Glory**
1978 *Coming Home**
1979 *Being There*
1981 *Second Hand Hearts*
1982 *Lookin' To Get Out; Let's Spend
The Night Together*
(documentary)
1983 *Time Is On Our Side*
(documentary)
1984 *The Slugger's Wife*
1985 *Eight Million Ways To Die*

## ASQUITH, Anthony
(1902–68) UK

1927 *Shooting Stars* (co-director)
1928 *Underground*
1929 *The Runaway Princess*
1930 *A Cottage On Dartmoor* (US:
*Escaped From Dartmoor*)
1931 *Tell England* (US: *Battle Of
Gallipoli*)
1932 *Dance Pretty Lady*
1933 *The Lucky Number*
1934 *Unfinished Symphony* (co-
director)
1935 *Moscow Nights; Brown On
Resolution* (co-director)
1938 *Pygmalion** (co-director)
1939 *French Without Tears; Guide
Dogs For The Blind*
(documentary)
1940 *Freedom Radio; Quiet Wedding;
Channel Incident* (documentary)
1941 *Cottage To Let; Rush Hour*
(documentary)

1942 *Uncensored*
1943 *The Demi-Paradise; We Dive At Dawn; Welcome To Britain* (co-director)
1944 *Fanny By Gaslight; Two Fathers* (documentary)
1945 *The Way To The Stars*
1946 *While The Sun Shines*
1948 *The Winslow Boy*
1950 *The Woman In Question*
1951 *The Browning Version*
1952 *The Importance Of Being Earnest*
1953 *The Final Test; The Net*
1954 *The Young Lovers; Carrington VC*
1955 *On Such A Night*
1958 *Orders To Kill*
1959 *Libel!; The Doctor's Dilemma*
1960 *The Millionairess; Zero* (documentary)
1961 *Two Living, One Dead*
1962 *Guns Of Darkness*
1963 *The VIPs; An Evening With The Royal Ballet* (co-director)
1964 *The Yellow Rolls-Royce*

## ATTENBOROUGH, Richard
(1923– ) UK

1969 *Oh! What A Lovely War*
1972 *Young Winston*
1977 *A Bridge Too Far*
1978 *Magic*
1982 *Gandhi\**
1985 *A Chorus Line*
1987 *Cry Freedom\**
1992 *Chaplin*
1993 *Shadowlands*

See also actors listing

## AVILDSEN, John G
(1936– ) USA

1963 *Greenwich Village Story* (actor only)
1964 *Smiles* (short); *Black Like Me* (assistant)
1965 *Mickey One* (assistant)
1967 *Light, Sound, Diffuse; Turn On To Love* (shorts)
1968 *Okay Bill; Sweet Dreams*

1969 *Guess What We Learned In School Today?*
1970 *Joe*
1971 *Cry Uncle* (UK: *Super Dick*)
1972 *The Stoolie*
1973 *Save The Tiger*
1974 *Foreplay* (co-director)
1975 *W W And The Dixie Dancekings*
1976 *Rocky\**
1978 *Slow Dancing In The Big City*
1980 *The Formula*
1981 *Neighbors*
1982 *Traveling Hopefully* (documentary)
1983 *A Night In Heaven*
1984 *The Karate Kid\**
1986 *The Karate Kid Part II*
1987 *Happy New Year*
1988 *For Keeps* (UK: *Maybe Baby*)
1989 *Lean On Me; The Karate Kid Part III*
1990 *Rocky V*
1992 *The Power Of One*

## AXEL, Gabriel
(19?– ) Denmark

1959 *Guld Og Gronne Skove*
1963 *Tre Piger I Paris*
1967 *Den Rodde Kappe*
1968 *Det Kaere Legetoj*
1971 *Med Kaerlig Hilsen*
1975 *Familien Gyldenkaal*
1976 *Alt Paa Et Braet*
1987 *Babettes Gastebud\** (UK: *Babette's Feast*)
1989 *Christian*

# B

## BABENCO, Hector
(1946– ) Argentina

1975 *Rei Da Noite* (UK: *King Of The Night*)
1978 *Lucio Flavio*
1981 *Pixote*
1985 *Kiss Of The Spiderwoman\**
1987 *Besame Mucho; Ironweed\**
1991 *At Play In The Fields Of The Lord*

## BACON, Lloyd
(1890–1955) USA

1923  *The Host* (short)
1924  *Don't Fail; The Wild Goose Chaser* (both shorts)
1925  *The Raspberry Romance; Merrymakers; Breaking The Ice; He Who Gets Smacked; Take Your Time; Good Morning Madam; The Window Dummy* (all shorts)
1926  *Wide Open Faces; Two Lips In Holland; Meet My Girl* (all shorts); *Broken Hearts Of Hollywood; Private Izzy Murphy*
1927  *Smith's Customer; Smith's Surprise; Smith's New Home* (all shorts); *The Heart Of Maryland; White Flannels; A Sailor's Sweetheart; Brass Knuckles*
1928  *The Question Of Today* (short); *Pay As You Enter; The Lion And The Mouse; Women They Talk About; The Singing Fool*
1929  *Stark Mad; Honky Tonk; No Defense; Say It With Songs; So Long Netty*
1930  *Moby Dick; The Other Tomorrow; She Couldn't Say No; A Notorious Affair; The Office Wife*
1931  *Fifty Million Frenchmen; Sit Tight; Gold Dust Gertie; Kept Husbands; Honor Of The Family*
1932  *Fireman Save My Child; The Famous Ferguson Case; Miss Pinkerton; Manhattan Parade; You Said A Mouthful; Crooner*
1933  *The Picture Snatcher; Son Of A Sailor; 42nd Street\*; Mary Stevens MD; Footlight Parade\**
1934  *Six Day Bike Rider; He Was Her Man; Wonder Bar; Here Comes The Navy; A Very Honorable Guy* (UK: *A Very Honourable Man*)
1935  *In Caliente; Devil Dogs Of The Air; Frisco Kid; Broadway Gondolier; The Irish In Us*
1936  *Sons O' Guns; Cain And Mabel; Gold Diggers Of 1937*
1937  *Ever Since Eve; Marked Woman; San Quentin; Submarine D-1*
1938  *Cowboy From Brooklyn* (UK: *Romance And Rythmn*); *Boy Meets Girl; Racket Busters; A Slight Case Of Murder*
1939  *The Oklahoma Kid; Wings Of The Navy; Invisible Stripes; Espionage Agent; Indianapolis Speedway* (UK: *Devil On Wheels*)
1940  *Three Cheers For The Irish; A Child Is Born; Brother Orchid; Knute Rockne — All American* (UK: *A Modern Hero*)
1941  *Honeymoon For Three; Affectionately Yours; Footsteps In The Dark; Navy Blues*
1942  *Larceny Inc; Wings For The Eagle; Silver Queen*
1943  *Action In The North Atlantic*
1944  *The Sullivans; Sunday Dinner For A Soldier*
1945  *Captain Eddie*
1946  *Home, Sweet Homicide; Wake Up And Dream*
1947  *I Wonder Who's Kissing Her Now*
1948  *You Were Meant For Me; Give My Regards To Broadway; Don't Trust Your Husband/An Innocent Affair*
1949  *Mother Is A Freshman* (UK: *Mother Knows Best*); *It Happens Every Spring; Miss Grant Takes Richmond* (UK: *Innocence Is Bliss*)
1950  *Kill The Umpire!; The Fuller Brush Girl* (UK: *The Affairs Of Sally*); *The Good Humor Man*
1951  *Call Me Mister; The Frogmen; Golden Girl*
1953  *The 'I Don't Care' Girl; The Great Sioux Uprising; Walking My Baby Home; She Couldn't Say No* (UK: *Beautiful But Dangerous*)
1954  *The French Line*

## BADHAM, John
(1943–   ) USA

1971  *The Impatient Heart* (TV)
1973  *Isn't It Shocking?* (TV)

1974　*The Law* (TV); *The Gun* (TV);
　　　*Reflections Of Murder* (TV); *The
　　　Godchild* (TV)
1976　*The Keegans* (TV); *The Bingo
　　　Long Travelling All Stars And
　　　Motor Kings*
1977　*Saturday Night Fever**
1979　*Dracula*
1981　*Whose Life Is It Anyway?*
1982　*Blue Thunder*
1983　*Wargames**
1985　*American Flyers*
1986　*Short Circuit*
1987　*Stakeout*
1989　*Disorganized Crime* (executive
　　　producer only)
1990　*Bird On A Wire**
1991　*The Hard Way*
1993　*Point Of No Return; Stakeout 2*

## BARRON, Steve
(1956–　) Ireland

1984　*Electric Dreams*
1990　*Teenage Mutant Ninja Turtles**
1993　*The Coneheads*

## BEATTY, Warren
(1937–　) USA

1978　*Heaven Can Wait** (co-director)
1981　*Reds**
1990　*Dick Tracy**

See also actors listing

## BEAUMONT, Harry
(1888–1966) USA

1915　*The Call Of The City*
1916　*The Truant Soul*
1917　*Skinner's Baby; Skinner's Dress
　　　Suit; Skinner's Bubble; Burning
　　　The Candle; Filling His Own
　　　Shoes* (all shorts)
1918　*Brown Of Harvard; Thirty A Week*
1919　*Wild Goose Chase; Little Rowdy;
　　　A Man And His Money; One Of
　　　The Finest; Heartsease; Toby's
　　　Bow; Go West,Young Man; City
　　　Of Comrades; Lord And Lady
　　　Algy; The Gay Lord Quex*

1920　*Stop Thief!; The Great Accident;
　　　Going Some; Officer 666; Dollars
　　　And Sense*
1921　*Glass Houses; The Fourteenth
　　　Lover*
1922　*Very Truly Yours; The Ragged
　　　Heiress; June Madness; They
　　　Like'Em Rough; Seeing's
　　　Believing; The Five Dollar Baby;
　　　Lights Of The Desert; Love In The
　　　Dark*
1923　*Crinoline And Romance; A Noise
　　　In Newboro; The Gold Diggers;
　　　Main Street*
1924　*Babbitt; Beau Brummell; The
　　　Lover Of Camille; Don't Doubt
　　　Your Husband; A Lost Lady*
1925　*Recompense; His Majesty Bunker
　　　Bean; Rose Of The Wild*
1926　*Sandy; Womanpower*
1927　*One Increasing Purpose*
1928　*Forbidden Hours; Our Dancing
　　　Daughters*
1929　*A Single Man; Speedway; The
　　　Broadway Melody**
1930　*Lord Byron Of Broadway* (UK:
　　　*What Price Melody?*) (co-director);
　　　*The Florodora Girl* (UK: *The Gay
　　　Nineties*); *Children Of Pleasure;
　　　Our Blushing Brides; Those Three
　　　French Girls*
1931　*Dance Fools Dance; The Great
　　　Lover; Laughing Sinners; West Of
　　　Broadway*
1933　*When Ladies Meet; Should Ladies
　　　Behave?; Made On Broadway*
　　　(UK: *The Girl I Made*)
1934　*Murder In The Private Car*
　　　(UK: *Murder On The Runaway
　　　Train*)
1935　*Enchanted April*
1936　*The Girl On The Front Page*
1937　*When's Your Birthday?*
1944　*Maisie Goes To Reno* (UK: *You
　　　Can't Do That To Me*)
1945　*Twice Blessed; Up Goes Maisie*
　　　(UK: *Up She Goes*)
1946　*The Show-Off*
1947　*Undercover Maisie* (UK:
　　　*Undercover Girl*)
1948　*Alias A Gentleman*

## BECKER, Harold
(1950– ) USA

1964 *Interview With Bruce Gordon* (short)
1972 *The Ragman's Daughter*
1979 *The Onion Field*
1980 *The Black Marble*
1981 *Taps*
1985 *Vision Quest*
1988 *The Boost*
1989 *Sea Of Love\**
1993 *Damage*

## BEINEIX, Jean-Jacques
(1946– ) France

1977 *Le Chien De Monsieur Michel* (short); *L'Animal* (assistant director)
1979 *French Postcards* (assistant director)
1981 *Diva\**
1983 *La Lune Dans Le Caniveau* (UK: *The Moon In The Gutter*)
1986 *37.2 Degrés Le Matin* (UK: *Betty Blue\**)
1989 *Roselyne Et Les Lions* (UK: *Roselyne And The Lions*)
1992 *IP5*

## BENEDEK, Laslo
real name: László Benedek
(1907–92) Hungary

1940 *A Little Bit Of Heaven* (editor only)
1948 *The Kissing Bandit*
1949 *Port Of New York*
1951 *Death Of A Salesman*
1952 *Storm Over Tibet* (uncredited)
1953 *The Wild One\**
1954 *Kinder, Mütter Und Ein General; Bengal Brigade* (UK: *Bengal Rifles*)
1957 *Affair In Havana*
1960 *Moment Of Danger* (US: *Malaga*); *Recours En Grace*
1966 *Namu The Killer Whale*
1968 *The Daring Game*
1971 *The Night Visitor*
1974 *Assault On Agathon*
1985 *King Kong's Faust* (actor only)

## BENNETT, Compton
real name: Robert Compton-Bennett
(1900–74) UK

1941 *Freedom Must Have Wings* (documentary)
1942 *Find, Fix And Strike* (documentary)
1944 *Men Of Rochdale* (documentary)
1945 *The Seventh Veil; Julius Caesar* (short)
1946 *The Years Between; Daybreak*
1948 *My Own True Love*
1949 *That Forsyte Woman* (UK: *The Forsyte Saga*)
1950 *King Solomon's Mines\** (co-director)
1952 *So Little Time; Gift Horse* (UK: *Glory At Sea*); *It Started In Paradise*
1953 *Desperate Moment*
1957 *That Woman Opposite; After The Ball; The Flying Scot*
1960 *Beyond The Curtain*
1961 *First Left Past Eden* (short)
1965 *How To Undress In Public Without Undue Embarrassment*

## BENTON, Robert Douglas
(1932– ) USA

1964 *A Texas Romance — 1909* (short)
1967 *Bonnie And Clyde\** (co-writer only)
1970 *There Was A Crooked Man* (co-writer only)
1972 *What's Up Doc?\** (co-writer only); *Bad Company*
1977 *The Late Show*
1978 *Superman\** (co-writer only)
1979 *Kramer Vs Kramer\**
1982 *Still Of The Night*
1984 *Places In The Heart\**
1987 *Nadine*
1991 *Billy Bathgate*

## BERESFORD, Bruce
(1940– ) Australia

1972 *The Adventures Of Barry Mackenzie*
1974 *Barry Mackenzie Holds His Own*

1975 *Side By Side*
1976 *Don's Party*
1977 *The Getting Of Wisdom*
1978 *Money Movers*
1980 *Breaker Morant; The Club*
1982 *Puberty Blues*
1983 *Tender Mercies**
1985 *King David; The Fringe Dwellers*
1986 *Crimes Of The Heart*
1987 *Aria* (co-director)
1989 *Driving Miss Daisy*; Her Alibi*
1990 *Mister Johnson*
1991 *The Black Robe*
1992 *Rich In Love*

## BERGER, Ludwig
real name: Ludwig Bamberger
(1892–1969) Germany

1922 *Ein Glas Wasser*
1923 *Verlorene Schuh*
1926 *Ein Walzertraum* (UK: *The Waltz Dream*)
1928 *Meister Von Nurnberg; The Woman From Moscow; Sins Of The Fathers*
1929 *Brennende Herz* (UK: *The Burning Heart*)
1930 *The Vagabond King; Playboy Of Paris*
1932 *Ich Bei Tag Und Du Bei Nacht*
1933 *Early To Bed; Walzerkrieg; Guerre Des Valses*
1937 *Pygmalion*
1938 *Trois Valses* (UK: *Three Waltzes*)
1940 *Ergens In Nederland; The Thief Of Bagdad** (co-director)
1950 *Ballerina*

## BERGMAN, Ernst Ingmar
(1918–   ) Sweden

1944 *Hets* (UK: *Torment*) (writer only)
1945 *Kris* (UK: *Crisis*)
1946 *Det Regnar På Vår Kärlek* (UK: *It Rains On Our Love*)
1947 *Skepp Till Indialand* (UK: *A Ship Bound For India*)
1948 *Musik I Mörker* (UK: *Music In Darkness*); *Hamnstad* (UK: *Port Of Call*)

1949 *Fängelse* (UK: *Prison*); *Törst* (UK: *Thirst*)
1950 *Till Glädye* (UK: *To Joy*); *Sånt Händes Inte Här* (UK: *High Tension*)
1951 *Sommarlek* (UK: *Summer Interlude*)
1952 *Kvinnors Väntan* (UK: *Secrets Of A Woman*)
1953 *Sommaren Med Monika* (UK: *Summer With Monika*); *Gycklarnas Afton* (UK: *Sawdust And Tinsel*)
1954 *En Lektion I Karlek* (UK: *A Lesson In Love*)
1955 *Kvinnodrom* (UK: *Journey Into Autumn*); *Sommarnattens Leende* (UK: *Smiles Of A Summer Night*)
1957 *Det Sjunde Inseglet** (UK: *The Seventh Seal*); *Smultronstallet** (UK: *Wild Strawberries*)
1958 *Nara Livet* (UK: *So Close To Life*); *Ansiktet* (UK: *The Face*)
1959 *Jungfrukallan* (UK: *The Virgin Spring*)
1960 *Djavulens Oga* (UK: *The Devil's Eye*)
1961 *Ssom I En Spegel* (UK: *Through A Glass Darkly*)
1963 *Nattvardsgasterna* (UK: *Winter Light*); *Tystnaden* (UK: *The Silence*)
1964 *For Att Inte Tala Om Alla Desse Kvinnor* (UK: *Now About These Women*)
1966 *Persona**
1967 *Stimulantia* (co-director)
1968 *Skammen* (UK: *The Shame*); *Vargtimmen* (UK: *Hour Of The Wolf*)
1969 *Riten* (UK: *The Rite*); *The Faro Document* (TV); *En Passion* (UK: *A Passion*)
1970 *Beroringen* (UK: *The Touch*)
1972 *Viskningar Och Rop** (UK: *Cries And Whispers*)
1973 *Scener Ur Ett Aktenskap* (UK: *Scenes From A Marriage*)
1974 *Der Zauberflote* (UK: *The Magic Flute*)

**BERGMAN, Ernst Ingmar** (cont.)

1975 *Ansikte Mot Ansikte* (UK: *Face To Face*)
1977 *Das Schangenei* (UK: *The Serpent's Egg*)
1978 *Herbsonnaten* (UK: *Autumn Sonata*)
1979 *Aus Dem Leben Der Marionettes* (UK: *From The Life Of The Marionettes*)
1982 *Fanny Och Alexander\** (UK: *Fanny And Alexander*)
1984 *After The Rehearsal*
1992 *Den Goda Viljan* (UK: *The Best Intentions*) (screenwriter only)

## BERKELEY, Busby
real name: Busby Berkeley William Enos (1895–1976) USA

1930 *Whoopee!* (choreographer only)
1931 *Kiki; Palmy Days* (both choreographer only)
1932 *The Kid From Spain* (choreographer only)
1933 *Roman Scandals\*; 42nd Street\*; Gold Diggers Of 1933\*; Footlight Parade\** (all choreographer only); *She Had To Say Yes* (co-director)
1934 *Fashions; Wonder Bar; Dames* (all choreographer only)
1935 *In Caliente; Stars Over Broadway* (both choreographer only); *Gold Diggers Of 1935; Go Into Your Dance* (UK: *Casino De Paree*); *Bright Lights* (UK: *Funnyface*); *I Live For Love* (UK: *I Live For You*)
1936 *Stage Struck; Gold Diggers Of 1937* (choreographer only)
1937 *The Singing Marine; Varsity Show* (both choreographer only); *The Go Getter; Hollywood Hotel*
1938 *Gold Diggers In Paris* (choreographer only); *Comet Over Broadway; Men Are Such Fools; Garden Of The Moon*
1939 *Broadway Serenade* (choreographer only); *Babes In Arms\*; Fast And Furious; They Made Me A Criminal*

1940 *Strike Up The Band; Forty Little Mothers*
1941 *Ziegfeld Girl; Lady Be Good; Born To Sing* (all choreographer only); *Babes On Broadway; Blonde Inspiration*
1942 *Calling All Girls* (short); *For Me And My Gal* (UK: *For Me And My Girl*)
1943 *Three Cheers For The Girls; Girl Crazy* (both choreographer only): *The Gang's All Here* (UK: *The Girls He Left Behind*)
1945 *All-Star Musical Revue* (co-director)
1946 *Cinderella Jones*
1949 *Take Me Out To The Ball Game* (UK: *Everybody's Cheering*)
1950 *Two Weeks With Love* (choreographer only)
1951 *Call Me Mister; Two Tickets To Broadway* (both choreographer only)
1952 *Million Dollar Mermaid* (UK: *The One-Piece Bathing Suit*) (choreographer only)
1953 *Small Town Girl; Easy To Love* (both choreographer only)
1962 *Jumbo* (choreographer only)

## BERRI, Claude
(1934– ) France

1960 *Les Bonnes Femmes* (actor only)
1962 *Les Sept Péchés Capitaux* (UK: *The Seven Deadly Sins*) (actor only)
1963 *Les Baisers*
1964 *Le Poulet* (short); *Behold A Pale Horse* (actor only)
1968 *Mazel Tov Ou Le Mariage* (UK: *Marry Me! Marry Me!*)
1971 *L'Oeuf; Taking Off* (both producer only)
1972 *Les Fous Du Stade* (producer only); *Le Sex Shop*
1973 *Je Sais Rien Mais Je Dirai Tout; Pleure Pas La Bouche Pleine* (both producer only)

1975 *Un Sac De Billes; Je T'Aime Moi Non Plus* (both producer only); *Le Male Du Siècle*
1976 *La Première Fois*
1977 *Un Moment D'Egarement*
1979 *Tess\** (producer only)
1980 *Inspecteur La Bavure* (producer only); *Je Vous Aime*
1982 *Deux Heures Moins Le Quart Avant Jesus Christ* (producer only)
1983 *L'Africain; Banzai; Garçon!; L'Homme Blessé* (all producer only); *Tchao Pantin*
1984 *Le Vengeance Du Serpent À Plumes* (producer only)
1985 *Scem De Guerra* (producer only)
1986 *Jean de Florette\*; Manon Des Sources\**
1987 *Hotel De France* (producer only)
1988 *L'Ours* (UK: *The Bear*); *Trois Places Pour Le 26; A Gauche En Sortant De L'Ascenseur* (all producer only)
1989 *Valmont* (producer only)
1990 *Stan The Flasher* (producer only); *Uranus*
1992 *L'Amant* (UK: *The Lover*) (producer only)
1993 *Germinal*

## BERTOLUCCI, Bernardo
(1940– ) Italy

1961 *Accattone* (assistant director)
1962 *La Commare Seca* (UK: *The Grim Reaper*)
1964 *Prime Della Rivoluzione* (UK: *Before The Revolution*)
1965 *Il Canale* (documentary)
1966 *La Via Del Petrolio* (TV) (documentary)
1968 *Partner; Cera Una Volta Il West* (UK: *Once Upon A Time In The West\**)
1969 *Amore E Rabbia* (UK: *Love And Anger*); *Le Strategia Del Ragno* (UK: *The Spider's Stratagem*)
1970 *Il Conformista* (UK: *The Conformist*)

1971 *La Saluta E Malato O I Poveri Muorioro Prima* (documentary)
1972 *Ultimo Tango A Parigi\** (UK: *Last Tango In Paris*)
1976 *Novecento* (UK: *1900\**)
1979 *La Luna*
1981 *La Tragedia Di Un Uomo Ridicolo* (UK: *The Tragedy Of A Ridiculous Man*)
1987 *The Last Emperor\**
1990 *The Sheltering Sky*
1993 *The Little Buddha*

## BESSON, Luc
(1959– ) France

1979 *Moonraker\** (assistant only)
1980 *The Nude Bomb; Gauguin — The Savage* (TV) (both assistant only); *Deux Lions Au Soleil; Court Circuit; Homme Libre, Tu Cheriras La Mer* (all assistant director)
1981 *Les Bidasses Aux Grandes Manoeuvres* (assistant director)
1983 *Le Grand Carnaval* (second unit director only); *Le Dernier Combat* (UK: *The Last Battle*)
1985 *Subway\**
1986 *Kamikaze* (screenwriter only)
1988 *Le Grand Bleu* (UK: *The Big Blue\**)
1990 *Nikita*
1991 *Atlantis*

## BIGELOW, Kathryn
(c1951– ) USA

1978 *Set-Up* (short)
1980 *Union City* (script supervisor)
1982 *The Loveless; Born In Flames* (actress only)
1987 *Near Dark*
1990 *Blue Steel*
1991 *Point Break\**
1993 *Company Of Angels*

## BLIER, Bertrand
(1939– ) France

1963 *Hitler? Connais Pas!*
1966 *La Grimace*

**BLIER, Bertrand** (cont.)
1967 *Si J'Etais Un Espion*
1970 *Laisse Aller, C'est Une Valse*
   (writer only)
1973 *Les Valseuses* (UK: *Making It*)
1975 *Calmos*
1978 *Préparez Vos Mouchoirs* (UK: *Get Out Your Handkerchiefs*)
1979 *Buffet Froid*
1981 *Beau-Père*
1982 *La Femme De Mon Pote* (UK: *My Best Friend's Girl*)
1984 *Notre Histoire* (UK: *Our Story*)
1986 *Tenue De Soirée*
1989 *Trop Belle Pour Toi!**
1991 *Merci La Vie*
1993 *Un Deux Trois Soleil*

**BOGART, Paul**
(c.1919–   ) USA

1968 *Halls Of Anger*
1969 *Marlowe*
1970 *In Search Of America* (TV)
1971 *The Skin Game*
1972 *Cancel My Reservation*
1973 *Class Of '44*
1974 *Tell Me Where It Hurts* (TV)
1975 *Mr Ricco; Winner Take All* (TV)
1984 *Oh God, You Devil!*
1988 *Torch Song Trilogy**
1992 *Neil Simon's Broadway Bound* (TV)

**BOGDANOVICH, Peter**
(1939–   ) USA

1966 *The Wild Angels* (2nd unit director); *Voyage To The Planet Of The Prehistoric Women* (various pseudonymous contributions)
1967 *The Trip* (actor only); *Targets*
1969 *Lion's Love* (actor only)
1970 *The Other Side Of The Wind* (actor only)
1971 *Directed By John Ford* (documentary); *The Last Picture Show**
1972 *What's Up Doc?**
1973 *Paper Moon**

1974 *Daisy Miller*
1975 *At Long Last Love*
1976 *Nickelodeon*
1977 *Opening Night* (actor only)
1979 *Saint Jack*
1981 *They All Laughed*
1985 *Mask*
1987 *Illegally Yours*
1990 *Texasville*
1992 *Noises Off*
1993 *The Thing Called Love*

**BOLESLAWSKI, Richard**
real name: Boleslaw Ryszart Srzednicki
(1889–1937) Poland

1915 *Tri Vstrechi/Three Meetings*
1918 *Khleb/Bread* (co-director)
1919 *Bohaterstwo Polskiego Skavto*
1920 *Cud Nad Wisla/The Miracle Of The Vistula*
1930 *Treasure Girl* (short); *The Grand Parade; The Last Of The Lone Wolf*
1931 *The Gay Diplomat; Woman Pursued*
1932 *Rasputin And The Empress* (UK: *Rasputin — The Mad Monk*)
1933 *Storm At Daybreak; Beauty For Sale* (UK: *Beauty*)
1934 *Fugitive Lovers; Men In White; Operator 13* (UK: *Spy 13*); *The Painted Veil; Hollywood Party* (co-director only)
1935 *O'Shaughnessy's Boy; Metropolitan; Clive Of India; Les Misérables**
1936 *Three Godfathers; The Garden Of Allah; Theodora Goes Wild*
1937 *The Last Of Mrs Cheyney* (co-director)

**BOORMAN, John**
(1933–   ) UK

1965 *Catch Us If You Can*
1967 *Point Blank**
1968 *Hell In The Pacific*
1970 *Leo The Last*
1972 *Deliverance**
1973 *Zardoz*

1977 *The Exorcist II: The Heretic*
1981 *Excalibur*
1984 *Dream One* (producer only)
1985 *The Emerald Forest*
1987 *Hope And Glory**
1990 *Where The Heart Is*
1991 *I Dreamt I Woke Up*
(documenatry)

## BORZAGE, Frank
(1893–1962) USA

1916 *Mammy's Rose; Life's Harmony*
(both co-director only); *Immediate
Lee; The Silken Spider; Nell
Dale's Menfolks; The Forgotten
Prayer; Nugget Jim's Partner;
Land O'Lizards; Pride And The
Man; Dollars Of Dross; The Code
Of Honor; That Gal Of Burke's;
The Courting Of Calliope Clew;
The Demon Of Fear;
Enchantment*
1917 *Wee Lady Betty* (co-director);
*Flying Colors; The Ghost Flower;
Until They Get Me; The Curse Of
Iku*
1918 *The Gun Woman; Shoes That
Danced; Innocent's Progress; An
Honest Man; Who Is To Blame?;
The Atom; Society For Sale*
1919 *Prudence Of Broadway; Toton;
Whom The Gods Would Destroy;
Ashes Of Desire*
1920 *Humoresque*
1921 *The Duke Of Chimney Butte; Get-
Rich-Quick Wallingford*
1922 *Hair Trigger Casey; Back Pay;
The Good Provider; Silent Shelby;
Billy Jim; The Valley Of Silent
Men; The Pride Of Palomar*
1923 *Children Of Dust; The Age Of
Desire; The Nth Commandment*
(UK: *The Higher Law*)
1924 *Secrets*
1925 *The Lady; Lazybones; Daddy's
Gone A-Hunting; Wages For
Wives; The Circle*
1926 *Marriage License?* (UK: *The
Pelican*); *The Dixie Merchant;
Early To Wed; The First Year*

1927 *Seventh Heaven*
1928 *Street Angel; The River*
1929 *Lucky Star; They Had To See
Paris*
1930 *Song O' My Heart; Liliom*
1931 *Doctors' Wives; Young As You
Feel; Bad Girl*
1932 *After Tomorrow; A Farewell To
Arms*; Young America* (UK: *We
Humans*)
1933 *Secrets; Man's Castle*
1934 *Little Man What Now?; Flirtation
Walk; No Greater Glory*
1935 *Stranded; Shipmates Forever;
Living On Velvet*
1936 *Hearts Divided; Desire*
1937 *Green Light; History Is Made At
Night; Big City*
1938 *Mannequin; Three Comrades;
The Shining Hour*
1939 *Disputed Passage*
1940 *The Mortal Storm; Strange Cargo;
Flight Command*
1941 *Smilin' Through; The Vanishing
Virginian*
1942 *Seven Sweethearts*
1943 *Stage Door Canteen; His Butler's
Sister*
1944 *Till We Meet Again*
1945 *The Spanish Main*
1946 *Magnificent Doll; I've Always
Loved You* (UK: *Concerto*)
1947 *That's My Man* (UK: *Will
Tomorrow Ever Come?*)
1948 *Moonrise*
1958 *China Doll*
1959 *The Big Fisherman*
1961 *Atlantis, The Lost Continent*
(uncredited co-director)

## BOULTING, John
(1913–85) UK

1945 *Journey Together*
1947 *Brighton Rock* (US: *Young
Scarface*)
1950 *Seven Days To Noon*
1951 *The Magic Box*
1954 *Seagulls Over Sorrento* (co-
director)
1955 *Private's Progress*

**BOULTING, John** (cont.)
1957 *Lucky Jim*
1959 *I'm All Right Jack\**
1960 *Suspect* (co-director)
1963 *Heavens Above!*
1965 *Rotten To The Core*

**BRANAGH, Kenneth**
(1960– ) UK

1989 *Henry V\**
1991 *Dead Again*
1992 *Peter's Friends\**
1993 *Much Ado About Nothing;*
*Frankenstein*

See also actors listing

**BRANDO, Marlon**
(1924– ) USA

1961 *One-Eyed Jacks\**

See also actors listing

**BRESSON, Robert**
(1907– ) France

1934 *Les Affaires Publiques*
1943 *Les Anges Du Péché*
1946 *Les Dames Du Bois De Boulogne*
1950 *Journal D'Un Curé De Campagne*
(UK: *Diary Of A Country Priest*)
1956 *Un Condamné À Mort S'Est*
*Échappe* (UK: *A Man Escaped*)
1959 *Pickpocket\**
1962 *Le Procès De Jeanne D'Arc* (UK:
*The Trial Of Joan Of Arc*)
1966 *Au Hasard, Balthazar* (UK:
*Balthazar*)
1967 *Mouchette*
1969 *Une Femme Douce* (UK: *A Gentle*
*Creature*)
1971 *Quatre Nuits D'Un Rêveur* (UK:
*Four Nights Of A Dreamer*)
1974 *Lancelot Du Lac*
1977 *Le Diable Probablement* (UK: *The*
*Devil, Probably*)
1983 *L'Argent*

**BREST, Martin**
(1951– ) USA

1977 *Hot Tomorrows*
1979 *Going In Style*
1982 *Fast Times At Ridgemont High*
(actor only)
1984 *Beverly Hills Cop\**
1985 *Spies Like Us* (actor only)
1988 *Midnight Run\**
1992 *Scent Of A Woman\**

**BRICKMAN, Paul**
(19?– )

1977 *The Bad News Bears In Breaking*
*Training; Citizens Band/Handle*
*With Care* (both scriptwriter only)
1983 *Deal Of The Century* (screenwriter
only); *Risky Business\**
1990 *Men Don't Leave*

**BRIDGES, James**
(1931– ) USA

1966 *The Appaloosa* (screenwriter only)
1968 *Faces* (actor only)
1970 *The Baby Maker; Colossus: The*
*Forbin Project* (screenwriter only)
1972 *Women In Limbo* (screenwriter
only)
1973 *The Paper Chase*
1978 *9-30-55*
1979 *The China Syndrome\**
1980 *Urban Cowboy\**
1982 *Mike's Murder*
1983 *Fire And Ice* (actor only)
1985 *Perfect*
1988 *Bright Lights, Big City*
1990 *White Hunter, Black Heart* (co-
producer only)

**BROOKS, James L**
(1940– ) USA

1978 *Real Life* (actor only)
1979 *Starting Over* (screenwriter only)
1981 *Modern Romance* (actor only)
1983 *Terms Of Endearment\**
1987 *Broadcast News\**
1988 *Big\** (co-producer only)

1989 *Say Anything* (executive producer only); *The War Of The Roses\** (co-producer only)
1993 *I'll Do Anything*

## BROOKS, Mel
real name: Melvin Kaminsky
(1926– ) USA

1963 *The Critic* (cartoon)
1966 *The Producers*
1970 *The Twelve Chairs*
1974 *Blazing Saddles\*; Young Frankenstein\**
1976 *Silent Movie*
1977 *High Anxiety*
1979 *The Muppet Movie\** (actor only)
1980 *The Elephant Man\** (executive producer only)
1981 *The History Of The World Part 1*
1983 *To Be Or Not To Be*
1985 *The Doctor And The Devils* (executive producer only)
1986 *The Fly\*; Solarbabies* (both executive producer only)
1987 *Spaceballs; 84 Charing Cross Road* (executive producer only)
1990 *Look Who's Talking Too* (voice only)
1991 *Life Stinks*
1993 *Robin Hood: Men In Tights*

## BROOKS, Richard
(1912–92) USA

1942 *Sin Town; Men Of Texas* (both co-writer only)
1943 *The White Savage; Cobra Woman; My Best Gal; Don Winslow Of The Coast Guard* (all co-writer only)
1946 *Swell Guy; The Killers\** (both co-writer only)
1947 *Brute Force* (co-writer only)
1948 *To The Victor; Key Largo\*; The Naked City* (all co-writer only)
1949 *Any Number Can Play* (co-writer only)
1950 *Storm Warning; Mystery Street* (both co-writer only); *Crisis*
1951 *The Light Touch*

1952 *Deadline USA* (UK: *Deadline*)
1953 *Battle Circus; Take The High Ground*
1954 *The Flame And The Flesh; The Last Time I Saw Paris*
1955 *The Blackboard Jungle\**
1956 *The Last Hunt; The Catered Affair* (UK: *Wedding Breakfast*)
1957 *Something Of Value*
1958 *The Brothers Karamazov; Cat On A Hot Tin Roof\**
1960 *Elmer Gantry\**
1962 *Sweet Bird Of Youth\**
1965 *Lord Jim*
1966 *The Professionals\**
1967 *In Cold Blood*
1969 *The Happy Ending*
1971 *$* (UK: *The Heist*)
1975 *Bite The Bullet*
1977 *Looking For Mr Goodbar*
1982 *Wrong Is Right* (UK: *The Man With The Deadly Lens*)
1985 *Fever Pitch*

## BROWN, Clarence
(1890–1987) USA

1920 *The Great Redeemer; The Last Of The Mohicans* (both co-director)
1921 *The Foolish Matrons* (co-director)
1922 *The Light In The Dark*
1923 *Don't Marry For Money; The Acquittal*
1924 *The Signal Tower; Butterfly; Smouldering Fires*
1925 *The Goose Woman; The Eagle*
1926 *Kiki*
1927 *The Flesh And The Devil*
1928 *A Woman Of Affairs*
1929 *The Trail Of '98; Wonder Of Women; Navy Blues*
1930 *Anna Christie\*; Romance*
1931 *Inspiration; A Free Soul; Possessed*
1932 *Emma; Letty Lynton; The Son-Daughter*
1933 *Looking Forward; Night Flight*
1934 *Sadie McKee; Chained*
1935 *Anna Karenina\*; Ah, Wilderness*
1936 *Wife Versus Secretary; The Gorgeous Hussy*

**BROWN, Clarence** (cont.)
1937 *Conquest*
1938 *Of Human Hearts*
1939 *Idiot's Delight; The Rains Came*
1940 *Edison The Man*
1941 *Come Live With Me; They Met In Bombay*
1943 *The Human Comedy*
1944 *The White Cliffs Of Dover; National Velvet\**
1946 *The Yearling\**
1947 *Song Of Love*
1949 *Intruder In The Dust; The Secret Garden* (producer only)
1950 *To Please A Lady*
1951 *Angels In The Outfield; It's A Big Country* (co-director only)
1952 *When In Rome; Plymouth Adventure*
1953 *Never Let Me Go* (producer only)


## BROWNING, Tod
(1880–1962) USA

1915 *The Lucky Transfer; The Living Death; The Highbinders; The Burned Hand; The Slave Girl; An Image Of The Past; The Story Of A Story; The Spell Of The Poppy; The Electrlc Alarm; The Woman From Warren's; Little Marie* (all shorts)
1916 *The Fatal Glass Of Beer; Everybody's Doing It; Puppets* (all shorts)
1917 *Jim Bludso; A Love Sublime; Hands Up!* (all shorts); *The Jury of Fate; Peggy, The Will O' The Wisp*
1918 *The Legion Of Death; Which Woman?; Revenge; The Deciding Kiss; The Eyes Of Mystery; The Brazen Beauty; Set Free*
1919 *The Unpainted Woman; The Wicked Darling; The Exquisite Thief; Bonnie, Bonnie Lassie; A Petal On The Current*
1920 *The Virgin Of Stamboul*
1921 *Outside The Law; No Woman Knows*

1922 *Under Two Flags; The Wise Kid; The Man Under Cover*
1923 *The Day Of Faith; Drifting; White Tiger*
1924 *The Dangerous Flirt* (UK: *A Dangerous Flirtation*); *Silk Stocking Sal*
1925 *Dollar Down; The Mystic; The Unholy Three*
1926 *The Blackbird; The Road To Mandalay*
1927 *The Unknown; The Show; London After Midnight* (UK: *The Hypnotist*)
1928 *The Big City; West Of Zanzibar*
1929 *Where East Is East; The Thirteenth Chair*
1930 *Outside The Law*
1931 *Dracula\*; The Iron Man*
1932 *Freaks*
1933 *Fast Workers*
1935 *Mark Of The Vampire*
1936 *The Devil-Doll*
1939 *Miracles For Sale*


## BUÑUEL, Luis
(1900–83) Spain

1928 *Un Chien Andalou*
1930 *L'Age D'Or*
1932 *Les Hurdes* (UK: *Land Without Bread*)
1935 *Don Quintin El Amargao; La Hija De Juan Simón* (both co-director)
1936 *Quién Me Quiere A Mi?; Centinela Allerta!* (both co-director)
1937 *Madrid 36* (uncredited)
1941 *El Vaticano De Pio XII*
1946 *Tampico/Gran Casino*
1949 *El Gran Calavera*
1950 *Los Olvidados* (UK: *The Young And The Damned*); *Susanna* (UK: *The Devil And The Flesh*)
1951 *La Hija Del Engano; Una Muja Sin Amor; Subida Al Cielo*
1952 *El Bruto; The Adventures Of Robinson Crusoe; El*
1953 *La Ilusion Viaja En Tranvía; Cumbres Borrascosas*
1954 *El Rio Y La Muerte*

1955 *La Vida Criminal De Archibaldo De La Cruz* (UK: *The Criminal Life Of Archibaldo De La Cruz*); *Cela S'Appelle L'Aurore; La Muerte En Este Jardina* (UK: *Evil Eden*)
1958 *Nazarín*
1959 *Los Ambiciosos*
1960 *La Joven* (UK: *Island Of Shame*)
1961 *Viridiana*
1962 *El Angel Exterminador* (UK: *The Exterminating Angel*)
1963 *Le Journal D'Une Femme De Chambre* (UK: *Diary Of A Chambermaid*)
1965 *Simon Del Desierto* (UK: *Simon Of The Desert*)
1967 *Belle De Jour\**
1968 *La Voie Lactée* (UK: *The Milky Way*)
1970 *Tristana*
1972 *Le Charme Discret De La Bourgeoisie* (UK: *The Discreet Charm Of The Bourgeoisie*)
1974 *Le Fantome De La Liberté* (UK: *The Phantom Of Liberty*)
1977 *Cet Oboour Objel Du Désir* (UK: *That Obscure Object Of Desire*)

## BURTON, Tim
(1958– ) USA

1982 *Vincent* (short)
1984 *Frankenweenie* (short)
1985 *Pee Wee's Big Adventure*
1988 *Beetlejuice\**
1989 *Batman\**
1990 *Edward Scissorhands\**
1992 *Batman Returns\**
1993 *Nightmare Before Christmas*

# C

## CACOYANNIS, Michael
real name: Mikhalis Kakogiannis
(1922– ) Greece

1953 *Windfall In Athens*
1954 *Stella*
1955 *The Girl In Black*
1957 *A Matter Of Dignity*

1959 *Eroica/Our Last Spring*
1960 *The Wastrel*
1961 *Electra*
1964 *Zorba The Greek\**
1967 *The Day The Fish Came Out*
1971 *The Trojan Women*
1974 *The Story Of Jacob And Joseph* (TV)
1975 *Attila 74* (documentary)
1977 *Iphigenia*
1986 *Sweet Country*

## CAIN, Christopher
(1943– ) USA

1984 *The Stone Boy*
1985 *That Was Then...This Is Now*
1986 *Where The River Runs Black*
1987 *The Principal*
1988 *Young Guns\**
1990 *Wheels Of Terror* (TV)
1992 *Pure Country*

## CAMERON, James
(1954– ) USA

1980 *Battle Beyond The Stars; Happy Birthday Gemini* (both assistant only)
1981 *Galaxy Of Terror* (second-unit director); *Piranha II: Flying Killers*
1984 *The Terminator\**
1985 *Rambo: First Blood Part II* (screenwriter only)
1986 *Aliens\**
1989 *The Abyss*
1991 *Terminator 2: Judgment Day\*; Point Break\** (executive producer only)

## CAMPION, Jane
(c1954– ) New Zealand

1982 *Peel* (short)
1983 *A Girl's Own Story* (short)
1984 *Passionless Moments*
1985 *Two Friends* (TV)
1989 *Sweetie*
1990 *An Angel At My Table\**
1993 *The Piano*

## CAPRA, Frank
(1897–1991) USA

1922 *Fultah Fisher's Boarding House*
1926 *The Strong Man*
1927 *Long Pants; For The Love Of Mike*
1928 *That Certain Thing; So This Is Love; The Matinee Idol; The Way Of The Strong; Say It With Sables; Submarine; The Power Of The Press; The Swim Princess; The Burglar*
1929 *The Younger Generation; The Donovan Affair; Flight*
1930 *Ladies Of Leisure; Rain Or Shine*
1931 *Dirigible; The Miracle Woman; Platinum Blonde*
1932 *Forbidden; American Madness*
1933 *The Bitter Tea Of General Yen; Lady For A Day\**
1934 *It Happened One Night\*; Broadway Bill*
1936 *Mr Deeds Goes To Town\**
1937 *Lost Horizon\**
1938 *You Can't Take It With You\**
1939 *Mr Smith Goes To Washington\**
1941 *Meet John Doe*
1942-45 *Why We Fight* (documentary series)
1944 *Tunisian Victory* (co-director); *Arsenic And Old Lace\**
1945 *Know Your Enemy: Japan* (documentary); *Two Down, One To Go* (documentary)
1946 *It's A Wonderful Life\**
1948 *State Of The Union*
1950 *Riding High*
1951 *Here Comes The Groom*
1959 *A Hole In The Head*
1961 *Pocketful Of Miracles*

## CARAX, Leos
real name: Alexandre Dupont
(1960– ) France

1980 *Strangulation Blues* (short)
1983 *Boy Meets Girl*
1986 *Mauvais Sang* (UK: *The Night Is Young*)
1987 *King Lear* (actor only)

1988 *Les Minstères De L'Art* (actor only)
1991 *Les Amants Du Pont Neuf\**

## CARDIFF, Jack
(1914– ) UK

1958 *Intent To Kill*
1959 *Beyond This Place*
1960 *Sons And Lovers\*; Scent Of Mystery* (UK: *Holiday In Spain*)
1962 *My Geisha; The Lion*
1964 *The Long Ships*
1965 *Young Cassidy*
1966 *The Liquidator*
1967 *The Mercenaries* (US: *Dark Of The Sun*)
1968 *Girl On A Motorcycle* (US: *Naked Under Leather*)
1973 *Penny Gold*
1974 *Mutations*

## CARNÉ, Marcel
(1909– ) France

1929 *Nogent, Eldorado Du Dimanche*
1936 *Jenny*
1937 *Drôle De Drame* (UK: *Bizarre, Bizarre*)
1938 *Quai Des Brumes; Hôtel Du Nord*
1939 *Le Jour Se Lève\** (UK: *Daybreak*)
1942 *Les Visiteurs Du Soir*
1944 *Les Enfants Du Paradis\** (UK: *Children Of Paradise*)
1946 *Les Portes De La Nuit* (UK: *Gates Of The Night*)
1949 *La Marie Du Port*
1951 *Juliette Ou La Clé Des Songes*
1953 *Thérèse Raquin*
1954 *L'Air De Paris*
1956 *Le Pays D'Ou Je Viens*
1958 *Les Tricheurs*
1960 *Terrain Vague*
1962 *Du Mouron Pour Les Petits Oiseaux*
1965 *Trois Chambres À Manhattan*
1967 *Les Jeunes Loups*
1971 *Les Assassins De L'Ordre*
1974 *La Merveilleuse Visite*
1976 *La Bible* (documentary)
1993 *Mouche*

## CASSAVETES, John
(1929–89) USA

1959 Shadows*
1961 Too Late Blues
1962 A Child Is Waiting
1968 Faces
1970 Husbands
1971 Minnie And Moskowitz
1974 A Woman Under The Influence
1976 The Killing Of A Chinese Bookie
1977 Opening Night
1980 Gloria
1983 Love Streams
1985 Big Trouble

See also actors listing

## CATON-JONES, Michael
(1957–   ) UK

1980 The Last Horror Film (assistant)
1986 Liebe Mutter; The Riveter (both shorts)
1987 Brond (TV)
1988 Lucky Sunil (TV)
1989 Scandal*
1990 Memphis Belle*
1991 'Doc' Hollywood
1993 This Boy's Life

## CHABROL, Claude
(1930–   ) France

1958 Le Beau Serge
1959 Les Cousins; A Double Tour (UK: Web Of Passion)
1960 Les Bonnes Femmes; Les Godelureaux
1961 L'Oeil Du Marin; The Seven Deadly Sins (co-director)
1962 Ophelia; Landru (UK: Bluebeard); Les Plus Belles Escroqueries Du Monde
1964 Le Tigre Aime La Chair Fraiche (UK: The Tiger Likes Fresh Blood); Paris Vu Par...(UK: Six in Paris) (co-director)
1965 Le Tigre Se Parfume A Dynamite (UK: An Orchid For The Tiger); Marie Chantal Contre Dr Kah

1966 Le Scandale (UK: The Champagne Murders); La Ligne De Démarcation
1967 La Route De Corinth (UK: The Road To Corinth)
1968 Les Biches; La Femme Infidèle
1969 Que La Bête Meure (UK: Killer); Le Boucher*
1970 La Rupture
1971 Juste Avant La Nuit
1972 La Décade Prodigieuse (UK: Ten Days' Wonder); Docteur Popaul (UK: Scoundrel In White)
1973 Les Noces Rouges (UK: Red Wedding); De Grey; Le Banc De Désolation
1974 NADA; Une Partie De Plaisir; Les Innocents Aux Mains Sales (UK: Innocents With Dirty Hands)
1975 Les Magiciens; Deux Et Deux Font Quatre(TV)
1976 Folie Bourgeoisies (UK: The Twist); Alice, Ou La Dernière Fugue
1977 Blood Relatives
1978 Violette Nozière
1979 Les Menteurs
1980 Le Cheval D'Orgeuil
1981 Les Fantômes De Chapelier
1983 Le Sang Des Autres
1984 Poulet De Vinaigre (UK: Cop Au Vin)
1985 Inspecteur Lavardin
1986 Masques
1987 Le Cri Du Hibou
1988 Une Affaire De Femmes
1990 Quiet Days In Clichy; Doctor M
1991 Madame Bovary
1992 Betty

## CHAPLIN, Sir Charles
(1889-1977) UK

1914 Caught In A Cabaret; Caught In The Rain; A Busy Day; The Fatal Mallet; Her Friend, The Bandit; Mabel's Busy Day; Mabel's Married Life; Laughing Gas; The Property Man; The Face On The Baroom Floor; The Masquerader; His New Profession; The

**CHAPLIN, Sir Charles** (cont.)
    *Rounders; The New Janitor;*
    *Those Love Pangs; Dough And*
    *Dynamite; Gentlemen Of Nerve;*
    *His Musical Career; His Trysting*
    *Place; Getting Acquainted; His*
    *Prehistoric Past*
1915  *His New Job; A Night Out; The*
    *Champion; In The Park; A Jitney*
    *Elopement; The Tramp; By The*
    *Sea; Work; A Woman; The Bank;*
    *Shanghaied; A Night In The*
    *Show*
1916  *Carmen; Police!; The*
    *Floorwalker; The Fireman; The*
    *Vagabond; One AM; The Count;*
    *The Pawnshop; Behind The*
    *Screen; The Rink*
1917  *Easy Street; The Cure; The*
    *Immigrant; The Adventurer*
1918  *A Dog's Life; The Bond; Triple*
    *Trouble; Shoulder Arms*
1919  *Sunnyside; A Day's Pleasure*
1921  *The Kid; The Idle Class; The Nut*
1922  *Pay Day; Nice And Friendly*
1923  *The Pilgrim; A Woman Of Paris;*
    *Souls For Sale*
1924  *The Gold Rush*
1926  *A Woman Of The Sea*
1928  *The Circus*
1931  *City Lights\**
1936  *Modern Times\**
1940  *The Great Dictator\**
1947  *Monsieur Verdoux*
1952  *Limelight\**
1957  *A King In New York*
1966  *A Countess From Hong Kong*

See also actors listing

**CIMINO, Michael**
(1940–  ) USA

1972  *Silent Running* (co-writer only)
1973  *Magnum Force* (co-writer only)
1974  *Thunderbolt And Lightfoot*
1978  *The Deer Hunter\**
1980  *Heaven's Gate\**
1985  *Year Of The Dragon*
1987  *The Sicilian*
1990  *Desperate Hours*

**CLAVELL, James**
(1922–  ) UK

1958  *Five Gates To Hell*
1960  *Walk Like A Dragon*
1962  *The Sweet And The Bitter*
1967  *To Sir With Love\**
1969  *Where's Jack?*
1971  *The Last Valley*

**CLAYTON, Jack**
(1921–  ) UK

1944  *Naples Is A Battlefield*
    (documentary)
1955  *The Bespoke Overcoat*
1959  *Room At The Top\**
1961  *The Innocents*
1964  *The Pumpkin Eater*
1967  *Our Mother's House*
1974  *The Great Gatsby*
1983  *Something Wicked This Way*
    *Comes*
1987  *The Lonely Passion Of Judith*
    *Hearne*
1992  *Momento Mori* (TV)

**CLEMENT, René**
(1913–  ) France

1931  *César Chez Les Galois*
    (documentary)
1936  *Soigne Ton Gauche* (short)
1937  *L'Arabie Interdite; Paris La Nuit*
    (both documentaries)
1938  *Flèche D'Argent*
1939  *La Bièvre; Energie Électrique;*
    *Histoire De Costume* (all
    documentaries)
1940  *Le Triage* (documentary)
1942  *Ceux Du Rail; Toulouse* (both
    documentaries)
1943  *Chefs de Matin; La Grande*
    *Pastorale* (both documentaries)
1944  *Mountain* (documentary)
1945  *La Bataille du Rail*
1946  *Le Père Tranquille; Les Maudits*
    (UK: *The Damned*)
1949  *Au Delà Des Grilles* (UK: *The*
    *Walls Of Malapaga*)
1950  *Le Chateau De Verre*

1952 *Les Jeux Interdits\** (UK: *Secret Games*)
1954 *Knave Of Hearts*
1955 *Gervaise*
1958 *The Sea Wall*
1959 *Plein Soleil* (UK: *Purple Noon*)
1961 *Quelle Joie De Vivre*
1962 *Le Jour Et L'Heure* (UK: *The Day And the Hour*)
1964 *Les Félins* (UK: *The Love Cage*)
1966 *Paris, Brûle T'Il?* (UK: *Is Paris Burning?*)
1969 *Rider On The Rain*
1971 *La Maison Sous Les Arbres* (UK: *The Deadly Trap*)
1972 *La Course Du Lièvre À Travers Les Champs* (UK: *And Hope To Die*)
1975 *Wanted: Baby-Sitter*

## CLIFFORD, Graeme
(19?– ) Australia

1972 *Images* (editor only)
1973 *Don't Look Now* (editor only)
1975 *The Rocky Horror Picture Show* (editor only)
1976 *The Man Who Fell To Earth* (editor only)
1978 *F\*I\*S\*T; Convoy* (both editor only)
1981 *The Postman Always Rings Twice\** (editor only)
1982 *Frances\**
1985 *Burke & Wills*
1988 *Gleaming The Cube*
1992 *Ruby Cairo*

## CLINE, Edward F 'Eddie'
(1892–1961) USA

1916 *The Winning Punch; His Busted Trust; Sunshine; His Bread And Butter; Her First Beau; Bubbles Of Trouble* (all shorts)
1917 *The Dogcatcher's Love; The Pawnbroker's Heart; A Bedroom Blunder; That Night; Villa Of The Movies* (all shorts)
1918 *The Kitchen Lady; Those Athletic Girls; His Smothered Love; The Summer Girls; Hide And Seek, Detectives; Whose Little Wife Are You?; Cupid's Day Off* (all shorts)
1919 *Hearts And Flowers; When Love Is Blond; A Schoolhouse Scandal* (all shorts); *East Lynne With Variations*
1920 *Mary's Little Lobster; Training For Husbands; Monkey Business; Ten Nights Without A Barroom* (all shorts); *One Week; Convict 13; The Scarecrow; Neighbors* (all shorts, all co-director); *Sheriff Nell's Comeback*
1921 *Who's Who?; His Meal Ticket; Singer Midget's Scandal; Singer Midget's Side Show* (all shorts); *The High Sign; The Haunted House; Hard Luck; The Golfer; The Boat; The Paleface*
1922 *Daydreams* (short); *Cops; The Frozen North; My Wife's Relations; The Electric House* (all shorts, all co-director)
1924 *Galloping Bungalows; Off His Trolley; The Plumber* (all shorts); *Captain January; When A Man's A Man; Little Robinson Crusoe; Good Bad Boy; Along Came Ruth*
1925 *Bashful Jim; Cold Turkey; Beloved Bozo; Love And Kisses; Tee For Two; Dangerous Curves Behind; The Soapsuds Lady; Hotsy Totsy* (all shorts); *The Rag Man; Old Clothes*
1926 *A Love Sundae; Goose Land; Puppy Lovetime; When A Man's A Prince; Smith's Vacation; The Gosh-Darn Mortgage; Flirty Four-Plushers; Spanking Breezes; The Ghost Of Folly; Alice Be Good; Smith's Baby; A Harem Knight; A Blonde's Revenge*
1927 *Hold That Pose; The Girl From Everywhere; The Jolly Jilter* (all shorts); *Let It Rain; Soft Cushions*

**CLINE, Edward F 'Eddie'** (cont.)
1928 *Love At First Sight* (short); *The Head Man; Broadway Fever; The Crash; Vamping Venus; Ladies Night In A Turkish Bath* (UK: *Ladies Night*)
1929 *His Lucky Day; The Forward Pass*
1930 *Hook, Line And Sinker; The Widow From Chicago; In The Next Room; Sweet Mama* (UK: *Conflict*); *Leathernecking* (UK: *Present Arms*); *Don't Bite Your Dentist; Take Your Medicine* (both shorts)
1931 *In Conference; No, No, Lady; Shove Off; Mlle Irene The Great* (all shorts); *The Girl Habit; Cracked Nuts*
1932 *The Door Knocker; His Weekend; The Mysterious Mystery; The Rookie* (all shorts); *Million Dollar Legs*
1933 *Detective Tom Howard Of The Suicide Squad; Uncle Jake* (both shorts); *So This Is Africa; Parole Girl*
1934 *Girl Trouble; Not Tonight Josephine; Morocco Nights* (all shorts); *The Dude Ranch; Peck's Bad Boy*
1935 *When A Man's A Man; It's A Great Life!; The Cowboy Millionaire*
1936 *Love In September* (short); *F-Man*
1937 *On Again — Off Again; Forty Naughty Girls; High Flyers*
1938 *Breaking The Ice; Hawaii Calls; Go Chase Yourself; Peck's Bad Boy With The Circus*
1940 *My Little Chickadee; The Villain Still Pursued Her; The Bank Dick\** (UK: *The Bank Detective*)
1941 *Cracked Nuts; Meet The Champ; Hello Sucker; Never Give A Sucker An Even Break* (UK: *What A Man*)
1942 *Private Buckaroo; Snuffy Smith, Yard Bird* (UK: *Snuffy Smith*); *What's Cookin?* (UK: *Wake Up And Dream*); *Behind The Eight Ball* (UK: *Off The Beaten Track*); *Give Out, Sisters*

1943 *Moonlight And Cactus; He's My Guy; Crazy House; Swingtime Johnny*
1944 *Ghost Catchers; Hat Check Honey; Penthouse Rhythm; Night Club Girl; Slightly Terrific*
1945 *See My Lawyer*
1946 *Bringing Up Father*
1947 *Jiggs And Maggie In Society*
1948 *Jiggs And Maggie In Court* (co-director)

## COCTEAU, Jean
(1889–1963) France

1925 *Jean Cocteau Fait Du Cinéma* (short)
1930 *Le Sang D'Un Poète*
1945 *La Belle Et La Bête*
1947 *L'Aigle A Deux Têtes* (UK: *The Eagle Has Two Heads*)
1948 *Les Parents Terribles*
1950 *Orphée\** (UK: *Orpheus*); *Coriolan* (short)
1952 *La Villa Santo-Sospir*
1956 *8 x 8* (co-director)
1959 *Le Testament D'Orphée*

## COEN, Joel
(1955– ) USA

1981 *Fear No Evil* (assistant editor only)
1982 *The Evil Dead\** (assistant editor only)
1984 *Blood Simple\**
1985 *Crime Wave* (screenwriter only); *Spies Like Us* (actor only)
1987 *Raising Arizona\**
1990 *Miller's Crossing\**
1991 *Barton Fink\**
1993 *The Hudsucker Proxy*

## COLUMBUS, Chris
(1959– ) USA

1984 *Reckless; Gremlins\** (both screenwriter only)
1985 *Young Sherlock Holmes; The Goonies* (both screenwriter only)
1987 *Adventures In Babysitting*

1988 *Heartbreak Hotel*
1990 *Home Alone\**
1991 *Only The Lonely*
1992 *Little Nemo: Adventures In Slumberland* (screenwriter only); *Home Alone 2: Lost In New York*
1993 *Mrs Doubtfire*

## CONWAY, Jack
(1887–1952) USA

1914 *Captain McLean*
1915 *The Old High Chair; The Way Of A Mother; The Price Of Power; The Mystical Jewel* (all shorts); *The Penitentes*
1916 *The Social Buccaneer; The Silent Battle; The Main Spring; Mary, Keep Your Feet Still; The Beckoning Trail; The Measure Of A Man*
1917 *A Jewel In Pawn; Her Soul's Inspiration; Come Through; The Bond Of Fear; Little Mary Fix-It; Polly's Redhead; The Little Orphan; The Charmer; Because Of A Woman*
1918 *Her Decision; Little Red Decides; Royal Democrat; You Can't Believe Everything; Lombardi Limited; A Diplomatic Mission; Desert Law*
1919 *Restless Souls*
1920 *Riders Of The Dawn/The Desert Of Wheat; The Dwelling Place Of Light; Servant In The House; The U P Trail; Lure Of The Orient; The Money Changers*
1921 *The Spenders; The Rage Of Paris; The Killer; The Millionaire; A Daughter Of The Law; Kiss*
1922 *Across The Deadline; Don't Shoot!; Another Man's Shoes; The Long Chance; Step On It!*
1923 *Trimmed In Scarlet; The Prisoner; Sawdust; What Wives Want; Quicksand; Flaming Passion/Lucretia Lombard*
1924 *The Trouble Shooter; The Heart Buster; The Roughneck* (UK: *Thorns Of Passion*

1925 *The Hunted Woman; The Only Thing*
1926 *Soul Mates; Brown Of Harvard*
1927 *Twelve Miles Out; The Understanding Heart*
1928 *Bringing Up Father; The Smart Set; While The City Sleeps*
1929 *Alias Jimmy Valentine; Untamed; Our Modern Maidens*
1930 *The Unholy Three; New Moon; They Learned About Women* (co-director)
1931 *The Easiest Way; Just A Gigolo* (UK: *The Dancing Partner*); *Five And Ten* (UK: *Daughter Of Luxury*) (co-director)
1932 *But The Flesh Is Weak; Red-Headed Woman; Arsene Lupin*
1933 *Hell Below; The Solitaire Man; The Nuisance* (UK: *Accidents Wanted*)
1934 *The Girl From Missouri* (UK: *100 Per Cent Pure*); *Viva Villa!* (co-director); *The Gay Bride*
1935 *A Tale Of Two Cities\*, One New York Night* (UK: *The Trunk Mystery*)
1936 *Libeled Lady*
1937 *Saratoga*
1938 *A Yank At Oxford; Too Hot To Handle*
1939 *Lady Of The Tropics; Let Freedom Ring*
1940 *Boom Town*
1941 *Honky Tonk; Love Crazy*
1942 *Crossroads*
1943 *Assignment In Brittany*
1944 *Dragon Seed* (co-director)
1947 *Desire Me* (co-director); *High Barbaree; The Hucksters\**
1948 *Julia Misbehaves*

## COOPER, Merian C
(1893–1973) USA

1926 *Grass* (co-director)
1927 *Chang* (co-director)
1929 *The Four Feathers*
1933 *King Kong\** (co-director)
1952 *This Is Cinerama* (co-director)

## COPPOLA, Francis Ford
(1939– ) USA

1962 *The Premature Burial* (assistant director); *Tower Of London* (dialogue director only); *The Magic Voyage Of Sinbad* (adaptor only); *The Playgirls And The Bellboy* (co-director); *Tonight For Sure*
1963 *Battle Beyond The Sun* (screenwriter only); *The Terror* (co-director); *Dementia 13*
1966 *This Property Is Condemned; Paris, Brûle T'Il?* (UK: *Is Paris Burning?*) (both co-writer only); *You're A Big Boy Now*
1967 *Reflections In A Golden Eye* (screenwriter only)
1968 *Finian's Rainbow*
1969 *The Rain People*
1970 *Patton** (co-writer only)
1972 *The Godfather**
1974 *The Great Gatsby* (screenwriter only); *The Conversation*; The Godfather, Part II**
1979 *Apocalypse Now*; The Black Stallion* (executive producer only)
1982 *Hammett; The Escape Artist* (both executive producer only); *One From The Heart*
1983 *The Black Stallion Returns* (executive producer only); *The Outsiders*; Rumblefish*
1984 *The Cotton Club*
1985 *Mishima: A Life In Four Chapters* (executive producer only)
1986 *Peggy Sue Got Married**
1987 *Tough Guys Don't Dance* (executive producer only); *Gardens Of Stone*
1988 *Tucker: The Man And His Dream**
1989 *New York Stories* (co-director)
1990 *The Godfather, Part III**
1992 *Bram Stoker's Dracula**

## CORNELIUS, Henry
(1913–58) UK

1947 *It Always Rains On Sundays* (co-writer only)
1948 *Passport To Pimlico*

1951 *The Galloping Major*
1953 *Genevieve**
1955 *I Am A Camera*
1957 *Next To No Time*
1958 *Law And Disorder*

## COSTA-GAVRAS, Konstantinos
(1933– ) Greece

1959 *L'Ambitieuse; Robinson Et Le Triporteur* (both assistant director)
1960 *Cresus; L'Homme A Femmes* (both assistant director)
1961 *Tout L'Or Du Monde* (assistant director)
1962 *Un Singe En Hiver* (assistant director)
1963 *La Baie Des Anges; Jour Et L'Heure* (assistant director)
1964 *Echappement Libre; Les Felins; Peau De Banane* (assistant director)
1965 *Compartiment Tueurs* (UK: *The Sleeping Car Murders*)
1966 *Un Homme De Trop* (UK: *Shock Troops*)
1968 *Z**
1969 *L'Aveu* (UK: *The Confession*)
1972 *État De Siège* (UK: *State Of Siege*)
1975 *Séction Spéciale*
1977 *La Vie Devant Soi* (UK: *Madame Rosa*) (actor only)
1979 *Clair De Femme*
1981 *Missing**
1983 *Hanna K*
1985 *Spies Like Us* (actor only); *Le Thé Au Harem D'Archimède* (producer only)
1986 *Conseil De Famille*
1988 *Betrayed*
1989 *The Music Box*

## COSTNER, Kevin
(1955– ) USA

1990 *Dances With Wolves**

See also actors listing

## COWARD, Noel
(1899–1973) UK

1931 *Private Lives* (original author)
1933 *Cavalcade\*; Tonight Is Ours; Bitter Sweet* (all original author)
1934 *Design For Living* (original author)
1942 *In Which We Serve\*; We Were Dancing* (original author)
1945 *Blithe Spirit\*; This Happy Breed; Brief Encounter\** (all original author)
1950 *Meet Me Tonight* (original author)

## CRAVEN, Wes
(1939– ) USA

1971 *Together* (assistant producer)
1972 *It Happened In Hollywood; You've Got To Walk It Like You Talk It Or You'll Lose That Beat* (both editor only)
1973 *Last House On The Left*
1977 *The Hills Have Eyes*
1981 *Deadly Blessing*
1982 *Swamp Thing*
1983 *The Hills Have Eyes Part II*
1984 *A Nightmare On Elm Street\*; Invitation To Hell* (TV)
1986 *A Nightmare On Elm Street 3: Dream Warriors* (co-writer only): *Deadly Friend*
1987 *Flowers In The Attic* (co-writer only); *The Serpent And The Rainbow*
1989 *Shocker*
1990 *Night Visions* (TV)
1991 *The People Under The Stairs*

## CRICHTON, Charles
(1910– ) UK

1944 *For Those In Peril*
1945 *Dead Of Night* (co-director); *Painted Boats*
1947 *Hue And Cry*
1948 *Against The Wind; Another Shore*
1949 *Train Of Events* (co-director)
1950 *Dance Hall*
1951 *The Lavender Hill Mob\**
1952 *Hunted*

1953 *The Titfield Thunderbolt*
1954 *The Love Lottery; The Divided Heart*
1956 *The Man In The Sky*
1958 *Law And Disorder; Floods Of Fear*
1959 *The Battle Of The Sexes*
1960 *The Boy Who Stole A Million*
1964 *The Third Secret*
1965 *He Who Rides A Tiger*
1968 *Tomorrow's Island* (short)
1970 *London — Through My Eyes* (documentary)
1983 *Perishing Solicitors* (short)
1988 *A Fish Called Wanda\**

## CROMWELL, John
real name: Elwood Cromwell
(1887–1979) USA

1929 *The Dance Of Life; Close Harmony* (both co-director); *The Mighty*
1930 *The Texan* (UK: *The Big Race*); *For The Defense; Street Of Chance; Tom Sawyer*
1931 *The Vice Squad; Scandal Sheet; Unfaithful; Rich Man's Folly*
1932 *The World And The Flesh*
1933 *Double Harness; Sweepings; The Silver Chord; Ann Vickers*
1934 *This Man Is Mine; Spitfire; The Fountain; Of Human Bondage*
1935 *Village Tale; Jalna; I Dream Too Much*
1936 *To Mary — With Love; Little Lord Fauntleroy; Banjo On My Knee*
1937 *The Prisoner Of Zenda\**
1938 *Algiers*
1939 *In Name Only; Made For Each Other*
1940 *Victory; Abe Lincoln In Illinois* (UK: *Spirit Of The People*)
1941 *So Ends Our Night*
1942 *Son Of Fury*
1944 *Since You Went Away\**
1945 *The Enchanted Cottage*
1946 *Anna And The King Of Siam*
1947 *Dead Reckoning; Night Song*
1950 *Caged; The Company She Keeps*
1951 *The Racket*
1958 *The Goddess*

363

**CROMWELL, John** (cont.)

1959 *The Scavengers*
1960 *De Sista Stegen* (UK: *A Matter Of Morals*)
1977 *Three Women* (actor only)
1978 *A Wedding* (actor only)

## CRONENBERG, David
(1943–   ) Canada

1966 *Transfer* (short)
1967 *From The Drain* (short)
1969 *Stereo*
1970 *Crimes Of The Future*
1975 *Shivers*
1976 *Rabid*
1978 *Fast Company*
1979 *The Brood*
1980 *Scanners*
1982 *Videodrome*
1983 *The Dead Zone*
1985 *Into The Night* (actor only)
1986 *The Fly**
1988 *Dead Ringers**
1989 *Nightbreed* (actor only)
1991 *The Naked Lunch*
1992 *Blue* (short, actor only)
1993 *M Butterfly*

## CROSLAND, Alan
(1894–1936) USA

1917 *Friends, Romans And Leo* (short); *Chris And The Wonderful Lamp; Knights Of The Square Table; The Apple-Tree Girl; Kidnapped; Light In The Darkness; The Little Chevalier; The Story That The Keg Told Me*
1918 *The Unbeliever; The Whirlpool*
1919 *The Country Cousin*
1920 *The Flapper; Greater Than Fame; The Point Of View; Youthful Folly; Broadway And Home*
1921 *Worlds Apart; Room And Board; Is Life Worth Living?*
1922 *The Prophet's Paradise; Why Announce Your Marriage?; Slim Shoulders; The Snitching Hour; Shadows Of The Sea; The Face In The Fog*

1923 *Under The Red Robe; The Enemies Of Women*
1924 *Miami; Unguarded Women; Sinners In Heaven; Three Weeks* (UK: *The Romance Of A Queen*)
1925 *Compromise; Contraband; Bobbed Hair*
1926 *Don Juan; When A Man Loves* (UK: *His Lady*)
1927 *The Beloved Rogue; Old San Francisco; The Jazz Singer**
1928 *Glorious Betsy; The Scarlet Lady* (UK: *The Scarlet Woman*)
1929 *On With The Show; General Crack*
1930 *Viennese Nights; Captain Thunder; Song Of The Flame; The Furies; Big Boy*
1931 *Children Of Dreams; The Silver Lining/Thirty Days*
1932 *Week-Ends Only*
1933 *Massacre*
1934 *Midnight Alibi; The Personality Kid; The Case Of The Howling Dog*
1935 *Mister Dynamite; It Happened In New York; The White Cockatoo; King Solomon Of Broadway; Lady Tubbs* (UK: *The Gay Lady*)
1936 *The Great Impersonation*

## CUKOR, George
full name: George Dewey Cukor
(1899–1983) USA

1929 *River Of Romance* (dialogue director)
1930 *All Quiet On The Western Front** (dialogue director); *Grumpy* (co-director); *The Virtuous Sin* (co-director); *The Royal Family Of Broadway* (co-director)
1931 *Tarnished Lady; Girls About Town*
1932 *What Price Hollywood?; A Bill Of Divorcement**; *Rockabye; One Hour With You* (uncredited co-director); *The Animal Kingdom* (uncredited co-director)
1933 *Our Betters; Dinner At Eight; Little Women**

1935  *David Copperfield\*; No More Ladies* (uncredited co-director)
1936  *Sylvia Scarlett; Romeo And Juliet; Camille\**
1938  *Holiday*
1939  *Zaza; The Women\*; Gone With The Wind\** (uncredited co-director)
1940  *Susan And God* (UK: *The Gay Mrs Trexel*); *The Philadelphia Story\**
1941  *A Woman's Face; Two-Faced Woman*
1942  *Her Cardboard Lover; The Keeper Of The Flame*
1944  *Gaslight\*; Winged Victory*
1945  *I'll Be Seeing You* (uncredited co-director)
1947  *A Double Life; Desire Me* (uncredited co-director)
1949  *Edward My Son; Adam's Rib\**
1950  *A Life Of Her Own; Born Yesterday\**
1951  *The Model And The Marriage Broker*
1952  *The Marrying Kind; Pat And Mike\**
1953  *The Actress*
1954  *It Should Happen To You; A Star Is Born\**
1956  *Bhowani Junction*
1957  *Les Girls; Wild Is The Wind*
1958  *Hot Spell* (uncredited co-director)
1960  *Heller In Pink Tights; Let's Make Love; Song Without End* (uncredited co-director)
1962  *The Chapman Report*
1964  *My Fair Lady\**
1969  *Justine*
1972  *Travels With My Aunt*
1975  *Love Among The Ruins* (TV)
1976  *The Bluebird*
1979  *The Corn Is Green* (TV)
1981  *Rich And Famous*

**CURTIZ, Michael**
real name: Mihály Kertész
(1888–1962) Hungary

1912  *Az Utolsó Bohém; Ma És Holnap*
1913  *Rablélek; Hazasodik Az Uram*
1914  *Princess Pongyola; Az Éjszaka Rabjai; Aranyásao; A Kölcsönkert Csecsemök; Bánk Bán; A Tolonc*
1915  *Akit Ketten Szeretnek*
1916  *The Black Rainbow; The Doctor; A Magyar Föld Ereje; Az Ezust Kescke; Farkus/The Wolf; The Carthusian; A Medikus; Seven Of Clubs*
1917  *A Föld Embere; A Kuruzslo; A Béke Utja; A Vörös Sámson; A Senke Fia; A Szentjóbi Erdö Titka; Arendás Zsidó; Az Utolsó Hajinal; Az Ezredes; Halálcsengö; Master Zoárd; Egy Krajcár Története; Tatárjárás; Tavasz A Telben*
1918  *A Csunya Fiu; Szamárbor; The Scorpion; Judás; Lulu; A Napraforgos Hölgy; A Wellington Rejtély; Az Ödög; Ninety Nine; Lu, The Coquette; Varázskeringö; The Merry Widow; Alraune* (co-director)
1919  *Jön Az Öcsem; Die Dame Mit Dem Schwarzen Handschuh*
1920  *Die Gottesgeisel; Boccaccio; Die Dame Mit Den Sonnenblumen; Der Stern Von Damaskus*
1921  *Mrs Tutti Frutti; Cherchez La Femme; Frau Dorothys Bekenntnis; Wege Des Schreckens*
1922  *Sodom Und Gomorrah, Part I; Sodom Und Gomorrah, Part II*
1923  *Die Lawine; Namelos/Der Scharlatan; Der Junge Medardus*
1924  *Harun El Raschid; Die Slavenkönigin*
1925  *Das Spielzeug Von Paris*
1926  *Fiaker Nummer 13; Der Goldene Schmetterling; The Third Degree*
1927  *The Desired Woman; A Million Bid; Good Time Charley*
1928  *Tenderloin*
1929  *Noah's Ark; The Gamblers; Madonna Of Avenue A; Glad Rag Doll; Hearts In Exile*
1930  *The Matrimonial Bed* (UK: *A Matrimonial Problem*); *Mommy; Under A Texas Moon; Bright Eyes; A Soldier's Plaything; River's End*

**CURTIZ, Michael** (cont.)
1931 *Mad Genius; God's Gift To Women* (UK: *Too Many Women*); *Dämon Des Meeres*
1932 *The Strange Love Of Molly Louvain; The Woman From Monte Carlo; Doctor X; Cabin In The Cotton; 20,000 Years In Sing Sing*
1933 *The Mystery Of The Wax Museum; Private Detective 62; Goodbye Again; The Kennel Murder Case; Keyhole; Female* (co-director)
1934 *The Key; Mandalay; Jimmy The Gent; British Agent*
1935 *Front Page Woman; The Case Of The Curious Bride; Little Big Shot; Captain Blood\*; Black Fury*
1936 *The Charge Of The Light Brigade; Mountain Justice; The Walking Dead*
1937 *Stolen Holiday; Kid Galahad; The Perfect Specimen*
1938 *Gold Is Where You Find It; The Adventures Of Robin Hood\** (co-director); *Four Daughters; Four's A Crowd; Angels With Dirty Faces\**
1939 *Dodge City; Sons Of Liberty; The Private Lives Of Elizabeth And Essex\*; Four Wives; Daughters Courageous*
1940 *Virginia City; The Sea Hawk\*; Santa Fe Trail*
1941 *The Sea Wolf; Dive Bomber*
1942 *Captains Of The Clouds; Yankee Doodle Dandy\*; Casablanca\**
1943 *Mission To Moscow; This Is The Army*
1944 *Passage To Marseille; Janie*
1945 *Roughly Speaking; Mildred Pierce\**
1946 *Night And Day\**
1947 *Life With Father\*; The Unsuspected*
1948 *Romance On The High Seas*
1949 *My Dream Is Yours; Flamingo Road; The Lady Takes A Sailor*
1950 *Young Man With A Horn* (UK: *Young Man Of Music*); *Bright Leaf; Breaking Point*

1951 *Jim Thorpe — All American; Force Of Arms*
1952 *I'll See You In My Dreams; The Story Of Will Rogers*
1953 *The Jazz Singer; Trouble Along The Way*
1954 *The Boy From Oklahoma; The Egyptian; White Christmas\**
1955 *We're No Angels*
1956 *The Scarlet Hour; The Vagabond King; The Best Things In Life Are Free*
1957 *The Helen Morgan Story*
1958 *The Proud Rebel; King Creole*
1959 *The Hangman; The Man In The Net*
1960 *The Adventures Of Huckleberry Finn; A Breath Of Scandal*
1961 *Francis Of Assisi*
1962 *The Commancheros*

# D

## DA COSTA, Morton
(1914–89) USA

1958 *Auntie Mame\**
1962 *The Music Man*
1963 *Island Of Love*

## DANTE, Joe
(1945–  ) USA

1976 *Hollywood Boulevard* (co-director)
1977 *Grand Theft Auto* (editor)
1978 *Piranha*
1979 *Rock'n'Roll High School*
1980 *The Howling*
1983 *Twilight Zone — The Movie* (co-director)
1984 *Gremlins\**
1985 *Explorers*
1987 *Innerspace; Amazon Women On The Moon* (co-director)
1989 *The 'burbs*
1990 *Gremlins 2: The New Batch*
1992 *Matinee*

## DAVIES, Terence
(1945–   ) UK

1974 *Children*
1980 *Madonna And Child*
1983 *Death And Transfiguration*
1988 *Distant Voices, Still Lives\**
1992 *The Long Day Closes\**


## DEARDEN, Basil
real name: Basil Dear
(1911–71) UK

1938 *It's In The Air; Penny Paradise*
(both co-director); *This Man Is
News* (co-writer)
1939 *Come On George*
1940 *Let George Do It* (co-writer);
*Spare A Copper* (associate
producer only)
1941 *Young Veteran* (assistant
director); *The Black Sheep Of
Whitehall* (co-director)
1942 *The Goose Steps Out* (co-
director)
1943 *The Bells Go Down; My Learned
Friend* (co-director)
1944 *The Halfway House; They Came
To A City*
1945 *Dead Of Night* (co-director)
1946 *The Captive Heart*
1947 *Frieda*
1948 *Saraband For Dead Lovers*
1949 *Train of Events* (co-director); *The
Blue Lamp*
1950 *Cage Of Gold; Pool Of London*
1951 *I Believe In You* (co-director)
1952 *The Gentle Gunman* (co-director)
1953 *The Square Ring* (co-director)
1954 *The Rainbow Jacket; Out Of The
Clouds* (both co-director)
1955 *The Ship That Died Of Shame;
Who Done It?* (both co-director)
1957 *Davy* (producer only)
1958 *The Smallest Show On Earth;
Violent Playground; Rockets
Galore* (producer only)
1959 *Sapphire; Desert Mice* (producer
only)
1960 *The League Of Gentlemen; The
Man In The Moon*

1961 *The Secret Partner; Victim\*; All
Night Long* (co-director)
1962 *Life For Ruth*
1963 *The Mind Benders; A Place To Go*
1964 *Woman Of Straw; Masquerade*
1966 *Khartoum*
1968 *Only When I Larf; The
Assassination Bureau*
1970 *The Man Who Haunted Himself*


## DEL RUTH, Roy
(1895–1961) USA

1920 *The Heart Snatcher; Hungry Lions
And Tender Hearts* (both shorts,
both co-director); *Should
Dummies Wed?; Through The
Keyhole; Farmyard Follies; His
Noisy Still; A Lightweight Lover;
The Jazz Bandits; Chase Me* (all
shorts)
1921 *Love And Doughnuts; Hard
Knocks And Love Taps; Be
Reasonable* (all shorts)
1922 *The Duck Hunter; Oh Daddy!; On
Patrol; When Summer Comes; By
Heck!; Gymnasium Jim; Ma And
Pa* (all shorts)
1923 *Nip And Tuck; Flip Flops; Asleep
At The Switch* (all shorts)
1924 *The Cat's Meow; A Deep Sea
Panic; The Hollywood Kid; The
Masked Marvel; Shanghaied
Lovers; His New Mamma; A Nip
Of Scotch* (all shorts)
1925 *House Of Flickers* (short, co-
director); *The Mysterious
Stranger; Head Over Heels* (both
shorts); *Eve's Lover; Hogan's
Alley; Three Weeks In Paris*
1926 *The Man Upstairs; The Little Irish
Girl; Across The Pacific;
Footloose Widows* (UK: *Fine
Feathers*)
1927 *Wolf's Clothing; The First Auto;
Ham And Eggs At The Front; If I
Were Single*
1928 *The Terror; Beware Of Bachelors;
Powder My Back; Five And Ten
Cent Annie* (UK: *Ambitious Annie*)

**DEL RUTH, Roy** (cont.)

1929  *Conquest; The Hottentot; The Desert Song; The Aviator; Gold Diggers Of Broadway*

1930  *The Life Of The Party; Hold Everything; The Second Floor Mystery; Three Faces East; Divorce Among Friends*

1931  *Side Show; My Past; The Maltese Falcon; Blonde Crazy* (UK: *Larceny Lane*)

1932  *Beauty And The Boss; Taxi!; Winner Takes All; Blessed Event*

1933  *Employees' Entrance; The Little Giant; The Mind Reader; Captured!; Bureau Of Missing Persons; Lady Killer*

1934  *Upperworld; Bulldog Drummond Strikes Back; Kid Millions*

1935  *Broadway Melody Of 1936; Thanks A Million; Folies Bergère* (UK: *The Man From The Folies Bergère*)

1936  *It Had To Happen; Born To Dance; Private Number* (UK: *Secret Interlude*)

1937  *On The Avenue; Broadway Melody Of 1938*

1938  *Tail Spin; Happy Landing; My Lucky Star*

1939  *The Star Maker; Here I Am Stranger*

1940  *He Married His Wife*

1941  *The Chocolate Soldier; Topper Returns*

1942  *Maisie Gets Her Man* (UK: *She Got Her Man*)

1943  *Broadway Rythmn; Du Barry Was A Lady*

1944  *Barbary Coast Gent; Ziegfeld Follies**

1947  *It Happened On Fifth Avenue*

1948  *The Babe Ruth Story*

1949  *Red Light; Always Leave Them Laughing*

1950  *The West Point Story* (UK: *Fine And Dandy*)

1951  *Starlift; On Moonlight Bay*

1952  *Stop, You're Killing Me; About Face*

1953  *Three Sailors And A Girl*

1954  *Phantom Of The Rue Morgue*

1959  *The Alligator People*

1960  *Why Must I Die?* (UK: *13 Steps To Death*)

## DE MILLE, Cecil Blount
(1881–1959)

1914  *The Squaw Man; Brewster's Millions; The Master Mind; The Man On The Box; The Only Son; The Ghost Breaker* (all co-director); *Ready Money; The Circus Man; Cameo Kirby* (all co-writer only); *The Call Of The North; The Virginian; What's His Name; The Man From Home; Rose Of the Rancho*

1915  *The Girl Of The Golden West; The Warrens Of Virginia; The Unafraid; The Captive; The Wild Goose Chase; The Arab; Chimmie Fadden; Kindling; Carmen; Chimmie Fadden Out West; The Cheat; The Golden Chance; The Goose Girl* (co-director); *The Country Boy; A Gentleman Of Leisure; The Governor's Lady; Snobs* (all co-writer only)

1916  *The Love Mask* (co-writer only); *Temptation; The Trail Of The Lonesome Pine; The Heart Of Nora Flynn; Maria Rose; The Dream Girl*

1917  *Betty To The Rescue* (co-writer only); *Joan The Woman; A Romance Of The Redwoods; The Little American; The Woman God Forgot; The Devil Stone; Lost And Won*

1918  *The Whispering Chorus; Old Wives For New; We Can't Have Everything; Till I Come Back To You; The Squaw Man* (remake)

1919  *Don't Change Your Husband; For Better, For Worse; Male And Female*

1920  *Why Change Your Wife?; Something To Think About*

1921 *Forbidden Fruit; The Affairs Of Anatol; Fool's Paradise*
1922 *Saturday Night; Manslaughter; Don't Tell Everything* (co-director)
1923 *Hollywood* (guest appearance); *Adam's Rib; The Ten Commandments*
1924 *Triumph; Feet Of Clay*
1925 *The Golden Bed; The Road To Yesterday*
1926 *The Volga Boatman*
1927 *The King Of Kings*
1929 *The Godless Girl; Dynamite*
1930 *Free And Easy* (guest appearance); *Madame Satan*
1931 *The Squaw Man* (remake)
1932 *The Sign Of The Cross*
1933 *This Day And Age*
1934 *Four Frightened People; Cleopatra*
1935 *The Crusades*
1936 *The Plainsman*
1938 *The Buccaneer*
1939 *Union Pacific*
1940 *North West Mounted Police*
1942 *Star Spangled Rythmn* (guest appearance); *Reap The Wild Wind**
1944 *The Story Of Dr Wassell*
1947 *Variety Girl* (guest appearance); *Unconquered*
1949 *Samson And Delilah**
1950 *Sunset Boulevard** (actor only)
1952 *Son Of Paleface* (guest appearance); *The Greatest Show On Earth**
1956 *The Ten Commandments**
1957 *The Buster Keaton Story* (guest appearance); *The Heart Of Show Business* (narrator)
1958 *The Buccaneer* (producer only)

## DEMME, Jonathan
(1944–  )

1970 *Eyewitness* (music coordinator only)
1972 *Angels Hard As They Come; The Hot Box* (both co-writer only)

1974 *Caged Heat*
1975 *Crazy Mama*
1976 *Fighting Mad*
1977 *Citizen's Band/Handle With Care*
1979 *The Last Embrace*
1980 *Melvin And Howard*
1984 *Swing Shift; Stop Making Sense* (documentary)
1986 *Something Wild*
1987 *Swimming To Cambodia* (documentary)
1988 *Married To The Mob*
1991 *The Silence Of The Lambs**
1992 *Cousin Bobby* (documentary)
1993 *Philadelphia*

## DE PALMA, Brian
(1940–  )

1961 *Icarus* (short) *660214, The Story Of An IBM Card* (short)
1963 *Woton's Wake* (short)
1964 *Jennifer* (short)
1965 *Bridge That Gap* (short)
1966 *Show Me A Strong Town And I'll Show You A Strong Bank* (short); *The Responsive Eye* (documentary)
1967 *Murder A La Mod*
1968 *Greetings*
1969 *The Wedding Party*
1970 *Dionysus In '69; Hi, Mom!*
1972 *Get To Know Your Rabbit*
1973 *Sisters*
1974 *Phantom Of The Paradise*
1975 *Obsession*
1976 *Carrie**
1978 *The Fury*
1979 *Home Movies*
1980 *Dressed To Kill*
1981 *Blow Out*
1983 *Scarface**
1984 *Body Double*
1986 *Wise Guys*
1987 *The Untouchables**
1989 *Casualties Of War*
1990 *The Bonfire Of The Vanities**
1992 *Raising Cain*

## DE SICA, Vittorio
(1902–74) Italy

1940 *Rose Scarlette* (co-director)
1941 *Maddelena Zero In Condotta; Teresa Venerdi*
1942 *Un Garibaldino Al Convento*
1943 *I Bambini Ci Guardano*
1946 *La Porta Del Cielo; Sciuscia* (UK: *Shoeshine*)
1948 *Ladri Di Biciclette\** (UK: *The Bicycle Thieves*)
1950 *Miracolo A Milano* (UK: *Miracle In Milan*)
1952 *Umberto D*
1954 *Stazione Termini* (UK: *Indiscretion Of An American Wife*); *L'Oro Di Napoli* (UK: *Gold Of Naples*)
1956 *Il Tetto*
1961 *La Ciociara\** (UK: *Two Women*); *Il Giudizio Universale*
1962 *Boccacio '70* (co-director); *I Sequestrati Di Altona* (UK: *The Condemned Of Altona*)
1963 *Il Boom; Ieri, Oggi, Domani* (UK: *Yesterday, Today And Tomorrow*)
1964 *Matrimonio All'Italiana* (UK: *Marriage — Italian Style*)
1965 *Un Monde Nouveau*
1966 *After The Fox; Le Streghe* (UK: *The Witches*) (co-director)
1967 *Woman Times Seven*
1968 *Amanti* (UK: *A Place For Lovers*)
1970 *Le Coppie* (co-director); *Il Giardino Dei Finzi Contini* (UK: *The Garden Of The Finzi Contini*); *I Girasoli* (UK: *Sunflower*)
1972 *Lo Chiameremo Andrea*
1973 *Una Breva Vacanza* (UK: *A Brief Vacation*)
1974 *Il Viaggio* (UK: *The Journey*)

## DE VITO, Danny
(1945– ) USA

1975 *Minestrone* (short)
1977 *The Sound Sleeper* (short)
1984 *The Ratings Game* (TV)
1987 *Throw Momma From The Train\**
1989 *The War Of The Roses\**
1992 *Hoffa\**

See also actors listing

## DIETERLE, William
real name: Wilhelm Dieterle
(1893–1972) Germany

1923 *Der Mensch Am Wege; Die Grüne Manuela* (co-director)
1924 *Das Wachsfigurenkabinett* (co-director)
1927 *Das Geheimnis Des Abbé X*
1928 *Die Heilige Und Ihr Narr; Geschlecht In Fesseln — Die Sexualnot Der Gefangenen*
1929 *Ich Liebe Für Dich; Frühlingsrauschen; Das Schweigen Im Walde*
1930 *Ludwig Der Zweite, König Von Bayern; Eine Stunde Glück; Der Tanz Geht Weiter; Dis Maske Fällt; Kismet; Dämon Des Meeres*
1931 *Die Heilige Flamme* (co-director); *The Last Flight; Her Majesty's Love*
1932 *Man Wanted; Jewel Robbery; Six Hours To Live!; The Crash; Scarlet Dawn*
1933 *Lawyer Man; Grand Slam; Adorable; The Devil's In Love; From Headquarters; Female* (co-director)
1934 *Fashions; Doctor Monica* (both co-director); *Madame Du Barry; Fog Over Frisco; The Firebird; The Secret Bride*
1935 *A Midsummer Night's Dream\** (co-director); *Dr Socrates*
1936 *The Story Of Louis Pasteur\*; The White Angel; Satan Met A Lady*
1937 *The Great O'Malley; Another Dawn; The Life Of Emile Zola\**
1938 *Blockade*
1939 *Juarez; The Hunchback Of Notre Dame\**
1940 *Dr Ehrlich's Magic Bullet; A Dispatch From Reuters*
1941 *All That Money Can Buy*
1942 *Syncopation; Tennessee Johnson*
1944 *Kismet; I'll Be Seeing You* (co-director)
1945 *This Love Of Ours; Love Letters*
1946 *Duel In The Sun\** (co-director); *The Searching Wind*

1948  *Paid In Full; The Accused*
1949  *Portrait Of Jennie; Rope Of Sand; Volcano*
1950  *September Affair; Dark City*
1952  *Red Mountain; Boots Malone; The Turning Point*
1953  *Salome*
1954  *Elephant Walk*
1956  *Magic Fire; One Against Many*
1957  *Peking Express; The Loves Of Omar Khayam*
1959  *Il Vendicatore*
1960  *Herrin Der Welt* (co-director); *Die Fastnachtsbeichte*
1965  *The Confession*

## DMYTRYK, Edward
(1908–   ) USA

1930  *Only Saps Work; The Royal Family Of Broadway* (editor only)
1932  *Milion Dollar Legs* (editor)
1934  *Belle Of The Nineties; College Rhythmn* (co-editor only)
1935  *Ruggles Of Red Gap\** (editor only); *The Hawk*
1936  *Too Many Parents; Three Cheers For Love; Three Married Men; Easy To Take* (all editor only)
1937  *Murder Goes To College; Turn Off The Moon; Double Or Nothing; Hold'Em Navy* (all editor only)
1938  *Bull Drummond's Peril; Prison Farm* (both editor only)
1939  *Zaza; Love Affair\*; Some Like It Hot* (all editor only); *Television Spy; Emergency Squad*
1940  *Golden Gloves; Mystery Sea Raider; Her First Romance*
1941  *The Devil Commands; Under Age; Sweethearts Of The Campus; The Blonde From Singapore; Secrets Of The Lone Wolf; Confessions Of Boston Blackie*
1942  *Counter Espionage; Seven Miles From Alcatraz*
1943  *Hitler's Children; The Falcon Strikes Back; Captive Wild Woman; Behind The Rising Sun; Tender Comrade*
1944  *Farewell, My Lovely*

1945  *Back To Bataan; Cornered*
1946  *Till The End Of Time*
1947  *Crossfire\*; So Well Remembered*
1949  *Obsession; Give Us This Day*
1952  *Mutiny; The Sniper; Eight Iron Men*
1953  *The Juggler; Three Lives*
1954  *The Caine Mutiny\*; Broken Lance*
1955  *The End Of The Affair; Soldier Of Fortune; The Left Hand Of God*
1956  *The Mountain; Bing Presents Orieste* (short)
1957  *Raintree County*
1958  *The Young Lions*
1959  *Warlock; The Blue Angel*
1961  *The Reluctant Saint*
1962  *Walk On The Wild Side*
1964  *The Carpetbaggers\*; Where Love Has Gone*
1965  *Mirage*
1966  *Alvarez Kelly*
1968  *Anzio; Shalako*
1972  *Bluebeard*
1975  *The 'Human' Factor*
1976  *He Is My Brother*

## DONALDSON, Roger
(1945–   ) Australia

1977  *Sleeping Dogs*
1981  *Smash Palace*
1984  *The Bounty\**
1985  *Marie*
1987  *No Way Out\**
1988  *Cocktail\**
1990  *Cadillac Man*
1992  *White Sands*

## DONEN, Stanley
(1924–   ) USA

1943  *Best Foot Forward* (choreographer only)
1944  *Hey Rookie; Jam Session; Kansas City Kitty; Cover Girl* (all choreographer only)
1945  *Anchors Aweigh\** (choreographer only)
1946  *Holiday In Mexico; No Leave, No Love* (both choreographer only)

**DONEN, Stanley** (cont.)
1947 *This Time For Keeps; Living In A Big Way; Killer McCoy* (all choreographer only)
1948 *A Date With Judy; The Big City; The Kissing Bandit* (all choreographer only)
1949 *Take Me Out To The Ball Game* (choreographer only); *On The Town** (co-director)
1951 *Royal Wedding* (UK: *Wedding Bells*)
1952 *Singin' In The Rain** (co-director); *Love Is Better Than Ever; Fearless Fagin*
1953 *Give A Girl A Break*
1954 *Seven Brides For Seven Brothers*; Deep In My Heart*
1955 *It's Always Fair Weather*
1956 *Funny Face**
1957 *The Pajama Game* (co-director); *Kiss Them For Me*
1958 *Indiscreet; Damn Yankees* (co-director)
1960 *Once More With Feeling; Surprise Package; The Grass Is Greener*
1963 *Charade**
1966 *Arabesque*
1967 *Two For The Road; Bedazzled*
1969 *Staircase*
1974 *The Little Prince*
1975 *Lucky Lady*
1978 *Movie, Movie*
1980 *Saturn 3*
1984 *Blame It On Rio*

**DONNER, Richard**
(1930–   ) USA

1961 *X-15*
1968 *Salt And Pepper*
1970 *Twinky*
1976 *The Omen**
1978 *Superman**
1980 *Inside Moves*
1981 *The Final Conflict* (executive producer only)
1982 *The Toy*
1985 *The Goonies; Ladyhawke*
1987 *Lethal Weapon*; The Lost Boys* (executive producer only)
1988 *Scrooged*
1989 *Lethal Weapon 2*
1992 *Radio Flyer; Lethal Weapon 3*

**DWAN, Allan**
real name: Joseph Aloysius Dwan
(1885–1981) USA

1911 *Branding A Bad Man; A Western Dreamer; A Daughter Of Liberty; A Trouper's Heart; Rattlesnakes And Gunpowder; The Ranch Tenor; The Sheepman's Daughter; The Sagebrush Phrenologist; The Elopements On Double L Ranch; $5,000 Reward — Dead Or Alive; The Witch Of The Range; The Cowboy's Ruse; Law And Order On Bar L Ranch; The Yiddisher Cowboy; The Broncho Buster's Bride; The Hermit's Gold; The Actress And The Cowboys; The Sky Pilot's Intemperance; A Western Waif; The Call Of The Open Range; The School Ma'am Of Snake; The Ranch Chicken; Cupid In Chaps; The Outlaw's Trail; The Ranchman's Nerve; When East Comes West; The Cowboy's Deliverance; The Cattle Thief's Brand; The Parting Trails; The Cattle Rustler's End; Cattle, Gold And Oil; The Ranch Girl; The Poisoned Flume; The Brand Of Fear; The Blotted Brand; Auntie And The Cowboys; The Western Doctor's Peril; The Smuggler And The Girl; The Cowboy And The Artist; Three Million Dollars; The Stage Robbers Of San Juan; The Mother Of The Ranch; The Gunman; The Claim Jumpers; The Circular Fence; The Rustler Sheriff; The Love Of The West; The Trained Nurse At Bar Z; The Miner's Wife; The Land Thieves; The Cowboy And The Outlaw; Three Daughters Of The West; Caves Of La Jolla; The Lonely Range; The Horse Thief's*

Bigamy; The Trail Of The Eucalyptus; The Stronger Man; The Water War; The Three Shell Game; The Mexican; The Eastern Cowboy; The Way Of The West; The Test; The Master Of The Vineyard; Sloppy Bill Of The Rollicking R; The Sheriff's Sisters; The Angel Of Paradise Ranch; The Smoke Of The 45; The Man Hunt; Santa Catalina, Magic Isle Of The Pacific; The Last Notch; The Gold Lust; The Duel Of The Candles; Bonita Of El Cajon; The Lawful Holdup; Battleships; Dams And Waterways

1912 A Midwinter Trip To Los Angeles; The Misadventures Of A Claim Agent; Broncho Busting For Flying A Pictures; The Winning Of La Mesa; The Locket; The Relentless Outlaw; Justice Of The Sage; Objections Overruled; The Mormon; Love And Lemons; The Best Policy; The Real Estate Fraud; The Grubstake Mortgage; Where Broadway Meets The Mountains; An Innocent Grafter; Society And Chaps; The Leap Year Cowboy; The Land Baron Of San Tee; An Assisted Elopement; From The Four Hundred To The Herd; The Broken Ties; After School; A Bad Investment; The Full Value; The Tramp's Gratitude; Fidelity; Winter Sports And Pastimes Of Coronado Beach; The Maid And The Man; The Cowboy Socialists; Checkmate; The Ranchman's Marathon; The Coward; The Distant Relative; The Ranch Detective; Driftwood; The Eastern Girl; The Pensioners; The End Of The Feud; The Wedding Dress; Mystical Maid Of Jamasha Pass; The Other Wise Man; The Haters; The Thread Of Life; The Wandering Gypsy; The Reward Of Valor; The Brand; The Green Eyed Monster; Cupid Through

Padlocks; For The Good Of Her Men; The Simple Love; The Weaker Brother; Fifty Mile Auto Contest; The Wordless Message; The Evil Inheritance; The Marauders; The Girl Back Home; Under False Pretences; Where There's A Heart; The Vanishing Race; The Fatal Mirror; Point Loma, Old Town; The Tell Tale Shells; Indian Jealousy; San Diego; The Canyon Dweller; It Pays To Wait; A Life For A Kiss; The Meddlers; The Girl And The Gun; The Battleground; The Bad Man And The Ranger; The Outlaw Colony; The Land Of Death; The Bandit Of Point Loma; The Jealous Rage; The Will Of James Waldron; The House That Jack Built; Curtiss's School Of Aviation; The Stepmother; The Odd Job Man; The Liar; The Greaser And The Weakling; The Stranger At Coyote; The Dawn Of Passion; The Vengeance That Failed; The Fear; The Foreclosure; White Treachery; Their Hero Son; Calamity Anne's Ward; Father's Favourite; Jack Of Diamonds; The Reformation Of Sierra Smith; The Promise; The New Cowpuncher; The Best Man Wins; The Good Love And The Bad; The Horse Thief; The Man From The East; Ranch Life On The Range; Paid In Full; The Loneliness Of Neglect; Blackened Hills; The Recognition; The Power of Love; The Daughters Of Sẽnor Lopez; Nell Of The Pampas; The Law Of God; The Animal Within; Pals; Her Own Country; Jack's Word; The Would-Be Heir; The Thief's Wife; The Intrusion At Lompoc; Man's Calling; God's Unfortunate; Maiden And Men; The Wanderer; One, Two, Three; The Wooers Of Mountain Kate

1913 The Fraud That Failed; Another Man's Wife; Calamity Anne's

**DWAN, Allan** (cont.)
Inheritance; Their Masterpiece;
His Old-Fashioned Mother; Where
Destiny Guides; The Silver-Plated
Gun; A Rose Of Old Mexico;
Building The Great Los Angeles
Aqueduct; Women Left Alone;
Andrew Jackson; Calamity Anne's
Vanity; The Fugitive; The
Romance; The Finer Things; Love
Is Blind; Then The Light Fails;
High And Low; The Greater Love;
The Jocular Winds; The
Transgression Of Manuel;
Calamity Anne, Detective; The
Orphan's Mine; When A Woman
Won't; An Eastern Flower; Cupid
Never Ages; Calamity Anne's
Beauty; The Renegade's Heart;
Matches; The Mute Witness;
Cupid Throws A Brick; Woman's
Honor; Suspended Sentence; In
Another's Nest; The Ways Of
Fate; Boobs And Bricks; Calamity
Anne's Trust; Oil On Troubled
Waters; The Road To Ruin; The
Brothers; Human Kindness; Youth
And Jealousy; Angel Of The
Canyons; The Great Harmony;
Her Innocent Marriage; Calamity
Anne Parcel Post; The Ashes Of
Three; On The Border; Her Big
Story; When Luck Changes; The
Wishing Seat; Hearts And Horses;
The Reward Of Courage; The
Soul Of A Thief; The Marine Law;
The Road To Success; The Spirit
Of The Flag; The Call To Arms;
Women And War; The Power
Flash Of Death; The Picket
Guard; Mental Suicide; Man's
Duty; The Animal; The Wall Of
Money; The Echo Of A Song;
Criminals; The Restless Spirit;
Jewels Of A Sacrifice; Back To
Life; Red Margaret; Moonshiner;
Bloodhounds Of The North; He
Called Her In; The Menace; The
Chase; The Battle Of Wills
1914 The Lie; The Honor Of The
Mounted; Remember Mary

Magdalene; Discord And
Harmony; The Menace To
Carlotta; The Embezzler; The
Lamb, The Woman, The Wolf;
The End Of The Feud; The
Tragedy of Whispering Creek;
The Unlawful Trade; The
Forbidden Room; The Hopes Of
Blind Alley; The Great Universal
Mystery; Richelieu; Wildflower;
The Country Chairman; The Small
Town Girl; The Straight Road; The
Conspiracy; The Unwelcome Mrs
Hatch; The Man On The Case
1915 The Dancing Girl; David Harum;
The Love Route; The
Commanding Officer; May
Blossom; The Pretty Sister Of
Jose; A Girl Of Yesterday; The
Foundling; Jordan Is A Hard Road
1916 Betty Of Greystone; The Habit Of
Happiness; The Good Bad Man;
An Innocent Magdalene; The Half-
Breed; Manhattan Madness; Fifty-
Fifty
1917 Panthea; The Fighting Odds; A
Modern Musketeer
1918 Mr Fix-It; Bound In Morocco; He
Comes Up Smiling
1919 Cheating Cheaters; Getting Mary
Married; The Dark Star; Soldiers
Of Fortune
1920 The Luck Of The Irish; The
Forbidden Thing
1921 A Perfect Crime; A Broken Doll;
The Scoffer; The Sin Of Martha
Queed; In The Heart Of A Fool
1922 The Hidden Woman; Superstition;
Robin Hood
1923 The Glimpses Of The Moon;
Lawful Larceny; Zaza; Big Brother
1924 A Society Scandal; Manhandled;
Her Love Story; Wages Of Virtue;
Argentine Love
1925 Night Life In New York; Coast Of
Folly; Stage Struck
1926 Sea Horses; Padlocked; Tin
Gods; Summer Bachelors
1927 The Music Master; West Point;
The Joy Girl; East Side, West
Side; French Dressing

1928 *The Big Noise*
1929 *The Iron Mask; Tide Of Empire; The Far Call; Frozen Justice; South Sea Rose*
1930 *What A Widow!; Man To Man*
1931 *Chances; Wicked*
1932 *While Paris Sleeps*
1933 *Her First Affaire; Counsel's Opinion*
1934 *The Morning After*
1935 *Black Sheep; Navy Wife*
1936 *Song And Dance Man; Human Cargo; High Tension; 15 Maiden Lane*
1937 *Woman-Wise; That I May Live; One Mile From Heaven; Heidi*
1938 *Rebecca Of Sunnybrook Farm; Josette; Suez*
1939 *The Three Musketeers; The Gorilla; Frontier Marshall*
1940 *Sailor's Lady; Young People; Trail Of The Vigilantes*
1941 *Look Who's Laughing; Rise And Shine*
1942 *Friendly Enemies; Here We Go Again*
1943 *Around The World*
1944 *Up In Mabel's Room; Abroad With Two Yanks*
1945 *Brewster's Milions; Getting Gertie's Garter*
1946 *Rendezvous With Annie*
1947 *Calendar Girl; Northwest Outpost; Driftwood*
1948 *The Inside Story; Angel In Exile*
1949 *Sands Of Iwo Jima\**
1950 *Surrender*
1951 *Belle Le Grand; The Wild Blue Yonder*
1952 *I Dream Of Jeannie; Montana Belle*
1953 *The Woman They Almost Lynched; Sweethearts On Parade*
1954 *Flight Nurse; Silver Lode; Passion; Cattle Queen Of Montana*
1955 *It's Always Sunday; Escape To Burma; Pearl Of The South Pacific; Tennessee's Partner*
1956 *Slightly Scarlet; Hold Back The Night*

1957 *The River's Edge; The Restless Breed*
1958 *Enchanted Island*
1961 *Most Dangerous Man Alive*

# E

## EASTWOOD, Clint
(1930– ) USA

1971 *Play Misty For Me\**
1972 *High Plains Drifter*
1973 *Breezy*
1975 *The Eiger Sanction*
1976 *The Outlaw Josey Wales\**
1977 *The Gauntlet*
1980 *Bronco Billy*
1982 *Firefox*
1983 *Honkytonk Man; Sudden Impact*
1985 *Pale Rider\**
1986 *Heartbreak Ridge*
1988 *Bird\*; Thelonius Monk: Straight No Chaser* (executive producer only)
1989 *Pink Cadillac*
1990 *White Hunter, Black Heart\*; The Rookie*
1992 *Unforgiven\**
1993 *Perfect World*

See also actors listing

## EDWARDS, Blake
real name: William B McEdwards
(1922– ) USA

1942 *Ten Gentlemen From West Point; Lucky Legs* (both actor only)
1943 *A Guy Named Joe* (actor only)
1944 *In The Meantime, Darling; Marshal Of Reno; See Here, Private Hargrove; Ladies Courageous; The Eve Of St Mark; Marine Raiders; Wing And A Prayer; My Buddy; The Unwritten Code; Thirty Seconds Over Tokyo; She's A Sweetheart* (all actor only)

**EDWARDS, Blake** (cont.)

1945 *This Man's Navy; A Guy, A Gal And A Pal; Gangs Of The Waterfront; What Next, Corporal Hargrove?; They Were Expendable; Tokyo Rose; Stranglers Of The Swamp* (all actor only)

1946 *The Strange Love Of Martha Ivers; Till The End Of Time; The Best Years Of Our Lives\** (all actor only)

1947 *The Beginning Or The End* (actor only); *Panhandle* (co-writer, actor)

1948 *Leather Gloves* (co-writer, actor)

1949 *Stampede* (co-writer)

1952 *Sound Off; Rainbow Round My Shoulder* (both writer only)

1953 *All Ashore; Cruisin' Down The River* (both writer only)

1954 *Drive A Crooked Road; The Atomic Kid* (both writer only)

1955 *My Sister Eileen* (writer only); *Bring Your Smile Along*

1956 *He Laughed Last*

1957 *Operation Mad Ball* (co-writer only)

1958 *This Happy Feeling*

1959 *The Perfect Furlough; Operation Petticoat\**

1960 *High Time*

1961 *The Couch* (co-scenarist only); *Breakfast At Tiffany's\**

1962 *The Notorious Landlady* (co-writer only); *Experiment In Terror; Days Of Wine And Roses\**

1963 *Soldier In the Rain* (co-writer only); *The Pink Panther\**

1964 *A Shot In The Dark*

1965 *The Great Race\**

1966 *What Did You Do In The War Daddy?*

1967 *Gunn*

1968 *The Party*

1969 *Inspector Clouseau* (screenwriter only)

1970 *Darling Lili*

1971 *The Wild Rovers*

1972 *The Carey Treatment*

1974 *The Tamarind Seed; The Return of The Pink Panther*

1976 *The Pink Panther Strikes Again*

1978 *Revenge Of The Pink Panther*

1979 *10\**

1981 *SOB*

1982 *Victor, Victoria; Trail Of The Pink Panther*

1983 *The Curse Of The Pink Panther; The Man Who Loved Women*

1984 *Micki And Maude*

1986 *A Fine Mess; That's Life*

1987 *Blind Date\**

1988 *Sunset; Justin Case* (TV)

1989 *Peter Gunn* (TV); *Skin Deep*

1991 *Switch*

1993 *Son Of The Pink Panther*

## EISENSTEIN, Sergei Mikhailovitch
(1898–1948) Russia

1923 *Kinodnevik Glumova* (UK: *Glumov's Film Diary*)

1925 *Stachka* (UK: *Strike*); *Bronenosets Potemkin* (UK: *The Battleship Potemkin*)

1928 *Oktiabr* (UK: *October*) (co-director)

1929 *Everyday* (actor only); *Staroe I Novoe* (UK: *The Old And The New*) (co-director)

1930 *Romance Sentimentale* (co-director)

1932 *Que Viva Mexico!* (unfinished)

1937 *Bezhin Meadow* (unfinished)

1938 *Aleksandr Nevskii\** (UK: *Alexander Nevsky*)

1940 *Mighty Stream*

1944 *Ivan Groznyi* (UK: *Ivan The Terrible Part One*)

1946 *Ivan Goznyi II: Boyarskii Zagovor* (UK: *Ivan The Terrible Part II: The Boyars' Plot*)

## ENDFIELD, Cy
(1914–83) South Africa

1944 *Nostradamus IV* (co-director); *Tale Of A Dog; Radio Bugs; Dancing Romeo* (all shorts)

1945 *The Great American Mug; Magic On A Stick* (both shorts)

1946 *Our Old Car* (short); *Gentleman Joe Palooka*
1947 *Stork Bites Man*
1948 *The Argyle Secrets*
1949 *Joe Palooka In The Big Night*
1950 *The Underworld Story; The Sound Of Fury* (UK: *Try And Get Me*)
1952 *Tarzan's Savage Fury*
1953 *The Limping Man; Colonel March Investigates*
1954 *Impulse; The Master Plan* (as Hugh Raker)
1955 *The Secret*
1956 *Child In The House* (supervising director)
1957 *Hell Drivers*
1958 *Sea Fury*
1959 *Jet Storm* (US: *The Killing Urge*)
1961 *Mysterious Island*
1963 *Zulu\*; Hide And Seek*
1965 *Sands Of The Kalahari*
1969 *De Sade* (co-director)
1971 *Universal Soldier*
1979 *Zulu Dawn* (screenwriter only)

# F

## FAIMAN, Peter
(19?–  ) Australia

1986 *'Crocodile' Dundee\**
1991 *Dutch* (UK: *Driving Me Crazy*)

## FARGO, James
(1938–  ) USA

1971 *Raid On Rommel* (assistant director)
1972 *High Plains Drifter; Joe Kidd; Duel* (TV) (all assistant director)
1973 *Breezy; Showdown* (both assistant director)
1974 *The Sugarland Express\** (assistant director)
1975 *The Eiger Sanction* (assistant director)
1976 *The Enforcer; The Outlaw Josey Wales\** (associate producer only)
1978 *Caravans; Every Which Way But Loose\**

1979 *Game For Vultures*
1982 *Forced Vengeance*
1988 *Born To Race*
1989 *Riding The Edge*

## FELLINI, Federico
(1920–  ) Italy

1939 *Lo Vedi Come...Lo Vedi Come Sei?!* (gagman only)
1940 *Non Me Lo Dire!; Il Pirata Sono Io!* (both gagman only)
1941 *Documento Z3* (uncredited co-writer only)
1942 *Avanti C'E Posto; Chi L'Ha Vistro?; Quarta Pagina* (all co-writer only)
1943 *Apparizione; Campo Dei Fiori; Tutta La Città Canta; L'Ultima Carrozzella* (all co-writer only)
1945 *Roma, Città Aperta\** (UK: *Rome—Open City*) (assistant director, co-writer only)
1946 *Paisà* (UK: *Paisan*) (assistant director, co-writor only)
1947 *Il Delitto Di Giovanni Episcopo; Il Passatore; La Fumeria D'Oppio; L'Ebreo Errante* (all co-writer only)
1948 *Il Mulino Del Po; In Nome Della Legge; Senza Pietà; La Città Dolente* (all co-writer only); *L'Amore* (assistant director, co-writer only)
1949 *Francesco, Giullare Di Dio* (co-writer, assistant director only)
1950 *Il Cammino Della Speranza; Persiane Chiuse* (both co-writer only); *Luci Del Varietà* (UK: *Lights Of Variety*)
1951 *La Città Si Difende; Cameriera Bella Presenza Offresi* (both co-writer only); *Lo Sceicco Bianco* (UK: *The White Sheik*)
1952 *Il Brigante Di Tacca Del Lupo; Europa 51* (both co-writer only)
1953 *I Vitelloni* (UK: *Spivs*); *Amore In Città* (co-director)
1954 *La Strada\**
1955 *Il Bidone* (UK: *The Swindlers*)
1957 *Le Notti Di Cabiria\** (UK: *Nights Of Cabiria*)

**FELLINI, Federico** (cont.)

1958 *Fortunella* (co-writer only)
1960 *La Dolce Vita\** (UK: *The Sweet Life*)
1962 *Boccaccio '70*
1963 *Otto E Mezzo\** (UK: *8½*)
1965 *Giulietta Degli Spiriti* (UK: *Juliet Of The Spirits*)
1967 *Il Viaggio Di G Mastona* (unfinished)
1968 *Histoires Extraordinaires* (UK: *Tales Of Mystery*) (co-director)
1969 *Fellini–Satyricon*
1970 *Alex In Wonderland* (actor only); *I Clowns* (UK: *The Clowns*)
1972 *Fellini's Roma*
1974 *C'Eravamo Tanto Amati* (guest appearance only); *Amarcord*
1976 *Fellini's Casanova*
1979 *Prova D'Orchestra* (UK: *Orchestra Rehearsal*)
1980 *La Città Delle Donne* (UK: *City Of Women*)
1983 *E La Nave Va* (UK: *And The Ship Sails On*)
1986 *Ginger And Fred*
1987 *Intervista* (UK: *The Interview*)
1990 *La Voce Della Luna* (UK: *Voices Of The Moon*)

**FISHER, Terence**
(1904–80) UK

1935 *Brown On Resolution* (assistant editor)
1936 *Tudor Rose; Jack Of All Trades; Where There's A Will; Everybody Dance; Windbag The Sailor* (all editor only)
1938 *Mr Satan* (editor only)
1939 *On The Night Of The Fire* (editor only)
1940 *George And Margaret* (editor only)
1941 *Atlantic Ferry; The Seventh Survivor* (both editor only)
1942 *Flying Fortress; The Peterville Diamond; Tomorrow We Live; The Night Invader* (all editor only)
1943 *The Dark Tower; The Hundred Pound Window; Candlelight In Algeria* (all editor only)

1944 *One Exciting Night; Flight From Folly* (both editor only)
1945 *The Wicked Lady* (editor only)
1947 *The Master Of Bankdam* (editor only); *To The Public Danger*
1948 *A Song For Tomorrow; Colonel Bogey; Portrait From Life*
1949 *Marry Me*
1950 *The Astonished Heart; So Long At The Fair* (both co-director)
1951 *Home To Danger*
1952 *The Last Page; Stolen Face; Distant Trumpet; Wings Of Danger*
1953 *Mantrap; Spaceways; Blood Orange; Three's Company* (co-director); *Four Sided Triangle*
1954 *The Stranger Came Home; Final Appointment; Face The Music; Mask Of Dust; Children Galore*
1955 *Stolen Assignment; The Flaw; Murder By Proxy*
1956 *The Gelignite Gang; The Last Man To Hang?; The Curse Of Frankenstein*
1957 *Kill Me Tomorrow*
1958 *Dracula\*; The Revenge Of Frankenstein*
1959 *The Hound Of The Baskervilles; The Mummy; The Stranglers Of Bombay; The Man Who Could Cheat Death*
1960 *The Brides Of Dracula; The Two Faces Of Dr Jekyll*
1961 *Sword Of Sherwood Forest; The Curse Of The Werewolf*
1962 *The Phantom Of The Opera; Sherlock Holmes Und Der Halsband Des Todes* (UK: *Sherlock Holmes And The Deadly Necklace*)
1963 *The Horror Of It All*
1964 *The Gorgon; The Earth Dies Screaming*
1965 *Dracula — Prince Of Darkness*
1966 *Island Of Terror*
1967 *Frankenstein Created Woman; Night Of The Big Heat*
1968 *The Devil Rides*
1969 *Frankenstein Must Be Destroyed*
1973 *Frankenstein And The Monster From Hell*

## FLEISCHER, Richard
(1916–   ) USA

1943  *This Is America; Flicker Flashbacks* (two series of shorts)
1944  *Memo For Joe* (short)
1946  *Child Of Divorce*
1947  *Design For Death* (documentary); *Banjo*
1948  *So This Is New York; Bodyguard*
1949  *The Clay Pigeon; Follow Me Quietly; Make Mine Laughs; Trapped*
1950  *Armored Car Robbery*
1951  *The Narrow Margin*
1952  *The Happy Time*
1953  *Arena*
1954  *20,000 Leagues Under The Sea\**
1955  *The Girl In The Red Velvet Swing; Violent Saturday*
1956  *Between Heaven And Hell; Bandido!*
1958  *The Vikings\*; These Thousand Hills*
1959  *Compulsion*
1960  *Crack In The Mirror; The Big Gamble*
1962  *Barabbas*
1966  *Fantastic Voyage*
1967  *Doctor Dolittle; Think 20th* (documentary)
1968  *The Boston Strangler*
1969  *Che!*
1970  *Tora! Tora! Tora!; 10 Rillington Place*
1971  *Blind Terror; The Last Run*
1972  *The New Centurions* (UK: *Precinct 45 — Los Angeles Police*)
1973  *The Don Is Dead; Soylent Green*
1974  *Mr Majestyk; The Spikes Gang*
1975  *Mandingo*
1976  *The Incredible Sarah*
1977  *The Prince And The Pauper*
1979  *Ashanti*
1980  *The Jazz Singer*
1982  *Tough Enough*
1983  *Amityville 3-D*
1984  *Conan The Destroyer*
1985  *Red Sonja*
1987  *Million Dollar Mystery*
1989  *Call From Space*

## FLEMING, Victor
(1883–1949) USA

1919  *When The Clouds Roll By* (co-director)
1920  *The Mollycoddle*
1921  *Mamma's Affair* (short); *Woman's Place*
1922  *Red Hot Romance; The Lane That Had No Turning; Anna Ascends*
1923  *Dark Secrets; Law Of The Lawless; To The Last Man; Call Of The Canyon*
1924  *Empty Hands; Code Of The Sea*
1925  *The Devil's Cargo; Adventure; A Son Of His Father; Lord Jim*
1926  *The Blind Goddess; Mantrap*
1927  *The Rough Riders* (UK: *The Trumpet Call*); *The Way Of All Flesh; Hula*
1928  *The Awakening*
1929  *Abie's Irish Rose; Wolf Song; The Virginian*
1930  *Common Clay; Renegades*
1931  *Around The World In Eighty Minutes*
1932  *The Wet Parade; Red Dust*
1933  *The White Sister; Bombshell* (UK: *Blonde Bombshell*)
1934  *Treasure Island*
1935  *Reckless; The Farmer Takes A Wife*
1937  *Captains Courageous\*; The Good Earth\** (uncredited co-director)
1938  *Test Pilot\*; The Great Waltz* (co-director)
1939  *The Wizard Of Oz\*; Gone With The Wind\** (both co-director)
1941  *Dr Jekyll And Mr Hyde*
1942  *Tortilla Flat*
1943  *A Guy Named Joe*
1945  *Adventure*
1948  *Joan Of Arc\**

## FORD, John
real name: Sean Aloysius O'Feeney
(1895–1973) USA

1917  *The Tornado; The Trail Of Hate; The Scrapper; The Soul*

**FORD, John** (cont.)
Herder; Cheyenne's Pal;
Straight Shooting; The Secret
Man; A Marked Man; Bucking
Broadway

1918 The Phantom Riders; Wild
Woman; Thieves' Gold; The
Scarlet Drop; Hell Bent; A
Woman's Fool; Three Mounted
Men

1919 Roped; The Fighting Brothers;
A Fight For Love; By Indian Post;
The Rustlers; Bare Fists; Gun
Law; The Gun Packer; Riders Of
Vengeance; The Last Outlaw; The
Outcasts Of Poker Flat; The Ace
Of The Saddle; The Rider Of The
Law; A Gun Fightin' Gentleman;
Marked Men

1920 The Prince Of Avenue A; The Girl
In Number 29; Hitchin' Posts; Just
Pals; The Big Punch

1921 The Freeze Out; Desperate Trails;
Action; Sure Fire; Jackie

1922 The Wallop; Little Miss Smiles;
The Village Blacksmith

1923 The Face On The Barroom Floor;
Three Jumps Ahead; Cameo
Kirby; North Of Hudson Bay;
Hoodman Blind

1924 The Iron Horse; Hearts Of Oak

1925 Lightnin'; Kentucky Pride; The
Fighting Heart; Thank You

1926 The Shamrock Handicap; Three
Bad Men; The Blue Eagle

1927 Upstream

1928 Mother Machree; Four Sons;
Hangman's House; Napoleon's
Barber; Riley The Cop

1929 Strong Boy; Salute; The Black
Watch

1930 Men Without Women; Born
Reckless; Up The River

1931 Seas Beneath; The Brat;
Arrowsmith*; Flesh

1933 Pilgrimage; Dr Bull

1934 The Lost Patrol; The World Moves
On; Judge Priest

1935 The Whole Town's Talking; The
Informer*; Steamboat Round The
Bend

1936 The Prisoner Of Shark Island;
Mary Of Scotland; The Plough
And The Stars

1937 Wee Willie Winkie; The
Hurricane*

1938 Four Men And A Prayer;
Submarine Patrol

1939 Stagecoach*; Drums Along The
Mohawk; Young Mr Lincoln

1940 The Grapes Of Wrath*; The Long
Voyage Home

1941 Tobacco Road; How Green Was
My Valley*; Sex Hygiene
(documentary)

1942 The Battle Of Midway; Torpedo
Squadron (both documentaries)

1943 December Seventh (co-director);
We Sail At Midnight (both
documentaries)

1945 They Were Expendable

1946 My Darling Clementine*

1947 The Fugitive

1948 Fort Apache; Three Godfathers

1949 She Wore A Yellow Ribbon

1950 When Willie Comes Marching
Home; Wagonmaster; Rio Grande

1951 This Is Korea! (documentary)

1952 What Price Glory?; The Quiet
Man*

1953 The Sun Shines Bright; Mogambo

1954 The Long Grey Line

1955 Mister Roberts* (co-director)

1956 The Searchers*

1957 The Wings Of Eagles; The Rising
Of The Moon

1958 The Last Hurrah

1959 Gideon Of Scotland Yard; The
Horse Soldiers

1960 Sergeant Rutledge

1961 Two Rode Together

1962 The Man Who Shot Liberty
Valance*; How The West Was
Won* (co-director)

1963 Donovan's Reef

1964 Cheyenne Autumn

1965 Young Cassidy (co-director)

1966 Seven Women

1970 Chesty: A Tribute To A Legend
(documentary)

1971 Vietnam! Vietnam! (executive
producer only)

## FORMAN, Milos
(1932–   ) Czechoslovakia

1958 *Laterna Magika* (co-director)
1960 *Laterna Magika II* (co-director)
1963 *Konkurs; Kdyby Ty Muziky Nebyly*
(UK: *If It Weren't For Music*)
1964 *Cerný Petr* (UK: *Peter And Pavla*)
1965 *Lásky Jedné Plavovlásky* (UK: *A Blonde In Love*)
1967 *Horí, Má Panenko* (UK: *The Fireman's Ball*)
1971 *Taking Off*
1973 *Visions Of Eight* (documentary, co-director)
1975 *One Flew Over The Cuckoo's Nest**
1979 *Hair*
1981 *Ragtime**
1984 *Amadeus**
1986 *Heartburn* (actor only)
1989 *New Year's Day* (actor only); *Valmont*

## FORSYTH, Bill
(1946–   ) UK

1978 *The Long Shot* (actor only)
1979 *That Sinking Feeling*
1980 *Gregory's Girl**
1981 *Andrina* (TV)
1983 *Local Hero**
1984 *Comfort And Joy*
1987 *Housekeeping*
1989 *Breaking In*
1993 *Being Human*

## FOSSE, Bob
real name: Robert Louis Fosse
(1927–1987) USA

1953 *The Affairs Of Dobie Gillis; Kiss Me Kate; Give A Girl A Break* (all actor only)
1955 *My Sister Eileen* (actor, choreographer only)
1957 *The Pajama Game* (choreographer only)
1958 *Damn Yankees* (UK: *What Lola Wants*) (actor, choreographer only)
1968 *Sweet Charity**

1972 *Cabaret**
1974 *The Little Prince* (actor only); *Lenny**
1976 *Thieves* (actor only)
1979 *All That Jazz**
1983 *Star 80*

## FRANK, T C
see **LAUGHLIN, Tom**

## FRANKENHEIMER, John
(1930–   ) USA

1957 *The Young Stranger*
1961 *The Young Savages; All Fall Down*
1962 *Birdman Of Alcatraz*; The Manchurian Candidate**
1963 *Seven Days In May**
1964 *The Train**
1966 *Seconds; Grand Prix**
1968 *The Extraordinary Seaman; The Fixer*
1969 *The Gypsy Moths*
1970 *I Walk The Line; The Horsemen*
1973 *The Impossible Object; The Iceman Cometh*
1974 *99 44/100% Dead* (UK: *Call Harry Crown*)
1975 *French Connection II*
1976 *Black Sunday*
1979 *Prophecy*
1982 *The Challenge*
1985 *The Holcroft Covenant*
1986 *52 Pick-Up*
1989 *Dead Bang*
1990 *The Fourth War*
1991 *The Year Of The Gun*

## FRANKLIN, Sidney Arnold
(1893–1972) USA

1914 *The Sheriff* (short, co-director)
1915 *Little Dick's First Case; The Baby; Little Dick's First Adventure; The Rivals; Her Filmland Hero; Pirates Bold; The Kid Magicians; The Runaways; The Little Cupids; Dirty Face Dan; A Ten Cent Adventure; The Straw Man; The Doll House Mystery* (all shorts, all co-director)

**FRANKLIN, Sidney Arnold** (cont.)

1916 *The Children In The House; The Little Schoolma'am; Let Katie Do It; Martha's Vindication; Gretchen The Greenhorn; A Sister Of Six* (all co-director)

1917 *Jack And The Beanstalk; Treasure Island; Babes In The Woods; Aladdin And His Wonderful Lamp; Going Straight* (all co-director)

1918 *Ali Baba And The 40 Thieves; Fan Fan* (both co-director); *Six Shooter Andy; The Bride Of Fear; Confession; The Safety Curtain; Her Only Way; The Forbidden City; The Heart Of Wetona*

1919 *The Probation Wife; Heart O' The Hills; The Hoodlum* (UK: *The Ragamuffin*)

1920 *Two Weeks; Unseen Forces*

1921 *Not Guilty; Courage*

1922 *Smilin' Through; East Is West; The Primitive Lover*

1923 *Brass; Dulcy; Tiger Rose*

1924 *Her Night Of Romance*

1925 *Her Sister From Paris; Learning To Love*

1926 *Beverly Of Graustark; The Duchess Of Buffalo*

1927 *Quality Street*

1928 *The Actress* (UK: *Trelawny Of The Wells*)

1929 *Devil May Care; Wild Orchids; The Last Of Mrs Cheyney*

1930 *The Lady Of Scandal* (UK: *The High Road*); *A Lady's Morals* (UK: *Jenny Lind*)

1931 *The Guardsman; Private Lives*

1932 *Smilin' Through* (remake)

1933 *Reunion In Vienna*

1934 *The Barretts Of Wimpole Street\**

1935 *The Dark Angel*

1937 *The Good Earth\** (co-director)

1939 *On Borrowed Time* (producer only)

1940 *Waterloo Bridge* (producer only)

1942 *Mrs Miniver\*; Random Harvest\** (both producer only)

1943 *Madame Curie\** (producer only)

1944 *The White Cliffs Of Dover* (producer only)

1946 *The Yearling\** (producer only)

1948 *Command Decision; Homecoming* (both producer only)

1950 *The Miniver Story* (producer only)

1953 *Young Bess; The Story Of Three Loves* (both producer only)

1957 *The Barretts Of Wimpole Street* (remake)

**FRAWLEY, James**
(1937– ) USA

1971 *The Christian Licorice Store*

1973 *Kid Blue*

1975 *Delancey Street* (TV)

1976 *The Big Bus*

1978 *The Deadly Prince Of Paradise* (TV) (UK: *Nightmare At Pendragon's Castle*)

1979 *The Muppet Movie\**

1980 *The Great American Traffic Jam* (TV)

1985 *Fraternity Vacation*

1988 *Spies, Lies And Naked Thighs* (TV)

1990 *The Secret Life Of Archie's Wife* (TV)

**FREARS, Stephen**
(1941– )

1966 *Morgan — A Suitable Case For Treatment* (assistant director)

1967 *If...; Charlie Bubbles* (both assistant director); *The Burning*

1971 *Gumshoe*

1973 *O Lucky Man!* (assistant director)

1978 *Long Shot* (actor only)

1979 *Bloody Kids* (TV)

1984 *The Hit*

1985 *My Beautiful Laundrette\**

1987 *Prick Up Your Ears\*; Sammy And Rosie Get Laid; Mr Jolly Lives Next Door*

1988 *Dangerous Liaisons\**

1990 *The Grifters\**

1992 *Hero* (UK: *Accidental Hero*)

1993 *The Snapper* (TV)

## FRIEDKIN, William
(1939– ) USA

1967 *Good Times*
1968 *The Birthday Party; The Night They Raided Minsky's*
1970 *The Boys In The Band*
1971 *The French Connection\**
1973 *The Exorcist\**
1977 *Sorcerer*
1978 *The Brinks Job*
1980 *Cruising*
1983 *The Deal Of The Century*
1985 *To Live And Die In LA*
1986 *CAT Squad* (TV) (aka *Stalking Danger*)
1987 *Rampage*
1988 *CAT Squad: Python Wolf* (TV)
1990 *The Guardian*

# G

## GARNETT, Tay
real name: William Taylor Garnett
(1895–1977) USA

1928 *Celebrity; The Spieler* (UK: *The Spellbinder*)
1929 *The Flying Fool; Oh, Yeah! (UK: No Brakes)* (co-director)
1930 *Her Man; Officer O'Brien*
1931 *Bad Company*
1932 *One Way Passage; Prestige; Okay America* (UK: *The Penalty Of Fame*)
1933 *SOS Iceberg; Destination Unknown*
1935 *China Seas; Professional Soldier; She Couldn't Take It* (UK: *Woman Tamer*)
1937 *Love Is News; Slave Ship; Stand-In*
1938 *Trade Winds; Joy Of Living*
1939 *Eternally Yours*
1940 *Slightly Honourable; Seven Sinners*
1941 *Cheers For Miss Bishop*
1942 *My Favorite Spy*
1943 *The Cross Of Lorraine; Bataan*
1944 *Mrs Parkington*

1945 *The Valley Of Decision*
1946 *The Postman Always Rings Twice\**
1947 *Wild Harvest*
1949 *A Connecticut Yankee In King Arthur's Court* (UK: *A Yankee In King Arthur's Court*)
1950 *The Fireball; Cause For Alarm!*
1951 *Soldiers Three*
1952 *One Minute To Zero*
1953 *Main Street To Broadway*
1954 *The Black Knight*
1955 *Seven Wonders Of The World* (co-director)
1960 *A Terrible Beauty* (US: *The Night Fighters*)
1963 *Cattle King* (UK: *Guns Of Wyoming*)
1970 *The Delta Factor*
1972 *Challenge To Be Free*
1973 *Timber Tramp*

## GILBERT, Lewis
(1920– ) UK

1944 *Sailors Do Care* (documentary)
1945 *The Ten Year Plan* (documentary)
1946 *Arctic Harvest; Under One Roof* (both documentaries)
1947 *Fishing Grounds Of The World* (documentary); *The Little Ballerina*
1950 *Once A Sinner*
1951 *It's A Small World; Scarlet Thread; There Is Another Sun*
1952 *Emergency Call; Cosh Boy; Time Gentlemen Please*
1953 *Johnny On The Run; Albert RN*
1954 *The Good Die Young; The Sea Shall Not Have Them*
1955 *Cast A Dark Shadow*
1956 *Reach For The Sun*
1957 *The Admirable Crichton* (US: *Paradise Lagoon*)
1958 *A Cry From The Streets; Carve Her Name With Pride*
1959 *Ferry To Hong Kong*
1960 *Sink The Bismarck! Light Up The Sky!*
1961 *The Greengage Summer* (US: *Loss Of Innocence*)

**GILBERT, Lewis** (cont.)

1962 *HMS Defiant* (US: *Damn The Defiant!)*
1964 *The Seventh Dawn*
1966 *Alfie\**
1967 *You Only Live Twice\**
1969 *The Adventurers*
1971 *Friends*
1974 *Paul And Michelle*
1975 *Operation Daybreak*
1976 *Seven Nights In Japan*
1977 *The Spy Who Loved Me\**
1979 *Moonraker\**
1983 *Educating Rita\**
1985 *Not Quite Jerusalem*
1989 *Shirley Valentine\**
1991 *Stepping Out*

**GILLIAM, Terry**
(1940–  ) USA

1971 *And Now For Something Completely Different* (co-writer, animator and performer)
1974 *Monty Python And The Holy Grail* (co-director and performer)
1976 *Jabberwocky*
1979 *Monty Python's Life Of Brian* (co-writer and performer)
1981 *Time Bandits\**
1982 *Monty Python Live At The Hollywood Bowl* (performer only)
1983 *Monty Python's Meaning Of Life* (co-writer, animator and performer)
1985 *Brazil\*; Into The Night* (performer only)
1988 *The Adventures Of Baron Munchhausen\**
1991 *The Fisher King*

**GLEN, John**
(1932–  ) UK

1981 *For Your Eyes Only\**
1983 *Octopussy\**
1985 *A View To A Kill\**
1987 *The Living Daylights\**
1989 *Licence To Kill\**
1992 *Aces: Iron Eagle III; Christopher Columbus — The Discovery*

**GLENVILLE, Peter**
(1913–  ) UK

1955 *The Prisoner*
1958 *Me And The Colonel*
1960 *Summer And Smoke*
1962 *Term Of Trial*
1964 *Becket\**
1966 *Hotel Paradiso*
1967 *The Comedians*

**GODARD, Jean-Luc**
(1930–  ) France

1954 *Opération Béton* (short)
1955 *Une Femme Coquette* (short)
1957 *Charlotte Et Véronique Ou Tous Les Garçons S'Appellent Patrick* (short)
1958 *Une Histoire D'Eau* (co-director); *Charlotte Et Son Jules* (both co-director)
1959 *A Bout De Souffle\** (UK: *Breathless*)
1960 *Le Petit Soldat* (UK: *The Little Soldier*)
1961 *Une Femme Est Une Femme; Les Sept Péchées Capitaux* (UK: *The Seven Deadly Sins*) (co-director)
1962 *Vivre Sa Vie* (UK: *It's My Life*); *RoGoPaG* (co-director)
1963 *Le Mépris* (UK: *Contempt*); *Les Carabiniers* (UK: *The Soldiers*); *Les Plus Belles Escroqueries Du Monde* (co-director)
1964 *Bande A Part* (UK *The Outsiders*); *La Femme Mariée* (UK: *A Married Woman*); *Reportage Sur Orly* (documentary); *Paris Vu Par* (UK: *Six In Paris*) (co-director)
1965 *Alphaville; Pierrot Le Fou*
1966 *Masculin–Féminin; Made In USA*
1967 *Le Plus Vieux Métier Du Monde* (UK: *The Oldest Profession*) (co-director); *Far From Vietnam* (both documentaries); *Deux Ou Trois Choses Que Je Sais D'Elle* (UK: *Two Or Three Things I Know*

About Her); *Week-End; Le Gai Savoir; La Chinoise*
1968 *Un Film Comme Les Autres; One Plus One/Sympathy For The Devil*
1969 *Amore E A Rabbia/Angelo 70* (co-director); *British Sounds; Pravda* (co-director); *Le Vent D'Est* (co-director); *Lotte In Italia* (co-director)
1970 *Jusqu'à La Victoire*
1971 *Vladimir Et Rosa* (co-director)
1972 *Tout Va Bien; A Letter To Jane*
1975 *Comment Ça Va; Ici Et Ailleurs* (both co-director); *Numero Deux*
1980 *Sauve Qui Peut La Vie*
1982 *Passion*
1983 *Prénom: Carmen*
1985 *Hail Mary; Detective*
1987 *Aria* (co-director); *Soigne Ta Droite; King Lear*
1990 *Nouvelle Vague*
1993 *Hélas Pour Moi*

## GORDON, Michael
(1909–    ) USA

1942 *Underground Agent; One Dangerous Night; Boston Blackie Goes Hollywood* (UK: *Blackie Goes Hollywood*)
1943 *Crime Doctor*
1947 *The Web*
1948 *Another Part Of The Forest; An Act Of Murder*
1949 *The Lady Gambles; Woman In Hiding*
1950 *Cyrano De Bergerac*
1951 *I Can Get It For You Wholesale* (UK: *This Is My Affair*); *The Secret Of Convict Lake*
1953 *Wherever She Goes*
1959 *Pillow Talk\**
1960 *Portrait In Black*
1962 *Boys' Night Out*
1963 *For Love Or Money; Move Over, Darling*
1965 *A Very Special Favor*
1966 *Texas, Across The River*
1968 *The Impossible Years*
1970 *How Do I Love Thee?*

## GORDON, Steve
(1938–82) USA

1978 *The One And Only* (screenwriter)
1981 *Arthur\**

## GOULDING, Edmund
(1891–1959) UK

1925 *Sun-Up; Sally, Irene And Mary*
1926 *Paris* (UK: *Shadows of Paris*)
1927 *Women Love Diamonds*
1928 *Love/Anna Karenina*
1929 *The Trespasser*
1930 *The Devil's Holiday; Paramount On Parade* (co-director)
1931 *Reaching For The Moon; The Night Angel*
1932 *Blondie Of The Follies; Grand Hotel\**
1934 *Riptide*
1935 *The Flame Within*
1937 *That Certain Woman*
1938 *White Banners; The Dawn Patrol*
1939 *Dark Victory\*; The Old Maid\*; We Are Not Alone*
1940 *'Til We Meet Again*
1941 *The Great Lie*
1943 *Forever And A Day* (co-director); *The Constant Nymph; Claudia*
1946 *Of Human Bondage; The Razor's Edge\*; The Shocking Miss Pilgrim* (part directed)
1947 *Nightmare Alley*
1949 *Everybody Does It*
1950 *Mr 880*
1952 *Down Among The Sheltering Palms; We're Not Married*
1956 *Teenage Rebel*
1958 *Mardi Gras*

## GREEN, Alfred E
(1889–1960) USA

1916 *The Temptation Of Adam*
1917 *Lost And Found; For Reward Of Service* (both shorts); *The Princess Of Patches; Little Lost Sister; The Lad And The Lion*
1918 *The Friendship Of Beaupère; Trials And Tribulations*

**GREEN, Alfred E** (cont.)

1919 *The Web Of Chance; Right After Brown*

1920 *A Double-Dyed Deceiver; Silk Husbands And Calico Wives; Just Out Of College; The Man Who Had Everything*

1921 *Little Lord Fauntleroy; Through The Back Door* (both co-director)

1922 *Our Leading Citizen; The Bachelor Daddy; The Ghost Breaker; The Man Who Saw Tomorrow; Back Home And Broke; Come On Over* (UK: *Darlin'*)

1923 *The Ne'er-Do-Well; Woman-Proof*

1924 *Pied Piper Malone; Inez From Hollywood* (UK: *The Good Bad Girl*); *In Hollywood With Potash And Perlmutter* (UK: *So This Is Hollywood*)

1925 *Sally The Talker; The Man Who Found Himself*

1926 *Irene; Ella Cinders; The Girl From Montmartre; It Must Be Love; Ladies At Play*

1927 *Two Girls Wanted; The Auctioneer; Is Zat So?: Come To My House*

1928 *Honor Bound*

1929 *Making The Grade; Disraeli*

1930 *The Green Goddess; The Man From Blankley's; Sweet Kitty Bellairs; Old English*

1931 *Smart Money; Men Of The Sky; The Road To Singapore*

1932 *The Dark Horse; Silver Dollar; It's Tough To Be Famous; The Rich Are Always With Us; Union Depot* (UK: *Gentleman For A Day*)

1933 *Parachute Jumper; The Narrow Corner; I Loved A Woman; Baby Face*

1934 *The Merry Frinks* (UK: *The Happy Family*); *Dar Hazard; Housewife; As The Earth Turns; Gentlemen Are Born; A Lost Lady; Side Streets* (UK: *Woman In Her Thirties*)

1935 *The Goose And The Gander; Sweet Music; Dangerous; The Girl From 10th Avenue* (UK: *Men On Her Mind*); *Here's To Romance*

1936 *They Met In A Taxi; Colleen; More Than A Secretary; The Golden Arrow; Two In A Crowd*

1937 *Mr Dodd Takes The Air; Let's Get Married; The League Of Frightened Men; Thoroughbreds Don't Cry*

1938 *The Duke Of West Point; Ride A Crooked Mile* (UK: *Escape From Yesterday*)

1939 *King Of The Turf; 20,000 Men A Year; The Gracie Allen Murder Case*

1940 *South Of Pago-Pago; Flowing Gold; Shooting High; East Of The River*

1941 *Badlands Of Dakota; Adventure In Washington* (UK: *Female Correspondent*)

1942 *Meet The Stewarts; The Mayor Of 44th Street*

1943 *Appointment In Berlin; There's Something About A Soldier*

1944 *Strange Affair; Mr Winkle Goes To War* (UK: *Arms And The Woman*)

1945 *A Thousand And One Nights*

1946 *Tars And Spars; The Jolson Story**

1947 *The Fabulous Dorseys; Copacabana*

1948 *The Girl From Manhattan; Four Faces West* (UK: *Thoy Passed This Way:*)

1949 *Cover-Up*

1950 *The Jackie Robinson Story; Sierra*

1951 *Two Gals And A Guy*

1952 *Invasion USA*

1953 *The Eddie Cantor Story; Paris Model*

1954 *Top Banana*

## GREENAWAY, Peter
(1942–   ) UK

1966 *Train; Tree* (shorts)

1967 *Revolution; Five Postcards From Capital Cities*

1969 *Intervals*

1971 *Erosion*

1973 *H Is For House*
1975 *Windows; Water; Water Wrackets*
1976 *Goole By Numbers*
1977 *Dear Phone*
1978 *1–100; A Walk Through H; Vertical Features Remake*
1980 *The Falls*
1981 *Act Of God; Zandra Rhodes*
1982 *The Draughtsman's Contract**
1983 *Four American Composers*
1984 *Making A Splash; A TV Dante — Canto 5*
1985 *Inside Rooms — The Bathroom; A Zed And Two Noughts*
1987 *The Belly Of An Architect*
1988 *Drowning By Numbers*
1989 *The Cook, The Thief, His Wife And Her Lover*; Death In The Seine* (short)
1991 *Prospero's Books*
1993 *The Baby Of Macon*

## GUILLERMIN, John
(1925– ) UK

1949 *Torment* (US: *Paper Gallows*)
1951 *Smart Alec; Two On The Tiles; Four Days*
1952 *Song Of Paris; Miss Robin Hood*
1953 *Operation Diplomat; Strange Stories* (co-director)
1954 *Adventure In The Hopfields; The Crowded Day*
1955 *Dust And Gold; Double Jeopardy; Thunderstorm*
1956 *Town On Trial!*
1957 *The Whole Truth*
1958 *I Was Monty's Double*
1959 *Tarzan's Greatest Adventure*
1960 *The Day They Robbed The Bank Of England; Never Let Go*
1962 *Waltz Of The Toreadors; Tarzan Goes To India*
1964 *Guns At Batasi*
1965 *Rapture*
1966 *The Blue Max*
1967 *PJ* (UK: *A New Face In Hell*)
1968 *House Of Cards*
1969 *The Bridge At Remagen*
1970 *El Condor*
1972 *Skyjacked*

1973 *Shaft In Africa*
1974 *The Towering Inferno**
1976 *King Kong**
1978 *Death On The Nile*
1980 *Mr Patman*
1983 *Crossover*
1984 *Sheena, Queen Of The Jungle*
1986 *King Kong Lives*
1988 *The Trackers* (TV)
1989 *The French Revolution*

# H

## HACKFORD, Taylor
(1944– ) USA

1978 *Teenage Father* (short)
1980 *The Idolmaker*
1982 *An Officer And A Gentleman**
1984 *Against All Odds*
1985 *White Nights*
1987 *Hail! Hail! Rock'n'Roll; La Bamba* (producer only)
1988 *Everybody's All-American* (UK: *When I Fall In Love*)
1989 *Rooftops* (executive producer only)
1990 *The Long Walk Home* (executive producer only)
1991 *Mortal Thoughts; Queen's Logic; Sweet Talker* (all executive producer only)
1992 *Blood In, Blood Out*

## HAINES, Randa
(19?– ) USA

1984 *Something About Amelia* (TV)
1986 *Children Of A Lesser God**
1990 *The Doctor*
1993 *Wrestling Ernest Hemingway*

## HALL, Alexander
(1894–1968) USA

1932 *Sinners In The Sun; Madame Racketeer* (UK: *The Sporting Widow*) (co-director)

**HALL, Alexander** (cont.)
1933 *Midnight Club; The Girl In 419; Torch Singer* (UK: *Broadway Singer*) (all co-director)
1934 *The Pursuit of Happiness; Limehouse Blues; Little Miss Marker* (UK: *Girl In Pawn*); *Miss Fane's Baby Is Stolen* (UK: *Kidnapped*) (co-director)
1935 *Goin' To Town, Annapolis Farewell* (UK: *Gentlemen Of The Navy*)
1936 *Give Us This Night; Yours For The Asking*
1937 *Exclusive*
1938 *There's Always A Woman; I Am The Law; There's That Woman Again* (UK: *What A Woman*)
1939 *Good Girls Go To Paris; The Lady's From Kentucky; The Amazing Mr Williams*
1940 *The Doctor Takes A Wife; He Stayed For Breakfast*
1941 *Bedtime Story; This Thing Called Love* (UK: *Married But Single*); *Here Comes Mr Jordan**
1942 *They All Kissed The Bride; My Sister Eileen*
1943 *The Heavenly Body*
1944 *Once Upon A Time*
1945 *She Wouldn't Say Yes*
1947 *Down To Earth*
1949 *The Great Lover*
1950 *Louisa; Love That Brute*
1951 *Up Front*
1952 *Because You're Mine*
1953 *Let's Do It Again*
1956 *Forever, Darling*

**HAMER, Robert**
(1911–63) UK

1945 *Dead Of Night* (co-director); *Pink String And Sealing Wax*
1947 *It Always Rains On Sundays*
1949 *Kind Hearts And Coronets**; *The Spider And The Fly*
1951 *His Excellency*
1952 *The Long Memory*
1954 *Father Brown*
1955 *To Paris With Love*

1959 *The Scapegoat*
1960 *School For Scoundrels*
1962 *55 Days At Peking* (screenwriter only)
1963 *A Jolly Bad Fellow* (screenwriter only)

**HAMILTON, Guy**
(1922–  ) UK

1952 *The Ringer*
1953 *The Intruder*
1954 *An Inspector Calls*
1955 *The Colditz Story*
1956 *Charley Moon*
1957 *Manuela*
1959 *The Devil's Disciple; A Touch Of Larceny*
1961 *The Best Of Enemies*
1962 *The Party's Over*
1964 *The Man In The Middle; Goldfinger**
1966 *Funeral In Berlin*
1969 *Battle Of Britain*
1971 *Diamonds Are Forever**
1973 *Live And Let Die**
1974 *The Man With The Golden Gun**
1978 *Force Ten From Navarone*
1980 *The Mirror Crack'd*
1982 *Evil Under The Sun*
1985 *Remo Williams, The Adventure Begins*
1989 *Sauf Votre Respect*

**HARVEY, Anthony**
(1931–  ) UK

1966 *Dutchman*
1968 *The Lion In Winter**
1971 *They Might Be Giants*
1973 *The Glass Menagerie* (TV)
1974 *The Abdication*
1976 *The Disappearance of Aimee* (TV)
1978 *Eagle's Wing*
1979 *Players*
1980 *Richard's Things* (TV)
1981 *An Act Of Love* (TV) (co-director)
1982 *Johnny Belinda* (TV)
1983 *Svengali* (TV)
1984 *The Ultimate Solution Of Grace Quigley*

## HATHAWAY, Henry
real name: Marquis Henri Leopold De
    Fiennes
(1898–1985)

1932  *Heritage Of The Desert; Wild
      Horse Mesa*
1933  *Under The Tonto Rim; Sunset
      Pass; Man Of The Forest; To The
      Last Man; The Thundering Herd*
1934  *The Last Round-Up; Come On
      Marines!; The Witching Hour; Now
      And Forever*
1935  *The Lives Of A Bengal Lancer\*;
      Peter Ibbetson*
1936  *Trail Of The Lonesome Pine; Go
      West, Young Man*
1937  *Souls At Sea; Lest We Forget*
1938  *Spawn Of The North*
1939  *The Real Glory*
1940  *Johnny Apollo; Brigham Young*
1941  *Sundown; The Shepherd Of The
      Hills*
1942  *Ten Gentlemen From West Point;
      China Girl*
1944  *Home In Indiana; Wing And A
      Prayer*
1945  *Nob Hill; The House On 92nd
      Street*
1946  *The Dark Corner; 13 Rue
      Madeleine*
1947  *Kiss Of Death*
1948  *Call Northside 777*
1949  *Down To The Sea In Ships*
1950  *The Black Rose; Rawhide*
1951  *You're In The Navy Now;
      Fourteen Hours; The Desert Fox*
      (UK: *Rommel—Desert Fox*)
1952  *Diplomatic Courier; O'Henry's Full
      House* (co-director)
1953  *White Witch Doctor; Niagara; The
      Coronation Parade* (short)
1954  *Prince Valiant; Garden Of Evil*
1955  *The Racers* (UK: *Such Men Are
      Dangerous*)
1956  *The Bottom Of The Bottle* (UK:
      *Beyond The River*); *23 Paces To
      Baker Street*
1957  *Legend Of The Lost*
1958  *From Hell To Texas* (UK:
      *Manhunt*)

1959  *Woman Obsessed; Seven
      Thieves*
1960  *North To Alaska*
1962  *How The West Was Won\** (co-
      director)
1964  *Circus World* (UK: *The
      Magnificent Showman*)
1965  *The Sons Of Katie Elder*
1966  *Nevada Smith*
1967  *The Last Safari*
1968  *Five Card Stud*
1969  *True Grit\**
1971  *Raid On Rommel; Shootout*
1974  *Hangup*

## HAWKS, Howard
full name: Howard Winchester Hawks
(1896–1977) USA

1926  *The Road To Glory; Fig Leaves*
1927  *Paid To Love; The Cradle
      Snatchers; Fazil*
1928  *A Girl In Every Port; The Air
      Circus* (co-director)
1929  *Trent's Last Case*
1930  *The Dawn Patrol*
1931  *The Criminal Code*
1932  *Scarface\*; The Crowd Roars;
      Tiger Shark*
1933  *Today We Live*
1934  *Twentieth Century*
1935  *Ceiling Zero; Barbary Coast*
1936  *The Road To Glory; Come And
      Get It* (co-director)
1938  *Bringing Up Baby\**
1939  *Only Angels Have Wings*
1940  *His Girl Friday\**
1941  *Sergeant York\*; Ball Of Fire\**
1943  *Air Force*
1944  *To Have And Have Not\**
1946  *The Big Sleep\**
1947  *A Song Is Born*
1948  *Red River\**
1949  *I Was A Male War Bride\**
1952  *The Big Sky; Monkey Business;
      O'Henry's Full House* (co-director)
1953  *Gentlemen Prefer Blondes\**
1955  *Land Of The Pharoahs*
1959  *Rio Bravo\**
1962  *Hatari!*
1963  *Man's Favourite Sport*

389

**HAWKS, Howard** (cont.)
1965 *Red Line 7000*
1967 *El Dorado*
1970 *Rio Lobo*


## HECKERLING, Amy
(1954– ) USA

1982 *Fast Times At Ridgemont High*
1984 *Johnny Dangerously*
1985 *National Lampoon's European Vacation; Into The Night* (actress only)
1989 *Look Who's Talking**
1990 *Look Who's Talking Too*


## HEERMAN, Victor
(1892– ) UK

1920 *Don't Ever Marry; The Poor Simp*
1921 *A Divorce Of Convenience; The Chicken In The Case*
1922 *My Boy; John Smith; Love Is An Awful Thing*
1923 *Rupert Of Hentzau; Modern Matrimony; The Dangerous Maid*
1924 *The Confidence Man*
1925 *Old Home Week; Irish Luck*
1926 *For Wives Only*
1927 *Ladies Must Dress; Rubber Heels*
1928 *Love Hungry*
1930 *Personality; Paramount On Parade; Animal Crackers*; Sea Legs*
1931 *Moonlight And Romance*
1932 *The Stolen Jools* (UK: *The Slippery Pearls*) (short)
1934 *The Little Minister* (screenwriter only)
1939 *Golden Boy* (screenwriter only)
1949 *Little Women* (screenwriter only)


## HEISLER, Stuart
(1894–1979) USA

1936 *Straight From The Shoulder*
1940 *The Biscuit Eater* (UK: *God Gave Him A Dog*)
1941 *The Monster And The Girl; Among The Living*

1942 *The Glass Key; The Remarkable Andrew*
1944 *The Negro Soldier* (documentary)
1945 *Along Came Jones*
1946 *Blue Skies**
1947 *Smash Up, The Story Of A Woman* (UK: *A Woman Destroyed*)
1949 *Tokyo Joe; Tulsa*
1950 *Dallas; Chain Lightning; Storm Warning*
1951 *Journey Into Light*
1952 *Saturday Island; The Star*
1954 *Beachhead; This Is My Love*
1955 *I Died A Thousand Times*
1956 *The Burning Hills; The Lone Ranger*
1961 *Hitler*


## HENRY, Buck
(1930– ) USA

1978 *Heaven Can Wait** (co-director)
1980 *First Family*


## HEREK, Stephen
(19?– ) USA

1986 *Critters*
1989 *Bill And Ted's Excellent Adventure**
1991 *Don't Tell Mom, The Babysitter's Dead*
1992 *The Mighty Ducks* (UK: *Champions*)


## HERZOG, Werner
real name: Werner Stipetic
(1942– ) Germany

1962 *Herakles* (short)
1964 *Spiel Im Sand* (short)
1966 *Der Beispiellose Verteidigung Der Festung Deutschkreutz* (UK: *The Unprecendented Defence Of The Fortress Deutschkreutz*) (short)
1967 *Letzte Worte* (UK: *Last Words*); *Lebenszeichen* (UK: *Signs Of Life*)

1969 *Massnahmen Gegen Fanatiker* (UK: *Measures Against Fanatics*) (documentary); *Die Fliegenden Ärtze Von Ostafrika* (UK: *The Flying Doctors Of East Africa*)
1970 *Auch Zwerge Haben Klein Angefangen* (UK: *Even Dwarfs Started Small*); *Fata Morgana*; *Behinderte Zukunft* (documentary)
1971 *Land Des Schweigens Und Der Dunkleheit* (UK: *Land Of Silence And Darkness*)
1972 *Aguirre, Der Zorn Gottes\** (UK: *Aguirre, Wrath Of God*)
1974 *Jeder Für Sich Und Gott Gegen Alle* (UK: *The Enigma Of Kasper Hauser*); *Die Grosse Ekstase Des Bildschnitzers Steiner* (UK: *The Great Ecstasy Of Woodcarver Steiner*)
1976 *How Much Wood Would A Woodchuck Chuck?*; *Mit Mir Will Keiner Spielen* (both shorts); *Herz Aus Glas* (UK: *Heart Of Glass*); *La Soufrière* (documentary)
1977 *Stroszek*
1979 *Nosferatu: Phantom Der Nacht* (UK: *Nosferatu The Vampyre*); *Woyzeck*
1980 *Glaube Und Wahrung; Huie's Predigt*
1982 *Fitzcarraldo; Burden Of Dreams* (documentary, participant only); *Chambre 666* (actor only)
1983 *Man Of Flowers* (actor only)
1984 *Wo Die Grünen Ameisen Traumen* (UK: *Where The Green Ants Dream*)
1985 *Ballade Vom Kleinen Soldaten; Gasherbrum — Der Leuchtende Berg; Tokyo-Ga* (actor only)
1987 *Cobra Verde*
1988 *Herdsmen Of The Sun; Lightning Over Braddock: A Rustbowl Fantasy* (actor only)
1989 *Gekauftes Glück; Hard To Be A God* (both actor only)
1990 *Echos Aus Einem Düsteren Reich*
1991 *Schrei Aus Stein* (UK: *Scream Of Stone*)

## HIBBS, Jesse
(1906–85) USA

1953 *The World's Most Beautiful Girls* (short); *The All-American* (UK: *The Winning Way*)
1954 *Ride Clear Of Diablo; Rails Into Laramie; Black Horse Canyon; The Yellow Mountain*
1955 *To Hell And Back\*; The Spoilers*
1956 *World In My Corner; Walk The Proud Land*
1957 *Joe Butterfly*
1958 *Ride A Crooked Trail*

## HIGGINS, Colin
(1941–88) USA

1971 *Harold And Maude* (screenwriter)
1976 *Silver Streak\** (screenwriter)
1978 *Foul Play\**
1980 *9 To 5\**
1982 *The Best Little Whorehouse In Texas\**
1985 *Into The Night* (actor only)
1987 *Out On A Limb* (TV) (co-writer only)

## HILL, George Roy
(1922– ) USA

1962 *Period Of Adjustment*
1963 *Toys In The Attic*
1964 *The World Of Henry Orient*
1966 *Hawaii*
1967 *Thoroughly Modern Millie\**
1969 *Butch Cassidy And The Sundance Kid\**
1972 *Slaughterhouse Five*
1973 *The Sting\**
1975 *The Great Waldo Pepper*
1977 *Slap Shot*
1979 *A Little Romance*
1982 *The World According To Garp*
1984 *The Little Drummer Girl*
1988 *Funny Farm*

## HILL, Walter
(1942– ) USA

1968 *The Thomas Crown Affair** (assistant director)
1969 *Take The Money And Run* (assistant director)
1972 *The Getaway; Hickey And Boggs* (both screenwriter only)
1973 *The Mackintosh Man; The Thief Who Came To Dinner* (both screenwriter only)
1975 *The Drowning Pool* (co-writer only); *Hard Times* (UK: *The Streetfighter*)
1978 *The Driver*
1979 *The Warriors; Alien** (producer only)
1980 *The Long Riders*
1981 *Southern Comfort*
1982 *48 Hrs**
1984 *Streets Of Fire*
1985 *Brewster's Millions*
1986 *Crossroads; Aliens** (executive producer only); *Blue City* (producer only)
1987 *Extreme Prejudice*
1988 *Red Heat*
1989 *Johnny Handsome*
1990 *Another 48 Hrs*
1992 *Alien 3* (producer only); *Trespass*

## HILLER, Arthur
(1923– ) Canada

1956 *Massacre At Sand Creek* (TV)
1957 *Homeward Borne* (TV); *The Careless Years*
1962 *This Rugged Land* (TV); *Miracle Of The White Stallions* (UK: *Flight Of The White Stallions*)
1963 *The Wheeler Dealers* (UK: *Separate Beds*)
1964 *The Americanization Of Emily*
1965 *Promise Her Anything*
1966 *Penelope*
1967 *Tobruk; The Tiger Makes Out*
1969 *Popi*
1970 *The Out-Of-Towners; Love Story**; *Plaza Suite; Confrontation* (short)
1971 *The Hospital*

1972 *Man Of La Mancha*
1974 *The Crazy World Of Julius Vrooder*
1975 *The Man In The Glass Booth*
1976 *W C Fields And Me; Silver Streak**
1979 *The In-Laws; Nightwing*
1981 *Making Love*
1982 *Author! Author!*
1983 *Romantic Comedy*
1984 *The Lonely Guy; Teachers*
1987 *Outrageous Fortune*
1989 *See No Evil Hear No Evil*
1990 *Taking Care Of Business*
1991 *Married To It*
1992 *The Babe*

## HITCHCOCK, Alfred Joseph
(1899–1980) UK

1922 *Number Thirteen* (uncompleted)
1923 *Always Tell Your Wife*
1926 *The Pleasure Garden; The Mountain Eagle; The Lodger*
1927 *Downhill; Easy Virtue; The Ring*
1928 *The Farmer's Wife; Champagne; The Manxman*
1929 *Blackmail**; *Juno And The Paycock*
1930 *Elstree Calling; Murder; An Elastic Affair* (short)
1931 *The Skin Game*
1932 *Rich And Strange; Number Seventeen*
1933 *Waltzes From Vienna*
1934 *The Man Who Knew Too Much*
1935 *The 39 Steps**
1936 *Secret Agent; Sabotage*
1937 *Young And Innocent*
1938 *The Lady Vanishes**
1939 *Jamaica Inn*
1940 *Rebecca**; *Foreign Correspondent**
1941 *Mr And Mrs Smith; Suspicion**
1942 *Saboteur*
1943 *Shadow Of A Doubt**
1944 *Lifeboat**; *Bon Voyage* (short); *Aventure Malgache* (short)
1945 *Spellbound**
1946 *Notorious**
1947 *The Paradine Case*
1948 *Rope*

1949 *Under Capricorn*
1950 *Stage Fright*
1951 *Strangers On A Train**
1953 *I Confess*
1954 *Dial M For Murder; Rear Window**
1955 *To Catch A Thief*; The Trouble With Harry*
1956 *The Man Who Knew Too Much; The Wrong Man*
1958 *Vertigo**
1959 *North By Northwest**
1960 *Psycho**
1963 *The Birds**
1964 *Marnie*
1966 *Torn Curtain*
1969 *Topaz*
1972 *Frenzy*
1976 *Family Plot*

## HODGES, Mike
(1932–  ) UK

1969 *Suspect* (TV)
1970 *Rumour* (TV)
1971 *Get Carter**
1972 *Pulp*
1974 *The Terminal Man*
1978 *Damien: Omen II* (screenwriter only)
1980 *Flash Gordon*
1983 *Squaring The Circle* (TV); *Missing Pieces* (TV)
1985 *Morons From Outer Space*
1986 *Florida Straits* (TV)
1987 *A Prayer For The Dying*
1989 *Black Rainbow*

## HOOPER, Tobe
(1943–  ) USA

1965 *The Heiress* (short)
1966 *Down Friday Street* (short)
1967 *A Way Of Learning* (short)
1970 *The Heisters*
1972 *Eggshells*
1974 *The Texas Chainsaw Massacre*
1976 *Eaten Alive* (UK: *Death Trap*)
1979 *Salem's Lot* (TV)
1980 *The Funhouse*
1982 *Poltergeist**
1985 *Lifeforce*

1986 *Invaders From Mars; The Texas Chainsaw Massacre 2*
1989 *Spontaneous Combustion*
1990 *I'm Dangerous Tonight* (TV)
1993 *Nightmare*

## HOPPER, Dennis
(1935–  ) USA

1969 *Easy Rider**
1971 *The Last Movie*
1980 *Out Of The Blue*
1988 *Colors**
1989 *Back Track* (UK: *Catchfire*)
1990 *The Hot Spot*

See also actors listing

## HORNE, James Wesley
(1881–1942) USA

1920 *The Third Eye*
1924 *American Manner*
1927 *College*
1929 *Liberty* (uncredited); *Big Business* (both shorts)
1931 *Chickens Come Home; Laughing Gravy; Our Wife; Come Clean; One Good Turn; Beau Hunks* (all shorts)
1932 *Any Old Port*
1935 *Thicker Than Water* (short); *Bonnie Scotland*
1936 *The Bohemian Girl* (co-director)
1937 *Way Out West**
1942 *Holt Of The Secret Service*

## HOWARD, Ron
(1954–  )

1977 *Grand Theft Auto*
1978 *Cotton Candy* (TV)
1980 *Skyward* (TV); *Leo And Loree* (executive producer only)
1981 *Through The Magic Pyramid* (TV)
1982 *Night Shift*
1984 *Splash**
1986 *Cocoon**
1986 *Gung Ho*
1987 *No Man's Land* (co-executive producer only); *Willow*

**HOWARD, Ron** (cont.)
1988  *Clean And Sober; Vibes* (both executive producer only)
1989  *The 'burbs\** (producer only); *Parenthood*
1991  *Backdraft\*; Closet Land* (executive producer only)
1992  *Far And Away*

**HOWARD, Leslie**
real name: Leslie Stainer
(1890–1943) UK

1938  *Pygmalion\** (co-director)
1941  *Pimpernel Smith*
1942  *The First Of The Few*
1943  *The Gentle Sex; The Lamp Still Burns* (producer only)

See also actors listing

**HUDSON, Hugh**
(1940–  ) UK

1977  *Fangio*
1978  *12 Squadron Buccaneers* (short); *Midnight Express\** (second-unit director)
1981  *Chariots Of Fire\**
1984  *Greystoke\**
1985  *Revolution\**
1989  *Lost Angels* (UK: *The Road Home*)

**HUGHES, Howard**
(1905–76) USA

1926  *Everybody's Acting; Swell Hogan* (both producer only)
1927  *Two Arabian Knights* (producer only)
1928  *The Mating Call; The Racket*
1930  *Hell's Angels*
1931  *The Age For Love; The Front Page* (both producer only)
1932  *Scarface\*; Sky Devils* (both producer only)
1943  *Outlaw\**
1947  *The Sin Of Harold Diddlebock* (UK: *Mad Wednesday*) (producer only)

1950  *Never A Dull Moment; Outrage; Vendetta* (all producer only)
1951  *His Kind Of Woman* (executive producer only); *Two Tickets To Broadway* (producer only)
1952  *Angel Face* (producer only)
1956  *The Conqueror* (producer only)

**HUGHES, John**
(1936–  ) USA

1982  *National Lampoon's Class Reunion* (screenwriter only)
1983  *National Lampoon's Vacation; Nate And Hayes* (UK: *Savage Islands*); *Mr Mom* (all screenwriter only)
1984  *Sixteen Candles*
1985  *The Breakfast Club; Weird Science; National Lampoon's European Vacation* (screenwriter only)
1986  *Ferris Bueller's Day Off; Pretty In Pink* (screenwriter only)
1987  *Planes, Trains And Automobiles\*; Some Kind Of Wonderful* (screenwriter only)
1988  *The Great Outdoors* (executive producer, screenwriter only); *She's Having A Baby*
1989  *National Lampoon's Christmas Vacation* (UK: *National Lampoon's Winter Holiday*) (producer, screenwriter only); *Uncle Buck*
1990  *Home Alone\** (screenwriter only)
1991  *Career Opportunities* (executive producer, screenwriter only); *Only The Lonely; Dutch* (UK: *Driving Me Crazy*) (both screenwriter only); *Curly Sue*
1992  *Home Alone 2\** (screenwriter only)
1993  *Black Cat Bone: The Return Of Huckleberry Finn; Dennis* (screenwriter, producer only)

**HUNT, Peter**
(1928–  ) UK

1969  *On Her Majesty's Secret Service\**
1974  *Gold*

1976 *Gulliver's Travels; Shout At The Devil*
1978 *The Beasts Are On The Streets* (TV); *Flying High* (TV)
1980 *Death Hunt*
1981 *Rendezvous Hotel* (TV)
1984 *The Last Days Of Pompeii* (TV)
1985 *Wild Geese II*
1986 *Hyper Sapien*
1987 *Assassination*
1990 *Desperate Hours* (supervising editor only)
1992 *Secrets* (TV)

## HUNTER, Tim
(19?– ) USA

1979 *Over The Edge* (screenwriter only)
1982 *Tex*
1985 *Sylvester*
1986 *The River's Edge**
1990 *Paint It Black*
1991 *Lies Of The Twins*
1993 *The Saint Of Fort Washington*

## HUSTON, John Marcellus
(1906–87) USA

1941 *The Maltese Falcon**
1942 *In This Our Life; Across The Pacific*
1943 *Report From The Aleutians; Tunisian Victory* (co-director)
1945 *The Battle Of San Pietro*
1946 *Let There Be Light*
1948 *On Our Merry Way* (co-director); *The Treasure Of The Sierra Madre**; *Key Largo**
1949 *We Were Strangers*
1950 *The Asphalt Jungle**
1951 *The Red Badge Of Courage**; *The African Queen**
1952 *Moulin Rouge**
1953 *Beat The Devil*
1956 *Moby Dick*
1957 *Heaven Knows Mr Allison*
1958 *The Barbarian And The Geisha; The Roots Of Heaven*
1960 *The Unforgiven; The Misfits**
1962 *Freud*

1963 *The List Of Adrian Messenger*
1964 *The Night Of The Iguana**
1966 *The Bible...In The Beginning**
1967 *Casino Royale* (co-director); *Reflections In A Golden Eye*
1969 *Sinful Davey; A Walk With Love And Death*
1970 *The Kremlin Letter*
1972 *Fat City; The Life And Times Of Judge Roy Bean*
1973 *The Mackintosh Man*
1975 *The Man Who Would Be King**
1976 *Independence* (short)
1979 *Wise Blood*
1980 *Phobia*
1981 *Escape To Victory*
1982 *Annie**
1984 *Under The Volcano*
1985 *Prizzi's Honor**
1987 *The Dead*
1988 *Mr North* (executive producer, screenwriter only)

## HUTTON, Brian G
(1935– ) USA

1964 *Wild Seed* (UK: *Fargo*)
1966 *The Pad (And How To Use It)*
1967 *Sol Madrid* (UK: *The Heroin Gang*)
1968 *Where Eagles Dare**
1970 *Kelly's Heroes*
1971 *Zee & Co*
1973 *Night Watch*
1980 *The First Deadly Sin*
1983 *High Road To China*

# I

## IVORY, James
(1928– ) USA

1957 *Venice: Themes And Variations* (documentary)
1959 *The Sword And The Flute*
1963 *The Householder*
1964 *The Delhi Way*
1965 *Shakespeare Wallah*
1968 *The Guru*
1970 *Bombay Talkie*

**IVORY, James** (cont.)
1971 *Adventures Of A Brown Man In Search Of Civilisation*
1972 *Savages*
1974 *The Wild Party*
1975 *Autobiography Of A Princess*
1977 *Roseland*
1979 *Hullabaloo Over Georgie And Bonnie's Pictures; The Europeans*
1980 *Jane Austen In Manhattan*
1981 *Quartet*
1982 *Courtesans Of Bombay*
1983 *Heat And Dust*
1984 *The Bostonians*
1985 *A Room With A View\**
1987 *Maurice*
1989 *Slaves Of New York*
1990 *Mr And Mrs Bridge*
1992 *Howard's End\**
1993 *Remains Of The Day*

# J

## JARMAN, Derek
(1942– ) UK

1971 *The Devils* (set designer only); *Studio Bankside; Miss Gaby; A Journey To Avebury* (all shorts)
1972 *Savage Messiah* (set designer only); *Broken English; Garden Of Luxor; Andrew Logan Kisses The Glitterati; Tarot* (all shorts)
1973 *The Art Of Mirrors; Building The Pyramids*
1975 *Ula's Fête; Picnic At Ray's; Sebastiane Wrap* (all shorts)
1976 *Gerald's Film; Sloane Square; A Room Of One's Own; Houston Texas* (all shorts); *Sebastiane\**
1977 *Jordan's Dance; Every Woman For Herself And All For Art* (both shorts); *Jubilee*
1978 *Nighthawks* (actor only)
1979 *The Tempest*
1981 *T G—Psychic Rally In Heaven* (short)
1982 *The Dream Machine; Waiting For Waiting For Godot* (both shorts)
1984 *Imagining October* (short)

1985 *Angelic Conversations*
1986 *Caravaggio*
1987 *Prick Up Your Ears\*; Ostia* (both actor only); *Aria* (co-director); *The Last Of England*
1988 *Cactus Land; Derek Jarman: You Know What I Mean* (both actor only); *War Requiem*
1990 *The Garden*
1991 *Edward II\**
1993 *Wittgenstein*

## JARROTT, Charles
(1927– ) UK

1962 *Time To Remember*
1969 *Anne Of The Thousand Days\**
1972 *Mary, Queen Of Scots*
1973 *Lost Horizon*
1974 *The Dove*
1976 *Escape From The Dark*
1977 *The Other Side Of Midnight*
1980 *The Last Flight Of Noah's Ark; Condorman*
1982 *The Amateur*
1986 *The Boy In Blue*
1987 *Poor Little Rich Girl: The Barbara Hutton Story* (TV)
1990 *Night Of The Fox* (TV)
1991 *Changes* (TV)

## JEFFRIES, Lionel
(1926– ) UK

1970 *The Railway Children\**
1972 *The Amazing Mr Blunden; Baxter*
1978 *The Water Babies; Wombling Free*

## JEWISON, Norman
(1926– ) Canada

1962 *Forty Pounds Of Trouble*
1963 *The Thrill Of It All*
1964 *Send Me No Flowers*
1965 *The Art Of Love; The Cincinnati Kid\**
1966 *The Russians Are Coming, The Russians Are Coming\**
1967 *In The Heat Of The Night\**
1968 *The Thomas Crown Affair\**

1969 *Gaily, Gaily*
1970 *The Landlord* (producer only)
1971 *Fiddler On The Roof*
1973 *Jesus Christ Superstar; Billy Two-Hats* (co-producer)
1975 *Rollerball*
1978 *FIST*
1979 *And Justice For All*
1980 *The Dogs Of War* (executive producer)
1982 *Best Friends*
1984 *A Soldier's Story; Iceman* (producer)
1985 *Agnes Of God**
1987 *Moonstruck**
1989 *In Country*
1991 *Other People's Money*

## JOFFE, Roland
(1945– ) UK

1984 *The Killing Fields**
1986 *The Mission*
1989 *Fat Man And Little Boy* (UK: *The Shadowmakers*)
1992 *City Of Joy*
1993 *The Super Mario Brothers* (producer only)

## JOHNSTON, Joe
(1950– ) USA

1989 *Honey I Blew Up the Kids*
1991 *The Rocketeer*
1993 *The Pagemaster*

## JONES, Terry
(1942– ) UK

1970 *And Now For Something Completely Different* (co-writer and performer only)
1974 *Monty Python And The Holy Grail* (co-director)
1976 *Pleasure At Her Majesty's; Jabberwocky* (both performer only)
1979 *Monty Python's Life Of Brian; The Secret Policeman's Ball* (performer only)

1982 *Monty Python Live At The Hollywood Bowl* (performer only)
1983 *Monty Python's Meaning Of Life*
1986 *Labyrinth* (screenwriter only)
1987 *Personal Services**
1989 *Erik The Viking*

## JORDAN, Neil
(1950– ) Ireland

1982 *Angel*
1984 *Company Of Wolves*
1986 *Mona Lisa**
1988 *High Spirits*
1989 *We're No Angels*
1991 *The Miracle*
1992 *The Crying Game**

# K

## KAPLAN, Jonathan
(1947– ) USA

1973 *The Slams; The Student Teachers*
1974 *Night Call Nurses; Truck Turner*
1975 *White Line Fever*
1976 *Cannonball; Hollywood Boulevard* (both actor only)
1977 *Mr Billion*
1979 *Over The Edge*
1981 *The Gentleman Bandit* (TV)
1982 *Heart Like A Wheel*
1983 *Girls Of The White Orchid* (TV) (aka *Death Ride To Osaka*)
1987 *Project X*
1988 *The Accused**
1989 *Immediate Family*
1991 *Love Field*
1992 *Unlawful Entry*

## KASDAN, Lawrence
(1949– ) USA

1980 *The Empire Strikes Back** (screenwriter only)
1981 *Continental Divide; Raiders Of The Lost Ark** (both screenwriter only); *Body Heat**
1983 *The Return Of The Jedi** (screenwriter only); *The Big Chill**

**KASDAN, Lawrence** (cont.)
1985 *Into The Night* (actor only);
*Silverado**
1987 *Cross My Heart* (producer only)
1988 *The Accidental Tourist**
1989 *Immediate Family* (executive
producer only)
1990 *I Love You To Death*
1991 *Grand Canyon*
1992 *The Bodyguard* (producer and
screenwriter only)

**KAUFMAN, Philip**
(1936– ) USA

1965 *Goldstein*
1969 *Fearless Frank*
1972 *The Great Northfield Minnesota
Raid*
1974 *The White Dawn*
1976 *The Outlaw Josey Wales**
(screenwriter only)
1978 *The Invasion Of The
Bodysnatchers*
1979 *The Wanderers*
1981 *Raiders Of The Lost Ark**
(screenwriter only)
1983 *The Right Stuff**
1988 *The Unbearable Lightness Of
Being*
1990 *Henry And June*
1993 *The Rising Sun*

**KAZAN, Elia**
real name: Elia Kazanjoglou
(1909– ) USA

1934 *Pie In The Sky* (actor only)
1937 *People Of The Cumberland*
(documentary)
1940 *City For Conquest* (actor only)
1941 *Blues In The Night* (actor only);
*It's Up To You* (documentary)
1945 *A Tree Grows In Brooklyn*
1946 *The Sea Of Grass*
1947 *Boomerang; Gentleman's
Agreement**
1949 *Pinky*
1950 *Panic In The Streets*
1951 *A Streetcar Named Desire**
1952 *Viva Zapata!*

1953 *Man On A Tightrope*
1954 *On The Waterfront**
1955 *East Of Eden**
1956 *Baby Doll*
1957 *A Face In The Crowd*
1960 *Wild River*
1961 *Splendor In The Grass*
1963 *America, America* (UK: *The
Anatolian Smile*)
1969 *The Arrangement*
1972 *The Visitors*
1976 *The Last Tycoon*

**KEIGHLEY, William**
(1889–1984) USA

1932 *The Match King* (co-director)
1933 *Easy To Love; Ladies They Talk
About* (co-director)
1934 *Journal Of A Crime; Dr Monica;
Big-Hearted Herbert; Kansas City
Princess; Babbitt*
1935 *G-Men; Special Agent; Stars Over
Broadway; Mary Jane's Place*
(UK: *Wanderlust*); *The Right To
Live* (UK: *The Sacred Flame*)
1936 *The Singing Kid; Bullets Or
Ballots; Green Pastures* (co-
director)
1937 *God's Country And The Woman;
The Prince And The Pauper;
Varsity Show*
1938 *Brother Rat; Valley Of The Giants;
Secrets Of An Actress; The
Adventures Of Robin Hood** (co-
director)
1939 *Yes, My Darling Daughter; Each
Dawn I Die*
1940 *The Fighting 69th; Torrid Zone;
No Time For Comedy*
1941 *Four Mothers; The Bride Came
COD; The Man Who Came To
Dinner*
1942 *George Washington Slept Here*
1944 *The Target For Today*
(documentary)
1947 *Honeymoon*
1948 *The Street With No Name*
1950 *Rocky Mountain*
1951 *Close To My Heart*
1953 *The Master Of Ballantrae*

## KELLOGG, Ray
(1906–76) USA

1959 *My Dog Buddy*
1963 *Cleopatra\** (second-unit director)
1964 *Cheyenne Autumn* (second-unit director)
1966 *Batman* (second-unit director)
1967 *Way, Way Out; Hombre* (both second-unit director)
1968 *The Green Berets\** (co-director)
1969 *Castle Keep* (second-unit director)
1970 *Tora! Tora! Tora!* (second-unit director)

A second-unit specialist, the above is a selective list of credits.

## KELLY, Gene
(1912–  ) USA

1949 *On The Town\** (co-director)
1952 *Singin' In The Rain\** (co-director)
1956 *Invitation To The Dance*
1957 *The Happy Road*
1958 *The Tunnel Of Love*
1962 *Gigot*
1967 *A Guide For The Married Man*
1969 *Hello Dolly!\**
1970 *The Cheyenne Social Club*
1976 *That's Entertainment Part Two*

See also actors listing

## KERSHNER, Irvin
(1923–  ) USA

1958 *Stakeout On Dope Street*
1959 *The Young Captives*
1961 *The Hoodlum Priest*
1963 *A Face In The Rain*
1964 *The Luck Of Ginger Coffey*
1966 *A Fine Madness*
1967 *The Flim Flam Man* (UK: *One Born Every Minute*)
1970 *Loving*
1972 *Up The Sandbox*
1974 *S\*P\*Y\*S*
1976 *The Return Of A Man Called Horse; Raid On Entebbe* (TV)
1978 *Eyes Of Laura Mars*
1980 *The Empire Strikes Back\**

1983 *Never Say Never Again\**
1988 *Wildfire* (executive producer only)
1990 *Robocop 2*

## KING, Henry
(1888–1982) USA

1915 *The Brand Of Man; Who Pays*
1916 *Little Mary Sunshine; The Oath Of Hate; The Sand Lark; Shadows And Sunshine; Joy And The Dragon*
1917 *Vengeance Of The Dead; Told At Twilight; Twin Kiddies; Souls In Pawn; The Unafraid; The Climber; Sunshine And Gold; The Bride's Silence; The Upper-Crust; The Mainspring; Scepter Of Suspicion; Southern Pride; A Game Of Wits; The Mate Of The Sally Ann*
1918 *Beauty And The Rogue; Mademoiselle Tiptoes; King Social Briars; The Locked Heart; Up Romance Road; The Ghost Of Rosy Taylor; Powers That Pray; Hearts Or Diamonds; All The World To Nothing; Hobbs In A Hurry; When A Man Rides Alone*
1919 *Some Liar; Brass Buttons; Where The West Begins; A Sporting Chance; Six Feet Four; This Hero Stuff; A Fugitive From Matrimony; Haunting Shadows; 23½ Hours Leave*
1920 *The White Dove; Uncharted Channels; One Hour Before Dawn; Dice Of Destiny; Help Wanted — Male*
1921 *Mistress Of Shenstone; When We Were 21; Salvage; Sting Of The Lash; Tol'able David*
1922 *The Seventh Day; The Bond Boy; Sonny; Fury*
1923 *The White Sister*
1924 *Romola*
1925 *Any Woman; Sackcloth And Scarlet; Stella Dallas*
1926 *Partners Again; The Winning Of Barbara Worth*
1927 *The Magic Flame*

**KING, Henry** (cont.)

1928 *The Woman Disputed* (co-director)
1929 *She Goes To War; Hell Harbor*
1930 *The Eyes Of The World; Lightnin'*
1931 *Merely Mary Ann; Over The Hill*
1932 *The Woman In Room 13*
1933 *State Fair; I Loved You Wednesday* (co-director)
1934 *Marie Galante; Carolina* (UK: *The House Of Connelly*)
1935 *One More Spring; Way Down East*
1936 *The Country Doctor; Ramona; Lloyds Of London*
1937 *Seventh Heaven*
1938 *Alexander's Ragtime Band\*; In Old Chicago\**
1939 *Jesse James\*; Stanley And Livingstone*
1940 *Little Old New York; Maryland; Chad Hanna*
1941 *Remember The Day; A Yank In The RAF*
1942 *The Black Swan*
1943 *The Song Of Bernadette\**
1944 *Wilson\**
1945 *A Bell For Adano*
1946 *Margie*
1947 *Captain From Castile*
1948 *Deep Waters*
1949 *Prince Of Foxes; Twelve O'Clock High\**
1950 *The Gunfighter*
1951 *I'd Climb The Highest Mountain; David And Bathsheba*
1952 *The Snows Of Kilimanjaro\*; O'Henry's Full House* (co-director); *Wait 'Til The Sun Shines Nellie*
1953 *King Of The Khyber Rifles*
1955 *Untamed; Love Is A Many Splendored Thing\**
1956 *Carousel*
1957 *The Sun Also Rises*
1958 *The Bravados*
1959 *This Earth Is Mine; Beloved Infidel*
1961 *Tender Is The Night*

**KLEISER, Randal**
(1946–  ) USA

1976 *Street People* (screenwriter only)
1978 *Grease\**
1980 *The Blue Lagoon\**
1981 *Rich And Famous* (actor only)
1982 *Summer Lovers*
1984 *Grandview USA*
1986 *Flight Of The Navigator*
1987 *North Shore* (executive producer only)
1988 *Big Top Pee-Wee*
1989 *Getting It Right*
1991 *White Fang; Return To The Blue Lagoon* (executive producer only)
1992 *Honey I Blew Up The Baby*

**KLOVES, Steve**
(1962–  ) USA

1989 *The Fabulous Baker Boys\**
1993 *Flesh And Bone*

**KORDA, Alexander**
real name: Sándor Kellner
(1893–1956) Hungary

1914 *A Bescapott Ùjságíró* (UK: *The Duped Journalist*); *Tutyu And Toto; Örhaz A Karpatokban* (UK: *Watchtower In The Carpathians*) (co-director)
1915 *Lyon Lea* (co-director); *A Tiszti Kardbojt* (UK: *The Officer's Sword*)
1916 *White Nights; A Nagymama* (UK: *The Grandmother*); *Mesék Az Írógépröl* (UK: *Typewriter Tales*); *A Ktszívü Férfi* (UK: *The Man With Two Hearts*); *As Egymillió Fontos Bankó* (UK: *The Million Pound Note*); *Ciklámen; Vergödö Szívek* (UK: *Fighting Hearts*); *A Nevetö Szaszkia* (UK: *Laughing Saskia*; *Mágnás Miska* (UK: *Miska The Great*)
1917 *Szent Péter Esernyöje* (UK: *St Peter's Umbrella*); *A Gólyakalifa* (UK: *The Stork Caliph*); *Mágia* (UK: *Magic*); *Harrison And Barrison*

1918 *Faun; Az Aranyember* (UK: *The Man With The Golden Touch*); *Mary Ann*
1919 *Ave Caesar!; Fehér Rósza* (UK: *The White Rose*); *Yamata; Se Ki, Se Be* (UK: *Not In, Or Out*); *Number III*
1920 *Seine Majestät Das Berrelkind* (UK: *The Prince And The Pauper*)
1921 *Heeren Der Neere* (UK: *Masters Of The Sea*)
1922 *Eine Versunkene Welt* (UK: *Vanished World*); *Samson And Delilah*
1923 *Das Unbekannte Morgen* (UK: *The Unknown Tomorrow*)
1924 *Jedermanns Frau* (UK: *Everybody's Woman*); *Tragödie Im Haus Hapsburg* (UK: *Mayerling*)
1925 *Der Tanzer Meiner Frau* (UK: *Dancing Mad*)
1926 *Madame Wünscht Keine Kinder* (UK: *Madame Wants No Children*)
1927 *Eine Dubarry Von Heute* (UK: *A Modern Dubarry*)
1928 *Yellow Lily; Night Watch*
1929 *Love And The Devil; The Squall; Her Private Life; Lilies Of The Field*
1930 *Women Everywhere; The Princess And The Plumber*
1931 *Rive Gauche* (aka *Die Männer Um Lucie*); *Marius; Service For Ladies*
1932 *Wedding Rehearsal*
1933 *The Girl From Maxim's; The Private Life Of Henry VIII**
1934 *The Private Life Of Don Juan*
1936 *Rembrandt*
1941 *That Hamilton Woman* (UK: *Lady Hamilton*)
1945 *Perfect Strangers*
1947 *An Ideal Husband*

1933 *Das Hässliche Mädchen; Peter*
1934 *Kleine Mutti/Little Mother*
1935 *Katharina Die Letzte/Catherine The Last; Das Tagebuch Der Geliebten/Marie Baschkirtzeff*
1936 *Three Smart Girls**
1937 *100 Men And A Girl**
1938 *The Rage Of Paris*
1939 *Three Smart Girls Grow Up; First Love*
1940 *Spring Parade*
1941 *It Started With Eve*
1942 *Between Us Girls*
1944 *Music For Millions*
1946 *Two Sisters From Boston*
1947 *The Unfinished Dance; The Bishop's Wife**
1948 *The Luck Of The Irish*
1949 *The Inspector General; Come To The Stable*
1950 *Wabash Avenue; Harvey*; My Blue Heaven*
1951 *Elopement; No Highway* (UK: *No Highway In The Sky*); *Mr Belvedere Rings The Bell*
1952 *My Cousin Rachel; O'Henry's Full House* (co-director); *Stars And Stripes Forever* (UK: *Marching Along*)
1953 *The Robe**
1954 *Desirée*
1955 *A Man Called Peter; The Virgin Queen; Good Morning Miss Dove*
1956 *The Power And The Prize; D-Day The Sixth Of June*
1957 *My Man Godfrey*
1958 *Fraulein*
1959 *The Naked Maja*
1960 *The Story Of Ruth*
1961 *Flower Drum Song*
1962 *Mr Hobbs Takes A Vacation*
1963 *Take Her She's Mine*
1965 *Dear Brigitte*
1966 *The Singing Nun*

## KOSTER, Henry
real name: Hermann Kosterlitz
(1905–88) Germany

1932 *Das Abenteuer Der Thea Roland* (UK: *Thea Roland*)

## KOTCHEFF, Ted
real name: William Theodore Kotcheff
(1931– ) Canada

1962 *Tiara Tahiti*
1965 *Life At The Top*

**KOTCHEFF, Ted** (cont.)

1968 *Two Gentlemen Sharing*
1970 *Outback*
1973 *Billy Two Hats*
1974 *The Apprenticeship Of Duddy Kravitz*
1976 *Fun With Dick And Jane*
1978 *Who Is Killing The Great Chefs Of Europe?* (UK: *Too Many Chefs*)
1979 *North Dallas Forty*
1981 *Split Image*
1982 *First Blood**
1983 *Uncommon Valor*
1985 *Joshua Then And Now*
1986 *The Check Is In The Mail* (producer only)
1988 *Switching Channels*
1989 *Weekend At Bernie's; Winter People*
1992 *Folks*


**KRAMER, Stanley Earl**
(1913– ) USA

1948 *So This Is New York* (producer only)
1949 *Champion; Home Of The Brave* (producer only)
1950 *The Men; Cyrano De Bergerac* (both producer only)
1952 *Death Of A Salesman; My Six Convicts; The Sniper; High Noon**; The Happy Time; The Four Poster; Eight Iron Men; The Member Of The Wedding* (all producer only)
1953 *The Juggler; The Five Thousand Fingers Of Dr T; The Wild One** (all producer only)
1954 *The Caine Mutiny** (producer only)
1955 *Not As A Stranger**
1957 *The Pride And The Passion*
1958 *The Defiant Ones**
1959 *On The Beach*
1960 *Inherit The Wind*
1961 *Judgement At Nuremberg**
1962 *Pressure Point; A Child Is Waiting* (both producer only)
1963 *It's A Mad, Mad, Mad, Mad World**

1964 *Invitation To A Gunfighter* (producer only)
1965 *Ship Of Fools**
1967 *Guess Who's Coming To Dinner**
1969 *The Secret Of Santa Vittoria*
1970 *RPM*
1971 *Bless The Beasts And Children*
1973 *Oklahoma Crude*
1977 *The Domino Principle* (UK: *The Domino Killings*)
1979 *The Runner Stumbles*


**KUBRICK, Stanley**
(1928– ) USA

1951 *Day Of The Fight; Flying Padre* (both documentaries)
1953 *The Seafarers* (documentary); *Fear And Desire*
1955 *Killer's Kiss*
1956 *The Killing**
1957 *Paths Of Glory**
1960 *Spartacus**
1962 *Lolita**
1964 *Dr Strangelove, Or How I Learned To Stop Worrying And Love The Bomb**
1968 *2001: A Space Odyssey**
1971 *A Clockwork Orange**
1975 *Barry Lyndon**
1980 *The Shining**
1987 *Full Metal Jacket**


**KUROSAWA, Akira**
(1910– ) Japan

1943 *Sugata Sanshiro* (UK: *Judo Saga*)
1944 *Ichiban Utsukushiku* (UK: *The Most Beautiful*); *Zoku Sugata Sanshiro* (UK: *Judo Saga II*)
1945 *Tora-No-O O Fumu Otokotachi* (UK: *They Who Tread On The Tiger's Tail*)
1946 *Asu O Tsukuru Hitobito* (UK: *Those Who Make Tomorrow*); *Waga Seishu Ni Kui Nashi* (UK: *No Regrets For Lost Youth*)
1947 *Subarashki Nichiyobi* (UK: *Wonderful Sunday*)
1948 *Yoidore Tenshi* (UK: *Drunken Angel*)

1949 *Shizukanaru Ketto* (UK: *The Silent Duel*)
1950 *Skyanduru* (UK: *Scandal*); *Rashomon**
1951 *Hakuchi* (UK: *The Idiot*)
1952 *Ikiru* (UK: *Living*)
1954 *Shichinin No Samurai** (UK: *Seven Samurai*)
1955 *Ikomono No Kioku* (UK: *I Live In Fear*)
1957 *Kumonosu-Jo** (UK: *Throne Of Blood*); *Donzoko* (UK: *The Lower Depths*)
1958 *Kakushi Toride No San-Akunin* (UK: *The Hidden Fortress*)
1960 *Warui Yatsu Hodo Yoku Nemuru*
1961 *Yojimbo*
1962 *Sanjuro*
1963 *Tengoku To Jigoku* (UK: *High And Low*)
1965 *Akahige* (UK: *Red Beard*)
1970 *Dodes'Ka-Den*
1975 *Dersu Uzala*
1980 *Kagemusha**
1985 *Ran**
1990 *Akira Kurosawa's Dreams*
1991 *Hachingatsu-No-Kyoshikoyku* (UK: *Rhapsody In August*)
1993 *Madadayo*

# L

## LA CAVA, Gregory
(1892–1952) USA

1917 *Der Kaptain's Valet; Der Kaptain Is Examined For Insurance* (both shorts)
1920 *Judge Rummy In Bear Facts* (short)
1922 *His Nibs*
1924 *Restless Wives; The New Schoolteacher*
1935 *Womanhandled*
1926 *Let's Get Married; Say It Again; So's Your Old Man*
1927 *Paradise For Two; Running Wild; The Gay Defender; Tell It To Sweeney*
1928 *Feel My Pulse; Half A Bride*

1929 *Big News; Saturday's Children*
1930 *His First Command*
1931 *Smart Woman; Laugh And Get Rich*
1932 *The Age Of Consent; The Half-Naked Truth; Symphony Of Six Million* (UK: *Melody Of Life*)
1933 *Gabriel Over The White House; Bed Of Roses; Gallant Lady*
1934 *The Affairs Of Cellini; What Every Woman Knows*
1935 *Private Worlds; She Married Her Boss*
1936 *My Man Godfrey*
1937 *Stage Door**
1939 *Fifth Avenue Girl*
1940 *Primrose Path*
1941 *Unfinished Business*
1942 *Lady In A Jam*
1947 *Living In A Big Way*

## LANDIS, John
(1950–   ) USA

1972 *Schlock*
1973 *Battle For The Planet Of The Apes* (actor only)
1975 *Death Race 2000* (actor only)
1977 *Kentucky Fried Movie*
1978 *National Lampoon's Animal House**
1979 *1941** (actor only)
1980 *The Blues Brothers**
1981 *An American Werewolf In London**
1983 *Trading Places*; The Twilight Zone* (co-director)
1984 *The Muppets Take Manhattan* (actor only)
1985 *Into the Night; Spies Like Us*
1986 *Three Amigos*
1987 *Amazon Women On The Moon* (co-director)
1988 *Coming To America**
1989 *Spontaneous Combination* (TV) (actor only)
1990 *Psycho IV* (TV); *Darkman* (both actor only)
1991 *Oscar*
1992 *Sleepwalkers* (actor only); *Innocent Blood*

**LANG, Fritz**
(1890–1976) Germany

1919 *Halbblut* (UK: *The Half-Breed*);
*Die Spinnen I: Der Goldene See;
Harakiri*
1920 *Die Spinnen II: Das Brillianten
Schiff; Das Wandernde Bild; Vier
Um Die Frau*
1921 *Der Müde Tod* (UK: *Destiny*)
1922 *Dr Mabuse, Der Spieler I: Ein Bild
Der Zeit; Dr Mabuse Der Spieler
II: Inferno*
1923 *Die Nibelungen I: Siegfrieds Tod;
Die Nibelungen II: Kriemhilds
Rache*
1926 *Metropolis*
1927 *Spione* (UK: *The Spy*)
1928 *Frau Im Mond* (UK: *The Girl In
The Moon*)
1931 *M\**
1932 *Das Testament Von Dr Mabuse*
(UK: *The Testament Of Dr
Mabuse*)
1933 *Liliom*
1936 *Fury*
1937 *You Only Live Once*
1938 *You And Me*
1940 *The Return Of Frank James*
1941 *Western Union; Man Hunt*
1943 *Hangmen Also Die*
1944 *Ministry Of Fear; The Woman In
The Window*
1945 *Scarlet Street*
1946 *Cloak And Dagger*
1948 *The Secret Beyond The Door*
1949 *House By The River*
1950 *An American Guerilla In The
Philippines* (UK: *I Shall Return*)
1952 *Rancho Notorious; Clash By Night*
1953 *The Blue Gardenia; The Big Heat\**
1954 *Human Desire*
1955 *Moonfleet; While The City Sleeps*
1956 *Beyond A Reasonable Doubt*
1958 *Der Tiger Von Eschnapur* (UK:
*The Tiger Of Bengal*); *Das
Indische Grabmal* (UK: *The Indian
Tomb*)
1960 *Die Tausend Augen Des Dr
Mabuse* (UK: *The Thousand Eyes
Of Dr Mabuse*)

1963 *Le Mépris* (UK: *Contempt*) (actor
only)

**LANG, Walter**
(1896–1972)

1925 *The Red Kimono*
1926 *The Carnival Girl; The Golden
Web; The Earth Woman; Money
To Burn*
1927 *By Whose Hand?; The College
Hero; Sally In Our Alley; The Satin
Woman; The Ladybird*
1928 *The Desert Bride; The Night Flyer;
Shadows Of The Past*
1929 *The Spirit Of Youth; Brothers* (UK:
*Two Sons*)
1930 *The Big Fight; Hello Sister; Cock
O' The Walk* (co-director); *The
Costello Case* (UK: *The Costello
Murder Case*)
1931 *Command Performance; Hell
Bound; Women Go On Forever*
1932 *No More Orchids*
1933 *The Warrior's Husband; Meet The
Baron*
1934 *The Mighty Barnum; The Party's
Over; When The Gods Destroy*
1935 *Hooray For Love; Carnival* (UK:
*Carnival Nights*)
1936 *Love Before Breakfast*
1937 *Wife, Doctor And Nurse; Second
Honeymoon*
1938 *The Baroness And The Butler; I'll
Give A Million*
1939 *The Little Princess*
1940 *Star Dust; The Bluebird; The
Great Profile; Tin Pan Alley*
1941 *Moon Over Miami; Week-End In
Havana*
1942 *Song Of The Islands; The
Magnificent Dope*
1943 *Coney Island*
1944 *Greenwich Village*
1945 *State Fair*
1946 *Sentimental Journey; Claudia And
David*
1947 *Mother Wore Tights*
1948 *Sitting Pretty; When My Baby
Smiles At Me*

1949 *You're My Everything*
1950 *Cheaper By The Dozen\*; The Jackpot*
1951 *On The Riviera*
1952 *With A Song In My Heart*
1953 *Call Me Madam*
1954 *There's No Business Like Showbusiness*
1956 *The King And I\**
1957 *The Desk Set* (UK: *His Other Woman*)
1959 *But Not For Me*
1960 *Can-Can; The Marriage Go-Round*
1961 *Snow White And The Three Stooges* (UK: *Snow White And The Three Clowns*)

## LAUGHTON, Charles
(1899–1962) UK

1955 *The Night Of The Hunter\**

See also actors listing

## LAUGHLIN, Tom
(1938– ) USA

1967 *Born Losers* (as T C Frank)
1971 *Billy Jack\** (as T C Frank)
1974 *The Trial Of Billy Jack*
1977 *Billy Jack Goes To Washington*

## LAUNDER, Frank
(1907– ) UK

1942 *Partners In Crime* (short, co-director)
1943 *Millions Like Us* (co-director)
1944 *2,000 Women*
1946 *I See A Dark Stranger*
1947 *Captain Boycott*
1948 *The Blue Lagoon*
1950 *The Happiest Days Of Your Life*
1951 *Lady Godiva Rides Again*
1952 *Folly To Be Wise*
1954 *The Belles Of St Trinians\**
1956 *Geordie*
1958 *Blue Murder At St Trinians*
1959 *The Bridal Path*
1960 *The Pure Hell Of St Trinians*
1965 *Joey Boy*

1966 *The Great St Trinians Train Robbery*
1980 *The Wildcats Of St Trinians*

## LEAN, David
(1908–91) UK

1942 *In Which We Serve\** (co-director)
1944 *This Happy Breed*
1945 *Blithe Spirit\*; Brief Encounter\**
1946 *Great Expectations\**
1948 *Oliver Twist\*; The Passionate Friends*
1950 *Madeleine*
1952 *The Sound Barrier*
1954 *Hobson's Choice*
1955 *Summer Madness*
1957 *The Bridge On The River Kwai\**
1962 *Lawrence Of Arabia\**
1965 *Doctor Zhivago\**
1970 *Ryan's Daughter\**
1984 *A Passage To India\**

## LEE, Spike
real name: Shelton Lee
(1956– ) USA

1977 *Last Hustle In Brooklyn* (short)
1980 *The Answer* (short)
1981 *Sarah* (short)
1982 *Joe's Bed-Stuy Barbershop: We Cut Heads* (short)
1986 *She's Gotta Have It\**
1988 *School Daze*
1989 *Do The Right Thing\**
1990 *Mo' Better Blues*
1991 *Jungle Fever\**
1992 *Malcolm X\**

## LEHMANN, Michael
(19?– ) USA

1989 *Heathers\**
1990 *Meet The Applegates*
1991 *Hudson Hawk*

## LEIGH, Mike
(1943– ) UK

1971 *Bleak Moments*
1983 *Meantime*
1984 *Four Days In July*

**LEIGH, Mike** (cont.)
1987 *The Short And Curlies* (short)
1988 *High Hopes\**
1991 *Life Is Sweet\**
1993 *Mike Leigh's Untitled '92*


**LEISEN, Mitchell**
(1897–1972) USA

1933 *Tonight Is Ours; The Eagle And The Hawk* (both associate director); *Cradle Song*
1934 *Death Takes A Holiday; Murder At The Vanities*
1935 *Behold My Wife; Four Hours To Kill; Hands Across The Table*
1936 *Thirteen Hours By Air; The Big Broadcast Of 1937*
1937 *Swing High, Swing Low; Easy Living*
1938 *Artists And Models Abroad* (UK: *Stranded In Paris*); *The Big Broadcast Of 1938*
1939 *Midnight*
1940 *Arise My Love; Remember The Night*
1941 *I Wanted Wings; Hold Back The Dawn\**
1942 *The Lady Is Willing; Take A Letter Darling* (UK: *The Green-Eyed Woman*)
1943 *No Time For Love*
1944 *Lady In The Dark; Frenchman's Creek; Practically Yours*
1945 *Masquerade In Mexico; Kitty*
1946 *To Each His Own*
1947 *Suddenly It's Spring; Golden Earrings*
1948 *Dream Girl*
1949 *Song Of Surrender; Bride Of Vengeance; Captain Carey USA* (UK: *After Midnight*)
1950 *No Man Of Her Own*
1951 *The Mating Season; Darling, How Could You?* (UK: *Rendezvous*)
1952 *Young Man With Ideas*
1953 *Tonight We Sing*
1955 *Bedevilled*
1957 *The Girl Most Likely*
1963 *Spree!*

**LELAND, David**
(1947– ) UK

1968 *1917* (actor only)
1970 *Julius Caesar; One Brief Summer* (both actor only)
1980 *Time Bandits\** (actor only)
1982 *The Missionary* (actor only)
1986 *Mona Lisa\** (screenwriter only)
1987 *Wish You Were Here\*; Personal Services\** (screenwriter only)
1989 *Checking Out*
1990 *The Big Man*


**LEONARD, Robert Z**
(1889–1968) USA

1914 *The Master Key*
1915 *A Boob's Romance; Idols Of Clay; Little Blonde In Black; Shattered Memories* (shorts); *The Silent Command; Heritage; Judge Not; The Woman Of Mona Diggins; The Crippled Hand*
1916 *The Silent Member; The Boob's Victory; The Evidence; The Silent Man Of Timber Gulch; The Winning Of Miss Construe; The Woman Who Followed Me* (all shorts); *The Eagle's Wings; Little Eva Egerton; The Plow Girl; Secret Love*
1917 *Christmas Memories; Life's Pendulum* (both shorts); *At First Sight; The Little Orphan; Princess Virtue; A Mormon Maid; The Primrose Ring; Face Value*
1918 *Her Body In Bond; The Bride's Awakening; Danger — Go Slow; Modern Love*
1919 *The Delicious Little Devil; The Big Little Person; What Am I Bid?; The Way Of A Woman; The Scarlet Shadow; Miracle Of Love; April Folly*
1920 *The Restless Sex*
1921 *The Gilded Lily; Heedless Moths; Peacock Alley*
1922 *Fascination; Broadway Rose*
1923 *Jazzmania; The French Doll; Fashion Row*

1924 *Circe The Enchantress;
Mademoiselle Midnight; Love's
Wilderness*
1925 *Cheaper To Marry; Bright Lights;
Time, The Comedian*
1926 *Dance Madness; The Waning
Sex; Mademoiselle Modiste*
1927 *A Little Journey; The Demi-Bride;
Adam And Evil; Tea For Three*
1928 *Baby Mine; The Cardboard Lover;
A Lady Of Chance*
1929 *Marianne*
1930 *In Gay Madrid; Let Us Be Gay;
The Divorcee*
1931 *The Bachelor Father; It's A Wise
Child; Susan Lenox, Her Fall And
Rise* (UK: *The Rise Of Helga*);
*Five And Ten* (UK: *Daughter Of
Luxury*)
1932 *Lovers Courageous; Strange
Interlude* (UK: *Strange Interval*)
1933 *Peg O' My Heart; Dancing Lady*
1934 *Outcast Lady* (UK: *A Woman Of
The World*)
1935 *After Office Hours; Escapade*
1936 *The Great Ziegfeld\*; Piccadilly
Jim*
1937 *The Firefly; Maytime*
1938 *The Girl Of The Golden West*
1939 *Broadway Serenade*
1940 *New Moon; Pride And Prejudice;
Third Finger, Left Hand*
1941 *Ziegfeld Girl; When Ladies Meet*
1942 *We Were Dancing; Stand By For
Action!* (UK: *Cargo Of Innocents*)
1943 *The Man From Down Under*
1944 *Marriage Is A Private Affair*
1945 *Weekend At The Waldorf*
1946 *The Secret Heart*
1947 *Cynthia* (UK: *The Rich, Full Life*)
1948 *B F's Daughter* (UK: *Polly
Fulton*)
1949 *The Bribe; In The Good Old
Summertime*
1950 *Nancy Goes To Rio; Duchess Of
Idaho; Grounds For Divorce*
1951 *Too Young To Kiss*
1952 *Everything I Have Is Yours*
1953 *The Clown; The Great Diamond
Robbery*
1954 *Her Twelve Men*

1955 *The King's Thief; Beautiful But
Dangerous*
1957 *Kelly And Me*

## LEONE, Sergio
(1929–89) Italy

1957 *Taxi...Signore?* (short)
1958 *Nel Segno Di Roma* (UK: *Sign Of
The Gladiator* (co-writer)
1959 *Gli Ultimi Giorni Di Pompeii* (UK:
*The Last Days Of Pompeii*) (co-
writer)
1961 *Le Sette Sfide* (writer only); *Il
Colosso Di Rodi* (UK: *The
Colossus Of Rhodes*)
1962 *Sodom And Gomorrah* (second-
unit director)
1963 *Duel Of The Titans; Le Verdi
Bandiere Di Allah* (both writer
only)
1964 *Per Un Pugno Di Dollari\** (UK: *A
Fistful Of Dollars*)
1965 *Per Qualche Dollaro In Più\** (UK:
*For A Few Dollars More*)
1966 *Il Buono, Il Brutto, Il Cattivo\** (UK:
*The Good, the Bad And The Ugly*)
1968 *C'era Una Volta Il West\** (UK:
*Once Upon A Time In The West*)
1972 *Giù La Testa* (UK: *Duck You
Sucker*)
1973 *Il Mio Nome E Nessuno* (UK: *My
Name Is Nobody*) (story idea only)
1975 *Un Genio Due Compari E Un
Pollo*
1978 *Il Gatto* (producer only)
1981 *Bianco Rosso E Verdone*
(producer only)
1983 *Once Upon A Time In America\**

## LEROY, Mervyn
(1900–87) USA

1927 *Her Primitive Mate/No Place To
Go*
1928 *Flying Romeos; Oh, Kay!; Harold
Teen; Naughty Baby* (UK:
*Reckless Rosie*)
1929 *Hot Stuff; Little Johnny Jones;
Broadway Babies* (UK: *Broadway
Daddies*)

**LEROY, Mervyn** (cont.)

1930 *Playing Around; Showgirl In Hollywood; Top Speed; Numbered Men; Little Caesar\**
1931 *Broadminded; Five Star Final\*; Gentleman's Fate; Too Young To Marry; Local Boy Makes Good; Tonight Or Never*
1932 *Heart Of New York; High Pressure; Two Seconds; Big City Blues; Three On A Match; I Am A Fugitive From A Chain Gang\**
1933 *Hard To Handle; Elmer The Great; Tugboat Annie\*; Gold Diggers Of 1933\*; The World Changes*
1934 *Heat Lightning; Hi, Nellie!; Happiness Ahead*
1935 *Page Miss Glory; I Found Stella Parrish; Sweet Adeline; Oil For The Lamps Of China*
1936 *Anthony Adverse; Three Men On A Horse*
1937 *The King And The Chorus Girl; They Won't Forget*
1938 *Fools For Scandal*
1940 *Waterloo Bridge; Escape*
1941 *Blossoms In The Dust; Unholy Partners; Johnny Eager*
1942 *Random Harvest\**
1943 *Madame Curie\**
1944 *Thirty Seconds Over Tokyo*
1945 *The House That I Live In* (short)
1946 *Without Reservations*
1948 *Homecoming*
1949 *Little Women; Any Number Can Play*
1950 *East Side, West Side*
1951 *Quo Vadis?\**
1952 *Lovely To Look At; Million Dollar Mermaid* (UK: *The One Piece Bathing Suit*)
1953 *Latin Lovers*
1954 *Rose Marie*
1955 *Strange Lady In Town; Mister Roberts\** (co-director)
1956 *The Bad Seed; Toward The Unknown* (UK: *Brink Of Hell*)
1958 *No Time For Sergeants; Home Before Dark*
1959 *The FBI Story*
1960 *Wake Me When It's Over*

1961 *The Devil At Four O'Clock; A Majority Of One*
1962 *Gypsy\**
1963 *Mary, Mary*
1965 *Moment To Moment*

## LESTER, Richard
(1932– ) USA

1961 *The Running, Jumping And Standing Still Film* (short)
1962 *It's Trad, Dad*
1963 *The Mouse On The Moon*
1964 *A Hard Day's Night*
1965 *Help!; The Knack And How To Get It*
1966 *A Funny Thing Happened On The Way To The Forum*
1967 *How I Won The War*
1968 *Petulia*
1969 *The Bed-Sitting Room*
1973 *The Three Musketeers\**
1974 *The Four Musketeers; Juggernaut*
1975 *Royal Flash*
1976 *Robin And Marian; The Ritz*
1979 *Butch And Sundance: The Early Days; Cuba*
1980 *Superman II*
1983 *Superman III*
1984 *Finders, Keepers*
1989 *The Return Of The Musketeers*
1991 *Get Back* (documentary)

## LEVINSON, Barry
(1932– ) USA

1974 *Street Girls* (screenwriter only)
1976 *Silent Movie* (screenwriter only)
1977 *High Anxiety* (screenwriter only)
1979 *And Justice For All* (screenwriter only)
1980 *Inside Moves* (screenwriter only)
1981 *History Of The World Part 1* (performer only)
1982 *Best Friends* (screenwriter only); *Diner*
1983 *Unfaithfully Yours* (screenwriter only)
1984 *The Natural*
1985 *The Young Sherlock Holmes*

1987 *Tin Men\*; Good Morning Vietnam\**
1988 *Rainman\**
1990 *Avalon*
1991 *Bugsy*
1992 *Toys*

## LITVAK, Anatole
real name: Mikhail Anatol Litwak
(1902–74) Russia

1924 *Tatiana*
1930 *Dolly Macht Karriere* (UK: *Dolly Gets Ahead*)
1931 *Nie Wieder Liebe* (UK: *No More Love*)
1932 *Coeur De Lilas; Be Mine Tonight*
1933 *Sleeping Car; Cette Vieille Canaille*
1935 *L'Equipage*
1936 *Mayerling*
1937 *Tovarich; The Woman I Love* (UK: *The Woman Between*)
1938 *The Sisters; The Amazing Dr Clitterhouse*
1939 *Confessions Of A Nazi Spy*
1940 *All This And Heaven Too; City For Conquest; Castle On The Hudson* (UK: *Years Without Days*)
1941 *Out Of The Fog; Blues In The Night*
1942 *This Above All; Prelude To War* (documentary)
1943 *The Nazis Strike; Divide And Conquer; The Battle Of Russia; Operation Titanic* (all documentaries)
1944 *The Battle Of China* (documentary)
1945 *War Comes To America* (documentary)
1947 *The Long Night*
1948 *The Snake Pit\*; Sorry, Wrong Number*
1951 *Decision Before Dawn*
1954 *Act Of Love*
1955 *The Deep Blue Sea*
1956 *Anastasia*
1959 *The Journey*
1961 *Aimez-Vous Brahms?* (UK: *Goodbye Again*)
1962 *Five Miles To Midnight*
1966 *10.30PM Summer*

1967 *The Night Of The Generals*
1970 *The Lady In The Car With Glasses And A Gun*

## LLOYD, Frank
(1888–1960) UK

1914 *Billie's Baby; For His Superior's Honor* (both shorts)
1915 *From The Shadows; Little Mr Fixer; In The Grasp Of The Law; The Little Girl Of The Attic; 10,000 Dollars; The Toll Of Youth; To Redeem An Oath; To Redeem A Value* (all shorts); *Eleven To One; Dr Mason's Temptation; An Arrangement With Fate; Jane; Fate's Alibi; The Bay Of Seven Islands; A Double Deal In Pork; His Last Trick; The Pinch; The Prophet Of The Hills; Paternal Love; Martin Lowe — Fixer; Their Golden Wedding; Trickery; The Source Of Happiness*
1016 *The Call Of The Cumberlands; The Gentleman From Indiana; The Tongues Of Men; Madame President; An International Marriage; The Code Of Marcia Gray; The Intrigue; The Making Of Maddalena; Sins Of Her Parents; The Stronger Love; David Garrick*
1917 *The Price Of Silence; The Heart Of A Lion; American Methods; A Tale Of Two Cities; When A Man Sees Red*
1918 *The Kingdom of Love; Les Misérables; The Blindness Of Divorce; True Blue; For Freedom*
1919 *The Rainbow Trail; Riders Of The Purple Sage; The Man Hunter; Pitfalls Of A Big City; The World And Its Women*
1920 *The Loves Of Letty; Madame X; The Silver Horde; The Woman In Room 13; The Great Lover*
1921 *A Tale Of Two Worlds; Roads Of Destiny; Voice In The Dark; The Man From Lost River; The Invisible Power; The Sin Flood; The Grim Comedian*

**LLOYD, Frank** (cont.)

1922 *The Eternal Flame; Oliver Twist*
1923 *Within The Law; Ashes Of Vengeance; The Voice From The Minaret*
1924 *Black Oxen; The Sea Hawk; The Silent Watcher*
1925 *Winds Of Chance; The Splendid Road; Her Husband's Secret*
1926 *The Wise Guy; The Eagle Of The Sea*
1927 *Children Of Divorce*
1928 *Adoration*
1929 *Weary River; The Divine Lady; Young Nowheres; Dark Streets; Drag* (UK: *Parasites*)
1930 *Son Of The Gods; The Way Of All Men* (UK: *Sin Flood*); *The Lash* (UK: *Adios*)
1931 *East Lynne; The Right Of Way; The Age For Love*
1932 *A Passport To Hell* (UK: *Burnt Offering*)
1933 *Cavalcade\*; Berkeley Square; Hoopla*
1934 *Servants' Entrance*
1935 *Mutiny On The Bounty\**
1936 *Under Two Flags*
1937 *Maid Of Salem; Wells Fargo*
1938 *If I Were King*
1939 *Rulers Of The Sea*
1940 *The Howard Of Virginia* (UK: *The Tree Of Liberty*)
1941 *The Lady From Cheyenne; This Woman Is Mine*
1943 *Forever And A Day* (co-director)
1945 *Blood On the Sun*
1954 *The Shanghai Story*
1955 *The Last Command*

**LOACH, Ken**
(1936–   ) UK

1967 *Poor Cow*
1969 *Kes*
1971 *Family Life*
1979 *Black Jack; The Gamekeeper* (TV)
1981 *Looks And Smiles*
1986 *Fatherland*

1990 *Hidden Agenda*
1991 *Riff-Raff\**
1993 *The Estate*

**LOGAN, Joshua**
(1908–88) USA

1938 *I Met My Love Again* (co-director)
1955 *Picnic\**
1956 *Bus Stop\**
1957 *Sayonara\**
1958 *South Pacific\**
1960 *Tall Story*
1961 *Fanny*
1964 *Ensign Pulver*
1967 *Camelot\**
1969 *Paint Your Wagon\**

**LOSEY, Joseph**
(1909–84) USA

1939 *Pete Roleum And His Cousins* (short)
1941 *A Child Went Forth; Youth Gets A Break* (both shorts)
1945 *A Gun In His Hand* (short)
1948 *The Boy With Green Hair*
1950 *The Lawless*
1951 *The Prowler; The Big Night; M*
1952 *Stranger On The Prowl*
1954 *The Sleeping Tiger*
1955 *A Man On The Beach* (short)
1956 *Intimate Stranger*
1957 *Time Without Pity; The Gypsy And The Gentleman*
1959 *Blind Date*
1960 *First On The Road* (short); *The Criminal*
1961 *The Damned*
1962 *Eve*
1963 *The Servant\**
1964 *King And Country*
1966 *Modesty Blaise*
1967 *Accident*
1968 *Boom; Secret Ceremony*
1970 *Figures In A Landscape*
1971 *The Go-Between*
1972 *The Assassination Of Trotsky*
1973 *A Doll's House*
1974 *Galileo*
1975 *The Romantic Englishwoman*

1976 *Mr Klein*
1978 *Les Routes Du Sud*
1979 *Don Giovanni*
1982 *La Truite* (UK: *The Trout*)
1984 *Steaming*

## LUBITSCH, Ernst
(1892–1947) Germany

1914 *Fräulein Seifenschaum* (short)
1915 *Blinde Kuh; Auf Eis Geführt; Lieutenant Auf Befiel; Zucker Und Zimt* (all shorts)
1916 *Wo Ist Mein Schatz?; Der Schwarze Moritz; Der Gemischte Frauenchor; Der GmbH; Der Erste Patient* (all shorts); *Als Ich Tot War; Schuhpalast Pinkus; Tenor*
1917 *Ossis Tagebuch; Der Blusekönig; Wenn Vier Dasselbe Tun; Ein Fideles Gefängnis; Der Kraftmeyer; Der Letze Anzug; Prinz Sami* (all shorts)
1918 *Der Rodelkavalier; Das Mädel Vom Ballet; Fuhrmann Henschel; Marionetten* (all shorts); *Der Fall Rosentopf* (UK: *The Rosentopf Case*); *Ich Möchte Kein Mann Sein; Carmen; Die Augen Der Mumie Ma* (UK: *The Eyes of The Mummy*)
1919 *Meier Aus Berlin; Schwabenmädel; Meine Frau, Die Filmschauspielerin* (all shorts); *Die Puppe* (UK: *The Doll*); *Die Austernprinzessin* (UK: *The Oyster Princess*); *Rausch* (UK: *Intoxication*); *Madame Dubarry*
1920 *Romeo Und Julia Im Schnee* (short); *Anna Boleyn* (UK: *Anne Boleyn*); *Sumurun* (UK: *One Arabian Night*); *Kohlhiesels Töchter* (UK: *His Two Daughters*)
1921 *Die Bergkätze* (UK: *The Mountain Cat*)
1922 *Das Weib Des Pharao* (UK: *The Loves Of Pharaoh*)
1923 *Rosita; Die Flamme* (UK: *Montmartre*)
1924 *The Marriage Circle; Three Women; Forbidden Paradise*

1925 *Kiss Me Again; Lady Windermere's Fan*
1926 *So This Is Paris*
1927 *The Student Prince*
1928 *The Patriot*
1929 *Eternal Love; The Love Parade**
1930 *Monte Carlo; Paramount On Parade* (co-director)
1931 *The Smiling Lieutenant*
1932 *One Hour With You; If I Had A Million* (both co-director); *Trouble In Paradise; Broken Lullaby* (UK: *The Man I Killed*)
1933 *Design For Living*
1934 *The Merry Widow*
1937 *Angel*
1938 *Bluebeard's Eighth Wife*
1939 *Ninotchka**
1940 *The Shop Around The Corner**
1941 *That Uncertain Feeling*
1942 *To Be Or Not To Be**
1943 *Heaven Can Wait**
1946 *Cluny Brown*
1948 *That Lady In Ermine* (completed by Otto Preminger (see p427))

## LUCAS, George
(1945–   ) USA

1965 *THX-1138; 4EB* (shorts)
1967 *Herbie; Anyone Lived In A Pretty Hometown* (shorts)
1968 *The Emperor*
1970 *THX-1138*
1973 *American Graffiti**
1977 *Star Wars**

## LUHRMANN, Baz
(1962–   )

1992 *Strictly Ballroom**

## LUMET, Sidney
(1924–   ) USA

1957 *Twelve Angry Men**
1958 *Stage Struck*
1959 *That Kind Of Woman*
1960 *The Fugitive Kind*
1961 *A View From The Bridge*
1962 *Long Day's Journey Into Night**

**LUMET, Sidney** (cont.)
1964 *Failsafe*
1965 *The Pawnbroker\*; The Hill*
1966 *The Deadly Affair; The Group*
1968 *Bye Bye Braverman; The Seagull*
1969 *The Appointment; Last Of The Mobile Hotshots*
1970 *King: A Filmed Record...Montgomery To Memphis* (documentary, co-director)
1971 *The Anderson Tapes*
1972 *Child's Play; The Offence*
1973 *Lovin' Molly; Serpico*
1974 *Murder On The Orient Express\**
1975 *Dog Day Afternoon\**
1976 *Network\**
1977 *Equus*
1978 *The Wiz*
1980 *Just Tell Me What You Want*
1981 *Prince Of The City*
1982 *Deathtrap; The Verdict\**
1983 *Daniel*
1984 *Garbo Talks*
1986 *The Morning After; Power*
1988 *Running On Empty*
1989 *Family Business\**
1990 *Q & A*
1992 *A Stranger Among Us*
1993 *Beyond Innocence*

**LYNCH, David**
(1946– ) USA

1968 *The Alphabet* (short)
1970 *The Grandmother* (short)
1977 *Eraserhead*
1980 *The Elephant Man\**
1984 *Dune*
1986 *Blue Velvet\**
1988 *Zelly And Me* (actor)
1990 *Wild At Heart\**
1991 *The Cabinet Of Dr Ramirez* (executive producer only)
1992 *Twin Peaks: Fire Walk With Me*

**LYNE, Adrian**
(1941– ) UK

1980 *Foxes*
1983 *Flashdance\**

1986 *9½ Weeks*
1987 *Fatal Attraction\**
1990 *Jacob's Ladder*
1993 *Indecent Proposal*

# M

**MACKENDRICK, Alexander**
(1912– ) UK

1948 *Whisky Galore\**
1951 *The Man In The White Suit\**
1952 *Mandy*
1954 *The Maggie*
1955 *The Ladykillers\**
1957 *Sweet Smell Of Success\**
1962 *Sammy Going South*
1965 *A High Wind In Jamaica*
1967 *Don't Make Waves*

**MACKENZIE, John**
(1932– ) UK

1970 *One Brief Summer*
1971 *Unman, Wittering And Zigo*
1972 *Made*
1980 *The Long Good Friday\**
1981 *A Sense Of Freedom* (TV)
1983 *The Honorary Consul*
1985 *The Innocent*
1986 *Act Of Vengeance* (TV)
1987 *The Fourth Protocol*
1989 *The Last Of The Finest*
1992 *Ruby*

**MALICK, Terence**
(1943– ) USA

1969 *Lanton Mills* (short, screenwriter only)
1970 *Deadhead Miles; Pocket Money* (both screenwriter only)
1973 *Badlands\**
1974 *The Gravy Train* (pseudonymous co-writer only)
1978 *Days Of Heaven\**

## MALLE, Louis
(1932– ) France

1955 *La Fontaine De Vaucluse; Station 307* (both short documentaries)
1956 *Le Monde Du Silence* (UK: *The Silent World*) (co-director)
1957 *Ascenseur Pour L'Echafaud* (UK: *Lift To The Scaffold*)
1958 *Les Amants* (UK: *The Lovers*)
1960 *Zazie Dans Le Métro* (UK: *Zazie*)
1962 *Vie Privée* (UK: *A Very Private Affair*); *Vive Le Tour* (documentary)
1963 *Le Feu Follet* (UK: *A Time To Live And A Time To Die*)
1964 *Bons Baisers De Bangkok* (documentary)
1965 *Viva Maria!; Le Voleur* (UK: *The Thief*)
1968 *Histoires Extraordinaires* (UK: *Tales Of Mystery*) (co-director)
1969 *Calcutta; Phantom India* (both documentaries)
1971 *Le Souffle Au Coeur* (UK: *Dearest Love*)
1972 *Humain, Trop Humain* (UK: *A Human Condition*) (documentary)
1973 *Place De La République* (documentary)
1974 *Lacombe Lucien*
1975 *Black Moon*
1978 *Pretty Baby*
1980 *Atlantic City**
1981 *My Dinner With André*
1983 *Crackers*
1985 *Alamo Bay; God's Country* (documentary)
1986 *And The Pursuit Of Happiness*
1987 *Au Revoir Les Enfants**
1990 *Milou En Mai*
1992 *Damage*

## MAMOULIAN, Rouben
(1897–1987) Russia

1929 *Applause*
1931 *City Streets; Dr Jekyll And Mr Hyde**
1932 *Love Me Tonight*
1933 *Song Of Songs; Queen Christina**

1934 *We Live Again*
1935 *Becky Sharp**
1936 *The Gay Desperado*
1937 *High, Wide And Handsome*
1939 *Golden Boy*
1940 *The Mark Of Zorro*
1941 *Blood And Sand*
1942 *Rings On Her Fingers*
1948 *Summer Holiday*
1957 *Silk Stockings*

## MANKIEWICZ, Joseph L
(1909–93) USA

1946 *Dragonwyck; Somewhere In The Night; The Late George Apley*
1947 *The Ghost And Mrs Muir*
1948 *Escape*
1949 *A Letter To Three Wives*; House Of Strangers*
1950 *No Way Out; All About Eve**
1951 *People Will Talk*
1952 *Five Fingers*
1953 *Julius Caesar**
1954 *The Barefoot Contessa**
1955 *Guys And Dolls**
1957 *The Quiet American*
1959 *Suddenly Last Summer**
1963 *Cleopatra**
1967 *The Honey Pot*
1970 *There Was A Crooked Man*
1972 *Sleuth**

## MANN, Anthony
real name: Emil Anton Bundsmann
(1906–67) USA

1942 *Moonlight In Havana; Dr Broadway*
1943 *Nobody's Darling*
1944 *Strangers In The Night; My Best Gal*
1945 *Two O'Clock Courage; The Great Flamarion; Sing Your Way*
1946 *Strange Impersonation; The Bamboo Blonde*
1947 *Desperate; Railroaded!; T-Men*
1948 *Raw Deal*
1949 *Reign Of Terror; Border Incident*
1950 *Side Street; The Devil's Doorway; Winchester'73; The Furies*

**MANN, Anthony** (cont.)

1951 *The Tall Target*
1942 *Bend Of The River* (UK: *Where The River Bends*)
1953 *The Naked Spur; Thunder Bay; The Glenn Miller Story**
1954 *The Far Country*
1955 *Strategic Air Command; The Man From Laramie; The Last Frontier*
1956 *Serenade*
1957 *Men In War; The Tin Star*
1958 *Man Of The West; God's Little Acre*
1960 *Cimarron*
1961 *El Cid**
1963 *The Fall Of The Roman Empire*
1965 *The Heroes Of Telemark*
1968 *A Dandy In Aspic* (completed by actor Laurence Harvey (see p189))

**MANN, Daniel**
(1912–  ) USA

1948 *The Counterfeiters*
1952 *Come Back, Little Sheba*
1954 *About Mrs Leslie*
1955 *I'll Cry Tomorrow*; The Rose Tattoo**
1956 *The Teahouse Of The August Moon**
1958 *Hot Spell*
1959 *The Last Angry Man*
1960 *The Mountain Road; Butterfield 8**
1961 *Ada*
1962 *Five Finger Exercise*
1963 *Who's Been Sleeping In My Bed?*
1965 *Judith*
1966 *Our Man Flint*
1968 *For Love Of Ivy*
1969 *A Dream Of Kings*
1971 *Willard; The Harness* (TV)
1972 *The Revengers*
1973 *Interval; Maurie*
1974 *Lost In The Stars*
1976 *Journey Into Fear*
1978 *Matilda*
1980 *The Incredible Mr Chadwick; Playing For Time* (TV)
1981 *The Day The Loving Stopped* (TV)
1987 *The Man Who Broke A 1,000 Chains* (TV)

**MANN, Delbert**
(1920–  ) USA

1955 *Marty**
1957 *The Bachelor Party*
1958 *Desire Under The Elms; Separate Tables**
1959 *Middle Of The Night*
1960 *The Dark At The Top Of The Stairs*
1961 *The Outsider; Lover Come Back*
1962 *That Touch Of Mink*
1963 *A Gathering Of Eagles*
1964 *Dear Heart*
1965 *Quick Before It Melts; Mister Buddwing* (UK: *Woman Without A Face*)
1967 *Fitzwilly*
1968 *The Pink Jungle; Heidi* (TV)
1969 *David Copperfield* (TV)
1971 *Kidnapped; She Waits* (TV); *Jane Eyre* (TV)
1972 *No Place To Run* (TV)
1973 *Man Without A Country* (TV)
1975 *A Girl Named Sonner* (TV)
1976 *Birch Interval; Francis Gary Powers* (TV)
1977 *Tell Me My Name* (TV)
1978 *Breaking Up* (TV); *Love's Dark Side* (TV); *Home To Stay* (TV); *Thou Shalt Not Commit Adultery* (TV)
1979 *Torn Between Two Lovers* (TV); *All Quiet On The Western Front* (TV)
1981 *Night Crossing; To Find My Son* (TV)
1983 *The Gift Of Love: A Christmas Story* (TV); *Bronte*
1984 *Love Leads The Way* (TV)
1985 *A Death In California* (TV)
1986 *The Last Days Of Patton* (TV)
1991 *Ironclads* (TV)

**MANN, Michael**
(1943–  ) USA

1979 *The Jericho Mile* (TV)
1981 *Thief*
1983 *The Keep*
1986 *Manhunter*

1987 *Band Of The Hand* (executive producer only)
1992 *The Last Of The Mohicans\**

## MARQUAND, Richard
(c1938–87) UK

1975 *Do Yourself Some Good* (short)
1976 *Beowulf* (actor only)
1978 *The Legacy*
1979 *The Birth Of The Beatles*
1981 *The Eye Of The Needle*
1983 *The Return Of The Jedi\**
1984 *Until September*
1985 *Jagged Edge\**
1987 *Hearts Of Fire*

## MARSHALL, Garry
(c1935–  ) USA

1968 *How Sweet It Is* (producer and screenwriter only); *Psych-Out* (actor only)
1970 *The Grasshopper* (producer and screenwriter only)
1982 *Young Doctors In Love*
1984 *The Flamingo Kid*
1986 *Nothing In Common*
1987 *Overboard*
1988 *Beaches\**
1990 *Pretty Woman\**
1991 *Soapdish* (actor only); *Frankie And Johnny*
1992 *A League Of Their Own* (actor only)

## MARSHALL, Penny
(1942–  ) USA

1968 *How Sweet It Is; The Savage Seven* (both actor only)
1975 *How Come Nobody's On Our Side* (actor only)
1979 *1941\** (actor only)
1985 *Movers And Shakers* (actor only)
1986 *Jumpin' Jack Flash*
1988 *Big\**
1990 *Awakenings\**
1992 *A League Of Their Own*

## MARTON, Andrew
(1904–92) Hungary

1929 *Two O'Clock In The Morning* (UK: *The Hour Of Fear*)
1931 *Die Nacht Ohne Pause* (co-director)
1932 *Nordpol Ahoi!* (UK: *SOS Iceberg*)
1934 *Der Dämon Der Berge* (UK: *Beast Of The Himalayas*)
1935 *Miss President*
1936 *Wolf's Clothing; The Secret Of Stamboul*
1937 *School For Husbands*
1940 *A Little Bit Of Heaven*
1945 *Gentle Annie*
1946 *Gallant Bess*
1950 *King Solomon's Mines\** (co-director)
1951 *The Red Badge Of Courage\** (second-unit director)
1952 *The Wild North; Storm Over Tibet* (co-director)
1953 *The Devil Makes Three; Mask Of The Himalayas* (documentary)
1954 *Gypsy Colt; Prisoner Of War; Men Of The Fighting Lady; Green Fire*
1956 *Seven Wonders Of The World* (co-director)
1957 *A Farewell To Arms* (second-unit director)
1958 *Underwater Warrior*
1959 *Ben-Hur\** (second-unit director)
1962 *55 Days At Peking* (second-unit director); *The Longest Day\** (co-director); *It Happened In Athens*
1963 *Cleopatra\** (second-unit director)
1964 *The Thin Red Line*
1965 *Crack In The World; Clarence The Cross-Eyed Lion; Around The World Under The Sea*
1966 *Birds Do It*
1967 *Africa — Texas Style*

## MAYO, Archie
(1891–1968) USA

1917 *Double Dukes* (co-director); *Kid Snatchers; The Nurse Of An Aching Heart* (all shorts)
1918 *Beaches And Peaches* (short)

**MAYO, Archie** (cont.)

1923 *Don't Play Hookey; Mama's Baby Boy; A Man Of Position; Spring Fever* (all shorts)

1924 *Short Change; High Gear; Husbands Wanted* (all shorts)

1925 *Good Spirits; The Imperfect Lover; Off His Beat; Oh Bridget; A Rarin' Romeo; Tender Feet; Why Hesitate?* (all shorts)

1926 *Weak But Willing* (short); *Johnny Get Your Haircut* (co-director); *Christine Of The Big Tops; Money Talks; Unknown Treasures*

1927 *Dearie; Quarantined Rivals; Slightly Used; The College Widow*

1928 *The Foreigner; Charles Rogers In The Movie Man; Henry B Walthall In Retribution* (all shorts); *The Crimson City; Beware Of Married Men; On Trial; My Man; Street Sadie* (UK: *The Girl From State Street*)

1929 *Sonny Boy; The Sap; The Sacred Flame; Is Everybody Happy?*

1930 *Vengeance; Courage; Oh! Sailor, Behave!; Wide Open; The Doorway To Hell* (UK: *A Handful Of Clouds*)

1931 *Svengali; Illicit; Bought*

1932 *Under 18; The Expert; Street Of Women; Two Against The World; Night After Night*

1933 *The Mayor Of Hell; Convention City; Ever In My Heart; The Life Of Jimmy Dolan* (UK: *The Kid's Last Fight*)

1934 *Gambling Lady; Desirable; The Man With Two Faces*

1935 *Go Into Your Dance; The Case Of The Lucky Legs; Bordertown*

1936 *The Petrified Forest\*; I Married A Doctor; Black Legion; Give Me Your Heart* (UK: *Sweet Aloes*)

1937 *Call It A Day; It's Love I'm After*

1938 *The Adventures Of Marco Polo; Youth Takes A Fling*

1939 *They Shall Have Music* (UK: *Melody Of Youth*)

1940 *Four Sons; The House Across The Bay*

1941 *The Great American Broadcast; Confirm Or Deny; Charley's Aunt* (UK: *Charley's American Aunt*)

1942 *Moontide; Orchestra Wives*

1943 *Crash Dive*

1944 *Sweet And Low Down*

1946 *Angel On My Shoulder; A Night In Casablanca*

**MAZURSKY, Paul**
real name: Irwin Mazursky
(1930– ) USA

1951 *Fear And Desire* (actor only)

1955 *Blackboard Jungle\** (actor only)

1966 *Deathwatch* (actor only)

1968 *I Love You Alice B Toklas* (screenwriter, co-executive producer only)

1969 *Bob & Carol & Ted & Alice\**

1971 *Alex In Wonderland*

1973 *Blume In Love*

1974 *Harry And Tonto*

1976 *A Star Is Born\** (actor only); *Next Stop, Greenwich Village*

1978 *An Unmarried Woman\**

1979 *A Man, A Woman, And A Bank* (actor only)

1980 *Willie And Phil*

1981 *The History Of The World—Part I* (actor only)

1982 *Tempest*

1984 *Moscow On The Hudson*

1985 *Into The Night* (actor only)

1986 *Down And Out In Beverly Hills*

1988 *Punchline\** (actor only); *Moon Over Parador*

1989 *Scenes From The Class Struggle In Beverly Hills* (actor only); *Enemies: A Love Story\**

1990 *Taking Care Of Business* (executive producer only)

1991 *Scenes From The Mall*

1993 *The Pickle*

**MCBRIDE, Jim**
(1941– ) USA

1968 *David Holzman's Diary*

1969 *My Girlfriend's Wedding*

1971 *Glen And Randa*

1974 *Hot Times*
1979 *The Last Embrace* (actor only)
1983 *Breathless*
1987 *The Big Easy**
1989 *Great Balls Of Fire!*

## MCCAREY, Leo
(1898–1969) USA

1921 *Society Secrets* (short)
1924 *All Wet* (short)
1925 *Bad Boy; Innocent Husbands* (both shorts)
1926 *Crazy Like a Fox; Dog Shy; Be Your Age* (all shorts)
1927 *We Faw Down* (short)
1928 *Came The Dawn; The Family Group; The Fight Pest; The Finishing Touch; Limousine Love; Should Women Drive?* (all shorts)
1929 *Liberty; Wrong Again* (both shorts); *The Sophomore; Red Hot Rythmn*
1930 *Let's Go Native; Wild Company; Part-Time Wife*
1931 *Indiscreet*
1932 *The Kid From Spain*
1933 *Duck Soup**
1934 *Six Of A Kind; Belle Of The Nineties*
1935 *Ruggles Of Red Gap**
1936 *The Milky Way*
1937 *Make Way For Tomorrow; The Awful Truth**
1939 *Love Affair**
1940 *My Favourite Wife*
1942 *Once Upon A Honeymoon*
1944 *Going My Way**
1945 *The Bells Of St Mary's**
1948 *Good Sam*
1952 *My Son John*
1957 *An Affair To Remember*
1959 *Rally Round The Flag Boys*
1962 *Satan Never Sleeps* (UK: *The Devil Never Sleeps*)

Listing of short films is selective

## MCLEOD, Norman Z
(1898–1964) USA

1928 *Taking A Chance*

1930 *Along Came Youth* (co-director)
1931 *Finn And Hattie* (co-director); *Monkey Business; The Miracle Man; Touchdown* (UK: *Playing The Game*)
1932 *Horse Feathers; If I Had A Million* (co-director); *The Miracle Man*
1933 *Alice In Wonderland; Mama Loves Papa; A Lady's Profession*
1934 *Melody In Spring; Many Happy Returns; It's A Gift*
1935 *Redheads On Parade; Coronado; Here Comes Cookie* (UK: *The Plot Thickens*)
1936 *Early To Bed; Pennies From Heaven*
1937 *Mind Your Own Business; Topper*
1938 *There Goes My Heart; Merrily We Live*
1939 *Topper Takes a Trip; Remember?*
1940 *Little Men*
1941 *The Trial Of Mary Dugan; Lady Be Good*
1942 *Jackass Mail; Panama Hattie*
1943 *The Powers Girl* (UK: *Hello! Beautiful*); *Swing Shift Maisie* (UK: *The Girl In Overalls*)
1946 *The Kid From Brooklyn*
1947 *The Secret Life Of Walter Mitty; Road To Rio*
1948 *The Paleface*; Isn't It Romantic*
1950 *Let's Dance*
1951 *My Favorite Spy*
1952 *Never Wave At A WAC* (UK: *The Private Wore Skirts*)
1954 *Casanova's Big Night*
1957 *Public Pigeon Number 1*
1959 *Alias Jesse James*

## MCTIERNAN, John
(1951–  ) USA

1985 *Nomads*
1986 *Death Of A Soldier* (actor only)
1988 *Die Hard**
1990 *The Hunt For Red October**
1991 *Flight Of The Intruder* (executive producer only)
1992 *Medicine Man*
1993 *The Last Action Hero*

## MEDAK, Peter
(19?– ) Hungary

1962 *The Phantom Of The Opera* (assistant director)
1966 *Funeral In Berlin* (second-unit director); *Kaleidoscope* (associate producer)
1968 *Negatives*
1972 *A Day In The Death Of Joe Egg; The Ruling Class*
1973 *Third Girl From The Left* (TV)
1974 *Ghost In The Noonday Sun*
1978 *The Odd Job*
1979 *The Changeling*
1981 *Zorro, The Gay Blade*
1982 *Mistress Of Paradise* (TV)
1986 *The Men's Club*
1990 *The Krays\**
1991 *Let Him Have It*
1993 *Romeo Is Bleeding*

## MILESTONE, Lewis
real name: Levis Milstein
(1895–1980) USA

1925 *Seven Sinners*
1926 *The New Klondike; The Caveman*
1927 *Two Arabian Knights*
1928 *The Garden Of Eden; The Racket*
1929 *The Betrayal; New York Nights*
1930 *All Quiet On The Western Front\**
1931 *The Front Page\**
1932 *Rain*
1933 *Hallelujah, I'm A Bum* (UK: *Hallelujah, I'm A Tramp*)
1934 *The Captain Hates The Sea*
1935 *Paris In Spring* (UK: *Paris Love Song*)
1936 *Anything Goes; The General Died At Dawn*
1939 *The Night Of Nights; Of Mice And Men\**
1940 *Lucky Partners*
1941 *My Life With Caroline*
1942 *Our Russian Frontier* (documentary, co-director)
1943 *Edge Of Darkness; The North Star*
1944 *The Purple Heart*
1945 *A Walk In The Sun*

1946 *The Strange Love Of Martha Ivers*
1948 *Arch Of Triumph; No Minor Vices*
1949 *The Red Pony*
1950 *Halls Of Montezuma*
1952 *Kangaroo; Les Misérables*
1953 *Melba; They Who Dare*
1954 *Le Vedova* (UK: *The Widow*)
1959 *Pork Chop Hill*
1960 *Ocean's Eleven\**
1962 *Mutiny On the Bounty\**

## MILLER, George
(1945– ) Australia

1971 *Violence In The Cinema, Part I* (short)
1973 *Devil In Evening Dress* (documentary); *Frieze, An Underground Film* (short, editor only)
1979 *Mad Max\**
1980 *Chain Reaction* (associate producer only)
1981 *Mad Max 2\**
1983 *The Twilight Zone — The Movie* (co-director)
1985 *Anzacs* (TV); *Mad Max — Beyond Thunderdome\** (co-director)
1987 *The Year My Voice Broke* (co-producer only); *The Witches Of Eastwick\**
1989 *Dead Calm* (co-producer only)
1992 *Lorenzo's Oil\**

## MINNELLI, Vincente
(c1910–86) USA

1942 *Panama Hattie* (uncredited co-director)
1943 *Thousand Cheer* (uncredited co-director); *Cabin In The Sky; I Dood It* (UK: *By Hook Or By Crook*)
1944 *Ziegfeld Follies\** (co-director); *Meet Me In St Louis\**
1945 *Yolanda And The Thief; The Clock* (UK: *Under The Clock*)
1946 *Undercurrent; Till The Clouds Roll By* (uncredited co-director)
1948 *The Pirate*
1949 *Madame Bovary*

1950  *Father Of The Bride\**
1951  *An American In Paris\*; Father's Little Dividend*
1952  *The Bad And The Beautiful\*; Lovely To Look At* (uncredited co-director)
1953  *The Band Wagon\*; The Story Of Three Loves* (co-director)
1954  *The Long, Long Trailer; Brigadoon*
1955  *Kismet; The Cobweb*
1956  *Lust For Life\*; Tea And Sympathy*
1957  *Designing Woman; The Seventh Sin* (co-director)
1958  *Gigi\*; The Reluctant Debutante; Some Came Running*
1960  *Home From The Hill; The Bells Are Ringing*
1961  *The Four Horsemen Of The Apocalypse*
1962  *Two Weeks In Another Town*
1963  *The Courtship Of Eddie's Father*
1964  *Goodbye Charlie*
1965  *The Sandpiper*
1970  *On A Clear Day You Can See Forever*
1976  *A Matter Of Time*

## MIZOGUCHI, Kenji
(1898–1956) Japan

1922  *Ai Ni Yomigaeru Hi; Seishun No Yumeji; Joen No Chimata; Furusato; Rupimono; 813: The Adventures Of Arsene Lupin; Haizan No Uta Wa Kanashi; Chi To Rei*
1923  *Yoru; Kiri No Minato; Haikyo No Naka; Toge No Uta; Kanto* (documentary)
1924  *Kanashiki Hakuchi; Gendai No Joo; Josei Wa Tsuyoshi; Schichmencho No Yukue; Samidare Zoshi; Jinkyo; Musen Fusen; Kanraku No Onna; Akatsuki No Shi*
1925  *Kyokubadan No Joo; Daichi Wa Hohoemu; Akai Yuki No Terasarete* (co-director); *Furusato No Uta; Ningen; Gaijo No Sukechi* (co-director); *Shirayuri Wa Nageku*

1926  *Nogi Taisho To Kuma-San; Doka O; Kaminingyo Haru No Sasayaki; Shin Ono Ga Tsumi* (UK: *My Fault*); *Kyoren No Onna Shisho; Kane; Kaikoko Danji*
1927  *Ko-On; Jihi Shincho*
1928  *Hito No Issho — Parts I, II, III*
1929  *Tokyo–Koshinkyoku; Asahi Wa Kagayaku* (co-director); *Nihombashi; Tokai Kokyogaku*
1930  *Furusato; Tojin Ikichi*
1931  *Shikamo Karera Wa Yuku — Parts I and II*
1932  *Toki No Ujigami; Mammo Kenkoku No Reimei*
1933  *Taki No Shiraito* (UK: *The Water Magician*); *Gion Matsuru; Kamikaze Ren; Jimpuren*
1934  *Aizo Togo; Orizuro Osen* (UK: *The Downfall*)
1935  *Maria No Oyuki* (UK: *Oyuki The Virgin*); *Gubijinso* (UK: *The Field Poppy*)
1936  *Naniwa Ereji* (UK: *Naniwa Elegy*); *Gion No Shimai* (UK: *Sisters Of The Gion*)
1937  *Aienkyo* (UK: *The Straits Of Love And Hate*)
1938  *Aa Furusato; Roei No Uta* (co-director)
1939  *Zangiku Monogatari* (UK: *The Story Of The Last Chrysanthemums*)
1940  *Naniwa Onna; Geido Ichidai Otoko*
1941  *Genroku Chushingura — Part I* (UK: *The Loyal 47 Of The Genroku Era*)
1942  *Musashi Miyamoto* (UK: *The Swordsman*); *Genroku Chushingura — Part II*
1944  *Danjuro Sandai*
1945  *Hisshoka; Meito Bijomaru* (UK: *The Sword*)
1946  *Josei No Shori* (UK: *The Victory Of Women*); *Utamaro O Meguro Gonin No Onna* (UK: *Five Women Around Utamarao*)
1947  *Joyu Sumako No Koi* (UK: *The Loves Of Actress Sumako*)
1948  *Yoru No Onnatachi* (UK: *Women Of The Night*)

**MIZOGUCHI, Kenji** (cont.)

1949 *Waga Koi Wa Moeru* (UK: *My Love Has Been Burning*)
1950 *Yuki Fujin Ezu* (UK: *Portrait Of Madame Yuki*)
1951 *Musashino Fujin* (UK: *Madame Musashino*); *Oyu-Sama* (UK: *Miss Oyu*)
1952 *Saikaku Ichidai Onna* (UK: *The Life Of Oharu*)
1953 *Ugetsu Monogatari\*; Gion Bayashi* (UK: *Gion Music Festival*)
1954 *Sansho Dayu* (UK: *Sansho The Bailiff*); *Chikamatsu Monogatari* (UK: *A Story From Chikamatsu*); *Uwasa No Onna* (UK: *A Woman Of Rumour*)
1955 *Yokihi* (UK: *The Empress Yang Kwei Fei*); *Shin-Heike Monogatari* (UK: *New Tales Of The Taira Clan*)
1956 *Agasen Chitai* (UK: *Street Of Shame*)
1957 *Osaka Monogatar* (co-director)

**MULCAHY, Russell**
(1953–   ) Australia

1982 *Derek And Clive Get The Horn*
1984 *Razorback*
1984 *Highlander\**
1991 *Highlander II: The Quickening; Ricochet*
1992 *Blue Ice*
1993 *The Real McCoy*

**MULLIGAN, Robert**
(1925–   ) USA

1957 *Fear Strikes Out*
1960 *The Rat Race*
1961 *The Great Imposter; Come September*
1962 *The Spiral Road; To Kill A Mockingbird\**
1963 *Love With The Proper Stranger*
1964 *Baby The Rain Must Fall*
1965 *Inside Daisy Clover*
1967 *Up The Down Staircase*
1968 *The Stalking Moon*
1970 *The Pursuit Of Happiness*

1971 *Summer Of '42*
1972 *The Other*
1974 *The Nickel Ride*
1978 *Bloodbrothers; Same Time, Next Year*
1982 *Kiss Me Goodbye*
1988 *Clara's Heart*
1991 *The Man In The Moon*

# N

**NARIZZANO, Silvio**
(1927–   ) Canada

1960 *Under Ten Flags* (co-director)
1965 *Fanatic*
1966 *Georgy Girl\**
1968 *Blue*
1970 *Loot*
1972 *Redneck*
1975 *The Sky Is Falling*
1976 *Why Shoot The Teacher?*
1978 *The Class Of Miss MacMichael*
1980 *Staying On* (TV)
1981 *Choices*

**NEAME, Ronald**
(1911–   ) UK

1947 *Take My Life*
1949 *The Golden Salamander*
1952 *The Card*
1953 *The Million Pound Note*
1956 *The Man Who Never Was*
1957 *The Seventh Sin* (co-director)
1958 *Windom's Way*
1959 *The Horse's Mouth*
1960 *Tunes Of Glory\**
1961 *Escape From Zahrain*
1963 *I Could Go On Singing*
1964 *The Chalk Garden*
1965 *Mister Moses*
1966 *Gambit; A Man Could Get Killed* (co-driector)
1969 *The Prime Of Miss Jean Brodie\**
1970 *Scrooge*
1972 *The Poseidon Adventure\**
1974 *The Odessa File*

1979  *Meteor*
1980  *Hopscotch*
1981  *First Monday In October*
1986  *Foreign Body*

## NEEDHAM, Hal
(1937–   ) USA

1963  *McLintock!* (actor only)
1967  *The Ballad Of Josie* (stunt coordinator only)
1968  *Bandolero!* (stunt coordinator only)
1971  *One More Train To Rob* (actor only)
1972  *The Culpepper Cattle Company* (actor and stunt coordinator only)
1974  *The Longest Yard\** (UK: *The Mean Machine*) (second-unit director); *Three The Hard Way* (stunt coordinator only)
1975  *W W And The Dixie Dancekings; French Connection II; Peeper* (all stunt coordinator only); *Take A Hard Ride* (second-unit director)
1976  *Gator* (second-unit director); *Jackson County Jail* (actor only); *Nickelodeon* (stunt coordinator)
1977  *Semi-Tough* (stunt coordinator); *Smokey And The Bandit\**
1978  *The End; Foul Play\** (both stunt coordinator); *Hooper*
1979  *The Villain* (UK: *Cactus Jack*)
1980  *Smokey And The Bandit II* (UK: *Smokey And The Bandit Ride Again*)
1981  *The Cannonball Run\**
1982  *Megaforce*
1983  *Cannonball Run II; Stroker Ace*
1985  *Southern Voices, American Dreams* (actor only)
1986  *Rad*
1987  *Body Slam*

## NEGULESCO, Jean
(1900–   ) USA

1937  *Expensive Husbands; Fight For Your Lady* (both co-writer only)
1938  *Beloved Brat; Swiss Miss* (both co-writer only)

1939  *Rio* (story only); *Three And A Day* (short)
1940  *The Flag Of Humanity; Alice In Movieland; Joe Reichman And His Orchestra; A Dog In The Orchard* (all shorts)
1941  *USC Band And Glee Club; Carioca Serenaders; Jan Garber And His Orchestra; Skinnay Ennis And His Orchestra; Cliff Edwards And His Buckaroos; Freddy Martin And His Orchestra; Marie Green And Her Merrie Men; Hal Kemp And His Orchestra; Those Good Old Days; At The Stroke Of Twelve* (all shorts); *Singapore Woman*
1942  *The Gay Parisian; Spanish Fiesta; California Junior Symphony; A Ship Is Born; Leo Reisman And His Orchestra; The Don Cossack Chorus; The Spirit Of West Point; Richard Kimber And His Orchestra; The Daughter Of Rosie O'Grady; Carl Hoff And His Band; Six Hits And A Miss; The Spirit Of Annapolis; Glen Gray And His Band; The Army Air Force Band; The US Marine Band; The Playgirls* (all shorts)
1943  *The Army Show; Women At War; The US Navy Band; Over The Wall; The US Army Band; The Voice That Thrilled The World; Ozzie Nelson And His Orchestra; All American Band; Childhood Days; US Service Bands; Sweetheart Serenade; Cavalcade Of The Dance* (all shorts)
1944  *Roaring Guns; South American Sway; Grandfather's Follies* (all shorts); *The Mask Of Dimitrios; The Conspirators*
1945  *All Star Melody Masters; Listen To The Bands; Borrah Minevitch And His Harmonica School; The Serenaders* (all shorts)
1946  *Three Strangers; Nobody Lives Forever; Humoresque*
1947  *Deep Valley*
1948  *Johnny Belinda\*; Road House*

**NEGULESCO, Jean** (cont.)
1949 *Britannia Mews*
1950 *Under My Skin; Three Came Home*
1951 *The Mudlark; Take Care Of My Little Girl*
1952 *Phone Call From A Stranger; O Henry's Full House; Lydia Bailey; Lure Of The Wilderness*
1953 *Titanic; Scandal At Scourie; How To Marry A Millionaire**
1954 *Three Coins In The Fountain*; Woman's World*
1955 *Daddy Long Legs; The Rains of Ranchipur*
1957 *Boy On A Dolphin*
1958 *The Gift Of Love; A Certain Smile*
1959 *Count Your Blessings; The Best Of Everything*
1961 *Jessica*
1964 *The Pleasure Seekers*
1969 *The Heroes*
1970 *Hello–Goodbye*

**NELSON, Gary**
(c1916–   ) USA

1974 *The Girl On The Late Late Show* (TV)
1975 *Medical Story* (TV); *Panache* (TV)
1976 *Freaky Friday*
1977 *Washington: Behind Closed Doors* (TV)
1978 *To Kill a Cop* (TV)
1979 *The Black Hole**
1981 *The Prise Of Jesse Hallam* (TV)
1983 *Jimmy The Kid; Murder Me, Murder You* (TV); *Murder In Coweta County* (TV)
1985 *Lady Blue*
1986 *Allan Quatermain And The Lost City Of Gold*
1988 *Shooter* (TV)
1989 *Get Smart, Again!* (TV)

**NELSON, Ralph**
(1916–87) USA

1962 *Requiem For A Heavyweight* (UK: Blood Money)

1963 *Soldier In The Rain; Lilies Of The Field**
1964 *Fate Is The Hunter; Father Goose*
1965 *Once A Thief*
1966 *Duel At Diablo*
1967 *Counterpoint*
1968 *Charly**
1969 *..tick...tick...tick*
1970 *Soldier Blue*
1971 *Flight Of The Doves*
1972 *The Wrath Of God*
1974 *The Wilby Conspiracy*
1976 *Embryo*
1977 *A Hero Ain't Nothing But A Sandwich*
1978 *Because He's My Friend; Lady Of The House* (TV) (co-director)
1979 *You Can't Go Home Again* (TV); *Christmas Lilies Of The Field*

**NEWMAN, Paul**
(1925–   ) USA

1959 *On The Harmfulness Of Tobacco* (short)
1968 *Rachel, Rachel**
1971 *Sometimes A Great Notion* (UK: Never Give An Inch)
1973 *The Effect Of Gamma Rays On Man-In-The-Moon Marigolds*
1980 *The Shadow Box* (TV)
1984 *Harry And Son*
1987 *The Glass Menagerie*

See also actors listing

**NICHOLS, Mike**
real name: Michael Peschowsky
(1931–   ) USA

1966 *Who's Afraid Of Virginia Woolf?**
1967 *The Graduate**
1970 *Catch-22**
1971 *Carnal Knowledge*
1973 *The Day Of The Dolphins*
1974 *The Fortune*
1980 *Gilda Live*
1983 *Silkwood**
1986 *The Long Shot* (executive producer only); *Heartburn*
1988 *Biloxi Blues; Working Girl**

1990 *Postcards From The Edge\**
1991 *Regarding Henry\**
1993 *Remains Of The Day* (producer only); *Wolf*

## NICHOLSON, Jack
(1937– ) USA

1971 *Drive He Said*
1978 *Goin' South*
1990 *The Two Jakes\**

See also actors listing

## NIMOY, Leonard
(1931– ) USA

1984 *Star Trek III—The Search For Spock*
1986 *Star Trek IV—The Voyage Home*
1987 *Three Men And A Baby\**
1988 *The Good Mother*
1990 *Funny About Love*

# O

## OLIVIER, Laurence
(1907–89) UK

1944 *Henry V\**
1948 *Hamlet\**
1955 *Richard III\**
1957 *The Prince And The Showgirl\**
1970 *The Three Sisters*

See also actors listing

## OLMI, Ermanno
(1931– ) Italy

1953 *La Digi Sul Ghiaccio* (short)
1954 *La Pattuglia Di Passo San Giacomo* (short)
1955 *Società Ovesticino-Dinamo; Cantiere D'Inverno; La Mia Valle; L'Onda; Boungirono Natura* (all shorts)
1956 *Michelino La B; Construzione Meccaniche Riva* (all shorts)

1958 *Tre Fili Fino A Milano; Giochi Di Colonia; Venezia Città Minore* (all shorts)
1959 *Il Tempo Si È Fermato* (UK: *Time Stood Still*)
1960 *Il Grande Paese D'Acciaio*
1961 *Le Grand Barrage; Un Metro Lungo Cinque* (both shorts); *Il Posto* (UK: *The Job*)
1962 *Una Storia Milanese* (actor only)
1963 *I Fidanzati* (UK: *The Engagement*)
1964 *E Venne Un Uomo* (UK: *A Man Named John*)
1969 *Un Certo Giorno* (UK: *One Fine Day*)
1970 *I Recuperanti* (UK: *The Scavengers*)
1971 *Durante L'Estate* (UK: *During The Summer*)
1974 *La Circostanza* (UK: *The Circumstance*)
1978 *L'Albero Degli Zoccoli\** (UK: *The Tree Of Wooden Clogs*)
1982 *Cammina, Cammina*
1983 *Milano '83* (documentary)
1987 *Lunga Vita Alla Signora* (UK: *Long Live The Lady!*)
1988 *La Leggenda Del Santo Bevitore* (UK: *The Legend Of The Holy Drinker*)
1990 *Lungo Il Fiume* (UK: *Down The River* (documentary)

## OSHIMA, Nagisa
(1932– ) Japan

1959 *Ai To Kibo No Machi; Asu No Taiyo* (short)
1960 *Seishun Zankoku Monogatori* (UK: *Cruel Story Of Youth*); *Taiyo No Hakaba; Nihon No Yoru To Kiri* (UK: *Night And Fog In Japan*)
1961 *Shiiku* (UK: *The Catch*)
1962 *Amusaka Shiro Tokisada* (UK: *The Rebel*)
1964 *I'm Here Bellett; A Child's First Adventure*
1965 *Etsuraku* (UK: *The Pleasures Of The Flesh*); *Yunbogi No Nikki* (UK: *The Diary Of Yunbogi*)

**OSHIMA, Nagisa** (cont.)

1966 *Hakuchu No Torima* (UK: *Violence At Noon*)

1967 *Ninja Beugeicho* (UK: *Tales Of The Ninja*); *Nihon Shunkako* (UK: *Sing A Song Of Sex*); *Muri-Shinju: Nihon No Natsu*

1968 *Daitoa Senso* (UK: *The Pacific War*); *Koshikei* (UK: *Death By Hanging*); *Kaeyyekita Yopparai* (UK: *Three Resurrected Drunkards*)

1969 *Mo Taku-To To Bunkadaika-Kumei; Shinjuku Dorobo Nikki* (UK: *Diary Of A Shinjuku Thief*); *Shonen* (UK: *Boy*)

1970 *Tokyo Senso Sengo Hiwa* (UK: *The Man Who Left His Will On Film*)

1971 *Gishiki* (UK: *The Ceremony*)

1972 *Natsu No Imoto* (UK: *Summer Soldiers*)

1976 *Ai No Corrida\** (UK: *Empire Of The Senses*)

1978 *Ai No Borei* (UK: *Empire Of Passion*)

1983 *Merry Christmas Mr Lawrence*

1986 *Max Mon Amour*

1991 *Kyoto, My Mother's Place* (documentary)

# OZU, Yasujiro

(1903–63) Japan

1925 *Gakuso O Idete* (UK: *Out Of College*)

1927 *Zange No Yaiba* (UK: *Sword Of Penitence*)

1928 *Nyobo Funshitsu* (UK: *Wife Lost*); *Kabocha* (UK: *Pumpkin*); *Wakado No Yume* (UK: *The Dreams Of Youth*); *Nikutaibi* (UK: *The Body Beautiful*); *Hikkoshi Fufu* (UK: *Two On The Move*)

1929 *Wakakihi; Wasei Kenka Tomodachi; Takara No Yama; Daigaku Wa Keredo* (UK: *I Passed But...*); *Tokkan Kozo; Kaishain Seikatsu* (UK: *The Life Of An Office Worker*)

1930 *Kekkon-Gaku Nyumon; Hogaraka Ni Ayume; Rakudai Wa Shita Kereda* (UK: *I Failed But...*); *Sono No Yo Tsuma; Erogami No Onryo; Ashi No Sawatta Koun; Shukujo To Hige; Ojosan*

1931 *Tokyo No Gassho* (UK: *Tokyo Chorus*); *Bijin Aishu* (UK: *Beauty's Sorrows*)

1932 *Haru Wa Gofujin Kara; Umarete Wa Mita Karedo* (UK: *I Was Born But...*); *Seishun No Yume Ima Izuko; Mata Au Hi Made* (UK: *Till We Meet Again*)

1933 *Tokyo No Onna* (UK: *Woman Of Tokyo*); *Hijosen No Onna* (UK: *Dragnet Girl*); *Dekigokoro* (UK: *Passing Fancy*)

1934 *Haha Ko Kowazuya* (UK: *A Mother Should Be Loved*); *Ukigusa Monogatori* (UK: *A Story Of Floating Weeds*)

1935 *Hakoiri Musumi* (UK: *An Innocent Maid*); *Tokyo Yoitoko* (UK: *Tokyo Is A Nice Place*); *Tokyo No Yado* (UK: *An Inn In Tokyo*)

1936 *Daigaku Yoitoko* (UK: *College Is A Nice Place*); *Hitori Musuko* (UK: *The Only Son*)

1937 *Shukujo Wa Nani O Wasuretaka* (UK: *What Did The Lady Forget?*)

1941 *Toda-Ke No Kyodai* (UK: *The Brothers And Sisters Of The Toda Family*)

1942 *Chichi Ariki* (UK: *There Was A Father*)

1947 *Nagaya Shinshi Roku* (UK: *Diary Of A Tenement Gentleman*); *Kazi No Naka No Mendori* (UK: *A Hen In The Wind*)

1949 *Banshun* (UK: *Late Spring*)

1950 *Munakata Shimei* (UK: *The Munakata Sisters*)

1951 *Bakushu* (UK: *Early Summer*)

1952 *Ochazuke No Aji* (UK: *The Flavour Of Green Tea Over Rice*)

1953 *Tokyo Monogatari\** (UK: *Tokyo Story*)

1956 *Soshun* (UK: *Early Spring*)

1957 *Tokyo Boshoku* (UK: *Twilight In Tokyo*)

1958 *Higanbana* (UK: *Equinox Flower*)
1959 *Ohayo* (UK: *Good Morning*);
*Ukigusa* (UK: *Floating Weeds*)
1960 *Akibiyori* (UK: *Late Autumn*)
1961 *Kohayagawa-Ke No Aki* (UK:
*Early Autumn*)
1962 *Samma No Aji* (UK: *An Autumn
Afternoon*)

# P

## PAKULA, Alan J
(1928– ) USA

1957 *Fear Strikes Out* (producer only)
1962 *To Kill A Mockingbird** (producer
only)
1963 *Love With The Proper Stranger*
(producer only)
1964 *Baby, The Rain Must Fall*
(producer only)
1965 *Inside Daisy Clover* (producer
only)
1967 *Up The Down Staircase* (producer
only)
1968 *The Stalking Moon* (producer
only)
1969 *The Sterile Cuckoo* (UK: *Pookie*)
1971 *Klute**
1972 *Love, Pain And The Whole
Damned Thing*
1974 *The Parallax View*
1976 *All The President's Men**
1978 *Comes A Horseman*
1979 *Starting Over*
1981 *Roll-Over*
1982 *Sophie's Choice**
1986 *Dream Lover*
1987 *Orphans*
1989 *See You In The Morning*
1990 *Presumed Innocent**
1992 *Consenting Adults*

## PARKER, Alan
(1944– ) UK

1970 *Melody* (screenwriter only)
1973 *Footsteps; Our Cissy* (both shorts)
1974 *The Evacuees* (TV)

1976 *No Hard Feelings* (TV); *Bugsy
Malone**
1978 *Midnight Express**
1980 *Fame*
1981 *Shoot The Moon*
1982 *Pink Floyd — The Wall*
1984 *Birdy*
1987 *Angel Heart*
1988 *Mississippi Burning**
1990 *Come See The Paradise*
1991 *The Commitments*

## PECKINPAH, Sam
(1926–84) USA

1956 *Invasion Of the Bodysnatchers**
(actor only)
1961 *The Deadly Companions*
1962 *Ride The High Country* (UK: *Guns
In The Afternoon*)
1965 *The Glory Guys* (screenwriter
only); *Major Dundee*
1968 *Villa Rides* (screenwriter only)
1969 *The Wild Bunch**
1970 *The Ballad Of Cable Hogue*
1971 *Straw Dogs*
1972 *Junior Bonner; The Getaway*
1973 *Pat Garrett And Billy The Kid*
1974 *Bring Me The Head Of Alfredo
Garcia*
1975 *The Killer Elite*
1977 *Cross Of Iron*
1978 *China 9, Liberty 37* (actor only);
*Convoy*
1979 *Il Visitatore* (UK: *The Visitor*)
(actor only)
1983 *The Osterman Weekend*

## PEERCE, Larry
(c1935– ) USA

1964 *One Potato, Two Potato*
1966 *The Big TNT Show*
1967 *The Incident*
1969 *Goodbye Columbus**
1971 *The Sporting Club*
1972 *A Separate Peace*
1973 *Ash Wednesday*
1974 *The Other Side Of The Mountain*
1976 *Two Minute Warning*

**PEERCE, Larry** (cont.)
1977 *The Other Side Of The Mountain, Part 2*
1979 *The Bell Jar*
1980 *Why Would I Lie?*
1982 *Love Child*
1983 *Hard To Hold*
1987 *Queenie* (TV)
1989 *Wired*

## PENN, Arthur
(1922– ) USA

1958 *The Left-Handed Gun*
1962 *The Miracle Worker*
1965 *Mickey One*
1966 *The Chase*
1967 *Bonnie And Clyde\**
1969 *Alice's Restaurant*
1970 *Little Big Man*
1973 *Visions Of Eight* (documentary, co-director)
1975 *Night Moves*
1976 *The Missouri Breaks*
1981 *Four Friends*
1985 *Target*
1987 *Dead Of Winter*
1989 *Penn And Teller Get Killed*
1992 *The Painting* (TV)

## POITIER, Sidney
(1924– ) USA

1972 *Buck And The Preacher*
1973 *A Warm December*
1974 *Uptown Saturday Night*
1975 *Let's Do It Again*
1977 *A Piece Of The Action*
1980 *Stir Crazy\**
1982 *Hanky Panky*
1985 *Fast Forward*
1990 *Ghost Dad*

See also actors listing

## POLANSKI, Roman
(1933– ) Poland

1955/57 *Rower/The Bicycle* (unfinished)
1958 *Morderstwo; Rozbijemy Zabawe; Lampa; Two Men And A Wardrobe* (all shorts)

1959 *Gdy Spadaja Anioly* (short)
1960 *Le Gros Et Le Maigre* (short)
1962 *Ssaki* (short); *Nóz W Wodzie* (UK: *Knife In The Water*)
1963 *Les Plus Belles Escroqueries Du Monde* (co-director)
1965 *Repulsion\**
1966 *Cul-De-Sac*
1967 *The Fearless Vampire Killers*
1968 *Rosemary's Baby\**
1971 *Macbeth*
1972 *What?*
1974 *Chinatown\**
1976 *Le Locataire* (UK: *The Tenant*)
1979 *Tess\**
1986 *Pirates*
1988 *Frantic\**
1992 *Bitter Moon*

## POLLACK, Sydney
(1934– ) USA

1962 *War Hunt* (actor only)
1965 *The Slender Thread*
1966 *This Property Is Condemned*
1968 *The Scalphunters*
1969 *Castle Keep; They Shoot Horses Don't They?\**
1972 *Jeremiah Johnson*
1973 *The Way We Were\**
1974 *The Yakuza*
1975 *Three Days Of The Condor\**
1977 *Bobby Deerfield*
1979 *The Electric Horseman\**
1980 *Honeysuckle Rose* (executive producer only)
1981 *Absence Of Malice\**
1982 *Tootsie\** (also actor)
1984 *Songwriter* (producer only)
1985 *Out Of Africa\**
1988 *Bright Lights, Big City* (producer only)
1989 *The Fabulous Baker Boys\*; Major League* (both executive producer only)
1990 *Presumed Innocent\** (producer only); *White Palace* (executive producer only); *Havana*
1991 *Dead Again; King Ralph* (both executive producer only)

1992 *The Player\*; Husbands And Wives; Death Becomes Her\** (all actor only)
1993 *The Firm*

## PONTECORVO, Gillo
(1919–  ) Italy

1955 *Die Windrose* (co-director)
1957 *La Grande Strada Azzurra* (UK: *The Long Blue Road*); *Il Medico E Lo Stregone*
1960 *Kapò*
1965 *La Battaglia Di Algeri\** (UK: *The Battle Of Algiers*)
1969 *Queimada* (UK: *Burn*)
1979 *Ogro*

## POWELL, Michael
(1905–90) UK

1931 *Two Crowded Hours; My Friend The King; Rynox; The Rasp; The Star Reporter*
1932 *Hotel Splendide; COD; His Lordship; Born Lucky*
1933 *The Fire Raisers*
1934 *The Night Of The Party; Red Ensign; Something Always Happens; The Girl In The Crowd*
1935 *Lazybones; The Love Test; The Phantom Light; The Price Of A Song; Someday*
1936 *Her Last Affaire; The Brown Wallet; Crown V Stevens; The Man Behind The Mask*
1937 *The Edge Of The World*
1939 *The Spy In Black; The Lion Has Wings*
1940 *Contraband; The Thief Of Bagdad\** (co-director)
1941 *An Airman's Letter To His Mother* (short); *49th Parallel\**
1942 *One Of Our Aircraft Is Missing*
1943 *The Volunteer* (short); *The Silver Fleet* (co-producer only); *The Life And Death Of Colonel Blimp\** (co-director)
1944 *A Canterbury Tale* (co-director)
1945 *I Know Where I'm Going* (co-director)

1946 *A Matter Of Life And Death\** (co-director)
1947 *Black Narcissus\** (co-director); *The End Of The River* (co-producer)
1948 *The Red Shoes\** (co-director)
1949 *The Small Back Room* (co-director)
1950 *Gone To Earth; The Elusive Pimpernel* (both co-director)
1951 *The Tales Of Hoffman* (co-director)
1955 *The Sorcerer's Apprentice* (short); *Oh, Rosalinda!* (co-director)
1956 *The Battle Of The River Plate; Ill Met By Moonlight* (both co-director)
1959 *Honeymoon; Peeping Tom\**
1961 *The Queen's Guards*
1964 *Bluebeard's Castle*
1966 *They're A Weird Mob*
1969 *Age Of Consent*
1972 *The Boy Who Turned Yellow*
1978 *Return To The Edge Of The World*
1983 *Pavlova—A Woman For All Time* (supervisor only)

## PREMINGER, Otto
(1906–86) USA

1931 *Der Grosse Liebe*
1936 *Under Your Spell*
1937 *Danger—Love At Work*
1943 *Margin For Error*
1944 *In The Meantime, Darling; Laura\**
1945 *A Royal Scandal* (UK: *Czarina*); *Fallen Angel*
1946 *Centennial Summer*
1947 *Forever Amber; Daisy Kenyon*
1948 *That Lady In Ermine* (co-director)
1949 *Whirlpool; The Fan* (UK: *Lady Windermere's Fan*)
1950 *Where The Sidewalk Ends*
1951 *The Thirteenth Letter*
1952 *Angel Face*
1953 *The Moon Is Blue; Stalag 17\** (actor only)
1954 *River Of No Return; Carmen Jones*

**PREMINGER, Otto** (cont.)
1955  *The Court Martial Of Billy Mitchell*
(UK: *One Man Mutiny*); *The Man
With The Golden Arm*
1957  *Saint Joan*
1958  *Bonjour Tristesse*
1959  *Porgy And Bess; Anatomy Of A
Murder**
1960  *Exodus**
1962  *Advise And Consent*
1963  *The Cardinal*
1965  *In Harm's Way; Bunny Lake Is
Missing*
1967  *Hurry Sundown*
1968  *Skidoo*
1969  *Tell Me That You Love Me Junie
Moon*
1971  *Such Good Friends*
1975  *Rosebud*
1979  *The Human Factor*

**PRESSBURGER, Emeric**
(1902–88) Hungary

1935  *La Vie Parisienne* (screenwriter
only)
1938  *The Challenge* (screenwriter only)
1939  *The Spy In Black* (screenwriter
only)
1940  *Contraband* (screenwriter only)
1941  *49th Parallel** (screenwriter only)
1942  *One Of Our Aircraft Is Missing*
(co-director)
1943  *The Silver Fleet* (co-producer
only); *The Life And Death Of
Colonel Blimp*; The Volunteer*
(both co-director)
1944  *A Canterbury Tale* (co-director)
1945  *I Know Where I'm Going* (co-
director)
1946  *A Matter Of Life And Death** (co-
director)
1947  *Black Narcissus** (co-director);
*The End Of The River* (co-
producer only)
1948  *The Red Shoes** (co-director)
1949  *The Small Back Room* (co-
director)
1950  *Gone To Earth; The Elusive
Pimpernel* (both co-director)

1951  *The Tales Of Hoffman* (co-
director)
1953  *Twice Upon A Time*
1955  *Oh, Rosalinda!* (co-director)
1956  *The Battle Of The River Plate; Ill
Met By Moonlight* (both co-
director); *Miracle In Soho*
(screenwriter only)
1965  *Operation Crossbow* (screenwriter
only)
1966  *They're A Weird Mob*
(screenwriter only)
1972  *The Boy Who Turned Yellow*
(screenwriter only)

**PUENZO, Luis**
(c1946–   ) Argentina

1973  *Light Of My Shoes*
1985  *La Historia Oficial* (UK: *The
Official Version*)
1989  *Old Gringo**
1992  *The Plague*

# R

**RAFELSON, Bob**
(1933–   ) USA

1968  *Head*
1969  *Easy Rider** (co-producer only)
1970  *Five Easy Pieces**
1971  *The Last Picture Show*; Drive He
Said* (both co-producer only)
1972  *The King Of Marvin Gardens*
1976  *Stay Hungry*
1981  *The Postman Always Rings
Twice**
1985  *Always* (actor only)
1987  *Black Widow*
1989  *The Mountains Of The Moon*
1992  *Man Trouble*

**RAIMI, Sam**
(1957–   ) USA

1982  *The Evil Dead**
1985  *Crimewave; Spies Like Us* (actor
only)

1987 *Evil Dead 2: Dead By Dawn;
Thou Shalt Not Kill...Except* (actor
only)
1988 *Maniac Cop* (actor only)
1989 *Intruder* (actor only); *Easy Wheels*
(executive producer only)
1990 *Darkman; Miller's Crossing\** (actor
only)
1992 *Innocent Blood* (actor only);
*Lunatics: A Love Story* (presenter
only); *Army Of Darkness: The
Medieval Dead*
1993 *Hard Target* (co-producer only)

## RAPPENEAU, Jean-Paul
(1932– ) France

1958 *Chronique Provinciale* (short)
1965 *La Vie De Chateau*
1971 *Les Mariés De L'An Deux* (UK:
*The Scoundrel*)
1975 *Le Sauvage* (UK: *The Savage*)
1982 *Tout Feu, Tout Flamme*
1990 *Cyrano De Bergerac\**

## RAPPER, Irving
(1898– ) USA

1941 *Shining Victory; One Foot In
Heaven*
1942 *The Gay Sisters; Now Voyager\**
1944 *The Adventures Of Mark Twain*
1945 *Rhapsody In Blue; The Corn Is
Green*
1946 *Deception*
1947 *The Voice Of The Turtle*
1949 *Anna Lucasta*
1950 *The Glass Menagerie*
1951 *Another Man's Poison*
1953 *Forever Female; Bad For Each
Other*
1956 *Strange Intruder; The Brave
One*
1958 *Marjorie Morningstar*
1959 *The Miracle*
1960 *Giuseppe Venduto Dei Fratelli*
(UK: *Sold Into Egypt*)
1961 *Pontius Pilate*
1970 *The Christine Jorgensen Story*
1978 *Born Again*

## RAY, Nicholas
real name: Ray Nicholas Kienzle
(1911-79) USA

1948 *They Live By Night*
1949 *A Woman's Secret; Knock On
Any Door*
1950 *Born To Be Bad; In A Lonely
Place*
1951 *Flying Leathernecks; On
Dangerous Ground* (co-director)
1952 *The Lusty Men*
1954 *Johnny Guitar*
1955 *Run For Cover; Rebel Without A
Cause\**
1956 *Bigger Than Life; Hot Blood*
1957 *Bitter Victory; The True Story Of
Jesse James* (UK:*The James
Brothers*)
1958 *Wind Across The Everglades;
Party Girl*
1959 *The Savage Innocents*
1961 *King Of Kings*
1962 *55 Days At Peking*
1073 *Wo Can't Go Homo Again*
1974 *Dreams Of Thirteen* (co-director)
1977 *Der Amerikanische Freund* (UK:
*The American Friend*) (actor only)
1979 *Hair* (actor only)
1980 *Lightning Over Water*
(documentary, co-director)

## RAY, Satyajit
(1921-92) India

1955 *Pather Panchali\**
1956 *Aparajito* (UK: *The Unvanquished*)
1957 *Paras Pathar* (UK: *The
Philosopher's Stone*)
1958 *Jalsaghar* (UK: *The Music Room*)
1959 *Apu Sansar* (UK: *The World Of Apu*)
1960 *Devi* (UK: *The Goddess*)
1961 *Rabindranath Tragore*
(documentary); *Teen Kanya* (UK:
*Two Daughters*)
1962 *Kanchanjanga; Abhijan*
1963 *Mahanagar* (UK: *The Big City*)
1964 *Charulata* (UK: *The Lonely Wife*)
1965 *Two* (short); *Kapurush-O-
Mahapurush* (UK: *The Coward
And The Holy Man*)

**RAY, Satyajit** (cont.)
1966  Nayak (UK: The Hero)
1967  Chiriakhana
1968  Goopy Gyne, Bagha Byne (UK: The Adventures Of Goopy And Bagha)
1969  Aranyer Din Ratri (UK: Days And Nights In The Forest)
1970  Pratidwandi (UK: The Adversary)
1971  Sikkim (documentary); Seemabaddha (UK: Company Limited)
1973  Ashanti Sanket (UK: Distant Thunder)
1974  The Inner Eye (short)
1975  Sonar Kella (UK: The Golden Fortress); Jane Aranya (UK: The Middle-Man)
1977  Shantranj Ke Kilhari (UK: The Chess Players)
1979  Joi Baba Felunath (UK: The Elephant God)
1980  Heerok Rajar Deshe (UK: The Kingdom Of Diamonds
1981  Sadgati (TV) (UK: Deliverance); Pikoo (TV) (short)
1982  Ghare Bahire (UK: Home And The World)
1989  Ganashatru (UK: An Enemy Of The People)
1990  Shakha Proshakha (UK: Branches Of The Tree)

**REDFORD, Robert**
(1937–  ) USA

1980  Ordinary People*
1987  The Milagro Beanfield War
1992  A River Runs Through It

See also actors listing

**REED, Sir Carol**
(1906–76) UK

1935  It Happened In Paris (co-director); Midshipman Easy
1936  Laburnum Grove; Talk Of The Devil
1937  Who's Your Lady Friend?
1938  Bank Holiday; Penny Paradise; Climbing High
1939  A Girl Must Live; The Stars Look Down
1940  Night Train To Munich; The Girl In The News
1941  Kipps; The Young Mr Pitt
1942  A Letter From Home; The New Lot (both documentaries)
1944  The Way Ahead
1945  The True Glory (documentary)
1946  Odd Man Out*
1948  The Fallen Idol
1949  The Third Man*
1950  National Playing Fields (documentary short)
1951  Outcast Of The Islands
1953  The Man Between
1955  A Kid For Two Farthings
1956  Trapeze*
1958  The Key
1960  Our Man In Havana
1963  The Running Man
1965  The Agony And The Ecstasy
1968  Oliver!*
1970  Flap (UK: The Last Warrior)
1971  Follow Me

**REINER, Carl**
(1923–  ) USA

1959  Happy Anniversary; The Gazebo (both actor only)
1961  Gidget Goes Hawaiian (actor only)
1963  It's A Mad, Mad, Mad, Mad World* (actor only); The Thrill Of It All (actor and screenwriter only)
1965  The Art Of Love (actor and screenwriter only)
1966  Alice Of Wonderland In Paris; Don't Worry We'll Think Of A Title; The Russians Are Coming, The Russians Are Coming* (all actor only)
1967  Enter Laughing; A Guide For The Married Man (actor only)
1969  The Comic; Generation (actor only)
1970  Where's Poppa?

1973 *10 From Your Show Of Shows* (actor only)
1975 *Medical Story* (TV) (actor only)
1977 *Oh, God!**
1978 *The One And Only; The End* (actor only)
1979 *The Jerk**
1982 *Dead Men Don't Wear Plaid*
1983 *The Man With Two Brains**
1984 *All Of Me**
1985 *Summer Rental*
1987 *Summer School*
1989 *Bert Rigby, You're A Fool*
1990 *Spirit Of '76* (actor only); *Sibling Rivalry*
1993 *Triple Indemnity*

## REINER, Rob
(1945– ) USA

1967 *Enter Laughing* (actor only)
1970 *Where's Poppa?; Halls Of Anger* (both actor only)
1971 *Summertree* (actor only)
1974 *Thursday's Game* (TV) (actor only)
1975 *How Come Nobody's On Our Side?* (actor only)
1977 *Fire Sale* (actor only)
1979 *More Than Friends* (TV) (actor and co-writer only)
1982 *Million Dollar Infield* (actor and co-writer only)
1984 *This Is Spinal Tap*
1985 *The Sure Thing*
1987 *Throw Momma From The Train** (actor only); *Stand By Me; The Princess Bride*
1989 *When Harry Met Sally**
1990 *Postcards From The Edge*; Spirit Of '76* (both actor only); *Misery**
1991 *Regarding Henry** (actor only)
1992 *A Few Good Men**

## REISZ, Karel
(1926– ) Czechoslovakia

1952 *Stars Who Made The Cinema* (documentary)
1955 *Momma Don't Allow* (co-director, documentary)

1957 *Every Day Except Christmas* (co-producer only)
1959 *We Are The Lambeth Boys* (documentary)
1960 *Saturday Night And Sunday Morning**
1963 *This Sporting Life* (producer only)
1964 *Night Must Fall*
1966 *Morgan—A Suitable Case For Treatment*
1968 *Isadora*
1974 *The Gambler*
1978 *Who'll Stop The Rain?* (UK: *Dog Soldiers*)
1981 *The French Lieutenant's Woman**
1985 *Sweet Dreams**
1990 *Everybody Wins*

## REITMAN, Ivan
(1946– ) Canada

1071 *Foxy Lady*
1972 *Cannibal Girls*
1975 *Shivers/They Came From Within/ The Parasite Murders* (co-producer only)
1976 *Death Weekend* (producer only); *Rabid* (co-executive producer only)
1978 *National Lampoon's Animal House** (producer only); *Et La Terreur Commence* (executive producer only)
1979 *Meatballs*
1981 *Heavy Metal* (producer); *Stripes*
1983 *Spacehunter: Adventures In The Forbidden Zone* (executive producer only)
1984 *Ghostbusters**
1986 *Legal Eagles; The Canadian Conspiracy* (actor only)
1987 *Big Shots* (executive producer only)
1988 *Casual Sex?; Feds* (both executive producer only); *Twins**
1989 *Ghostbusters II*
1990 *Kindergarten Cop**
1993 *Dave*

## RENE, Norman
(19?–   ) USA

1990  *Longtime Companion\**
1992  *Prelude To A Kiss*


## RENOIR, Jean
(1894–1979) France

1924  *Une Fille Sans Joie; La Fille De L'Eau* (UK: *Whirlpool Of Fate*)
1926  *Nana*
1927  *Charleston; Marquita*
1928  *La Petite Marchande D'Allumettes* (UK: *The Little Match-Seller*); *Tire-Au-Flanc*
1929  *Le Tournoi; Le Bled*
1930  *On Purge Bébé*
1931  *La Chienne*
1932  *La Nuit Du Carrefour; Boudu Sauvé Des Eaux* (UK: *Boudu Saved From Drowning*)
1933  *Chotard Et Cie*
1934  *Madame Bovary; Toni*
1935  *Le Crime De Monsieur Lange*
1936  *La Vie Est À Nous; Une Partie De Campagne* (UK: *A Day In The Country*)
1937  *La Grande Illusion\*; La Marseillaise; Terre D'Espagne* (documentary); *Les Bas-Fonds* (UK: *The Lower Depths*)
1938  *La Bête Humaine* (UK: *Judas Was A Woman*)
1939  *La Règle Du Jeu\** (UK: *The Rules Of The Game*)
1940  *La Tosca* (co-director)
1941  *Swamp Water* (UK: *The Man Who Came Back*)
1943  *This Land Is Mine*
1944  *Salute To France* (documentary)
1945  *The Southerner*
1946  *The Diary Of A Chambermaid*
1947  *The Woman On The Beach*
1951  *The River*
1952  *La Carrozza D'Oro* (UK: *The Golden Coach*)
1955  *French Cancan*
1956  *Élena Et Les Hommes* (UK: *The Night Does Strange Things*);

*L'Album De Famille De Jean Renoir* (documentary)
1959  *Le Testament Du Docteur Cordelier* (UK: *Experiment In Evil*); *Le Déjeuner Sur L'Herbe* (UK: *Lunch On The Grass*)
1962  *Le Caporal Epinglé*
1968  *La Direction D'Acteur Par Jean Renoir* (documentary)
1969  *Le Petit Théatre De Jean Renoir*


## REYNOLDS, Kevin
(1953–   ) USA

1980  *Proof* (short—student film)
1985  *Fandango*
1988  *The Beast*
1991  *Robin Hood: Prince Of Thieves\**
1993  *Rapa Nui*


## RICHARDSON, Tony
real name: Cecil Antonio Richardson
(1928–91) UK

1955  *Momma Don't Allow* (co-director)
1959  *Look Back In Anger*
1960  *The Entertainer\**
1961  *Sanctuary; A Taste Of Honey*
1962  *The Loneliness Of The Long Distance Runner*
1963  *Tom Jones\**
1965  *The Loved One*
1966  *Mademoiselle*
1967  *Red And Blue* (short)
1968  *The Charge Of The Light Brigade*
1969  *Laughter In The Dark; Hamlet*
1970  *Ned Kelly*
1973  *A Delicate Balance*
1974  *Dead Cert*
1977  *Joseph Andrews*
1978  *A Death In Canaan* (TV)
1982  *The Border*
1984  *The Hotel New Hampshire*
1985  *Turning A Blind Eye* (documentary)
1986  *Penalty Phase* (TV)
1988  *Shadows On The Sun* (TV)
1990  *The Phantom Of The Opera* (TV)
1991  *Blue Sky*

## RITCHIE, Michael
(1938– ) USA

1967 *The Outsider* (TV); *Cry Hard, Cry Fast* (TV)
1968 *The Sound Of Anger(TV)*
1969 *Downhill Racer*
1972 *Prime Cut; The Candidate*
1975 *Smile*
1976 *The Bad News Bears**
1977 *Semi-Tough*
1978 *The Bad News Bears Go To Japan* (producer only)
1979 *An Almost Perfect Affair*
1980 *The Island; Divine Madness*
1983 *The Survivors*
1985 *Fletch*
1986 *The Golden Child; Wildcats*
1988 *The Couch Trip*
1989 *Fletch Lives*
1992 *Diggstown* (UK: *Midnight Sting*)
1993 *Cops And Robbersons*

## RITT, Martin
(1914–90) USA

1944 *Winged Victory* (actor only)
1956 *Edge Of The City* (UK: *A Man Is Ten Feet Tall*)
1957 *No Down Payment*
1958 *The Long, Hot Summer*
1959 *The Sound And The Fury; The Black Orchid; Five Branded Women*
1961 *Paris Blues*
1962 *Hemingway's Adventures Of A Young Man*
1963 *Hud**
1964 *The Outrage*
1965 *The Spy Who Came In From The Cold*
1967 *Hombre*
1968 *The Brotherhood*
1969 *The Molly Maguires*
1970 *The Great White Hope*
1972 *Sounder*; Pete'n' Tillie*
1974 *Conrack*
1975 *Der Richter Und Sein Henker* (UK: *End Of The Game*) (actor only)
1976 *The Front*
1977 *Casey's Shadow*

1979 *Norma Rae**
1981 *Back Roads*
1983 *Cross Creek*
1985 *The Slugger's Wife*
1986 *Murphy's Romance*
1987 *Nuts**
1989 *Stanley And Iris*

## ROBBINS, Jerome
real name: Jerome Rabinowitz
(1918– ) USA

1956 *The King And I** (choreographer only)
1961 *West Side Story** (co-director)

## ROBBINS, Tim
(1958– ) USA

1992 *Bob Roberts**

See also actors listing

## ROBINSON, Phil Alden
(1950– ) USA

1984 *All Of Me*; Rhinestone* (both screenwriter only)
1987 *In The Mood* (UK: *The Woo Woo Kid*)
1989 *Field Of Dreams**
1992 *Sneakers*

## ROBSON, Mark
(1913–78) USA

1943 *The Seventh Victim; The Ghost Ship*
1944 *Youth Runs Wild*
1945 *Isle Of The Dead*
1946 *Bedlam*
1948 *Roughshod*
1949 *Champion; Home Of The Brave; My Foolish Heart*
1950 *Edge Of Doom* (UK: *Stronger Than Fear*); *Bright Victory* (UK: *Lights Out*)
1951 *I Want You*
1953 *Return To Paradise*
1954 *Hell Below Zero; Phffft!; The Bridges At Toko-Ri*

**ROBSON, Mark** (cont.)
1955 *A Prize Of Gold; Trial*
1956 *The Harder They Fall*
1957 *The Little Hut; Peyton Place\**
1958 *The Inn Of The Sixth Happiness*
1960 *From The Terrace\**
1962 *Nine Hours To Rama*
1963 *The Prize*
1965 *Von Ryan's Express*
1967 *Valley Of The Dolls*
1969 *Daddy's Gone A-Hunting*
1971 *Happy Birthday, Wanda June*
1972 *Limbo*
1974 *Earthquake\**
1979 *Avalanche Express*

## ROEG, Nicolas
(1928–  ) UK

1958 *A Woman Possessed; Moment Of Indiscretion; The Man Inside* (all camera operator only)
1959 *The Great Van Robbery; Passport To Shame; The Child And The Killer* (all camera operator only)
1960 *The Trials Of Oscar Wilde; The Sundowners\*; Jazz Boat* (all camera operator only)
1961 *Information Received* (camera operator only)
1962 *Lawrence Of Arabia\** (second-unit photographer)
1963 *Dr Crippen; The System; The Caretaker; Just For Fun* (all cinematographer only)
1964 *The Masque Of The Red Death; Nothing But The Best; Every Day's A Holiday; Code 7, Victim 5* (all cinematographer only)
1965 *Judith* (second-unit director)
1966 *A Funny Thing Happened On The Way To The Forum; Fahrenheit 451* (both cinematographer only)
1967 *Far From The Madding Crowd; Casino Royale* (both cinematographer only)
1968 *Petulia* (cinematographer only)
1970 *Performance* (co-director)
1971 *Walkabout; The Glastonbury Fair* (short)
1973 *Don't Look Now*

1976 *The Man Who Fell To Earth*
1980 *Bad Timing\**
1982 *Eureka*
1985 *Insignificance*
1987 *Castaway; Aria* (co-director)
1988 *Track 29*
1989 *Sweet Bird Of Youth* (TV); *The Witches*
1990 *Without You I'm Nothing* (executive producer only); *Cold Heaven*

## ROMERO, George A
(1940–  ) USA

1954 *The Man From The Meteor* (short)
1955 *Gorilla* (short)
1956 *Earthbottom* (documentary)
1958 *Curly; Slant* (both shorts)
1962 *Expostulations*
1968 *Night Of The Living Dead\**
1972 *There's Always Vanilla/The Affair*
1973 *Jack's Wife/Hungry Wives; The Crazies*
1976 *Martin*
1978 *Zombies* (UK: *Zombies — Dawn Of The Dead*)
1981 *Knightriders*
1982 *Creepshow*
1985 *Day Of The Dead*
1987 *Creepshow 2* (screenwriter only)
1988 *Monkey Shines: An Experiment In Fear*
1990 *Night Of The Living Dead* (executive producer only); *Two Evil Eyes* (co-director); *Tales From The Darkside — The Movie* (co-writer)
1991 *The Dark Half; The Silence Of The Lambs* (actor only)

## ROSENBERG, Stuart
(1925–  ) USA

1960 *Murder Inc* (co-director)
1961 *Question 7*
1965 *Memorandum For A Spy* (TV)
1966 *Fame Is The Name Of The Game* (TV); *The Faceless Man* (TV)
1967 *Cool Hand Luke\**

1969 *The April Fools*
1970 *WUSA; Move*
1972 *Pocket Money*
1973 *The Laughing Policeman* (UK: *An Investigation Of Murder*)
1975 *The Drowning Pool*
1976 *Voyage Of The Damned*
1978 *Love And Bullets*
1979 *The Amityville Horror**
1980 *Brubaker*
1984 *The Pope Of Greenwich Village*
1987 *Let's Get Harry*
1991 *My Heroes Have Always Been Cowboys*

## ROSS, Herbert
(1927– ) USA

1954 *Carmen Jones* (choreographer only)
1961 *The Young Ones* (choreographer only)
1962 *Summer Holiday* (choreographer only)
1967 *Doctor Dolittle* (choreographer only)
1968 *Funny Girl** (choreographer only)
1969 *Goodbye Mr Chips*
1970 *The Owl And The Pussycat**
1971 *T R Baskin* (UK: *A Date With A Lonely Girl*)
1972 *Play It Again, Sam**
1973 *The Last Of Sheila*
1975 *Funny Lady; The Sunshine Boys*
1976 *The Seven-Per-Cent Solution*
1977 *The Turning Point*; The Goodbye Girl**
1978 *California Suite**
1980 *Nijinsky*
1981 *Pennies From Heaven*
1982 *I Ought To Be In Pictures*
1983 *Max Dugan Returns*
1984 *Footloose; Protocol*
1987 *Dancers; The Secret Of My Success*
1989 *Steel Magnolias**
1990 *My Blue Heaven*
1991 *True Colors*
1993 *Undercover Blues*

## ROSSELLINI, Roberto
(1906–77) Italy

1936 *Daphne* (short)
1938 *Prelude A L'Après-Midi D'Un Faune* (short); *Luciano Serra Pilota* (co-director)
1939 *Fantasia Sottomarino; Il Tachino Prepotente; La Vispa Teresa* (all shorts)
1941 *Il Ruscello Di Ripasottile* (short); *La Nave Bianca*
1942 *Una Pilota Ritorna*
1943 *L'Uomo Della Croce; Desiderio* (co-director)
1945 *Roma, Città Aperta** (UK: *Rome—Open City*)
1946 *Paisà*
1947 *Germania, Anno Zero* (UK: *Germany: Year Zero*)
1948 *L'Amore* (UK: *Ways Of Love*); *Il Miracolo; La Macchina Ammazzacattivi*
1949 *Stromboli*
1950 *Francesco—Giullaro Di Dio*
1952 *Europa'51* (UK: *No Greater Love*); *The Seven Deadly Sins* (co-director); *Siamo Donne* (UK: *We The Women*) (co-director)
1953 *Dov'è La Liberta?*
1954 *Viaggio In Italia* (UK: *Journey To Italy*); *Giovanna D'Arco Al Rogo* (UK: *Joan Of Arc At The Stake*); *Die Angst* (UK: *Fear*); *Amori Di Mezzo Secolo* (co-director)
1958 *India* (documentary)
1959 *Il Generale Della Rovere*
1960 *Viva L'Italia!; Era Notte A Roma* (UK: *It Was A Night In Rome*)
1961 *Vanina Vanini* (UK: *The Betrayer*); *Torino Nei Centi Anni* (documentary)
1962 *Anima Nera; RoGoPaG* (co-director)
1964 *L'Età Del Ferro* (documentary)
1966 *La Prise De Pouvoir De Louis XIV* (TV)
1967 *Idea Di Un'Isola* (TV)
1968 *Atti Degli Apostoli* (TV) (UK: *Acts Of The Apostles*)
1970 *Socrates* (TV)

**ROSSELLINI, Roberto** (cont.)

1971 *Blaise Pascal* (TV)
1972 *Agostino Di Ippona*
1973 *L'Età Di Cosimo De Medici* (TV)
1974 *Descartes* (TV)
1975 *Anno Uno* (UK: *Year One*)
1977 *Il Messia* (UK: *The Messiah*)

## ROSSEN, Robert
(1908–66) USA

1937 *Marked Woman; They Won't Forget* (both co-writer only)
1938 *Racket Busters* (co-writer only)
1939 *Dust Be My Destiny; The Roaring Twenties\** (both screenwriter only)
1940 *A Child Is Born* (screenwriter only)
1941 *Blues In The Night; The Sea Wolf; Out Of The Fog* (all screenwriter only)
1943 *Edge Of Darkness* (screenwriter only)
1946 *A Walk In The Sun; The Strange Love Of Martha Ivers*
1947 *Desert Fury* (screenwriter only); *Johnny O'Clock; Body And Soul*
1949 *The Undercover Man* (screenwriter only); *All The King's Men\**
1951 *The Brave Bulls*
1955 *Mambo*
1956 *Alexander The Great*
1957 *Island In The Sun*
1959 *They Came To Cordura*
1961 *The Hustler\**
1964 *Lilith*

## RUBEN, Joseph
(1951–  ) USA

1975 *The Sister-In-Law*
1976 *The Pom Pom Girls*
1977 *Joyride*
1978 *Our Winning Season*
1980 *GORP*
1984 *Dreamscape*
1987 *The Stepfather*
1989 *True Believer*
1991 *Sleeping With The Enemy\**
1993 *The Good Son*

## RUGGLES, Wesley
(1889–1972) USA

1917 *Bobby, The Pacifist; Bobby's Bravery; Bobby, Philanthropist; Bobby, Movie Director* (all shorts); *For France*
1918 *The Blind Adventure*
1919 *The Winchester Woman*
1920 *Sooner Or Later; Piccadilly Jim; The Desperate Hero; Love; The Leopard Woman*
1921 *The Greater Claim; Uncharted Seas; Over The Wire*
1922 *Wild Honey; If I Were Queen; Slippery McGee*
1923 *Mr Billings Spends His Dime; The Remittance Woman; The Heart Raider*
1924 *The Age Of Innocence*
1925 *Welcome Granger; He Who Gets Rapped; Merton Of The Goofies; The Great Decide; The Fast Male; The Covered Flagon; Madam Sans Gin; Three Bases East; What Price Gloria?; Don Coo-Coo* (all shorts)
1926 *A Man Of Quality; The Kick-Off*
1927 *Beware Of Widows; Silk Stockings*
1928 *The Fourflusher; Finders Keepers*
1929 *Street Girl; Girl Overboard; Condemned* (UK: *Condemned To Devil's Island*); *Scandal* (UK: *High Society*)
1930 *Honey; The Sea Bat*
1931 *Cimarron\*; Are These Our Children?*
1932 *Roar Of The Dragon; No Man Of Her Own*
1933 *The Monkey's Paw; College Humor; I'm No Angel\**
1934 *Bolero; Shoot The Works* (UK: *Thank Your Stars*)
1935 *The Gilded Lily; Accent On Youth; The Bride Comes Home*
1936 *Valiant Is The Word For Carrie*
1937 *I Met Him In Paris; True Confession*
1938 *Sing, You Sinners*
1939 *Invitation To Happiness*

1940 *Too Many Husbands* (UK: *My Two Husbands*)
1941 *Arizona; You Belong To Me* (UK: *Good Morning, Doctor*)
1942 *Somewhere I'll Find You*
1943 *Slightly Dangerous*
1944 *See Here, Private Hargrove*
1946 *London Town*

## RUSSELL, Ken
(1927–  ) UK

1957 *Peepshow* (short)
1958 *Amelia And The Angel* (short); *Lourdes* (documentary)
1964 *French Dressing*
1967 *Billion Dollar Brain*
1968 *Song Of Summer* (TV)
1969 *Women In Love\**
1970 *Dance Of the Seven Veils* (TV); *The Music Lovers*
1971 *The Devils; The Boyfriend*
1972 *Savage Messiah*
1974 *Mahler; Tommy*
1975 *Lisztomania*
1977 *Valentino*
1978 *Clouds Of Glory* (TV)
1980 *Altered States*
1984 *Crimes Of Passion*
1986 *Gothic*
1987 *Aria* (co-director)
1988 *The Lair Of The White Worm; Salome's Last Dance*
1989 *The Rainbow*
1990 *The Russia House* (actor only)
1991 *Whore; Prisoner Of Honor* (TV)

## RYDELL, Mark
(1934–  ) USA

1956 *Crime In The Streets* (actor only)
1968 *The Fox\**
1969 *The Reivers*
1972 *The Cowboys*
1973 *The Long Goodbye* (actor only); *Cinderella Liberty*
1976 *Harry And Walter Go To New York*
1979 *The Rose\**
1981 *On Golden Pond\**
1984 *The River*

1988 *Punchline\** (actor only)
1990 *Havana* (actor only)
1991 *For The Boys*
1993 *Intersection*

# S

## SAKS, Gene
(1921–  ) USA

1965 *A Thousand Clowns* (actor only)
1967 *The Odd Couple\*; Barefoot In The Park\**
1969 *Cactus Flower\**
1972 *Last Of The Red Hot Lovers*
1974 *Mame*
1975 *The Prisoner Of Second Avenue* (actor only)
1978 *The One And Only* (actor only)
1983 *Lovesick* (actor only)
1984 *The Goodbye People* (actor only)
1988 *Funny* (actor only); *Brighton Beach Memoirs*

## SANDRICH, Mark
(1900–45) USA

1926 *Jerry The Giant* (co-director); *Napoleon Junior* (short)
1927 *A Midsummer Night's Steam; Brave Cowards; Careless Hubby; First Prize; Hello Sailor; Hold Fast; Hold That Bear; Hot Soup; The Movie Hound; Night Owls; Shooting Wild; Some Scout*
1928 *Bear Knees; A Cow's Husband; High Strung; A Lady Lion; Sword Points* (all shorts); *Love Is Blonde* (co-director); *Runaway Girls*
1931 *The County Seat; Cowslips; The Gay Nighties; Many A Sip; A Melon-Drama; Scratch As Catch Can; The Strife Of The Party; The Way Of All Fish; The Wife O'Riley; False Roomers* (all shorts)
1932 *Ex-Rooster; A Hurry Call; The Iceman's Ball; Jitters, The Butler; The Millionaire Cat; A Slip At The Switch; When Summons Comes; So This Is Harris* (all shorts)

**SANDRICH, Mark** (cont.)

1933 *The Druggist's Dilemma; Hokus Focus; Private Wives; Thru Thin And Thicket, Or Who's Zoo In Africa* (all shorts); *Melody Cruise; Aggie Appleby, Maker Of Men* (UK: *Cupid In The Rough*)
1934 *Hips Hips Hooray; Cockeyed Cavaliers; The Gay Divorcee\** (UK: *The Gay Divorce*)
1935 *Top Hat\**
1936 *Follow The Fleet; A Woman Rebels*
1937 *Shall We Dance?*
1938 *Carefree*
1939 *Man About Town*
1940 *Buck Benny Rides Again; Love Thy Neighbour*
1941 *Skylark*
1942 *Holiday Inn\**
1943 *So Proudly We Hail!*
1944 *Here Come The Waves; I Love A Soldier*

## SAYLES, John
(1950–　) USA

1978 *Piranha* (screenwriter)
1979 *The Lady In Red* (screenwriter only); *The Return Of The Secaucus Seven\**
1980 *Alligator; Battle Beyond The Stars; The Howling; A Perfect Match* (TV) (all screenwriter only)
1982 *Lianna; The Challenge* (screenwriter only)
1983 *Baby, It's You; Enormous Changes At The Last Minute* (co-screenwriter only)
1984 *Hard Choices* (actor only); *The Brother From Another Planet*
1986 *Unnatural Causes* (TV) (actor and screenwriter only); *The Clan Of The Cave Bear* (screenwriter only); *Something Wild* (actor only)
1987 *Matewan; Wild Thing* (screenwriter only)
1988 *Eight Men Out*
1989 *Shannon's Deal* (TV); *Breaking In* (screenwriter only); *Untamagiru* (actor only)

1990 *Little Vegas* (actor only)
1991 *City Of Hope*
1992 *Straight Talk* (actor only); *Passion Fish*
1993 *My Life's In Turnaround* (actor only); *The Secret Of Roan And Inish*

## SCHAFFNER, Franklin J
(1920–89) USA

1963 *The Stripper* (UK: *Woman Of Summer*)
1964 *The Best Man*
1965 *The War Lord*
1967 *The Double Man; Planet Of The Apes\**
1970 *Patton\**
1971 *Nicholas And Alexandra*
1973 *Papillon\**
1976 *Islands In The Stream*
1978 *The Boys From Brazil*
1980 *Sphinx*
1982 *Yes Giorgio*
1987 *Lionheart*
1989 *Welcome Home*

## SCHEPISI, Fred
full name: Frederic Alan Schepisi
(1939–　) Australia

1970 *The Party* (short)
1973 *Libido* (co-director)
1976 *The Devil's Playground*
1978 *The Chant Of Jimmie Blacksmith*
1982 *Barbarosa*
1984 *Iceman*
1985 *Plenty*
1987 *Roxanne\**
1988 *A Cry In The Dark\**
1990 *The Russia House*
1992 *Mr Baseball*
1993 *Six Degrees Of Separation*

## SCHERTZINGER, Victor
(1880–1941) USA

1917 *The Millionaire Vagrant; The Clodhopper; Sudden Jim; The Pinch Hitter*

1918 *The Son Of His Father; Hired Man; His Mother's Boy; The Family Skeleton; Playing The Game; His Own Home Town; The Claws Of The Hun; A Nine O'Clock Town*

1919 *Hard Boiled; Home Breaker; The Lady Of Red Butte; Other Men's Wives; The Sheriff's Son; String Beans; Extravagance; Quicksands; The Peace Of Roaring River; When Doctors Disagree; Upstairs*

1920 *Pinto; The Jinx; The Blooming Angel; The Slim Princess*

1921 *Made In Heaven; What Happened To Rosa; The Concert; Beating The Game; Mr Barnes Of New York; Head Over Heels; Bootlegger's Daughter; Scandalous Tongues*

1923 *The Lonely Road; The Scarlet Lily; Refuge; Dollar Devils; The Kingdom Within; The Man Next Door; Chastity; Long Live The King; The Man Life Passed By*

1924 *Bread; A Boy Of Flanders*

1925 *Thunder Mountain; Frivolous Sal; Man And Maid; The Wheel; The Golden Strain*

1926 *Siberia; The Return Of Peter Grimm; The Lily*

1927 *Stage Madness; The Secret Studio; The Heart Of Salome*

1928 *The Showdown; Forgotten Faces; Manhattan Cocktail*

1929 *Fashions in Love; The Wheel Of Life; Redskin; Nothing But The Truth; The Laughing Lady*

1930 *Safety In Numbers; Heads Up; Paramount On Parade* (co-director)

1931 *Friends And Lovers; The Woman Between* (UK: *Madame Julie*)

1932 *Strange Justice; Uptown New York*

1933 *The Cocktail Hour; The Constant Woman; My Woman*

1934 *Beloved; One Night Of Love*

1935 *Let's Live Tonight; Love Me Forever* (UK: *On Wings Of Song*)

1936 *The Music Goes Round*

1937 *Something To Sing About*

1939 *The Mikado*

1940 *Rhythm On The River; Road To Singapore**

1941 *Birth Of The Blues; Road To Zanzibar; Kiss The Boys Goodbye*

1942 *The Fleet's In*

## SCHLESINGER, John
(1926– ) UK

1950 *The Starfish* (documentary)

1956 *Sunday In The Park* (documentary)

1959 *The Innocent Eye* (documentary)

1960 *Terminus* (documentary)

1961 *The Class* (documentary)

1962 *A Kind Of Loving*

1963 *Billy Liar**

1965 *Darling**

1967 *Far From The Madding Crowd*

1969 *Midnight Cowboy**

1971 *Sunday, Bloody Sunday**

1973 *Visions Of Eight* (co-director)

1975 *The Day Of The Locust*

1979 *Yanks*

1981 *Honky Tonk Freeway*

1983 *An Englishman Abroad* (TV)

1985 *The Falcon And The Snowman*

1987 *The Believers*

1988 *Madame Sousatzka*

1990 *Pacific Heights*

1991 *102 Boulevard Haussman* (TV)

1992 *The Lost Language Of Cranes* (TV) (actor only)

1993 *The Innocent*

## SCHLÖNDORFF, Volker
(1939– ) Germany

1960 *Wenn Kummert's* (short)

1966 *Young Törless; Mord Und Totschlag* (UK: *A Degree Of Murder*)

1969 *Michael Kohlhaas*

1970 *Baal*

1971 *Rio Da Mortes* (TV); *Der Plötzliche Reichtum Der Armen Leute Von Kombach* (UK: *The*

**SCHLÖNDORFF, Volker** (cont.)
   *Sudden Fortune Of The Poor People Of Kombach)*
1972 *Die Ehegattin; Die Moral Der Ruth Halbfass; Strohfeuer* (UK: *Summer Lightning)*
1974 *Übernächtung In Tirol*
1975 *Die Verlorene Ehre Der Katharina Blum* (UK: *The Lost Honour Of Katharina Blum*) (co-director)
1976 *Der Fangschuss*
1977 *Coup De Grace*
1978 *Deutschland Im Herbst* (co-director)
1979 *Der Blechtrommel\** (UK: *The Tin Drum)*
1980 *Kaleidoscope*
1981 *Die Fälschung* (UK: *Circle Of Deceit)*
1983 *Krieg Und Frieden*
1984 *Un Amour De Swann* (UK: *Swann In Love*)
1985 *Death Of A Salesman* (TV)
1987 *A Gathering Of Old Men; Vermischte Nachrichten* (UK: *Odds And Ends*) (co-director)
1990 *The Handmaid's Tale*
1991 *Voyager*

**SCHOEDSACK, Ernest Beaumont**
(1893–1979) USA

1924 *Golden Prince/The Lost Empire* (documentary)
1926 *Grass* (documentary, co-director)
1927 *Chang* (documentary, co-director)
1929 *The Four Feathers* (co-director)
1931 *Rango* (documentary)
1932 *The Most Dangerous Game* (UK: *The Hounds Of Zaroff*) (co-director)
1933 *King Kong\*; Son Of Kong* (both co-director); *Blind Adventure*
1935 *The Last Days Of Pompeii*
1937 *Trouble In Morocco; Outlaws Of The Orient*
1940 *Dr Cyclops*
1949 *Mighty Joe Young*
1952 *This Is Cinerama* (uncredited co-director)

**SCHRADER, Paul**
(1946– ) USA

1970 *For Us, The Cinema Is The Most Important Of The Arts* (short)
1974 *The Yakuza* (screenwriter only)
1975 *Obsession* (screenwriter only)
1976 *Taxi Driver\** (screenwriter only)
1977 *Rolling Thunder* (screenwriter only)
1978 *Old Boyfriends* (screenwriter only); *Blue Collar*
1979 *Hardcore* (UK: *The Hardcore Life*)
1980 *Raging Bull\** (screenwriter); *American Gigolo\**
1982 *Cat People*
1985 *Mishima: A Life In Four Chapters*
1986 *The Mosquito Coast* (screenwriter only)
1987 *Light Of Day*
1988 *Patty Hearst; The Last Temptation Of Christ\** (screenwriter only)
1990 *The Comfort Of Strangers*
1991 *Light Sleeper*

**SCHROEDER, Barbet**
(1941– ) Iran

1963 *Les Carabiniers* (actor only)
1965 *Paris Vu Par...* (actor, producer only)
1966 *La Collectionneuse* (producer only)
1969 *Ma Nuit Chez Maud* (UK: *My Night At Maud's*) (producer only); *More*
1972 *L'Amour, L'Après-Midi* (UK: *Chloe In The Afternoon*) (producer only); *La Vallée*
1973 *Céline Et Julie Vont En Bateau* (UK: *Céline And Julie Go Boating*) (actor, executive producer only)
1974 *General Idi Amin Dada*
1975 *Maitresse*
1978 *Koko, Le Gorilla Qui Parle; Perceval Le Gallois* (producer only); *Roberte* (actor only)
1983 *Les Tricheurs; Mauvaise Conduite* (producer only)
1985 *The Charles Bukowski Tapes*
1987 *Barfly*

1989 *Wait Until Spring Bandini* (actor only)
1990 *The Golden Boat* (actor only); *Reversal Of Fortune**
1992 *Single White Female*

## SCORSESE, Martin
(1943– ) USA

1964 *What's A Nice Girl Like You Doing In A Place Like This?* (short)
1965 *It's Not Just You, Murray* (short)
1967 *The Big Shave* (short)
1968 *Who's That Knocking At My Door?*
1970 *Woodstock* (co-assistant director, co-editor only)
1971 *Medicine Ball Caravan* (associate producer only)
1972 *Elvis On Tour* (supervising editor only); *Boxcar Bertha*
1973 *Mean Streets**
1974 *Alice Doesn't Live Here Anymore**
1975 *Italianamerican* (documentary)
1976 *Cannonball* (actor only); *Taxi Driver**
1977 *American Boy* (documentary); *New York, New York**
1978 *The Last Waltz*
1980 *Raging Bull**
1982 *The King Of Comedy**
1983 *Pavlova* (actor only)
1985 *After Hours*
1986 *The Color Of Money**; *Round Midnight* (actor only)
1988 *The Last Temptation Of Christ**
1989 *New York Stories* (co-director)
1990 *Goodfellas**; *Akira Kurosawa's Dreams* (actor only); *The Grifters** (producer only)
1991 *Guilty By Suspicion* (actor only); *Cape Fear**
1993 *Age Of Innocence*

## SCOTT, Ridley
(1939– ) UK

1977 *The Duellists*
1979 *Alien**
1982 *Blade Runner**
1985 *Legend*

1987 *Someone To Watch Over Me*
1989 *Black Rain*
1991 *Thelma And Louise**
1992 *1492: The Conquest Of Paradise*

## SCOTT, Tony
(19?– ) UK

1983 *The Hunger*
1986 *Top Gun**
1987 *Beverly Hills Cop 2*
1990 *Days Of Thunder; Revenge*
1991 *The Last Boy Scout*
1993 *True Romance*

## SEATON, George
(1911–1979) USA

1945 *Billy Rose's Diamond Horseshoe* (UK: *Diamond Horseshoe*); *Junior Miss*
1946 *The Shocking Miss Pilgrim*
1947 *Miracle On 34th Street** (UK: *The Big Heart*)
1948 *Apartment For Peggy*
1949 *Chicken Every Sunday*
1950 *The Big Lift; For Heaven's Sake*
1952 *Anything Can Happen*
1953 *Little Boy Lost*
1954 *The Country Girl**
1956 *The Proud And The Profane*
1957 *Williamsburg: The Story Of A Patriot*
1958 *Teacher's Pet*
1961 *The Pleasure Of His Company*
1962 *The Counterfeit Traitor*
1963 *The Hook*
1964 *36 Hours*
1968 *What's So Bad About Feeling Good?*
1969 *Airport**
1973 *Showdown*

## SELTZER, David
(1940– ) USA

1971 *The Hellstrom Chronicle*
1972 *King, Queen, Knave; One Is A Lonely Number* (both screenwriter only)

**SELTZER, David** (cont.)
1974 *The Other Side Of The Mountain* (screenwriter only)
1976 *The Omen\** (screenwriter only)
1979 *Prophecy* (screenwriter only)
1982 *Six Weeks* (screenwriter only)
1983 *Table For Five* (screenwriter only)
1986 *Lucas*
1988 *Punchline\**
1990 *Bird On A Wire\** (screenwriter only)

**SHELTON, Ron**
(1945– ) USA

1981 *The Pursuit Of DB Cooper* (screenwriter only)
1983 *Under Fire\** (second-unit director, screenwriter only)
1986 *The Best Of Times* (screenwriter only)
1988 *Bull Durham\**
1989 *Blaze*
1992 *White Men Can't Jump*

**SHERIDAN, Jim**
(1949– ) Ireland

1989 *My Left Foot\**
1990 *The Field*
1992 *Into The West* (screenwriter only)

**SHERMAN, Lowell**
(1885–1934) USA

1933 *She Done Him Wrong\**

**SIDNEY, George**
(1911– ) USA

1936 *Polo* (short documentary)
1937 *Sunday Night At The Trocadero; Pacific Paradise* (both shorts)
1938 *Billy Rose's Casa Manana Revue; Party Fever; Men In Fright; Football Romeo; Practical Jokers; Alfalfa's Aunt* (all shorts)
1939 *Tiny Troubles; Love On Tap; Duel Personalities; Clown Princes; Cousin Wilbur; Hollywood Hobbies; Dog Daze* (all shorts)

1941 *Flicker Memories; Willie And The Mouse; Of Pups And Puzzles* (all shorts); *Free And Easy*
1942 *Pacific Rendezvous*
1943 *Pilot No 5; Thousands Cheer*
1944 *Bathing Beauty*
1945 *Anchors Aweigh\**
1946 *Holiday In Mexico; The Harvey Girls\**
1947 *Cass Timberlane*
1948 *The Three Musketeers\**
1949 *The Red Danube*
1950 *Key To The City; Annie Get Your Gun\**
1951 *Showboat\**
1952 *Scaramouche*
1953 *Kiss Me Kate; Young Bess*
1955 *Jupiter's Darling*
1956 *The Eddy Duchin Story*
1957 *Jeanne Eagels; Pal Joey*
1959 *Who Was That Lady?*
1960 *Pepe*
1963 *Bye, Bye Birdie; A Ticklish Affair*
1964 *Viva Las Vegas* (UK: *Love In Las Vegas*)
1966 *The Swinger*
1967 *Half A Sixpence*

**SIEGEL, Don**
(1912–91) USA

1945 *Hitler Lives; Star In the Night* (both shorts)
1946 *The Verdict*
1949 *Night Unto Night; The Big Steal*
1952 *The Duel At Silver Creek; No Time For Flowers*
1953 *China Venture; Count The Hours* (UK: *Every Minute Counts*)
1954 *Riot In Cell Block 11; Private Hell 36*
1955 *Annapolis Story* (UK: *The Blue And The Gold*)
1956 *Invasion Of The Bodysnatchers\*; Crime In The Streets*
1957 *A Spanish Affair; Baby Face Nelson*
1958 *The Line-Up; The Gun Runners*
1959 *Edge Of Eternity; Hound Dog Man*
1960 *Flaming Star*
1962 *Hell Is For Heroes!*

1964 *The Killers; The Hanged Man* (TV)
1967 *Stranger On The Run* (TV)
1968 *Madigan; Coogan's Bluff*
1969 *Death Of A Gunfighter; Two Mules For Sister Sara*
1970 *The Beguiled*
1971 *Dirty Harry\**
1973 *Charley Varrick*
1974 *The Black Windmill*
1976 *The Shootist\**
1977 *Telefon*
1978 *Invasion Of The Bodysnatchers* (actor only)
1979 *Escape From Alcatraz*
1980 *Rough Cut*
1982 *Jinxed!*
1985 *Into The Night* (actor only)

## SILVERSTEIN, Elliot
(1927–  ) USA

1962 *Belle Sommers* (TV)
1965 *Cat Ballou\**
1966 *The Happening*
1969 *A Man Called Horse*
1977 *The Car*
1987 *Night Of Courage* (TV)
1990 *Rich Men, Single Women* (TV)

## SINGLETON, John
(1967–  ) USA

1991 *Boyz 'n' The Hood\**
1993 *Poetic Justice*

## SIODMAK, Robert
(1900–73) USA

1929 *Menschen Am Sonntag* (UK: *People On Sunday*) (co-director)
1930 *Abschied; Der Kampf Mit Dem Drachen* (short)
1931 *Der Mann, Der Seinen Mörder Sucht; Voruntersuchung; Stürme Der Leidenschaft* (UK: *Tempest*)
1932 *Quick*
1933 *Brennendes Geheimnis; Le Sexe Faible* (UK: *The Weaker Sex*)
1934 *La Crise Est Finie*
1936 *La Vie Parisienne; Mister Flow; Le Chemin de Rio* (UK: *Woman Racket*)

1937 *Mollenard*
1938 *Ultimatum* (co-director)
1939 *Pièges* (UK: *Snares*)
1941 *West Point Widow*
1942 *The Night Before The Divorce; My Heart Belongs To Daddy; Fly By Night* (UK: *Secret Of G 32*)
1943 *Someone To Remember; Son Of Dracula*
1944 *Cobra Woman; Phantom Lady; Christmas Holiday*
1945 *The Suspect; Uncle Harry/The Strange Affair Of Uncle Harry; The Spiral Staircase*
1946 *The Dark Mirror; The Killers\**
1947 *Time Out Of Mind*
1948 *Cry Of The City; Criss Cross*
1949 *The Great Sinner; Thelma Jordan* (UK: *The File On Thelma Jordan*)
1950 *Deported*
1951 *The Whistle At Eaton Falls* (UK: *Richer Than The Earth*)
1952 *The Crimson Pirate*
1954 *Le Grand Jeu* (UK: *Flesh And The Woman*)
1955 *Die Ratten*
1956 *Mein Vatter Der Schauspieler*
1957 *Nachts, Wenn Der Teufel Kam*
1958 *Dorothea Angemann*
1959 *The Rough And The Smooth*
1960 *Katja; Mein Schulfreund*
1961 *L'Affaire Nina B*
1962 *Tunnel 28* (UK: *Escape From East Berlin*)
1964 *Der Schutz* (UK: *The Yellow Devil*); *Der Schatz Der Azteken*
1965 *Die Pyramide Des Sonnengottes*
1967 *Custer Of The West*
1968 *Der Kampf Um Rom I*
1969 *Der Kampf Um Rom II*

## SIRK, Douglas
real name: Claus Detlev Sierk
(1900–87) Denmark

1935 *April, April; Das Mädchen Vom Moorhof; Stützen Der Gesellschaft* (UK: *The Pillars Of Society*)
1936 *Das Hofkonzert; Schlussakkord* (UK: *Final Accord*)

**SIRK, Douglas** (cont.)
1937 *La Habanera; Liebling Der Matrosen; Zu Neuen Ufern* (UK: *To New Shores*)
1938 *Die Heimat Ruft*
1939 *Boef Je*
1942 *Hitler's Madman*
1944 *Summer Storm*
1946 *A Scandal In Paris*
1947 *Lured* (UK: *Personal Column*)
1948 *Sleep My Love*
1949 *Shockproof; Slightly French*
1950 *Mystery Submarine; The First Legion*
1951 *The Lady Pays Off; Weekend With Father; Thunder On The Hill* (UK: *Bonaventure*)
1952 *Has Anybody Seen My Gal?; No Room For The Groom; Meet Me At The Fair*
1953 *Take Me To Town; All I Desire*
1954 *Taza, Son Of Cochise; Magnificent Obsession*; Sign Of The Pagan; Captain Lightfoot*
1955 *All That Heaven Allows*
1956 *There's Always Tomorrow; Written On The Wind*
1957 *Battle Hymn; The Tarnished Angels; Interlude*
1958 *A Time To Love And A Time To Die*
1959 *Imitation of Life**
1975 *Talk To Me Like The Rain*
1977 *Sylvesternacht*
1979 *Bourbon Street Blues*

**SODERBERGH, Steven**
(1963– ) USA

1989 *sex, lies and videotape**
1991 *Kafka*
1993 *King Of The Hill*

**SONNENFELD, Barry**
(19?– ) USA

1982 *In Our Water* (cinematographer only)
1984 *Blood Simple*; Violated* (cinematographer only)

1985 *Compromising Positions* (cinematographer only)
1986 *Wisdom* (cinematographer only)
1987 *Raising Arizona*; Throw Momma From The Train*; Three O'Clock High* (all cinematographer only)
1988 *Big** (cinematographer only)
1989 *When Harry Met Sally** (cinematographer only)
1990 *Miller's Crossing*; Misery** (cinematographer only)
1991 *The Addams Family**
1993 *For Love Or Money; Addams Family Values*

**SPHEERIS, Penelope**
(1945– ) USA

1978 *Real Life* (producer only)
1980 *The Decline Of Western Civilization*
1983 *Suburbia*
1985 *The Boys Next Door*
1986 *Hollywood Vice Squad; Summer Camp Nightmare* (screenwriter only)
1987 *Dudes*
1988 *The Decline Of Western Civilization Part II, The Metal Years; Calling the Shots* (actor only)
1990 *Wedding Band* (actor only)
1991 *Prison Stories: Women On The Inside* (TV) (co-director)
1992 *Wayne's World**
1993 *The Beverly Hillbillies*

**SPIELBERG, Steven**
(1947– ) USA

1960 *Escape To Nowhere*
1963 *Firefight*
1969 *Amblin'* (short); *Night Gallery* (TV)
1970 *Four In One* (TV)
1971 *Murder By The Book* (TV); *Duel* (TV)
1972 *Something Evil* (TV)
1973 *Savage* (TV); *Ace Eli And Rodger Of The Skies* (story only)
1974 *The Sugarland Express*
1975 *Jaws**

1977 *Close Encounters Of The Third Kind\**

1978 *I Want To Hold Your Hand* (producer only)

1979 *1941\**

1980 *Used Cars* (producer only); *The Blues Brothers\** (actor only)

1981 *Continental Divide* (co-executive producer only); *Raiders Of The Lost Ark\**

1982 *ET\**; *Poltergeist\** (producer only)

1983 *The Twilight Zone — The Movie* (co-director)

1984 *Gremlins\** (producer only); *Indiana Jones And The Temple Of Doom\**

1985 *Back To The Future\**; *Young Sherlock Holmes*; *The Goonies* (all executive producer only); *The Color Purple\**

1986 *An American Tail*; *The Money Pit* (both co-executive producer only)

1987 *batteries not included*; *Innerspace\** (both co-executive producer only); *Empire Of The Sun\**

1988 *The Land Before Time*; *Who Framed Roger Rabbit\** (both co-executive producer only)

1989 *Back To The Future II*; *Dad* (both co-executive producer only); *Indiana Jones And The Temple Of Doom\**; *Always\**

1990 *Joe Versus The Volcano*; *Arachnophobia*; *Gremlins 2: The New Batch*; *Back To The Future III* (all co-executive producer only)

1991 *An American Tail — Feivel Goes West* (producer only); *Hook\**

1993 *Jurassic Park*; *Schindler's List*

## SPOTTISWOODE, Roger
(1943– ) UK

1971 *Straw Dogs* (editor only)

1972 *The Getaway* (editor only)

1973 *Pat Garrett And Billy The Kid* (editor only)

1974 *The Gambler* (editor only)

1975 *Hard Times* (UK: *The Streetfighter*) (editor only)

1978 *Who'll Stop The Rain* (UK: *Dog Soldiers*) (executive producer)

1980 *Terror Train*

1981 *The Pursuit Of DB Cooper*

1982 *The Renegade* (TV); *48 Hrs\** (screenwriter only)

1983 *Under Fire\**

1985 *Baby...Secret Of The Lost Legend* (executive producer)

1986 *The Best Of Times*

1987 *The Last Innocent Man* (TV)

1988 *Shoot To Kill* (UK: *Deadly Pursuit*)

1989 *Turner And Hooch\**

1990 *Air America*

1992 *Stop, Or My Mom Will Shoot!*

## STEVENS, George Cooper
(1904–75) USA

1930 *Blood And Thunder*; *Ladies Last* (shorts)

1931 *Air Tight*; *Call A Cop!*; *High Gear*; *The Kick-Off*; *Mama Loves Papa!*

1932 *Boys Will Be Boys*; *Who, Me?*; *Family Troubles*

1933 *What Fur?*; *Grin And Bear It*; *A Divorce Courtship*; *Flirting In The Park*; *Quiet Please*; *Rock-A-Bye Cowboy*; *Room Mates*; *Should Crooners Marry?*; *Walking Back Home* (shorts); *The Cohens And Kellys In Trouble*

1934 *Bridal Bail*; *Cracked Shots*; *Ocean Swells*; *Rough Necking*; *Strictly Fresh Yeggs*; *The Undie-World* (all shorts); *Bachelor Bait*; *Kentucky Kernels* (UK: *Triple Trouble*)

1935 *Alice Adams*; *Annie Oakley*

1936 *Swing Time\**

1937 *Quality Street*; *A Damsel In Distress*

1938 *Vivacious Lady*

1939 *Gunga Din*

1940 *Vigil In The Night*

1941 *Penny Serenade*

1942 *Woman Of The Year\**; *The Talk Of The Town*

1943 *The More The Merrier*

1948 *I Remember Mama*

1951 *A Place In The Sun\**

**STEVENS, George Cooper** (cont.)

1952 *Something To Live For*
1953 *Shane\**
1956 *Giant\**
1959 *The Diary Of Anne Frank\**
1965 *The Greatest Story Ever Told*
1969 *The Only Game In Town*

## STEVENSON, Robert
(1905–86) UK

1932 *Happy Ever After* (co-director)
1933 *Falling For You* (co-director)
1935 *Jack Of All Trades*
1936 *The Man Who Changed His Mind; Tudor Rose*
1937 *King Solomon's Mines; Non-Stop New York; Owd Bob*
1939 *The Ware Case; Young Man's Fancy; Return To Yesterday*
1940 *Tom Brown's Schooldays*
1941 *Back Street*
1942 *Joan Of Paris*
1943 *Forever And A Day* (co-director)
1944 *Jane Eyre*
1946 *The American Creed* (documentary)
1947 *Dishonored Lady*
1948 *To The Ends Of The Earth*
1949 *I Married A Communist* (UK: *The Woman On Pier 13*)
1950 *Walk Softly Stranger*
1951 *My Forbidden Past*
1952 *The Las Vegas Story*
1957 *Johnny Tremain; Old Yeller*
1959 *Darby O'Gill And The Little People*
1960 *Kidnapped; The Absent-Minded Professor*
1962 *In Search Of The Castaways*
1963 *Son Of Flubber; The Misadventures Of Merlin Jones*
1964 *Mary Poppins\**
1965 *The Monkey's Uncle; That Darn Cat*
1967 *The Gnome Mobile*
1968 *Blackbeard's Ghost*
1969 *The Love Bug\**
1971 *Bedknobs And Broomsticks*
1974 *Herbie Rides Again; The Island At The Top Of The World*

1975 *One Of Our Dinosaurs Is Missing*
1976 *The Shaggy DA*

## STONE, Oliver
(1946– ) USA

1970 *Street Scenes 1970*
1974 *Seizure*
1978 *Midnight Express\** (screenwriter only)
1981 *The Hand*
1982 *Conan The Barbarian* (screenwriter only)
1983 *Scarface\** (screenwriter only)
1985 *The Year Of The Dragon* (screenwriter only)
1986 *8 Milion Ways To Die* (screenwriter only); *Salvador\*; Platoon\**
1987 *Wall Street\**
1988 *Talk Radio*
1989 *Born On The 4th Of July\**
1990 *Blue Steel; Reversal Of Fortune\** (both producer only)
1991 *Iron Maze* (executive producer only); *The Doors; JFK\**
1993 *Heaven And Earth*

## STREISAND, Barbra
(1943– ) USA

1983 *Yentl\**
1991 *The Prince Of Tides\**

See also actors listing

## STURGES, John
(1911–92) USA

1946 *The Man Who Dared; Shadowed; Alias Mr Twilight*
1947 *For The Love Of Rusty; Thunderbolt* (co-director); *Keeper Of The Bees*
1948 *Best Man Wins; The Sign Of The Ram*
1949 *The Walking Hills*
1950 *The Capture; Mystery Street; Right Cross*

1951 *The Magnificent Yankee* (UK: *The Man With 30 Sons*); *Kind Lady; The People Against O'Hara; It's A Big Country* (co-director)
1952 *The Girl In White* (UK: *So Bright The Flame*)
1953 *Jeopardy; Fast Company; Escape From Fort Bravo*
1954 *Bad Day At Black Rock\**
1955 *Underwater; The Scarlet Coat*
1956 *Backlash*
1957 *Gunfight At The OK Corral*
1958 *The Law And Jake Wade; The Old Man And The Sea*
1959 *Last Train From Gun Hill; Never So Few*
1960 *The Magnificent Seven\**
1961 *By Love Possessed*
1962 *Sergeants Three; A Girl Named Tamiko*
1963 *The Great Escape\**
1965 *The Satan Bug; The Hallelujah Trail*
1967 *Hour Of The Gun*
1968 *Ice Station Zebra*
1969 *Marooned*
1972 *Joe Kidd*
1973 *Valdez, The Halfbreed* (UK: *The Valdez Horses*)
1974 *McQ*
1976 *The Eagle Has Landed*

## STURGES, Preston
real name: Edmond Preston Biden
(1898–1959) USA

1930 *The Big Pond; Fast And Loose* (co-screenwriter only)
1931 *Strictly Dishonourable* (screenwriter only)
1933 *The Power And The Glory; Child Of Manhattan* (screenwriter only)
1934 *Thirty Day Princess; We Live Again* (co-screenwriter only)
1935 *The Good Fairy; Diamond Jim* (both screenwriter only)
1937 *Hotel Haywire; Easy Living* (both screenwriter only)
1938 *Port Of Seven Seas; If I Were King* (both screenwriter only)

1940 *Remember The Night* (screenwriter only); *The Great McGinty* (UK: *Down Went McGinty*); *Christmas In July*
1941 *Sullivan's Travels\*; The Lady Eve\**
1942 *The Palm Beach Story\**
1943 *The Great Moment*
1944 *Hail The Conquering Hero; The Miracle Of Morgan's Creek*
1946 *The Sin Of Harold Diddlebock* (UK: *Mad Wednesday*)
1948 *Unfaithfully Yours*
1949 *The Beautiful Blonde From Bashful Bend*
1956 *The Diary Of Major Thompson*
1958 *Paris Holiday* (actor only)

## SZABÓ, István
(1936– ) Hungary

1961 *Koncert* (UK: *Concert*); *Variációk Egy Témára* (UK: *Variations On A Theme*) (both shorts)
1963 *Te* (UK: *You*) (short)
1964 *Álmodozások Kora* (UK: *The Age Of Daydreaming*)
1966 *Apa* (UK: *Father*)
1967 *Kegyelet* (UK: *Piety*)
1970 *Szerelmesfilm* (UK: *Love Film*)
1971 *Budapest, Amiért Szeretem* (UK: *Budapest, Why I Love It*) (series of shorts)
1973 *Tüzoltó Utca 25* (UK: *25 Fireman's Street*)
1974 *Ösbemutató* (UK: *Premiere*)
1976 *Budapesti Mesék* (UK: *Budapest Tales*)
1977 *Várostérkép* (UK: *City Map*) (short)
1979 *Bizalom* (UK: *Confidence*); *Der Grüne Vogel* (UK: *The Green Bird*)
1980 *Mephisto\**
1984 *Bali*
1985 *Redl Ezredes* (UK: *Colonel Redl*)
1988 *Hanussen*
1991 *Meeting Venus*
1992 *Édes Emma, Drága Böbe* (UK: *Sweet Emma, Dear Böbe*)

# T

## TARKOVSKY, Andrei
(1932–86) Russia

1959 *There Will Be No Leave Today* (short)
1960 *Katok I Skripka* (UK: *The Steamroller And The Violin*)
1962 *Ivanovo Detstvo* (UK: *Ivan's Childhood*)
1966 *Andrei Rublev\**
1971 *Solyaris* (UK: *Solaris*)
1974 *Zerkalo* (UK: *The Mirror*)
1979 *Stalker*
1983 *Nostalghia* (UK: *Nostalgia*)
1986 *Offret\** (UK: *The Sacrifice*)

## TATI, Jacques
real name: Jacques Tatischeff
(1908–82) France

1932 *Oscar, Champion De Tennis* (screenwriter, actor only)
1934 *On Demande Une Brute* (co-screenwriter, actor only)
1935 *Gai Dimanche* (co-screenwriter, actor only)
1936 *Soigne Ton Gauche* (actor only)
1938 *Retour A La Terre* (screenwriter, actor only)
1945 *Sylvie Et Le Fantôme* (actor only)
1946 *Le Diable Au Corps* (actor only)
1947 *L'Ecole Des Facteurs*
1949 *Jour De Fête*
1952 *Les Vacances De Monsieur Hulot\** (UK: *Monsieur Hulot's Holiday*)
1958 *Mon Oncle*
1967 *Playtime*
1971 *Traffic*
1973 *Parade*

## TAUROG, Norman
(1899–1981) USA

1920 *The Fly Cop; The Suitor; The Stage Hand; School Days* (co-director, all shorts)
1921 *The Fall Guy; The Hick; The Bakery; The Bell Hop; The Rent Collector; The Sawmill* (co-director, all shorts)

1922 *The Show; A Pair Of Kings* (co-director, both shorts)
1923 *The Four Flusher; The Mummy* (both shorts)
1924 *Pain As You Enter; Rough And Ready; Fast And Furious; What A Night* (all shorts)
1925 *Below Zero; Cheap Skates; Going Great; Hello Goodbye; Hello Hollywood; Motor Mad; Pleasure Bound; Spot Light; Step Lightly* (all shorts)
1926 *Teacher Teacher; Jolly Tars; Careful Please; Creeps; Here Comes Charlie; Honest Injun; The Humdinger; Mr Cinderella; Move Along; Movieland; Nobody's Business; Nothing Matters; On Edge* (all shorts)
1927 *Up In Arms; At Ease; Kilties; Breezing Along; Drama De Luxe; The Draw-Back; Goose Flesh; Her Husky Hero; His Better Half; Howdy Duke; The Little Rube; New Wrinkles; Papa's Boy; Plumb Dumb; Somebody's Fault* (all shorts)
1928 *At It Again; Blazing Away; Always A Gentleman; Blondes Beware; Cutie; A Home Made Man; Listen Children; Rah!Rah!Rah!; Slippery Road* (all shorts); *The Farmer's Daughter*
1929 *All Steamed Up; Knights Out; Detectives Wanted; Hired And Fired; The Medicine Man* (all shorts); *Lucky Boy; Troopers Three* (both co-director); *In Holland; The Diplomats*
1930 *The Fatal Card; Just A Pal; Meet The Boyfriend; Oh, Teddy; The Patient; Sing, You Dancers; Song Service* (all shorts); *Sunny Skies; Hot Curves; Follow The Leader*
1931 *Cab Waiting; The Great Pants Mystery; Simply Killing* (all shorts); *Finn And Hattie* (co-director); *Skippy; Huckleberry Finn; Sooky; Newly Rich* (UK: *Forbidden Adventure*)

1932 *Hold 'Em Jail!; The Phantom President; If I Had A Million* (co-director)
1933 *A Bedtime Story; The Way To Love*
1934 *Mrs Wiggs Of The Cabbage Patch; We're Not Dressing; College Rhythm*
1935 *The Big Broadcast Of 1936*
1936 *Strike Me Pink; Rhythm On The Range; Reunion* (UK: *Heart In Reunion*)
1937 *Fifty Roads To Town; You Can't Have Everything*
1938 *The Adventures Of Tom Sawyer; Boys' Town\*; Mad About Music; The Girl Downstairs*
1939 *Lucky Night*
1940 *Young Tom Edison; Broadway Melody Of 1940; Little Nellie Kelly*
1941 *Men Of Boys' Town; Design For Scandal*
1942 *Are Husbands Necessary?; A Yank At Eton*
1943 *Presenting Lily Mars; Girl Crazy*
1946 *The Hoodlum Saint*
1947 *The Beginning Or The End*
1948 *The Bride Goes Wild; Words And Music*
1949 *That Midnight Kiss*
1950 *Mrs O'Malley And Mr Malone; Please Believe Me; The Toast Of New Orleans*
1951 *Rich, Young And Pretty; Room For One More*
1952 *The Stooge; Jumping Jacks*
1953 *The Caddy; The Stars Are Singing*
1954 *Living It Up*
1955 *You're Never Too Young*
1956 *Bundle Of Joy; Pardners; The Birds And The Bees*
1957 *The Fuzzy Pink Nightgown*
1958 *Onionhead*
1959 *Don't Give Up The Ship*
1960 *Visit To A Small Planet; GI Blues*
1961 *All Hands On Deck; Blue Hawaii*
1962 *Girls! Girls! Girls!*
1963 *Palm Springs Weekend; It Happened At The World's Fair*
1965 *Tickle Me; Sergeant Deadhead; Dr Goldfoot And The Bikini Machine* (UK: *Dr G And The Bikini Machine*)
1966 *Double Trouble; Spinout* (UK: *California Holiday*)
1968 *Speedway; Live A Little, Love A Little*

## TEAGUE, Lewis
(1941– ) USA

1974 *Cockfighter; Dirty O'Neil; The Forgotten Island Of Santosha; Summer Run* (all editor only)
1975 *Crazy Mama* (editor only); *Death Race 2000* (second-unit director)
1977 *Thunder And Lightning* (second-unit director)
1978 *Avalanche* (editor only); *Fast Charlie — The Moonbeam Rider* (second-unit director)
1979 *The Lady In Red*
1980 *Alligator; The Big Red One* (second-unit director)
1982 *Fighting Back*
1983 *Cujo*
1985 *The Jewel Of The Nile\*; Stephen King's Cat's Eye*
1989 *Shannon's Deal* (TV)
1990 *Collision Course; Navy SEALS*
1991 *Deadlock* (TV)

## TEMPLE, Julien
(1953– ) UK

1979 *The Great Rock'n'Roll Swindle*
1981 *The Secret Policeman's Other Ball*
1983 *Undercover*
1984 *Mantrap*
1985 *Running Out Of Luck*
1986 *Absolute Beginners\**
1987 *Aria* (co-director)
1989 *Earth Girls Are Easy*

## THOMAS, Gerald
(1920– ) UK

1956 *Circus Friends*
1957 *Time Lock; The Vicious Circle*

**THOMAS, Gerald** (cont.)
1958 *Chain Of Events; The Solitary Child; The Duke Wore Jeans; Carry On Sergeant\**
1959 *Carry On Nurse; Carry On Teacher; Please Turn Over*
1960 *Carry On Constable; Watch Your Stern; No Kidding*
1961 *Carry On Regardless; Raising The Wind*
1962 *Carry On Cruising; Twice Round The Daffodils; The Iron Maiden*
1963 *Nurse On Wheels; Carry On Cabby; Carry On Cleo*
1964 *Carry On Jack; Carry On Spying*
1965 *The Big Job; Carry On Cowboy*
1966 *Carry On Screaming; Don't Lose Your Head*
1967 *Follow That Camel*
1968 *Carry On Doctor; Carry On Camping*
1969 *Carry On Up The Khyber; Carry On Again Doctor*
1970 *Carry On Up The Jungle; Carry On Loving*
1971 *Carry On At Your Convenience; Carry On Henry*
1972 *Carry On Matron; Carry On Abroad*
1973 *Carry On Girls; Bless This House*
1974 *Carry On Dick*
1975 *Carry On Behind*
1976 *Carry On England*
1977 *That's Carry On!*
1978 *Carry On Emmannuelle*
1992 *Carry On Columbus*

**THOMPSON, J Lee**
(1914–   ) UK

1950 *Murder Without Crime*
1952 *The Yellow Balloon*
1953 *The Weak And The Wicked*
1954 *For Better, For Worse*
1955 *As Long As They're Happy; An Alligator Named Daisy*
1956 *Yield To The Night*
1957 *The Good Companions; Woman In A Dressing Gown*
1958 *Ice Cold In Alex*
1959 *No Trees In The Street; Tiger Bay; Northwest Frontier*

1960 *I Aim At The Stars*
1961 *The Guns of Navarone\**
1962 *Cape Fear\*; Taras Bulba*
1963 *Kings Of The Sun*
1964 *What A Way To Go!; John Goldfarb, Please Come Home*
1965 *Return From The Ashes*
1966 *Eye Of The Devil*
1968 *Mackenna's Gold*
1969 *The Chairman; Country Dance*
1972 *Conquest Of The Planet Of The Apes; A Great American Tragedy (TV)*
1973 *Battle For The Planet Of The Apes; The Blue Knight (TV)*
1974 *Huckleberry Finn; The Reincarnation Of Peter Proud*
1975 *Widow (TV)*
1976 *St Ives*
1977 *The White Buffalo*
1978 *The Greek Tycoon; The Passage*
1980 *Cabo Blanco*
1981 *Happy Birthday To Me*
1983 *Ten To Midnight*
1984 *The Ambassador; The Evil That Men Do*
1985 *King Solomon's Mines*
1986 *Firewalker; Murphy's Law*
1987 *Death Wish 4: The Crackdown*
1988 *Messenger Of Death*
1989 *Kinjite: Forbidden Subjects*

**THORPE, Richard**
real name: Rollo Thorpe
(1896–1991) USA

1923 *Three O'Clock In The Morning; That's That*
1924 *Battling Buddy; Bringin' Home The Bacon; Hard Hittin' Hamilton; Fast And Fearless; Walloping Wallace (all shorts); Gold And Grit; Rarin' To Go; Rough Ridin'*
1925 *Double Action Daniels; On the Go; Fast Fightin' (all shorts); The Desert Demon; Saddle Cyclone; Full Speed*
1926 *Rawhide; The Bandit Buster; The Fighting Cheat; Double Daring; College Days; Josselyn's Wife*

1927 *The Cyclone Cowboy; Between Dangers; The Desert Of The Lost; The Soda Water Cowboy; White Pebbles; The First Night*

1928 *The Flyin' Buckaroo* (short); *The Galloping Gobs; Valley Of Hunted Men; Vultures Of The Sea; The Vanishing West; The Cowboy Cavalier; Desperate Courage*

1929 *The Fatal Warning; King Of The Kongo; The Bachelor Girl*

1930 *The Lone Defender; Border Romance; Wings Of Adventure; The Utah Kid; Under Montana Skies; The Dude Wrangler* (UK: *Feminine Touch*); *The Thoroughbred* (UK: *Rising To Win*)

1931 *The Sky Spider; Neck And Neck; The Devil Plays; King Of The Wild; Grief Street* (UK: *Stage Whispers*); *The Lawless Woman; The Lady From Nowhere; Wild Horse* (co-director)

1932 *Slightly Married; The Thrill Of Youth; The King Murder; Beauty Parlor; Forbidden Company; Cross Examination; Forgotten Women; Murder At Dawn* (UK: *The Death Ray*); *Probation* (UK: *Second Chances*); *Midnight Lady* (UK: *Dream Mother*); *Escapade* (UK: *Dangerous Ground*)

1933 *Rainbow Over Broadway; Man Of Sentiment; I Have Lived; Notorious But Nice; Strange People; Forgotten; Women Won't Tell; The Secrets Of Wu Sin; Love Is Dangerous* (UK: *Women Are Dangerous*)

1934 *The Quitter; City Park; Stolen Sweets; Green Eyes; Cheating Cheaters; Murder On The Campus* (UK: *At The Stroke Of Nine*)

1935 *Secret Of The Chateau; Strange Wives; Last Of The Pagans*

1936 *The Voice Of Bugle Ann; Tarzan Escapes!*

1937 *Dangerous Number; Double Wedding; Night Must Fall*

1938 *The First Hundred Years; Man Proof; Love Is A Headache; Three Loves Has Nancy; The Crowd Roars; The Toy Wife* (UK: *Frou Frou*)

1939 *The Adventures Of Huckleberry Finn; Tarzan Finds A Son!*

1940 *The Earl Of Chicago; Twenty Mule Team; Wyoming* (UK: *Bad Man Of Wyoming*)

1941 *Barnacle Bill; Tarzan's Secret Treasure; The Bad Man* (UK: *Two-Gun Cupid*)

1942 *Apache Trail; White Cargo; Tarzan's New York Adventure; Joe Smith, American* (UK: *Highway To Freedom*)

1943 *Three Hearts For Julia; Above Suspicion; Cry Havoc!*

1944 *Two Girls And A Sailor; The Thin Man Goes Home*

1945 *Thrill Of A Romance; What Next, Corporal Hargrove?; Her Highness And The Bellboy*

1947 *Fiesta; This Time For Keeps*

1948 *A Date With Judy; On An Island With You*

1949 *Big Jack; The Sun Comes Up; Challenge To Lassie; Malaya* (UK: *East Of The Rising Sun*)

1950 *Black Hand; Three Little Words*

1951 *The Great Caruso; Vengeance Valley; The Unknown Man; It's A Big Country* (co-director)

1952 *Carbine Williams; Ivanhoe\*; The Prisoner Of Zenda*

1953 *The Girl Who Had Everything; All The Brothers Were Valiant*

1954 *Knights Of The Round Table; Athena; The Student Prince; The Flame And The Flesh*

1955 *The Adventures Of Quentin Durward* (UK: *Quentin Durward*)

1957 *Ten Thousand Bedrooms; Jailhouse Rock; Tip On A Dead Jockey* (UK: *Time For Action*)

1959 *The House Of The Seven Hawks; Killers Of Kilimanjaro*

1960 *The Tartars*

1961 *The Honeymoon Machine*

1962 *The Horizontal Lieutenant*

**THORPE, Richard** (cont.)
1963 *Follow The Boys; Fun In Acapulco*
1964 *The Golden Head; The Truth About Spring*
1965 *That Funny Feeling*
1966 *The Scorpio Letters* (TV)
1967 *The Last Challenge* (UK: *The Pistolero Of Red River*)


## TORNATORE, Giuseppe
(1956– ) Italy

1986 *Il Camorrista*
1989 *Nuovo Cinema Paradiso** (UK: *Cinema Paradiso*)
1990 *Stanno Tutti Bene* (UK: *Everybody's Fine*)
1991 *La Domenica Specialmente* (UK: *Especially On Sunday*) (co-director)
1993 *A Simple Formality*


## TOWNE, Robert
(1936– ) USA

1960 *The Last Woman On Earth* (screenwriter only)
1965 *The Tomb Of Ligeia* (screenwriter only)
1967 *Bonnie And Clyde** (screenwriting consultant)
1968 *Villa Rides* (screenwriter only)
1971 *Drive, He Said* (actor only)
1973 *The Last Detail* (screenwriter only)
1974 *Chinatown** (screenwriter only)
1975 *Shampoo*; The Yakuza* (both screenwriter only)
1982 *Personal Best*
1984 *Greystoke: The Legend Of Tarzan, Lord Of The Apes** (screenwriter only)
1987 *The Pick-Up Artist* (actor only); *Tough Guys Don't Dance* (assistance only); *The Bedroom Window* (screenwriter, executive producer only)
1988 *Tequila Sunrise**
1990 *Days Of Thunder** (screenwriter only)


## TROELL, Jan
(1931– ) Sweden

1962 *Barnvagnen* (cinematographer only)
1966 *Har Har Du Ditt Liv*
1967 *Ole Dole Doff*
1971 *Utvandrarna** (UK: *The Emigrants*)
1972 *Nybyggarna* (UK: *The New Land*)
1974 *Zandy's Bride*
1977 *Bang*
1979 *Hurricane*
1982 *Ingenjor Andrees Luftfard*
1986 *Sagolandet*
1991 *Il Capitano*


## TRUFFAUT, François
(1932–84) France

1955 *Une Visite* (short)
1957 *Les Mistons* (UK: *The Mischief Makers*) (short)
1958 *Une Histoire D'Eau* (short, co-director)
1959 *Les Quatre Cents Coups** (UK: *The 400 Blows*)
1960 *Tirez Sur Le Pianiste* (UK: *Shoot The Pianist*)
1961 *Jules Et Jim** (UK: *Jules And Jim*); *L'Amour A Vingt Ans* (UK: *Love At Twenty*) (co-director)
1964 *La Peau Douce* (UK: *Silken Skin*)
1966 *Fahrenheit 451*
1967 *La Mariée Etait En Noir* (UK: *The Bride Wore Black*)
1968 *Baisers Volés* (UK: *Stolen Kisses*)
1969 *L'Enfant Sauvage* (UK: *The Wild Child*); *La Sirène Du Mississippi*
1970 *Domicile Conjugale* (UK: *Bed And Board*)
1971 *Les Deux Anglaises Sur Le Continent* (UK: *Anne And Muriel*)
1972 *Une Belle Fille Comme Moi* (UK: *A Gorgeous Bird Like Me*)
1973 *La Nuit Américaine** (UK: *Day For Night*)
1975 *L'Histoire D'Adèle H* (UK: *The Story Of Adèle H*)
1976 *L'Argent De Poche* (UK: *Small Change*)

1977 *L'Homme Qui Aimait Les Femmes* (UK: *The Man Who Loved Women*); *Close Encounters Of The Third Kind** (actor only)
1978 *La Chambre Verte* (UK: *The Green Room*)
1979 *L'Amour En Fuite* (UK: *Love On The Run*)
1980 *Le Dernier Métro* (UK: *The Last Metro*)
1981 *La Femme D'A Coté* (UK: *The Woman Next Door*)
1983 *Vivement Dimanche!*

## TUTTLE, Frank
(1892–1963) USA

1922 *The Cradle Buster*
1923 *Puritan Passions; Second Fiddle; Youthful Cheaters*
1924 *Peter Stuyvesant; The Puritans* (both shorts); *Grit; Dangerous Money*
1925 *The Manicure Girl; A Kiss In The Dark; Miss Bluebeard; Lucky Devil; Lovers In Quarantine*
1926 *The Untamed Lady; The American Venus; Kid Boots; Love 'Em And Leave 'Em*
1927 *Blind Alleys; Time To Love; The Spotlight; One Woman To Another*
1928 *Easy Come, Easy Go; His Private Life; Love And Learn; Varsity; Something Always Happens*
1929 *Marquis Preferred; The Studio Murder Mystery; Sweetie; The Greene Murder Case; Men Are Like That*
1930 *The Benson Murder Case; Only The Brave; True To The Navy; Love Among The Millionaires; Her Wedding Night; Paramount On Parade* (co-director)
1931 *No Limit; It Pays To Advertise; Dud Ranch; This Is The Night*
1932 *This Reckless Age; The Big Broadcast*
1933 *Dangerously Yours; Roman Scandals*; *Pleasure Cruise*

1934 *Ladies Should Listen; Here Is My Heart; Springtime For Henry*
1935 *All The King's Horses; The Glass Key; Two For Tonight*
1936 *College Holiday*
1937 *Waikiki Wedding*
1938 *Doctor Rythmn*
1939 *Paris Honeymoon; I Stole A Million; Charlie McCarthy — Detective*
1942 *This Gun For Hire; Lucky Jordan*
1943 *Hostages*
1944 *The Hour Before The Dawn*
1945 *Don Juan Quilligan; The Great John L* (UK: *A Man Called Sullivan*)
1946 *Suspense; Swell Guy*
1950 *Le Traqué* (UK: *Gunman In The Streets*)
1951 *Magic Face*
1955 *Hell On Frisco Bay*
1956 *A Cry In The Night*
1959 *Island Of Lost Women*

# U

## UNDERWOOD, Ron
(19?–   ) USA

1989 *Tremors*
1991 *City Slickers**
1993 *Heart And Souls*

# V

## VADIM, Roger
real name: Roger Vadim Plémiannikov
(1927–   ) France

1951 *Blackmailed* (screenwriter only)
1956 *Cette Sacré Gamine* (screenwriter only); *Et Dieu Créa La Femme** (UK: *And God Created Woman*)
1957 *Sait-On Jamais?* (UK: *When The Devil Drives*); *Les Bijoutiers Du Clair De Lune* (UK: *Heaven Fell That Night*)
1959 *Les Liaisons Dangereuses*
1960 *Et Mourir De Plaisir* (UK: *Blood And Roses*)

**VADIM, Roger** (cont.)
1961 *La Bride Sur Le Cou* (UK: *Please, Not Now!*); *Le Sept Pechées* (UK: *The Seven Deadly Sins*) (co-director)
1962 *La Vice Et La Vertu* (UK: *Vice And Virtue*); *Le Repos Du Guerrier* (UK: *Warrior's Rest*)
1963 *Chateau En Suède*
1964 *La Ronde*
1966 *La Curée* (UK: *The Game Is Over*)
1967 *Histoires Extraordinaires* (UK: *Tales Of Mystery*) (co-director)
1968 *Barbarella\**
1971 *Pretty Maids All In A Row*
1972 *Hellé*
1973 *Don Juan 1973 Ou Si Don Juan Etait Une Femme* (UK: *Don Juan, Or If Don Juan Were A Woman*)
1974 *Charlotte*
1976 *Une Femme Fidèle* (UK: *When A Woman In Love...*)
1979 *Night Games*
1981 *The Hot Touch*
1982 *Comeback*
1983 *Surprise Party*
1985 *Into The Night* (actor only)
1987 *And God Created Woman* (remake)

# VAN DYKE II, Woodbridge Strong
(1889–1943) USA

1917 *Her Good Name; Clouds; Mother's Ordeal; The Land Of Long Shadows; The Range Boss; The Open Places; Sadie Goes To Heaven; The Gift O'Gab; Men Of The Desert*
1918 *The Lady Of The Dugout*
1919 *Daredevil Jack*
1920 *The Hawk's Trail; Double Adventure*
1921 *The Avenging Arrow; White Eagle*
1922 *According To Hoyle; The Boss Of Camp 4; Forget-Me-Not; The Milky Way*
1923 *The Little Girl Next Door/You Are In Danger; The Destroying Angel; The Miracle Makers*

1924 *Loving Lies; The Beautiful Sinner; Half-A-Dollar Bill; Winner Takes All; The Battling Fool; Gold Heels; Barriers Burned Away* (UK: *The Chicago Fire*)
1925 *Hearts And Spurs; The Trail Rider; The Timber Wolf; The Ranger Of The Big Pines; The Desert's Price*
1926 *The Gentle Cyclone; War Paint*
1927 *Winners Of The Wilderness; Heart Of the Yukon; California; Eyes Of The Totem; Foreign Devils; Spoilers Of The West*
1928 *Under The Black Eagle; Wyoming* (UK: *The Rock Of Friendship*); *White Shadows In The South Seas* (uncredited)
1929 *The Pagan*
1931 *Trader Horn; Never The Twain Shall Meet; Guilty Hands; Cuban Love Song*
1932 *Tarzan The Apeman\*; Night Court* (UK: *Justice For Sale*)
1933 *Penthouse* (UK: *Crooks In Clover*); *The Prizefighter And The Lady* (UK: *Everywoman's Man*)
1934 *Laughing Boy; The Thin Man\*; Forsaking All Others; Hide-Out; Manhattan Melodrama; Eskimo* (UK: *Mala The Magnificent*)
1935 *Naughty Marietta; I Live My Life*
1936 *Rose Marie\*; San Francisco\*; After The Thin Man; Love On The Run; His Brother's Wife* (UK: *Lady Of The Tropics*); *The Devil Is A Sissy* (UK: *The Devil Takes Account*)
1937 *They Gave Him A Gun; Rosalie; Personal Property* (UK: *The Man In Possession*)
1938 *Marie Antoinette; Sweethearts*
1939 *Stand Up And Fight; It's A Wonderful World; Another Thin Man; Andy Hardy Gets Spring Fever*
1940 *I Take This Woman; I Love You Again; Bitter Sweet*
1941 *Rage In Heaven; The Feminine Touch; Shadow Of The Thin Man;*

*Dr Kildare's Victory* (UK: *The Doctor And The Debutante*)
1942  *I Married An Angel; Cairo; Journey For Margaret*

## VAN SANT, Gus
(c1952–  ) USA

1978  *Property* (sound only)
1985  *Mala Noche*
1987  *Five Ways To Kill Yourself; Ken Death Gets Out Of Prison; My New Friends* (all shorts)
1988  *Junior* (short)
1989  *Drugstore Cowboy*
1990  *Thanksgiving Prayer* (short)
1991  *My Own Private Idaho**
1993  *Even Cowgirls Get The Blues*

## VARNEL, Marcel
(1894–1947) UK

1932  *Chandu, The Magician* (co-director); *The Silent Witness*
1933  *Infernal Machine*
1934  *Freedom Of The Seas; Girls Will Be Boys*
1935  *Dance Band; I Give My Heart; No Monkey Business*
1936  *All In; Public Nuisance No 1; Good Morning Boys*
1937  *Oh! Mr Porter*; Okay For Sound*
1938  *Alf's Button Afloat; Hey!Hey!USA; Old Bones Of The River*
1939  *Ask A Policeman; Band Wagon; The Frozen Limits; Where's That Fire*
1940  *Gasbags; Neutral Port; Let George Do It*
1941  *Hi! Gang; I Thank You; Turned Out Nice Again; The Ghost Of St Michael's; South American George*
1942  *King Arthur Was A Gentleman; Much Too Shy*
1943  *Get Cracking; Bell Bottom George*
1944  *He Snoops To Conquer*
1945  *I Didn't Do It*
1946  *George In Civvy Street; This Man Is Mine*

## VERHOEVEN, Paul
(1938–  ) Holland

1960  *Een Hagedis Teveel* (UK: *A Lizard Too Much*) (short)
1963  *Feest* (UK: *Let's Have A Party*) (short)
1966  *Hets Korps Mariniers* (UK: *The Dutch Marine Corps*) (short)
1968  *Mussert* (TV)
1971  *Wat Zien Ik* (UK: *Business Is Business*)
1973  *Oh Jonathan, Oh Jonathan* (actor only); *Turks Fruit* (UK: *Turkish Delight*)
1975  *Keetje Tippel* (UK: *Cathy Tippel*)
1977  *Soldaat Van Oranje* (UK: *Soldier Of Orange*)
1980  *Spetters*
1983  *De Vierde Man* (UK: *The Fourth Man*)
1985  *Flesh And Blood*
1987  *Robocop**
1990  *Total Recall**
1992  *Basic Instinct**

## VIDOR, Charles
(1900–59) USA

1931  *The Bridge* (short)
1933  *Sensation Hunters*
1934  *Double Door; Strangers All*
1935  *The Arizonian; His Family Tree*
1936  *Muss'Em Up* (UK: *House Of Fate*)
1937  *A Doctor's Diary; The Great Gambini; She's No Lady*
1939  *Romance Of The Redwoods; Blind Alley; Those High Gray Walls* (UK: *The Gates Of Alcatraz*)
1940  *My Son, My Son!; The Lady In Question*
1941  *Ladies In Retirement; New York Town*
1942  *The Tuttles Of Tahiti*
1943  *The Desperadoes*
1944  *Cover Girl; Together Again*
1945  *A Song To Remember; Over 21*
1946  *Gilda**
1948  *The Loves Of Carmen*
1951  *It's A Big Country* (co-director)
1952  *Hans Christian Andersen*

**VIDOR, Charles** (cont.)
1953 *Thunder In The East*
1954 *Rhapsody*
1955 *Love Me Or Leave Me**
1956 *The Swan*
1957 *The Joker Is Wild; A Farewell To Arms*
1960 *Song Without End* (co-director)


**VIDOR, King Wallis**
(1894–1982) USA

1913 *Hurricane In Galveston* (co-director, short)
1914 *Sugar Manufacture; In Tow* (both shorts)
1915 *Fort Worth Robbery* (short)
1917 *Judge Brown's Justice* (short)
1919 *The Turn In The Road; Better Times; The Other Half; Poor Relations*
1920 *The Family Honor; The Jack-Knife Man*
1921 *The Sky Pilot; Love Never Dies; The Real Adventure*
1922 *Woman, Wake Up!; Dusk To Dawn; Conquering The Woman; Peg O' My Heart*
1923 *The Woman Of Bronze; Three Wise Fools*
1924 *Wild Oranges; Happiness; The Wine Of Youth; Wife Of The Centaur; His Hour*
1925 *Proud Flesh; The Big Parade*
1926 *La Bohème; Bardleys The Magnificent*
1928 *The Crowd; Show People; The Patsy* (UK: *The Politic Flapper*)
1929 *Hallelujah*
1930 *Not So Dumb; Billy The Kid*
1931 *The Champ*; Street Scene*
1932 *Bird Of Paradise; Cynara*
1933 *The Stranger's Return*
1934 *Our Daily Bread* (UK: *The Miracle Of Life*)
1935 *The Wedding Night; So Red The Rose*
1936 *The Texas Rangers*
1937 *Stella Dallas**
1938 *The Citadel**

1939 *The Wizard Of Oz** (uncredited co-director)
1940 *Northwest Passage; Comrade X*
1941 *HM Pulham Esq*
1944 *An American Romance*
1946 *Duel In The Sun**
1948 *A Miracle Can Happen*
1949 *The Fountainhead; Beyond The Forest*
1951 *Lightning Strikes Twice*
1952 *Japanese War Bride; Ruby Gentry*
1954 *Man Without A Star*
1956 *War And Peace**
1959 *Solomon And Sheba*
1964 *Truth And Illusion: An Introduction To Metaphysics; Metaphor* (both documentary shorts)
1982 *Love And Money* (actor only)


**VIGO, Jean**
(1905–34) France

1929 *A Propos De Nice*
1931 *Taris* (short)
1932 *Zéro De Conduite*
1934 *L'Atalante**


**VISCONTI, Luchino**
real name: Count Don Luchino Visconti Di Modrone
(1906–76) Italy

1936 *Les Bas-Fonds; Une Partie De Campagne* (both assistant director)
1940 *La Tosca* (assistant director)
1942 *Ossessione**
1945 *Giorni Di Gloria* (assistant director); *Giorni Di Gloria* (documentary, co-director)
1948 *La Terra Trema*
1951 *Bellissima; Appunti Su Un Fatto Di Cronaca* (short documentary)
1953 *Siamo Donne* (UK: *We The Women*) (co-director)
1954 *Senso* (UK: *The Wanton Countess*)
1957 *Le Notte Bianchi* (UK: *White Nights*)
1960 *Rocco E I Suoi Fratelli* (UK: *Rocco And His Brothers*)

1962 *Boccaccio '70* (co-director); *Il Gattopardo\** (UK: *The Leopard*)
1965 *Vaghe Stelle Dell'Orsa* (UK: *Of A Thousand Delights*)
1966 *Le Streghe* (UK: *The Witches*) (co-director)
1967 *Lo Straniero* (UK: *The Stranger*)
1969 *La Caduta Degli Dei\** (UK: *The Damned*)
1970 *Alla Ricerca Di Tadzio*
1971 *Morte A Venezia\** (UK: *Death In Venice*)
1972 *Ludwig*
1974 *Gruppo Di Famiglia In Un Interno* (UK: *Conversation Piece*)
1976 *L'Innocente* (UK: *The Innocent*)

## VON STERNBERG, Josef

real name: Jonas Sternberg
(1894–1969) Austria

1919 *The Mystery Of The Yellow Room; By Divine Right; Vanity's Price* (all assistant director)
1925 *The Salvation Hunters; The Exquisite Sinner; The Masked Bride*
1926 *A Woman Of The Sea/The Sea Gull* (never released)
1927 *It; Children Of Divorce* (both uncredited); *Underworld*
1928 *The Last Command; The Docks Of New York; The Drag Net*
1929 *The Case Of Lena Smith; Thunderbolt*
1930 *Der Blaue Engel\** (UK: *The Blue Angel*); *Morocco*
1931 *Dishonored; An American Tragedy*
1932 *Shanghai Express; Blonde Venus; I Take This Woman*
1934 *The Scarlet Empress*
1935 *The Devil Is A Woman; Crime And Punishment*
1936 *The King Steps Out*
1937 *I Claudius* (uncompleted)
1938 *The Great Waltz* (uncredited contribution)
1939 *Sergeant Madden*
1940 *I Take This Woman* (uncredited contribution)

1941 *The Shanghai Gesture*
1943 *The Town* (documentary short)
1950 *Jet Pilot*
1952 *Macao* (co-director)
1953 *Anatahan* (UK: *The Saga Of Anatahan*)

# W

## WAJDA, Andrzej
(1926– ) Poland

1950 *Zly Chlopiec* (UK: *The Bad Boy*): *Keidy Ty Śpisz* (UK: *While You Sleep*) (both shorts)
1951 *Ceramika Ilzecka* (UK: *The Pottery Of Ilzecka*)
1955 *Ide Ku Slóncu* (UK: *Towards The Sun*) (short); *Pokolenie* (UK: *A Generation*)
1957 *Kanal*
1958 *Popiol I Diamanti\** (UK: *Ashes And Diamonds*)
1959 *Lotna*
1960 *Niewinni Czarodzieje* (UK: *Innocent Sorcerers*)
1961 *Samson*
1962 *Sibirska Ledi Magbet* (UK: *The Siberian Lady Macbeth*); *L'Amour A Vingt Ans* (UK: *Love At Twenty*) (co-director)
1965 *Popioly* (UK: *Ashes*)
1967 *Bramy Raju* (UK: *Gates To Paradise*)
1968 *Wszytko Na Sprzedaz* (UK: *Everything For Sale*); *Roly-Poly* (TV) (short)
1969 *Polowanie Na Muchy* (UK: *Hunting Flies*)
1970 *Krajobraz Po Bitwie* (UK: *Landscape After Battle*)
1971 *Brzezina* (UK: *The Birch Wood*)
1972 *Wesle* (UK: *The Wedding*)
1973 *Pilatus Und Andere* (UK: *Pilate And Others*)
1974 *Ziemia Obiecana* (UK: *Land Of Promise*)
1976 *Smuga Cienia* (UK: *The Shadow Line*)

**WAJDA, Andrzej** (cont.)
1977  *Czlowiek Z Marmuru* (UK: *Man Of Marble*)
1978  *Bez Zwie Czulenia* (UK: *Rough Treatment*); *The Dead Class*
1979  *Panxiy Z Wilko* (UK: *The Young Girls Of Wilko*); *Noc Listopadowa* (UK: *November Night*)
1980  *Dyrygent* (UK: *The Conductor*)
1981  *Czlowiek Z Zelaza* (UK: *Man Of Iron*)
1982  *Danton*
1983  *Land Of Promise*
1985  *A Love In Germany*
1986  *Kronika Wypadkow Milosnych* (UK: *Chronicle Of A Love Affair*)
1987  *Les Possédés* (UK: *The Possessed*)
1990  *Korczak*

# WALSH, Raoul
(1887–1981) USA

1910  *The Banker's Daughter; A Mother's Love; Paul Revere's Ride* (all actor only)
1912  *The Life Of General Villa* (co-director); *Outlaw's Revenge*
1913  *The Double Knot; The Hindu Image/The Mystery Of The Hindu Image; The Gunman*
1914  *Sierra Jim's Reformation; The Final Verdict*
1915  *Birth Of A Nation* (actor only); *The Death Dice; His Return; The Greaser; The Fatal Black Beau; Carmen; The Fencing Master; Man For All That; 11.30 PM; The Celestial Code; The Buried Hand; A Bad Man And Others; The Regeneration; Home From The Sea; The Lone Cowboy*
1916  *Blue Blood And Red; Pillars Of Society; The Serpent*
1917  *The Conqueror; The Honor System; Betrayed; The Innocent Sinner; The Silent Lie; The Pride Of New York; This Is The Life*
1918  *On the Jump; The Woman And*

The Law; The Prussian Cur; Every Mother's Son; I'll Say So*
1919  *Should A Husband Forgive?; Evangeline; The Strongest*
1920  *From Now On; The Deep Purple*
1921  *The Oath; Serenade*
1922  *Kindred Of the Dust*
1923  *Lost And Found On A South Sea Island*
1924  *The Thief Of Bagdad*
1925  *East Of Suez; The Wanderer; The Spaniard* (UK: *Spanish Love*)
1926  *The Lucky Lady; What Price Glory?; The Lady of The Harem*
1927  *The Monkey Talks; The Loves Of Carmen*
1928  *Sadie Thompson; Me, Gangster; The Red Dance* (UK: *The Red Dancer Of Moscow*)
1929  *In Old Arizona; The Cockeyed World; Hot For Paris*
1930  *The Big Trail\**
1931  *The Man Who Came Back; Women Of All Nations; Yellow Ticket* (UK: *The Yellow Passport*)
1932  *Wild Girl* (UK: *Salomy Jane*); *Me And My Gal* (UK: *Pier 13*)
1933  *Sailor's Luck; The Bowery; Going Hollywood*
1934  *Under Pressure*
1935  *Every Night At Eight; Baby Face Harrington*
1936  *Klondike Annie; Big Brown Eyes; Spendthrift*
1937  *OHMS; Jump For Glory; Hitting A New High; Artists And Models*
1938  *College Swing* (UK: *Swing, Teacher, Swing*)
1939  *St Louis Blues; The Roaring Twenties\**
1940  *The Dark Command; They Drive By Night* (UK: *The Road To Frisco*)
1941  *Manpower; High Sierra\*; The Strawberry Blonde; They Died With Their Boots On*
1942  *Desperate Journey; Gentleman Jim*
1943  *Background To Danger; Northern Pursuit*
1944  *Uncertain Glory*

1945 *The Horn Blows At Midnight; Salty O'Rourke; Objective Burma!*
1946 *The Man I Love*
1947 *Pursued; Cheyenne*
1948 *Fighter Squadron; One Sunday Afternoon; Silver River*
1949 *White Heat\*; Colorado Territory*
1950 *Montana; The Enforcer* (UK: *Murder Inc*) (uncredited contributions)
1951 *Along The Great Divide; Distant Drums; Captain Horatio Hornblower RN* (UK: *Captain Horatio Hornblower*)
1952 *The World In His Arms; Blackbeard The Pirate; The Lawless Breed; Glory Alley*
1953 *Gun Fury; A Lion Is In The Streets; Sea Devils*
1954 *Saskatchewan* (UK: *O'Rourke Of The Royal Mounted*)
1955 *Battle Cry; The Tall Men*
1956 *The Revolt Of Mamie Stover; The King And Four Queens*
1957 *Band Of Angels*
1958 *The Naked And The Dead; The Sheriff Of Fractured Jaw*
1959 *A Private Affair*
1960 *Esther And The King*
1961 *Marines Let's Go!*
1964 *A Distant Trumpet*

## WALTERS, Charles
(1911–82) USA

1942 *Seven Days Leave* (choreographer only)
1943 *DuBarry Was A Lady; Presenting Lily Mars; Best Foot Forward; Girl Crazy* (all choreographer only)
1944 *Broadway Rythmn; Three Men In White; Ziegfeld Follies\*; Meet Me In St Louis\** (all choreographer only)
1945 *Thrill Of A Romance; Her Highness And The Bellboy; Weekend At The Waldorf; The Harvey Girls\*; Abbott And Costello In Hollywood* (all choreographer only); *Spreadin' The Jam* (short)

1947 *Good News*
1948 *Easter Parade\**
1949 *The Barkleys Of Broadway*
1950 *Summer Stock* (UK: *If You Feel Like Singing*)
1951 *Texas Carnival; Three Guys Named Mike*
1952 *The Belle Of New York*
1953 *Lili; Dangerous When Wet; Easy To Love; Torch Song*
1955 *The Glass Slipper; The Tender Trap*
1956 *High Society\**
1957 *Don't Go Near The Water*
1959 *Ask Any Girl*
1960 *Please Don't Eat The Daisies*
1961 *Two Loves* (UK: *Spinster*)
1962 *Jumbo; Summer Holiday* (choreographer only)
1964 *The Unsinkable Molly Brown*
1966 *Walk, Don't Run*

## WAYNE, John
real name: Michael Marion Morrison (1907–79)

1960 *The Alamo\**
1968 *The Green Berets\**

See also actors listing

## WEIR, Peter
(1944– ) Australia

1967 *Count Vim's Last Exercise* (short)
1968 *The Life And Times Of The Rev Buck Shotte* (short)
1970 *Three To Go* (co-director)
1971 *Homesdale* (documentary)
1972 *Incredible Floridas* (documentary)
1973 *What Ever Happened To Green Valley?* (documentary)
1974 *The Cars That Ate Paris*
1975 *Picnic At Hanging Rock\**
1977 *The Last Wave*
1978 *The Plumber* (TV)
1980 *Gallipoli\**
1982 *The Year Of Living Dangerously\**

**WEIR, Peter** (cont.)
1985 *Witness*
1986 *The Mosquito Coast*
1989 *Dead Poets Society\**
1990 *Green Card\**
1993 *Fearless*


## WELLES, Orson
(1915–85) USA

1934 *The Hearts Of Age* (short, co-director)
1938 *Too Much Johnson*
1941 *Citizen Kane\**
1942 *The Magnificent Ambersons\*; Journey Into Fear* (co-director); *It's All True* (uncompleted)
1946 *The Stranger*
1948 *The Lady From Shanghai\*; Macbeth*
1951 *Othello*
1955 *Confidential Report; Don Quixote* (uncompleted)
1958 *Touch Of Evil\**
1962 *The Trial*
1966 *Chimes At Midnight*
1968 *The Immortal Story*
1969 *The Deep* (uncompleted)
1972 *The Other Side Of The Wind* (unreleased)
1973 *F For Fake*

See also actors listing


## WELLMAN, William Augustus
(1896–1975) USA

1920 *The Twins From Suffering Creek*
1923 *The Man Who Won; Second Hand Love; Cupid's Fireman; Big Dan*
1924 *Not A Drum Was Heard; The Vagabond Trail; The Circus Cowboy*
1925 *When Husbands Flirt*
1926 *The Boob* (UK: *The Yokel*); *The Cat's Pajamas; You Never Know Women*
1927 *Wings*
1928 *Legion Of The Condemned; Ladies Of The Mob; Beggars Of Life*

1929 *Chinatown Nights; The Man I Love; Woman Trap*
1930 *Dangerous Paradise; Maybe It's Love; Young Eagles*
1931 *Night Nurse; Star Witness; Other Men's Women/Steel Highway; The Public Enemy\** (UK: *Enemies Of The Public*); *Safe In Hell* (UK: *The Lost Lady*)
1932 *The Conquerors; So Big; The Purchase Price; Love Is A Racket; The Hatchet Man* (UK: *The Honourable Mr Wong*); *Frisco Jenny* (UK: *The Common Ground*)
1933 *Lily Turner; Heroes For Sale; Midnight Mary; Central Airport; Wild Boys Of The Road* (UK: *Dangerous Days*); *College Coach* (UK: *Football Coach*)
1934 *Stingaree; Looking For Trouble*
1935 *Call Of The Wild; The President Vanishes* (UK: *Strange Conspiracy*)
1936 *Small Town Girl; Robin Hood Of Eldorado*
1937 *Nothing Sacred; A Star Is Born\**
1938 *Men With Wings*
1939 *Beau Geste\*; The Light That Failed*
1941 *Reaching For The Sun*
1942 *Thunder Birds; Roxie Hart; The Great Man's Lady*
1943 *The Ox-Bow Incident\** (UK: *Strange Incident*); *Lady Of Burlesque* (UK: *Striptease Lady*)
1944 *Buffalo Bill*
1945 *This Man's Navy; The Story Of GI Joe*
1946 *Gallant Journey*
1947 *Magic Town*
1948 *Yellow Sky; The Iron Curtain*
1949 *Battleground*
1950 *The Happy Years; The Next Voice You Hear*
1951 *It's A Big Country* (co-director); *Across The Wide Missouri; Westward The Women*
1952 *My Man And I*
1953 *Island In The Sky*
1954 *The High And The Mighty\*; Track Of The Cat*

1955 *Blood Alley*
1956 *Goodbye, My Lady*
1958 *Darby's Rangers* (UK: *The Young Invaders*); *Lafayette Escadrille* (UK: *Hell Bent For Glory*)

## WENDERS, Wim
(1945– ) Germany

1967 *Schauplätze; Same Player Shoots Again* (both shorts)
1968 *Silver City; Polizeifilm* (both shorts)
1969 *Alabama—2000 Light Years; Drei Amerikanische LPs* (both shorts)
1970 *Summer In The City*
1971 *Die Angst Des Tormanns Beim Elfmeter* (UK: *The Goalkeeper's Fear Of The Penalty*)
1972 *Der Scharlachrote Buchstabe* (UK: *The Scarlet Letter*)
1974 *Alice In Den Städten* (UK: *Alice In The Cities*)
1975 *Falsche Bewegung* (UK: *Wrong Movement*)
1976 *Im Lauf Der Zeit* (UK: *Kings Of The Road*)
1977 *Der Amerikanische Freund* (UK: *The American Friend*)
1980 *Lightning Over Water* (co-director)
1982 *Hammett; Der Stand Der Dinge* (UK: *The State Of Things*)
1984 *Paris, Texas\*; Room 666* (documentary)
1985 *Tokyo-Ga* (documentary)
1987 *Der Himmel Über Berlin* (UK: *Wings Of Desire*)
1989 *Aufzeichnungen Zu Kleidern Unde Städten* (UK: *Notebook On Cities And Clothes*) (documentary)
1991 *Until The End Of The World*
1993 *Im Weiter Ferne, So Nah*

## WHALE, James
(1889–1957) UK

1929 *The Love Doctor* (dialogue director only)
1930 *Hell's Angels* (dialogue director only); *Journey's End*

1931 *Waterloo Bridge; Frankenstein\**
1932 *The Impatient Maiden; The Old Dark House*
1933 *The Kiss Before The Mirror; The Invisible Man; By Candlelight*
1934 *One More River* (UK: *Over The River*)
1935 *Remember Last Night?; Bride Of Frankenstein\**
1936 *Showboat*
1937 *The Road Back; The Great Garrick*
1938 *Sinners In Paradise; Port Of Seven Seas; Wives Under Suspicion*
1939 *The Man In The Iron Mask*
1940 *Green Hell*
1941 *They Dare Not Love*
1949 *Hello Out There*

## WHELAN, Tim
(1893–1957) USA

1928 *Adam's Apple*
1929 *When Knights Were Bold*
1933 *It's A Boy; Aunt Sally*
1934 *The Camels Are Coming*
1935 *The Murder Man; The Perfect Gentleman*
1936 *Two's Company; Smash And Grab*
1937 *The Mill On The Floss; Farewell Again; Action For Slander* (co-director)
1938 *The Divorce Of Lady X; St Martin's Lane*
1939 *Q Planes; Ten Days In Paris*
1940 *The Thief Of Bagdad\** (co-director); *The Mad Doctor* (UK: *A Date With Destiny*)
1941 *International Lady*
1942 *Twin Beds; Nightmare; Seven Days' Leave*
1943 *Higher And Higher*
1944 *Swing Fever; Step Lively*
1946 *Badman's Territory*
1948 *This Was A Woman*
1955 *Rage At Dawn; Texas Lady*

## WHORF, Richard
(1906–66) USA

1945 *The Hidden Eye*
1946 *Till The Clouds Roll By**
1947 *It Happened In Brooklyn; Love From A Stranger*
1948 *Luxury Liner*
1950 *Champagne For Caesar*

## WILDER, Billy
real name: Samuel Wilder
(1906–  ) Austria/USA

1929 *Menschen Am Sonntag* (UK: *People On Sunday*); *Der Teufelsreporter* (both co-writer only)
1930 *Seitensprünge* (writer only)
1931 *Ihre Hoheit Befiehlt; Der Falsche Ehemann; Emil Und Die Detektive* (UK: *Emil And The Detectives*); *Mann Der Seinen Mörder Sucht* (UK: *Looking For His Murderer*) (all co-writer only)
1932 *Es War Einmal Ein Walzer; Ein Blonder Traum; Scampolo, Ein Kind Der Strasse; Das Blaue Von Himmel* (all co-writer only)
1933 *Mauvaise Graine* (co-director); *Madame Wünscht Keine Kinder; Was Frauen Träumen; Adorable* (all co-writer only)
1934 *Music In The Air; One Exciting Adventure* (both co-writer only)
1935 *Lottery Lover* (co-writer only)
1937 *Champagne Waltz* (co-writer only)
1938 *Bluebeard's Eighth Wife* (co-writer only)
1939 *Midnight; What A Life; Ninotchka** (all co-writer only)
1940 *Arise My Love* (co-writer only)
1941 *Hold Back The Dawn*; Ball Of Fire** (both co-writer only)
1942 *The Major And The Minor*
1943 *Five Graves To Cairo*
1944 *Double Indemnity**
1945 *The Lost Weekend**
1948 *The Emperor Waltz; A Foreign Affair*
1950 *Sunset Boulevard**

1951 *The Big Carnival* (UK: *Ace In The Hole*)
1953 *Stalag 17**
1954 *Sabrina* (UK: *Sabrina Affair*)
1955 *The Seven Year Itch**
1957 *Love In The Afternoon; The Spirit Of St Louis*
1958 *Witness For The Prosecution**
1959 *Some Like It Hot**
1960 *The Apartment**
1961 *One Two Three*
1963 *Irma La Douce**
1964 *Kiss Me Stupid*
1966 *The Fortune Cookie** (UK: *Meet Whiplash Willie*)
1970 *The Private Life Of Sherlock Holmes*
1972 *Avanti!**
1974 *The Front Page*
1978 *Fedora*
1981 *Buddy, Buddy*

## WILSON, Hugh
(1943–  ) USA

1983 *Stroker Ace* (co-writer only)
1984 *Police Academy**
1985 *Rustler's Rhapsody*
1987 *Burglar*
1993 *Guarding Tess*

## WISE, Robert
(1914–  ) USA

1939 *Bachelor Mother; Fifth Avenue Girl; The Hunchback Of Notre Dame** (all editor only)
1940 *Dance, Girl Dance; My Favorite Wife* (both editor only)
1941 *Citizen Kane*; The Devil And Daniel Webster* (both editor only)
1942 *The Magnificent Ambersons*; Seven Days Leave* (both editor only)
1943 *Bombadier; The Fallen Sparrow; The Iron Major* (all editor only)
1944 *The Curse Of The Cat People* (co-director); *Mademoiselle Fifi*
1945 *The Body Snatcher; A Game Of Death*
1946 *Criminal Court*

1947 *Born To Kill* (UK: *Lady Of Deceit*)
1948 *Mystery In Mexico; Blood On The Moon*
1949 *The Set-Up*
1950 *Two Flags West; Three Secrets*
1951 *The House On Telegraph Hill; The Day The Earth Stood Still*
1952 *Something For The Birds; The Captive City*
1953 *The Desert Rats; Destination Gobi; So Big*
1954 *Executive Suite*
1955 *Helen Of Troy*
1956 *Tribute To A Bad Man; Somebody Up There Likes Me*
1957 *Until They Sail; This Could Be The Night*
1958 *Run Silent, Run Deep; I Want To Live!\**
1959 *Odds Against Tomorrow*
1961 *West Side Story\**
1962 *Two For The Seesaw*
1963 *The Haunting*
1965 *The Sound Of Music\**
1966 *The Sand Pebbles\**
1968 *Star!*
1970 *The Andromeda Strain*
1973 *Two People*
1975 *The Hindenburg*
1977 *Audrey Rose*
1979 *Star Trek — The Motion Picture\**
1989 *Rooftops*

## WOOD, Sam
full name: Samuel Grosvenor Wood
(1883–1949) USA

1919 *Double Speed*
1920 *The Dancin' Fool; Excuse My Dust; Sick Abed; What's Your Hurry?; A City Sparrow; Her Beloved Villain; The Snob; Her First Elopement*
1921 *The Great Moment; Peck's Bad Boy; Under The Lash; Don't Tell Everything*
1922 *Her Husband's Trademark; Beyond The Rocks; Her Gilded Cage; The Impossible Mrs Bellew; My American Wife*

1923 *Bluebeard's Eighth Wife; Prodigal Daughters; His Children's Children*
1924 *The Next Corner; Bluff; The Female; The Mine With The Iron Door*
1925 *The Re-Creation Of Brian Kent*
1926 *Fascinating Youth; One Minute To Play*
1927 *A Racing Romeo; Rookies; The Fair Co-Ed*
1928 *The Latest From Paris; Telling The World*
1929 *So This Is College; It's A Great Life*
1930 *The Girl Said No; They Learned About Women* (co-director); *Sins Of The Children* (UK: *The Richest Man In The World*); *Paid* (UK: *Within The Law*)
1931 *A Tailor Made Man; The New Adventures Of Get-Rich-Quick Wallingford; The Man In Possession*
1932 *Prosperity; Huddle* (UK: *Impossible Lover*)
1933 *Hold Your Man; Christopher Bean; The Barbarian* (UK: *A Night In Cairo*)
1934 *Stamboul Quest*
1935 *A Night At The Opera\*; Let 'Em Have It* (UK: *False Faces*)
1936 *Whipsaw; The Unguarded Hour*
1937 *Navy Blue And Gold; A Day At The Races; Madame X*
1938 *Stablemates; Lord Jeff* (UK: *The Boy From Barnardo's*)
1939 *Goodbye Mr Chips\**
1940 *Raffles; Our Town\*; Rangers Of Fortune; Kitty Foyle\**
1941 *The Devil And Miss Jones*
1942 *King's Row\*: The Pride Of The Yankees\**
1943 *For Whom The Bell Tolls\*; The Land Is Bright* (documentary)
1944 *Casanova Brown*
1945 *Guest Wife; Saratoga Trunk*
1946 *Heartbeat*
1947 *Ivy*
1948 *Command Decision*
1949 *The Stratton Story; Ambush*

## WYLER, William
(1902–81) Germany

1925  *Crook Buster* (short)
1926  *Don't Shoot; The Fire Barrier; The Gunless Bad Man; The Horse Trader; Martin Of The Mounted; The Two Fister* (all shorts); *Ridin' For Love; The Stolen Ranch; Lazy Lightning*
1927  *Daze Of The West; Galloping Justice; The Haunted Homestead; Gun Justice; The Home Trail; Kelcy Gets Her Man; The Lone Star; The Ore Raiders; The Phantom Outlaw; The Square Shooter; Tenderfoot Courage; The Silent Partner* (all shorts); *Hard Fists; The Border Cavalier; Desert Dust; Thunder Riders; Straight Shootin'* (UK: *Range Riders*)
1928  *The Shakedown; Anybody Here Seen Kelly?*
1929  *The Love Trap; Hell's Heroes*
1930  *The Storm*
1931  *A House Divided*
1932  *Tom Brown Of Culver*
1933  *Her First Mate; Counsellor At Law*
1934  *Glamour*
1935  *The Good Fairy; The Gay Deception*
1936  *These Three; Dodsworth*; Come And Get It* (co-director)
1937  *Dead End**
1938  *Jezebel**
1939  *Wuthering Heights**
1940  *The Letter*; The Westerner*
1941  *The Little Foxes**
1942  *Mrs Miniver**
1944  *The Memphis Belle; The Fighting Lady* (both documentaries)
1946  *The Best Years Of Our Lives**
1947  *Thunderbolt* (documentary, co-director)
1949  *The Heiress**
1951  *The Detective Story*
1952  *Carrie*
1953  *Roman Holiday**
1955  *The Desperate Hours*

1956  *Friendly Persuasion**
1958  *The Big Country**
1959  *Ben-Hur**
1962  *The Children's Hour* (UK: *The Loudest Whisper*)
1965  *The Collector*
1966  *How To Steal A Million*
1968  *Funny Girl**
1970  *The Liberation Of LB Jones*

# Y

## YATES, Peter
(1929–  ) UK

1960  *The Entertainer*; Sons And Lovers** (both assistant director)
1961  *The Guns Of Navarone*; The Roman Spring Of Mrs Stone; A Taste Of Honey* (all assistant director)
1962  *Summer Holiday*
1964  *One Way Pendulum*
1967  *Robbery*
1968  *Bullitt**
1969  *John And Mary*
1970  *Murphy's War*
1972  *The Hot Rock* (UK: *How To Steal A Diamond In Four Uneasy Lessons*)
1973  *The Friends Of Eddie Coyle*
1974  *For Pete's Sake*
1975  *Mother, Jugs And Speed*
1977  *The Deep**
1979  *Breaking Away**
1981  *Eyewitness* (UK: *The Janitor*)
1983  *The Dresser*; Krull*
1985  *Eleni*
1987  *Suspect**
1988  *The House On Carroll Street*
1989  *An Innocent Man*
1992  *The Year Of The Comet*

## YIMOU, Zhang
(1950–   )

1984  Huang Tudi (cinematographer only)
1985  Yi Ge Yu Ba Ge (cinematographer only)
1986  Da Yue Bing (cinematographer only)
1987  Hong Gaoliang* (UK: Red Sorghum); Lao Jing (actor, cinematographer only)
1989  Judou*
1990  The Terra-Cotta Warrior (actor, producer only)
1991  Dahong Denglong Gaogao Gua (UK: Raise The Red Lantern)
1992  Qiu Ju Da Guansi (UK: The Story Of Qiu Ju)
1993  The Secret Coffin

## YOUNG, Shaun Terence
(1915–   ) UK

1944  Men Of Arnhem (documentary, co-director)
1948  Corridor Of Mirrors; Woman Hater; One Night With You
1950  They Were Not Divided
1951  Valley Of The Eagles
1952  Tall Headlines
1953  The Red Beret
1954  That Lady
1955  Storm Over The Nile (co-director)
1956  Safari; Zarak
1957  Action Of The Tiger; No Time To Die!
1959  Serious Charge
1960  Black Tights; Too Hot To Handle
1961  Orazi E Curiazzoi (UK: Duel Of Champions)
1962  Dr No*
1963  From Russia With Love*
1965  La Guerre Secrète (UK: The Dirty Game); The Amorous Adventures Of Moll Flanders; Thunderball*
1966  The Poppy Is Also A Flower (UK: Danger Grows Wild); Triple Cross
1967  Wait Until Dark; L'Avventuriero (UK: The Rover)

1968  Mayerling
1969  The Christmas Tree
1970  Cold Sweat
1971  Red Sun
1972  The Valachi Papers
1973  The Amazons
1974  The Klansman
1976  Jackpot (unfinished)
1979  Bloodline
1980  Inchon!
1983  The Jigsaw Man
1984  Where Is Parsifal? (executive producer only)
1993  L'Arbre Metallique

# Z

## ZEFFIRELLI, Franco
(1923–   ) Italy

1947  Angelina (actor only)
1948  La Terra Trema (assistant director)
1951  Bellisima (assistant director)
1954  Senso (assistant director)
1957  Camping
1966  Florence — Days Of Destruction (documentary)
1967  The Taming Of The Shrew*
1968  Romeo And Juliet*
1972  Fratelli Sole Sorella Luna (UK: Brother Sun, Sister Moon)
1977  Jesus Of Nazareth (TV)
1979  The Champ
1981  Endless Love
1983  La Traviata; Strasphere (documentary)
1986  Otello
1988  Il Giovane Toscanini (UK: Young Toscanini)
1990  Hamlet*
1993  Storia Di Una Capinera

## ZEMECKIS, Robert
(1951– ) USA

1973 *Field Of Honor* (short)
1978 *I Wanna Hold Your Hand*
1979 *1941** (screenriter only)
1980 *Used Cars*
1984 *Romancing The Stone**
1985 *Back To The Future**
1988 *Who Framed Roger Rabbit**
1989 *Back To The Future II*
1990 *Back To The Future III*
1992 *Death Becomes Her**

## ZIEFF, Howard
(1943– ) USA

1973 *Slither*
1975 *Hearts Of The West* (UK:
       *Hollywood Cowboy*)
1978 *House Calls*
1979 *The Main Event*
1980 *Private Benjamin**
1983 *Unfaithfully Yours*
1989 *The Dream Team*
1991 *My Girl*
1993 *My Girl 2*

## ZINNEMANN, Fred
(1907– ) Austria

1927 *La Marche Des Machines*
       (assistant cameraman)
1929 *Ich Küsse Ihre Hand, Madame;
       Sprengbagger 1010; Menschen
       Am Sonntag* (UK: *People On
       Sunday*) (all assistant cameraman
       only)
1930 *Man Trouble* (assistant director);
       *All Quiet On The Western Front**
       (actor only)
1931 *The Spy* (assistant director)
1932 *The Wiser Sex; The Man From
       Yesterday; The Kid From Spain*
       (all assistant director)
1934 *The Wave* (documentary, co-
       director)
1937 *Friend Indeed* (short)
1938 *Tracking The Sleeping Death;
       Weather Wizards; The Story Of Dr*

*Carver; That Mothers Might Live;
       They Live Again* (all shorts)
1939 *While America Sleeps; Help
       Wanted!; The Ash Can Fleet; One
       Against The World; Forgotten
       Victory* (all shorts)
1940 *Stuffie; The Way In The
       Wilderness; The Old South; The
       Great Meddler* (all shorts)
1941 *Forbidden Passage; Your Last Act*
       (both shorts)
1942 *The Lady Or The Tiger?* (short);
       *Kid Glove Killer; Eyes In The
       Night*
1944 *The Seventh Cross*
1945 *Little Mr Jim*
1946 *My Brother Talks To Horses*
1948 *The Search; Act Of Violence*
1950 *The Men*
1951 *Teresa; Benjy* (documentary)
1952 *High Noon*; The Member Of The
       Wedding*
1953 *From Here To Eternity**
1956 *Oklahoma!**
1957 *A Hatful Of Rain*
1959 *The Nun's Story**
1960 *The Sundowners**
1964 *Behold A Pale Horse*
1966 *A Man For All Seasons**
1973 *The Day Of The Jackal**
1977 *Julia**
1982 *Five Days In Summer*
1989 *Stand Under The Dark Clock*
       (documentary, appearance only)

## ZUCKER, David
(1947– ) USA

1977 *The Kentucky Fried Movie* (actor,
       screenwriter only)
1980 *Airplane!** (co-director)
1984 *Top Secret!* (co-director)
1986 *Ruthless People* (co-director)
1988 *The Naked Gun—From The Files
       Of Police Squad!**
1991 *The Naked Gun 2½—The Smell
       Of Fear*
1993 *Naked Gun 33 ⅓*

## ZUCKER, Jerry
(1950–  ) USA

1977  *The Kentucky Fried Movie* (actor, screenwriter only)
1979  *Rock'n'Roll High School* (second-unit director)
1980  *Airplane!** (co-director)
1984  *Top Secret!* (co-director)
1986  *Ruthless People* (co-director)
1988  *The Naked Gun — From The Files Of Police Squad!** (executive producer, screenwriter only)
1990  *Ghost**
1991  *The Naked Gun 2½ — The Smell Of Fear* (co-executive producer only)

## ZWICK, Ed
(1952–  ) USA

1982  *Paper Dolls* (TV)
1983  *Special Bulletin* (TV)
1986  *About Last Night*
1989  *Glory**
1991  *Leaving Normal*